Allusions—
Cultural, Literary, Biblical, and Historical: A Thematic Dictionary

Related Gale Titles

Dictionary of Collective Nouns and Group Terms. 2nd edition. Furnishes definitions, usage examples, and source notes for 1,800 terms. Ancient phrases, general terms, modern punning terms, and terms of quantity and number are covered.

Idioms and Phrases Index. Contains over 400,000 entries identifying some 140,000 idioms, phrases, and expressions in the English language. Each entry guides users to one or more of 30 dictionaries that define the term.

Modifiers. Presents some 16,000 English adjectives derived from, or relating to, over 4,000 selected common and technical nouns.

Mottoes. An extensive collection of more than 9,000 mottoes - familial, personal, institutional - from around the world and throughout history. Arranged under nearly 400 thematic categories with alphabetical indexes, each motto is identified as to source. Foreign mottoes are translated into English.

Slogans. This work collects more than 6,000 slogans, rallying cries, and other exhortations from such fields as advertising, politics, and everyday speech, and arranges them under appropriate thematic headings, along with a discussion of each slogan's origin and use.

-Ologies and -Isms. 3rd edition. A lexicon of more than 15,000 words containing such suffixes as -ology, -ism, -ic, -cide, -phobia, -mancy, etc., that are not easily accessible in standard dictionaries. Words are arranged under thematic headings.

Picturesque Expressions: A Thematic Dictionary. 2nd edition. Explains 7,000 expressions. Entries give the expression, an explanation of its origin, its approximate date of appearance in written English, and, in most cases, usage notes and illustrative quotations.

Prefixes and Other Word-Initial Elements of English. For each of 3,000 common and technical prefixes, the dictionary gives examples of use, a description of its origin and meaning, and variant and related forms.

Suffixes and Other Word-Final Elements of English. Provides definitions, usage notes, examples, and variant and related forms of 1,500 suffixes.

The Private Lives of English Words. Identifies and explains the etymologies of some 400 words that exemplify various processes of linguistic change. Most of these words have had their meanings drastically changed over the course of their history.

Allusions—
Cultural, Literary, Biblical, and Historical: A Thematic Dictionary

---

SECOND EDITION

Laurence Urdang
and Frederick G. Ruffner, Jr.
Editors

David M. Glixon
Associate Editor

GALE RESEARCH COMPANY • BOOK TOWER
DETROIT, MICHIGAN 48226

Editorial Staff

Gale Research Company

Library of Congress Cataloging-in-Publication Data

Allusions--cultural, literary, biblical, and historical.

Bibliography: p.
Includes index.
1. Allusions. I. Urdang, Laurence. II. Ruffner, Frederick G. III. Glixon, David M.
PN43.A4 1986 081 86-9981
ISBN 0-8103-1828-8

Data Processing and Composition by
Alexander Typesetting, Inc., Indianapolis, Indiana

Typographic and System Design by Laurence Urdang Inc.

Printed in the United States of America

Contents

Preface to the Second Edition

When *Allusions* was first published, in 1982, it was generally well received, providing sufficient encouragement for the preparation of this Second Edition, containing more than 8,700 entries, an increase of nearly 25 percent over the First Edition.

As with many books that attempt to break new ground, the First Edition contained a number of flaws, which we have sought to correct in this Second Edition. Among them, alas, was my failure to make it clear that we generally avoided the inclusion of real people unless they were felt to epitomize a particular characteristic that appears as a Thematic Category. The reason for that decision lay in the fact that it is impossible to list all of the **POETS, ARTISTS,** etc. who might be deemed worthy of entry, because they are considered proverbially great (like Milton), because they are an important referent for a certain style of poem (like Meredith, for "shaped" poetry), or for any other reason. A few have been retained (**Leonardo** under **INVENTIVENESS** and **VERSATILITY**, for example), though only those with specific attributes—for instance, Michelangelo does not appear.

A number of people have written to us with suggestions for additions, deletions, and shifts of entries from one category to another, and we have taken all of these offerings under serious consideration. Because of the enormous diversity of interests and expertness among contributors, we have received many suggestions that the editors felt to be too specialized for a work of general reference; in other cases, we have felt embarrassed at having missed some of the more obvious allusions. Sometimes, though a suggested entry may have been quite valid, its referent was far too general to allow its inclusion: for example, an attribute of a character who is not named in a work of fiction or whose name is extremely unlikely to be known and therefore cannot be classified into the present structure of the book has been eliminated from consideration. In other cases, the attribute or attributes of a character are too vague to admit entry. Also omitted are characters that are relatively obscure or, though prominent, appear in relatively obscure works of literature, even though those works might have been created by well-known authors.

In short, as we wrote in the First Edition,

> Not everything is here, of course. There are probably hundreds of thousands of allusions. . . . Any reader of this book can find inclusions that may not be to his taste and omissions that he considers heinously unforgivable. We have attempted a broad coverage of a subject so vast and so mercurial that it is doubtful its documentation can ever be complete.

Those statements are still valid, and they are likely to remain so regardless of the number of editions of this book that might follow.

Some comment has focused on the presentation of the source material, both at the entry and in the Bibliography, chiefly at the decision to use a modern edition as a source. The decision to use secondary sources and modern editions was taken deliberately, for they are the sources most conveniently and most readily found on the shelves of libraries. Thus, reference is made, for example, to a 1970 edition of the Old Testament published by Oxford University Press, to a 1947 edition, also by O.U.P., of *Hamlet*, and to a 1965 Atheneum edition of *Golden Boy*, by Clifford Odets. Moreover, there are many references to secondary sources, like *The Reader's Encyclopedia*, by William Rose Benét (Crowell, 1965), *The New Columbia Encyclopedia* (Columbia U.P., 1975), and the *Encyclopaedia Britannica* (EB, 1977). It seemed obvious to the editors that secondary sources, recognized as such, would be more readily available than original documents and other original sources on which they were based and, likewise, that no reasoning user of *Allusions* would think that we were suggesting that Old Testament, *Hamlet*, and *Golden Boy* were originally published in, respectively, 1970, 1947, and 1965.

The idea that, where practical, original publication dates be included somewhere in the Bibliography or at each entry is a good one, and we may be able to include them in a Third Edition; but there was not sufficient time to include them in the Second, and users will have to rely on other bibliographical sources for that information, which is easily found in many library catalogues.

We have been fortunate in obtaining the editorial expertise of David M. Glixon, who added more than 1,500 new entries and did considerable housekeeping on existing material. Paul Falla has provided valuable insight in his analysis of the First Edition and his suggestions for additions to the Second. And we are grateful to Elizabeth Chapman Hewitt, who has culled a great number of sources to provide suggestions for new entries. As always, however, the responsibility for the results rests on the editors, who, in their own wisdom (or lack of it) must assume that burden.

Laurence Urdang

Essex, Connecticut
March 1986

Preface to the First Edition

If language can be considered a fabric, then the warp are its words, the weft its grammar. There are plain-weave fabrics with little color and elaborate tapestries that are works of art. Much of literary language falls into the latter category. Yet we cannot ignore the poetry and the rhetorical devices used by those of us who are not poets. Language is by nature metaphoric.

With a few exceptions, dictionaries persist in ignoring the most productive, evocative, emotive, descriptive aspects of language. They pay scant attention to the creative genius of its users, whether they be poets or peasants. Rather, they are concerned with a sterile distillate which robs the lexicon of its intimations of creativity. Lexicographers by tradition or discipline ignore the innate ability of speakers to perceive relationships between the realities of life and the symbolism of myth, literature, culture, and language. The rationale is that dictionaries record denotation, not connotation. Even cursory examination of any desk (or larger) dictionary will show that such a claim is errant, arrant nonsense: one need only read through a few longer entries like *take, run,* or *set* to see how false that position is, how many metaphoric senses are listed.

Lexicographers, it must be acknowledged, are (almost) human, too: no matter how disciplined the mind, it cannot avoid metaphor or allusion. Language is not a plain weave, an ecru fustian; it is a colorful tapestry. Depending on the weaver, it may not always turn out to be a panoramic work of art, but colorful it often is, frequently realistic in some areas and abstract in others. Even the "scientific" lexicographer succumbs to its magic, unable to separate his work from his nature: there can be no objectivity in the description of one's own language.

Nevertheless, that does not keep lexicographers from trying to be objective, chiefly by the arbitrary elimination of certain classes of words and meanings and the inclusion—just as arbitrary—of others. We may ask why, for example, the word *Superman* (in reference to the comic-strip character) is omitted: surely, it has not only denotative meaning but also a host of useful connotations and metaphoric senses that are far more familiar to (American) English speakers than are the kinds of obscure entries that one customarily finds in dictionaries.

There are thousands of such references that constantly occur in our language. Some may be drawn from the comic strips, as in the case of *Superman*; many are drawn from literature (*Babbitt, Scrooge*), from legend or mythology (*Midas, Hercules, Paul Bunyan*), from brand names (*Edsel, Coca-*

Cola [Coke]), from symbols (*closed book, yin-yang*), from real people (*Shakespeare, Rockefeller*—on a formula like, "He's a regular Rockefeller"), from events (*Watergate, Boston Tea Party*), from the names of places, buildings, or the like (*Loch Ness, Empire State Building*), from music and the other arts (*Star-spangled Banner, Mona Lisa*), from animals (*dolphin, leopard, mule, rabbit*—all have their attributes), and from every other classification of information associated with culture. By what criteria may such references be omitted from a dictionary that purports to contain "all of the common words and meanings of English"? Even so-called "unabridged" dictionaries don't list them.

These lexical items cannot be omitted on the grounds of lack of frequency: they are often more frequent than words that are listed. They cannot be omitted because "everyone already knows them": a (general) dictionary is supposed to be "a description of the lexicon, or word stock of a language," and they clearly are a part of the lexicon. Many words, now spelled with small letters, were once allusive referents—*thersitical, pander*. Some are listed in dictionaries with capitals—*Midas, Jonah, Adam, Gargantuan*. Capitalization is an empty criterion if we consider language as primarily spoken, with any distinction between capital and small letters obviously inaudible. (It may be true that some proper names and adjectives are identifiable from their syntactic relationships, even in oral discourse, but that is not true of all: we speak of *Shakespeare*, "the" *George Washington Bridge*, and so on; but how can one analyze *a Shakespeare* 'a genius,' or *a Scrooge* 'a miser,' or *a Rockefeller* 'a wealthy man' as distinct from the senses for which they are equivalents? These are preceded by indefinite articles, hence are used metaphorically.)

Because we feel these words should be documented in their metaphoric senses, we have compiled this book. *Allusions—Cultural, Literary, Biblical, and Historical: A Thematic Dictionary*, contains more than 7,000 such references: to the Bible, Shakespeare, Dickens; to Greek, Roman, Scandinavian, and other mythologies; to American, European, Eastern, and other legends; to music, the arts, industry, comics, motion pictures, television, radio—in fact, to all of the divers elements that make up what we classify under the general rubric of culture. These are our familiar, everyday references, the things we talk about and the things we use when we speak English, the veritable fabric of our lives, gathered in a single work for easy reference. Not everything is here, of course. There are probably hundreds of thousands of allusions (if they could all be counted), always arriving, always departing. Any reader of this book can find inclusions that may not be to his taste and omissions that he considers heinously unforgivable. We have attempted a broad coverage of a subject so vast and so mercurial that it is doubtful its documentation can ever be complete. We should be grateful for readers' comments, addenda, and corrigenda.

Laurence Urdang

Essex, Connecticut
August 1981

How to Use This Book

Allusions is a thematic dictionary, with more than 8,700 entries organized under 712 thematic categories, each of which has one or (sometimes many) more appropriate entries listed beneath it. The 712 categories are presented in the text in alphabetic order by the name of the category heading (e.g. AMBITION, FRIENDSHIP, SLEUTHING); a complete list, including cross references, is given in the **Table of Thematic Categories**, pp. 13–27.

If you are seeking a set of allusions that deal with a particular theme, say **IRASCIBILITY**, then you will find it in the text as a category, no. 384. Under it will be a number of allusions listed alphabetically and numbered, e.g.:

384. IRASCIBILITY (See also ANGER, EXASPERATION, SHREWISHNESS.)

1. **Caius, Dr.** irritable physician. [Br. Lit.: *Merry Wives of Windsor*]
2. **Donald Duck** cantankerousness itself. [Comics: Horn, 216–217]
3. **Elisha** sics bears on boys for their jibing. [O.T.: II Kings 2:23–24]
4. **Findlay, Maude** out-spoken, oft-married, liberated woman. [TV: "Maude" in Terrace, II, 79–80]

Each entry contains an allusion (in **bold face** type), a brief definition, then other information within square brackets:

(a) A broad category that provides another focus on the allusion (e.g., for **1.**, "Br. Lit."; for **2.**, "Comics"; for **3.**, "O.T."; for **4.**, "TV").
Note: See the list of abbreviations at the end of this section to identify the broad categories designated.

(b) A secondary source reference for further background (e.g., for **2.** "Horn, 216–217"; for **4.** "Terrace, II, 79–80") or a primary reference (e.g., for **1.** *"Merry Wives of Windsor"*; for **3.** "II Kings 2:23–24").
Note: Source designations given within brackets refer to the **Bibliography**, pp. 537–574, where they are more fully identified.

If you are seeking information on a particular allusion encountered in reading, study, conversation, etc., you may consult the **Index**, pp. 577–634, where all allusions from the text are listed alphabetically, including cross references and variant forms.

Abbreviations Used in This Book

Am.	American	**Hagiog.**	Hagiography	**O.T.**	Old Testament
Arab.	Arabic	**Hist.**	History	**Pers.**	Persian
Arg.	Argentinian	**Hung.**	Hungarian	**Phil.**	Philosophy
Arth.	Arthurian	**Iconog.**	Iconography	**Pop.**	Popular
Aust.	Austrian	**Ind.**	Indian	**Port.**	Portuguese
Babyl.	Babylonian	**Ital.**	Italian	**Rel.**	Religion
Br.	British	**Jap.**	Japanese	**Ren.**	Renaissance
Can.	Canadian	**Jew.**	Jewish	**Rom.**	Roman
Class.	Classical	**Jour.**	Journalism	**Russ.**	Russian
Czech.	Czechoslovakian	**Lit.**	Literature	**Scot.**	Scottish
Dan.	Danish	**Mex.**	Mexican	**Span.**	Spanish
Egypt.	Egyptian	**Misc.**	Miscellaneous	**Swed.**	Swedish
Eur.	European	**Myth.**	Mythology	**Theol.**	Theology
Flem.	Flemish	**Nor.**	Norwegian	**Trad.**	Tradition
Fr.	French	**N.T.**	New Testament	**TV**	Television
Ger.	German	**Nurs. Rhyme**	Nursery Rhyme	**Yid.**	Yiddish
Gk.	Greek				

Table of Thematic Categories

Categories used in the text are in **CAPITAL LETTERS** and are numbered in their alphabetic sequence. Also included, but not numbered and appearing with only their initial letter capitalized, are synonyms referring to actual categories, e.g., Adversity (See **FAILURE.**).

A

1. **ABANDONMENT** (See also **ORPHAN.**)
2. **ABDUCTION**
3. **ABUNDANCE** (See also **FERTILITY.**)
4. **ACTING**
5. **ADOLESCENCE**
6. **ADULTERY** (See also **CUCKOLDRY, FAITHLESSNESS.**)
7. **ADVENTUROUSNESS** (See also **JOURNEY, QUEST, WANDERING.**)

Adversity (See **FAILURE.**)
Advice (See **COUNSEL.**)
Affectation (See **PRETENSION.**)
Affliction (See **SUFFERING.**)

8. **AGE, OLD**
9. **AGELESSNESS** (See also **IMMORTALITY.**)

Aggressiveness (See **CONQUEST.**)

10. **AID, GOVERNMENTAL** (See also **GENEROSITY.**)
11. **AID, ORGANIZATIONAL** (See also **GENEROSITY.**)

Aimlessness (See **WANDERING.**)

12. **AIR**

Alarm (See **WARNING.**)

13. **ALCOHOLISM** (See also **DRUNKENNESS.**)

Allurement (See **TEMPTATION.**)

14. **ALOOFNESS**
15. **AMBIGUITY**
16. **AMBITION**
17. **AMERICA**
18. **ANDROGYNY**
19. **ANGEL**
20. **ANGER** (See also **EXASPERATION, IRASCIBILITY, RANTING.**)
21. **ANNUNCIATION**
22. **ANTI-HEROISM**
23. **ANTIMILITARISM** (See also **PEACE, PEACEMAKING.**)
24. **ANTIQUARIANS**
25. **ANTI-SEMITISM** (See also **BIGOTRY, GENOCIDE.**)
26. **ANTISLAVERY**
27. **APHRODISIACS**
28. **APOCALYPSE**
29. **APOSTASY** (See also **SACRILEGE.**)
30. **APPEARANCES, DECEIVING** (See also **ILLUSION.**)
31. **APPLE**
32. **ARCHITECTS**
33. **ARGUMENTATIVENESS**
34. **ARISTOCRACY**
35. **ARRIVISM** (See also **PHILISTINISM.**)

36. **ARROGANCE** (See also **BOASTFULNESS, CONCEIT, EGOTISM.**)
Artfulness (See **CUNNING.**)
37. **ARTISTIC SKILL**
Artlessness (See **INNOCENCE, NAÏVETÉ.**)
38. **ASCENSION**
39. **ASCETICISM** (See also **AUSTERITY, DISCIPLINE.**)
40. **ASS**
41. **ASSASSINATION** (See also **MURDER.**)
42. **ASTROLOGY** (See also **ZODIAC.**)
43. **ASTRONAUTICS**
44. **ASTRONOMY**
45. **ATHLETICISM**
46. **ATONEMENT**
47. **AUSTERITY** (See also **ASCETICISM, DISCIPLINE.**)
48. **AUTHORITY**
49. **AUTHORSHIP**
Autobiography (See **BIOGRAPHY and AUTOBIOGRAPHY.**)
50. **AUTUMN**
51. **AVIATION**
52. **AWKWARDNESS** (See also **INEPTITUDE.**)

B

53. **BACHELORDOM**
Badness (See **EVIL.**)
54. **BALDNESS**
55. **BALLOONING** (See also **AVIATION.**)
56. **BANISHMENT**
57. **BANKRUPTCY** (See also **POVERTY.**)
58. **BAPTISM**
59. **BARRENNESS**
Bashfulness (See **TIMIDITY.**)
60. **BATTLE** (See also **WAR.**)
61. **BEAUTY**
62. **BEAUTY, FEMININE** (See also **BEAUTY, SENSUAL.**)
63. **BEAUTY, LASTING**
64. **BEAUTY, MASCULINE** (See also **VIRILITY.**)
65. **BEAUTY, RUSTIC**
66. **BEAUTY, SENSUAL** (See also **BEAUTY, FEMININE; SEX SYMBOL.**)
67. **BESTIALITY** (See also **PERVERSION.**)
68. **BETRAYAL** (See also **TREACHERY.**)
69. **BIGOTRY** (See also **ANTI-SEMITISM.**)
70. **BIOGRAPHY and AUTOBIOGRAPHY**
71. **BIRDS**
Birth (See **CHILDBIRTH.**)
72. **BIRTHSTONES**
73. **BLACKMAIL** (See also **BRIBERY.**)
Blackness (See **NIGHT.**)
Blasphemy (See **APOSTASY.**)
74. **BLINDNESS**
75. **BOASTFULNESS** (See also **ARROGANCE, CONCEIT, EGOTISM.**)
76. **BOHEMIANISM**
77. **BOREDOM** (See also **FUTILITY.**)
78. **BORESOMENESS**
Boxing (See **PUGILISM.**)
79. **BOYISHNESS** (See also **MANNISHNESS.**)
80. **BRAVERY** (See also **HEROISM.**)
81. **BRAWNINESS** (See also **STRENGTH, VIRILITY.**)
82. **BREVITY**
83. **BRIBERY** (See also **BLACKMAIL.**)
84. **BRIDGE**
85. **BRIGHTNESS**
86. **BRITAIN**

87. **BRUTALITY** (See also **CRUELTY, MUTILATION.**)
88. **BULL**
89. **BULLYING**
90. **BUREAUCRACY**
91. **BURIAL ALIVE**
92. **BURIAL GROUND**
93. **BUTLER** (See also **SERVANT.**)
94. **BUXOMNESS**

C

95. **CANNIBALISM**
96. **CARELESSNESS** (See also **FORGETFULNESS, IRRESPONSIBILITY, LAZINESS.**)
97. **CASTAWAY**
98. **CASTRATION**
99. **CATS**

Cemetery (See **BURIAL GROUND.**)

100. **CENSORSHIP**
101. **CHANCE** (See also **FATE.**)

Charity (See **GENEROSITY.**)

102. **CHARMS**
103. **CHASTITY** (See also **MODESTY, PURITY, VIRGINITY.**)
104. **CHAUVINISM** (See also **BIGOTRY, PATRIOTISM.**)
105. **CHEERFULNESS** (See also **GAIETY, JOVIALITY, OPTIMISM.**)
106. **CHILDBIRTH**

Childlessness (See **BARRENNESS.**)

107. **CHILDREN** (See also **YOUTH.**)
108. **CHIVALRY**
109. **CHRIST** (See also **PASSION OF CHRIST.**)
110. **CHRISTMAS**
111. **CIRCUMCISION**
112. **CLEANLINESS** (See also **ORDERLINESS.**)

Cleverness (See **CUNNING.**)

113. **CLOCKS**
114. **CLOWNS**

Clumsiness (See **AWKWARDNESS, INEPTITUDE.**)

115. **COARSENESS**
116. **COCKNEY**
117. **COLDNESS**
118. **COLONIZATION**

Comedy (See **ZANINESS.**)
Comeuppance (See **LAST LAUGH.**)
Comfort (See **LUXURY.**)
Commerce (See **FINANCE.**)
Companionship (See **FRIENDSHIP.**)
Compassion (See **KINDNESS.**)
Compromise (See **PEACEMAKING.**)

119. **CONCEALMENT** (See also **REFUGE.**)
120. **CONCEIT** (See also **ARROGANCE, BOASTFULNESS, EGOTISM.**)
121. **CONDEMNATION**
122. **CONFUSION**
123. **CONQUERORS**
124. **CONSCIENCE**
125. **CONSERVATISM**
126. **CONSPIRACY** (See also **INTRIGUE.**)

Constancy (See **LOYALTY.**)

127. **CONTEMPLATION**
128. **CONTENTMENT**
129. **CONTROVERSY** (See also **SCANDAL.**)
130. **CONVENTIONALITY**
131. **COOPERATION**
132. **COUNSEL** (See also **GUIDANCE.**)

Courage (See **BRAVERY.**)

133. **COURTESANSHIP** (See also **MISTRESSES, PROSTITUTION.**)
134. **COURTESY**

E

F

248. **FAREWELL**
249. **FARMING**
250. **FASCISM**
251. **FASHION**
252. **FASTIDIOUSNESS** (See also **PUNCTUALITY.**)
253. **FATE** (See also **CHANCE.**)
254. **FATHERHOOD**
255. **FATNESS**
256. **FEARSOMENESS**
257. **FEAST** (See also **EPICUREANISM.**)
258. **FEMALE POWER**
259. **FEMININITY**
260. **FEMINISM** (See also **EQUALITY.**)
261. **FERRYING**
262. **FERTILITY** (See also **ABUNDANCE.**)
263. **FESTIVAL, FILM**
264. **FESTIVAL, MUSIC**
   Fierceness (See **SAVAGERY.**)
265. **FILTH** (See also **DIRTINESS.**)
266. **FINANCE** (See also **MONEY.**)
267. **FIRE**
268. **FIRSTS**
   Flamboyance (See **ELEGANCE.**)
269. **FLATTERY**
270. **FLIRTATIOUSNESS** (See also **SEDUCTION.**)
271. **FLOWER or PLANT, NATIONAL** (See also **FLOWER, STATE.**)
272. **FLOWER, STATE** (See also **FLOWER or PLANT, NATIONAL.**)
273. **FLOWERS**
274. **FLYING**
275. **FOLLY**
   Foolishness (See **DIMWITTEDNESS, STUPIDITY.**)
   Fools (See **CLOWNS.**)
276. **FOPPISHNESS**
277. **FORGERY** (See also **FRAUDULENCE, HOAX.**)
278. **FORGETFULNESS** (See also **CARELESSNESS.**)
279. **FORGIVENESS**
280. **FORTITUDE** (See also **BRAVERY.**)
   Fratricide (See **MURDER.**)
281. **FRAUDULENCE** (See also **FORGERY, HOAX.**)
282. **FREEDOM** (See also **DELIVERANCE.**)
283. **FRENZY**
284. **FRIENDSHIP** (See also **LOYALTY.**)
285. **FRIVOLITY**
286. **FRONTIER**
287. **FRUSTRATION** (See also **EXASPERATION, FUTILITY.**)
288. **FUNERAL**
289. **FUTILITY** (See also **DESPAIR, FRUSTRATION.**)

G

290. **GAIETY** (See also **CHEERFULNESS, JOVIALITY, JOY.**)
   Gallantry (See **CHIVALRY.**)
291. **GAMBLING**
292. **GANGSTERISM** (See also **OUTLAWRY.**)
293. **GENERATION GAP**
294. **GENEROSITY** (See also **AID, ORGANIZATIONAL; KINDNESS.**)
295. **GENIUS** (See also **WISDOM.**)
296. **GENOCIDE** (See also **BRUTALITY, MASSACRE.**)
297. **GENTLENESS**
298. **GENUINENESS**
299. **GHOST**
300. **GIANTISM** (See also **TALLNESS.**)
301. **GLOOMINESS**

302. GLUTTONY (See also **GREED.**)
303. GOD
304. GOODNATUREDNESS (See also **CHEERFULNESS.**)
Goodness (See **KINDNESS.**)
305. GOSSIP (See also **SLANDER.**)
Gourmandism (See **EPICUREANISM, GLUTTONY.**)
Graciousness (See **COURTESY, HOSPITALITY.**)
306. GRATITUDE
307. GREED (See also **STINGINESS.**)
308. GRIEF
309. GROWTH
310. GUARDIANSHIP (See also **PROTECTIVENESS.**)
311. GUIDANCE (See also **COUNSEL.**)
312. GUIDE
313. GULLIBILITY (See also **DUPERY.**)

H

314. HAIR
Happiness (See **JOY.**)
315. HARMONY
316. HARSHNESS
317. HATRED
Haughtiness (See **ARROGANCE.**)
318. HEADLESSNESS (See also **DECAPITATION.**)
319. HEALING (See also **MEDICINE.**)
320. HEALTH
321. HEARTLESSNESS (See also **CRUELTY, RUTHLESSNESS.**)
322. HEAVEN (See also **PARADISE.**)
Height (See **GIANTISM, TALLNESS.**)
323. HELL (See also **UNDERWORLD.**)
324. HELPFULNESS (See also **KINDNESS.**)
325. HENPECKED HUSBANDS
Heresy (See **APOSTASY.**)
326. HEROISM (See also **BRAVERY.**)
327. HIGHSPIRITEDNESS
328. HIGHWAYMEN (See also **OUTLAWRY, THIEVERY.**)
329. HOAX
330. HOLY DAYS and PERIODS
331. HOMECOMING
332. HOMOSEXUALITY
333. HONESTY (See also **RIGHTEOUSNESS, VIRTUOUSNESS.**)
334. HOPE (See also **OPTIMISM.**)
Hopelessness (See **DESPAIR.**)
335. HORROR
336. HORSE
337. HORSERACE
338. HOSPITALITY
339. HOUSES, FATEFUL
Hugeness (See **GIANTISM.**)
340. HUMBUGGERY (See also **FRAUDULENCE, TRICKERY.**)
341. HUMILITY (See also **MODESTY.**)
Humorousness (See **WITTINESS.**)
342. HUNGER
343. HUNTING
344. HYPOCHONDRIA
345. HYPOCRISY (See also **PRETENSION.**)

I

346. IDEALISM
347. IDENTIFICATION
348. IDOLATRY
349. IGNORANCE (See also **STUPIDITY.**)
350. ILLEGITIMACY

J

437. **MELANCHOLY** (See also **GRIEF.**)
438. **MEMORY**
  Mercy (See **FORGIVENESS.**)
439. **MESSENGER**
440. **MIDDLE CLASS**
441. **MILITARISM** (See also **SOLDIERING.**)
442. **MIMICRY**
443. **MIRACLE**
444. **MIRROR**
445. **MISANTHROPY**
  Misbehavior (See **MISCHIEVOUSNESS.**)
446. **MISCHIEVOUSNESS** (See also **JOKE, PRACTICAL.**)
447. **MISERLINESS** (See also **STINGINESS.**)
448. **MISSIONARY**
449. **MISTRESSES** (See also **COURTESANSHIP, PROSTITUTION.**)
450. **MOCKERY**
451. **MODESTY** (See also **CHASTITY, HUMILITY.**)
452. **MONEY** (See also **FINANCE.**)
453. **MONSTERS**
454. **MOON**
455. **MOTHERHOOD**
  Motivation (See **INDUCEMENT.**)
  Mourning (See **GRIEF.**)
456. **MURDER** (See also **ASSASSINATION, INFANTICIDE, PATRICIDE.**)
457. **MUSIC**
458. **MUTENESS**
459. **MUTILATION** (See also **BRUTALITY, CRUELTY.**)
  Mutiny (See **REBELLION.**)
460. **MYSTERY**
461. **MYSTICISM**

N

462. **NAÏVETÉ** (See also **INEXPERIENCE, INNOCENCE.**)
463. **NATIVITY** (See also **CHRISTMAS.**)
  Neglectfulness (See **CARELESSNESS.**)
  Nervousness (See **INSECURITY.**)
464. **NIGHT**
465. **NIHILISM**
466. **NOBLE SAVAGE**
467. **NOBLEMINDEDNESS**
  Noise (See **LOUDNESS.**)
  Nonchalance (See **INDIFFERENCE.**)
468. **NOSE**
  Nosiness (See **GOSSIP.**)
469. **NOSTALGIA**
470. **NUDITY**
471. **NURSING**
472. **NYMPH**

O

  Obesity (See **FATNESS.**)
473. **OBSESSIVENESS**
474. **OBSTINACY**
  Obtuseness (See **DIMWITTEDNESS.**)
  Oddness (See **ECCENTRICITY.**)
  Oldness (See **AGE, OLD.**)
475. **OMEN** (See also **PROPHECY.**)
476. **OMNIPRESENCE** (See also **UBIQUITY.**)
477. **OMNISCIENCE**
478. **OPPORTUNISM**
479. **OPTIMISM** (See also **HOPE.**)
480. **ORDERLINESS** (See also **CLEANLINESS.**)
481. **ORPHAN** (See also **ABANDONMENT.**)

482. **OUTLAWRY** (See also **HIGHWAYMEN, THIEVERY.**)

P

483. **PACIFICATION**
Pain (See **SUFFERING.**)
484. **PARADISE** (See also **HEAVEN, UTOPIA.**)
485. **PARADOX**
486. **PASSION OF CHRIST** (See also **CHRIST.**)
487. **PASSION, SENSUAL**
488. **PASSWORD**
489. **PASTORALISM**
490. **PATIENCE** (See also **LONGSUFFERING.**)
491. **PATRICIDE**
492. **PATRIOTISM** (See also **CHAUVINISM, LOYALTY.**)
493. **PATRONAGE** (See also **PHILANTHROPY.**)
494. **PEACE**
495. **PEACEMAKING** (See also **ANTIMILITARISM.**)
496. **PEDANTRY**
497. **PENITENCE**
498. **PERFECTION**
499. **PERJURY** (See also **DECEIT.**)
500. **PERMANENCE**
501. **PERSECUTION**
502. **PERSEVERANCE** (See also **DETERMINATION.**)
503. **PERVERSION** (See also **BESTIALITY.**)
504. **PESSIMISM** (See also **CYNICISM, SKEPTICISM.**)
505. **PHILANTHROPY** (See also **GENEROSITY, PATRONAGE.**)
506. **PHILISTINISM**
507. **PHILOSOPHY**
508. **PIANO**
Piety (See **RIGHTEOUSNESS.**)
509. **PIRACY**
Pitilessness (See **HEARTLESSNESS, RUTHLESSNESS.**)
Plague (See **DISEASE.**)
510. **POETRY** (See also **INSPIRATION.**)
511. **POISON**
512. **POISONING**
Politeness (See **COURTESY.**)
Politeness, Excessive (See **COURTESY, EXCESSIVE.**)
513. **POLITICS**
514. **POLYGAMY**
515. **POMPOSITY**
516. **POSSESSION** (See also **ENCHANTMENT.**)
517. **POVERTY**
518. **POWER**
519. **PRECOCIOUSNESS**
520. **PREDICAMENT**
521. **PRETENSION** (See also **HYPOCRISY.**)
Prey (See **QUARRY.**)
Pride (See **BOASTFULNESS, EGOTISM, VANITY.**)
522. **PRIZE**
Prodigality (See **DISSIPATION.**)
523. **PROFLIGACY** (See also **DEBAUCHERY, LUST, PROMISCUITY.**)
524. **PROLIFICNESS**
525. **PROMISCUITY** (See also **PROFLIGACY.**)
526. **PROPAGANDA**
527. **PROPHECY** (See also **OMEN.**)
Prosperity (See **SUCCESS.**)
528. **PROSTITUTION** (See also **COURTESANSHIP, MISTRESSES.**)
529. **PROTECTION** (See also **CHARMS.**)
530. **PROTECTIVENESS** (See also **GUARDIANSHIP.**)
531. **PRUDENCE**
532. **PRUDERY**

T

635. **TEMPTATION**
Terror (See **HORROR.**)
636. **TERRORISM**
637. **TEST**
638. **THEATER**
639. **THIEVERY** (See also **GANGSTERISM, HIGHWAYMEN, OUTLAWRY.**)
640. **THINNESS**
641. **THIRST**
642. **THUNDER** (See also **LIGHTNING.**)
643. **TIME**
Timelessness (See **AGELESSNESS, IMMORTALITY.**)
644. **TIME TRAVEL**
645. **TIMIDITY** (See also **COWARDICE.**)
646. **TORTURE**
647. **TOTALITARIANISM**
648. **TOUGHNESS**
649. **TOURING**
650. **TRANSFORMATION**
651. **TRANSVESTISM**
652. **TREACHERY** (See also **TREASON.**)
653. **TREASON** (See also **TREACHERY.**)
654. **TREASURE**
655. **TREES**
656. **TRIAL**
657. **TRICKERY** (See also **CUNNING, DECEIT, HUMBUGGERY.**)
658. **TRINITY**
659. **TRUMPET**
Truth (See **HONESTY.**)
660. **TURNING POINT**
661. **TWINS** (See also **DOUBLES.**)
662. **TYRANNY**

U

663. **UBIQUITY** (See also **OMNIPRESENCE.**)
664. **UGLINESS**
665. **UNATTAINABILITY** (See also **IMPOSSIBILITY.**)
666. **UNDERWORLD** (See also **HELL.**)
Unfaithfulness (See **FAITHLESSNESS.**)
Ungratefulness (See **INGRATITUDE.**)
Unkindness (See **CRUELTY, INHOSPITALITY.**)
667. **UNSCRUPULOUSNESS** (See also **TRICKERY.**)
668. **UNSELFISHNESS** (See also **DEDICATION.**)
669. **UNSOPHISTICATION** (See also **NAÏVETÉ.**)
Unworldliness (See **ASCETICISM.**)
Uselessness (See **FUTILITY.**)
670. **USURPATION**
671. **USURY**
672. **UTOPIA** (See also **HEAVEN, PARADISE, WONDERLAND.**)

V

Valor (See **BRAVERY.**)
673. **VANITY** (See also **CONCEIT, EGOTISM.**)
674. **VENGEANCE**
675. **VERBOSITY**
676. **VERSATILITY**
677. **VICTORY**
678. **VILLAINY** (See also **EVIL, WICKEDNESS.**)
Vindictiveness (See **VENGEANCE.**)
Violence (See **BRUTALITY, CRUELTY.**)
679. **VIOLIN**
680. **VIRGINITY** (See also **CHASTITY, PURITY.**)
681. **VIRILITY** (See also **BEAUTY, MASCULINE; BRAWNINESS.**)

Allusions

A

1. **ABANDONMENT** (See also **ORPHAN.**)

1. **Ariadne** deserted by her lover Theseus at Naxos. [Gk. Myth.: Benét 48]
2. **Auburn** agricultural village which loses inhabitants with onslaught of industry. [Br. Lit.: "The Deserted Village" in *Traveller*]
3. **Cio-Cio-San** deserted by family for renouncing her religion. [Ital. Opera: Puccini, *Madama Butterfly,* Westerman, 357]
4. **Hauser, Caspar** foundling, in solitary confinement till sixteen, then thrown into the world, claimed as a royal scion, and assassinated. [Ger. Lit.: Wassermann *Caspar Hauser* in Benét, 446]
5. **Helmer, Nora** deserts family to find "whole woman" identity. [Nor. Lit.: *A Doll's House*]
6. **Henchard-Newson, Susan** Michael Henchard's deserted wife. [Br. Lit.: *The Mayor of Casterbridge,* Magill I, 571–573]
7. **Mary Celeste** brigantine found drifting with no hands aboard. [Br. Folklore: Leach, 683]
8. **Meeber, Carrie** deserted by her first lover, she deserts her second. [Am. Lit.: *Sister Carrie* in Magill I, 895]
9. ***Patna*** ship, carrying Moslem pilgrims, abandoned by captain and crew in a storm. [Br. Lit.: Joseph Conrad *Lord Jim*]
10. **Perdita** abandoned as an infant by the king, her father, secretly raised by a shepherd. [Br. Drama: Shakespeare *The Winter's Tale*]
11. **Philoctetes** Greek hero abandoned for ten years by his comrades because of the smell of his wound. [Gk. Drama: Sophocles *Philoctetes* in Benét, 783]
12. **Santuzza** deserted by Turiddu after yielding to his advances. [Ital. Opera: Mascagni, *Cavalleria Rusticana,* Westerman, 3387 339]
13. **Smike** boy deserted and forgotten at Dotheboys Hall. [Br. Lit.: *Nicholas Nickleby*]
14. **Snow White** deserted in forest; found by seven dwarfs. [Ger. Fairy Tale: Grimm, 184]
15. **Tatiana** gives her love to Onegin, who scorns it and leaves her. [Russ. Lit.: *Eugene Onegin*]

16. **Thursday, Margaret** left on church doorstep as baby. [Children's Lit.: *Margaret Thursday,* Fisher, 199–200]

2. ABDUCTION

1. **Balfour, David** expecting inheritance, kidnapped by uncle. [Br. Lit.: *Kidnapped*]
2. **Bertram, Henry** kidnapped at age five; taken from Scotland. [Br. Lit.: *Guy Mannering*]
3. **Bonnard, Sylvestre** to save an orphan girl from cruel treatment, removes her from school by trickery and becomes her guardian. [Fr. Lit.: France *The Crime of Sylvestre Bonnard* in Magill II, 196]
4. **Cephalus** carried off in lusting Aurora's chariot. [Rom. Myth.: Hall, 36]
5. **Conway, Hugh** kidnapped to the lamasery called Shangri-la. [Br. Lit.: *Lost Horizon*]
6. **Europa** maiden carried off to Crete by Zeus in the form of a white bull. [Gk. Myth.: Benét, 327]
7. **Gilda** abducted by Duke of Mantua's courtiers. [Ital. Opera: Verdi, *Rigoletto,* Westerman, 299–300]
8. **Helen** carried off by Paris, thus precipitating Trojan war. [Gk. Lit.: *Iliad,* Hall, 147]
9. **Hylas** boy beloved by Heracles is carried off by the nymphs after he draws water from their fountain. [Gk. Myth.: Brewer *Dictionary*, 476]
10. **Lyudmilla** princess carried off on her wedding night by the wizard Chernomor. [Russ. Poetry: *Ruslan and Lyudmilla* in Haydn & Fuller, 653]
11. ***Prisoner of Zenda, The*** King of Ruritania is held captive in castle of Zenda. [Br. Lit.: *The Prisoner of Zenda*]
12. **Proserpina** (Gk. **Persephone**) whisked away by lustful Pluto in chariot. [Rom. Lit.: *Metamorphoses; Fasti;* Art: Hall, 260]
13. **Raid of Ruthven** James VI kidnapped for ten months by Protestant nobles (1582–1583). [Scot. Hist.: Grun, 258]
14. **Resurrection Men** 1800s "body snatchers"; supplied cadavers for dissection. [Br. Hist.: Brewer *Note-Book,* 756]
15. **Sabine Women** menfolk absent, Romans carry off women for wives. [Rom. Hist.: Brewer *Dictionary,* 948; Flem. Art: Rubens, "Rape of the Sabine Women"]
16. **virgins of Jabesh-gilead** abducted by Israelites while dancing at Shiloh. [O.T.: Judges 21:12–24]

3. ABUNDANCE (See also FERTILITY.)

1. **Amalthea's horn** horn of Zeus's nurse-goat which became a cornucopia. [Gk. Myth.: Walsh *Classical,* 19]
2. **cornucopia** conical receptacle which symbolizes abundance. [Rom. Myth.: Kravitz, 65]
3. **Copia** goddess of abundance. [Rom. Myth.: Kravitz, 65]
4. **Cubbins, Bartholomew** head sports abundant supply of hats. [Children's Lit.: *The Five Hundred Hats of Bartholomew Cubbins*]
5. **Dagon (Dāgan)** fish-corn god symbolizing fertility and abundance. [Babyl. Myth.: Parrinder, 72; Jobes, 410]
6. **Daikoku** god has inexhaustible sack of useful articles. [Jap. Myth.: *LLEI,* I: 325]
7. **Dhisana** Vedic goddess of abundance. [Hinduism: Jobes, 439]
8. **Doritis** epithet of Aphrodite, meaning "bountiful." [Gk. Myth.: Zimmerman, 25]
9. **Goshen** Egyptian fertile land; salvation for Jacob's family. [O.T.: Genesis 46:28]
10. **land of milk and honey** land of fertility and abundance. [O.T.: Exodus 3:8, 33:3; Jeremiah 11:5]
11. **Thanksgiving Day** American holiday celebrating abundant harvest; originally observed by Pilgrims (1621). [Am. Culture: *NCE,* 2726]
12. **wheat ears, garland of** symbol of agricultural abundance and peace. [Western Folklore: Jobes, 374]

4. ACTING

1. **Berma** great actress, whom the narrator sees in her prime and in her decline. [Fr. Lit.: Proust *Remembrance of Things Past*, in Benét, 99]
2. **Meeber, Carrie** small-town girl finds work on chorus line and matures into a successful actress. [Am. Lit.: *Sister Carrie* in Magill I, 895]
3. **Players, the** acting troupe employed by Hamlet. [Br. Drama: Shakespeare *Hamlet*]
4. **Thespis** first individual Greek performer; whence *thespian.* [Gk. Drama: Espy, 46]
5. **Trelawny, Rose** young actress sees married life as dull and returns to the stage. [Br. Drama: Arthur Wing Pinero *Trelawny of the "Wells"* in Benét, 1022]
6. **Vitus, St.** patron saint of actors. [Christian Hagiog.: Brewster, 291]

7. **Woffington, Peg** married and unmarried men admire her stage talents and fall in love with her. [Br. Lit.: *Peg Woffington* in Magill I, 724]

5. ADOLESCENCE

1. ***Seventeen*** novel of young love. [Am. Lit.: Booth Tarkington *Seventeen* in Magill I, 882]

6. ADULTERY (See also CUCKOLDRY, FAITHLESSNESS.)

1. **Alcmena** unknowingly commits adultery when Jupiter impersonates her husband. [Rom. Lit.: *Amphitryon*]
2. **Alison** betrays old husband amusingly with her lodger, Nicholas. [Br. Lit.: *Canterbury Tales,* "Miller's Tale"]
3. **Andermatt, Christiane** eventually has child by lover, not husband. [Fr. Lit.: *Mont-Oriol,* Magill I, 618–620]
4. **Bathsheba** pressured by David to commit adultery during husband's absence. [O.T.: II Samuel 11:4]
5. **Bloom, Molly** sensual wife of Leopold has an affair with Blazes Boylan. [Irish Lit.: Joyce *Ulysses* in Magill I, 1040]
6. **Bovary, Emma** acquires lovers to find rapture marriage lacks. [Fr. Lit.: *Madame Bovary,* Magill I, 539–541]
7. **Brant, Capt. Adam** fatefully falls for general's wife. [Am. Lit.: *Mourning Becomes Electra*]
8. **Buchanan, Tom** even with Daisy's knowledge, deliberately has affairs. [Am. Lit.: *The Great Gatsby*]
9. **Chatterley, Connie** takes the gameskeeper of her impotent husband as her lover. [Br. Lit.: D. H. Lawrence *Lady Chatterley's Lover* in Benét, 559]
10. **Clytemnestra** takes Aegisthus as paramour. [Gk. Lit.: *Orestes*]
11. ***Couples*** group of ten husbands sleep with each others' wives. [Am. Lit.: Weiss, 108]
12. **Cunizza** amours with Sordello while married to first husband. [Br. Lit.: *Sordello*]
13. **currant** symbol of infidelity. [Flower Symbolism: Jobes, 398]
14. **de Lamare, Julien** Jeanne's young philandering husband, who has affairs with her foster-sister and their neighbor's wife. [Fr. Lit.: Maupassant *A Woman's Life* in Magill I, 1127]
15. **Dimmesdale, Rev. Arthur** Puritan minister who commits adultery. [Am. Lit.: Hawthorne *The Scarlet Letter*]
16. **Guinevere** King Arthur's unfaithful wife. [Br. Lit.: *Le Morte d'Arthur*]
17. **Herzog** insatiable husband plays the field. [Am. Lit.: *Herzog*]

18. **Julia, Donna** Alfonso's wife; gives herself to Don Juan. [Br. Lit.: "Don Juan" in Magill I, 217–219]
19. **Karenina, Anna** commits adultery with Count Vronsky; scandalizes Russian society. [Russ. Lit.: *Anna Karenina*]
20. **Lancelot** enters into an adulterous relationship with Guinevere. [Br. Lit.: Malory *Le Mort d'Arthur*]
21. **Mannon, Christine** conspires with lover to poison husband; discovered, commits suicide. [Am. Lit.: *Mourning Becomes Electra*]
22. **Moechus** personification of adultery. [Br. Lit.: *The Purple Island,* Brewer *Handbook,* 715]
23. **Pozdnishef, Madame** bored with husband, acquires Trukhashevsky as lover. [Russ. Lit.: *The Kreutzer Sonata,* Magill I, 481–483]
24. **Prynne, Hester** adulterous woman in Puritan New England; condemned to wear a scarlet letter. [Am. Lit.: *The Scarlet Letter*]
25. **scarlet letter** "A" for "adultery" sewn on Hester Prynne's dress. [Am. Lit.: *The Scarlet Letter*]
26. **Tonio** after Nedda's repulsion, tells husband of her infidelities. [Ital. Opera: Leoncavallo, *Pagliacci,* Westerman, 341–342]
27. **Wicked Bible** misprint gives Commandment: "Thou shalt commit adultery." [*sic*] [Br. Hist.: Brewer *Dictionary,* 108]

7. ADVENTUROUSNESS (See also JOURNEY, QUEST, WANDERING.)

1. **Adverse, Anthony** leads adventurous and romantic life in Italy, France, and America in the Napoleonic era. [Am. Lit.: Haydn & Fuller, 36]
2. **Baggins, Bilbo** hobbit-protagonist; has escapades with dwarfs. [Br. Lit.: *The Hobbit*]
3. **Blas, Gil** picaresque victimizer and victim who encounters all the social classes of 18th-century Spain. [Fr. Lit.: *Gil Blas*; Benét, 395]
4. **Bond, James** secret agent 007, whose exploits feature futuristic technology. [Br. Lit.: Herman, 27]
5. **Boob McNutt** schlemiel has wild adventures among fabulous beasts on tropical isles. [Comics: Horn, 125]
6. **Bunny, Benjamin** Peter Rabbit's thrill-seeking cousin. [Children's Lit.: *The Tale of Benjamin Bunny*]
7. **Clarke, Micah** helps in Monmouth's unsuccessful attempt to wrest the throne from King James. [Br. Lit.: Doyle *Micah Clarke* in Magill I, 585]

8. **Crusoe, Robinson** experiences adventures among pirates, cannibals, and slavers. [Br. Lit.: Defoe *Robinson Crusoe*]
9. **Deadwood Dick** hero of Wild West dime novels. [Am. Folklore: Walsh *Modern*, 115]
10. **Eulenspiegel, Till** wanders the Low Countries, living by his wits and avenging the evil deeds of King Philip. [Belg. Lit.: Benét, 325]
11. **Fabio** 19th-century young runaway becomes gaucho; Argentinian Huckleberry Finn. [Arg. Lit.: *Don Segundo Sombra*]
12. **Fabrizio del Dongo** partisan of Napoleon, involved in love, intrigue, a duel, and ends up as a Carthusian monk. [Fr. Lit.: Stendhal *The Charterhouse of Parma* in Magill I, 135]
13. **Finn, Huckleberry** 19th-century picaresque teenager travels down the Mississippi on a raft. [Am. Lit.: *Huckleberry Finn*]
14. **Flanders, Moll** amoral adventuress of many liasons. [Br. Lit.: Defoe *Moll Flanders* in Benét, 678]
15. **Fogg, Phileas** gentleman undertakes world trip on wager. [Fr. Lit.: *Around the World in Eighty Days]*
16. **Gilliatt** battles storms, disaster, and a giant octopus in order to salvage a ship's engine and win a bride. [Fr. Lit.: *Toilers of the Sea* in Magill II, 1037]
17. **Gordon, Flash** constantly launches into apparently hopeless adventures to combat evil powers. [Comics: Berger, 133]
18. **Gulliver, Lemuel** 17th-century hero travels to fanciful lands on extraordinary voyages. [Br. Lit.: *Gulliver's Travels*]
19. **Hajji Baba** shrewd rascal travels around Persia. [Fr. Lit.: *Hajji Baba of Ispahan* in Magill I, 343]
20. **Hannay, Richard** traced and hounded by enemies of England, has several narrow escapes. [Br. Lit. and Cinema: Buchan *The 39 Steps* in Magill I, 972]
21. **Hawkins, Jim** cabin boy on pirate ship. [Br. Lit.: *Treasure Island*]
22. **Hornblower, Horatio** gallant warship captain in Napoleonic era. [Br. Lit.: *Captain Horatio Hornblower*]
23. **Huon of Bordeaux** as penance for killing a prince, submits to perilous journey to the East. [Ger. Lit.: Benét, 487; Ger. Opera: *Oberon*]
24. **Jason** leader of Argonauts in successful quest for the Golden Fleece. [Gk. Legend: Brewer *Dictionary*, 500]

25. ***Kidnapped*** caught in the intrigues of Scottish factions, David Balfour and Alan Breck are shipwrecked, escape from the king's soldiers, and undergo great dangers. [Br. Lit.: R. L. Stevenson *Kidnapped*]
26. **Kim** orphan wanders streets of India with lama. [Br. Lit.: *Kim*]
27. ***Kon-Tiki*** tale of raft trip taken to prove sea-borne migration of peoples and culture. [Pacific Hist.: *Kon-Tiki*]
28. **Krull, Felix** has adventures in Germany, France, and Portugal under a succession of names and professions. [Ger. Lit.: Mann *The Confessions of Felix Krull* in Magill III, 218]
29. **Lawrence of Arabia** T. E. Lawrence (1888–1935), legendary hero, led Arab revolt against Turkey. [Br. Hist.: Benét, 572]
30. ***Lazarillo de Tormes*** 16th-century picaresque novel about a runaway youth who lives by his wits serving, in succession, a blind beggar and several unworthy ecclesiastics. [Span. Lit.: Haydn & Fuller, 415]
31. **Lismahago, Lieutenant Obadiah** 19th-century sportsman with quixotic tales. [Br. Lit.: *Humphry Clinker*, Magill I, 394–397]
32. **Münchhausen, Baron** picaresque traveler and teller of tall tales. [Ger. Lit.: *Baron Münchhausen*]
33. **Mowgli** infant lost in the Indian forest is brought up by a wolf pack. [Children's Lit.: Kipling *The Jungle Books* in Magill I, 461]
34. ***Nautilus*** submarine in which its builder, Captain Nemo, cruises around the world. [Fr. Lit.: Jules Verne *Twenty Thousand Leagues Under the Sea*]
35. **Nemo, Captain** travels throughout the world in the *Nautilus*, a submarine of his own invention. [Fr. Lit.: Jules Verne *Twenty Thousand Leagues under the Sea*]
36. **Odysseus (Ulysses)** varied adventures after the Trojan War kept him away from Ithaca for ten years. [Gk. Myth.: *Odyssey*]
37. **Pickle, Peregrine** young rogue experiences escapades in England and on the Continent. [Br. Lit.: *Peregrine Pickle* in Magill I, 731-4]
38. **Polo, Marco** 13th-century Venetian merchant; brought Oriental wonders to Europe. [Eur. Hist.: Bishop, 222–224]
39. **Pym, Arthur Gordon** journeys include mutiny, shipwreck, savages, and the supernatural. [Am. Lit.: Poe, "The Narrative of Arthur Gordon Pym" in Magill I, 640–643]
40. **Quatermain, Allan** undertakes a dangerous African expedition in search of a lost diamond mine. [Br. Lit.: H. Rider Haggard *King Solomon's Mines* in Magill I, 475]

41. **Random, Roderick** exiled for killing in a duel, goes to sea, endures shipwreck and battles, and discovers his wealthy father. [Br. Lit.: *Roderick Random*, Haydn & Fuller, 644]
42. **Ruslan** undergoes many adventures to regain his abducted bride. [Russ. Poetry: *Ruslan and Lyudmilla* in Haydn & Fuller, 653]
43. **Sawyer, Tom** classic 19th-century adventuresome, all-American boy. [Am. Lit.: *Tom Sawyer*]
44. ***Simplicissimus*** from callowness to audacity on 17th-century battlefields. [Ger. Lit.: *Simplicissimus*]
45. **Sindbad the Sailor** has scores of adventures in the course of seven voyages. [Arab. Lit.: *Arabian Nights*]
46. **Tartarin** 19th-century French Quixote acts out his dreams of travel. [Fr. Lit.: *Tartarin de Tarascon*]
47. **Tarzan** jungle man leads adventurous life. [Am. Lit.: *Tarzan of the Apes*]
48. ***Time Machine, The*** inventor travels into future; sees degeneration of life. [Br. Lit.: *The Time Machine*]
49. ***Tom Jones*** picaresque novel of a young man in 18th-century England. [Br. Lit.: Haydn & Fuller, 745]

Adversity (See FAILURE.)

Advice (See COUNSEL.)

Affectation (See PRETENSION.)

Affliction (See SUFFERING.)

8. AGE, OLD

1. **Alberich** 500 years old, but still child-sized. [Ger. Legend: Walsh *Classical*, 13]
2. **Chuffey** old clerk. [Br. Lit.: *Martin Chuzzlewit*]
3. **Cumaean sibyl** was granted long life by Apollo; when she rejected his love, he withheld eternal youth and she withered away. [Gk. Myth.: *Metamorphoses*, 14]
4. **Darby and Joan** happily settled elderly couple. [Br. Ballad: Brewer *Dictionary*, 300]
5. **Elli** personification of Old Age, he out-wrestled Thor. [Norse Myth.: Edith Hamilton *Mythology*]
6. **Ezekiel** portrayed with flowing white beard. [Art: Hall, 118]
7. **Father Time** personification of the old year. [Folklore: Misc.]
8. **Geritol** leading brand of tonic for geriatric health. [Trademarks: Crowley *Trade*, 230]

9. **Matlock, Lucinda** vigorous old woman dies at 96, scorning the degeneracy around her. [Am. Poetry: Masters *Spoon River Anthology*]
10. **Methuselah** oldest man mentioned in Bible. [O.T.: Genesis 5:27]
11. **Parr, Thomas** husbandman; lived through reigns of ten sovereigns. [Br. Hist.: Brewer *Dictionary*, 805]
12. **Philemon and Baucis** fabled aged couple. [Rom. Lit.: *Metamorphoses*]
13. **Prufrock, J. Alfred** "I grow old, I grow old." [Br. Lit.: "The Love Song of J. Alfred Prufrock" in Hart, 497]
14. **Rabbi Ben Ezra** Browning's poem about old age. [Br. Poetry: Benét, 836]
15. **Storks' Law** obliged children to maintain their needy parents in old age. [Rom. Hist.: Brewer *Dictionary*, 862]
16. ***Superannuated Man, The*** Charles Lamb's essay on his growing infirmities and subsequent retirement. [Br. Lit.: Lamb, Charles in Benét, 563]
17. **Tithonus** granted immortality but not eternal youth; continually got older. [Gk. Myth.: Kravitz]

9. AGELESSNESS (See also IMMORTALITY.)

1. **Endymion** man kept immortally youthful through eternal sleep. [Gk. Myth.: Howe, 91; Br. Lit.: "Endymion" in Harvey, 271]
2. **Gray, Dorian** artist Basil Hallward's "ideal of youth" remains young as his portrait ages. [Br. Lit.: *The Picture of Dorian Gray*, Magill I, 746–748]
3. **Grecian urn** lovers depicted on it will be forever young. [Br. Poetry: Keats "Ode on a Grecian Urn"]
4. **Little Orphan Annie** teenage heroine who has not aged since strip started (1938). [Comics: "Little Orphan Annie" in Horn, 459]

Aggressiveness (See CONQUEST.)

10. AID, GOVERNMENTAL (See also GENEROSITY.)

1. **Berlin Airlift** free world's circumvention of Soviet blockade (1948–1949). [Eur. Hist.: Van Doren, 519]
2. **G.I. Bill** WWII U.S. veterans' educational subsidy by government. [Am. Hist.: Van Doren, 499]
3. **Lend-Lease Act** provision of American materiel to beleaguered Allies in WWII. [Am. Hist.: Van Doren, 480]

4. **Marshall Plan** U.S.-led project to rebuild post-WWII Europe. [Eur. Hist.: Van Doren, 515]
5. **Medicare** U.S. program of health insurance for the aged. [Am. Hist.: *EB,* VI: 747]
6. **New Frontier** President John F. Kennedy's legislative program, encompassing such areas as civil rights, the economy, and foreign relations. [Am. Hist.: *WB,* K:212]
7. **Peace Corps** U.S. agency devoted to assisting underdeveloped nations. [Am. Hist.: Van Doren, 575–576]
8. **Social Security Act** U.S. legislation providing for old-age benefits financed by payroll taxes; later expanded to include more extensive coverage. [Am. Hist.: *EB,* IX: 314]
9. **VISTA** (Volunteers in Service to America), government agency which fights poverty in the U.S. [Am. Hist.: *WB,* 1: 27]
10. **WPA (1935–43)** provided work for unemployed construction and theater workers, artists, writers, and youth. [U.S. Hist.: *NCE,* 3006]

11. AID, ORGANIZATIONAL (See also GENEROSITY.)

1. **Boy Scouts** organization of boys dedicated to community service and character building. [Am. and Br. Hist.: *NCE,* 350]
2. **CARE** agency devoted to channeling relief to needy people abroad. [Am. Hist.: *NCE,* 456]
3. **Girl Scouts** recreational and service organization for girls. [Am. and Br. Hist.: *NCE,* 1089]
4. **National Guard** military reserve units frequently help in civil disturbances and natural disasters. [Am. Hist.: *NCE,* 1885]
5. **Red Cross** international philanthropic organization devoted to the alleviation of human suffering. [World Hist.: *NCE,* 2288]
6. **Salvation Army** nonsectarian Christian organization for philanthropic and evangelical work. [World Hist.: *NCE,* 2408–2409]
7. **UNRRA (1943–49)** supplied funds and personnel to areas freed from the Axis. [Eur. Hist.: *NCE,* 2832]

Aimlessness (See WANDERING.)

12. AIR

1. **Aeolus** god of the winds. [Gk. Myth.: Zimmerman, 9]
2. **Aether** god of whole atmosphere. [Gk. Myth.: Jobes, 42]
3. **Aurae** winged nymphs of breezes. [Rom. Myth.: *LLEI,* I: 323]
4. **Juno** in allegories of elements, personification of air. [Art: Hall, 128]

5. **sylph** spirit inhabiting atmosphere in Rosicrucian philosophy. [Medieval Hist.: Brewer *Dictionary,* 1055]

Alarm (See WARNING.)

13. ALCOHOLISM (See also DRUNKENNESS.)

1. **Alcoholics Anonymous (AA)** society of ex-alcoholics who help alcoholics to stop drinking. [Am. Hist.: Flexner, 356]
2. **Bowery, the** area in New York City known for its destitute and drunken population. [Am. Culture: Misc.]
3. **Brick** dipsomaniac; drinks until he feels a "click." [Am. Lit.: *Cat on a Hot Tin Roof*]
4. **Emery, Stan** drinking as only means to adjust to world. [Am. Lit.: *The Manhattan Transfer*]
5. **English, Julian** aristocratic drunkard mistreats his beloved wife, quarrels with everyone, and kills himself after a drunken bout. [Am. Lit.: *Appointment in Samarra*]
6. **Flyte, Sebastian** drinks to escape from his family, most of whom he detests. [Br. Lit.: Evelyn Waugh *Brideshead Revisited* in Magill I, 83]
7. ***Iceman Cometh, The*** portrayal of Harry Hope's rundown saloon which harbors alcoholics. [Am. Lit.: *The Iceman Cometh*]
8. **L'Assommoir** study of the demoralizing effects of alcohol. [Fr. Lit.: *L'Assommoir*]
9. ***Lost Weekend, The*** study of Don Birnam, an unsuccessful writer who drinks too much. [Am. Lit.: *The Lost Weekend,* Magill I, 531–532]
10. **Prohibition** resurgence of American puritanism (1920–1933). [Am. Hist.: Allen, 14–15]
11. **skid row** a run-down area frequented by alcoholics. [Am. Culture: Misc.]

Allurement (See TEMPTATION.)

14. ALOOFNESS

1. **Bartleby** refuses to associate with others or even to mingle with other employees. [Am. Lit.: Melville *Bartleby the Scrivener*]
2. **Chapin, Joseph** successful attorney blinded by his emotional coldness and his need for propriety and respectability. [Am. Lit.: John O'Hara *Ten North Frederick* in Benét, 732]
3. **de Coverly, Major** so aloof that nobody dares to ask him his first name. [Am. Lit.: *Catch-22*]

4. **Gatsby, Jay** enigmatic and aloof from intimacy; addressed others as "old sport." [Am. Lit.: *The Great Gatsby*]
5. **Hatteras, Captain** paranoid sea captain remains incognito for half a voyage. [Fr. Lit.: *Captain Hatteras*]
6. **Havisham, Miss** eccentric lady who resents men; maintains a detached attitude toward Pip. [Br. Lit.: *Great Expectations*]
7. **Miriam** mysteriously reluctant to reveal her past. [Am. Lit.: *The Marble Faun*]
8. **Morgan, Captain** officious officer; will not talk with enlisted men. [Am. Lit.: *Mister Roberts,* Magill I, 605–607]
9. **Trot, Dame** "not troubled with other folks' strife." [Nurs. Rhyme: *Mother Goose,* 13]
10. **Winterbourne** distant from even his own feelings about Daisy. [Am. Lit.: *Daisy Miller*]

15. AMBIGUITY

1. **Delphic oracle** ultimate authority in ancient Greece; often speaks in ambiguous terms. [Gk. Hist.: Leach, 305]
2. **Iseult's vow** pledge to husband has double meaning. [Arth. Legend: *Tristan*]
3. **Loxias** epithet of Apollo, meaning "ambiguous" in reference to his practically uninterpretable oracles. [Gk. Myth.: Zimmerman, 26]
4. **Pooh-Bah** different opinion for every one of his offices. [Br. Opera: *The Mikado,* Magill I, 591–592]

16. AMBITION

1. **Alger, Horatio** author of a series of rags-to-riches stories. [Am. Lit.: *Ragged Dick*]
2. **Bart, Lily** sacrifices her principles and her chance for love in schemes to climb the social ladder. [Am. Lit.: *The House of Mirth* in Hart, 385]
3. **Chardon, Lucien (de Rubempré)** young writer determined to achieve fame and wealth. [Fr. Lit.: Balzac *Lost Illusions* in Magill II, 595]
4. **Claudius** murders to gain throne; plots to keep it. [Br. Lit.: *Hamlet*]
5. **Constance** ambitious for her son Arthur. [Br. Lit.: *King John*]
6. **Faustus, Doctor** makes a pact with the devil to further his own ambitions. [Br. Lit.: *The Tragical History of Doctor Faustus*]
7. ***Golden Boy*** talented young violinist gives up musical career for the sake of wealth and fame as a boxer. [Am. Lit.: Odets *Golden Boy* in Magill III, 422]

8. **hollyhock** traditional symbol of ambition. [Flower Symbolism: *Flora Symbolica,* 174]
9. **John, King** aspiring, self-assertive king of mediocre character. [Br. Lit.: *King John*]
10. **Macbeth** aspires to political power. [Br. Lit.: *Macbeth*]
11. **Macbeth, Lady** stops at nothing to gain political power for husband. [Br. Lit.: *Macbeth*]
12. **mountain laurel** traditional symbol of ambition. [Flower Symbolism: *Flora Symbolica,* 175]
13. **Ragged Dick** hero of a Horatio Alger rags-to-riches story. [Am. Lit.: *Ragged Dick*]
14. **Roxana** sleeps with the rich to get ahead in world. [Br. Lit.: *Roxana, The Fortunate Mistress*]
15. **Sejanus** chief minister of Emperor Tiberius uses seduction, conspiracy, and poisoning to gain the throne. [Br. Drama: Benét, 912]
16. **Slope, Rev. Obadiah** vainly strives to advance himself in objectionable ways. [Br. Lit.: Trollope *Barchester Towers* in Magill I, 55]
17. **Sutpen, Thomas** from poor origins, tries to gain aristocratic status. [Am. Lit.: Faulkner *Absalom, Absalom* in Magill I, 5]
18. **Tamburlaine** Scythian bandit becomes king of Persia and ruler of Turkey and Babylon. [Br. Drama: *Tamburlaine the Great* in Magill I, 950]
19. ***What Makes Sammy Run*** a dynamic but vicious opportunist attains success. [Am. Lit.: *What Makes Sammy Run*]

17. AMERICA

1. **apple pie** typical, wholesome American dessert. [Am. Culture: Flexner, 68]
2. **bald eagle** national bird of the U.S.; native only to North America. [Am. Culture: *EB,* I: 753]
3. **baseball** traditional American sport and pastime. [Am. Sports: *EB,* I: 850]
4. **Brother Jonathan** the original Uncle Sam. [Am. Hist.: Hart, 110]
5. **Crossing of the Delaware** Washington's beleaguered army attacks Trenton; famous event in American history (1776). [Am. Hist.: Jameson, 138]
6. **e pluribus unum** motto of the U.S.: Latin 'one out of many.' [Am. Culture: *RHD,* 481]

7. **Fourth of July** Independence Day; traditional U.S. holiday; anniversary of adoption of Declaration of Independence (July 4, 1776). [Am. Culture: *EB,* V: 326]
8. **Liberty Bell** symbol of American freedom; at Independence Hall, Philadelphia. [Am. Hist.: Jameson, 284]
9. **Mayflower** ship that brought the founding Puritans. [Am. Hist.: Jameson, 313]
10. **melting pot** America as the home of many races and cultures. [Am. Pop. Culture: Misc.]
11. ***Old Ironsides*** the frigate *Constitution*, symbol of U.S. success in War of 1812, now preserved as a museum. [Am. Hist.: Benét, 733]
12. **Peoria** typical mid-American town. [Am. Culture: Misc.]
13. **Pledge of Allegiance** statement of loyalty to the U. S., inaugurated in 1892 upon 400th anniversary of the discovery of America. [Am. Hist.: *WB,* P: 508]
14. **Plymouth Rock** site of Pilgrim landing in Massachusetts (1620). [Am. Hist.: Jameson, 395–396]
15. **pumpkin pie** traditional dish, especially at Thanksgiving. [Am. Culture: Flexner, 68]
16. **Red, White, and Blue** the colors of the U. S. flag, used in reference to the flag itself and ideals of patriotism. [Am. Hist.: Misc.]
17. **Silent Majority** average Americans of middle class. [Am. Culture: Flexner, 375]
18. **Star-Spangled Banner, The** U.S. national anthem. [Am. Hist.: *EB,* IX: 532]
19. **Stars and Stripes** nickname for the U.S. flag. [Am. Hist.: Brewer *Dictionary*, 8567]
20. **Statue of Liberty** great symbolic structure in New York harbor. [Am. Hist.: Jameson, 284]
21. **Thanksgiving** annual U.S. holiday celebrating harvest and yearly blessings; originated with Pilgrims (1621). [Am. Culture: *EB,* IX: 922]
22. **Uncle Sam** personifies people or government of the United States. [Am. Hist.: Hart, 870–871]
23. **Vespucci, Amerigo** (1454–1512) Italian navigator-explorer from whose name *America* is derived. [Am. Hist.: *EB,* X: 410]
24. **Washington, D.C.** focus of U.S. government, policies, etc. [Am. Hist.: Hart, 899]

25. **Washington, George** (1732–1799) "the Father of our country"; first U.S. President (1789–1797). [Am. Hist.: Jameson, 535–536]
26. **White House** official residence of the president of the U.S. in Washington, D.C. [Am. Culture: *EB*, X: 656]
27. **Yankee** to an American, a New Englander; to a Southern American, any Northerner; to a foreigner, any American. [Am. Hist.: Hart, 953]

18. ANDROGYNY

1. **Hermaphroditus** half-man, half-woman; offspring of Hermes and Aphrodite. [Gk. Myth.: Hall, 153]
2. **Iphis** Cretan maiden reared as boy because father ordered all daughters killed. [Gk. Myth.: Howe, 143]
3. **Tiresias** prophet who lived as man and a woman. [Gk. Myth.: Zimmerman, 255–256]

19. ANGEL

1. **Abaddon** angel in charge of Sheol's bottomless pit. [N.T.: Revelation 9:11; 20:1–3]
2. **Abdiel** faithful seraph who withstood Satan when urged to revolt. [Br. Lit.: *Paradise Lost*]
3. **Arcade** acquires knowledge of science, loses faith in God, and conspires to take over Heaven for Satan. [Fr. Lit.: *The Revolt of the Angels* in Magill I, 821]
4. **Azrael** watches over the dying and takes the soul; will himself be the last to die. [Islamic Myth.: Brewer *Dictionary*, 60]
5. **cherubim** four-winged, four-faced angels inspired Ezekiel to carry God's message to the people. [O.T.: Ezek. 1:15]
6. **Gabriel** angel of the annunciation; tells Mary she will bear Christ child. [N.T.: Luke 1:26–38]
7. **guardian angel** believed to protect a particular person. [Folklore: Misc.]
8. **Jordan, Mr.** heavenly messenger has to find a new body for a boxer who died before his earthly time was up. [Am. Drama and Cinema: *Here Comes Mr. Jordan*]
9. **Lucifer** archangel; Satan's name before his fall from Heaven. [Christian Hagiog.: *Collier's*, XII, 143]
10. **Michael** leader of angels against Satan. [N.T.: Revelation 12:7–9; Br. Lit.: *Paradise Lost*]
11. **Raphael** God's healer and helper in Book of Tobit. [Apocrypha: Tobit]

12. **seraphim** six-winged angels of the highest order, distinguished by their zeal and love. [O.T.: Isaiah 6:2; Benét, 915]
13. **Uriel** sent by God to instruct prophet Esdras. [Apocrypha: II Esdras 4]
14. **Zadkiel** angel of the planet Jupiter. [Jew. Myth.: Brewer *Handbook*, 1237]

20. ANGER (See also EXASPERATION, IRASCIBILITY, RANTING.)

1. **Allecto** one of the three Furies, vengeful deities who punish evil-doers. [Gk. Myth.: Zimmerman, 274]
2. **Almeira** scorned woman like whom “hell hath no fury.” [Br. Drama: *The Mourning Bride*]
3. **Belinda** furious over loss of lock of hair. [Br. Lit.: *Rape of the Lock*]
4. **Bernardo** enraged that member of a rival street-gang is making advances to his sister. [Am. Musical: *West Side Story*]
5. **Brunhild** furiously vengeful concerning Kriemhild’s accusations of promiscuity. [Ger. Lit.: *Nibelungenlied*]
6. **Erinyes (the Furies)** angry and avenging deities who pursue evil-doers. [Gk. Myth.: Leach, 347]
7. **Fudd, Elmer** hapless man seethes over Bugs Bunny’s antics. [Comics: “Bugs Bunny” in Horn, 140]
8. **Hera** (Rom. **Juno**) angry at Zeus’s illicit sexual pleasure. [Gk. Myth.: Leach, 563]
9. **Herod** angry at wise men’s disobedience, orders slaughter of male infants. [N.T.: Matthew 2:16–17]
10. **Hulk, the** character whose anger transforms him into monster. [Comics: Horn, 324–325]
11. **Megaera** one of the three Furies, vengeful deities who punish evil-doers. [Gk. Myth.: Zimmerman, 274]
12. **Nemesis** goddess of vengeance. [Gk. Myth.: Zimmerman, 173]
13. **Oronte** takes offense at Alceste’s criticism of sonnet. [Fr. Lit.: *The Misanthrope*]
14. **Othello** smothers wife, Desdemona, in paroxysm of rage over her suspected adultery. [Br. Lit.: *Othello*]
15. **Rumpelstiltskin** stamps ground in rage over lass’s discovery of his name. [Ger. Fairy Tale: *Rumpelstiltskin*]
16. **Tisiphone** one of the three Furies, vengeful deities who punish evil-doers. [Gk. Myth.: Zimmerman, 274]
17. **Volumnia** “in anger, Junolike.” [Br. Lit.: *Coriolanus*]
18. **whin** indicates fury. [Flower Symbolism: *Flora Symbolica*, 178]

21. ANNUNCIATION

1. **dove and lily** pictured with Virgin and Gabriel. [Christian Iconography: Brewer *Dictionary,* 645]
2. **Elizabeth** Mary's old cousin; bears John the Baptist. [N.T.: Luke 1:36–80]
3. **Gabriel** messenger angel; tells Mary she will bear Christ child. [N.T.: Luke 1:26–38]
4. **Hail, Mary** prayer adapted from the words of Gabriel to Mary announcing the coming birth of Christ. [N.T.: Luke 1:26–36]

22. ANTI-HEROISM

1. **Bloom, Leopold** his ineffectual wandering about Dublin is contrasted with Ulysses' epic adventures. [Irish Lit.: James Joyce *Ulysses* in Magill I, 1040]
2. **Bluntschli, Capt.** Swiss officer prefers eating chocolates and making love to fighting. [Br. Drama: Shaw *Arms and the Man* in Benét, 51]
3. **Brown, Charlie** bumbling boy with low self-esteem. [Comics: "Peanuts" in Horn, 542–543]
4. **Cooke, Ebenezer** his every move denies all things heroic. [Am. Lit.: *The Sot-Weed Factor*]
5. **Hoover, Dwayne** materially successful car dealer whose only friend is his dog. [Am. Lit.: *Breakfast of Champions]*
6. **Meursault** the 20th-century indifferent man to whom things happen because he allows them to. [Fr. Lit.: Camus *The Stranger* in Weiss, 445]
7. **Rosewater, Eliot** unemployed heir who spends day buying drinks for volunteer firemen. [Am. Lit.: *God Bless You, Mr. Rosewater*]
8. **Spade, Sam** semi-literate, tough-talking private eye; lacks culture. [Am. Lit.: *The Maltese Falcon*]

23. ANTIMILITARISM (See also PEACE, PEACEMAKING.)

1. ***All Quiet on the Western Front*** unromanticized novel of WWI and its unsung heroes. [Ger. Lit.: *All Quiet on the Western Front*]
2. **Arjuna** called upon by duty to be a warrior, he refuses to join the fratricidal battle. [Hindu Lit.: *The Bhagavad-Gita* in Benét, 103]
3. ***Arms and the Man*** satirizes romantic view of war. [Br. Lit.: *Arms and the Man*]
4. ***Farewell to Arms, A*** novel of lovers who flee from war's horrors. [Am. Lit.: *A Farewell to Arms*]

5. **Quakers** known for service to peace. [Am. Hist.: *EB*, 7: 743–745]
6. **Sherston, George** refuses to continue taking part in a war being wrongfully prolonged. [Br. Lit.: *Memoirs of an Infantry Officer* in Magill I, 579]
7. **Undershaft, Barbara** fights her father's involvement in munitions manufacture. [Br. Drama: Shaw *Major Barbara* in Magill III, 617]

24. ANTIQUARIANS

1. **Clutterbuck, Cuthbert** retired captain, devoted to study of antiquities. [Br. Lit.: *The Monastery*]
2. **Oldbuck, Jonathan** learned and garrulous antiquary. [Br. Lit.: *The Antiquary*]
3. **Teufelsdroeckh, Herr** eccentric German philosopher and professor. [Br. Lit.: *Sartor Resartus;* Brewer *Handbook*, 1088]

25. ANTI-SEMITISM (See also BIGOTRY, GENOCIDE.)

1. **Agobard** (799–840) Lyonnais archbishop, father of medieval anti-Jewish racism. [Fr. Hist.: Wigoder, 15]
2. **Anti-Defamation League** B'nai B'rith organization which fights anti-Semitism. [Am. Hist.: Wigoder, 33]
3. **Armleder** medieval bands; ravaged Alsatian Jewish communities. [Ger. Hist.: Wigoder, 41]
4. **Ashkenazi, Simcha and Jacob** discover the tenuousness of their position when anti-Semitism spreads in Poland. [Yiddish Lit.: *Brothers Ashkenazi*]
5. **Babi Yar** Russian site of WWII German massacre of the Jews. [Russ. Hist.: Wigoder, 56]
6. **Bernheim Petition** 1933 petition exposed Nazi treatment of Jews. [Jew. Hist.: Wigoder, 83]
7. **Black Death pogroms** plague blamed on Jews who were later murdered. [Jew. Hist.: Bishop, 382]
8. **Black Hundreds** early 20th-century armed squads ravaged Jews. [Russ. Hist.: Wigoder, 92]
9. **blood libel** trials of Jews who allegedly murdered non-Jews for Passover blood. [Jew. Hist.: Wigoder, 95]
10. **Bok, Yakov** victim of Russian anti-Semitism; falsely accused of murder. [Am. Lit.: *The Fixer*]
11. **Final Solution** Nazi plan to exterminate Jewish race. [Ger. Hist.: *Hitler*, 1037–1061]

12. **Frank, Anne** (1929–1945) young Dutch girl found and killed by Nazis after years in hiding. [Dutch Lit.: *Diary of Anne Frank*]
13. ***Gentleman's Agreement*** indictment of anti-Semiticism. [Am. Lit.: *Gentleman's Agreement*]
14. **Haman** convinces king to issue decree for Jewish extermination. [O.T.: Esther 3:1–11]
15. **Hep Hep riots** Jewish pogroms Germany (1819). [Ger. Hist.: Wigoder, 251]
16. **Hitler, Adolf** (1889–1945) Nazi dictator of Germany; eclipsed all predecessors' hatred for Jews. [World Hist.: *Hitler*]
17. ***Jacobowsky and the Colonel*** anti-Semitic Polish colonel refuses to recognize his rescuer because he is Jewish. [Ger. Lit.: *Jacobowsky and the Colonel*]
18. **Kishinev** Moldavian city; scene of pogroms and WWII genocide. [Jew. Hist.: Wigoder, 344]
19. **Kristallnacht** destruction of Jews' property anticipated later atrocities (November 9–10, 1938). [Ger. Hist.: *Hitler,* 689–694]
20. ***Mein Kampf*** Adolf Hitler's autobiography, including his theories on treatment of the Jews. [Ger. Hist.: *Mein Kampf*]
21. **Nuremberg Laws** stripped Jews of citizenship and civil rights (1935). [Ger. Hist.: Wigoder, 458]
22. ***Protocols of the Elders of Zion*** forged tract revealing Jewish conspiracy to control world. [Jew. Hist.: Wigoder, 170]
23. **swastika** symbol of German anti-Semitism since 1918; became emblem of Nazi party. [Ger. Hist.: *Collier's,* XVIII, 78]
24. **Torquemada, Tomás de** (1420–1498) head of Spanish Inquisition; instrumental in expelling Jews from Spain (1492). [Span. Hist.: Wigoder, 600]
25. **Untermenschen** subhumans; Nazi conception of Jews and Slavs. [Ger. Hist.: Shirer, 1223]
26. **Volkischer Beobachter** Nazi party organ featuring Jew-baiting articles. [Ger. Hist.: Shirer, 75–78]

26. ANTISLAVERY

1. **Abolitionists** activist group working to free slaves. [Am. Hist.: Jameson, 1]
2. **Emancipation Proclamation** edict issued by Abraham Lincoln freeing the slaves (1863). [Am. Hist.: *EB,* III: 869]
3. **Free Soil Party** Abolitionist political party before Civil War. [Am. Hist.: Flexner, 3]

4. **Jayhawkers** antislavery guerrillas fighting on Union side in Civil War. [Am. Hist.: Jameson, 256]
5. **Laus Deo!** poem written to celebrate emancipation of slaves. [Am. Lit.: "Laus Deo!" in Hart, 460]
6. ***Liberator*** William Lloyd Garrison's virulently Abolitionist newspaper. [Am. Hist.: Van Doren, 142]
7. **Lincoln, Abraham** (1809–1865) sixteenth U.S. president; issued Emancipation Proclamation, freeing the slaves. [Am. Hist.: Jameson, 286–287]
8. ***North Star*** newspaper supporting emancipation founded by Frederick Douglass. [Am. Hist.: Hart, 607]
9. **Shelby, George** vows to devote self to freeing slaves. [Am. Lit.: *Uncle Tom's Cabin*]
10. **Stowe, Harriet Beecher** (1811–1896) author of *Uncle Tom's Cabin*, influential Abolitionist novel. [Am. Hist.: Jameson, 481]
11. ***Uncle Tom's Cabin*** highly effective, sentimental Abolitionist novel. [Am. Lit.: Jameson, 513]
12. **Underground Railroad** system which helped slaves to escape to the North. [Am. Hist.: *EB*, X: 255]

27. APHRODISIACS

1. **cestus** Aphrodite's girdle made by Hephaestus; magically induces passion. [Gk. Myth.: Benét, 183]
2. **ginseng** induces passion. [Plant Symbolism: *EB*, IV: 549]
3. **lupin** leguminous plant; arouses passion. [Plant Folklore: Boland, 9]
4. **mandrake** a narcotic that arouses passion. [Western Folklore: Boland, 13]
5. **marjoram** used on bedsheets; Venus used it with Ascanius. [Rom. Myth.: Boland, 11–12]
6. **periwinkle, worms, and houseleek** combination induces passion. [Plant Folklore: Boland, 9]
7. **raw oysters** food consumed as a love potion. [Popular Folklore: Misc.]
8. **Spanish fly** preparation made of green blister beetles and used to incite cattle to mate. [Insect Symbolism: *EB*, IX: 399]
9. **willow seeds** taken in water, produce only sons. [Western Folklore: Boland, 11]

28. APOCALYPSE

1. **behemoth** king of animals whose flesh will provide feast for chosen when Messiah comes. [Jew. Tradition: Leach, 132]

2. **Four Horsemen of the Apocalypse** four riders symbolizing pestilence, war, famine, and death. [N.T.: Revelation 6:1–8]
3. **Gog and Magog** giant leaders in ultimate battle against God's people. [N.T.: Revelation 20:8]
4. **Götterdämmerung** day of great battle between Teutonic gods and forces of evil. [Ger. Folklore: Leach, 461]
5. **leviathan** sea monster; symbol of apocalypse. [Jew. Tradition: Leach, 67]
6. **Revelation** final book of the New Testament discussing the coming of the world's end. [N.T.: Revelation]

29. APOSTASY (See also SACRILEGE.)

1. **Aholah and Aholibah** symbolize Samaria's and Jerusalem's abandonment to idols. [O.T.: Ezekiel 23:4]
2. **Albigenses** heretical sect; advocated Manichaean dualism. [Fr. Hist.: *NCE,* 53]
3. **Arians** 4th-century heretical sect; denied Christ's divinity. [Christian Hist.: Brewer *Note-Book,* 43]
4. **Big-endians** heretical group; always break eggs unlawfully at large end. [Br. Lit.: *Gulliver's Travels*]
5. **Cathari** heretical Christian sect in 12th and 13th centuries; professed a neo-Manichaean dualism. [Christian Hist.: *EB,* II: 639]
6. **Donatists** Christian group in North Africa who broke with Catholicism (312). [Christian Hist.: *EB,* III: 618]
7. **Ebionites** 2nd- and 3rd-century Christian ascetic sect that retained a Jewish emphasis. [Christian Hist.: *EB,* III: 768]
8. **Erastianism** doctrine declaring state is superior to the church in ecclesiastical affairs (1524–1543). [Christian Hist.: *EB,* III: 937]
9. **Fires of Smithfield** Marian martyrs burnt at stake as heretics. [Br. Hist.: Brewer *Dictionary,* 1013]
10. **Gnosticism** heretical theological movement in Greco-Roman world of 2nd century. [Christian Hist.: *EB,* IV: 587]
11. **Inquisition** Roman Catholic tribunal engaged in combating and suppressing heresy. [Christian Hist.: *NCE,* 1352]
12. **Jansenism** unorthodox Roman Catholic movement of the 17th and 18th centuries led by Cornelius Jansen. [Christian Hist.: *EB,* V: 515]
13. **Julian the Apostate (331–363)** Roman emperor, educated as a Christian but renounced Christianity when he became emperor. [Rom. Hist.: Benét, 533]

14. **Lollards** in late medieval England, a name given to followers of unorthodox philosopher John Wycliffe. [Christian Hist.: *EB,* VI: 306]
15. **min** appellation of any heretic, Jew or non-Jew. [Judaism: Wigoder, 417]
16. **Monophysites** heretical Christian sect who questioned the divine and human nature of Jesus. [Christian Hist.: *EB,* VI: 1003]
17. **Montanism** 2nd-century heretical Christian movement led by prophet Montanus. [Christian Hist.: *EB,* VI: 1012]
18. **Sabellianism** 3rd-century Christian heresy led by Sabellius. [Christian Hist.: *EB,* VIII: 747]

30. APPEARANCES, DECEIVING (See also ILLUSION.)

1. **Baldwin, George** "good" lawyer having affair with client's wife. [Am. Lit.: *The Manhattan Transfer*]
2. **Clinker, Humphry** admirable character concealed by shabby exterior. [Br. Lit.: *Humphry Clinker*]
3. **Cory, Richard** man "with everything" commits suicide. [Am. Lit.: "Richard Cory" in Hart, 711]
4. **daffodil** beautiful, but narcotic. [Plant Symbolism: *Flora Symbolica,* 168]
5. **Gray, Dorian** his portrait becomes the record of his life. [Br. Lit.: *The Picture of Dorian Gray*]
6. **Little Buttercup** apparently dumpy woman , once "young and charming." [Br. Opera: *H.M.S. Pinafore*]
7. **Phaedra** pretends unkindness to Hippolytus to hide her passion for him. [Fr. Drama: *Phaedra,* Magill I, 741–742]
8. **Sawyer, Tom** hoodwinks friends into white-washing fence by pretending chore is a reward, not a punishment. [Am. Lit.: *Tom Sawyer*]
9. **Tchitchikoff** swindler-adventurer, outwardly a philanthropist. [Russ. Lit.: *Dead Souls*]
10. **Valancourt** his gambling not a vice but attempt to secure money to aid friends. [Br. Lit.: *The Mysteries of Udolpho,* Magill I, 635–638]
11. **Venus's-flytrap** lures insects with sweet odor. [Flower Symbolism: *Flora Symbolica,* 178]

31. APPLE

1. **Adam and Eve** original couple tempted to eat forbidden fruit. [O.T.: Genesis 2:17]

2. **Apple Annie** nickname for women who sold apples on street corners during the Depression. [Am. Culture: Flexner, 11]
3. **Appleseed, Johnny** (John Chapman, 1774–1845), missionary nurseryman who supplied apple seeds to pioneers. [Am. Folklore: *EB,* II: 746]
4. **Big Apple** nickname for New York City. [Am. Folklore: Misc.]
5. **forbidden fruit** fruit that God forbade Adam and Eve to eat; byword for tempting object. [O.T.: Genesis 3:1–6]
6. **golden apples of the Hesperides** a wedding gift to Hera; Hercules stole some in the course of his labors. [Gk. Myth.: Brewer *Dictionary,* 451]
7. **golden apples** given by Venus to Hippomenes to distract Atalanta and win his race with her. [Class. Myth.: *Metamorphoses*]
8. **Newton, Isaac** (1642–1727) English mathematician whose observation of apple's fall led to treatise on gravitation. [Br. Hist.: *EB,* 13: 16–21]
9. **Tell, William** Swiss folk hero condemned to shoot apple from atop son's head. [Swiss Folklore: *EB,* IX: 872]

32. ARCHITECTS

1. **Daedalus** mythical Greek architect said to have built the labyrinth for King Minos of Crete. [Gk. Myth.: *EB,* III: 342]
2. **Roecus** architect of the early temple of Hera at Samos. [Architecture: *NCE,* 1799]
3. **Thomas, St.** patron saint of architects. [Christian Hagiog.: *Saints and Festivals,* 30]

33. ARGUMENTATIVENESS

1. **Absolute, Sir Anthony** warm-hearted but testy; always blames others. [Br. Drama.: *The Rivals*]
2. **Caterpillar** peevishly disputes with Alice. [Br. Lit.: *Alice's Adventures in Wonderland*]
3. **Lessways, Hilda** husband Edwin could never agree with her. [Br. Lit.: *The Clayhanger Trilogy*]
4. **Naggleton, Mr. and Mrs.** contentious and fault finding couple. [Br. Lit.: *Punch,* 1864–1865; Brewer *Handbook,* 742]

34. ARISTOCRACY

1. **Almanach de Gotha** German social register. [Ger. Lit.: Benét, 26]
2. **Beaucaire, Monsieur** portrays English aristocracy as shallow, inept snobs. [Am. Lit.: *Monsieur Beaucaire,* Magill I, 616–617]

3. **blue blood** said to flow in the veins of the nobility. [Western Cult.: Brewer *Dictionary*]
4. **Brahmin** appellation accorded members of old, "aristocratic" New England families. [Am. Hist.: *EB*, II: 226]
5. ***Cabala, The*** portrays wealthy esoterics, mysteriously influential in governmental affairs. [Am. Lit.: *The Cabala*]
6. **First Families of Virginia** elite families of prestigious rank. [Am. Usage: Misc.]
7. **Four Hundred, the** social elite; the number of people Mrs. Astor could accommodate in her ballroom. [Am. Usage: Misc.]
8. **gold on white** symbol of elite class. [Chinese Art: Jobes, 357]
9. **Junkers** Prussian elite. [Ger. Hist.: *Hitler*, 387]
10. ***Social Register*** book listing names and addresses of social elite. [Am. Usage: Misc.]
11. **St. Aubert, Emily** young French woman of wealth and position. [Br. Lit.: *The Mysteries of Udolpho*, Magill I, 635–638]
12. **Winthrop** English upper-class family; America's parliamentary governors. [Am. Hist.: Hart, 937–938]

35. ARRIVISM (See also PHILISTINISM.)

1. ***Beverly Hillbillies, The*** hillbillies transplanted by wealth to Beverly Hills. [TV: Terrace, I, 93–94]
2. **Gatsby, Jay** nouveau riche entrepreneur displays wealth on Long Island. [Am. Lit.: *The Great Gatsby*]
3. **Jefferson, George** bumptious black who thinks money is everything. [TV: "The Jeffersons" in Terrace, I, 409–410]
4. **Jiggs and Maggie** they flounder in seas of sudden wealth. [Comics: "Bringing up Father" in Horn, 132]
5. **Jourdain, Monsieur** elderly tradesman who spends wealth trying to raise his social status. [Fr. Lit.: *Le Bourgeois Gentilhomme*]
6. **Newman, Christopher** nouveau riche entrepreneur feels he deserves an aristocratic wife. [Am. Lit.: *The American*]

36. ARROGANCE (See also BOASTFULNESS, CONCEIT, EGOTISM.)

1. **amber** traditional symbol of arrogance. [Gem Symbolism: Jobes, 81]
2. **Arachne** presumptuously challenges Athena to weaving contest; transformed into spider. [Gk. Myth.: Leach, 69]
3. **Catherine de Bourgh, Lady** arrogant, vulgar woman. [Br. Lit.: *Pride and Prejudice*]

4. **Citizen Kane** rich and powerful man drives away friends by use of power. [Am. Cinema: Halliwell, 149]
5. **Coriolanus** class-conscious and contemptuous leader. [Br. Lit.: *Coriolanus*]
6. **Darcy, Fitz William** proud of superior station. [Br. Lit.: *Pride and Prejudice*]
7. **Duck, Donald** overbearing comic strip character with a chip on his shoulder. [Comics: Horn, 216–217]
8. **Dundreary, Lord** his aristocratic haughtiness a trademark. [Br. Lit.: *Our American Cousin*]
9. **Ferrara, Duke of** has had his wife murdered for too little appreciation of her place. [Br. Poetry: Browning *My Last Duchess* in Magill IV, 247]
10. **Humpty Dumpty** arbitrarily gives his own meanings to words, and tolerates no objections. [Br. Lit.: Lewis Carroll *Through the Looking-Glass*]
11. **Lucifer** rebel archangel who challenged God's supremacy. [Christian Hagiog.: *Collier's*, XII, 143]
12. **Lucy** know-it-all cartoon character gives advice to other children. [Comics: "Peanuts" in Horn, 543]
13. **Niobe** for boasting of superiority, her children are killed. [Gk. Myth.: Hall, 224; Rom. Lit.: *Metamorphoses*]
14. **rue** traditional symbol of arrogance. [Flower Symbolism: *Flora Symbolica,* 177]
15. **tall sunflower** indicates haughtiness. [Flower Symbolism: *Flora Symbolica,* 177]
16. **Uzziah** king of Judah assumed priests' function of burning incense; punished with leprosy. [O.T.: II Chronicles 26:16-19]
17. **veni, vidi, vici** Caesar's dispatch describing his subjugation of Pharnaces (47 B.C.). [Rom. Hist.: Brewer *Note-Book,* 923]
18. **Volumnia** magisterial mother of Coriolanus; molds his character. [Br. Lit.: *Coriolanus*]
19. **yellow carnation** traditional symbol of arrogance. [Flower Symbolism: Jobes, 291]
20. **yellow sultan** traditional symbol of arrogant contempt. [Flower Symbolism: *Flora Symbolica,* 177]

Artfulness (See CUNNING.)

37. ARTISTIC SKILL

1. **Myron** Greek sculptor (5th century B.C.) of Discobolus and other works acclaimed for extraordinary lifelikeness. [Gk. Art: *NCE,* 1870]

2. **Phidias** Greek sculptor (468–432 B.C.), epitome of classical art. [Gk. Art: Benét]
3. **Pygmalion** carved so beautiful and lifelike a statue that he fell in love with it. [Gk. Myth.: Benét]
4. **Zeuxis** Greek artist (420–390 B.C.) so skilled that birds reputedly flew to his painting of a bunch of grapes. [Gk. Art: *EB* (1963)]

Artlessness (See INNOCENCE, NAÏVETÉ.)

38. ASCENSION

1. **Assumption of Virgin Mary** belief that Mary was assumed bodily into heaven. [Christian Tradition: *NCE,* 1709]
2. **crescent moon** Mary often depicted standing on or above moon. [Christian Iconog.: Brewer *Dictionary,* 726]
3. **Elijah** transported to heaven in fiery chariot. [O.T.: II Kings 2:11]
4. **Helen of Troy** soars away into the air from the cave in which Menelaus left her. [Gk. Drama: Euripides *Helen*]
5. **Jesus Christ** 40 days after Resurrection, ascended into heaven. [N.T.: Acts 1:1–11]
6. **Marguerite** borne to heaven by angels. [Fr. Opera: *Faust,* Westerman, 183–185]
7. **mi'raj** Muhammad's night journey to paradise. [Islam: Leach, 731]
8. **Romulus** taken to the heavens by Mars in a fiery chariot. [Rom. Myth: Brewer *Dictionary,* 775]
9. **stars, garland of** emblem associated with the Assumption of the Virgin Mary. [Christian Iconog.: Jobes, 374]

39. ASCETICISM (See also AUSTERITY, DISCIPLINE.)

1. **Albigenses** heretical and ascetic Christian sect in France in 12th and 13th centuries. [Christian Hist.: *EB,* I: 201]
2. **Alexis, St.** patron saint of beggars and hermits. [Christian Hagiog.: Brewer *Dictionary,* 22]
3. **Anthony, St.** founder of monasticism. [Christian Hagiog.: Attwater, 49]
4. **Béguines** 12th-century French mendicant order. [Fr. Hist.: Espy, 98–99]
5. **Cathari** heretical and ascetic Christian sect in Europe in 12th and 13th centuries. [Christian Hist.: *EB,* II: 639]
6. **Cistercians** Roman Catholic monastic order observing strict asceticism, founded in 1098. [Christian Hist.: *EB,* II: 948]

7. **Clare, St.** founder of mendicant Order of Poor Clares. [Christian Hagiog.: Hall, 69]
8. **Crazy Ivar** lived in hole on side of river bed. [Am. Lit.: *O Pioneers!*, Magill I, 663–665]
9. **Diogenes** (412–323 B.C.) despised worldly possessions; made his home in a tub. [Gk. Hist.: Hall, 104]
10. **Fakirs** fanatical mendicant sects found primarily in India. [Asian Hist.: Brewer *Note-Book*, 310]
11. **Franciscans** 13th-century religious order whose members lived in poverty. [Christian Hist.: *EB*, IV: 273]
12. **Gandhi, Mohandas K.** (1869–1948) Indian spiritual leader; embodied Hindu abstemiousness. [Indian Hist.: *NCE*, 1042]
13. **Jerome, St.** Christian monastic leader who searched for peace as hermit in desert. [Christian Hist.: *EB*, V: 545]
14. **Manichaean Sabbath** Manichaean observance of Sunday, demanding abstinence from food and sex. [Christian Hist.: *EB*, VIII: 746]
15. **Paul of Thebes, St.** first Christian hermit; cave-dweller most of life. [Christian Hagiog.: Attwater, 268]
16. **Priscillianism** rigorously ascetic Christian sect found in Europe until the 6th century. [Christian Hist.: *EB*, VIII: 219]
17. **Stoicism** philosophical school in Greco-Roman antiquity advocating rationality and austerity. [Gk. Hist.: *EB*, VIII: 746]
18. **Stylites, St. Simeon** Christian monk whose philosophy was so ascetic that he dwelt atop a column to meditate. [Christian Hist.: *EB*, IX: 216]
19. **Timon of Athens** lost wealth, lived frugally; became misanthropic when deserted by friends. [Br. Lit.: *Timon of Athens*]
20. **Trappist monks** order with austere lifestyle. [Rom. Cath. Hist.: *NCE*, 2779]
21. **Waldenses** members of 12th-century French religious movement living in poverty. [Christian Hist.: *EB*, X: 519]
22. **Xenocrates** temperate philosopher, noted for contempt of wealth. [Gk. Hist.: Brewer *Dictionary*, 1169]

40. ASS

1. **Balaam's ass** ass which rebukes Balaam who then blesses the Israelites. [O.T.: Numbers 22:22–35]
2. **Bottom, Nick** oaf upon whom Puck fixes ass's head. [Br. Lit.: *Midsummer Night's Dream*]
3. **Dapple** Sancho's ass. [Span. Lit.: *Don Quixote*]

4. **Democratic Party** donkey; symbol of Democratic Party in U.S. politics. [Am. Culture: Misc.]
5. **Golden Ass, The** Lucius, transformed into donkey, observes foibles of mankind. [Rom. Lit.: Benét, 44]
6. **Midas** for judging Pan winner of flute contest, his ears are changed to ass's ears. [Gk. Myth.: Leach, 83]
7. **Pinocchio and Lampwick** naughtiness causes them to sprout donkey's ears and tails. [Ital. Lit.: *Pinocchio*]

41. ASSASSINATION (See also MURDER.)

1. **assassins** Fanatical Moslem sect that smoked hashish and murdered Crusaders (11th–12th centuries). [Islamic Hist.: Brewer *Note-Book*, 52]
2. **Brutus** conspirator and assassin of Julius Caesar. [Br. Lit.: *Julius Caesar*]
3. **Caesar, Julius** (102–44 B.C.) murdered by conspirators. [Br. Lit.: *Julius Caesar*]
4. **Gorboduc** king killed by the people, who were horrified at his murderous family. [Br. Legend and Lit.: Benét, 410]
5. **Harmodius** assassinated Hipparchus, brother of the tyrant Hippias. [Gk. Hist.: *EB* (1963) XI, 198]
6. **Ides of March** Caesar killed by opposing factions (44 B.C.). [Rom. Hist.: *EB*, 3: 575–580]

42. ASTROLOGY (See also ZODIAC.)

1. **Chaldea** ancient Mesopotamian land where study of astrology developed. [Ancient Hist.: *NCE*, 499]
2. **Ecclitico** manipulator and false astrologer; dupes Buonafede. [Ger. Opera: Haydn, *The World of the Moon*, Westermark, 68–69]
3. **Mannering, Guy** cast fateful horoscope for young Bertram. [Br. Lit.: *Guy Mannering*]
4. **Nostradamus** (1503–1566) French astrologer/seer; wrote *Centuries* (1555), famous book of prognostications. [Fr. Hist.: *NCE*, 1969]
5. **Urania** muse of astrology. [Gk. Myth.: Brewer *Dictionary*, 1119]

43. ASTRONAUTICS

1. **Flash Gordon** space-traveling hero. [Am. Comics and Cin.: Halliwell]

2. ***From the Earth to the Moon*** Verne tale of a group who have a monster gun cast to shoot them to the moon. [Fr. Lit.: *WB* 13:650]
3. **Kennedy Space Center (Cape Canaveral)** U.S. launch site for manned space missions. [U.S. Hist.: *WB*, So:562]
4. **Pfaal, Hans** to escape his creditors, constructs a balloon and travels to the moon. [Am. Lit.: *The Unparalleled Adventures of One Hans Pfaal* in Poe]
5. **Ransom, Dr. Elwin** kidnapped and taken to Malacandra (Mars), he escapes with the help of its wise inhabitants. [Br. Lit.: C. S. Lewis *Out of the Silent Planet* in Weiss, 437]
6. **Rogers, Buck** early spaceman in fantasy comics. [Comics: Horn, 137–138]
7. **space shuttle** U.S. spacecraft capable of reuse, making travel more practical. [U.S. Hist.: *WB*, So:561]

44. ASTRONOMY

1. **Aristarchus of Samos** (fl. c. 270 B.C.) Greek astronomer; first to maintain that Earth rotates and revolves around Sun. [Gk. Hist.: *EB*, I: 514]
2. **Copernicus, Nicholas** (1453–1543) Polish astronomer; author of the Copernican theory that planets orbit the sun. [Polish Hist.: *NCE*, 652]
3. **Galileo** (1564–1642) Italian mathematician, astronomer, and physicist. [Ital. Hist.: *EB*, IV: 388]
4. **Halley, Edmond** (1656–1742) British mathematician and astronomer; calculated orbit of comet named after him. [Br. Hist.: *EB*, IV: 860]
5. **Hipparchus** (fl. 146–127 B.C.) astronomer who calculated the year and discovered the precession of the equinoxes. [Turkish Hist.: *EB*, V: 55]
6. **Ptolemy** (85–165) eminent Greek astronomer. [Gk. Hist.: Hall, 255]
7. **Urania** muse of astronomy. [Gk. Myth.: Jobes, 374]

45. ATHLETICISM

1. **Leander** swims the mile-wide Hellespont every night to court Hero. [Gk. Myth.: Hamilton, 432]
2. **marathon** modern races, more than 26 miles, commemorate feat of Pheidippides. [World Sports: Benét, 633]
3. **Pheidippides** ran over 20 miles to Athens to announce victory at Marathon in 490 B.C., then died of exhaustion. [Gk. Legend: *Collier's*, XIII, 369]

46. ATONEMENT

1. **Murgatroyd, Sir Despard** atones for each of his daily crimes by performing a good deed every afternoon. [Br. Opera: Gilbert and Sullivan *Ruddigore*]

47. AUSTERITY (See also ASCETICISM, DISCIPLINE.)

1. **Amish** conservative Christian group in North America noted for its simple, orderly life and nonconformist dress. [Am. Hist.: *EB,* I: 316]
2. **Borromeo, Charles** archbishop; lived thriftily; gave money to poor. [Ital. Hist.: Hall, 65]
3. **Cato, Marcus Porcius** (234–149 B.C.) Roman statesman known for conservatism; taxed luxuries. [Rom. Hist.: *EB,* II: 645]
4. **Clennam, Mrs.** ascetic woman; wears only black. [Br. Lit.: *Little Dorrit*]
5. **common thistle** indicates starkness. [Flower Symbolism: *Flora Symbolica,* 178]
6. **Dotheboys Hall** Mr. Squeers's school: no extras, no vacations. [Br. Lit.: *Nicholas Nickleby*]
7. **Puritanism** 16th- and 17th-century religious reform movement noted for its moral earnestness and austerity. [Br. and Am. Hist.: *EB,* VIII: 309]
8. **Shakers** celibate religious sect flourishing in 19th-century U.S. [Am. Hist.: *EB,* IX: 105]
9. **Spartans** residents of Greek city known for its stern dedication to militarism. [Gk. Hist.: *EB,* IX: 403]

48. AUTHORITY

1. **cathedra** throne indicative of religious power. [Folklore: Jobes, 307]
2. **crook** staff carried as a symbol of office and authority. [Western Culture: Misc.]
3. **crosier** bishop's staff signifying his ruling power. [Christian Symbolism: Appleton, 21]
4. **cross and ball** signifies that spiritual power is above temporal. [Heraldry: Jobes, 387]
5. **crown** headpiece worn as symbol of royal authority. [Western Culture: Misc.]
6. **double bar cross** signifies archbishops, cardinals, and patriarchs. [Christian Iconog.: Jobes, 386]
7. **eagle** attribute of Zeus, thus of authority. [Art: Hall, 109]
8. **fasces** rods bundled about ax; emblem of magistrates, Fascists. [Rom. Hist.: Hall, 119; Ital. Hist.: Brewer *Dictionary,* 399]

9. **gavel** small mallet used by judge or presiding officer to signal order. [Western Culture: Misc.]
10. **globe** in Christ child's hands signifies power and dominion. [Christian Symbolism: de Bles, 25]
11. **Hoyle** authoritative rules for playing cards and other games. [Misc.: Barnhart, 590]
12. **keys** symbolic of St. Peter's spiritual authority. [Christian Symbolism: N.T.: Matthew 16:19]
13. **Lord's Anointed, the** Jewish or other king by divine right. [Judaism: O.T.: I Samuel 26:9]
14. **mace** ceremonial staff carried as a symbol of office and authority. [Western Culture: Misc.]
15. **miter** bishop's headdress signifying his authority. [Christian Symbolism: *EB VI*]
16. **nimbus** cloud of light signifying might, divinely imparted. [Gk. Lit.: *Iliad*]
17. **Ozymandias** king of ancient Egypt, evoked by Shelley as an example of the perishability of power. [Br. Lit.: Benét, 749]
18. **pectoral cross** worn by prelates on chain around neck. [Christian Iconog.: Child, 255; Jobes, 386]
19. **purple** color worn by persons of high rank. [Western Culture: Misc.]
20. **rod** wand or staff carried as a symbol of office and authority. [Western Culture: Misc.]
21. **scepter** symbol of regal or imperial power and authority. [Western Culture: Misc.]
22. **Stone of Scone** coronation stone where kings of Scotland were crowned. [Br. Hist.: Brewer *Dictionary*, 970]
23. **throne** seat of political or religious authority. [Western Folklore: Jobes, 1567]
24. **triple cross** three upper arms; symbolizes authority of the pope. [Christian Iconog.: Jobes, 386]

49. AUTHORSHIP

1. **Eden, Martin** laborer who becomes a famous writer. [Am. Lit.: *Martin Eden*]

Autobiography (See **BIOGRAPHY and AUTOBIOGRAPHY.**)

50. AUTUMN

1. **Autumnus** personification; portrayed as mature and manly. [Rom. Myth.: *LLEI*, I: 322]
2. **Bacchus** god of this season. [Rom. Myth.: Hall, 130]

3. **Carpo** goddess of autumn and corn season. [Gk. Myth.: Kravitz, 53]
4. **cornucopia** conical receptacle full of the fruits of the harvest. [World Culture: Misc.]
5. **grapes and vine leaves** symbolize harvest of vineyards for wine. [Art: Hall, 130]
6. **Indian summer** a period of mild, dry weather occurring in U.S. and Canada in late autumn. [Am. Culture: Misc.]

51. AVIATION

1. **Kitty Hawk** site of first manned, powered flight (1903). [Am. Hist.: Jameson, 563]
2. **Lafayette Escadrille** American aviators assisting Allies in WWI. [Am. Hist.: Jameson, 273]
3. ***Night Flight*** relates the harrowing experiences of early airmail pilots on South American routes. [Fr. Lit.: Magill III, 687]
4. **Red Baron** nickname given to Baron Richthofen. [Aviation: *EB,* VIII: 574]
5. **Smilin' Jack** comic strip pilot who solves crimes. [Comics: "Smilin' Jack" in Horn, 624–625]
6. **Spirit of St. Louis** Charles Lindbergh's plane. [Am. Hist.: Jameson, 287]
7. **Wright brothers** creators-aviators of first manned aircraft (1903). [Am. Hist.: Jameson, 563]

52. AWKWARDNESS (See also INEPTITUDE.)

1. **Clouseau, Inspector Jacques** bungling detective who inadvertently but always gets his man. [Am. Cinema: "The Pink Panther" in Halliwell, 565–566]
2. **Crane, Ichabod** lanky Yankee schoolmaster who loves Katrina. [Am. Lit.: *The Legend of Sleepy Hollow*]
3. **Dobbin, Captain William** tall, uncouth, awkward fellow with large feet. [Br. Lit.: *Vanity Fair*]
4. **Goofy** bumbling, awkward dog; originally named Dippy Dawg. [Comics: "Mickey Mouse" in Horn, 492]
5. **Gringoire** a penniless, stupid, and oafish poet. [Fr. Lit.: *The Hunchback of Notre Dame*]
6. **Li'l Abner** ungainly comic strip oaf with height of six foot three. [Comics: Horn, 450]
7. **Small, Lennie** simple-minded, clumsy giant; parasite of George. [Am. Lit.: *Of Mice and Men*]
8. **White Knight** falls off his horse every time it stops. [Br. Lit.: Lewis Carroll *Through the Looking-Glass*]

B

53. BACHELORDOM

1. **bachelor's button** celibacy symbol. [Flower Symbolism: Jobes, 171]
2. **Dillon, Matt** bachelor U.S. marshal fights for law and order in Old West. [TV: "Gunsmoke" in Terrace, I, 331–332]
3. **laurel** symbol of unmarried scholar; whence, *baccalaureate.* [Flower Symbolism: Emboden, 25]
4. **Mason, Perry** bachelor lawyer. [TV: Terrace, II, 199]
5. **Morgan, Rex** bachelor doctor stars in comic strip. [Comics: "Rex Morgan, M.D." in Horn, 580–581]
6. ***Odd Couple, The*** pair of bachelors living the good life in New York. [Am. Lit. and TV: Terrace, II, 160–161]
7. **Pumblechook** eminently "available" uncle of Joe Gargery. [Br. Lit.: *Great Expectations*]

Badness (See EVIL.)

54. BALDNESS

1. **Aeschylus** mistaking his bald head for a rock, an eagle dropped a tortoise on it, thus killing him. [Gk. Legend: Brewer *Dictionary*, 13]
2. **Mowgli** (the Frog) name given infant by wolves for hairlessness. [Children's Lit.: *The Jungle Book*]
3. **bald eagle** U.S. national bird whose white head looks bald. [Am. Hist.: *EB,* I: 753]

55. BALLOONING (See also AVIATION.)

1. ***Balloon Hoax, The*** 1844 news story falsely reports that eight men have crossed the Atlantic in a balloon. [Am. Lit.: *The Balloon Hoax* in Poe]
2. **Ferguson, Samuel** embarks with two others on air-borne journey over Africa. [Fr. Lit.: *Five Weeks in a Balloon*]
3. **Wizard of Oz** reaches and departs from Oz in circus balloon. [Children's Lit.: *The Wonderful Wizard of Oz*]

56. BANISHMENT

1. **Acadians** America's lost tribe; suffered expulsion under British. [Am. Hist.: Jameson, 2; Am. Lit.: "Evangeline" in Hart, 263]

2. **Adam and Eve** banished from the Garden of Eden for eating forbidden fruit. [O.T.: Genesis 3:23–24]
3. **anemone** ordered from Flora's court. [Gk. Myth.: *Flora Symbolica,* 172]
4. **Bolingbroke, Henry** banished, along with Mowbray, by King Richard. [Br. Lit.: Shakespeare *Richard II*]
5. **Cain** cast out from homeland for murdering Abel. [O.T.: Genesis 4:12]
6. **Devil's Island** former French penal colony off French Guiana. [Fr. Hist.: *NCE,* 754]
7. **Elba** site of Napoleon's first exile (1814). [Fr. Hist.: *NCE,* 854]
8. **fire and water** Roman symbol of exile. [Rom. Hist.: Brewer *Note-Book,* 451]
9. **Hagar and Ishmael** Sarah orders Abraham to drive them out. [O.T.: Genesis 21:9–13]
10. **Ivanhoe** disinherited by father, Cedric the Saxon. [Br. Lit.: *Ivanhoe*]
11. **Jenik** banished by jealous stepmother. [Czech. Opera: Smetana, *Bartered Bride,* Westerman, 404]
12. **Nolan, Philip** treasonous man sentenced to live remainder of life at sea. [Am. Lit.: *Man Without a Country*]
13. **Oedipus** exiles himself for killing father and marrying mother. [Gk. Lit.: *Oedipus Rex*]
14. **Patmos** island of exile for St. John. [N.T.: Revelation 1:9]
15. **Posthumus** marries Cymbeline's daughter; Cymbeline banishes him. [Br. Lit.: *Cymbeline*]
16. **Pride's Purge** Cromwell's ejection of royalist MPs (1648). [Br. Hist.: Brewer *Handbook,* 871]
17. **Rosalind** her sylvan exile sets scene for comedy. [Br. Lit.: *As You Like It*]
18. **Saint Helena** place of Napoleon's second exile (1815). [Fr. Hist.: *NCE,* 2397]
19. **Siberia** place of banishment and exile. [Geography. *NCE,* 2509–2510]
20. **Trail of Tears** forced march of 18,000 Cherokees westward to Indian Territory (Oklahoma); 4,000 die of disease and exposure (winter, 1838–1839). [Am. Hist.: *EB,* 2: 808]
21. **Tristram** expelled from Cornwall by King Mark for ten years. [Br. Lit.: *Le Morte d'Arthur*]
22. **Untouchables** lowest caste in India; social outcasts. [Ind. Culture: Brewer *Dictionary,* 1118]

57. BANKRUPTCY (See also POVERTY.)

1. **Birotteau, César** ruined by bad speculations and dissipated life. [Fr. Lit.: *Greatness and Decline of César Birotteau,* Walsh *Modern,* 58]
2. **Black Friday** day of financial panic (1869). [Am. Hist.: *RHDC*]
3. **Black Tuesday** day of stock market crash (1929). [Am. Hist.: Allen, 238]
4. **green cap** symbol of bankruptcy. [Eur. Hist.: Brewer *Note-Book,* 390–391]
5. **Harland, Joe** drunk who loses fortune on Wall Street. [Am. Lit.: *The Manhattan Transfer*]
6. **Hassan, Abu** pretends to be dead to avoid debts. [Ger. Opera: von Weber, *Abu Hassan,* Westerman, 138–139]
7. **Henchard, Michael** loses business and social standing through bad financial planning. [Br. Lit.: *Mayor of Casterbridge*]
8. **Lydgate, Tertius** driven deeper into debt on daily basis. [Br. Lit.: *Middlemarch*]
9. **Panic of 1873** bank failures led to extended depression. [Am. Hist.: Van Doren, 267–268]
10. **Queer Street** condition of financial insolvency. [Am. Usage: Misc.]

58. BAPTISM

1. **Aenon** where St. John performed rites. [N.T.: John 3:23]
2. **Cornelius** Roman centurion baptized by Peter. [N.T.: Acts 10, 11]
3. **John the Baptist** prophet who baptized crowds and preached Christ's coming. [N.T.: Matthew 3:1–13]
4. **scallop shell** vessel used for conferral of sacrament. [Christian Symbolism: Appleton, 88]

59. BARRENNESS

1. **Andermatt, Christiane** takes series of baths hoping to cure childlessness. [Fr. Lit.: *Mont-Oriol,* Magill I, 618–620]
2. ***Barren Ground*** novel portraying a woman's emotional sterility and her harsh labor on a farm. [Am. Lit.: *Barren Ground*]
3. **brown** symbol of unfruitfulness. [Color Symbolism: Jobes, 357]
4. **Death Valley** sterile, arid basin in Nevada and California. [Geography: *EB,* III: 417]
5. **Elizabeth** Virgin's kinswoman, blessed with pregnancy as old woman. [N.T.: Luke 1:5–25]

6. **Empty Quarter** vast desert in the Arabian peninsula. [Geography: *EB,* VIII: 703]
7. **Hannah** Elkanah's barren wife; prays to Lord who grants her a son, Samuel. [O.T.: I Samuel 1:6]
8. **Sahara** vast north African desert. [Geography: *EB,* VIII: 768]
9. **Sarah** Abraham's wife; unable to bear children. [O.T.: Genesis 11:30]
10. **Waste Land, The** portrays sterility and chaos of the contemporary world. [Br. Lit.: "The Waste Land" in Hart, 899–900]

Bashfulness (See TIMIDITY.)

60. BATTLE (See also WAR.)

1. **Actium** Octavian's naval defeat of Antony and Cleopatra (31 B.C.). [Rom. Hist.: *NCE,* 15]
2. **Agincourt** longbow helps British defeat French (1415). [Br. Lit.: *Henry V;* Br. Hist.: Harbottle *Battles,* 5]
3. **Alamo** fort at San Antonio that was site of Mexican massacre of Texans (1836). [Am. Hist.: Jameson, 8]
4. **Antietam** indecisive battle of the Civil War (1862). [Am. Hist.: Harbottle *Battles,* 15]
5. **Arbela** Alexander's rout of Darius (331 B.C.). [Classical Hist.: Harbottle *Battles,* 17]
6. **Armageddon** final battle between forces of good and evil. [N.T.: Revelation 16:16]
7. **Austerlitz** Napoleon's brilliant success over Austro-Russian coalition (1805). [Fr. Hist.: Harbottle *Battles,* 23–24]
8. **Balaclava** fought between Russians and British during Crimean War (1854). [Russ. Hist.: Harbottle *Battles,* 25–26]
9. **Battle of the Bulge** unsuccessful attempt by Germans to push Allies back from German territory (1944–1945). [Ger. Hist.: *EB,* II: 360–361]
10. **Belleau Wood** locale of significant American triumph in WWI (1918). [Am. Hist.: Jameson, 47]
11. ***Bhagavad-Gita*** Sanskrit epic relates the great fratricidal battle between two noble families. [Hindu Lit.: *Bhagavad-Gita* in Benét, 103]
12. **Bull Run** site of two important battles of the Civil War (1861) (1862). [Am. Hist.: Jameson, 68]
13. **Bunker Hill** "Don't shoot until you see the whites of their eyes"; American Revolutionary battle (1775). [Am. Hist.: Worth, 22]

14. **Cannae** perhaps Hannibal's greatest victory (216 B.C.). [Rom. Hist.: Harbottle *Battles,* 48]
15. **Coral Sea** first naval engagement exclusively involving planes versus ships (1942). [Am. Hist.: Van Doren, 488]
16. **Crécy** English over French; preeminence of longbow established (1346). [Fr. Hist.: Bishop, 382–385]
17. **Fort Sumter** site of opening blow of Civil War (1861). [Am. Hist.: Jameson, 486–487]
18. **Gettysburg** site of Pyrrhic victory for North in Civil War (1863). [Am. Hist.: Harbottle *Battles,* 97]
19. **Guadalcanal** Marines triumphed in first major U.S. offensive of WWII (1942–1943). [Am. Hist.: Van Doren, 490]
20. **Hastings** battle that determined the Norman Conquest of England (1066). [Br. Hist.: Harbottle *Battles,* 107]
21. **Iwo Jima** inspiring American triumph in the Pacific (1945). [Am. Hist.: Leonard, 472–480]
22. **Jutland** established British WWI naval supremacy (1916). [Br. Hist.: *EB,* 19: 954–955]
23. **Lexington** opening engagement of the American Revolution (1775). [Am. Hist.: Jameson, 283]
24. **Lindisfarne** object of first major Viking raid in Britain (792). [Br. Hist.: Grun, 86]
25. **Lucknow** Indian mutiny put down by British (1858). [Ind. Hist.: Harbottle *Battles,* 143]
26. **Marathon** plain near Athens where Greeks defeated Persians in 490 B.C. [Gk. Hist.: Benét, 633]
27. **Midway** site of decisive battle between Japanese and Americans in WWII (1942). [Am. Hist.: *EB,* VI: 877–878]
28. **Mount Badon** here Arthur soundly defeated the Saxons (c. 520). [Arthurian Legend: Benét, 72]
29. **New Orleans** end of War of 1812; fought after treaty had been signed (1815). [Am. Hist.: Worth, 22]
30. **Normandy Invasion** Allied invasion of Europe during WWII; D-Day (June 6, 1944). [Eur. Hist.: *EB,* VII: 391]
31. **Okinawa** scene of American amphibian operations during WWII (1945). [Am. Hist.: *EB,* VII: 505]
32. **Orléans** Joan of Arc's inspired triumph over English (1429). [Fr. Hist.: Bishop, 392]
33. **Pearl Harbor** site of Japanese surprise attack (December 7, 1941). [Am. Hist.: *EB,* VII: 822]
34. **Plains of Abraham** English victory decided last of French and Indian wars (1759). [Br. Hist.: *NCE,* 7]

35. **Ravenna** site of battle between Byzantines and an Italian force under Pope Gregory II. Byzantines were routed (729). [Gk. Hist.: Harbottle *Battles,* 207]
36. **Salamis** Xerxes' horde repulsed by numerically inferior Greek navy (480 B.C.). [Class. Hist.: Harbottle *Battles,* 219]
37. **Samarkand** Arabs defeated Chinese (751); adopted some of Chinese technology and culture. [Chinese Hist.: Grun, 78]
38. **Saratoga (Stillwater)** fought between Americans and British during Revolution (1777). [Am. Hist.: Harbottle *Battles,* 237–238]
39. **Sedan** decisive battle of the Franco-German War (1870). [Fr. Hist.: Harbottle *Battles,* 225]
40. **Stalingrad** unsuccessful German assault on Stalingrad, Russia (1942–1943). [Ger. Hist.: *EB,* IX: 517]
41. **Thermopylae** 300 Spartans hold off Xerxes' horde (480 B.C.). [Classical Hist.: Harbottle *Battles,* 248]
42. **Trafalgar** defeat of French and Spanish; zenith of British naval history (1805). [Br. Hist.: Harbottle *Battles,* 252–253]
43. **Trenton** Washington's brilliant surprise attack galvanized American morale (1776). [Am. Hist.: Jameson, 508]
44. **Valmy** battle fought between French and Prussians (1792). [Eur. Hist.: Harbottle *Battles,* 259]
45. **Verdun** site of numerous battles. [Fr. Hist.: *EB,* X: 395]
46. **Vicksburg** city held by Confederates; besieged several times (1862, 1863). [Am. Hist.: Harbottle *Battles,* 261–262]
47. **Waterloo** site of Napoleon's defeat (1815). [Fr. Hist.: Harbottle *Battles,* 266]
48. **Yorktown** site of American victory over British, ending Revolutionary War (1781). [Am. Hist.: Harbottle *Battles,* 271]

61. BEAUTY

1. **Aglaia** one of the Graces; embodiment of comeliness. [Gk. Myth.: Brewer *Dictionary,* 481]
2. **Blodenwedd** created from oak flowers and meadowsweet. [Welsh Lit.: *Mabinogion*]
3. **cowslip** symbol of beauty. [Flower Symbolism: Jobes, 377]
4. **Euphrosyne** one of the Graces; epitome of beauty in joy. [Gk. Myth.: Brewer *Dictionary,* 481]
5. **Graces** three daughters of Zeus and Eurynome; goddesses of charm and beauty. [Gk. Myth.: Howe, 61]
6. **hibiscus** symbol of beauty. [Flower Symbolism: *Flora Symbolica,* 174]

7. **Hora Quirini** goddess of loveliness. [Rom. Myth.: Kravitz, 44]
8. **lilies of the field** more splendidly attired than Solomon. [N.T.: Matthew 6:28–29; Luke 12:27–31]
9. **Monday's child** fair of face. [Nurs. Rhyme: Opie, 309]
10. **peri** beautiful fairylike creatures, guided way to heaven. [Pers. Myth.: Brewer *Dictionary,* 822]
11. **Thalia** one of the Graces; bestowed charm on others. [Gk. Myth.: Brewer *Dictionary,* 481]
12. **Ugly Duckling** scorned as unsightly, grows to be graceful swan. [Dan. Fairy Tale: *Andersen's Fairy Tales*]
13. **white camellia** symbol of beauty. [Flower Symbolism: Jobes, 281]

62. BEAUTY, FEMININE (See also BEAUTY, SENSUAL.)

1. **Amoret (Amoretta)** typical of female loveliness. [Br. Lit.: *Faerie Queene,* Brewer *Dictionary,* 30]
2. **Annabel Lee** poet's beautiful beloved. [Am. Lit.: "Annabel Lee" in *Portable Poe*]
3. **Aphrodite** (Rom. **Venus**) archetype of feminine beauty. [Gk. Myth.: Parrinder, 24]
4. **Astarte** beautiful goddess of fertility and sexual love. [Phoenician Myth.: Zimmerman, 33]
5. **Bathsheba** king David killed to gain her. [O.T.: II Samuel 11]
6. **Beauty** beautiful woman married to an enchanted beast who turns into a prince. [Fr. Fairy Tale: "Beauty and the Beast" in Walsh *Classical,* 49]
7. **Cleopatra** beautiful queen of Egypt; wins Marc Antony's heart. [Br. Lit.: *Antony and Cleopatra*]
8. **crabapple blossom** traditional symbol. [Chinese Flower Symbolism: Jobes, 377]
9. **Deirdre** prophesied to become the most beautiful woman in Ireland. [Irish Legend: Benét, 259]
10. **Doone, Lorna** her good looks stir John Ridd and others. [Br. Lit.: *Lorna Doone,* Magill I, 524–526]
11. **Dorothy la Désirée** Jurgen's childhood sweetheart; when he finds her again in a magic garden she has retained the beauty he had praised in his poems. [Am. Lit.: *Jurgen* in Magill I, 464]
12. **Duchess of Alba** Goya's lover and model, immortalized on canvas. [Span. Art: Wallechinsky, 192]
13. **Etain** most beautiful woman in Ireland. [Irish Folklore: Briggs, 123–125]

14. **Freya** goddess of love, beauty, and fecundity; beautiful, blue-eyed blonde. [Norse Myth.: Leach, 425]
15. **Galatea** statue so striking, Venus grants sculptor Pygmalion's wish that it live. [Gk. Myth.: *LLEI,* I: 286]
16. **Gibson girl** classic, comely woman of illustrations (1890s). [Am. Hist.: Flexner, 283]
17. **Golden Bells** epitome of the beautiful Chinese woman. [Irish Lit.: *Messer Marco Polo,* Magill I, 584–585]
18. **Hebe** beautiful cupbearer to the gods. [Gk. Myth.: Zimmerman, 117]
19. **Helen of Troy** beautiful woman kidnapped by smitten Paris, precipitating Trojan war. [Gk. Lit.: *Iliad; Trojan Women;* Euripides, *Helene*]
20. **Hypatia** (c. 370–415) Greek philosopher, renowned for beauty and wit. [Gk. Hist.: *NCE,* 1302]
21. **Kriemhild** Burgundian princess's beauty known throughout Europe. [Ger. Lit.: *Nibelungenlied*]
22. **Marcella** farmer's daughter; every bachelor fancies her. [Span. Lit.: *Don Quixote*]
23. **Marie Antoinette** (1755–1793) beautiful queen consort of King Louis XVI of France. [Fr. Hist.: *EB,* VI: 620]
24. **Miss America** annually selected most beautiful young woman in America. [Am. Hist.: Allen, 56–57]
25. **O'Hara, Scarlett** epitome of a beautiful Southern belle. [Am. Lit.: *Gone With the Wind*]
26. **Simonetta** Botticelli's hauntingly beautiful young model. [Ital. Art: Wallechinsky, 190]
27. **Snow White** snow-toned flesh, ebony hair, blood-red lips. [Ger. Fairy Tale: Grimm, 184]
28. **Teal Eye** "Her beauty remained forever in Boone's memory." [Am. Lit.: *The Big Sky*]
29. **Tehani** lovely Tahitian girl loved by Byam. [Br. Lit.: *Mutiny on the Bounty*]
30. **Van Tassel, Katrina** rich farmer's daughter, pursued by Ichabod Crane and Brom Bones. [Am. Lit.: *The Legend of Sleepy Hollow*]
31. ***Venus de Milo*** armless statue of pulchritudinous goddess. [Gk. Art: Brewer *Dictionary,* 1126]

63. BEAUTY, LASTING

1. **Célimène** beauty not diminished by character or age. [Fr. Drama: *The Misanthrope*]

2. **Mona Lisa** *La Gioconda,* da Vinci's enchanting portrait. [Ital. Art: Wallechinsky, 190]
3. **My Last Duchess** poem about a wife whose beauty is frozen in portrait. [Br. Lit.: "My Last Duchess" in Norton, 757–758]
4. **stock** symbolizes enduring loveliness. [Flower Symbolism: *Flora Symbolica,* 177]
5. **unravished bride** her portrait fixed in clay, she cannot fade but will be forever fair. [Br. Poetry: Keats "Ode on a Grecian Urn"]

64. BEAUTY, MASCULINE (See also VIRILITY.)

1. **Absalom** flawlessly handsome. [O.T.: II Samuel 14:25]
2. **Adonis** beautiful youth. [Gk. Myth.: Brewer *Dictionary,* 11]
3. **Andrews, Joseph** handsome, virtuous man admired by many ladies. [Br. Lit.: *Joseph Andrews*]
4. **Apollo** god of manly beauty. [Gk. Myth.: Leach, 67]
5. **Balder** god of light and joy; known for his beauty. [Norse Myth.: Leach, 106]
6. **Chateaupers, Phoebus de** gallant, handsome horseman eternally loved by Esmeralda. [Fr. Lit.: *The Hunchback of Notre Dame*]
7. ***David*** sculpture by Michelangelo depicting figure epitomizing male beauty. [Art: Osborne, 718]
8. **Glaucus** handsome, wealthy young Greek pursued by various ladies. [Br. Lit.: *The Last Days of Pompeii,* Magill I, 490–492]
9. **Hylas** Hercules' servant; so captivates Naiads, they abduct him. [Gk. Myth.: Hall, 158]
10. **Hyperion** one of the Titans; known for his beauty. [Gk. Myth.: Zimmerman, 132]
11. **Narcissus** beautiful youth who falls in love with his own reflection. [Gk. Myth.: Zimmerman, 171–172]
12. **Tadzio** handsome Polish boy exerts a fatal attraction for an elderly writer. [Ger. Lit.: Thomas Mann *Death in Venice*]

65. BEAUTY, RUSTIC

1. **Amaryllis** a favorite subject of pastoral poets. [Rom. Lit.: *Eclogues*]
2. **Chloë** beautiful shepherdess beloved by Daphnis. [Rom. Lit.: "Daphne and Chloë" in Brewer *Handbook,* 204]
3. **Dulcinea** beautiful peasant woman idealized by Don Quixote. [Span. Lit.: *Don Quixote*]
4. **Pocahontas** natural beauty embodied in an Indian maiden. [Am. Hist.: *EB,* VIII: 57]

5. **Ragmaid** no one but the prince sees through her dishevelment. [Br. Fairy Tale: "The Little Ragmaid" in Macleod, 39–44]
6. **Tess of the D'Urbervilles** beautiful country girl. [Br. Lit.: *Tess of the D'Urbervilles*]
7. **Thestylis** embodiment of peasant prettiness. [Br. Lit.: *L'Allegro,* Brewer *Dictionary,* 1074]

66. BEAUTY, SENSUAL (See also BEAUTY, FEMININE; SEX SYMBOL.)

1. **Angelica** infidel princess of exquisite grace and charm. [Ital. Lit.: *Orlando Innamorato; Orlando Furioso*]
2. **Borgia, Lucrezia** (1480–1519) her beauty was as legendary as her rumored vices and heartlessness. [Ital. Hist.: Plumb, 59]
3. **Buchanan, Daisy** Jay Gatsby's femme fatale. [Am. Lit.: *The Great Gatsby*]
4. **Cleopatra** seductive queen of Egypt; beloved by Marc Antony. [Br. Lit.: *Antony and Cleopatra*]
5. **Helen of Troy** Faust's desire to possess her makes him faint. [Ger. Lit.: *Faust*]
6. **Jezebel** Phoenician princess; enemy of the prophets; name is a byword for wicked woman. [O.T.: I Kings 16:21, 31; II Kings 9:1–10, 30–37]
7. **Lolita** precociously seductive 12-year-old. [Am. Lit.: *Lolita*]
8. **Madeline** gazed at in awe by Porphyro. [Br. Lit.: "The Eve of St. Agnes" in Magill I, 263–264]
9. **Montez, Lola** (c. 1818–1861) Irish singer and dancer; mistress to famous men. [Irish Hist.: *NCE,* 1821]
10. **Phryne** courtesan, acquitted of charge by baring bosom. [Gk. Hist.: Brewer *Dictionary,* 830]
11. **Playmate of the Month** nude girl provocatively gracing *Playboy's* centerfold. [Am. Culture: Flexner, 285]
12. **Queen of Sheba** sultry Biblical queen who visits Solomon. [O.T.: I Kings 10]
13. **Salome** seductive dancer who obtains head of John the Baptist as reward. [N.T.: Matthew 14:3, 11]
14. **Vye, Eustacia** capricious, seductive, trouble-making heroine. [Br. Lit.: *Return of the Native,* Harvey, 690]

67. BESTIALITY (See also PERVERSION.)

1. **Asterius** Minotaur born to Pasiphaë and Cretan Bull. [Gk. Myth.: Zimmerman, 34]
2. **Leda** raped by Zeus in form of swan. [Gk. Myth.: Zimmerman, 149]

3. **Lucius** transformed into ass, makes love with harlot. [Rom. Lit.: *The Golden Ass*]
4. **Pasiphaë** positioned inside hollow cow, consummates lust for bull. [Gk. Myth.: Hall, 234; Gk. Lit.: *Imagines* 1:16]
5. **Zeus** in form of a swan, seduces and impregnates Leda. [Gk. Myth.: Zimmerman, 149]

68. BETRAYAL (See also TREACHERY.)

1. **Judas Iscariot** apostle who betrays Jesus. [N.T.: Matthew 26:15]
2. **Proteus** though engaged, steals his friend Valentine's beloved, reveals his plot and effects his banishment. [Br. Drama: Shakespeare *Two Gentlemen of Verona*]

69. BIGOTRY (See also ANTI-SEMITISM.)

1. **Beaumanoir, Sir Lucas de** prejudiced ascetic; Grand Master of Templars. [Br. Lit.: *Ivanhoe*]
2. **Bunker, Archie** middle-aged bigot in television series. [TV: "All in the Family" in Terrace, I, 47–48]
3. **fiery cross** used as symbolic threat by Ku Klux Klan. [Am. Hist.: Jobes, 387]
4. **Hitler, Adolf** (1889–1945) German dictator; his New Order excluded non-Aryans, e.g., Jews, Slavs. [Ger. Hist.: *Hitler*]
5. **Jim Crow** Negro stereotype popularized by 19th-century minstrel shows. [Am. Hist.: Van Doren, 138]
6. **John Birch Society** ultra-conservative, anti-Communist U.S. organization founded in 1958. [Am. Hist.: *NCE,* 1421]
7. **Ku Klux Klan** anti-Negro terrorist organization, started in southern U.S. [Am. Hist.: Allen, 46–49]
8. **Lebenshorn** Himmler's adoption/breeding scheme to produce master race. [Ger. Hist.: *Hitler,* 1046]
9. ***Light in August*** study of race problem in South. [Am. Lit.: *Light in August*]
10. **Little Rock, Arkansas** required military intervention to desegregate schools (1957–1958). [Am. Hist.: Van Doren, 556–557]
11. ***Native Son*** pictures underprivileged Negro as either churchgoer or criminal. [Am. Lit.: *Native Son,* Magill I, 643–645]
12. **Nazi** *Nazionalsozialist;* rabid anti-Semite member of Hitler's party. [Ger. Hist.: Shirer]
13. **New Order** partially fulfilled Nazification of Europe. [Eur. Hist.: *Hitler,* 935, 1055]

70. BIOGRAPHY and AUTOBIOGRAPHY

1. **Boswell, James** (1740–1793) Scottish author and devoted biographer of Samuel Johnson. [Br. Hist.: *NCE,* 341]
2. **Cellini, Benvenuto** (1500–1571) Italian sculptor and author of important autobiography. [Ital. Lit.: *NCE,* 488]
3. ***Confessions*** Rousseau (1712–1778) reveals details of an erratic and rebellious life. [Fr.Lit.: Benét, 218]
4. ***Confessions of St. Augustine, The*** St. Augustine tells of his life and conversion. [Christian Hagiog.: Hayden & Fuller, 153]
5. **Driffield, Edward** novelist whose life story is examined by Kear and Ashenden. [Br. Lit.: Maugham *Cakes and Ale* in Magill I, 99]
6. ***Education of Henry Adams, The*** intellectual autobiography traces the thought processes and moral degeneration of modern man. [Am. Lit.: *The Education of Henry Adams*; Magill I, 238]
7. **Franklin, Benjamin** (1706–1790) American statesman; author of famous autobiography. [Am. Lit.: *NCE,* 1000]
8. ***Lives of the Caesars*** biographies by Suetonius of the first twelve Roman Emperors. [Rom. Hist.: Benét, 973]
9. ***Memoirs of George Sherston, The*** fictional autobiography of a poet as country gentleman, soldier, and pacifist. [Br. Lit.: Magill I, 575, 579]
10. **Pepys, Samuel** (1633–1703) English public official; author of diary. [Br. Lit.: *NCE,* 2103]
11. **Plutarch** (c. 46–c. 120) Greek biographer known for his *Lives,* a collection of biographies of Greek and Roman leaders. [Gk. Lit.: *NCE,* 2170]
12. **Toklas, Alice B.** fictive author of an autobiography by Gertrude Stein. [Am. Lit.: Stein *The Autobiography of Alice B. Toklas* in Benét, 66]
13. **Venerable Bede** (c. 673–735) Benedictine monk; wrote memorable biographies of English saints. [Br. Hist.: *NCE,* 257]

71. BIRDS

1. **Birdman of Alcatraz** (Robert Stroud, 1890–1963) from jailbird to famous ornithologist. [Am. Hist.: Worth, 28]
2. ***Birds, The*** Hitchcock film in which birds turn on the human race and terrorize a town. [Am. Cinema: Halliwell, 51]
3. **Blue Bird of Happiness** symbolizes the goal of the two children in Maeterlinck play. [Belg. Lit.: *The Blue Bird* in Haydn & Fuller, 94]

4. **Cloud-cuckoo-land** (**Nephelococcygia**) city in which all power is to be vested in the birds. [Gk. Drama: Aristophanes *Birds*]
5. **cranes of Ibycus** called on by the dying poet to bear witness against his murderers, they lead to the murderers' conviction. [Gk. Myth.: *NCE*, 1307]
6. **Gripp** talking raven, beloved pet of half-wit Barnaby Rudge. [Br. Lit.: Dickens *Barnaby Rudge*]
7. **Halitherses** Ithacan seer; ornithologist. [Gk. Myth.: Kravitz, 46]
8. **phoenix** fabulous Arabian bird; sings a dirge, burns itself to ashes, and rises to a new life. [Gk. Myth.: Brewer *Dictionary*, 699]
9. **Polynesia** wise old parrot who teaches Dr. Dolittle the languages of birds and animals. [Children's Lit.: Hugh Lofting *Dr. Dolittle*]
10. **raven** bird of ill omen visits the despairing poet. [Am. Lit.: Poe *The Raven*]
11. **Seagull, Jonathan Livingston** ambitious seagull is determined to improve its flying techniques and achieve greater speeds. [Am. Lit.: Richard Bach *Jonathan Livingston Seagull*]

Birth (See **CHILDBIRTH.**)

72. BIRTHSTONES

1. **amethyst** February. [Am. Gem Symbolism: Kunz, 319–320]
2. **aquamarine** March alternate birthstone. [Am. Gem Symbolism: Kunz, 319]
3. **bloodstone** March. [Am. Gem Symbolism: Kunz, 319–320]
4. **diamond** April. [Am. Gem Symbolism: Kunz, 319–320]
5. **emerald** May. [Am. Gem Symbolism: Kunz, 319–320]
6. **garnet** January. [Am. Gem Symbolism: Kunz, 319–320]
7. **moonstone** June alternate birthstone. [Am. Gem Symbolism: Kunz, 319]
8. **opal** October. [Am. Gem Symbolism: Kunz, 319–320]
9. **pearl** June. [Am. Gem Symbolism: Kunz, 319–320]
10. **peridot** August alternate birthstone. [Am. Gem Symbolism: Kunz, 319]
11. **ruby** July. [Am. Gem Symbolism: Kunz, 319–320]
12. **sapphire** September. [Am. Gem Symbolism: Kunz, 319–320]
13. **sardonyx** August. [Am. Gem Symbolism: Kunz, 319–320]
14. **topaz** November. [Am. Gem Symbolism: Kunz, 319–320]
15. **tourmaline** October alternate birthstone. [Am. Gem Symbolism: Kunz, 320]

16. **turquoise** December. [Am. Gem Symbolism: Kunz, 319–320]

73. BLACKMAIL (See also BRIBERY.)

1. **Rigaud** adventurer and extortionist. [Br. Lit.: *Little Dorrit*]
2. **Rudge** extorts to achieve personal ends. [Br. Lit.: *Barnaby Rudge*]
3. **Sextus** threatens murder and dishonor to bed Lucretia. [Rom. Lit.: *Fasti; Livy;* Br. Lit.: *The Rape of Lucrece*]
4. **Wegg, Silas** attempts to blackmail Boffin. [Br. Lit.: *Our Mutual Friend*]

Blackness (See NIGHT.)

Blasphemy (See APOSTASY.)

74. BLINDNESS

1. **Agib** dervish who lost an eye. [Arab. Lit.: *Arabian Nights*]
2. **Anchises** blinded by lightning. [Gk. Myth.: Walsh *Classical*, 22]
3. **Blind Pew** David, the blind beggar. [Br. Lit.: *Treasure Island*]
4. **Braille, Louis** (1809–1852) teacher of blind; devised raised printing which is read by touch. [Fr. Hist.: *NCE*, 354]
5. **Cratus** Titan who blinded Prometheus. [Gk. Myth.: Kravitz, 67–68]
6. **Demodocus** blind bard rewarded by Odysseus. [Gk. Lit.: *Odyssey* VIII]
7. **Ephialtes** giant deprived of his left eye by Apollo and of his right eye by Hercules. [Gk. Myth.: Brewer *Dictionary*, 333]
8. **Gloucester** cruelly blinded by those he served. [Br. Lit.: *King Lear*]
9. **the Graeae** share one eye among them. [Gk. Myth.: Gayley, 208–210]
10. **Heldar, Dick** artist who gradually goes blind and is abandoned by his sweetheart. [Br. Lit.: *The Light that Failed* in Benét, 586]
11. **Homer** sightless writer of *Iliad* and *Odyssey*. [Gr. Hist.: Wallechinsky, 13]
12. **Justice** personified as a blindfolded goddess, token of impartiality. [Rom. Tradition: Jobes II, 898]
13. **Keller, Helen** (1880–1968) Achieved greatness despite blindness and deafness. [Am. Hist.: Wallechinsky, 13]
14. **Lucy, St.** vision restored after gouging out of eyes. [Christian Hagiog.: Brewster, 20–21]

15. **mole** said to lack eyes. [Medieval Animal Symbolism: White, 95–96]
16. **Nydia** beautiful flower girl lacks vision but "sees" love. [Br. Lit.: *The Last Days of Pompeii,* Magill I, 490–492]
17. **Odilia, St.** recovered vision; shrine, pilgrimage for visually afflicted. [Christian Hagiog.: Attwater, 257]
18. **Oedipus** blinded self on learning he had married his mother. [Gk. Lit.: *Oedipus Rex*]
19. **Paul, St.** blinded by God on road to Damascus. [N.T.: Acts 9:1–19]
20. **Peeping Tom** stricken blind for peeping as the naked Lady Godiva rode by. [Br. Legend: Brewer *Dictionary*]
21. **Plutus** blind god of Wealth. [Gk. Lit.: *Plutus*]
22. **Polyphemus** Cyclops blinded by Odysseus. [Gk. Myth.: *Odyssey*]
23. **Rochester, Edward** blinded when his home burns down, depends on the care of Jane Eyre. [Br. Lit.: Charlotte Brontë *Jane Eyre*]
24. **Samson** Israelite hero treacherously blinded by Philistines. [O.T.: Judges 16:4–21]
25. **Stagg** sightless roomkeeper. [Br. Lit.: *Barnaby Rudge*]
26. **three blind mice** sightless rodents; lost tails to farmer's wife. [Nurs. Rhyme: Opie, 306]
27. **Tiresias** made sightless by Athena for viewing her nakedness. [Gk. Myth.: Brewer *Dictionary,* 1086]
28. **Tobit** sparrow guano falls into his eyes while sleeping. [Apocrypha: Tobit 2:10]
29. **Zedekiah** eyes put out for revolting against Nebuchadnezzar. [O.T.: II Kings 25:7]

75. BOASTFULNESS (See also ARROGANCE, CONCEIT, EGOTISM.)

1. **Aglaonice** Thessalian who claimed power over moon. [Gk. Legend: Brewer *Dictionary,* 16]
2. **Ajax (the greater)** archetypal *Miles Gloriosus.* [Br. Lit.: *Troilus and Cressida*]
3. **Anchises** Trojan prince; crippled for boasting of intimacy with Aphrodite. [Gk. Myth.: Zimmerman, 22]
4. **Armado** verbose braggart and pedant. [Br. Lit.: *Love's Labour's Lost*]
5. **Basilisco** knight renowned for foolish bragging. [Br. Lit.: *Solomon and Persida,* Brewer *Dictionary,* 83]

6. **Bessus** braggart soldier in the *Miles Gloriosus* tradition. [Br. Lit.: Walsh *Modern*, 55]
7. **Bluffe, Captain** blustering braggart and spurious war veteran. [Br. Lit.: *The Old Batchelour*]
8. **Bobadill, Captain** blustering braggadocio of yellow stripe. [Br. Lit.: *Every Man in His Humour*]
9. **Braggadocchio** empty braggart. [Br. Lit.: *Faerie Queene*]
10. **Capaneus** struck dead by a thunderbolt for boasting that not even Jove could stop him from scaling the wall of Thebes. [Gk. Myth.: Benét, 166]
11. **Drawcansir** blustering bully, known for his extravagantly boastful speeches. [Br. Lit.: *The Rehearsal*]
12. **Falstaff** jovial knight and rascal of brazen braggadocio. [Br. Lit.: *Merry Wives of Windsor; I Henry IV; II Henry IV*]
13. **Gascon** inhabitant of Gascony, France; people noted for their bragging. [Fr. Hist.: *NCE*, 1049]
14. **Glendower, Owen** Welsh ally of the Percys; his boastfulness antagonizes Hotspur. [Br. Lit.: *I Henry IV*]
15. **Háry János** peasant hero of fanciful adventures. [Hung. Lit. and Opera: Osborne *Opera*, 148]
16. **Kay, Sir** rude and vainglorious knight of the Round Table. [Br. Lit.: *Le Morte d'Arthur; Idylls of the King*]
17. **Mahon, Christopher** runaway boy tells stories with self as epitome of bravery. [Irish Lit.: *The Playboy of the Western World*, Magill I, 758–759]
18. **Parolles** cowardly braggart and wastrel. [Br. Lit.: *All's Well That Ends Well*]
19. **Pistol** knight of the "killing tongue and quiet sword." [Br. Lit.: *II Henry IV*]
20. **Rodomont** gallant but blustering Saracen leader. [Ital. Lit.: *Orlando Furioso; Orlando Innamorato*]
21. **Roister Doister, Ralph** well-to-do dolt brags loud and long of bravery. [Br. Lit.: *Ralph Roister Doister*]
22. **Sacripant** noisy braggart. [Ital. Lit.: *Secchia Rapita*, Brewer *Handbook*, 945]
23. **Scaramouche** talks a good fight; never does. [Ital. Lit.: Espy, 125]
24. **Tartarin** tells tall tales of his fantastic adventures. [Fr. Lit.: *Tartarin de Tarascon*]
25. **Texan** resident of second largest U.S. state; known for his tall tales. [Am. Culture: Misc.]
26. **Thraso** swaggering but foolish soldier. [Rom. Lit.: *The Eunuch*]

27. **Vicar of Bray** declared that he would retain his office regardless of the reigning king's religion. [Br. Balladry: Walsh *Classical,* 61]

76. BOHEMIANISM

1. ***Autobiography of Alice B. Toklas, The*** Gertrude Stein's memoir of Paris' Bohemia. [Am. Lit.: Stein *The Autobiography of Alice B. Toklas* in Benét, 66]
2. **Bloomsbury** section of London where, in the first half of the 20th century, a group of artists and intellectuals frequently congregated. [Br. Culture: Benét, 115]
3. **Greenwich Village** area of southern Manhattan long identified with artists and writers. [Am. Culture: Misc.]
4. **Haight-Ashbury** neighborhood in San Francisco associated with beatnicks and "flower people" in the 1960s. [Am. Culture: Misc.]
5. **Latin Quarter** section of Paris on left bank of the Seine; home of students, artists, and writers. [Fr. Culture: *EB,* VI: 71–72]
6. **Olenska, Countess Ellen** often considers divorce; likes "unacceptable" people. [Am. Lit.: *The Age of Innocence*]
7. **SoHo** bohemian neighborhood So(uth of) Ho(uston Street), New York City. [Am. Culture: Misc.]

77. BOREDOM (See also FUTILITY.)

1. **Aldegonde, Lord St.** bored nobleman, empty of pursuits. [Br. Lit.: *Lothair*]
2. **Baudelaire, Charles** (1821–1867) French poet whose dissipated lifestyle led to inner despair. [Fr. Lit.: *NCE,* 248]
3. **Bovary, Emma** housewife suffers from ennui. [Fr. Lit.: *Madame Bovary*]
4. **Des Esseintes, Jean** in dissipation and isolation, develops morbid ennui. [Fr. Lit.: *Against the Grain*]
5. **Harthouse, James** thorough gentleman, weary of everything. [Br. Lit.: *Hard Times*]
6. **Oblomov, Ilya** Russian landowner; embodiment of physical and mental sloth. [Russ. Lit.: *Oblomov*]
7. **Povey, Constance Baines** uneventful thoughts, marriage best described as routine. [Br. Lit.: *The Old Wives' Tale,* Magill I, 684–686]

78. BORESOMENESS

1. **Bellenden, Lady Margaret** tiresomely repeats story of Charles II's visit. [Br. Lit.: *Old Mortality*]

2. **Bovary, Charles** "dull-witted husband reeked of medicine and drugs." [Fr. Lit.: *Madame Bovary*]
3. **Dryasdust, Rev.** imaginary preface writer with wooden style. [Br. Lit.: Wheeler, 108]
4. **Warburton, Lord** Isabel's kindly, thoughtful, but overly boring suitor. [Am. Lit.: *The Portrait of a Lady,* Magill I, 766–768]
5. **Welland, May** "correct but unexciting personality." [Am. Lit.: *The Age of Innocence*]

Boxing (See PUGILISM.)

79. BOYISHNESS (See also MANNISHNESS.)

1. **Drew, Nancy** tall, slender, boyish, girl detective. [Children's Lit.: *Bungalow Mystery*]
2. **Jo** tall, awkward tomboy in March family. [Am. Lit.: *Little Women*]
3. **Oakley, Annie** (1860–1926) American markswoman with boyish style. [Am. Hist.: *Century Cyclopedia,* 2993]

80. BRAVERY (See also HEROISM.)

1. **Achilles** foremost Greek hero of Trojan War; brave and formidable warrior. [Gk. Hist.: *NCE,* 12]
2. **Adrastus** courageous Indian prince; Rinaldo's enemy. [Ital. Lit.: *Jerusalem Delivered*]
3. **Agenor** Antenor's son; distinguished for his valor in battle. [Gk. Myth.: Zimmerman, 12]
4. **Bajazet** fierce, reckless, indomitable Sultan of Turkey; Tamerlane's captive. [Br. Lit.: *Tamerlane,* Walsh *Modern,* 39]
5. **Beowulf** singlehandedly fights firebreathing dragon. [Br. Lit.: *Beowulf*]
6. **Birch, Harvey** at great risk spies on British. [Am. Lit.: *The Spy*]
7. **black agate** makes athletes brave and invincible. [Gem Symbolism: Jobes, 45]
8. **black poplar** symbol of bravery. [Plant Symbolism: *Flora Symbolica,* 176]
9. **Boadicea (Boudicca)** British queen and female warrior; slew 80,000 Romans. [Br. Hist.: Walsh *Classical,* 58]
10. **Bold Beauchamp** 14th-century champion; British generic for *warrior.* [Br. Hist.: Walsh *Classical,* 49]
11. **Breck, Alan** while evading enemies, risks his life to save others. [Br. Lit.: *Kidnapped*]
12. **bull** heraldic symbol of courage. [Heraldry: Halberts, 21]

13. **carp** a pictorial symbol of bravery. [Chinese and Jap. Folklore: Jobes, 292]
14. **Clorinda** Amazonian, battles in armor. [Ital. Lit.: *Jerusalem Delivered*]
15. **David** audaciously stands before and slays Goliath. [O.T.: I Samuel 17:48–51]
16. **French willow** indicates courage. [Flower Symbolism: *Flora Symbolica,* 178]
17. **Fritchie, Barbara** her bravery impressed Stonewall Jackson. [Am. Lit.: "Barbara Fritchie" in Hart, 57]
18. **Gawain** bravery in the Castle of Wonders. [Arth. Legend: *Parsival*]
19. **Hale, Nathan** (1755–1776) Revolutionary war hero, calmly accepted fate. [Am. Hist.: Jameson, 215]
20. **Havelok** right makes might as gallant prince triumphs. [Dan. Lit.: *Havelok the Dane*]
21. **Hawkeye** scout and woodsman who risks his life to save English girls from hostile Indians. [Am. Lit.: Cooper *The Last of the Mohicans* in Magill I, 494]
22. **Hector** captain and chief hero of Trojan forces. [Rom. Lit.: *Aeneid; Metamorphoses*]
23. **Horatius** holds off Etruscan forces while Romans burn bridge. [Rom. Hist.: *Livy*]
24. **Iron Cross** German medal awarded for outstanding bravery in wartime. [Ger. Hist.: Misc.]
25. **Joan of Arc, St.** peasant leader of French rout of British. [Christian Hagiog.: Attwater, 187]
26. **larch** symbol of bravery. [Tree Symbolism: *Flora Symbolica,* 175]
27. **Medal of Honor** highest American military decoration for wartime gallantry. [Am. Hist.: Misc.]
28. **Nicephorus, St.** layman voluntarily executed to prevent priest's apostasy. [Christian Hagiog.: Attwater, 249]
29. **Pitcher, Molly** (1744–1832) took husband's place in battle during American Revolution. [Am. Hist.: Jameson, 393]
30. ***Profiles in Courage*** John F. Kennedy's anthology of biographies of brave statesmen. [Am. Lit.: *Profiles in Courage*]
31. **Purple Heart** U.S. medal awarded to those wounded in military action. [Am. Hist.: Misc.]
32. **red badge** symbol of the conquest of fear. [Am. Lit.: *Red Badge of Courage*]

33. **Richard the Lion-Hearted** (1159–1199) romantic warrior-king renowned for his bravery and prowess. [Br. Hist.: Bishop, 49]
34. **Roland** brave French hero of medieval chansons de geste. [Fr. Lit.: *NCE,* 2344]
35. **Samson** strong, brave judge of Israel; strength was in his hair. [O.T.: Judges 13–16]
36. **St. Paul** as a missionary he fearlessly confronts the "perils of waters, of robbers, in the city, in the wilderness." [N.T.: II Cor. 11:26]
37. **Theseus** displays bravery in facing Minotaur; against Procrustes. [Gk. Myth.: *Odyssey; Metamorphoses*]
38. **Victoria Cross** highest British military award for valor. [Br. Hist.: Brewer *Dictionary,* 1129]
39. **York, Sergeant Alvin** (1887–1964) hero of WWI; captured hundreds of Germans. [Am. Culture: Misc.]

81. BRAWNINESS (See also STRENGTH, VIRILITY.)

1. **Atlas, Charles** (1893–1972) American muscleman; successful selling body-building by mail order. [Am. Culture: Misc.]
2. **Big John** brawny, strapping miner who saves others in mine collapse. [Am. Music: Jimmy Dean, "Big Bad John"]
3. **Browdie, John** big Yorkshireman. [Br. Lit.: *Nicholas Nickleby*]
4. **Bunyan, Paul** lumberjack performs mighty deeds. [Am. Folklore: *The Wonderful Adventures of Paul Bunyan*]
5. **Goliath** gigantic, sinewy Philistine killed by David's slingshot. [O.T.: I Samuel 17; 21:9, 22:10; II Samuel 21:19]
6. **the Hulk** huge, raging, green-skinned strongman into which Dr. Banner is transformed. [Comics: Horn, 324–325]
7. **McTeague** brawn his chief asset; accompanied with little brains. [Am. Lit.: *McTeague*]
8. **Popeye** sailor who owes his incredible muscle-power to a diet of canned spinach. [Comics: Horn, 658]
9. **Tarzan** muscular English lord, reared by African apes, hero of novels and films. [Am. Lit.: *Tarzan of the Apes* (1914); Am. Cinema: Rovin, 105–106]

82. BREVITY

1. **Adonis' garden** of short life. [Br. Lit.: *I Henry IV*]
2. **bubbles** symbolic of transitoriness of life. [Art: Hall, 54]
3. **cherry fair** cherry orchards where fruit was briefly sold; symbolic of transience. [Folklore: Brewer *Dictionary,* 217]

4. **Gettysburg Address** terse but famous speech given by President Lincoln at dedication of national cemetery. (Gettysburg, Penn., 1863). [Am. Hist.: *EB*, IV: 515]
5. **Grey, Lady Jane** (1537–1554) queen of England for nine days. [Br. Hist.: *NCE*, 1146]
6. **night-blooming cereus** symbol of fading loveliness; blooms briefly. [Flower Symbolism: *Flora Symbolica*, 176]
7. **Six-Day War** Arab-Israeli war (1967). [Near East. Hist.: *EB*, I: 470]

83. BRIBERY (See also BLACKMAIL.)

1. **Black Sox Scandal** star White Sox players sold out to gamblers (1919). [Am. Sports: Turkin, 478]
2. **Frollo, Claude** offers to save Esmeralda if she will be his. [Fr. Lit.: *The Hunchback of Notre Dame*]
3. **Joel and Abiah** intent on gain, pervert justice as Israel judges. [O.T.: I Samuel 8:2–3]
4. **Judas Iscariot** betrays Jesus for a bribe of thirty pieces of silver. [N.T.: Matthew 26:15]
5. **Maltese Falcon, The** though he rejects large bribe, detective becomes involved in crime. [Am. Lit.: *The Maltese Falcon*, Magill I, 551–553]
6. **Menahem** pays off Assyrian king to avoid Israel. [O.T.: II Kings 15:20]
7. **mess of pottage** hungry Esau sells birthright for broth. [O.T.: Genesis 25:29–34]
8. **Shemaiah** suborned to render false prophecy to Nehemiah. [O.T.: Nehemiah 6:10–14]
9. **Tweed Ring** bribery is their essential method for corrupting officials (1860–1871). [Am. Hist.: Jameson, 511]

84. BRIDGE

1. **Al Sirat** fine as razor's edge, over which all must pass to enter paradise. [Islam: *Koran*]
2. **Amaurote** Utopian crossing; means "faintly seen." [Br. Lit.: *Utopia*]
3. **Bifrost** rainbow of water and fire for gods' passage from Asgard to Midgard. [Norse Myth.: Leach, 139]
4. **Bridge of San Luis Rey** rope bridge in Andes which breaks, killing five people. [Am. Lit.: *Bridge of San Luis Rey*]
5. **Brooklyn Bridge** suspension bridge spanning the East River from Manhattan to Brooklyn. [Am. Hist.: *EB*, II: 301]

6. **Golden Gate Bridge** suspension bridge in San Francisco spanning the Golden Gate. [Am. Hist.: *EB*, IV: 607]
7. **London Bridge** a bridge spanning the Thames at London; (not the Tower Bridge). [Br. Hist.: *EB*, VI: 311]
8. **River Kwai Bridge** bridge built by British POWs under Japanese orders. [Jap. Hist.: *Bridge Over the River Kwai*]
9. **Xerxes** constructed famed pontoon crossing of Hellespont. [Gk. Hist.: Brewer *Dictionary*, 1169]

85. BRIGHTNESS

1. **Alpha Centauri** brightest star in Centaurus constellation; closest star to Earth. [Astronomy: *NCE*, 74]
2. **diamond** April birthstone, most reflective of gems. [Gem Symbolism: Jobes, 440–441]
3. **North Star** bright star visible to naked eye and nearest to the north celestial pole. [Astronomy: *EB*, VIII: 79]
4. **Sirius** dog star; brightest star in the heavens. [Astronomy: *EB*, IX: 238]
5. **St. Elmo's fire** glow of electrical discharge appearing on towers and ships' masts. [Physics: *EB*, VIII: 780]
6. **Venus** bright planet, second from the Sun. [Astronomy: *EB*, X: 392]

86. BRITAIN

1. **Albion** poetic name for England. [Br. Lit.: Benét, 19]
2. **beefeater** yeoman of the English royal guard, esp. at the Tower of London; slang for Englishman. [Br. Culture: Misc.]
3. **Bull, John** personification of Britain. [Br. Folklore: Benét, 45]
4. **Court of St. James's** British royal court. [Br. Hist.: Misc.]
5. **George, St.** patron saint of Britain. [Br. Hist.: *Golden Legend*]
6. **God Save the Queen** British national anthem. [Br. Culture: Scholes, 408]
7. **Nation of Shopkeepers** name disdainfully given to Britain by Napoleon Bonaparte. [Fr. Hist.: Wheeler, 256]
8. **Rule Britannia!** patriotic song of Britain. [Br. Culture: Scholes, 897–898]
9. **10 Downing Street** the British government; refers to location of Prime Minister's residence [Br. Culture: Benét, 286]
10. **Union Jack** British national flag. [Br. Culture: Misc.]
11. **Whitehall** many government offices on this street; synonymous with government. [Br. Hist.: *NCE*, 2970]

87. BRUTALITY (See also CRUELTY, MUTILATION.)

1. **Black Prince** angered by Limoges' resistance, massacred three hundred inhabitants (1370). [Eur. Hist.: Bishop, 75]
2. **Caracalla** Roman emperor (211–217) massacred many thousands [Rom. Hist.: *EB* (1963) IV, 825]
3. **Cenci, Count** he delighted in making people suffer. [Br. Lit.: "The Cenci" in Magill I, 131–133]
4. **Crown** a stevedore who deals with people by physical force. [Am. Lit.: *Porgy,* Magill I, 764–766]
5. **Drancy** concentration camp; France's largest Jewish deportation center. [Jew. Hist.: Wigoder, 161]
6. **Eichmann, Adolph** (1906–1962) Nazi SS officer; directed "Final Solution" in Europe. [Jew. Hist.: Wigoder, 167]
7. **Enlil** ordered wholesale destruction of humanity by flood. [Babylonian Myth.: *Gilgamesh*]
8. **Gestapo** German secret police under Nazi regime. [Ger. History: *RHD,* 595]
9. **Grimes, Peter** fisherman suspected of ill-treating his apprentices. [Br. Opera: *Peter Grimes* in Osborne *Opera,* 240]
10. **Herod Antipas** presents John the Baptist's head to Salome. [N.T.: Mark 6:17–28]
11. **Himmler, Heinrich** (1900–1945) architect of the "Final Solution" to exterminate Jews. [Ger. Hist.: *Hitler*]
12. **Hitler, Adolf** (1889–1945) Nazi dictator; architect of "Final Solution" to exterminate Jews. [Ger. Hist.: *Hitler*]
13. **Jael** drove tent-peg through skull of Sisera. [O.T.: Judges 4:19–21]
14. **Koch, Ilse** "Bitch of Buchenwald"; had inmates skinned for lampshades (WWII). [Ger. Hist.: Shirer, 1280]
15. **Kramer, Josef** "Beast of Belsen"; camp exterminator (WWII). [Ger. Hist.: Shirer, 878]
16. **Mengele, Dr. Joseph** Auschwitz concentration camp doctor; experimented on inmates (WWII). [Ger. Hist.: Wallechinsky, 83]
17. **Nazi** Jew-baiting, murderous Aryan supremacist under Hitler. [Ger. Hist.: Shirer]
18. **Nero** coarse, conceited, brutal emperor of Rome (37–68). [Polish Lit.: *Quo Vadis,* Magill I, 797–799]
19. **Procrustes** robber; stretches or amputates limbs of victims to fit his bed. [Class. Myth.: Zimmerman, 221]
20. **Reign of Terror** all roads led to the guillotine (1793–1794). [Fr. Hist.: *EB,* IX: 904]

21. **S.S.** ruthless corps implemented Nazi atrocities. [Germ. Hist.: Brewer *Dictionary*]
22. **SAVAK** Iranian secret police [Iranian History: *Facts* (1979), 125]
23. **St. Evremonde, Marquis** ruthless aristocrat deliberately killed two people and ran over a child. [Br. Lit.: Dickens *A Tale of Two Cities*]

88. BULL

1. **Apis** bull of Memphis, created in Osiris' image. [Egypt. Myth.: Benét, 41]
2. **Buchis** black bull worshiped as chief city god. [Egypt. Rel.: Parrinder, 52]
3. **Cretan bull** sacred to Poseidon; sent to Minos. [Gk. Myth.: Kravitz, 68]
4. **Ferdinand** daydreaming bull who refuses to fight in ring. [Children's Lit.: *The Story of Ferdinand*]
5. **Minotaur** fabulous monster of Crete, half-bull, half-man. [Gk. Myth.: *EB,* VI: 922]
6. **Taurus** constellation of the zodiac symbolized by the bull. [Astrology: *EB,* IX: 844]

89. BULLYING

1. **Chowne, Parson Stoyle** terrorizes parish; kidnaps children. [Br. Lit.: *The Maid of Sker,* Walsh *Modern,* 94–95]
2. **Claypole, Noah** bully; becomes thief in Fagin's gang. [Br. Lit.: *Oliver Twist*]
3. **Curley** he picks on feeble-minded Lennie. [Am. Lit.: *Of Mice and Men*]
4. **Flashman, Harry** unconscionably impudent and overbearing coward. [Br. Lit.: *Flashman; Tom Brown's Schooldays*]
5. **hector** street gang member (early 1600s). [Br. Hist.: Espy, 40]
6. **Kowalski, Stanley** crude humor, animal maleness. [Am. Lit.: *A Streetcar Named Desire*]
7. **McTeague** forbidden to practice dentistry, he becomes mean and surly. [Am. Lit.: *McTeague*]

90. BUREAUCRACY

1. **Brid'oison, Judge** jurist who loves red tape. [Fr. Lit.: *Marriage of Figaro*]
2. ***Catch-22*** concerned with the frustration of red-tape mechanisms. [Am. Lit.: *Catch-22*]

3. **Circumlocution Office, the** department of efficient bureaucratic evasiveness. [Br. Lit.: *Little Dorrit*]
4. ***Inspector General, The*** drama highlighting foibles of petty officialdom. [Russ. Lit.: *The Inspector General*]
5. ***M*A*S*H*** bitter farce on bungling bureaucracy in a Korean Army hospital. [Am. Cinema and TV: Halliwell, 474–475]
6. **red tape** excessive formality; bureaucratic paperwork. [Am. and Br. Usage: Misc.]
7. **Secretary, the** repeatedly refuses permission to see the Consul. [Am. Opera: Menotti, *The Consul,* Westerman, 552–553]
8. ***Trial, The*** novel of individual accused of crime by impersonal bureaucracy. [Ger. Lit.: *The Trial*]

91. BURIAL ALIVE

1. **Antigone** condemned to be buried alive, she thwarts Creon's order by killing herself. [Gk. Lit.: *Antigone*]
2. **Fortunato** walled up in a catacomb by the man he had wronged. [Am. Lit.: Poe "The Cask of Amontillado"]
3. **Lafourcade, Victorine** found alive in her tomb by her rejected suitor. [Am. Lit.: Poe "The Premature Burial"]
4. **Sindbad** entombed, by custom, upon his wife's death, he manages to escape. [Arab. Lit.: *Arabian Nights*; Magill II, 50]
5. **Usher, Madeline** breaks out of vault in which she had been buried alive. [Am. Lit.: Poe "Fall of the House of Usher"]

92. BURIAL GROUND

1. **Aceldama** potter's field; burial place for strangers. [N.T.: Matthew 27:6–10, Acts 1:18–19]
2. **Alloway graveyard** where Tam O'Shanter saw witches dancing among opened coffins. [Br. Lit.: Burns *Tam O'Shanter* in Benét, 985]
3. **Arlington National Cemetery** final resting place for America's war heroes. [Am. Hist.: Flexner, 95]
4. **Boot Hill** Tombstone, Arizona's graveyard, where gunfighters are buried. [Am. Hist.: Flexner, 178]
5. **Campo Santo** famous cemetery in Pisa, with Gothic arcades and Renaissance frescoes. [Ital. Hist.: *Collier's*, XV, 433]
6. **Castel Sant'Angelo** built in Rome by Hadrian as an imperial mausoleum. [Rom. Hist.: *Collier's*, XVI, 539]
7. **Catacombs of St. Calixtus** in Rome, one of the largest of subterranean burial places, with eleven miles of galleries. [Ital. Hist.: *Collier's*, IV, 458]

8. **Escorial** former monastery in central Spain; mausoleum of Spanish sovereigns. [Span. Hist.: *NCE*, 890]
9. **Flanders Field** immortalized in poem; cemetery for WWI dead. [Eur. Hist.: Jameson, 176]
10. **Gettysburg** site of Civil War battle; cemetery for war dead. [Am. Culture: *EB*, IV: 515]
11. **God's Acre** Moravian graveyard in Winston-Salem, N.C., with 3,000 identical marble markers. [Am. Hist.: *Collier's*, XIX, 471]
12. **Grant's Tomb** New York City burial place of General Ulysses S. Grant. [Am. Culture: *EB*, IV: 680]
13. **Great Pyramid of Cheops** enormous Egyptian royal tomb. [World Hist.: Wallechinsky, 255]
14. **Holy Sepulcher** Jerusalem cave where body of Jesus is said to have lain. [Christ. Tradition: Brewer *Dictionary*, 814]
15. **Machpelah** cave where Abraham, Sarah, Isaac, Jacob are buried. [O.T.: Genesis 23:19, 25:9, 49:30, 50:13]
16. **potter's field** burial ground purchased with Judas's betrayal money. [N.T.: Matthew 27:6–8]
17. **Stoke Poges** village whose churchyard is thought to be the scene of Gray's "Elegy." [Br. Lit.: Benét, 966]
18. **Taj Mahal** fabulous tomb built by Shah Jahan for wife. [Ind. Hist.: Wallechinsky, 317]
19. **Tomb of Mausolus** Queen Artemisia's spectacular memorial to husband. [World Hist.: Wallechinsky, 256]
20. **Tomb of the Unknowns** in Arlington National Cemetery; commemorates nameless war dead. [Am. Hist.: Brewer *Dictionary*, 1118]
21. **Westminster Abbey** abbey filled with tombs and memorials of famous British subjects. [Br. Hist.: *EB*, X: 632–633]

93. BUTLER (See also SERVANT.)

1. **Balderstone, Caleb** archetypal faithful servant of the Ravenswoods. [Br. Lit.: *Bride of Lammermoor*]
2. **Bunter** Lord Peter Wimsey's foil and jack-of-all-trades. [Br. Lit.: *The Nine Tailors*]
3. **Crichton** resourceful servant proves more than equal to his employers when household is marooned. [Br. Lit.: *The Admirable Crichton*]
4. **Davy** Justice Shallow's varlet; assumes identity of master. [Br. Lit.: *Henry IV*]
5. **Face** Lovewit's house servant; connives to make profit by alchemy. [Br. Lit.: *The Alchemist*]

6. **French, Mr.** gentleman's gentleman for architect and motherless children. [TV: "Family Affair"in Terrace, I, 254]
7. **Godfrey** when the impecunious socialite is hired as a butler, he and his mistress fall in love. [Am. Cinema: *My Man Godfrey* in Halliwell]
8. **Hudson, Mr.** nostalgic, punctilious master of "downstairs." [Br. TV: *Upstairs, Downstairs*]
9. **Jeeves** manservant who frequently rescues his master. [Br. Lit.: novels of P. G. Wodehouse; Espy, 337]
10. **Lurch** Addams's zombielike, extremely tall butler. [TV: "The Addams Family" in Terrace, I, 29]
11. **Passepartout** bungling foil to the punctilious Fogg. [Fr. Lit.: *Around the World in Eighty Days*]

94. BUXOMNESS

1. **Daisy Mae** Dogpatch beauty with enviable figure. [Comics: "Li'l Abner" in Horn, 450]
2. **Little Annie Fanny** buxom version of Little Orphan Annie. [Comics: *Playboy*, Horn, 442]
3. **Morpho** epithet of Aphrodite, meaning "shapely." [Gk. Myth.: Zimmerman, 25]
4. **West, Mae** (1892–1980) voluptuous American leading lady; archetypal sex symbol. [Am. Cinema: Halliwell, 759–760]
5. **Wife of Bath** well-endowed, lusty teller of tales. [Br. Lit.: *Canterbury Tales*]

C

95. CANNIBALISM

1. **Alive** account of cannibalism among air crash survivors. [Am. Lit.: *Alive*]
2. **Antiphates** chieftain of Laestrygones, man-eating giants of Italy. [Gk. Lit.: *Odyssey;* Rom. Lit.: *Metamorphoses*]
3. **Beane, Sawney** highwayman who fed his gang on victims' flesh. [Br. Culture: Misc.]
4. **black giants** kill, roast, and devour Sindbad's companions. [Arab. Lit.: *Arabian Nights* in Magill II, 50]
5. **Caliban** his name is anagram of *cannibal.* [Br. Lit.: *The Tempest*]
6. **Clymenus** eats child who is product of incestuous union with daughter Harpalyce. [Gk. Myth.: Howe, 114]
7. **Cronos** swallowed his children at birth; they lived again when he was forced by Zeus to disgorge them. [Gk. Myth.: *EB* (1963) VI, 747]
8. **Donner Party** of 89 emigrants to California, 47 survive by eating others (1846–1847). [Am. Hist.: *EB,* III: 623]
9. **Hansel and Gretel** fattened up for child-eating witch. [Ger. Fairy Tale: Grimm, 56]
10. **Laestrygones** man-eating giants encountered by Odysseus. [Gk. Lit.: *Odyssey*]
11. **Lamia** female spirit in serpent form; devours children. [Gk. Myth.: Zimmerman, 146; Br. Lit.: "Lamia" in Benét, 563]
12. **Lycaon** turned to wolf for cannibalistic activities; whence, *lycanthropy.* [Gk. Myth.: Espy, 37]
13. **Modest Proposal, A** Swift's satire suggesting that children of the poor be used as food for the rich (1729). [Br. Lit.: "A Modest Proposal" in Harvey, 793]
14. **Narrative of Arthur Gordon Pym, The** for four days, survivors feed on Parker's flesh. [Am. Lit.: Poe, "The Narrative of Arthur Gordon Pym" in Magill I, 640–643]
15. **Pelops** cut up and served as meal to gods. [Gk. Myth.: Brewer *Dictionary,* 817]
16. **Tereus** wife Procne murders son Itys and serves him to Tereus. [Gk. Myth.: Howe, 144]
17. **Thyestean banquet** banquet where Atreus serves Thyestes' sons to him as food. [Gk. Myth.: Brewer *Dictionary,* 1081]

18. **Ugolino** when his children die of starvation in prison, he devours them. [Ital. Poetry: *Inferno*]

96. CARELESSNESS (See also FORGETFULNESS, IRRESPONSIBILITY, LAZINESS.)

1. **Grasshopper** sings through summer, overlooking winter preparations. [Gk. Lit.: *Aesop's Fables*, "Ant and the Grasshopper"]
2. **Little Bo-peep** lost her sheep; found them tailless. [Nurs. Rhyme: Baring-Gould, 93]
3. **Little Boy Blue** sleeps while the sheep's in the corn. [Nurs. Rhyme: Baring-Gould, 46]
4. **Locket, Lucy** misplaced her pocket. [Nurs. Rhyme: *Mother Goose*, 23]
5. **Prism, Miss** nursemaid who misplaces manuscript and infant in railroad station. [Br. Lit.: *Importance of Being Earnest*]
6. **Theseus** neglects to hoist the sail to signal his safety to his father Aegeus, who despairingly throws himself into the sea. [Gk. Myth.: Brewer *Dictionary*, 12]

97. CASTAWAY

1. **Arden, Enoch** shipwrecked sailor; lost for eleven years. [Br. Lit.: "Enoch Arden" in Benét, 316]
2. **Bligh, Captain** commander of H.M.S. *Bounty* who was cast adrift by mutinous crew. [Am. Lit.: *Mutiny on the Bounty*]
3. **Byam, Roger** crew member of the *Bounty* cast onto South Sea island. [Am. Lit.: *Mutiny on the Bounty*]
4. **Crichton** resourceful butler who leads master and his family through difficulties on deserted island. [Br. Lit.: *Admirable Crichton*]
5. **Crusoe, Robinson** shipwreck victim who lives on desert island with savage he names Friday. [Br. Lit.: *Robinson Crusoe*]
6. **Gilligan's Island** comedy about a party shipwrecked on a South Pacific island. [TV: Terrace, I, 312–313]
7. **Gunn, Ben** marooned pirate, helps secure treasure hidden on island. [Br. Lit.: *Treasure Island*]
8. **Lost in Space** family is shipwrecked in space. [TV: Terrace, II, 38–39]
9. **Selkirk, Alexander** real-life prototype of *Robinson Crusoe*. [Br. Hist.: *EB*, IX: 45]
10. **Smith, Cyrus** knowledgeable engineer makes life bearable for castaway party on deserted island. [Fr. Lit.: *Mysterious Island*]
11. ***Swiss Family Robinson*** family shipwrecked on a deserted island. [Br. Lit.: *Swiss Family Robinson*]

98. CASTRATION

1. **Abélard, Peter** castrated by irate father of lover, Héloise. [Fr. Lit.: *Héloise and Abélard*]
2. **Barnes, Jake** castrated journalist whom Brett Ashley loves. [Am. Lit.: *The Sun Also Rises*]
3. **Cybele** hermaphroditic goddess honored orgiastically, usually by emasculation. [Phrygian Myth.: Parrinder, 68]

99. CATS

1. **cat, Dick Whittington's** sent to Morocco, its purchase by the king gives the future Lord Mayor his stake to success. [Br. Legend: Benét, 1088]
2. **Felix** lonely star-crossed fantasist, fights against fate in strange worlds. [Comics: "Felix the Cat" in Horn, 246]
3. **Garfield** lazy gourmand, impudent to its master. [Amer. Comics: *Garfield*]
4. **Heathcliff** aggressive cat, hoodwinks fishmongers and upsets milkmen. [Amer. Comics: *Heathcliff*]
5. **Krazy Kat** perennially involved in conflict with his friend Ignatz the mouse. [Comics: Horn, 436]
6. **Macavity** mysterious feline, "Napoleon of crime." [Br. Lit.: T. S. Eliot *Old Possum's Book of Practical Cats* in Drabble, 714]
7. **Mehitabel** unladylike cat; its motto, "toujours gai." [Am. Lit.: *archy and mehitabel* in Hart, 525]
8. **Old Deuteronomy** elderly cat whose comfort is seen to by the entire village. [Br. Lit.: T. S. Eliot *Old Possum's Book of Practical Cats* in Drabble, 714]
9. **Pluto** pet of a brutal alcoholic who mutilates and hangs it, with dire consequences to himself. [Am. Lit.: Poe "The Black Cat"]
10. **Puss in Boots** cleverly secures a fortune for its penniless master. [Fr. Fairy Tale: "Puss in Boots" in Benét, 829]
11. **Tobermory** taught to speak fluently, it proves insolent and catty. [Br. Lit.: *The Short Stories of Saki* in Magill IV, 1148]

Cemetery (See **BURIAL GROUND.**)

100. CENSORSHIP

1. **blue laws** restrict personal action to improve community morality. [Am. Hist.: Hart, 87]
2. **Boston** arbiter of Puritanical taste as reflected in phrase "banned in Boston." [Am. Usage: Misc.]
3. **Bowdler, Thomas** (1754–1825) expurgated Shakespeare and Gibbon for family editions. [Br. Hist.: Wallechinsky, 164]

4. **Comstock, Anthony** (1844–1915) in *comstockery,* immortalized advocate of blue-nosed censorship. [Am. Hist.: Espy, 135]
5. ***Fahrenheit 451*** describes a future America in which books are prohibited and burned. [Am. Lit.: Bradbury *Fahrenheit 451* in Weiss, 289]
6. **Hays, Will** (1879–1954) clean-minded arbiter of 1930s Hollywood tastes. [Am. Cinema: Griffith, 182]
7. **imprimatur** license given by Roman Catholic Church to publish a book. [Christian Hist.: Misc.]
8. **Index librorum prohibitorum** list of forbidden books compiled by Roman Catholic Church. [Christian Hist.: *NCE,* 1323]
9. **nihil obstat** Roman Catholic Church's inscription in books denoting no objection to literary content. [Christian Hist.: Misc.]
10. ***Tropic of Cancer*** novel noted for its sexual frankness and use of obscenity, long banned in the U.S. [Am. Lit.: Henry Miller *Tropic of Cancer*]
11. ***Ulysses*** Joyce novel long banned in U.S. for its sexual frankness. [Irish Lit.: Benét, 1037]
12. **Unigenitus** papal bull condemning Quesnel's Jansenist book (1713). [Christian Hist.: Brewer *Dictionary,* 1115]

101. CHANCE (See also FATE.)

1. **Bridoison, Taiel de** judge who casts dice to decide cases. [Fr. Lit.: *Pantagruel*]
2. **Fata Morgana** lake-dwelling sorceress and personification of chance. [Ital. Lit.: *Orlando Innamorato*]
3. **Fortuna** goddess of chance. [Rom. Myth.: Kravitz, 58]
4. **Jimmy the Greek** renowned American oddsmaker. [Am. Culture: Wallechinsky, 468]
5. **Russian roulette** suicidal gamble involving a six-shooter, loaded with one bullet. [Folklore: Payton, 590]
6. **Sors** god of chance. [Rom. Myth.: Espy, 42–43]
7. **Three Princes of Serendip** always make discoveries by accident. [Br. Lit.: *Three Princes of Serendip*]
8. **Urim and Thummin** oracular gems used for casting lots, set in Aaron's breastplate. [O.T.: Exodus 28:30; Leviticus 8:8]

Charity (See GENEROSITY.)

102. CHARMS

1. **Abracadabra** cabalistic charm used as an antidote for ague, toothache, etc. [Medieval Folklore: Brewer *Dictionary,* 3]

2. **alectoria** crystalline stone, having talismanic power, found in the stomach of cocks. [Gk. Myth.: Brewer *Dictionary*, 20]
3. **mezuza** doorpost ornament, thought by primitive Jews to protect them from harm. [Judaism: Rosten, 239]
4. **talisman** amulet with which Saladin cures Richard the Lion-Hearted. [Br. Lit.: *The Talisman*]

103. CHASTITY (See also MODESTY, PURITY, VIRGINITY.)

1. **Agnes, St.** virgin saint and martyr. [Christian Hagiog.: Brewster, 76]
2. **Artemis** (Rom. **Diana**) moon goddess; virgin huntress. [Gk. Myth.: Kravitz, 36]
3. **Bona Dea** goddess; so chaste no one but husband sees her after marriage. [Rom. Myth.: Zimmerman, 43]
4. **Britomart** embodiment of purity. [Br. Lit.: *Faerie Queene*]
5. **Claudia** proves innocence by rescuing goddess' ship. [Rom. Myth.: Hall, 70]
6. **Cunegunda** proves innocence by walking unharmed on hot ploughshares. [Christian Hagiog.: Hall, 86]
7. **Gawain, Sir** remained chaste despite the temptations offered him each night by his hostess. [Br. Lit.: *Sir Gawain and the Green Knight* in Benét, 934]
8. **Joseph** resisted the advances of Potiphar's wife. [O.T.: Gen. 39]
9. **lapis lazuli** emblem of sexual purity. [Gem Symbolism: Kunz, 370]
10. **mirror of Alasnam** by clearness or opacity shows woman's purity. [Arab. Lit.: *Arabian Nights,* "The Tale of Zayn Alasnam"]
11. **orange blossoms** symbolic of chastity when used in wedding ceremonies. [Flower Symbolism: *Flora Symbolica,* 176]
12. **phoenix** in Middle Ages, attribute of chastity personified. [Art: Hall, 246]
13. **sapphire** emblem of sexual purity. [Gem Symbolism: Kunz, 370]
14. **tortoise** symbol of sexual purity. [Animal Symbolism: Mercatante, 21]
15. **unicorn** capturable only by virgins; thus, a test of chastity. [Christian Symbolism: Appleton, 105]
16. **Venus Verticordia** Venus invoked to make women pure once more. [Rom. Myth.: Brewer *Dictionary,* 1126]

104. CHAUVINISM (See also BIGOTRY, PATRIOTISM.)

1. **Chauvin, Nicolas** soldier who passionately admired Napoleon; whence, ultranationalism. [Fr. Hist.: *NCE,* 518]
2. **Helmer, Torvald** treats wife Nora as an inferior being. [Nor. Lit.: *A Doll's House*]
3. **Jingo** legendary second-century empress of Japan, victorious invader of Korea and hence the conjectural eponym of jingoism. [Jap. Hist.: *EB* (1963) XIII, 69]
4. **Jingoes** nickname of 19th-century English pro-war party. [Br. Hist.: *EB* (1963) XIII, 69]
5. **male chauvinist pig** denigrating designation for a man who treats women as inferiors. [Am. Pop. Culture: Misc.]

105. CHEERFULNESS (See also GAIETY, JOVIALITY, OPTIMISM.)

1. **blood** humor effecting temperament of sanguineness. [Medieval Physiology: Hall, 130]
2. **coreopsis** symbol of cheerfulness because of its bright yellow flowers. [Flower Symbolism: Jobes, 371]
3. **crocus** symbol of cheerfulness. [Flower Symbolism: Jobes, 383]
4. **L'Allegro** pastoral idyll; title means the cheerful or merry one. [Br. Lit.: "L'Allegro" in Benét, 24–25]
5. **Pollyanna** the "glad child," extraordinarily optimistic. [Children's Lit.: *Pollyanna*]
6. **Raggedy Ann** good-natured despite misadventures; doll with perpetual smile. [Children's Lit.: *Raggedy Ann Stories*]
7. **Sabbath's (Sunday's) child** bonny and blithe, good and gay. [Nurs. Rhyme: Opie, 309]
8. **Silver, Mattie** Zeena's cousin-companion; brightens Frome's gloomy house. [Am. Lit.: *Ethan Frome*]
9. **Singin' in the Rain** downpour doesn't dampen singer's spirits. [Pop. Music: Fordin, 355]
10. **Tapley, Mark** Martin's ever-jovial companion. [Br. Lit.: *Martin Chuzzlewit*]
11. **xeranthemum** symbolizes good-naturedness in adversity. [Flower Symbolism: *Flora Symbolica,* 178]

106. CHILDBIRTH

1. **Artemis** (Rom. **Diana**) goddess of childbirth. [Gk. Myth.: Kravitz, 59]
2. **Asclepius** saved by his father Apollo from the body of pregnant Coronis when Apollo slays her for infidelity. [Gk. Myth.: Benét, 57]

3. **Athena** sprang from the head of Zeus when Hephaestus split it open with an axe. [Gk. Myth.: Benét, 60]
4. **Auge** Arcadian goddess of childbirth. [Arcadian Myth.: Kravitz, 59]
5. **Carmenta** one of Camenae; protectress of women in confinement. [Rom. Rel.: Zimmerman, 50]
6. **Dionysus** unborn god is saved from his dead mother and sewn into Zeus's thigh, from which he is later born. [Gk. Myth.: Benét, 273]
7. **dittany** symbol of childbirth. [Herb Symbolism: *Flora Symbolica,* 173]
8. **Egeria** goddess of childbirth; protectress of the unborn. [Rom. Myth.: Avery, 425–426]
9. **Eileithyia** ancient Greek goddess of childbirth. [Gk. Myth.: Zimmerman, 92]
10. **Hera** (Rom. **Juno**) goddess of childbirth. [Gk. Myth.: Kravitz, 59]
11. **Lilith** demon; dangerous to women in childbirth. [Jew. Trad.: Benét, 586]
12. **Lucina** goddess of childbirth. [Rom. Myth.: Kravitz, 59]
13. **Mater Matuta** goddess of childbirth. [Rom. Myth.: Howe, 160]
14. **Parca** ancient Greek goddess of childbirth. [Gk. Myth.: Kravitz, 59]
15. **test-tube baby** Louise Brown; first successful fertilization outside the body (1978). [Br. Hist.: *Facts* (1978), 596–597]
16. **Themis** goddess of childbirth. [Gk. Myth.: Kravitz, 53]

Childlessness (See BARRENNESS.)

107. CHILDREN (See also YOUTH.)

1. **Pan, Peter** determined always to remain a little boy. [Br. Lit.: J.M. Barrie *Peter Pan*]
2. **Pancras, St.** boy saint, patron of young boys. [Christian Hagiog.: Brewer *Dictionary,* 799]
3. **olive branches** humorous appellation for children. [O.T.: Psalms 128:3]
4. **snaps, snails, and puppy-dogs' tails** "what little boys are made of." [Nurs. Rhyme: *Mother Goose,* 108]
5. **sugar and spice** "what little girls are made of." [Nurs. Rhyme: *Mother Goose,* 108]

108. CHIVALRY

1. **Amadis of Gaul** personification of chivalric ideals: valor, purity, fidelity. [Span. Lit.: Benét, 27]
2. **Arthur, King** king of England; head of the Round Table. [Br. Lit.: *Le Morte d'Arthur*]
3. **Bevis** chivalrous medieval knight, righting wrongs in Europe. [Br. Lit.: *Bevis of Hampton*]
4. **Book of the Courtier** Castiglione's discussion of the manners of the perfect courtier (1528). [Ital. Lit.: *EB*, II: 622]
5. **Calidore, Sir** personification of courtesy and chivalrous actions. [Br. Lit.: *Faerie Queene*]
6. **Camelot** capital of King Arthur's realm, evokes the romance of knightly activity. [Br. Legend: *Collier's* IV, 224]
7. **Cid, El** Spanish military leader who becomes a national hero through chivalrous exploits. [Span. Lit.: *Song of the Cid*]
8. **Courtenay, Miles** dashing and chivalrous Irishman. [Br. Lit.: *King Noanett*, Walsh *Modern*, 108]
9. **Coverley, Sir Roger de** ideal, early 18th-century squire. [Br. Lit.: "Spectator" in Wheeler, 85]
10. **D'Artagnan** Dumas's ever-popular chivalrous character. [Fr. Lit.: *The Three Musketeers*]
11. **Dantes, Edmond** chivalrous adventurer. [Fr. Lit.: *Count of Monte-Cristo*]
12. **Edward III, King** when a countess dropped her garter, he put it on to reproach the sniggering courtiers, and instituted the Order of the Garter. [Br. Legend: Benét, 383]
13. **Eglamour, Sir** "a knight well-spoken, neat, and fine." [Br. Lit.: *Two Gentlemen of Verona*]
14. **Galahad, Sir** gallant, chivalrous knight of the Round Table. [Br. Lit.: *Le Morte d'Arthur*]
15. **Gareth** knight who, though Lynette scorns him as only a kitchen hand, successfully accomplishes rescuing her sister. [Br. Poetry: Tennyson *Idylls of the King*]
16. **Gawain, Sir** King Arthur's nephew; model of knightly perfection and chivalry. [Br. Lit.: *Sir Gawain and the Green Knight*]
17. **Ivanhoe** the epitome of chivalric novels. [Br. Lit.: *Ivanhoe*]
18. **Knights Templars** protected pilgrims to the Holy Land and fought the Saracens. [Medieval Hist.: *NCE*, 1490]
19. **Knights of the Round Table** chivalrous knights in King Arthur's reign. [Br. Lit.: *Le Morte d'Arthur*]
20. **Lancelot, Sir** knight in King Arthur's realm; model of chivalry. [Br. Lit.: *Le Morte d'Arthur*]

21. ***Morte d'Arthur, Le*** monumental work of chivalric romance. [Br. Lit.: *Le Morte d'Arthur*]
22. **Orlando** gallant and steadfast hero of medieval romance. [Ital. Lit.: *Orlando Furioso; Orlando Inammorato; Morgante Maggiore*]
23. **Quixote, Don** knight-errant ready to rescue distressed damsels. [Span. Lit.: *Don Quixote*]
24. **Raleigh, Sir Walter** drops his cloak over a puddle to save Queen Elizabeth from wetting her feet. [Br. Lit.: Scott *Kenilworth* in Magill I, 469]
25. **Richard the Lion-Hearted** (1159–1199) king known for his gallantry and prowess. [Br. Hist.: *EB*, 15: 827]
26. **Roland** paragon of chivalry; unyielding warrior in Charlemagne legends. [Fr. Lit.: *Song of Roland*]
27. **sweet william** symbolizes chivalry. [Flower Symbolism: *Flora Symbolica*, 181]
28. **Valiant, Prince** comic strip character epitomizes chivalry. [Comics: Horn, 565]

109. CHRIST (See also PASSION OF CHRIST.)

1. **Agnus Dei** lamb of god. [Christian Tradition: Brewer *Dictionary*, 17]
2. **bread** symbol of Christ's body in Eucharist. [Christian Tradition: Luke 22:19]
3. **chi rho** monogram of first two letters of Christ's name in Greek. [Christian Symbolism: Appleton, 111]
4. **Emmanuel** Jesus, especially as the Messiah. [N.T.: Matthew 1:23]
5. **fish** Greek acronym for Jesus Christ, Son of God, Saviour. [Christian Symbolism: Child, 210]
6. **Galilee** Jesus's area of activity. [Christianity: Wigoder, 203]
7. **Good Shepherd** [N.T.: John 10:11–14]
8. **ichthys** Greek for 'fish'; early Christian symbol and mystical charm. See **fish**. [Christian Symbolism: Brewer *Dictionary*, 478]
9. **I.N.R.I.** acronym of *Iesus Nazarenus, Rex Iudaeorum* 'Jesus of Nazareth, King of the Jews,' inscription affixed to Christ's cross as a mockery. [Christianity: Brewer *Note-Book*, 450]
10. **IHS (I.H.S.)** first three letters of Greek spelling of *Jesus*; also taken as acronym of *Iesus Hominum Salvator* 'Jesus, Savior of Mankind.' [Christian Symbolism: Brewer *Dictionary*, 480]
11. **King of Kings** appellation for Jesus Christ. [N.T.: Revelation 17:14]

12. **lamb** the Lord as the sacrificial animal. [Christian Symbolism: O.T.: Isaiah 53:7; N.T.: John 1:29]
13. **lion** symbol expressing power and courage of Jesus. [Christian Symbolism: N.T.: Revelation 5:5]
14. **Lord of the Dance** "At Bethlehem I had my birth." [Br. Folk Music: Carter, "Lord of the Dance" in Taylor, 128]
15. **Lord's Anointed, the** designation for Christ or the Messiah. [Christian Tradition: O.T.: I Samuel 26:9]
16. **Man of Sorrows** epithet for the prophesied Messiah. [O.T.: Isaiah 53:3]
17. **Messiah** expected leader who will deliver the Jews from their enemies; applied by Christians to Jesus. [O.T., N.T.: Brewer *Dictionary*, 602]
18. **Piers the Plowman** English plowman who becomes allegorical figure of Christ incarnate. [Br. Lit.: *The Vision of William, Concerning Piers the Plowman*, Magill III, 1105–1107]
19. **star** token of the Lord and his coming. [Christian Symbolism: O.T.: Numbers, 24:17; N.T.: Revelation 22:16]
20. **vine** gives nourishment to branches or followers. [Christian Symbolism: Appleton, 107; N.T.: John 15:5]
21. **wine** symbol of Christ's blood in Eucharist. [Christian Tradition: "Eucharist" in Cross, 468–469]

110. CHRISTMAS

1. **Amahl and the Night Visitors** lame shepherd boy gives crutch as gift for Christ Child; first opera composed for television (1951). [Am. Opera: *EB,* VI: 792–793]
2. **Befana** fairy fills stockings with toys on Twelfth Night. [Ital. Legend: *LLEI,* I: 323]
3. **carols** custom originating in England of singing songs at Christmas. [Christian Tradition: *NCE,* 552]
4. ***Child's Christmas in Wales, A*** nostalgic remembrance of Welsh Christmases. [Brit. Lit.: *A Child's Christmas in Wales*]
5. **Christmas** feast of the nativity of Jesus Christ (December 25). [Christian Tradition: *NCE,* 552]
6. **Christmas tree** custom originating in medieval Germany of decorating an evergreen tree at Christmas. [Christian Tradition: *NCE,* 552]
7. **Christmas, Father** legendary bringer of gifts; another name for Santa Claus. [Children's Lit.: *Father Christmas*]

8. **Deck the Halls with Boughs of Holly** traditional Christmas carol. [Western Culture: "Deck the Halls with Boughs of Holly" in Rockwell, 146–147]
9. **First Noel, The** traditional Christmas carol. [Western Culture: "The First Noel" in Rockwell, 136–137]
10. **Gift of the Magi, The** O. Henry's Christmas story of love and self-sacrifice. [Am. Lit.: Rockwell, 77–80]
11. **gold, frankincense, and myrrh** given to the infant Jesus by the three Wise Men. [N.T.: Matthew 2:1–11]
12. **Grinch** hating the delights of Yuletide, he steals Christmas presents but eventually relents and joins in the merriment. [Children's Lit.: Seuss *How the Grinch Stole Christmas* in Weiss, 210]
13. **Hark! the Herald Angels Sing** traditional Christmas carol. [Western Culture: "Hark! the Herald Angels Sing" in Rockwell, 132–133]
14. **holly** symbol of Christmas. [Flower Symbolism: *Flora Symbolica,* 174; Kunz, 331
15. **Jingle Bells** yuletide song composed by J. S. Pierpont. [Pop. Music: Van Doren, 200]
16. **Joy to the World!** traditional Christmas carol. [Western Culture: "Joy to the World!" in Rockwell, 138]
17. **Kringle, Kris** Santa Claus in Germany. [Ger. Folklore: *LLEI,* I: 277]
18. **Lord of Misrule** formerly, person chosen to lead Christmas revels and games. [Br. Folklore: Misc.]
19. ***Miracle on 34th Street*** film featuring benevolent old gentleman named Kris Kringle. [Am. Cinema: Halliwell, 493]
20. **mistletoe** traditional yuletide sprig under which kissing is obligatory. [Br. and Am. Folklore: Leach, 731]
21. **Night Before Christmas, The** poem celebrating activities of Christmas Eve. [Am. Lit.: "The Night Before Christmas"]
22. **O Come, All Ye Faithful** traditional Christmas carol. [Western Culture: "O Come, All Ye Faithful" in Rockwell, 142–143]
23. **O Little Town of Bethlehem** traditional Christmas carol. [Western Culture: "O Little Town of Bethlehem" in Rockwell, 120–121]
24. **red and green** traditional colors of Christmas. [Christian Tradition: Misc.]
25. **Rudolph, the Red-Nosed Reindeer** his nose lights Santa on his way. [Am. Music: "Rudolph, the Red-Nosed Reindeer"]

26. **Santa Claus** jolly, gift-giving figure who visits children on Christmas Eve. [Christian Tradition: *NCE*, 1937]
27. **Scrooge, Ebenezer** the great miser during season of giving. [Br. Lit.: *A Christmas Carol*]
28. **Silent Night** traditional Christmas carol. [Western Culture: "Silent Night" in Rockwell, 130–131]
29. **Star of Bethlehem** announces birth of the Christ child. [Christianity: N.T.: Matthew 2:2]
30. **yule log** log burned at Christmas. [Western Tradition: *NCE*, 552]
31. **We Three Kings of Orient Are** traditional Christmas carol. [Western Culture: "We Three Kings of Orient Are" in Rockwell, 122–123]

111. CIRCUMCISION

1. **Abraham** initiated rite in covenant with God. [O.T.: Genesis 17:11–14]
2. **Berith** Jewish rite of circumcising male child eight days after birth. [Judaism: Misc.]
3. **Elijah** traditionally represented at ceremony by empty chair. [Judaism: Wigoder, 172]
4. **Gibeath-haaraloth** Hill of Foreskins; where Joshua circumcised Israelites. [O.T.: Joshua 5:3]
5. **Shandy, Tristram** accidentally circumcised by a loose window in a sash. [Br. Lit.: *Tristram Shandy* in Magill I, 1027]

112. CLEANLINESS (See also ORDERLINESS.)

1. **Berchta** unkempt herself, demands cleanliness from others, especially children. [Ger. Folklore: Leach, 137]
2. **cat** continually "washes" itself. [Animal Symbolism: Jobes, 296]
3. **Clean, Mr.** brand of household cleaner. [Trademarks: Crowley *Trade*, 379]
4. **hyssop** Biblical herb used for ceremonial sprinkling. [Flower Symbolism: O.T. Psalms 51:7]
5. **Mary Mouse** constantly sweeping and dusting. [Children's Lit.: *Mary Mouse and the Doll's House*, Fisher, 216]
6. **Spic and Span** brand of household cleaner. [Trademarks: Crowley *Trade*, 546]
7. **Wag-at-the-Wa'** brownie who is strict about neatness of houses. [Br. Folklore: Briggs, 425–426]

Cleverness (See **CUNNING.**)

113. CLOCKS

1. **Big Ben** bell of Houses of Parliament clock in London keeps Britons punctual. [Br. Culture: Misc.]
2. **Nuremberg Egg** first watch; created by Peter Henlein (1502). [Ger. Hist.: Grun, 223]
3. **Strasbourg cathedral clock** famous clock in Strasbourg Cathedral. [Fr. Culture: *NCE,* 581]

114. CLOWNS

1. **Bardolph** "coney-catching rascal"; follower of Falstaff. [Br. Lit.: *Merry Wives of Windsor*]
2. **Bertoldo** medieval jester, butt, and buffoon. [Ital. Folklore: Walsh *Classical,* 54–55]
3. **Dagonet** fool at the court of King Arthur, who knighted him. [Br. Lit.: Barnhart, 303]
4. **Feste** playful fool. [Br. Lit.: *Twelfth Night*]
5. **Geddes** jester in the court of Mary Queen of Scots. [Scot. Hist.: Brewer *Handbook,* 380]
6. **Gobbo, Launcelot** a "wit-snapper," a "merry devil." [Br. Lit.: *Merchant of Venice*]
7. **harlequin** comic character in commedia dell'arte; dressed in multicolored tights in a diamond-shaped pattern. [Ital. Drama: *NCE,* 1194]
8. **Hop-Frog** deformed dwarf; court fool. [Am. Lit.: "Hop-Frog" in *Portable Poe,* 317–329]
9. **Jocus** Cupid's companion and fool. [Rom. Lit.: *Psychomachia*]
10. **Joey** after Joseph Grimaldi, famous 19th-century clown. [Am. Hist.: Espy, 45]
11. **Jupe** a clown in Sleary's circus. [Br. Lit.: *Hard Times*]
12. **Kelly, Emmett** (1897–1979) foremost silent, sad-faced circus clown. [Am. Hist.: Flexner, 83]
13. **McDonald, Ronald** hamburger chain's Pied Piper. [Am. Culture: *Grinding*]
14. **Merry-Andrew** Andrew Borde, Henry VIII's physician. [Br. Hist.: Wheeler, 241]
15. **Pagliacci** clown Canio stabs his unfaithful wife and her lover. [Ital. Opera: Osborne *Opera,* 233]
16. **Patch** court fool of Elizabeth, wife of Henry VII. [Br. Hist.: Brewer *Handbook,* 380]

17. **Touchstone** a "motley-mined," "roynish" court jester. [Br. Lit.: *As You Like It*]
18. **Yorick** jester in the court of Denmark. [Br. Lit.: *Hamlet*]

Clumsiness (See **AWKWARDNESS, INEPTITUDE.**)

115. COARSENESS

1. **Billingsgate** site of a London fishmarket, known for foul and abusive language. [Br. Hist.: Brewer *Dictionary*, 106]
2. **Branghtons, the** Evelina's rude, coarse cousins. [Br. Lit.: *Evelina*]
3. **Crawley, Sir Pitt** vulgar aristocrat. [Br. Lit.: *Vanity Fair*]
4. **Goops** naughty, balloon-headed children. [Am. Lit.: *Goops and How To Be Them,* Hart, 323]
5. **Neanderthal man** early form of man, Caucasoid and strongly built. [Anthropology: *NCE,* 1900]
6. **Ochs, Baron** vulgar, lecherous nobleman. [Aust. Opera: R. Strauss, *Rosenkavalier,* Westerman, 423–425]
7. **Pike** "he expectorates vehemently " [Am. Lit.: *At Home and Abroad,* Hart, 655]
8. **Tearsheet, Doll** prostitute with vitriolic vocabulary. [Br. Lit.: *II Henry IV*]
9. **Troglodytes** race of uncivilized cave dwellers. [Gk. Hist.: Brewer *Dictionary,* 1103]
10. **xanthium** symbolizes bad manners and rudeness. [Flower Symbolism: *Flora Symbolica,* 178]
11. **Yahoos** loutish, abusive brutes in shape of men. [Br. Lit.: *Gulliver's Travels*]

116. COCKNEY

1. **Bow Bells** famous bell in East End of London; "only one who is born within the bell's sound is a true Cockney." [Br. Hist.: *NCE,* 347]
2. **Doolittle, Eliza** Cockney girl taught by professor to imitate aristocracy. [Br. Lit.: *Pygmalion*]
3. **Weller, Tony and Samuel** father and son, coachman and bootblack, with colorful lingo. [Br. Lit.: Dickens *Pickwick Papers*]

117. COLDNESS

1. **Acis** blood turned into a "river of ice." [Gk. Myth.: *Metamorphoses*]
2. **Antarctica** continent of constant cold. [Geography: *WB*, A:495]

3. **Arctic** area of constant cold. [Geography: *WB*, A:600]
4. **Frost, Jack** personification of freezing cold. [Am. and Br. Folklore: Misc.]
5. **Hyperboreans** fabulous people living beyond North Wind, traditionally near North Pole. [Rom. Myth.: Zimmerman, 132]
6. **Lapland** northern region of Scandinavian peninsula, mostly within Arctic Circle. [Geography: Misc.]
7. **Lower Slobbovia** cartoon land of perpetual cold. [Comics: "Li'l Abner" in Horn, 450–451]

118. COLONIZATION

1. **Evander** Arcadian, founded settlement in Italy. [Gk. Myth.: Kravitz, 100]
2. **Jamestown, Virginia** first permanent English settlement in New World (1607). [Am. Hist.: Jameson, 255]
3. **Mayflower** ship which brought Pilgrims to New World (1620). [Am. Hist.: *NCE*, 1730]
4. **Plymouth Plantation** first English settlement in New England (1620). [Am. Hist.: *Major Bradford's Town*]
5. **thirteen original colonies** earliest settlements became first states in U.S. [Am. Hist.: *NCE*, 2733]
6. **Williamsburg** monument of American colonial period; settled in 1632. [Am. Hist.: Hart, 930]

Comedy (See **ZANINESS.**)

Comeuppance (See **LAST LAUGH.**)

Comfort (See **LUXURY.**)

Commerce (See **FINANCE.**)

Companionship (See **FRIENDSHIP.**)

Compassion (See **KINDNESS.**)

Compromise (See **PEACEMAKING.**)

119. CONCEALMENT (See also REFUGE.)

1. **Ali Baba** 40 thieves concealed in oil jars. [Arab. Lit.: *Arabian Nights*]
2. **ark of bulrushes** Moses hidden in basket to escape infanticide. [O.T.: Exodus 2:1–6]
3. **Holgrave** hides his identity as the builder's descendant and finds the concealed deed to the land. [Am. Lit.: Hawthorne *The House of the Seven Gables*]

4. **Hooper, Parson** wears a black veil as a symbol of secret sorrow and sin. [Am. Lit.: Hawthorne "The Minister's Black Veil" in Benét, 672]
5. **Inigo and Gonsalve** Concepción's would-be lovers; hides them in her husband's clocks. [Fr. Opera: Ravel, *The Spanish Hour*, Westerman, 198]
6. **Man in the Iron Mask** forced to perpetually wear an iron mask to conceal his indentity. [Br. Lit. and Fr. Hist.: Benét 628]
7. **Polonius** Hamlet stabs him through the arras. [Br. Lit.: *Hamlet*]
8. **sealed book** symbolic of impenetrable secrets. [Christian Symbolism: Appleton, 13]
9. **veil of Isis** never lifted to reveal the face of the goddess. [Anc. Egypt. Myth.: Brewer *Dictionary* 492]
10. **wilderness of Maon** where David sought refuge from Saul's pursuit. [O.T.: I Samuel 23:25–29]
11. **wilderness of Ziph** where David hid to escape Saul's search. [O.T.: I Samuel 23:14]

120. CONCEIT (See also ARROGANCE, BOASTFULNESS, EGOTISM.)

1. **Ajax (the lesser)** boastful and insolent; drowns due to vanity. [Gk. Myth.: Kravitz, 14]
2. **Bunthorne, Reginald** fleshly poet; "aesthetically" enchants the ladies. [Br. Lit.: *Patience*]
3. **Butler, Theodosius** thinks he is a wonderful person. [Br. Lit.: *Sketches by Boz*]
4. **Collins, Mr.** pompous, self-satisfied clergyman who proposes to Elizabeth Bennet. [Br. Lit.: Jane Austen *Pride and Prejudice*]
5. **Dalgetty, Rittmaster Dugald** self-aggrandizing, pedantic soldier-of-fortune. [Br. Lit.: *Legend of Montrose*]
6. **Dedlock, Sir Leicester** contemplates his own greatness. [Br. Lit.: *Bleak House*]
7. **Dogberry and Verges** ignorant and bloated constables. [Br. Lit.: *Much Ado About Nothing*]
8. **Grosvenor, Archibald** idyllic poet of no imperfections. [Br. Lit.: *Patience*]
9. **Henry VIII** inflated self-image parallels bloated body. [Br. Lit.: *Henry VIII*]
10. **Horner, Little Jack** pats his back with "What a good boy am I!" [Nurs. Rhyme: *Mother Goose*, 90]

11. **Keefe, Jack** baseball pitcher is a chronic braggart and self-excuser suffering from an exaggerated sense of importance. [Am. Lit.: Lardner *You Know Me Al* in Magill III, 1159]
12. **Lewis** self-important coxcomb full of hollow, ostentatious valor. [Br. Lit.: *Henry V*]
13. **Malvolio** Olivia's grave, self-important steward; "an affectioned ass." [Br. Lit.: *Twelfth Night*]
14. **Montespan, Marquis de** regards exile and wife's concubinage as honor. [Br. Opera: *The Duchess of la Vallière,* Brewer *Handbook,* 721]
15. **narcissus** flower of conceit. [Plant Symbolism: *Flora Symbolica,* 170; Gk. Myth.: Zimmerman, 171–172]
16. **nettle** symbol of vanity and pride. [Flower Symbolism: *Flora Symbolica,* 176]
17. **Orion** scorpion stung him to death for his boasting. [Rom. Myth.: Brewer *Dictionary,* 971]
18. **Prigio, Prince** too clever prince; arrogance renders him unpopular. [Children's Lit.: *Prince Prigio*]
19. **Slurk, Mr.** had a "consciousness of immeasurable superiority" over others. [Br. Lit.: *Pickwick Papers*]
20. **Tappertit, Simon** boasted he could subdue women with eyes. [Br. Lit.: *Barnaby Rudge*]

121. CONDEMNATION

1. **bell, book, and candle** symbols of Catholic excommunication rite. [Christianity: Brewer *Note-Book,* 85]
2. **Bridge of Sighs** passage from Doge's court to execution chamber in Renaissance Venice. [Ital. Hist.: Brewer *Note-Book,* 121]
3. **Eurydice** doomed to eternal death when Orpheus disobeys Hades. [Gk. Myth.: Kravitz, 97]
4. **lions' mouths** Venetian receptacles for denunciations, character assassinations. [Ital. Hist.: Plumb, 259–260]
5. **Prometheus** a Titan condemned by Zeus for giving fire to mortals. [Gk. Lit.: *Prometheus Bound,* Magill I, 786–788]

122. CONFUSION

1. **Babel** where God confounded speech of mankind. [O.T.: Genesis 11:7–9]
2. **bedlam** from Hospital of St. Mary of Bethlehem, former English insane asylum. [Br. Folklore: Jobes, 193]

3. **Cia** amnesia victim whose identity becomes doubtful when the same identity is claimed by an insane woman. [Ital. Drama: Pirandello *As You Desire Me* in Sobel, 35]
4. ***Comedy of Errors, The*** two pairs of identical twins wreak social havoc in Ephesus. [Br. Drama: Shakespeare *The Comedy of Errors*]
5. **Corybantes** half-divine priests of Cybele; celebrated noisy festivals in her honor. [Gk. Myth.: Howe, 67]
6. **Jude** "the other Judas, not Iscariot." [N.T.: John 14:22]
7. **Labyrinth** maze at Knossos where Minotaur lived. [Gk. Myth.: Hall, 185]
8. **Pandemonium** Milton's capital of the devils. [Br. Lit.: *Paradise Lost*]
9. **Pantagruelian Law Case** not understanding the defense, judge gives incomprehensible verdict.[Fr. Lit.: *Pantagruel*]
10. **Serbonian Bog** Egyptian morass, "where armies whole have sunk." [Br. Lit.: *Paradise Lost*]
11. **Star-Splitter, The** "We've looked and looked, but after all where are we?" [Am. Lit.: "The Star-Splitter" in Hart, 799]

123. CONQUERORS

1. **Agricola** (40–93) enlightened governor and general; subdued all Britain. [Rom. Hist.: *NCE,* 35]
2. **Alaric** (c. 370–410) Visigoth chief; sacked Rome. [Eur. Hist.: Bishop, 14]
3. **Alexander the Great** (356–323 B.C.) Macedonian king and conqueror of much of Asia. [Gk. Hist.: *NCE,* 61]
4. **Attila** (d. 453) king of Huns. [Eur. Hist.: *NCE,* 182]
5. **Batu Khan** (d. 1255) Mongol conqueror of 13th century; grandson of Genghis Khan. [Asian Hist.: *NCE,* 248]
6. **Caesar, Julius** (102–44 B.C.) Roman statesman and general; reduced all of Gaul and Britain to Roman control. [Rom. Hist.: *NCE,* 416]
7. **Canute** (995–1035) Norseman; subjugator of England. [Br. Hist.: Bishop, 42]
8. **Charlemagne** (742–814) established the Carolingian empire. [Fr. Hist.: *NCE,* 507]
9. **Charles V** (1500–1558) Holy Roman Emperor; last to sack Rome (1527). [Ital. Hist.: Plumb, 43, 406–407]
10. **Cortés, Hernando** (1485–1547) annihilated Aztec culture, claiming Mexico for Spain. [Span. Hist.: *EB,* 5: 194–196]

11. **Cyrus II (the Great)** (d. 529 B.C.) creator of Persian empire (553–529). [Class. Hist.: Grun]
12. **Genghis Khan** (1167–1227) Mongol chieftain overran most of Asia and eastern Europe (1206–1227). [Asian Hist.: *EB,* 7: 1013–1016]
13. **Genseric** (c. 390–477) Vandal king; controlled large portion of Mediterranean. [Rom. Hist.: *NCE,* 1034]
14. **Golden Horde** 13th-century Mongol overlords of Russia. [Russ. Hist.: Grun, 170]
15. **Hitler, Adolf** (1889–1945) led Germany to conquer or destroy most of Europe. [Ger. Hist.: *Hitler*]
16. **Mohammed II** (1429–1481) Ottoman conqueror of Constantinople (1453). [Eur. Hist.: Plumb, 292–293]
17. **Napoleon** (1769–1821) vanquished most of Europe. [Fr. Hist.: Harvey, 570]
18. **Nebuchadnezzar** (d. 562 B.C.) subjugated Jews, initiating Babylonian captivity (597–5 B.C.). [O.T.: Daniel 1:1–2]
19. **Pizarro, Francisco** (c. 1476–1541) with small force, destroyed Incan empire. [Span. Hist.: *EB,* 14: 487–488]
20. **Tamerlane** (1336–1405) Tartar; vanquished Persia and India. [Asian Hist.: Brewer *Dictionary,* 1061]
21. **William the Conqueror** (1027–1087) commanded Normans in conquest of Britain; victor at Hastings (1066). [Br. Hist.: Bishop, 42–46]

124. CONSCIENCE

1. **Aidos** ancient Greek personification of conscience. [Gk. Myth.: Zimmerman, 14]
2. **Clamence** haunted by guilt because he failed to respond when aware that a girl had jumped or fallen into the Seine. [Fr. Lit.: Camus *The Fall*]
3. **Cricket, Jiminy** dapper mite guides the callow Pinocchio. [Am. Cinema: *Pinocchio* in *Disney Films,* 32–37]
4. ***Elder Statesman, The*** Lord Claverton ponders the shame of his past, personified by ghosts of his victims. [Br. Drama: T. S. Eliot *The Elder Statesman* in Magill IV, 262]
5. **Godunov, Boris** Tsar suffers pangs of conscience for having murdered the Tsarevitch in order to seize the throne. [Russ. Drama and Opera: *Boris Godunov*]
6. **Karamazov, Ivan** guilt for wishing his father's death culminates in hallucinatory conversations with the Devil. [Russ. Lit.: Dostoevsky *The Brothers Karamazov*]

7. **Solness, Halvard** plagued by awareness of his past ruthlessness and the guilt of defying God's will. [Nor. Drama: Ibsen *The Master Builder* in Magill II, 643]
8. **Valdes and Cornelius** Good Angel and Evil Angel; symbolize Faustus's inner conflict. [Br. Lit.: *Doctor Faustus*]
9. **Wilson, William** his Doppelgänger irrupts at occasions of duplicity. [Am. Lit.: "William Wilson" in *Portable Poe,* 57–82]

125. CONSERVATISM

1. **Apley, George** scion of an old Boston society family, he exemplifies its traditions and remains in old-fashioned mediocrity. [Am. Lit.: *The Late George Apley* in Magill I, 499]
2. **Conservative party** British political party, once called the Tory party. [Br. Hist.: *NCE,* 632]
3. **Daughters of the American Revolution (D.A.R)** conservative society of female descendants of Revolutionary War soldiers. [Am. Hist.: Jameson, 132]
4. **elephant** symbol of the Republican party. [Am. Hist.: Misc.]
5. **John Birch Society** ultraconservative, anti-Communist organization. [Am. Hist.: *NCE,* 1421]
6. **laissez-faire** political doctrine that an economic system functions best without governmental interference. [Politics: Misc.]
7. **Luddites** arch-conservative workmen; smashed labor-saving machinery (1779). [Br. Hist.: Espy, 107]
8. **Republican Party** U.S. political party, generally espousing a conservative platform. [Am. Hist.: Jameson, 424]
9. **Warbucks, Daddy** espouses a reactionary law-and-order society threatened by decadence, bureaucracy, and loss of Puritan virtues. [Comics: Berger, 84]

126. CONSPIRACY (See also INTRIGUE.)

1. **Babington Plot** abortive plot to assassinate Elizabeth I; sealed Mary Stuart's fate (1586). [Br. Hist.: *NCE,* 202]
2. **Black Friday** (September 24, 1869) gold speculation led to financial panic. [Am. Hist.: Van Doren, 259]
3. **Brutus** plotted against Caesar with Cassius and Casca. [Br. Lit.: *Julius Caesar*]
4. **Cassius** intriguer and accomplice in plot against Caesar. [Br. Lit.: *Julius Caesar*]
5. **Cinq-Mars** conspires against Cardinal Richelieu. [Fr. Lit.: *Cinq-Mars*]

6. **Cointet brothers** use a corrupt lawyer to ruin a young printer and cheat him of his invention. [Fr. Lit.: Balzac *Lost Illusions* in Magill II, 595]
7. **Doctors' Plot** physicians falsely tried for trying to poison Stalin. [Jew. Hist.: Wigoder, 160]
8. **Duke of Buckingham** Richard III's "counsel's consistory"; assisted him to throne. [Br. Lit.: *Richard III*]
9. **Fawkes, Guy** (1570–1606) leader of Gunpowder Plot to blow up Houses of Parliament (1605). [Br. Hist.: *EB, IV:* 70, 801]
10. **Gunpowder Plot** See **Fawkes, Guy.**
11. **Joseph's brothers** sold him into slavery out of envy and hatred. [O.T.: Genesis 37:18–28]
12. **Pontiac** (1720–1769) brains behind widespread American Indian uprising (1762). [Am. Hist.: Jameson, 398]
13. **Shallum** plots and successfully executes overthrow of Zechariah. [O.T.: II Kings 15:10]
14. **Watergate** political intrigue leading to resignation of Pres. Nixon. [Am. Hist.: *EB,* X: 568–569]
15. ***Woman in White, The*** Laura Fairlie is unjustly confined to an insane asylum in a plot to obtain her money. [Br. Lit.: Magill I, 1125]

Constancy (See LOYALTY.)

127. CONTEMPLATION

1. ***Compleat Angler, The*** Izaak Walton's classic treatise on the *Contemplative Man's Recreation.* [Br. Lit.: *The Compleat Angler*]
2. ***Thinker, The*** sculpture by Rodin, depicting contemplative man. [Fr. Art: Osborne, 988]

128. CONTENTMENT

1. **Aglaos** poor peasant said by the Delphic oracle to be happier than the king because he was contented. [Gk. Myth.: Benét, 15]

129. CONTROVERSY (See also SCANDAL.)

1. **Avignon** location of alternate papacy (1309–1377). [Fr. Hist.: Bishop, 376]
2. ***Birth of a Nation, The*** film elicits emotional response (1915). [Am. Cinema: Griffith, 36–39]
3. **Chicago 8 trial** alleged ringleaders of Chicago riots tried in circus atmosphere (1969). [Am. Hist.: Van Doren, 630]

4. **Dred Scott decision** Supreme Court decision concerning freedom of slaves (1857). [Am. Hist.: Jameson, 151–152]
5. ***Origin of Species, The*** once revolutionary theory of evolution and natural selection (1859). [Br. Science: *The Origin of Species*]
6. **Pentagon Papers** Defense Department's Vietnam policy papers leaked to press. [Am. Hist.: Flexner, 376]
7. ***Rite of Spring, The*** Stravinsky's score caused riot at premiere (1913). [Music Hist.: Thompson, 1900]
8. **Sacco and Vanzetti** (Nicola, 1891–1927) (Bartolomeo, 1888–1927) Italian immigrants tried and executed for murder in witch-hunt for anarchists. [Am. Hist.: *Sacco-Vanzetti Case: A Transcript*]
9. **Scopes trial** concerning the teaching of evolution in public schools (1925). [Am. Hist.: Allen, 142–146]
10. **Scottsboro Case** cause célèbre concerning nine Negro men, two white girls (1931). [Am. Hist.: Hart, 753]
11. **scrap of paper** pre-WWI Belgian neutrality; German disregard precipitated British involvement. [Am. Hist.: Jameson, 450]
12. **Stamp Act** legislative development contributing to American Revolution (1765). [Am. Hist.: Jameson, 475]
13. **Tonkin Gulf** disputed N. Vietnamese attacks escalated U.S. war effort (1964). [Am. Hist.: Van Doren, 595]
14. **Warren Report** government's much disputed conclusion that President Kennedy's assassin acted alone. [Am. Hist.: Van Doren, 594]

130. CONVENTIONALITY

1. **Archer, Newland** too bound by conventional mores to seek happiness with his wife's cousin. [Am. Lit.: *The Age of Innocence*]

131. COOPERATION

1. **Achaean League** federation of Greek cities formed in 280 B.C. to resist Macedonian domination. [Gk. Hist.: Brewer *Dictionary*, 6]
2. **Allies, the 1.** in World War I, nations, initially Russia, France, and Great Britain, allied against the Central Powers. **2.** in World War II, those allied against the Axis, including Great Britain, Russia, and U.S. [Eur. Hist.: *Collier's*, VIII, 457]
3. **Axis** in World War II, the alliance of Germany, Italy, Japan, etc., opposing the Allies. [Eur. Hist.: *Collier's*, VIII, 457]

4. **Central Powers** in World War I, the alliance of Hungary, Germany, Bulgaria, and Turkey. [Eur. Hist.: *NCE*, 493]
5. **Common Market** association of western European countries designed to facilitate free trade among members. [Eur. Hist.: *EB*, III: 1001]
6. **Confederacy** the eleven Southern states that seceded from the U.S. and banded together. [Am. Hist.: *NCE*, 623]
7. **Entente Cordiale** agreement between Great Britain and France to settle their disagreements over colonies as diplomatic partners. [Eur. Hist.: *WB*, 21: 367]
8. **Helsinki accord** agreement between Soviet bloc and the West for economic, commercial, and scientific cooperation and for respect of human rights and fundamental freedoms. [World Hist.: *News Directory* (1977), 177–179]
9. **League of Nations** world organization for international cooperation. [World Hist.: *EB*, 6: 102]
10. **NATO** free-world mutual security pact against Soviet bloc. [World Hist.: Van Doren, 520]
11. **Nazi-Soviet Pact** nonaggression treaty freed Hitler to invade Poland. [Ger. Hist.: Shirer, 685–705]
12. **OPEC** cartel of nations whose economic livelihood depends upon the export of petroleum. [World Hist.: *WB*, 14: 646]
13. **Pact of Steel** German-Italian treaty established common cause in future undertakings. [Eur. Hist.: Shirer, 646–648]
14. **Potsdam Conference** unconditional Japanese surrender demanded; war crimes trials planned (July, 1945). [World Hist.: Van Doren, 507]
15. **SEATO** organization formed to assure protection against communist expansion in Southeast Asia (1955–1976). [World Hist.: *EB*, IX: 377]
16. **Tinker to Evers to Chance** legendary baseball double-play combination (1902–1910). [Am. Sports: Turkin, 474]
17. **Triple Entente** association among Great Britain, France, and Russia; nucleus of the Allied Coalition in WWI. [World Hist.: *EB*, 10: 128]
18. **United Nations** world organization for international discussion and peacekeeping. [World Hist.: Brewer *Dictionary*, 1116]
19. **Yalta Conference** Allies developed plan for reconstruction of Europe (February, 1945). [World Hist.: Van Doren, 504]

132. COUNSEL (See also **GUIDANCE.**)

1. **Achitophel** sage adviser to David; subsequently to Absalom. [O.T.: II Samuel 16:23]

2. **Antenor** counselor; advised Priam to return Helen to Menelaus. [Gk. Myth.: Zimmerman, 23]
3. **Areopagus** hill near the Acropolis used for Athenian council deliberations. [Gk. Hist.: Benét, 46]
4. **Chesterfield, Lord (1694–1773)** wrote *Letters to His Son* to educate him in the ways of the world. [Br. Lit.: Magill III, 565]
5. **Consus** god of councils and advice; agricultural god. [Rom. Myth.: Kravitz, 65; Parrinder, 66]
6. **Egeria** wife, instructress, and advisor of emperor Numa. [Rom. Myth.: Jobes, 491; Avery, 426]
7. **Krishna** Hindu god acts as spiritual and military counselor to Arjuna and his family. [Hindu Lit.: *Mahabharata*]
8. **Laurence, Friar** adviser to the lovers. [Br. Lit.: *Romeo and Juliet*]
9. **Mentor** Odysseus's adviser; entrusted with care and education of Telemachus. [Gk. Lit.: *Odyssey*]
10. **Nestor** a sage old counselor to the Greeks in the Trojan War. [Gk. Myth.: *Iliad*]
11. **Polonius** gives Laertes rules of conduct. [Br. Drama: Shakespeare *Hamlet*]
12. **Poseidon Hippios** god of counsel and councils. [Gk. Myth.: Kravitz, 67]
13. **Proverbs** precepts for living according to God's law and common sense. [O.T.: Proverbs]
14. ***Way to Wealth, The*** maxims intended to inculcate virtue and frugality. [Am. Lit.: Benjamin Franklin *Poor Richard's Almanack* in Benét, 803]

Courage (See **BRAVERY.**)

133. COURTESANSHIP (See also MISTRESSES, PROSTITUTION.)

1. **Aspasia** mistress of Pericles; byword for cultured courtesan. [Gk. Hist.: Benét, 58]
2. **Camille** beautiful courtesan, the toast of Paris. [Fr. Lit.: *Camille*]
3. **Lais** celebrated Thessalonian courtesan, so beautiful the townswomen kill her out of jealousy. [Gk. Hist.: Benét, 561]
4. **Lescaut, Manon** lives well by giving affections to noblemen. [Fr. Lit.: *Manon Lescaut*]
5. **Marneffe, Madame** as courtesan for barons, she obtains wealth. [Fr. Lit.: *Cousin Bette,* Magill I, 166–168]
6. **Phryne** (4th century B.C.) wealthy Athenian hetaera of surpassing beauty. [Gk. Hist.: Benét, 784]

7. **Rosette** D'Albert's pliable, versatile, talented, acknowledged bedmate. [Fr. Lit.: *Mademoiselle de Maupin.* Magill I, 542–543]
8. **Thaïs** Alexandrian courtesan, converts to Christianity. [Medieval Legend: Walsh *Classical,* 307]
9. **Vasantasena** lovely courtesan whose many adventures culminate in an edict freeing her from her courtesan status. [Sanskrit Lit.: *The Little Clay Cart* in Haydn & Fuller, 432]
10. **Violetta** prosperous courtesan in fashionable Paris. [Ital. Opera: Verdi *La Traviata* in Benét, 1022]

134. COURTESY

1. **Boy Scouts** youth organization, ever ready to perform good deeds. [Am. Hist.: Jameson, 59]
2. **Castiglione, Baldassare** (1478–1529) author of *The Courtier,* Renaissance bible of etiquette. [Ital. Lit.: Plumb, 316–319]
3. **Dickon** one of "nature's gentlemen." [Children's Lit.: *The Secret Garden*]
4. **Post, Emily** (1873–1960) etiquette book author; preaches "consideration for others." [Am. Hist.: Flexner, 277]
5. **Shem and Japheth** cover father's nakedness without looking at him. [O.T.: Genesis 9:23–27]

135. COURTESY, EXCESSIVE

1. **Alphonse and Gaston** personifications of overdone politeness. [Comics: Horn, 77–78]
2. **Haskell, Eddie** hypocritical teenager, gracious toward adults, pugnacious toward children. [TV: "Leave It to Beaver" in Terrace, II, 18–19]
3. **Petruchio** his excessive courtesy a stratagem to break Katharina. [Br. Lit.: *The Taming of the Shrew*]

Covetousness (See GREED.)

136. COWARDICE (See also BOASTFULNESS, TIMIDITY.)

1. **Acres, Bob** a swaggerer lacking in courage. [Br. Lit.: *The Rivals*]
2. **Bobadill, Captain** vainglorious braggart, vaunts achievements while rationalizing faintheartedness. [Br. Lit.: *Every Man in His Humour*]
3. **chicken** slang insult used toward the timid. [Western Folklore: Jobes, 322]
4. **Conachar** pathetically lacks courage. [Br. Lit.: *The Fair Maid of Perth*]

5. **Coup de Jarnac** to hit a man while he is down. [Fr. Folklore: Espy, 62]
6. **Cowardly Lion** king of the forest has yellow streak up back. [Am. Lit.: *The Wonderful Wizard of Oz*]
7. **Duke of Plaza-Toro** always leads the retreat and is the first to hide from the enemy. [Br. Opera: Gilbert and Sullivan *The Gondoliers*]
8. **Falstaff, Sir John** "the better part of valor is discretion." [Br. Lit.: *I Henry IV*]
9. **Fleming, Henry** young recruit, in his first battle, runs away in terror. [Am. Lit.: Stephen Crane *The Red Badge of Courage*]
10. **Indiana Volunteers** during Mexican war, ran when action began. [Am. Hist.: Espy, 183]
11. **Martano** poltroon claiming credit for another's feat. [Ital. Lit.: *Orlando Furioso*]
12. **Panurge** rogue who in several adventures proves to be a great coward. [Fr. Lit.: Rabelais *Gargantua and Pantagruel*]
13. **Panza, Sancho** always removes himself a safe distance from his master's combats. [Span. Lit.: Cervantes *Don Quixote*]
14. **Police, the** homeloving and fearful of death, reluctant to combat the pirate band. [Br. Opera: Gilbert and Sullivan *The Pirates of Penzance*]
15. **Rogue's March** played in British Army to expel dishonored soldier. [Br. Music: Scholes, 885]
16. **Roister Doister, Ralph** foolish suitor repulsed by widow with household utensil. [Br. Lit.: *Ralph Roister Doister*]
17. **Scaramouche** stock character in commedia dell'arte; boastful poltroon. [Ital. Drama: Brewer *Dictionary*, 967]
18. **yellow** color symbolizing cowardice. [Western Culture: Misc.]

137. CRAFTSMANSHIP

1. **Alcimedon** a first-rate carver in wood. [Rom. Lit.: Vergil *Eclogues*, iii. 37.]
2. **Argus** skillful builder of Jason's Argo. [Gk. Myth.: Walsh *Classical*, 29]
3. **Athena** (Rom. **Minerva**) protector of craftsmen. [Gk. Myth.: Kravitz, 67]
4. **Bezalel and Oholiab** called to make tabernacle and accouterments for Moses. [O.T.: Exodus 31:1–11]
5. **Cyclopes** one-eyed, unruly giants; excellent metals craftsmen. [Gk. Myth.: Parrinder, 68]

6. **Dactyls** fabulous smiths; discovered iron and how to work with it. [Gk. Myth.: Leach, 273]
7. **Daedalus** great craftsman; built Labyrinth and Pasiphaë's cow. [Gk. Myth.: Leach, 273]
8. **Epeius** designer and builder of the Trojan Horse. [Rom. Lit.: *Aeneid*]
9. **Hephaestus** (Rom. **Vulcan**) god of fire and metalworkers. [Gk. Myth.: Zimmerman, 121]
10. **Hiram** expert brazier commissioned by Solomon for temple work. [O.T.: I Kings 7:13–14]
11. **Joseph** storied carpenter and foster-father of Jesus. [N.T.: Matthew 1:18–25; Hall, 177]
12. **Pygmalion** sculpts beautiful image which comes to life. [Rom. Lit.: *Metamorphoses*]
13. **Sidonians** known for timber-felling skill. [O.T.: I Kings 5:6]
14. **Tubal-cain** master of copper and iron smiths. [O.T.: Genesis 4:22]

138. CREATION

1. **Adam and Eve** first man and woman. [O.T.: Genesis 1:26, 2:21–25]
2. **Allah** made man from flowing blood. [Islam: Koran, 96:2]
3. **Apsu** primeval waters, origin of all things. [Babyl. Myth.: Leach, 68]
4. **Aruru** goddess pinched man, Enkidu out of clay. [Assyrian Myth.: Gaster, 9; Babyl. Myth.: *Gilgamesh*]
5. **Askr** first man; created from ash tree. [Norse Myth.: Benét, 58]
6. **Ea** made man from primordial ocean clay. [Babyl. Myth.: Gaster, 9]
7. **Embla** first woman on earth. [Norse Myth.: Benét, 58]
8. **Frankenstein's monster** living man created by a physiology student from body parts. [Br. Lit.: Mary Shelley *Frankenstein*]
9. **Genesis** Old Testament book dealing with world's creation. [O.T.: Genesis]
10. **God** created the world in six days. [O.T.: Genesis 1]
11. **the Hatchery** mass produces everything, including human beings. [Br. Lit.: *Brave New World*]
12. **Khnum** ram god, created man from clay on potter's wheel. [Egypt. Rel.: Parrinder, 155]
13. **Prometheus** molded man of clay, animated him with fire. [Gk. Myth.: Wheeler, 304]

14. **Shiva** Lord of creation; danced to begin life. [Hinduism: Binder, 23]
15. **Star Maker, the** the creator and destroyer of the universe, depicted primarily as an artist detached from it. [Sci. Fi.: Stapledon *Star Maker* in Weiss, 248]
16. **Tocupacha** molded man from clay. [Aztec Myth.: Gaster, 18]

139. CRIME FIGHTING (See also SLEUTHING.)

1. **Batman** devotes his life to fighting Gotham City's criminals. [Comics: Berger, 160]
2. **Canadian Mounties** (Royal Canadian Mounted Police) corps which gained a romantic reputation for daring exploits and persistence in trailing criminals. [Can. Hist.: *NCE,* 2367]
3. **Dragnet** radio show in which justice is always served. [Radio: Buxton, 73]
4. **Earp, Wyatt** (1848–1929) law officer and gunfighter of American West. [Am. Hist.: *NCE,* 819]
5. **Kojak** hard-boiled, Manhattan plainclothes detective. [TV: Terrace, I, 445]
6. **Lone Ranger** arch foe of criminals in early west. [Radio: "The Lone Ranger" in Buxton, 143–144; Comics: Horn, 460; TV: Terrace, II, 34–35]
7. **McGarrett, Steve** implacable nemesis of Hawaiian wrongdoers. [TV: "Hawaii Five-O" in Terrace, I, 342]
8. **Ness, Eliot** G-man successfully subdues Prohibition gangsters. [TV: "The Untouchables" in Terrace, II, 402–403]
9. **Peel, Sir Robert** (1788–1850) reorganized British police; established Irish constabulary. [Br. Hist.: Flexner, 276]
10. **Purvis, Melvin** gunned down Dillinger outside Chicago theater (1934). [Am. Hist.: Wallechinsky, 464]
11. **Scotland Yard** Criminal Investigation Department of Metropolitan Police. [Br. Hist.: Brewer *Dictionary,* 97]
12. **Starsky and Hutch** plainclothes L.A. detectives break cases and hearts. [TV: Terrace, II, 317]
13. **Superman** invincible scourge of crime. [Comics: Horn, 642–643]
14. **Texas Rangers** 19th-century constabulary thwarting villains. [Am. Hist.: Brewer *Dictionary,* 1071]
15. **Tracy, Dick** comic book cop. [Comics: Horn, 206–207]

140. CRIMINALITY (See also OUTLAWRY.)

1. **Murgatroyd, Sir Despard** baronet forced by his ancestors to perform a crime a day. [Br. Opera: Gilbert and Sullivan *Ruddigore*]
2. ***Newgate Calendar*** popular volumes on notorious crimes, published from 1773 to 1826. [Br. Lit.: Barnhart, 810]

141. CRITICISM

1. ***Blackwood's Magazine*** Scottish literary magazine founded in 1817, notorious for its Tory bias and vicious criticism. [Br. Lit.: Benét 111]
2. **Bludyer, Mr.** a "slashing" book reviewer with savage humor. [Br. Lit.: *Pendennis*]
3. **Bolo, Miss** "looked a small armoury of daggers" at those who made mistakes. [Br. Lit.: *Pickwick Papers*]
4. **Dutch uncle** strict elder who scolds and moralizes. [Br. Slang: Lurie, 122–123]
5. ***Edinburgh Review*** influential literary and political review, founded in 1802, inaugurating new literary standards. [Br. Lit.: Barnhart, 375]
6. **Eliphaz, Bildad, and Zophar** rebuke Job for his complaints. [O.T.: Job 4–31]
7. ***Essay on Criticism*** didactic poem on rules by which a critic should be guided. [Br. Lit.: Pope *Essay on Criticism* in Magill IV, 287]
8. **Joab** admonishes David for ingratitude to troops and servants. [O.T.: II Samuel 19:1–8]
9. **Michal** David's wife; castigates him for boyish exulting. [O.T.: II Samuel 6:20]
10. **Monday morning quarterback** football spectator who, in hindsight, points out where team went wrong. [Am. Sports and Folklore: Misc.]
11. **Sanballat and Tobiah** jeered Jews' attempt to rebuild Jerusalem's walls. [O.T.: Nehemiah 4:1–3]
12. **Theon** satirical poet of trenchant wit. [Rom. Lit.: Brewer *Dictionary*, 1073]
13. **Zoilus** malicious and contentious rhetorician; "Homer's scourge." [Gk. Hist.: Brewer *Dictionary*, 1175]

142. CRONYISM

1. **Tammany Hall** Manhattan Democratic political circle notorious for spoils system approach. [Am. Hist.: Jameson, 492]

143. CRUELTY (See also BRUTALITY.)

1. **Achren** mean, spiteful enchantress of Spiral Castle. [Children's Lit.: *The Castle of Llyr*]
2. **Allan, Barbara** spurned her dying sweetheart because of a fancied slight. [Br. Balladry: Benét, 78]
3. **Blackbeard** nickname of pirate, Edward Teach (d. 1718). [Am. Hist.: Hart, 84]
4. **Bligh, Captain** tyrannical master of the ship *Bounty*. [Am. Lit.: *Mutiny on the Bounty*]
5. **Bumble, Mr.** abusive beadle, mistreats Oliver and other waifs. [Br. Lit.: *Oliver Twist*]
6. **bull** symbolizes cruelty in Picasso's *Guernica*. [Span. Art.: Mercatante, 99]
7. **Cipolla** magician who hypnotizes and brutally humiliates members of the audience. [Ger. Lit.: *Mario and the Magician* in Benét, 636]
8. **Conchis** his psychological experiments cause repeated emotional anguish among his subjects. [Br. Lit.: John Fowles *The Magus* in Weiss, 279]
9. **Creakle, Mr.** headmaster at Salem House; enjoys whipping boys. [Br. Lit.: *David Copperfield*]
10. **cuscuta** symbol of cruelty. [Flower Symbolism; Jobes, 399]
11. **Diocletian** Roman emperor (284–305); instituted general persecutions of Christians. [Rom. Hist.: *EB*, 5: 805–807]
12. **Guilbert, Brian de Bois** dissolute and cruel commander of the Knights Templars. [Br. Lit.: *Ivanhoe*]
13. **Job's comforters** maliciously torment Job while ostensibly attempting to comfort him. [O.T.: Job]
14. **Legree, Simon** harsh taskmaster; slavetrader. [Am. Lit.: *Uncle Tom's Cabin*]
15. **leopard** represents meanness, sin, and the devil. [Animal Symbolism: Mercatante, 56]
16. **Margaret of Anjou** hard, vicious, strong-minded, imperious woman. [Br. Lit.: *II Henry VI*]
17. **Mezentius** Etrurian king put his subjects to death by binding them to dead men and letting them starve. [Rom. Legend: Benét, 664]
18. **Murdstone, Edward** harsh and cruel husband of widow Copperfield. [Br. Lit.: *David Copperfield*]
19. **painted bird, the** painted by peasants and released, it is rejected and killed by its original flock. [Pol. Tradition: Weiss, 345]

20. **Slout, Mr.** punished Oliver for asking for more gruel. [Br. Lit.: *Oliver Twist*]
21. **Squeers, Wackford** brutal, abusive pedagogue; starves and maltreats urchins. [Br. Lit.: *Nicholas Nickleby*]
22. **Totenkopfverbande** tough Death's Head units maintaining concentration camps in Nazi Germany. [Ger. Hist.: Shirer, 375]
23. **Vlad the Impaler** (c. 980–1015) prince of Walachia; called Dracula; ruled barbarously. [Eur. Hist.: *NCE,* 2907]

144. CRYING

1. **Bokim** Hebrew toponym: 'Weepers'; Israelites bewail their wrong doings. [O.T.: Judges 2:1–5]
2. **Heraclitus** the weeping philosopher; melancholic personality. [Gk. Phil.: Hall, 98]
3. **Mary Magdalene** tearfully washes Christ's feet. [N.T.: Luke 7:37–38]
4. **Niobe** weeps when her children are slain, even after Zeus turns her to stone. [Gk. Myth.: *RHDC*]
5. **Rachel weeping for her children** Israel, for children slain by order of Herod. [N.T.: Matthew 2:16–18]
6. **tears of Eos** dewdrops; teardrops shed for slain son. [Gk. Myth.: Brewer *Dictionary,* 1065]

145. CUCKOLDRY (See also ADULTERY, FAITHLESSNESS.)

1. **Actaeon's horns** symbol of cuckoldry. [Medieval and Ren. Folklore: Walsh *Classical,* 5]
2. **antlers** metaphorical decoration for deceived husband. [Western Folklore: Jobes, 395]
3. **Arveragus** delivers wife to adulterer to keep promise. [Br. Lit.: *Canterbury Tales,* "The Franklin's Tale"]
4. **Boylan, Blazes** cuckolds Leopold Bloom. [Irish Lit.: James Joyce *Ulysses* in Magill I, 1040]
5. **Cabot, Ephraim** Abbie, his young wife, seduces his youngest son Eben. [Am. Drama: Eugene O'Neill *Desire Under the Elms*]
6. **Chatterley, Sir Clifford** cripple whose wife has a prolonged affair with his gamekeeper. [Br. Lit.: D. H. Lawrence *Lady Chatterley's Lover* in Benét, 559]
7. **cuckoo** symbolizes adulterous betrayal by wife. [Western Folklore: Jobes, 395; Mercatante, 164]
8. **del Sarto, Andrea** cuckolded Florentine painter; protagonist of Browning's poem. [Art Hist.: Walsh *Modern,* 19–20; Br. Lit.: "Andrea del Sarto" in Norton, 778–783]

9. **Hildebrand, Old** sent away while wife and preacher play. [Ger. Fairy Tale: Grimm, 333]
10. **Mannon, Ezra** kindly general deceived by adulterous wife and murdered. [Am. Lit.: *Mourning Becomes Electra*]
11. **Mark, King** by Tristan after May-December marriage to Isolde. [Ger. Opera: Wagner, *Tristan and Isolde,* Westerman, 220]
12. **Menelaus** his wife, Helen, was also Paris's lover. [Gk. Lit.: *Iliad*]
13. **Rubin, Maximiliano** sickly pharmacist; wife's infidelities begin on wedding night. [Span. Lit.: *Fortunata and Jacinta*]
14. **Trusotsky** learns from his dead wife's letters that she had numerous lovers and that he is not the father of his child. [Russ. Lit.: Dostoevsky *The Eternal Husband*]
15. **Uriah the Hittite** while he is at war, his wife sleeps with David. [O.T.: II Samuel 11:6]

146. CUNNING (See also TRICKERY.)

1. **Adler, Irene** cleverly foiled Sherlock Holmes and the King of Bohemia. [Br. Lit.: Doyle "A Scandal in Bohemia" in *Sherlock Holmes*]
2. **Artful Dodger** nickname for the sly pickpocket, John Dawkins. [Br. Lit.: *Oliver Twist*]
3. **Asmodeus** clever, hell-born hero. [Fr. Lit.: *Le Diable Boîteux,* Walsh *Modern,* 31]
4. **Autolycus** craftiest of thieves; stole neighbors' flocks by changing marks. [Gk. Myth.: *NCE,* 192]
5. **Bamber, Jack** law clerk with "strange wild slyness." [Br. Lit.: *Pickwick Papers*]
6. **Bolingbroke, Henry** cleverness and timing bring him England's crown. [Br. Lit.: *Richard II*]
7. **Borgia, Cesare** (1476–1507) unscrupulously plotted against friend and foe. [Ital. Hist.: Plumb, 59–61]
8. **Brer Fox** sly trickster; outwits everyone. [Children's Lit.: *Uncle Remus*]
9. **Bunny, Bugs** for whom no trap is too tricky. [Comics: Horn, 140]
10. **cheetah** pounces without warning on prey. [Western Folklore: Jobes, 320]
11. **Cleopatra** manipulates Antony through her "infinite variety." [Br. Lit.: *Antony and Cleopatra*]
12. **crow** symbolizes one who lives by his wits. [Western Folklore: Jobes, 388]

13. **Dido** contracts for as much land as can be enclosed by an ox-hide; by cutting it into a strip she obtains enough to found a city. [Rom. Legend: *Collier's* VI, 259]
14. **Dolius** epithet of Hermes, meaning 'crafty.' [Gk. Myth.: Zimmerman, 124]
15. **Fabius** delayed meeting Hannibal's troops; wore them down; hence, *fabian.* [Rom. Hist.: Espy, 177]
16. **Figaro** ingeniously contrives means to his own ends. [Fr. Lit.: *Barber of Seville; Marriage of Figaro*]
17. **fox** symbol of cleverness and deceit. [Animal Symbolism: Mercatante, 84–85]
18. **Foxy Grandpa** shrewd old man always turns the table on mischievous kids. [Comics: Horn, 602]
19. **Helena** tricks husband into fulfilling marital duties. [Br. Lit.: *All's Well That Ends Well*]
20. **Hippomenes** beat the swift Atalanta in a race by distracting her with golden apples. [Gk. Myth.: Bulfinch]
21. **Isabella** frustrates captor while pretending compliance. [Ital. Opera: Rossini, *Italian Girl in Algeria,* Westerman, 118–119]
22. **jackal** outwits the tiger; imprisons him. [Hindu Folklore: Mercatante, 55]
23. **Little Claus** grows rich by tricks and extortions. [Dan. Lit.: *Andersen's Fairy Tales*]
24. **Malengin** carries net on back to "catch fools with." [Br. Lit.: *Faerie Queene*]
25. **Marion, Francis** (1732–1795) Revolutionary general, nick-named the "Swamp Fox." [Am. Hist.: Jameson, 308]
26. **Morgiana** female slave cleverly dispatches 40 thieves. [Arab. Lit.: *Arabian Nights,* "Ali Baba and the Forty Thieves"]
27. **Odysseus** wily and noble hero of the *Odyssey.* [Gk. Lit.: *Odyssey*]
28. **Oriol, Father** shrewd landowner with admirable bargaining ability. [Fr. Lit.: *Mont-Oriol,* Magill I, 618–620]
29. **Panurge** "received answers in twelve known and unknown tongues." [Fr. Lit.: *Gargantua and Pantagruel*]
30. **Philadelphia lawyer** clever at finding fine points and technicalities. [Am. Usage: Misc.]
31. **Road Runner** thrives on outwitting Wile E. Coyote. [Comics: "Beep Beep the Road Runner" in Horn, 105]
32. **Sawyer, Tom** hoodwinks friends into painting fence. [Am. Lit.: *Tom Sawyer*]

33. **Scheherazade** escapes being put to death by telling stories for 1001 nights. [Arab. Lit.: *Arabian Nights*]
34. **serpent** subtly deceives Eve in the Garden. [O.T.: Genesis 3:1]
35. **Sinon** induces Trojans to take in wooden horse. [Rom. Lit.: *Aeneid*]
36. **spider ophrys** indicates cleverness. [Flower Symbolism: *Flora Symbolica*, 177]
37. **third little pig** outwits Wolf; lures him into boiling water. [Children's Lit.: Bettelheim, 41–45]
38. **Weller, Samuel** ingeniously rescues his master, Mr. Pickwick, from many scrapes. [Br, Lit.: Dickens *Pickwick Papers*]
39. **Whipple, Molly** outwits ferocious giant and gains his talismanic possessions. [Br. Fairy Tale: "Molly Whipple" in Macleod, 58–64]
40. **wolf** symbol on coats of arms. [Heraldry: Halberts, 16]

147. CURIOSITY

1. **Anselmo** so assured of wife's fidelity, asks friend to try to corrupt her; friend is successful. [Span. Lit.: *Don Quixote*]
2. **Cupid and Psyche** her inquisitiveness almost drives him away forever. [Gk. Myth.: Espy, 27]
3. **Curious George** inquisitive, mischievous monkey. [Children's Lit.: *Curious George*]
4. **Fatima** Bluebeard's 7th and last wife; her inquisitiveness uncovers his murders. [Fr. Fairy Tale: Harvey, 97–98]
5. **Faustus, Doctor** makes demonic compact to sate thirst for knowledge. [Br. Lit.: *Doctor Faustus*]
6. **Harker, Jonathan** uncovers vampiric and lycanthropic activities at Castle Dracula. [Br. Lit.: *Dracula*]
7. **Lot's wife** ignores God's command; turns to salt upon looking back. [O.T.: Genesis 19:26]
8. **Lucius** his insatiable curiosity involves him in magic and his accidental transformation into an ass. [Rom. Lit.: *The Golden Ass*]
9. **Nosy Parker** after a meddlesome Elizabethan Archbishop of Canterbury. [Br. Hist.: Espy, 169]
10. **Odysseus' companions** to determine its contents, they open the bag Aeolus had given Odysseus, thus releasing winds that blow the ship off course. [Gk. Lit.: *Odyssey*]
11. **Pandora** inquisitively opens box of plagues given by Zeus. [Gk. Myth.: Zimmerman, 191]

12. **Pry, Paul** overly inquisitive journalist. [Br. Lit.: *Paul Pry;* Espy, 135]
13. **sycamore** symbolizes inquisitiveness. [Flower Symbolism: *Flora Symbolica,* 177]
14. **Vathek** journeys to Istakhar where world's secrets are revealed. [Br. Lit.: *Vathek*]

148. CURLYHEADEDNESS

1. **Little Orphan Annie** red, curly hair. [Comics: Horn, 459]
2. **Temple, Shirley** (1928–) blonde, curly-headed darling of America. [Am. Cinema: Browne, 100–111]

149. CURSE

1. **Ancient Mariner** cursed by the crew because his slaying of the albatross is causing their deaths. [Br. Poetry: Coleridge *The Rime of the Ancient Mariner*]
2. **Andvari** king of the dwarfs; his malediction spurs many events in the *Nibelungenlied.* [Norse Myth.: Bulfinch]
3. **Atreus, house of** cursed by Thyestes, whose children Atreus had served to him in a stew. [Gk. Legend: Benét, 61]
4. **Cain** cursed by God for murdering Abel. [O. T.: Genesis 4:11]
5. **Eriphyle** dying at the hand of her son Alcmaeon, she curses any land that would shelter him. [Gk. Myth.: Benét, 20]
6. ***Family Reunion, The*** the Eumenides haunt a decaying English family because the head of the house had plotted to kill his pregnant wife. [Br. Drama: Magill II, 321]
7. **Flying Dutchman** sea captain condemned to sail unceasingly because he had invoked the Devil's aid in a storm. [Maritime legend: Brewer *Dictionary*]
8. **Harmonia's necklace** brought disaster to all who possessed it. [Gk. Myth.: Benét, 442]
9. **Maule, Matthew** about to be executed as a wizard, laid a bloody doom on the Pyncheons. [Am. Lit.: Hawthorne *The House of the Seven Gables*]
10. **Melmoth the Wanderer** doomed by a curse to roam the earth for 150 years after his death. [Br. Lit.: *Melmoth the Wanderer*]
11. **moonstone** wrested by an English officer from Buddhist priests, who place a curse on all who possess it. [Br. Lit.: Collins *The Moonstone* in Benét, 683]
12. **Murgatroyd, Sir Rupert** he and all future lords of Ruddigore are doomed by a witch to commit a crime a day forever. [Br. Opera: Gilbert and Sullivan *Ruddigore*]

13. **Thyestes** cursed the house of Atreus, who had served him his sons in a stew. [Gk. Myth. & Drama: "Atreus," Benét, 61]
14. **Tutankhamen's tomb** its opening supposed to have brought a curse upon its excavators, some of whom died soon after. [Pop. Cult.: Misc.]

150. CUTENESS

1. **Bambi** adorable deer grows rhapsodically in beautiful forest. [Am. Cinema: *Bambi* in *Disney Films,* 53–56]
2. **teddy bear** cuddly commodity named after President Theodore Roosevelt. [Am. Hist.: Frank, 46]
3. **Thumper** Bambi's huggable rabbit sidekick. [Am. Cinema: *Bambi* in *Disney Films,* 53–56]

151. CYNICISM (See also PESSIMISM.)

1. **Antisthenes** (444–371 B.C.) Greek philosopher and founder of Cynic school. [Gk. Hist.: *NCE,* 121]
2. **Apemantus** churlish, sarcastic advisor of Timon. [Br. Lit.: *Timon of Athens*]
3. **Backbite, Sir Benjamin** sarcastic would-be poet and wit. [Br. Lit.: *School for Scandal*]
4. **Bierce, Ambrose** (1842–1914) acerbic journalist for *San Francisco Examiner;* nicknamed "Bitter Bierce." [Am. Lit.: Hart, 77]
5. **Diogenes** (412–323 B.C.) frustratedly looked everywhere for an honest man. [Gk. Hist.: Avery, 395]
6. **Ferdinand** rogue drifter views all his experiences with profound cynicism. [Fr. Lit.: *Journey to the End of the Night* in Magill I, 453]
7. **Lescaut** assured Geronte sister will succumb to his money. [Ital. Opera: Puccini, *Manon Lescaut,* Westerman, 346]
8. **Pandarus** jaded about good graces of women. [Br. Lit.: *Troilus and Cressida*]

D

152. DANCE

1. **Carmichael, Essie** untalented girl who goes into her ballet routine with little or no encouragement. [Am. Drama: Kaufman and Hart *You Can't Take It with You* in Hart, 955]
2. **Esmerelda** gypsy girl whose street dancing captivates onlookers. [Fr. Lit.: Victor Hugo *The Hunchback of Notre Dame*]
3. **"Red Shoes, The"** bewitched shoes force Karen to dance unceasingly. [Danish Lit.: Andersen "The Red Shoes" in Magill II, 27]
4. **Rockettes** precision dancers; a fixture at New York's Radio City Music Hall. [Am. Dance: Payton, 576]
5. **Roseland Ballroom** New York dance hall. [Pop. Culture: Misc.]
6. **Salome** danced to obtain head of John the Baptist. [N.T.: Matthew 14:6–11]
7. **St. Denis, Ruth, and Ted Shawn** (1877–1968) (1891–1972) husband-and-wife team, founders of Denishawn dance schools. [Am. Dance: *NCE*, 2395]
8. **Terpsichore** muse of dancing. [Gk. Myth.: Brewer *Dictionary*, 849]
9. **Vitus, St.** patron saint of dancers. [Christian Hagiog: *Saints and Festivals*, 291]
10. **Ziegfeld Follies** beautiful dancing girls highlighted annual musical revue on Broadway (1907–1931). [Am. Theater: *NCE*, 3045]

153. DANGER

1. **Geiger counter** radiation detector named for inventor. [Am. Hist.: Flexner, 12]
2. **Mayday** international radiotelephone distress signal. [Maritime Hist.: Misc.]
3. ***Perils of Pauline*** cliff-hangers in which Pauline's life is recurrently in danger. [Am. Cinema: Halliwell, 559]
4. **red alert** final alert; attack believed imminent. [Military: Misc.]
5. **red flag** symbol of peril. [Folklore: Jobes, 413]
6. **rhododendron** symbol of approaching pitfalls. [Flower Symbolism: *Flora Symbolica*, 177]
7. **rhubarb** symbol of approaching pitfalls. [Flower Symbolism: *Flora Symbolica*, 177]

8. **Scylla and Charybdis** rocks and whirlpool, respectively, opposite each other in the Strait of Messina. [Classical Myth.: Zimmerman, 59, 235–236]
9. **skull and crossbones** alerts consumers to presence of poison; represents death. [Folklore: Misc.]
10. **SOS** Morse code distress signal. [World Culture: Flexner, 359]
11. **Symplegades** "Clashing Cliffs" at the entrance to the Black Sea, said to crush vessels. [Classical Myth.: *New Century,* 1043]
12. **Syrtes** quicksands off the coast of northern Africa; any part of the sea dangerous to ships because of natural phenomena. [Rom. Myth.: Zimmerman, 251]
13. **sword of Damocles** signifies impending peril; blade suspended over banqueter by a hair. [Gk. Myth.: Brewer *Dictionary,* 297]
14. **thin ice** universal symbol of possible danger. [Folklore: Misc.]
15. **Yuck, Mr.** pictorial symbol denoting poison; grimacing face with tongue sticking out. [Am. Culture: Misc.]

Darkness (See NIGHT.)

154. DAWN

1. **Aarvak** one of the horses of the sun. [Norse Myth.: Leach, 1]
2. **Aurora** goddess of dawn whose tears provide dew. [Rom. Myth.: Kravitz, 42]
3. **Daphne** Apollo's attempted rape represents dawn fleeing daylight. [Gk. Myth.: Parrinder, 72; Jobes, 414]
4. **Eos** goddess of dawn; announces Helios each morning. [Gk. Myth.: Kravitz, 89]
5. **Heimdall** god of dawn and protector of rainbow bridge, Bifrost. [Norse Myth.: Leach, 488]
6. **laughing jackass** bird whose cry brings in daylight. [Euahlayi Legend: *How the People Sang The Mountains Up,* 19]
7. **Octa** mountain from which sun rises. [Rom. Folklore: Wheeler, 7]
8. **rays, garland of** emblem of Aurora, dawn goddess. [Gk. Myth.: Jobes, 374]
9. **rooster** its crowing at dawn heralds each new day. [Western Folklore: Leach, 329]

155. DEADLINESS

1. **anaconda** South American boa constrictor; longest and deadliest of its kind. [Zoology: *NCE,* 317]
2. **basilisk** monstrous reptile; has fatal breath and glance. [Gk. Folklore: Jobes, 184]

3. **black widow spider** poisonous spider; consumes her mate after mating. [Zoology: *NCE,* 308]
4. **boa constrictor** largest of all snakes; squeezes its victims in a deadly grip. [Zoology: *NCE,* 317]
5. **cobra** bite believed to mean certain death. [Folklore: Jobes, 352]
6. **copperhead** deadly pit viper in eastern U.S. [Zoology: *NCE,* 652]
7. **coral snake** its bite is deadly. [Zoology: *NCE,* 654]
8. **Gila monster** small but venomous lizard found in U.S. desert. [Zoology: *NCE,* 1084]
9. **Humbaba** one-eyed, fire- and plague-breathing monster whose eye could strike men dead. [Babyl. Myth.: *Gilgamesh*; Benét, 485]
10. **Hydra's gall** deadly; Hercules dipped his arrows in it. [Gk. and Rom. Myth.: Hall, 149]
11. **piranha** South American carnivorous fish. [Zoology: *EB,* VIII: 1]
12. **Portuguese man-of-war** a long-tentacled jellyfish whose sting can be deadly. [Zoology: *NCE,* 1408]
13. **python** nonvenomous jungle snake crushes its victims. [Zoology: *NCE,* 2252]
14. **rattlesnake** venomous snake, often deadly. [Zoology: *NCE,* 2281]
15. **shark** large and ferocious fish, sometimes man-eating. [Zoology: *NCE,* 2493]
16. **tarantula** spider with a deadly venom. [Zoology: *NCE,* 2695]
17. **upas** Asian and East Indian tree juice, extremely poisonous. [Eur. Myth.: Brewer *Dictionary,* 926]
18. **viper (or adder)** poisonous snake family; puff adder is deadliest of all. [Zoology: *NCE,* 2898]
19. **water moccasin** (also **cottonmouth**) highly poisonous snake found in southern U.S. [Zoology: *NCE,* 2490]

156. DEAFNESS

1. **Aged P.** Wemmick's deaf father. [Br. Lit.: *Great Expectations*]
2. **Bell, Alexander Graham** (1847–1922) telephone inventor; renowned for studies of deafness. [Am. Hist.: *NCE,* 265]
3. **Keller, Helen** (1880–1968) overcame handicap of deafness as well as blindness. [Am. Hist.: *NCE,* 1462]

4. **Quasimodo** rendered totally deaf by his occupation as bellringer at Notre Dame Cathedral. [Fr. Lit.: Victor Hugo *The Hunchback of Notre Dame*]

157. DEATH

1. **Ah Puch** deity of doom; represented as bloated corpse or skeleton. [Maya Myth.: Leach, 30]
2. **Ankou** gaunt driver of spectral cart; collects the dead. [Brittany Folklore: Leach, 62]
3. **Anubis** god and guardian of the dead. [Ancient Egyptian Rel.: Parrinder, 10]
4. **Arrow of Azrael** angel of death's way of summoning dead. [Islamic Myth.: Jobes, 129]
5. ***As I Lay Dying*** Bundren family ordeal after Addie's death. [Am. Lit.: Faulkner *As I Lay Dying*]
6. **asphodel flower** bloom growing in Hades. [Gk. Myth.: Kravitz, 37]
7. **Atropos** Fate who cuts thread of life. [Gk. and Rom. Myth.: Hall, 302]
8. **Azrael** angel of death; separates the soul from the body. [Islamic Myth.: Walsh *Classical,* 41]
9. **banshee** female specter, harbinger of death. [Irish and Welsh Myth.: Walsh *Classical,* 45]
10. **bell** passing bell; rung to indicate demise. [Christian Tradition: Jobes, 198]
11. **black** Western color for mourning. [Christian Color Symbolism: Leach, 242; Jobes, 357]
12. **Bodach Glas** gray specter; equivalent to Irish banshee. [Scot. Myth.: Walsh *Classical,* 45]
13. **Bran** god whose cauldron restored dead to life. [Welsh Myth.: Jobes, 241]
14. ***Bury the Dead*** six dead soldiers cause a rebellion when they refuse to be buried. [Am. Drama: Haydn & Fuller, 768]
15. **Calvary (Golgotha)** where Christ was crucified. [N.T.: Luke 23:33]
16. **Cer** goddess of violent death. [Gk. Myth.: Kravitz, 75]
17. **Charun** god of death. [Etruscan Myth.: Jobes, 315]
18. **Conqueror Worm** the worm ultimately vanquishes man in grave. [Am. Lit.: "Ligeia" in *Tales of Terror*]
19. ***Dance of Death*** Holbein woodcut, one of many medieval examples of the death motif. [Eur. Culture: Bishop, 363-367]

20. **danse macabre** Dance of Death; procession of all on their way to the grave. [Art: Osborne, 299–300, 677]
21. **dust and ashes** "I am become like dust and ashes." [O.T.: Job 30:19]
22. ***Endgame*** blind and chair-bound, Hamm learns that nearly everybody has died; his own parents are dying in separate trash cans. [Anglo-Fr. Drama: Beckett *Endgame* in Weiss, 143]
23. **Ereshkigal** goddess of death; consort of Nergal. [Sumerian and Akkadian Myth.: Parrinder, 93]
24. **extreme unction** Roman Catholic sacrament given to a person in danger of dying. [Christianity: *RHD*, 506]
25. **Gibbs, Emily** dying in childbirth, welcomed by the other spirits in the graveyard, she tries to relive her twelfth birthday. [Am. Drama: Thornton Wilder *Our Town* in Benét, 747]
26. **Grim Reaper** name given to personification of death. [Pop. Culture: Misc.]
27. **handful of earth** symbol of mortality. [Folklore: Jobes, 486]
28. **horse** symbol of agents of destruction. [Christian Tradition: N.T.: Revelation 6; Mercatante, 65]
29. **Ilyitch, Ivan** afflicted with cancer, he becomes irritable, visits many doctors, gradually disintegrates, and dies almost friendless. [Russ. Lit.: Tolstoy *The Death of Ivan Ilyitch* in Magill III, 256]
30. **Kali** Hindu goddess to whom Thug sacrificed victims. [Hinduism: Brewer *Dictionary*, 600]
31. **Krook** rag dealer dies spectacularly and horribly of "spontaneous combustion." [Br. Lit.: Dickens *Bleak House*]
32. **Lenore** "saintly soul floats on the Stygian river." [Am. Lit.: "Lenore" in Hart, 468]
33. **Lord of the Flies** showing man's consciousness and fear of dying. [Br. Lit.: *Lord of the Flies*]
34. **manes** spirits of the dead. [Rom. Rel.: Leach, 672]
35. **Mania** ancient Roman goddess of the dead. [Rom. Myth.: Zimmerman, 159]
36. **Niflheim** dark, cold region to which were sent those who died of disease or old age. [Scand. Myth.: Brewer *Dictionary* 642]
37. **nightingale** identified with mortality. [Animal Symbolism: Mercatante, 163]
38. ***On Borrowed Time*** an old man chases "Death" up a tree and keeps him there until the old man is ready to die. [Am. Drama: Sobel, 517]

39. **pale horse** fourth horse of Apocolypse, ridden by Death personified. [N.T.: Revelation 7:7–8]
40. ***Pardoner's Tale, The*** seeking to slay death, three rioters are told he is under a certain tree; there they find gold and kill each other over it. [Br. Lit.: Chaucer "The Pardoner's Tale" in *Canterbury Tales*]
41. **Requiem** religious mass (music or spoken) for the dead. [Christianity: Payton, 568]
42. **"Rime of the Ancient Mariner, The"** when Death wins the toss of the dice, the two hundred crew members drop dead. [Br. Poetry: Coleridge "The Rime of the Ancient Mariner"]
43. **Sacco Benedetto** yellow robe worn going to the stake during Inquisition. [Span. Hist.: Brewer *Dictionary*, 948]
44. **scythe** carried by the personification of death, used to cut life short. [Art.: Hall, 276]
45. **skeleton** visual representation of death. [Western Folklore: Cirlot, 298]
46. **skull** representation of body's dissolution. [Christian Symbolism: Appleton, 92]
47. **skull and crossbones** symbolizing mortality; sign on poison bottles. [World Culture: Brewer *Dictionary*, 1009]
48. **Styx** river which must be crossed to enter Hades. [Gk. Myth.: Howe, 259]
49. **Thanatos (Mors)** god of death; brother of Somnos (sleep). [Gk. Myth.: Gayley, 54]
50. **Thoth** record-keeper of the dead. [Egyptian Myth.: Leach, 1109]
51. **Valdemar, M.** in hypnotic trance, recounts impressions from other side of death. [Am. Lit.: "The Facts in the Case of M. Valdemar" in *Portable Poe*, 268–280]
52. **viaticum** Eucharist given to one who is dying. [Christianity: Brewer *Dictionary*, 1128]

158. DEATH, ACCIDENTAL

1. **Aeschylus** dramatist killed when an eagle dropped a turtle on his bald head, thinking it a rock. [Gk. Legend: Brewer *Dictionary*, 13]
2. **Ahab, Captain** whipped out of his boat by a flying harpoon-line. [Am. Lit.: Melville *Moby Dick*]
3. **Bosinney, Philip** distraught by a revelation, is run over in a London fog. [Br. Lit.: *The Forsyte Saga*]

4. ***Bridge of San Luis Rey*** primitive bridge in Peru breaks, hurling five people to their deaths. [Am. Lit.: *Bridge of San Luis Rey*]
5. **Havisham, Miss** burned to death in her old house. [Br. Lit.: Dickens *Great Expectations*]
6. **Sikes, Bill** fleeing pursuers, hangs himself with the rope he was using to escape. [Br. Lit.: Dickens *Oliver Twist*]
7. **Solness, Halvard** becomes dizzy on the tower of his new home and falls to his death. [Nor. Drama: Ibsen *The Master Builder* in Magill II, 643]
8. **Wilson, Myrtle** escaping from the house where she has been locked up by her husband, she is killed by a speeding car. [Am. Lit.: Fitzgerald *The Great Gatsby*]
9. **Yeobright, Eustacia** falls into a lake and drowns, as does Wildeve in an attempt to save her. [Br. Lit.: Hardy *The Return of the Native*]

159. DEATH, PREMATURE (See also LOVE, TRAGIC)

1. **Adonis** beautiful youth beloved by Venus, killed by a boar. [Gk. Myth.: Benét, 10]
2. **L'Aiglon** Napoleon's son dies before he can rouse the French to follow him. [Fr. Drama: *L'Aiglon* in Magill II, 551]
3. **Byron, Lord** (1788–1824) English poet died of fever at 36. [Br. Lit.: Harvey, 129]
4. **Dean, James** (1931–1955) leader of restless youth cult in early 50s. [Am. Cinema: *NCE*, 730]
5. **Dombey, Paul** dies at the age of seven, destroying the hopes of his merchant father. [Br. Lit.: Dickens *Dombey and Son*]
6. **Frank, Anne** (1929–1945) young Dutch diarist, died in Bergen-Belsen camp during WWII. [Jew. Hist.: Wigoder, 196]
7. **Grey, Lady Jane** (1537–1554) English queen at 15; died at 17. [Br. Hist.: *NCE*, 1146]
8. **Hope, Evelyn** died at sixteen, unaware how deeply she was loved by an older man who still mourns her. [Br. Poetry: Browning "Evelyn Hope"]
9. **Keats, John** (1795–1821) English poet died of consumption at 25. [Br. Lit.: Harvey, 443]
10. **Little Father Time** despondent boy kills two babies and himself. [Br. Lit.: Hardy *Jude the Obscure*]
11. **March, Beth** dies young; sensitive girl. [Children's Lit.: *Little Women*]

12. **Marvellous Boy, The** Thomas Chatterton (1752–1770), English poetic genius killed himself at seventeen. [Br. Hist.: Benét, 188]
13. **Romeo and Juliet** star-crossed lovers die as teenagers. [Br. Lit.: *Romeo and Juliet*]
14. **Schubert, Franz** (1797–1828) brilliant composer, died at 31. [Music Hist.: Thompson, 1968]
15. **Shelley, Percy Bysshe** (1792–1822) English poet drowned at 30. [Br. Lit.: Harvey, 748]
16. **Valentino, Rudolph** (1895–1926) matinée idol; his death caused several suicides. [Am. Cinema: Halliwell, 734]

160. DEBAUCHERY (See also DISSIPATION, PROFLIGACY.)

1. **Alexander VI** Borgia pope infamous for licentiousness and debauchery. [Ital. Hist.: Plumb, 219–220]
2. **Bacchus** (Gk. **Dionysus**) god of wine; honored by Bacchanalias. [Gk. Myth.: Howe, 83]
3. **Behan, Brendan** (1923–1964) uninhibited Irish playwright who lived wildly. [Irish Lit.: *NCE,* 261]
4. **Bowery** Manhattan district, once notorious for brothels and gambling halls. [Am. Hist.: Hart, 97]
5. **Hell-fire Club** 18th-century British clique devoted to debauchery. [Br. Hist.: Brewer *Note-Book,* 411]
6. **Nero** (A.D. 37–68) hated as Roman emperor; led life of debauchery. [Rom. Hist.: *NCE,* 1909]
7. **Pandarus** a "honey-sweet lord"; go-between for lovers. [Br. Lit.: *Troilus and Cressida*]
8. **Pornocracy** period of unparalleled papal decadence (early 10th century). [Christian Hist.: Grun, 106]
9. **Rasputin** (1871–1916) debauchee who preached and practised doctrine mixing religious fervor with sexual indulgence. [Russ. Hist.: *NCE,* 1770]
10. **Saturnalia** licentious December 17th feast honoring Saturn. [Rom. Myth.: Espy, 19]
11. **Satyricon** tales of vice and luxury in imperial Rome. [Rom. Lit.: *Satyricon*]
12. **Sergius III** instituted the Pornocracy. [Christian Hist.: Grun, 106]
13. **Sodom and Gomorrah** ancient cities destroyed by God because of their wickedness. [O.T.: Genesis 19:1–29]

Debt (See **BANKRUPTCY, POVERTY.**)

161. DECADENCE

1. **Buddenbrooks** portrays the downfall of a materialistic society. [Ger. Lit.: *Buddenbrooks*]
2. **cherry orchard** focal point of the declining Ranevsky estate. [Russ. Drama: Chekhov *The Cherry Orchard* in Magill II, 144]
3. **Diver, Dick** dissatisfied psychiatrist goes downhill on alcohol. [Am. Lit.: *Tender is the Night*]
4. **Gray, Dorian** beautiful youth whose hedonism leads to vice and depravity. [Br. Lit.: Oscar Wilde *The Picture of Dorian Gray*]
5. **Great Gatsby, The** 1925 novel by F. Scott Fitzgerald symbolizes corruption and decadence. [Am. Lit.: *The Great Gatsby*]
6. **House of Usher** eerie, decayed mansion collapses as master dies. [Am. Lit.: "Fall of the House of Usher" in *Tales of Terror*]
7. **Lonigan, Studs** Chicago Irishman whose life is one of physical and moral deterioration (1935). [Am. Lit.: *Studs Lonigan: A Trilogy,* Magill III, 1028–1030]
8. **Manhattan Transfer** novel portraying the teeming greed of the city's inhabitants. [Am. Lit.: *Manhattan Transfer*]
9. **Nana** indictment of social decay during Napoleon III's reign (1860s). [Fr. Lit.: *Nana,* Magill I, 638–640]
10. ***Remembrance of Things Past*** records the decay of a society. [Fr. Lit.: Haydn & Fuller, 630]
11. ***Satyricon*** novel by Petronius depicting social excesses in imperial Rome. [Rom. Lit.: Magill II, 938]
12. ***Sun Also Rises, The*** moral collapse of expatriots. [Am. Lit.: *The Sun Also Rises*]
13. ***Sound and the Fury, The*** Faulkner novel about an old Southern family gone to seed: victims of lust, incest, suicide, and idiocy. [Am. Lit.: Magill I, 917]
14. **Warren, The** Haredale's house, "mouldering to ruin. " [Br. Lit.: *Barnaby Rudge*]
15. **Yoknapatawpha County** northern Mississippi; decadent setting for Faulkner's novels. [Am. Lit.: Hart, 955]

162. DECAPITATION (See also HEADLESSNESS.)

1. **Antoinette, Marie** (1755–1793) queen of France beheaded by revolutionists. [Fr. Hist.: *NCE,* 1697]
2. **Argus** lulled to sleep and beheaded by Hermes. [Gk. Myth.: *Metamorphoses,* I]

3. **Boleyn, Anne** (1507–1536) beheaded by husband, Henry VIII, for adultery and incest. [Br. Hist.: *NCE,* 325]
4. **Gawain, Sir** challenged by the Green Knight, Gawain cuts off his head. [Br. Lit.: *Sir Gawain and the Green Knight* in Benét, 934]
5. **Grey, Lady Jane** (1537–1554) English queen beheaded at 17. [Br. Hist.: *NCE,* 1146]
6. **Guillotin, Joseph** (1738–1814) physician; advocated humane method of capital punishment. [Fr. Hist.: Wallechinsky, 164]
7. **Holofernes** Assyrian commander-in-chief beheaded by Judith. [*Apocrypha: Judith* 13:4–10]
8. **Hydra** nine-headed serpent beheaded by Heracles. [Gk. Myth.: Benét, 489]
9. **John the Baptist** head presented as gift to Salome. [N.T.: Mark 6:25–28]
10. **Medusa** beheaded by Perseus. [Gk. Myth.: Hall, 206; Rom. Lit.: *Metamorphoses*]
11. **More, Sir Thomas** (1478–1535) English statesman beheaded by King Henry VIII. [Br. Hist.: *NCE,* 1830]
12. **Queen of Hearts** constantly orders beheadings. [Br. Lit.: Lewis Carroll *Alice's Adventures in Wonderland*]

163. DECEIT

1. **Aimwell** pretends to be titled to wed into wealth. [Br. Lit.: *The Beaux' Stratagem*]
2. **Ananias** lies about amount of money received for land. [N.T.: Acts 5:1–6]
3. **Ananias Club** all its members are liars. [Am. Lit.: Worth, 10]
4. **angel of light** false apostles are like Satan in masquerade. [N.T.: II Corinthians 11:14]
5. **Apaturia** epithet of Athena, meaning 'deceitful.' [Gk. Myth.: Zimmerman, 36]
6. **apples of Sodom** outwardly sound fruit; inwardly rotten. [Class. Myth.: Jobes, 114]
7. **Arbaces** priest who frames Glaucus. [Br. Lit.: *The Last Days of Pompeii,* Magill I, 490–492]
8. **Archimago** uses sorcery to deceive people. [Br. Lit.: *Faerie Queene*]
9. **Arnolphe** plans marriage to ward; maintains guardianship under alias. [Fr. Lit.: *L'Ecole des Femmes*]
10. **bilberry** symbol for falsehood. [Flower Symbolism: *Flora Symbolica,* 172]

11. **Brunhild** outdone in athletic competition by Gunther with invisible assistance. [Ger. Myth.: *Nibelungenlied*]
12. **Buttermilk, Little Johnny** fools witch by substituting china for self in sack. [Br. Fairy Tale: Macleod, 21–24]
13. **Camilla, Mrs.** practises deception on Pip. [Br. Lit.: *Great Expectations*]
14. **clematis** symbol of deception. [Flower Symbolism: Jobes, 347; *Flora Symbolica,* 173]
15. **Conchis** for his psychological experiments he baits subjects with apparently seducible young women. [Br. Lit.: John Fowles *The Magus* in Weiss, 279]
16. **dogbane** symbol for deceit. [Flower Symbolism: Jobes, 458]
17. **Hlestakov, Ivan Alexandrovich** dissimulating gentleman hoodwinks town dignitaries as tsar's inspector. [Russ. Lit.: *The Inspector General*]
18. **hocus-pocus** magician's parody of *Hoc Est Corpus Domini.* [Western Folklore: Espy, 76]
19. **Jingle, Alfred** pretends to be a person of influence and elopes with an old maid for her money. [Br. Lit.: Dickens *Pickwick Papers*]
20. **Judas goat** decoy for luring animals to slaughter. [Western Folklore: Espy, 80]
21. **Latch, William** Esther's betrayer; seduces her on marriage pretense. [Br. Lit.: *Esther Waters,* Magill I, 254–256]
22. **Mak** Falstaffian figure; categorically maintains his innocence. [Br. Lit.: *The Second Shepherds' Play*]
23. **Malengin** personification of craftiness. [Br. Lit.: *Faerie Queene*]
24. **mask** a disguise; hence, symbol of deception. [Art: Hall, 204]
25. **Mme. St. Pé** feigns paralysis for seventeen years to keep her husband away from the woman he loves. [Fr. Drama: Jean Anouilh *The Waltz of the Toreadors* in *On Stage,* 383]
26. **Moncrieff, Algernon, and Jack Worthing** both assume fictitious name "Ernest" in wooing belles. [Br. Lit.: *The Importance of Being Earnest*]
27. **Montoni, Signor** marries Emily's aunt to secure her property. [Br. Lit.: *The Mysteries of Udolpho,* Magill I, 635–638]
28. **nightshade** poisonous flower; symbol of falsehood. [Flower Symbolism: *Flora Symbolica,* 176]
29. **Nimue** cajoles Merlin to reveal secret of power. [Arth. Romance: *History of Prince Arthur,* Brewer *Handbook,* 756]
30. **Nixon, Richard** (1913–) 37th U.S. president (1969–1974); nicknamed "Tricky Dicky." [Am. Hist.: Kane, 523]

31. **Pinocchio** wooden nose lengthens when he lies. [Ital. Lit.: *Pinocchio*]
32. **Sinon** convinced Trojans to accept wooden horse. [Rom. Lit.: *Aeneid*]
33. **Trojan Horse** hollow horse concealed soldiers, enabling them to enter and capture Troy. [Gk. Myth.: *Iliad*]
34. **white flytrap** lures insects with sweet odor. [Flower Symbolism: *Flora Symbolica,* 178]
35. **winter cherry** inedible fruit symbolizes falsehood. [Plant Symbolism: Jobes, 319]

164. DEDICATION

1. **Quixote, Don** spends his life redressing the wrongs of the whole world. [Sp. Lit.: Cervantes *Don Quixote*]
2. **Rieux, Dr.** remains in Algeria to care for plague victims and loses his wife to it. [Fr. Lit.: Albert Camus *The Plague*]

165. DEFEAT

1. **Appomattox Courthouse** scene of Lee's surrender to Grant (1865). [Am. Hist.: Jameson, 22]
2. **Armada, Spanish** defeat by English fleet marked Spain's decline and England's rise as a world power (1588). [Eur. Hist.: *EB,* 1: 521–522]
3. **Austerlitz** defeat of Austro-Russian coalition by Napoleon (1805). [Fr. Hist.: Harbottle *Battles,* 23–24]
4. **Bataan** Philippine peninsula where U.S. troops surrendered to Japanese (1942). [Am. Hist.: *NCE,* 245]
5. **Battle of the Boyne** sealed Ireland's fate as England's vassal state (1690). [Br. Hist.: Harbottle *Battles,* 39]
6. **Battle of the Bulge** final, futile German WWII offensive (1944–1945). [Eur. Hist.: *Hitler,* 1148–1153, 1154–1155]
7. **Caudine Forks** mountain pass where Romans were humiliatingly defeated by the Samnites. [Rom. Hist.: Brewer *Dictionary,* 186]
8. **Culloden** consolidated English supremacy; broke clan system (1746). [Br. Hist.: Harbottle *Battles,* 70]
9. **Dien Bien Phu** Vietminh rout of French paved way for partition of Vietnam (1954). [Fr. Hist.: Van Doren, 541]
10. **Gallipoli** poorly conceived and conducted battle ending in British disaster (1915). [Br. Hist.: Fuller, III, 240–261]
11. **Little Bighorn** scene of General Custer's "last stand" (1876). [Am. Hist.: Van Doren, 274]

12. **Pearl Harbor** Japan's surprise attack destroys U.S. fleet (1941). [Am. Hist.: *NCE,* 2089]
13. **Pyrrhic victory** a too costly victory; "Another such victory and we are lost." [Rom. Hist.: "Asculum I" in Eggenburger, 30–31]
14. **Salt River** up which losing political parties travel to oblivion. [Am. Slang: *LLEI,* I: 312]
15. **Sedan** decisive German defeat of French (1870). [Fr. Hist.: Harbottle *Battles,* 225]
16. **Stalingrad** German army succumbs to massive Soviet pincer movement (1942–1943). [Ger. Hist.: Fuller, III, 531–538]
17. **Waterloo** British victory in Belgium signals end of Napoleon's domination (1815). [Fr. Hist.: Harbottle *Battles,* 266]
18. **white flag** a sign of surrender. [Western Folklore: Misc.]

166. DEFENDER

1. **Bryan, William Jennings** (1860–1925) defended Creationism in famous Scopes trial. [Am. Hist.: *NCE,* 383–384]
2. **Canisius, St. Peter** Jesuit theologian; buttressed Catholic faith against Protestantism. [Christian Hagiog.: Attwater, 276]
3. **Daniel** halts Susanna's execution; gets her acquitted. [Apocrypha: Daniel and Susanna]
4. **Darrow, Clarence** (1857–1938) lawyer; Bryan's nemesis in Scopes trial (1925). [Am. Hist.: Jameson, 131]
5. **Defender of the Faith** Henry VIII as defender of the papacy against Martin Luther (1521). [Br. Hist.: *EB,* 8: 769–772]
6. **Defenders, The** father-son lawyer team in early 1960s. [TV: Terrace, I, 197]
7. **Donatello** Miriam's ardent friend ever ready to defend her. [Am. Lit.: *The Marble Faun*]
8. **Hector** bravely defended Troy against Greek siege for ten years. [Gk. Lit.: *Iliad*]
9. **Mason, Perry** detective novels and TV series feature courtroom drama by lawyer. [Am. Lit.: Gardner, Erle Stanley, in *EB,* IV: 416; Radio: Buxton, 186–187; TV: Terrace, II, 199]
10. **Ridd, John** defender of the parish of Oare in Somerset. [Br. Lit.: *Lorna Doone,* Magill I, 524–526]
11. **Zola, Emile** (1840–1902) attacked Army cover-up of Dreyfus affair in *J'accuse* (1898). [Fr. Hist.: Wallechinsky, 60]

167. DEFIANCE

1. **Becket, Thomas à (c. 1118–1170)** uncompromisingly defended the rights of the Church against King Henry II. [Br. Hist.: *NCE,* 2735]

2. **Mahon, Christopher** defies his father twice, knocking him out with a blow on the head. [Irish Drama: J. M. Synge *The Playboy of the Western World* in Magill I, 758]
3. ***Man for All Seasons, A*** Sir Thomas More (1478–1535) refuses to acknowledge Henry VIII as supreme head of the church. [Br. Hist.: Benét, 686; Br. Drama: Robert Bolt *A Man for All Seasons* in *On Stage*, 439]
4. **Tell, William** Swiss patriot refused to salute the Austrian governor's cap. [Swiss Legend: Brewer *Dictionary*, 885]

168. DEFORMITY (See also LAMENESS.)

1. **Calmady, Sir Richard** born without lower legs. [Br. Lit.: *Sir Richard Calmady,* Walsh *Modern,* 84]
2. **Carey, Philip** embittered young man with club foot seeks fulfillment. [Br. Lit.: *Of Human Bondage*]
3. **Cyclopes** one-eyed monsters. [Gk. Lit.: *Odyssey*]
4. **Elephant Man, the** Joseph Merrick, whose deformed face was said to resemble an elephant's. [Br. Cinema: *The Elephant Man*]
5. ***Freaks*** 1930s macabre movie about sideshow people. [Am. Cinema: Halliwell, 278]
6. **Gwynplaine** his disfigured face had a perpetual horrible grin. [Fr. Lit.: Hugo *The Man Who Laughs* in Benét, 632]
7. **Mayeux** deformed man, both brave and witty. [Fr. Folklore: Wheeler *Dictionary,* 237]
8. **Priapus** son of Aphrodite and Dionysus; grotesque man with huge phallus. [Gk. Myth.: Howe, 233]
9. **Quasimodo** hunchbacked bell-ringer. [Fr. Lit.: *Hunchback of Notre Dame*]
10. **Richard III** crook-back king. [Br. Lit.: Shakespeare *Richard III*]
11. **Sarn, Prudence** harelipped girl is servant on brother's farm. [Br. Lit.: *Precious Bane,* Magill I, 778–780]
12. **thalidomide** supposedly harmless sedative resulted in disfigured babies. [Am. Hist.: Van Doren, 582–583]
13. **Thersites** deformed Greek officer at the siege of Troy, famed for his malevolence. [Gk. Lit.: *Iliad*]
14. **Toulouse-Lautrec, Henri de** (1864–1901) crippled and stunted; became great artist. [Fr. Hist.: Wallechinsky, 13]

169. DELIVERANCE (See also FREEDOM.)

1. **Aphesius** epithet of Zeus, meaning 'releaser.' [Gk. Myth.: Zimmerman, 292–293]

2. **Bolívar, Simón** (1783–1830) the great liberator of South America. [Am. Hist.: *NCE,* 325]
3. **Boru, Brian** freed Ireland from the Danes. [Irish Myth.: Walsh *Classical,* 61–62]
4. **Brown, John** (1800–1859) abolitionist; attempted to liberate slaves. [Am. Hist.: Jameson, 64]
5. **Ehud** freed Israelites from Moabites by murdering king. [O.T.: Judges 3:15]
6. **Emancipation Proclamation** Lincoln's declaration freeing the slaves (1863). [Am. Hist.: Jameson, 161]
7. **Gideon** with 300 men, saved Israel from Midianites. [O.T.: Judges 6:14, 7:19–21]
8. **Jephthah** routed the Ammonites to save Israelites. [O.T.: Judges 11:32]
9. **Lincoln, Abraham** (1809–1865) 16th U.S. president; the Great Emancipator. [Am. Hist.: Jameson, 286–287]
10. **Messiah** expected leader sent by God to exalt Israel. [Judaism: Brewer *Dictionary*]
11. **Moses** led his people out of bondage. [O.T.: Exodus]
12. **Othniel** freed Israelites from bondage of Cushan-rishathaim. [O.T.: Judges 3:9]
13. **Parsifal** deliverer of Amfortas and the Grail knights. [Ger. Opera: Wagner, *Parsifal,* Westerman, 250]
14. **Passover** festival commemorating Exodus. [Judaism: Wigoder, 472; O.T.: Exodus 12]
15. **Purim** Jewish festival commemorating salvation from Haman's destruction. [O.T.: Esther 9:20–28]

170. DELUSION

1. **Borkman, John Gabriel** suffers from delusions of power. [Nor. Lit.: *John Gabriel Borkman*]
2. **Bowles, Sally** night-club entertainer thinks she has the makings of a great film actress. [Br. Lit.: Isherwood *Berlin Stories* in Drabble, 498]
3. **Clamence, Jean-Baptiste** living with his own good and evil. [Fr. Lit.: *The Fall*]
4. **Dubois, Blanche** felt she and Mitch were above others. [Am. Lit.: *A Streetcar Named Desire*]
5. **Jones, Brutus** self-styled island emperor experiences traumatic visions. [Am. Lit.: *Emperor Jones*]
6. **Lockit, Lucy** steals jailer-father's keys to free phony husband. [Br. Lit.: *The Beggar's Opera*]

7. **Pan, Peter** little boy, refuses to grow up; resides in Never Never Land. [Children's Lit.: *Peter Pan*]
8. **opium of the people** Marx's classic metaphor for religion. [Ger. Hist.: *Critique of Hegel's "Philosophy of Right"*]
9. **ostrich** hides head, thinking itself concealed. [Animal Symbolism: Brewer *Dictionary*, 788]

171. DEMAGOGUERY

1. **Hague, Frank** (1876–1956) corrupt mayor of Jersey City, N.J., for 30 years. [Am. Hist.: *NCE*, 1173]
2. **Long, Huey P.** (1893–1935) infamous "Kingfish" of Louisiana politics. [Am. Hist.: *NCE*, 1607]
3. **Pendergast, Thomas J.** (1872–1945) political boss in Kansas City, Mo.: convicted of income tax evasions. [Am. Hist.: *NCE*, 2096]
4. **Savonarola** (1452–1498) rabble-rousing bane of Renaissance Florence. [Ital. Hist.: Plumb, 141–142, 166–167]
5. **Stark, Willie** rises to top as graft-dealing political boss. [Am. Lit.: *All the King's Men*]
6. **Tweed, "Boss" William** (1823–1878) powerful Tammany Hall leader in New York City. [Am. Hist.: *NCE*, 2810]

172. DEMON (See also DEVIL.)

1. **Aello** Harpy; demon carrying people away, personifying a whirlwind. [Gk. Myth.: Jobes, 40]
2. **afreet** or **afrit** gigantic jinn, powerful and malicious. [Muslim Myth.: Benét, 13]
3. **Apophis** the snake god; most important of demons. [Ancient Egypt. Rel.: Parrinder, 24]
4. **Ashmedai** king of fiends. [Hebrew Myth.: Leach, 83]
5. **Asmodeus** king of the devils. [Talmudic Legend: Benét, 58]
6. **bat** bird that is the devil incarnate. [Western Folklore: Mercatante, 181]
7. **cat** evil being, demonic in nature. [Animal Symbolism: Mercatante, 46]
8. **crocodile** feared as spirit of evil. [African Folklore: Jobes, 382; Mercatante, 9]
9. **Demogorgon** mere mention of his name brings death and destruction. [Western Folklore: Benét, 263]
10. **Dives** ferocious spirits under sovereignty of Eblis. [Persian Myth.: *LLEI*, I: 326]
11. **Fideal** evil water spirit; dragged men under water. [Scot. Folklore: Briggs, 175]

12. **Great Giant of Henllys** ghost of dead man turned demon. [Br. Folklore: Briggs, 199–200]
13. **incubus** demon in the form of a man. [Western Folklore: Briggs, 232]
14. **jinn (genii)** class of demon assuming animal/human form. [Arab. Myth.: Benét, 13, 521]
15. **Old Bogy** nursery fiend invoked to frighten children. [Br. Folklore: Wheeler, 265]
16. **succubus** demon in the form of a woman. [Western Folklore: Briggs, 232]
17. **whale** former symbol of demonic evil. [Animal Symbolism: Mercatante, 26]

173. DESPAIR (See also FUTILITY.)

1. **Achitophel** hanged himself from despair when his advice went unheeded. [O.T.: II Samuel 17:23]
2. **Aram, Eugene** scholar murders from pressure of poverty. [Br. Lit.: *Eugene Aram*]
3. **Bowery, the** Manhattan skid row for alcoholics. [Am. Hist.: Hart, 97]
4. **Giant Despair** imprisons Christian and Hopeful in Doubting Castle. [Br. Lit.: *Pilgrim's Progress*]
5. **Hrothgar** Danish king desperately distressed by warrior-killing monster. [Br. Lit.: *Beowulf*]
6. **Maurya** mother loses six sons in the sea. [Br. Lit.: *Riders to the Sea*]
7. **Melusina** fairy who despaired when husband discovered secret. [Fr. Folklore: Brewer *Handbook*, 695]
8. **Narcissus** wastes away yearning to kiss reflection of himself. [Gk. Myth.: Brewer *Handbook*, 745; Rom. Lit.: *Metamorphoses*]
9. **Slough of Despond** bog enmiring and discouraging Christian. [Br. Lit.: *Pilgrim's Progress*]
10. **Sullivan brothers** mother despairs over losing her five sons in WWII (1942). [Am. Hist.: *Facts* (1943), 106]
11. **Tristram** or **Tristan** falsely told that Iseult is not coming to save him from fatal poisoning, he dies of despair. [Medieval Legend: Brewer *Dictionary*]
12. ***Waiting for Godot*** tramps consider hanging themselves because Godot has failed to arrive to set things straight. [Anglo-French Drama: Samuel Beckett *Waiting for Godot* in Magill III, 1113]

Detection, Crime (See **SLEUTHING.**)

Destiny (See **FATE.**)

174. DESTRUCTION

1. **Abaddon** angel of the abyss; king of locusts. [N.T.: Revelation 9:11]
2. **abomination of desolation** epithet for the destructive or hateful. [Western Folklore: Benét, 3]
3. **atomic bomb (A-bomb)** fission device of enormous destructive power. [Am. Sci.: *EB*, I: 628]
4. **Armageddon** final battle between forces of good and evil. [N.T.: Revelation 16:16]
5. **Bikini and Eniwetok** Pacific atolls, sites of H-bomb testing. [Am. Hist.: Flexner, 12]
6. **Doomsday device** superpower nuclear capability to destroy the world if attacked. [Brit. Cinema: *Dr. Strangelove*]
7. **Dresden, bombing of** allied incendiary bombs reduced city to inferno (February 13, 1945). [Ger. Hist.: *Hitler*, 1165; Am. Lit.: *Slaughterhouse-Five*]
8. **Enlil** storm god responsible for deluge. [Babyl. Myth.: Parrinder, 91]
9. **Enola Gay** B-52 that dropped the Hiroshima A-bomb. [U.S. Hist.: *WB*, W:405]
10. **firebranded foxes** Samson unlooses them to scorch cornfields. [O.T.: Judges 15:3–6]
11. **Four Horsemen of the Apocalypse** allegorical figures representing pestilence, war, famine, death. [N.T.: Revelation 6:1–8]
12. **Götterdämmerung** great final battle between Teutonic pantheon and forces of evil. [Ger. Myth.: Leach, 461]
13. **Hiroshima** Japanese city destroyed by A-bomb (1945). [Am. Hist.: Fuller, III,
14. **Hormah** Judah and his men level this Canaanite city. [O.T.: Judges 1:17]
15. **Hundred Years War** reduced much of France to wasteland (1337–1453). [Eur. Hist.: Bishop, 382–395]
16. **hydrogen bomb (H-bomb)** thermonuclear device more destructive than A-bomb. [Am. Sci.: *EB*, IX: 949]
17. **Jericho, Walls of** razed on the seventh blowing of trumpets. [O.T.: Joshua 6]
18. **Jerusalem** destroyed in 586 B.C. by Nebuchadnezzar, and in A.D. 70 by Titus. [Jew. Hist.: *Collier's*, XI, 16, 17]

19. **Juggernaut** (**Jagannath**) huge idol of Krishna drawn through streets annually, occasionally rolling over devotees. [Hindu Rel.: *EB,* V: 499]
20. **Krakatoa** volcano in southwest Pacific which violently exploded in 1883, destroying the island. [Asian Hist.: *NCE,* 1500]
21. **Kristallnacht** Nazi rampage against property of German Jews (November 9–10, 1938). [Ger. Hist.: *Hitler,* 689–694]
22. **Lidice** Czech town obliterated by Nazis (June 10, 1942). [Eur. Hist.: Van Doren, 489]
23. **Mt. St. Helens** volcanic eruption that devastated huge area in 1980. [U. S. Hist.: *WB*, M:735]
24. **Nagasaki** Japanese city destroyed by A-bomb (1945). [Am. Hist.: Fuller, III: 626]
25. **neutron bomb** causes limited havoc: kills people, preserves property. [World Hist.: *Facts* (1978), 103]
26. ***On the Beach*** describes search for survivors after entire population on North America has been wiped out by nuclear war. [Br. Lit.: Weiss, 332]
27. **Ragnarok** destruction of gods and all things in final battle with evil. [Norse Myth.: *NCE,* 1762]
28. **Rome, Sack of** destroyed by the German-Spanish army under Charles V (1527). [Ital. Hist.: Plumb, 43, 406–407]
29. **Sherman's "March to the Sea"** Confederate heartland ravaged by marauding Union army (1864). [Am. Hist.: Jameson, 307]
30. **Sodom and Gomorrah** Biblical cities destroyed by fire for wicked ways. [O.T.: Genesis 10:19; 13; 14; 18; 19]
31. **Thirty Years War** world war prototype reduced Germany to wasteland (1618–1648). [Eur. Hist.: *EB,* 18: 333–344]
32. **Vesuvius** volcano in Italy which erupted in A.D. 79, burying Pompeii and Herculaneum. [Rom. Hist.: *NCE,* 2187]
33. **Vials of Wrath** seven plagues precipitating end of world. [N.T.: Revelation 16:1–17]
34. **Vulcan** god of destruction, placated by gifts of captured weapons. [Rom. Myth.: Howe, 294]

175. DETERMINATION (See also PERSEVERANCE.)

1. **Agathocles** (361–289 B.C.) Syracusan king; "burned his ships behind him" in attacking Carthage. [Gk. Hist.: Walsh *Classical,* 9]
2. **Balboa, Rocky** determined prize fighter takes on impossible dream. [Am. Cinema: *Rocky* in *EB* (1978), 552]

3. **bulldog** bred for doggedly refusing to let go. [Dog Breeding: Misc.]
4. **Dry Guillotine** book by French escapee from Devil's Island. [Fr. Lit.: *Dry Guillotine*]
5. **Ignatz** tenaciously refuses Krazy Kat's advances. [Comics: "Krazy Kat" in Horn, 436–437]
6. **Jones, John Paul** (1747–1792) Revolutionary War naval hero; remembered for saying; "I have not yet begun to fight!" [Am. Hist.: Jameson, 260–261]
7. **Keller, Helen** (1880–1968) though blind and deaf, becomes noted author and lecturer. [Am. Hist.: Hart, 439–440]
8. **Little Engine That Could** succeeds when others refuse to help. [Children's Lit.: *The Little Engine That Could*]
9. ***Message to Garcia*, A** against great odds, American officer makes his way to Cuban general leading a revolt against Spain. [Am. Lit. and Hist.: Benét, 662]
10. **Papillon** wily prisoner endeavors repeatedly to escape from Devil's Island. [Fr. Lit.: *Papillon*]
11. **Santiago** struggles long and hard for great fish. [Am. Lit.: *Old Man and the Sea*]
12. **tortoise** slow and steady, it wins the race against the hare. [Animal Symbolism: Mercatante, 22; Gk. Lit.: Aesop, "The Tortoise and the Hare"]
13. **Tovesky, Marie** outgoing and friendly, despite husband's insane jealousy. [Am. Lit.: *O Pioneers!*, Magill I, 663–665]

176. DEVIL (See also DEMON.)

1. **Adramalech** leader of fallen angels. [Br. Lit.: *Paradise Lost*]
2. **adversary** traditional appellation of Satan [O.T.: Job 1:6; N.T.: I Peter 5:8]
3. **Amaimon** king of eastern portion of hell. [Medieval Legend: Brewer *Dictionary*, 28]
4. **Apollyon** Biblical name for Satan. [N.T.: Revelation 9:11]
5. **Applegate, Mr.** devil to whom aging Joe Boyd sells his soul to become a youthful champion outfielder. [Am. Lit.: Wallop *The Year the Yankees Lost the Pennant; Damn Yankees*]
6. **Auld Ane** literally, 'old one'; nickname for demon. [Scot. Folklore: Walsh *Modern*, 35]
7. **Auld Hornie** Scottish appellation for the devil. [Scot. Folklore: Leach, 353]
8. **Azazel** Satan's standard bearer. [Br. Lit.: *Paradise Lost*]
9. **Beelzebub** prince of demons. [N.T.: Matthew 12:24]

10. **Belial** chief of fiends. [O.T.: I Samuel 2:12]
11. **Cathleen** sells her soul to the devil in exchange for the souls of starving Irish peasants. [Irish Drama: Yeats *Countess Cathleen* in Benét, 228]
12. **Clootie** Scottish appellation for the devil. [Scot. Folklore: Leach, 353]
13. **Darkness, Prince of** "The Prince of Darkness," alias the Devil. [Br. Lit.: *All's Well That Ends Well*]
14. **the Deuce** New England appellation for the devil. [Am. Folklore: Leach, 353]
15. **Devils, Prince of the** biblical equivalent for Satan. [N.T.: Matthew 9:34]
16. **divis** devils shown as cat-headed men with horns and hooves. [Pers. Myth.: Barber & Riches]
17. **Eblis** devil and father of devils, called Azazel before his fall. [Islam: Brewer *Dictionary* 319]
18. **Faust (Dr. Faustus)** sells his soul to the devil in order to comprehend all experience. [Ger. Lit.: Goethe *Faust*; Br. Drama: Marlowe *Doctor Faustus*]
19. **Iblis (Eblis)** Moslem prince of darkness; chief evil spirit. [Islam: Leach, 513]
20. **Lucifer** a Biblical name for Satan. [O.T.: Isaiah 14:12]
21. **Master Leonard** grand-master of sabbats and orgies. [Medieval Demonology: Brewer *Handbook*, 684]
22. **Mephistopheles** fiend to whom Faust sells his soul. [Ger. Lit.: *Faust*]
23. ***Mysterious Stranger, The*** devil appears as a pleasant stranger, convinces a boy of the falseness of morals and the nonexistence of God. [Am. Lit.: Twain *The Mysterious Stranger* in Benét, 697]
24. **Nickie-Ben** a Scottish name for Satan. [Scot. Folklore: Wheeler, 258]
25. **Old Nick** Satan himself. [Western Folklore: Brewer *Dictionary*, 755]
26. **Old Scratch** Satan. [Eng. Usage: Brewer *Dictionary*, 973; Am. Lit.: "The Devil and Daniel Webster"]
27. **Peter, Meister** German euphemism alluding to the devil. [Ger. Folklore: Leach, 353]
28. **Satan** the devil himself, source of all evil. [O.T.: Job 1–2]

Devotion (See **FAITHFULNESS.**)

177. DICTION, FAULTY

1. **Ace, Jane** (1905–1974) radio personality, remembered for sayings such as "up at the crank of dawn." [Radio: "Easy Aces" in Buxton, 74–75]
2. **Amos 'n' Andy** early radio buffoons who distorted language: "I'se regusted!" [Radio: Buxton, 13–14]
3. **Bottom, Nick** tradesman-actor who constantly misuses words. [Br. Drama: Shakespeare *A Midsummer Night's Dream*]
4. **Claudius** because he stammered, held in little esteem as emperor. [Br. Lit.: *I, Claudius*]
5. **Clouseau, Inspector Jacques** infamous, tongue-tripping French detective. [Am. Cinema: *The Pink Panther* in Halliwell, 565]
6. **Dean, Dizzy** (1911–1974) famous baseball pitcher turned sports announcer: "He slud inta t'ird." [Radio: Buxton, 223]
7. **Dean, James** (1931–1955) actor whose inarticulateness epitomized the anti-eloquence of American youth in the 1950s. [Am. Cinema: Griffith, 423]
8. **Demosthenes** (384–322 B.C.) learned proper diction by practicing with mouth full of pebbles. [Gk. Hist.: *NCE*, 744]
9. **Dogberry** constable who garbles every phrase he speaks. [Br. Drama: Benét, 277]
10. **Doolittle, Eliza** Cockney flower girl transformed from guttersnipe to lady via better English. [Br. Lit.: *Pygmalion*]
11. **Ephraimites** identified as enemy by mispronunciation of "shibboleth." [O.T.: Judges 12:6]
12. **Fudd, Elmer** disgruntled little man, stammers out his frustration at impish rabbit. [TV: "The Bugs Bunny Show" in Terrace, I, 125]
13. **Malaprop, Mrs.** eponymous blunderer in word usage. [Br. Drama: Benét, 623]
14. **Partington, Mrs.** foolish old lady who constantly misuses words. [Am. Lit.: Brewer *Dictionary*, 681]
15. **Pig, Porky** stuttering porcine character in film cartoons. [Comics: Horn, 562–563]
16. **Pip** how orphan Philip Pirrup says his name. [Br. Lit.: *Great Expectations*]
17. **Spooner, Rev. W. A.** (1844–1930) legendary for transposing initial sounds: "our queer dean Mary"; hence, *spoonerism*. [Br. Hist.: Brewer *Dictionary*, 1029]

18. **Sylvester** the lisping feline star of film cartoons. [TV: "The Bugs Bunny Show" in Terrace, I, 125]

178. DIGNITY (See also NOBLEMINDEDNESS.)

1. **cherub** celestial being symbolizing dignity, glory, and honor. [Heraldry: Halberts, 23]
2. **cloves** symbolic of stateliness. [Plant Symbolism and Folklore: Jobes, 350]
3. **dahlia** symbol of dignity. [Flower Symbolism: Jobes, 406]
4. **ermine** fur which represents nobility. [Heraldry: Halberts, 13]
5. **strawberry** symbolizes esteem. [Flower Symbolism: *Flora Symbolica,* 177]

179. DILEMMA

1. **Buridan's ass** placed exactly between two equal haystacks, could not decide which to turn to in his hunger. [Fr. Philos.: Brewer *Dictionary*, 154]

180. DIMWITTEDNESS (See also STUPIDITY.)

1. **Allen, Gracie** (1906–1964) American comedienne who projected a scatterbrained image. [Radio, TV, Am. Cinema: Halliwell, 14]
2. **Bodine, Jethro** oafish mental midget of millionaire hillbilly family. [TV: "The Beverly Hillbillies" in Terrace, I, 93]
3. **Bullwinkle** dimwitted moose with penchant for pedantry. [TV: "Rocky and His Friends" in Terrace, II, 252–253]
4. **Bunker, Edith** Archie's lovable "dingbat." [TV: "All in the Family" in Terrace, I, 47–48]
5. **Compson, Benjy** 33-year-old idiot loved and protected by his sister and both calmed and distracted by pictures that flow through his mind. [Am. Lit.: Faulkner *The Sound and the Fury* in Magill I, 917]
6. **Costello, Lou** (1906–1959) dumpy American comedian; used dimwittedness to spark humor. [Am. Cinema: Halliwell, 171]
7. **Drummle, Bentley** "heavy in comprehension"; suspicious of new ideas. [Br. Lit.: *Great Expectations*]
8. **Elspeth** Flashman's air-headed but beguiling wife. [Br. Lit.: *Flashman*]
9. **Happy Hooligan** simple and harmless tramp, serene and optimistic despite constant bad luck. [Comics: Horn, 302]
10. **Jeff** boob who usually bungles Mutt's schemes. [Comics: Berger, 48]

11. **Laurel, Stan** (1890–1965) bumbling foil for Oliver Hardy. [Am. Cinema: Halliwell, 425]
12. **Moose** the epitome of "the obtuse jock," or dimwitted athlete. [Comics: "Archie" in Horn, 87]
13. **Palooka, Joe** semi-literate boxer, wholesome and bungling. [Comics: Horn, 343–344]
14. **Rudge, Barnaby** grotesquely dressed, retarded son of a murderer. [Br. Lit.: *Barnaby Rudge*]
15. **Zero** army private whose name and IQ are almost equivalent. [Comics: "Beetle Bailey" in Horn, 105–106]

181. DIRTINESS (See also FILTH.)

1. **Daw, Margery** sold her bed and slept on dirt. [Nurs. Rhyme: Opie, 297]
2. **Madison, Oscar** disheveled and sloppy sportswriter for *New York Herald.* [Am. Drama: *The Odd Couple;* TV: "The Odd Couple" in Terrace, II, 160]
3. **Pig Pen** "a walking dust storm." [Comics: "Peanuts" in Horn, 542–543]
4. **hoopoe** filthy bird; lines nest with dung. [Medieval Animal Symbolism: White, 150]

182. DISAPPEARANCE (See also ABDUCTION.)

1. **Arden, Enoch** missing for many years after being shipwrecked, returns to find his wife remarried. [Br. Poetry: "Enoch Arden"]
2. **Atlantis** submerged legendary island kingdom; never located. [Classical Folklore: Walsh *Classical,* 37]
3. **Bermuda Triangle** area of mysterious disappearance of ships and planes at sea. [Am. Hist.: *The Bermuda Triangle*]
4. **Bierce, Ambrose** (1842–1914?) journalist and short story writer; disappeared into Mexico in 1913. [Am. Hist.: *NCE,* 294]
5. **Crater, Judge** (Joseph Force Crater, 1889–1930?) Judge of N. Y. Supreme Court; vanished August 6, 1930. [Am. Hist.: *RHD*]
6. **Drood, Edwin** nephew of John Jasper; mysteriously vanishes. [Br. Lit.: *Edwin Drood*]
7. **Earhart, Amelia** (1897–1937?) aviatrix vanished in 1937 amid speculation and gossip. [Am. Hist.: *NCE,* 819]
8. **Hoffa, Jimmy** (1913–1975?) Teamsters' boss kidnapped and presumed dead. [Am. Hist.: *Facts* (1975), 573]
9. **Louis XVII** (1793–1795?) "lost dauphin"; heir to French kingship imprisoned and probably abducted. [Fr. Hist.: *NCE,* 1617]

10. **Mister Keen** tracer of lost persons. [Radio: "Keen" in Sharp, IV, 354]
11. **Prospero's banquet** vanishes after being shown to the hungry castaways. [Br. Drama: Shakespeare *The Tempest*]
12. **Roanoke** Carolina settlement that twice vanished, leaving no trace (1587). [Am. Hist.: Jameson, 430]

183. DISASTER (See also SHIPWRECK.)

1. **Amoco Cadiz** oil tanker broke up off Britanny coast; 1.6 million barrels spilled (1978). [Fr. Hist.: *Facts* (1978), 201, 202]
2. **Angur-boda** Utgard giantess, worker of disaster; literally, 'anguish-boding.' [Norse Myth.: Leach, 58]
3. **Chicago fire** conflagration destroyed most of city (1871). [Am. Hist.: Jameson, 94]
4. **Deluge** earth-covering flood that destroyed all but Noah's family and animals in the ark. [O.T.: Genesis 6–8]
5. **Deucalion's Flood** the Deluge of Greek legend. [Gk. Myth.: Benét, 266]
6. **Evangeline** concerns peaceful village vacated and destroyed during war. [Am. Lit.: "Evangeline" in Magill I, 261–263]
7. **Fatal Vespers** 2 Jesuits and 100 others killed in collapse of lecture hall. [Br. Hist.: Brewer *Dictionary*, 1127]
8. **Gilgamesh epic** Babylonian legend contains pre-Biblical account of Flood. [Near East. Myth.: *EB*, IV: 542]
9. **Hindenburg, the** German airship blew up upon mooring in New Jersey (1937). [Am. Hist.: *NCE*, 43]
10. **Johnstown Flood** Pennsylvania city destroyed by flood (May 31, 1889); 2,200 lives lost. [Am. Hist.: *NCE*, 1427]
11. ***Lusitania*** British luxury liner sunk by German submarine in World War I. [Br. Hist.: *EB* (1963) XX, 518]
12. **Pompeii** Roman city buried by eruption of Mt. Vesuvius (79). [Rom. Hist.: *NCE*, 2187]
13. **red cloud** indicates disaster is impending. [Eastern Folklore: Jobes, 350]
14. **San Francisco earthquake** disaster claiming many lives and most of city (1906). [Am. Hist.: Jameson, 443–444]
15. **Titanic** British passenger ship sinks on maiden voyage (1912). [Br. Hist.: *NCE*, 2753]

184. DISBELIEF (See also SKEPTICISM.)

1. **Capys** Trojan who mistrusted Trojan Horse; cautioned against bringing it into the city. [Gk. Myth.: Zimmerman, 50]

2. **Cassandra** no one gave credence to her accurate prophecies of doom. [Gk. Myth.: Zimmerman, 51]
3. **Gerstein, Kurt** anti-Nazi German; nobody credited his story of atrocities. [Ger. Hist.: Wigoder, 210]

185. DISCIPLINE

1. **chicken** indicates martinetish authority. [Military Slang: Wentworth, 98]
2. **Patton, General George** (1885–1945) U.S. Army general known for imposing rigid discipline on his troops. [Am. Hist.: *NCE*, 2083]
3. **Puritans** strictly religious and morally disciplined colonists. [Am. Hist.: Payton, 551]
4. **spare the rod and spoil the child** axiomatic admonition. [O.T.: Proverbs 13:24]
5. **Spartans** Doric people noted for bravery, frugality, and stern self-discipline. [Gk. Hist.: Payton, 640]
6. **West Point** U.S. Military Academy focusing on discipline as part of training. [Am. Hist.: Payton, 729]

186. DISCORD (See also CONFUSION.)

1. **Andras** demon of discord. [Occultism: Jobes, 93]
2. **discord, apple of** caused conflict among goddesses; Trojan War ultimate result. [Gk. Myth.: Benét, 43]
3. **Discordia** goddess of strife and discord. [Gk. Myth.: Kravitz, 83]
4. **Eris** goddess of discord; threw apple of discord among Peleus's wedding guests. [Gk. Myth.: Howe, 95]
5. **54-40 or Fight!** slogan alluding to disputed borders of Oregon territory under joint British and U.S. occupation. [Am. Hist.: Payton, 241]
6. **Gaza Strip** small coastal desert on borders of Egypt and Israel, the control of which has been in continual dispute. [Middle East. Hist.: Payton, 264]
7. **Great Schism, the** Catholic Church divided over papal succession (1378–1417). [Eur. Hist.: Bishop, 376–379]
8. **onyx** provokes disagreement and separates lovers. [Gem. Symbolism: Kunz, 98–99]

187. DISCOVERY

1. **Archimedes** (287–212 B.C.) discovered fluid displacement principle while bathing. [Gk. Hist.: Wallechinsky, 272]

2. **Blue Nile** its source discovered by James Bruce, c. 1773. [Br. Hist.: *NCE*]
3. **Dead Sea scrolls** ancient manuscripts of Biblical commentaries found in cave. [Jew. Hist.: Wigoder, 152]
4. **Eureka!** exclaimed Archimedes, on discovering specific gravity principle. [Gk. Hist.: *NCE*, 137]
5. **Franklin, Benjamin** (1706–1790) used a simple kite to identify lightning as electricity. [Science: *NCE*, 1000]
6. **Kaldi** Arabian goatherd; alleged discoverer of coffee (850). [Arab. Hist.: Grun, 97]
7. **New World** Christopher Columbus's expeditions to Americas from 1492 led to further exploration and development. [Eur. Hist.: Jameson, 107–108]
8. **Newton, Sir Isaac** (1642–1727) a falling apple said to have inspired theory of gravitation. [Science: *NCE*, 1929]
9. **Pacific Ocean** Its American coast discovered by Vasco Nuñez de Balboa in 1513. [Amer. Hist.: *NCE*, 213]
10. **Philippines** discovered by Magellan during his attempted circumnavigation of the globe. [World Hist.: Benét, 618]
11. **Rosetta Stone** inscribed in three languages; key to hieroglyphics. [Fr. Hist.: Brewer *Dictionary*, 935]
12. **San Salvador** Bahamian island, Columbus's first landfall in his discovery of America. [Am. Hist.: Benét, 214]
13. **Sutter's Mill** where James Marshall discovered California gold (1848). [Am. Hist.: *NCE*, 2662]
14. **Tutankhamun's tomb** incredible archaeological find unlocks the past. [Egypt. Hist.: *NCE*, 2809]

Discretion (See PRUDENCE.)

188. DISEASE

1. **AIDS** mysterious new disease, incurable and usually fatal. [U.S. Hist.: *WB*, A:153]
2. **Black Death** killed at least one third of Europe's population (1348–1349). [Eur. Hist.: Bishop, 379–382]
3. **bubonic plague** ravages Oran, Algeria, where Dr. Rieux perseveres in his humanitarian endeavors. [Fr. Lit.: *The Plague*]
4. ***Cancer Ward, The*** novel set in cancer ward of a Russian hospital. [Russ. Lit.: *The Cancer Ward* in Weiss, 64]
5. **Decameron, The** tales told by young people taking refuge from the black death ravaging Florence. [Ital. Lit.: Magill II, 231]
6. **Fiacre, St.** intercession sought by sick. [Christian Hagiog.: Attwater, 130]

7. **influenza epidemic** caused 500,000 deaths in U.S. alone (1918–1919). [Am. Hist.: Van Doren, 403]
8. **Joram** suffered for abandoning God's way. [O.T.: II Chronicles 21:15, 19]
9. ***Journal of the Plague Year*** Defoe's famous account of bubonic plague in England in 1665. [Br. Lit.: Benét, 529]
10. **Lazarus** leper brought back to life by Christ. [N.T.: John 11:1–44]
11. **Legionnaires' disease** 28 American Legion conventioneers die of flu-like disease in Philadelphia (1976). [Am. Hist.: *Facts* (1976), 573, 656]
12. **Molokai** Hawaiian island; site of government leper colony. [Am. Hist.: *NCE*, 1807]
13. **Naaman** leprous Syrian commander healed by Elisha. [O.T.: II Kings 5]
14. **red death, the** pestilence, embodied in a masque, fatally penetrates Prince Prospero's abbey. [Am. Lit.: Poe *The Masque of the Red Death*]
15. **Rock, St.** legendary healer of plague victims. [Christian Hagiog.: Attwater, 299]
16. **Sennacherib, army of** besieging Jerusalem, Assyrian force must withdraw after an outbreak of plague. [O.T.: II Kings 19:35; Br. Lit.: Byron *The Destruction of Sennacherib* in Benét, 266]
17. **seven plagues, the** visited upon the earth to signify God's wrath. [N.T.: Revelation]
18. **St. Anthony's Fire** horrific 11th-century plague. [Eur. Hist.: Brewer *Note-Book*, 34]
19. ***Syphilis*** Fracastoro's epic concerning *Syphilis*, mythical first victim. [Ital. Lit.: *RHD*, 1443; Plumb, 342]
20. **ten plagues, the** inflicted upon Egypt when Pharaoh refuses to let the Israelites emigrate. [O.T.: Exodus 7-12]
21. **Typhoid Mary** (Mary Mallon, 1870–1938) unwitting carrier of typhus; suffered 23-year quarantine. [Am. Hist.: Van Doren, 354]

189. DISGUISE

1. **Abigail** enters nunnery as convert to retrieve money. [Br. Lit.: *The Jew of Malta*]
2. **Achilles** disguised as a woman to avoid conscription. [Gk. Legend: Brewer *Handbook*, 642 (Lycomedes)]

3. **Aspatia** disguised as a man, engages a nobleman in a duel and dies of her wounds. [Br. Drama: Beaumont and Fletcher *The Maid's Tragedy* in Sobel, 444]
4. **Athena** assumes Mentor's form to persuade Telemachus to search for his father. [Gk. Lit.: *Odyssey*]
5. **Babbie** a young lady of good blood runs about in the dress and manners of a gypsy. [Br. Lit.: Barrie *The Little Minister* in Magill I, 513]
6. **Batman** millionaire Bruce Wayne dresses in his batlike cape and cowl. [Comics: Horn, 101]
7. **Beaucaire, Monsieur** to escape marriage, nobleman pretends to be a barber. [Am. Lit.: *Monsieur Beaucaire*]
8. **Biron** masks self as Muscovite; woos wrong woman. [Br. Lit.: *Love's Labour's Lost*]
9. **Blakeney, Percy** outwits his opponents by his ingenious disguises. [Br. Lit.: *Scarlet Pimpernel*]
10. **Bones, Brom** impersonates Headless Horseman to scare off rival suitor. [Am. Lit.: *The Legend of Sleepy Hollow*]
11. **Brainworm** impersonates variety of characters in his trickery. [Br. Lit.: *Every Man in His Humour*]
12. **Burchell, Mr.** baronet passes himself off as beggar. [Br. Lit.: *The Vicar of Wakefield*]
13. **Burlingame, Henry** man with a thousand faces. [Am. Lit.: *The Sot-Weed Factor*]
14. ***Charley's Aunt*** man poses as a woman in order to get his pal out of a jam. [Br. Drama: Barnhart, 228]
15. **Cléonte** masquerades as Grand Turk to win pretentious man's daughter. [Fr. Lit.: *Le Bourgeois Gentilhomme*]
16. **Cupid** disguised as Ascanius, son of Aeneas. [Gk. Myth.: *Aeneid*]
17. **Demara, Ferdinand, Jr.,** "Great Impostor"; posed in professional roles. [Am. Hist.: Wallechinsky, 484]
18. **Despina** disguised doctor who supposedly restores lovers to life. [Ger. Opera: Mozart, *Cosi fan tutte*, Westerman, 98]
19. **Elaine** disguises herself as Guinevere in order to seduce Lancelot. [Br. Lit.: Malory *Le Mort d'Arthur*]
20. **Eugenia, St.** dressed as male, becomes abbot of Egyptian monastery. [Christian Hagiog.: Attwater, 120]
21. **Finn, Huckleberry** after his supposed death, he dons a girl's dress and goes into town to gain information. [Am. Lit.: Mark Twain *Huckleberry Finn*]

22. **Ford** assumes pseudonym to uncover adulterer. [Br. Lit.: *Merry Wives of Windsor*]
23. **Gareth** queen requires him to disguise himself as a kitchen hand before he may seek knighthood. [Br. Poetry: Tennyson *Idylls of the King*]
24. **Gustavus, King** he and his lover Amelia are in disguises when he is killed by her husband. [Ital. Opera: *Un Ballo in Maschera* in Osborne *Opera*]
25. **Hardcastle, Kate** wins her suitor by pretending to be a barmaid. [Br. Drama: Goldsmith *She Stoops to Conquer* in Benét, 926]
26. **Hautdesert, Sir Bercilak de** disguised as Green Knight, challenges Gawain's valor. [Br. Lit.: *Sir Gawain and the Green Knight*]
27. **Helena** disguises herself as a pilgrim in order to follow her husband from France to Italy. [Br. Drama: Shakespeare *All's Well That Ends Well*]
28. **Holmes, Sherlock** returns in disguise after his supposed death to surprise his enemies. [Br. Lit.: Doyle *The Return of Sherlock Holmes* in *Sherlock Holmes*]
29. **Imogen** dresses in boy's clothes to escape her husband's murder plot. [Br. Drama: Shakespeare *Cymbeline*]
30. **Jacob** dressed as Esau to obtain father's blessing. [O.T.: Genesis 27:15–16]
31. **Joker, the** master of disguise confounds Batman. [Comics: "Batman" in Horn, 101]
32. **Julia** masks self as page. [Br. Lit.: *Two Gentlemen of Verona*]
33. **Köpenick** tailor disguised as a captain, takes over city. [Ger. Lit.: *Captain from Köpenick*, Espy, 173]
34. **Kenneth, Sir** as Richard's slave, saves king from assassination. [Br. Lit.: *The Talisman*]
35. **Leonora** dressed as a man, elopes with Alvaro and takes refuge in a hermit's cave. [Ital. Opera: *La Forza del Destino* in Osborne *Opera*]
36. **Leonora** masks as Fidelio to save imprisoned husband. [Ger. Opera: Beethoven, *Fidelio*, Scholes, 352–353]
37. **Leucippus** youth disguised as girl to be near Daphne; killed upon discovery. [Gk. Myth.: Zimmerman, 150]
38. **Lone Ranger** masked crime fighter hides true identity. [Radio: Buxton, 143–144; Comics: Horn, 460; TV: Terrace, II, 34–35]

39. **Maupin, Madelaine de** dresses and acts like a man in order to go among men and see them as they really are. [Fr. Lit.: *Mademoiselle de Maupin* in Magill I, 542]
40. ***Merry Wives of Windsor, The*** Mr. Ford disguises himself in order to thwart Falstaff's designs on Mrs. Ford. [Br. Drama: Shakespeare *The Merry Wives of Windsor*]
41. **Nanki-Poo** emperor's son disguised as a minstrel. [Br. Opera: *The Mikado,* Magill I, 591–592]
42. **Octavian** to spare his mistress, dresses as a chambermaid; Baron Ochs flirts with "her". [Ger. Opera: Strauss *Der Rosenkavalier* in Benét, 877]
43. **Odysseus** changed by Athena into an old beggar to avoid his recognition by Penelope's suitors. [Gk. Lit.: *Odyssey*]
44. **Paolo, Don** political agitator dressed incognito as priest. [Ital. Lit.: *Bread and Wine*]
45. **Paris** disguised as priest of Venus to free Helen. [Fr. Operetta: Offenbach, *La Belle Hélène,* Westerman, 272–273]
46. **Pierre, Maître** a French merchant; in reality, King Louis XI. [Br. Lit.: *Quentin Durward,* Magill I, 795–797]
47. **Portia** heiress disguises herself as a lawyer and wins a case for her fiancé's friend. [Br. Drama: Shakespeare *The Merchant of Venice*]
48. **Rodolph, Grand Duke** roams the streets in disguise, befriending the unfortunate. [Fr. Lit.: Sue *The Mysteries of Paris* in Magill I, 632]
49. **Rosalind** disguises herself as a male. [Br. Lit.: *As You Like It*]
50. **Saladin** Saracen leader, in doctor's garb, cures Richard's illness. [Br. Lit.: *The Talisman*]
51. **Serannes, Theodore de** "young man" in reality Mademoiselle de Maupin. [Fr. Lit.: *Mademoiselle de Maupin,* Magill I, 542–543]
52. **Siegfried** disguised as Gunther, steals gold ring from Brunhild. [Ger. Opera: Wagner, *Götterdämmerung,* Westerman, 244]
53. **Spina, Pietro** antifascist patriot disguises himself as a priest. [Ital. Lit.: *Bread and Wine*]
54. **Superman** superhero under guise of Clark Kent, mild-mannered reporter. [Comics: Horn, 642]
55. **Thousandfurs** king's daughter works anonymously, cloaked in manypelted coat. [Ger. Fairy Tale: Grimm, 245]
56. **Toad of Toad Hall** passes as washerwoman to escape from jail. [Children's Lit.: *The Wind in the Willows*]

57. **Toinette** disguises herself as a doctor and prescribes radical treatment for a hypochondriac. [Fr. Drama: Molière *Le Malade Imaginaire* in Sobel, 445]
58. **Vicentio** masquerades as Friar Lodowick. [Br. Lit.: *Measure for Measure*]
59. **Viola** masquerades as Cesario. [Br. Lit.: *Twelfth Night*]
60. **Zeus** disguises himself as: satyr to lie with Antiope, Amphitryon with Alcmena, Artemis with Callisto, shower of gold with Danaë, white bull with Europa, swan with Leda, flame of fire with Aegina, and cuckoo with Hera. [Gk. Myth.: Jobes, 1719; *New Century,* 1158; Zimmerman, 293]
61. **Zorro** masked swordsman, defender of weak and oppressed. [Am. Lit.: comic strip (1919); Am. Cinema: Halliwell, 794; TV: Terrace, II, 461–462]

Dishonesty (See DECEIT.)

190. DISILLUSIONMENT

1. **Adams, Nick** loses innocence through WWI experience. [Am. Lit.: "The Killers"]
2. **Angry Young Men** disillusioned postwar writers of Britain, such as Osborne and Amis. [Br. Lit.: Benét, 37]
3. **Blaine, Amory** world-weary youth, typical of the lost generation that finds life unfulfilling. [Am. Lit.: *This Side of Paradise*]
4. **Chardon, Lucien (de Rubempré)** young poet realizes he is not destined for success. [Fr. Lit.: Balzac *Lost Illusions* in Magill II, 595]
5. **Chuzzlewit, Martin** swindled, becomes disillusioned with Americans. [Br. Lit.: *Martin Chuzzlewit*]
6. **de Lamare, Jeanne** heartbroken by her husband's neglect and the discovery of his infidelities. [Fr. Lit.: Maupassant *A Woman's Life* in Magill I, 1127]
7. **Dodsworth, Sam** disillusioned with wife, European tour, and American situation. [Am. Lit.: *Dodsworth*]
8. **Eden, Martin** attains success as a writer but loses desire to live when isolated from former friends and disenchanted with new ones. [Am. Lit.: *Martin Eden*]
9. ***Journey to the End of the Night*** exposing the philosophy of post-war disillusionment. [Fr. Lit.: *Journey to the End of the Night,* Magill I, 453–455]
10. **Kennaston, Felix** learns in middle age that his life of romantic dreams was baseless. [Am. Lit.: *The Cream of the Jest* in Magill I, 168]

11. **Krasov, Kuzma Ilich** frustrated writer considers life complete waste. [Russ. Lit.: *The Village*]
12. **Loman, Willy** salesman victimized by own and America's values. [Am. Lit.: *Death of a Salesman*]
13. **Lost Generation** intellectuals and aesthetes, rootless and disillusioned, who came to maturity during World War I. [Am. Lit.: Benét, 600]
14. **March, Augie** "everyone got bitterness in his chosen thing." [Am. Lit.: *The Adventures of Augie March*]
15. **Melody, Cornelius** a failing tavern-keeper, flamboyantly boasts of his past. [Am. Drama: Eugene O'Neill *A Touch of the Poet* in Benét, 737]
16. ***Mysterious Stranger, The*** naive youth is convinced by the devil that morals are false, God doesn't exist, and there is no heaven or hell. [Am. Lit.: Benét, 697]
17. **O'Hanlon, Virginia** (1890–1971) *N.Y. Sun* editorial dispels her disillusionment about Santa Claus (1897). [Am. Hist.: Rockwell, 188]
18. **Pococurante** wealthy count who has lost his taste for most literature, art, music, and women. [Fr. Lit.: *Candide*]
19. ***Rasselas*** prince and his companions search in vain for greater fulfillment than is possible in their Happy Valley. [Br. Lit.: *Rasselas* in Magill I, 804]
20. **Smith, Winston** clerk loses out in totalitarian world. [Br. Lit.: *1984*]
21. **Webber, George** finds his native Southern town has degenerated morally and that his idealized, romantic Germany is corrupted. [Am. Lit.: Thomas Wolfe *You Can't Go Home Again*]

191. DISOBEDIENCE

1. **Achan** defies God's ban on taking booty. [O.T.: Joshua 7:1]
2. **Adam and Eve** eat forbidden fruit of Tree of Knowledge. [O.T.: Genesis 3:1–7; Br. Lit.: *Paradise Lost*]
3. **Antigone** despite Creon's order, she buries Polynices. [Gk. Lit.: *Antigone*]
4. **Bartleby** copyist in Wall Street office; refuses to do anything but copy documents. [Am. Lit.: "Bartleby the Scrivener"]
5. **Brunhild** disobeys father's order to let Siegmund die. [Ger. Opera: Wagner, *Valkyrie*, Westerman, 237]
6. **Saul** contravening God, takes spoils from conquered Amalekites. [O.T.: I Samuel 15:17–19]

7. **Vashti, Queen** loses queenship for not submitting to king's demands. [O.T.: Esther 1:10–22]

Disorder (See CONFUSION.)

192. DISSIPATION (See also DEBAUCHERY.)

1. **Breitmann, Hans** lax indulger. [Am. Lit.: *Hans Breitmann's Ballads*]
2. **Burley, John** wasteful ne'er-do-well. [Br. Lit.: *My Novel,* Walsh *Modern,* 79]
3. **Camors** leads selfish, shameless life. [Fr. Lit.: *M. de Camors,* Walsh *Modern,* 84]
4. **Carton, Sydney** wasteful bohemian; does not use his talents. [Br. Lit.: *A Tale of Two Cities*]
5. **Castlewood, Francis Esmond** gambles away living. [Br. Lit.: *Henry Esmond*]
6. **Christian II** sybaritic king. [Fr. Lit.: *Kings in Exile,* Walsh *Modern,* 96]
7. **Chuzzlewit, Jonas** dissipated, wasteful person. [Br. Lit.: *Martin Chuzzlewit*]
8. **Clavering, Sir Francis** dissipated gambling baronet. [Br. Lit.: *Pendennis*]
9. **Dalgarno, Lord Malcolm of** wasteful and ruinous; destroys several people. [Br. Lit.: *Fortunes of Nigel*]
10. **Fitzgerald, F. Scott** (1896–1940) American novelist whose works reflect a life of dissipation. [Am. Lit.: *NCE,* 957]
11. **Jeshurun** citizens abandon God; give themselves up to luxury. [O.T.: Deuteronomy 32:15]
12. **Mite, Sir Matthew** dissolute merchant; displays wealth ostentatiously. [Br. Lit.: *The Nabob,* Brewer *Handbook,* 713]
13. **Pheidippides** his extravagant bets ruin father's wealth. [Gk. Lit.: *The Clouds*]
14. **prodigal son** squanders share of money in reckless living. [N.T.: Luke 15:13]

193. DISTRACTION

1. **Porlock** a "person from Porlock" interrupted Coleridge while he was recollecting the dream on which he based "Kubla Khan". [Br. Lit.: *Poems of Coleridge* in Magill IV, 756]

Divination (See **OMEN.**)

194. DOGS

1. **Argos** Odysseus' pet, recognizes him after an absence of twenty years. [Gk. Lit.: *Odyssey* 17:298]
2. **Asta** the thin man's dog. [Am. Lit.: *The Thin Man*]
3. **Balthasar** almost a Pomeranian, companion of Jolyon Forsyte at Robin Hill. [Br. Lit.: "Indian Summer of a Forsyte"]
4. **barghest** monstrous goblin-dog, a nocturnal specter portending death. [Br. Folklore: *EB* (1963) III, 110]
5. **Boatswain** Byron's favorite dog. [Br. Hist.: Harvey, 239]
6. **Buck** after murder of his master, leads wolf pack. [Am. Lit.: *The Call of the Wild*]
7. **Bullet** Roy Rogers' dog. [TV: "The Roy Rogers Show" in Terrace, II, 260]
8. **Bull's-eye** Bill Sykes's dog. [Br. Lit.: *Oliver Twist*]
9. **Cerberus** three-headed beast guarding gates of hell. [Classical Myth.: Zimmerman, 55–56]
10. **Charley** elderly poodle that accompanied Steinbeck on trip across U.S. [Am. Lit.: John Steinbeck *Travels with Charley* in Weiss, 471]
11. **Checkers** Richard Nixon's cocker spaniel; used in his defense of slush fund (1952). [Am. Hist.: Wallechinsky, 126]
12. **Diogenes** Dr. Blimber's clumsy dog. [Br. Lit.: *Dombey and Son*]
13. **Dominic** hound who travels widely. [Children's Lit.: *Dominic*]
14. **Fala** Franklin Roosevelt's dog. [Am. Hist.: Wallechinsky, 126]
15. **Flopit** small, majestically self-important, and smelling of violets. [Am. Lit.: Booth Tarkington *Seventeen* in Magill I, 882]
16. **Flush** Elizabeth Barrett Browning's spaniel, subject of a biography. [Br. Lit.: Woolf *Flush* in Barnhart, 446]
17. **Gelert** greyhound slain by its master for killing his baby; he discovers that Gelert had killed a wolf menacing the child, who is found safe. [Eng. Ballad: *Beddgelert* in Brewer *Dictionary*, 93]
18. **Hound of the Baskervilles** gigantic "fiend dog" of Sir Arthur Conan Doyle's tale. [Br. Lit.: *The Hound of the Baskervilles*]
19. **Jip** Dora's little pet, lives in a tiny pagoda. [Br. Lit.: Dickens *David Copperfield*]
20. **Lassie** canine star of popular film and TV series. [TV: Terrace, II, 13–15; Radio: Buxton, 135]

21. **Marmaduke** floppy, self-centered, playful Great Dane. [Comics: *Marmaduke*]
22. **Mauthe Doog** ghostly black spaniel that haunted Peel Castle. [Br. Folklore: Benét, 649]
23. **Montmorency** companion on Thames boat trip. [Br. Lit.: Jerome *Three Men in a Boat* in Magill II, 1018]
24. **Nana** Newfoundland, nurse to the children. [Br. Lit.: J. M. Barrie *Peter Pan*]
25. **Peritas** Alexander the Great's dog. [Gk. Hist.: Harvey, 239]
26. **Rin-Tin-Tin** early film hero; German shepherd. [Radio: Buxton, 200]
27. **Sandy** Little Orphan Annie's dog. [Comics: "Little Orphan Annie" in Horn, 459]
28. **Snoopy** world's most famous beagle. [Comics: "Peanuts" in Horn, 542]
29. **Spot** dog accompanying Sally, Dick, and Jane in primers. [Am. Cult.: Misc.]
30. **Toto** pet terrier who accompanies Dorothy to Oz. [Am. Lit.: *The Wonderful Wizard of Oz*]

195. DOMESTICITY (See also WIFELINESS.)

1. **Crocker, Betty** leading brand of baking products; byword for one expert in homemaking skills. [Trademarks: Crowley *Trade*, 56]
2. **Dick Van Dyke Show, The** series on the vicissitudes of middle-class living. [TV: Terrace, I, 208–209]
3. **Donna Reed Show, The** joys and sorrows of a pediatrician and his family. [TV: Terrace, I, 220]
4. **Flintstones, The** family life in the Stone Age. [TV: Terrace, I, 271–273]
5. **hearth** symbol of home life. [Folklore: Jobes, 738]
6. **Honeymooners, The** nuts and bolts of American working-class life. [TV: Terrace, I, 365–366]
7. **Keep the Home Fires Burning** song of love of home popular during World War I. [Music: Scholes, 549]
8. **Leave It To Beaver** tranquil life in suburbia (1957–1963). [TV: Terrace II, 18]
9. **March, Meg** devoted wife and mother. [Children's Lit.: *Little Women*]
10. **Martha, St.** patroness of housewives and cooks. [Christian Hagiog.: Brewster, 345]

11. **My Three Sons** trials and tribulations of womanless household. [TV: Terrace, II, 131–132]
12. **Ozzie and Harriet** depicting home life, American style. [TV: "The Adventures of Ozzie and Harriet" in Terrace, I, 34–35]
13. **sage** symbolizes domestic virtue. [Flower Symbolism: *Flora Symbolica,* 177]
14. **silky** female spirit who does household chores. [Br. Folklore: Briggs, 364–365]

196. DOUBLES (See also TWINS.)

1. **Amphitryon and Jupiter** god assumes man's form to lie with his wife. [Rom. Lit.: *Amphitryon*]
2. **Darnay, Charles** physical duplicate of Carton. [Br. Lit.: *A Tale of Two Cities*]
3. **fetch** a Doppelgänger. [Irish Folklore: Leach, 376]
4. ***My Double and How He Undid Me*** story of a lazy minister who has his look-alike impersonator do all his chores. [Am. Lit.: Hayden & Fuller, 456]
5. **Prince of Wales** switches places with his double, poor boy Tom Canty. [Am. Lit.: *The Prince and the Pauper*]
6. **Sam and Eric** their identities merge as "Samneric." [Br. Lit.: *Lord of the Flies*]
7. **Sosia and Mercury** god assumes slave's identity. [Rom. Lit.: *Amphitryon*]
8. **Wilson, William** his Doppelgänger ultimately kills him. [Am. Lit.: "William Wilson" in *Portable Poe,* 57–82]

197. DREAMING

1. **Alice** dreams of falling down a rabbit-hole and experiencing strange adventures. [Br. Lit.: Lewis Carroll *Alice's Adventures in Wonderland*]
2. **Caedmon** 7th-century English religious poet supposed to have heard his verses in a dream. [Br. Lit.: Benét, 156]
3. **Calpurnia** dreams that a statue of Julius Caesar is spouting blood from a hundred wounds. [Br. Drama: Shakespeare *Julius Caesar*]
4. ***Finnegan's Wake*** Joyce novel based around the dreams and nightmares of H. C. Earwicker. [Br. Lit.: Joyce *Finnegans Wake*]
5. **Ibbetson, Peter** learns how to "dream true" and return to the scenes of childhood and the times of his ancestors. [Br. Lit. & Am. Opera: G. duMaurier *Peter Ibbetson* in Magill I, 736]

6. **"Kubla Khan"** poem supposedly composed by Coleridge from an opium dream. [Br. Lit.: Benét, 555]
7. **Little Nemo** dreams every night of Slumberland, a place of story-book palaces and fairy-tale landscapes. [Comics: Horn, 458]
8. **Morpheus** god of dreams. [Gk. Myth.: Benét, 688]
9. **Pharaoh** had dreams of cattle and corn by which Joseph was able to foretell the future. [O.T.: Genesis 41]
10. ***Pilgrim's Progress, The*** Bunyan dreamed this allegory of Christian's adventures while in prison. [Br. Lit.: Bunyan *Pilgrim's Progress*]
11. **Quixote, Don** falls into a trance and has visions of Montesinos and other heroes. [Sp. Lit.: Cervantes *Don Quixote*]
12. ***Under Milk Wood*** the commonplace inhabitants of a Welsh village voice their dreams. [Br. Drama: Dylan Thomas *Under Milk Wood* in Magill IV, 1247]

198. DRUG ADDICTION

1. ***Confessions of an English Opium-Eater*** Thomas de Quincy tells of his opium addiction, his nightmarish experiences, and the sufferings of withdrawal. [Br. Lit.: Haydn & Fuller, 155]
2. **Holmes, Sherlock** the famous sleuth, addicted to cocaine. [Br. Lit.: Benét, 473]
3. ***Man with the Golden Arm, The*** Chicagoan Frankie Machine, a failure, takes to morphine, murders his supplier, and hangs himself. [Am. Lit.: Benét, 632]
4. **Tyrone, Mary** addicted to morphine after childbirth, thanks to her husband's choice of a quack doctor. [Am. Lit.: O'Neill *Long Day's Journey into Night* in Sobel, 431]
5. ***Valley of the Dolls*** portrays self-destruction of drug-addicted starlets. [Am. Lit.: *Valley of the Dolls*]

199. DRUNKENNESS (See also ALCOHOLISM.)

1. **Acrasia** self-indulgent in the pleasures of the senses. [Br. Lit.: *Faerie Queene*]
2. **Admiral of the red** a wine-bibber. [Br. Folklore: Brewer *Dictionary*, 11]
3. **Bacchus, priest of** a toper, perhaps originally because of ceremonial duties. [Western Folklore: Brewer *Dictionary*, 65]
4. **Barleycorn, John** humorous personification of intoxicating liquor. [Am. and Br. Folklore: Misc.]
5. **Booze** sold cheap whiskey in a log-cabin bottle. [Am. Hist.: Espy, 152–153]

6. **Capp, Andy** archetypal British working-class toper. [Comics: Horn, 82–83]
7. **Gambrinus** mythical Flemish king; reputed inventor of beer. [Flem. Myth.: *NCE,* 1041]
8. **Magnifico, Don** appointed Prince's butler, oversamples his wines. [Ital. Opera: Rossini, *Cinderella,* Westerman, 120–121]
9. **Noah** inebriated from wine, sprawls naked in tent. [O.T.: Genesis 9:20–23]
10. **Silenus** one of Bacchus's retinue; fat, always inebriated. [Gk. Myth.: Hall, 283]
11. **Sly, Christopher** identity changes during drunken stupor. [Br. Lit.: *Taming of the Shrew*]
12. **Tam O'Shanter** stumbling home from the tavern sees witches dancing around open coffins in the graveyard. [Br. Lit.: Burns *Tam O'Shanter* in Benét, 985]
13. **Vincent, St.** patron saint of drunks. [Christian Hagiog.: Brewer *Dictionary,* 1129]

200. DUPERY (See also GULLIBILITY)

1. **Blake, Franklin** doped with laudanum, he is an unconscious accessory to the theft of the moonstone. [Br. Lit.: *The Moonstone* in Magill I, 263]
2. **Bobchinsky and Dobchinsky** town squires bamboozled by inspector-impostor. [Russ. Lit.: *The Inspector General*]
3. **Buonafede** tricked into financing and approving daughters' marriages. [Ger. Opera: Haydn, *The World of the Moon,* Westerman, 68–69]
4. **Calandrino** duped by friends into believing heliotrope confers invisibility. [It. Lit.: *Decameron,* "Calandrino and the Heliotrope"]
5. **Dapper** lawyer's clerk; swindled into believing himself perfect gambler. [Br. Lit.: *The Alchemist*]
6. **Drugger, Abel** cozened by rogues in hopes of future riches. [Br. Lit.: *The Alchemist*]
7. **Fenella** mute beauty tricked, imprisoned, and abandoned by Alfonso. [Fr. Opera: Auber, *Dumb Girl of Portici,* Westerman, 163–164]
8. **Iago** dupes Othello, Cassio, et al. [Br. Lit.: *Othello*]
9. **Matthew, Master** "the town gull." [Br. Lit.: *Every Man in His Humour*]
10. **Pelleas** used by Ettarre; betrayed by Gawain. [Br. Lit.: *Idylls of the King,* "Pelleas and Ettarre"]

11. **Roderigo** foppish dupe and tool of Iago. [Br. Lit.: *Othello*]
12. **Skvoznik-Dmukhanovsky, Anton Antonovich** prefect kowtows to supposed inspector for good impression. [Russ. Lit.: *The Inspector General*]

201. DWARFISM (See also SMALLNESS.)

1. **Alberich** king of dwarfs; lives in subterranean palace. [Norse Myth.: Leach, 33; Ger. Lit.: *Nibelungenlied*]
2. **Andvari** sometimes considered king of dwarfs; guarded Nibelung treasure. [Norse Myth.: Leach, 56]
3. **Dvalin** inventor of runes. [Norse Myth.: Leach, 330]
4. **Elbegast** king of dwarfs; dwelt in underground palace. [Norse Myth.: *LLEI,* I: 327]
5. **Hop-Frog** crippled, deformed court fool. [Am. Lit.: "Hop-Frog" in *Portable Poe,* 317–329]
6. **Matzerath, Oskar** deliberately remains at the age of three physically. [Ger. Lit.: Günter Grass *The Tin Drum* in Magill IV, 1220]
7. **Nibelungs** race of dwarfs who possess a hoard of gold. [Norse Myth.: Payton, 477]
8. **Oakmen** squat, dwarfish people with red caps. [Br. Folklore: Briggs, 313–314]
9. **Rumpelstiltskin** homunculus spins gold in exchange for lass's first child. [Ger. Fairy Tale: Grimm, 196]
10. **Seven Dwarfs** Doc, Happy, Sleepy, Sneezy, Bashful, Grumpy, Dopey. [Am. Cinema: *Snow White and the Seven Dwarfs* in *Disney Films,* 25–32]

202. DYSTOPIA

1. ***Brave New World*** Aldous Huxley's grim picture of the future, where scientific and social developments have turned life into a tragic travesty. [Br. Lit.: Magill I, 79]
2. **Erewhon** inhabitants worship superficiality, unreason, inconsistency, and evasion: a lampoon of 19th-century society. [Br. Lit.: *Erewhon* in Haydn & Fuller, 239]

E

Eagerness (See **ZEAL.**)

203. EARTH

1. **Bona Dea** "goddess of earthly creatures." [Rom. Myth.: Parrinder, 48]
2. **Bona Mater** Fauna, goddess of wildlife. [Rom. Myth.: Kravitz, 24]
3. **Demogorgon** tyrant-genius of soil and life of plants. [Medieval Eur. Myth.: *LLEI,* I: 326]
4. **Dyava-Matar** Hindu earthmother, equivalent of Demeter. [Hindu Myth.: Jobes, 480]
5. **Frigga** Odin's wife; symbolizes the earth. [Norse Myth.: *LLEI,* I: 328]
6. **Gaea** goddess of the earth; mother of the mountains. [Gk. Myth.: Howe, 104]
7. **gnome** ground-dwelling spirit in Rosicrucian philosophy. [Medieval Hist.: Brewer *Dictionary,* 468]
8. **Midgard** region between heaven and hell where men live. [Norse Myth.: Wheeler, 242]
9. **Mother Nature** epitome of the earth, especially its more benevolent phenomena. [Pop. Cult.: Misc.]
10. **Tapio** Finnish woodland god; realm described in Sibelius' *Tapiola.* [Music Hist.: Thompson, 2239]
11. **Tellus Mater** in allegories of elements, personification of earth. [Art: Hall, 128]
12. **two circles linked** symbol of earth as bride of heaven. [Christian Tradition: Jobes, 343]
13. **Vertumnus** god of changing seasons. [Rom. Myth.: Kravitz, 58]

204. EASTER

1. **basket** filled with treats, representative of feast on Easter Sunday. [Folklore: Misc.]
2. **bonnet** usually worn along with new clothes on Easter Sunday. ("Oh, I could write a sonnet about your Easter bonnet.") [Christian Tradition: Misc.; Am. Music: Irving Berlin, "Easter Parade"]
3. **bunny** delivers chocolates, etc., to children. [Western Folklore: Jobes, 487]

4. **daisy** a flower traditionally displayed in homes during Easter season. [Christian Tradition: Jobes, 487]
5. **egg** colored eggs as symbol of new life, adopted to reflect Resurrection. [Christian Tradition: Brewer *Dictionary,* 361]
6. **jelly beans** traditional treat for children on Easter Sunday; symbolize eggs. [Pop. Culture: Misc.]
7. **parade** of finery; most notable ones in New York and Atlantic City on Easter Sunday. [Pop. Culture: Misc.]
8. **purple and yellow** traditional colors seen in churches during Easter season. [Christian Color Symbolism: Jobes, 487]
9. **spring flowers** a token of Christ's resurrection. [Christian Tradition: Jobes, 487]
10. **white lily** symbol of Resurrection. [Christian Tradition: Jobes, 487]
11. **white and green** signifies color of Easter holidays. [Christian Color Symbolism: Jobes, 487]

205. EAVESDROPPING (See also CURIOSITY, VOYEURISM.)

1. **Andret** eavesdrops through keyhole on Tristan and Isolde's conversation. [Arthurian Legend: Walsh *Classical,* 22]
2. **Polonius** lurking behind arras, he is killed accidentally by Hamlet. [Br. Lit.: *Hamlet*]
3. **Pry, Paul** inquisitive, meddlesome character who "eavesdrops on everyone." [Br. Drama: *Paul Pry,* Payton, 514]
4. **Rumpelstiltskin** his name overheard by queen's messenger, allowing spell to be broken. [Ger. Fairy Tale: Grimm, 19]

206. ECCENTRICITY

1. **Addams Family** weird family, presented in grotesque domesticity. [TV: Terrace, I, 29]
2. **Boynton, Nanny** travels with set of *Encyclopaedia Britannica* to settle disputes. [Am. Lit.: "Percy" in *Stories,* 634–644]
3. **Dick, Mr.** odd but harmless old gentleman. [Br. Lit.: *David Copperfield*]
4. **Doolittle, Doctor** veterinarian who talks to animals. [Children's Lit.: *Dr. Doolittle*]
5. **Flite, Miss** "ancient" ward in Chancery. [Br. Lit.: *Bleak House*]
6. **Great-Aunt Dymphna** outlandish dresser who pointedly doesn't eat meat. [Children's Lit.: *The Growing Summer,* Fisher 124–127]
7. **Havisham, Miss** jilted bride turns into witchlike old woman. [Br. Lit.: *Great Expectations*]

8. **Longstocking, Pippi** outrageous, rebellious, imaginative child. [Children's Lit.: *Pippi Longstocking*]
9. **Madeline** individualist; only girl "out of line." [Children's Lit.: *Madeline,* Fisher, 196]
10. **Madwoman of Chaillot** delightfully pixilated old woman manages to exploit the Parisian exploiters. [Fr. Lit.: *The Madwoman of Chaillot,* Benét, 618]
11. **Pickwick, Mr. (Samuel)** jolly "conformist" who understands anything but the obvious. [Br. Lit.: *Pickwick Papers*]
12. **Poppins, Mary** English nanny who practises levitation, flies up chimneys, etc. [Children's Lit.: *Mary Poppins,* Fisher, 218]
13. **Salus, St. Simeon** behaved queerly to share outcasts' contempt. [Christian Hagiog.: Attwater, 311]

207. EDUCATION (See also TEACHING.)

1. **Academy, the** Plato's school in Athens. [Gk. Hist.: Benét, 5]
2. **Cadmus** introduced the alphabet to the Greeks. [Gk. Myth.: Brewer *Dictionary,* 161]
3. **Cambridge** one of two leading British universities (since 1231); consists of 24 colleges. [Br. Education: Payton, 116]
4. **Catherine of Alexandria, St.** patroness of education. [Christian Hagiog.: Hall, 58]
5. ***Education of Henry Adams, The*** autobiography describing intellectual influences on the author. [Am. Lit.: Hart, 249]
6. ***Émile*** Rousseau's treatise on education of children (1762). [Fr. Lit.: *Émile,* Magill III, 330–333]
7. **Feverel, Sir Austen** rears his son by a scientific system in which women were a minor factor. [Br. Lit.: Meredith *The Ordeal of Richard Feverel* in Magill I, 692]
8. **Gradgrind, Thomas** raises and educates children on materialistic principles. [Br. Lit.: Dickens *Hard Times*]
9. **Grand Tour, the** European tour as necessary part of education for British aristocrats. [Eur. Hist.: Plumb, 414]
10. **Instructions to a Son** papyrus document; one of earliest preserved writings (c. 2500 B.C.). [Classical Hist.: Grun, 2]
11. **Ivy League** select group of colleges: Brown, Columbia, Cornell, Dartmouth, Harvard, Pennsylvania, Princeton, Yale. [Am. Education: Payton, 343]
12. **Lyceum** a gymnasium where Aristotle taught in ancient Athens. [Gk. Hist.: Hart, 502]

13. **McGuffey Readers** sold 122,000,000 copies and exerted profound moral and cultural effect in mid 19th-century America. [Am. Hist.: Hart, 509]
14. **mortarboard** closefitting cap with flat square piece and tassel; part of academic costume. [Am. and Br. Culture: Misc.]
15. **Oxford** one of two leading British universities (c. 1167); consists of 34 colleges. [Br. Education: Payton, 502]
16. **Phi Beta Kappa** honorary scholarship society. [Am. Hist.: Hart, 651]
17. **Seven Sisters** select group of colleges: Barnard, Bryn Mawr, Mount Holyoke, Radcliffe, Smith, Vassar, Wellesley. [Am. Education: Payton, 615]
18. **Sorbonne** University of Paris; long esteemed as educational center. [Fr. Hist.: Brewer *Dictionary*, 1019]
19. **Wanderjahr** a year's absence from one's schooling as period to reflect on learning. [Eur. Hist.: Plumb, 414]

208. EFFEMINACY

1. **Blue Boy** Gainsborough painting depicting princely lad with sissyish overtones. [Br. Art.: Misc.]
2. **Fauntleroy, Little Lord** title-inheriting, yellow-curled sissy in velvet. [Am. Lit.: *Little Lord Fauntleroy*]
3. **Percy** personification of "sissy." [Pop. Culture: Misc.]

209. EGOTISM (See also ARROGANCE, CONCEIT, INDIVIDUALISM.)

1. **Baxter, Ted** TV anchorman who sees himself as most important news topic. [TV: "The Mary Tyler Moore Show" in Terrace, II, 70]
2. **cat** symbol of egotism because of its aloofness and independence. [Animal Symbolism: Mercatante, 49]
3. **Milvain, Jasper** sees himself as extremely important in literary world. [Br. Lit.: *New Grub Street,* Magill I, 647–649]
4. **narcissus** symbol of self-centeredness. [Flower Symbolism: *Flora Symbolica,* 176]
5. **Narcissus** falls in love with his reflection in pond. [Gk. Myth.: Brewer *Handbook,* 745; Rom. Lit.: *Metamorphoses*]
6. ***Number One*** portraying politician Crawford; self-gain as tour de force. [Am. Lit.: *Number One*]
7. **Patterne, Sir Willoughby** epitome of vanity and self-centeredness, tries to dominate all around him. [Br. Lit.: *The Egoist* in Magill I, 241]

8. **Patterne, Sir Willoughby** his egotism spelled his defeat. [Br. Lit.: *The Egoist,* Magill I, 241-242]
9. **Skimpole, Horace** egocentric, wily fraud. [Br. Lit.: *Bleak House*]
10. **Templeton** self-centered rat. [Children's Lit.: *Charlotte's Web*]

210. ELEGANCE

1. **After Six, Inc.** makers of men's formal wear and accessories. [Trademarks: Crowley *Trade,* 9]
2. **Archer, Isabel** American heiress undergoes process of refinement amid European culture. [Am. Lit.: *The Portrait of a Lady*]
3. **Ashley, Lady Brett** heroine "as charming when drunk as when sober." [Am. Lit.: *The Sun Also Rises*]
4. **dahlia** represents elegance. [Flower Symbolism: Jobes, 406]
5. **Darlington, Lord** epitome of London's man about town (1800s). [Br. Lit.: *Lady Windermere's Fan,* Magill I, 488–490]
6. **locust** tree representing elegance. [Tree Symbolism: *Flora Symbolica,* 175]
7. **Petronius** called by Roman historian Tacitus "a man of refined luxury," and "the arbiter of elegance"; lived in the reign of the emperor Nero. [Rom. Hist.: *EB* (1963) XVII 681]

211. ELF

1. **cluricaune** small creature who appears as an old man; knows about hidden treasure. [Irish Folklore: Brewer *Dictionary,* 213]

212. ELOPEMENT

1. **Carker, James** with Dombey's wife. [Br. Lit.: *Dombey and Son*]
2. **Leonora** with Alvaro, rejected as suitor by her father. [Ital. Opera: Verdi, *La Forza del Destino,* Westerman, 315–317]
3. **Little Emily** with Steerforth, although engaged to Ham. [Br. Lit.: *David Copperfield*]
4. **Madeline** with Porphyro, who appears in dream. [Br. Lit.: "The Eve of St. Agnes" in Magill I, 263–264]
5. **Wardle, Rachel** elopes with the imposter Alfred Jingle. [Br. Lit.: Dickens *Pickwick Papers*]

213. ELOQUENCE

1. **Ambrose, St.** bees, prophetic of fluency, landed in his mouth. [Christian Hagiog: Brewster, 177]
2. **Antony, Mark** gives famous speech against Caesar's assassins. [Br. Lit.: *Julius Caesar*]

3. **Arnall, Father** his sermons fill Stephen with the fear of hell-fire. [Br. Lit.: Joyce *Portrait of the Artist as a Young Man*]
4. **bees on the mouth** pictorial and verbal symbol of eloquence. [Folklore and Christian Iconog.: Brewster, 177]
5. **Bragi** god of poetry and fluent oration. [Norse Myth.: *LLEI,* I: 324]
6. **Calliope** chief muse of poetic inspiration and oratory. [Gk. Myth.: Brewer *Dictionary,* 177]
7. **Churchill, Winston** (1874–1965) statesman whose rousing oratory led the British in WWII. [Br. Hist.: *NCE,* 556]
8. **Cicero** (106–43 B.C.) orator whose forcefulness of presentation and melodious language is still imitated. [Rom. Hist.: *NCE,* 558]
9. **Demosthenes** (382–322 B.C.) generally considered the greatest of the Greek orators. [Gk. Hist.: *NCE,* 559]
10. **Gettysburg Address** Lincoln's brief, moving eulogy for war dead (1863). [Am. Hist.: Jameson, 286–287]
11. **King, Martin Luther, Jr.** (1929–1968) civil rights leader and clergyman whose pleas for justice won support of millions. [Am. Hist.: *NCE,* 1134]
12. **lotus** symbol of eloquence. [Plant Symbolism: *Flora Symbolica,* 175]
13. **Mapple, Father** preaches movingly and ominously on Jonah. [Am. Lit.: Melville *Moby Dick*]
14. **Paine, Thomas** (1737–1809) powerful voice of the colonies; wrote famous "Common Sense." [Am. Hist.: Jameson, 369–370]
15. **Webster, Daniel** (1782–1852) noted 19th-century American orator-politician. [Am. Hist.: Jameson, 539]

214. ENCHANTMENT (See also FANTASY, MAGIC.)

1. **Alidoro** fairy godfather to Italian Cinderella. [Ital. Opera: Rossini, *Cinderella,* Westerman, 120–121]
2. **Bottom** under spell, grows ass's head. [Br. Lit.: *A Midsummer Night's Dream*]
3. **Cinderella** enchantment lasts only till midnight. [Fr. Fairy Tale: *Cinderella*]
4. **Circe** enchantress who changes Odysseus's men into swine. [Gk. Lit.: *Odyssey;* Rom. Lit.: *Aeneid*]
5. **Geraldine, Lady** evil spirit who, by casting a spell, induces Christabel to bring her into her father's castle. [Br. Lit.: S.T. Coleridge "Christabel" in Benét, 195]

6. **Land of Oz** bewitching realm of magic and mystery. [Am. Lit.: *The Wonderful Wizard of Oz*]
7. **Lorelei** water nymph of the Rhine; lured sailors to their doom with her singing. [Ger. Folklore: Leach, 645]
8. **Maugis** enchanter; one of Charlemagne's paladins. [Fr. Folklore: Harvey, 526]
9. **Miracle, Dr.** bewitches Antonia into singing despite doctor's orders. [Fr. Opera: Offenbach, *Tales of Hoffmann,* Westerman, 275–276]
10. **Oberon** fairy king orders love charm placed on wife. [Br. Lit.: *A Midsummer Night's Dream*]
11. **Orpheus** his singing opens the gates of the underworld. [Ger. Opera: Gluck, *Orpheus and Euridyce,* Westerman, 72]
12. **Pied Piper** charms children of Hamelin with music. [Children's Lit.: "The Pied Piper of Hamelin" in *Dramatic Lyrics,* Fisher, 279–281]
13. **pishogue** Irish fairy spell that distorts reality. [Irish Folklore: Briggs, 327–328]
14. **Quixote, Don** ascribes all his misfortunes to the machinations of enchanters. [Span. Lit.: Cervantes *Don Quixote*]
15. **Scheherazade** spins yarns for Sultan for 1001 nights. [Arab. Lit.: *Arabian Nights*]
16. **Schwanda** Czech Orpheus; bagpipe music moves even Queen Iceheart. [Czech Opera: Weinberger, *Schwanda,* Westerman, 412]
17. **Sirens** with song, bird-women lure sailors to death. [Gk. Myth.: *Odyssey*]
18. **Sleeping Beauty** sleeps for 100 years. [Fr. Fairy Tale, *The Sleeping Beauty*]
19. **Titania** experiences spell-induced fascination over Bottom. [Br. Lit.: *A Midsummer Night's Dream*]
20. **Van Winkle, Rip** returns to village after sleep of 20 years. [Am. Lit.: *The Sketch Book of Geoffrey Crayon, Gent.*]
21. **vervain** indicates bewitching powers. [Flower Symbolism: *Flora Symbolica,* 178]
22. **Vivian** the Lady of the Lake, enchantress and mistress of Merlin. [Br. Lit.: Barnhart, 1118]

215. END

1. **Armageddon** battleground of good and evil before Judgment Day. [N.T.: Revelation 16:16]

2. **checkmate** end of game in chess: folk-etymology of *Shah-mat*, 'the Shah is dead.' [Br. Folklore: Espy, 217]
3. **fatal raven** indicates defeat or victory by arranging its wings. [Norse Legend: *Volsung Saga*]
4. **Judgment Day** final trial of all mankind. [N.T.: Revelation]
5. **Last Supper** Passover dinner the night before Christ died. [N.T.: Matthew 26:26–29; Mark 14:22–25; Luke 22:14–20]

216. ENDURANCE (See also LONGEVITY.)

1. **Atalanta** feminine name denotes power of endurance. [Gk. Myth.: Jobes, 148]
2. **Boston marathon** famous 26-mile race held annually for long-distance runners. [Am. Pop. Culture: Misc.]
3. **cedrala tree** symbol of longevity and endurance. [Eastern Folklore and Plant Symbolism: Jobes, 301]
4. **Denisovich, Ivan** prisoner persists through travails of Soviet camp. [Russ. Lit.: *One Day in the Life of Ivan Denisovich*]
5. **dromedary** able to cover a hundred miles in one day. [Medieval Animal Symbolism: White, 80–81]
6. **ironman triathlon** event combines swimming, bicycling, marathon run. [Pop. Cult.: Misc.]
7. **marathon dancing** dance contest with endurance as chief factor. [Am. Hist.: Sann, 57–69]
8. **Prometheus** epitome of stoic endurance. [Gk. Myth.: Gayley, 10–15]
9. **Steadfast Tin Soldier** one-legged toy survives multiple calamities; ultimately immolated. [Dan. Lit.: *Andersen's Fairy Tales*]
10. **Yossarian** always creating new ways to stay alive through long war. [Am. Lit.: *Catch-22*]

217. ENEMY

1. **Amalekites** Israel's hereditary foe and symbol of perpetual hatred. [Jew. Hist.: Wigoder, 24]
2. **Antichrist** principal antagonist of Christ. [Christianity: *NCE*, 117]
3. **Armilus** legendary name of anti-Messiah. [Judaism: Wigoder, 41]
4. **Satan** also called the Adversary or the Devil. [Christianity: Misc.]

218. ENLIGHTENMENT

1. **ball and cross** symbol of gradual universal evangelism. [Christian Tradition: Jobes, 176]

2. **Bodhisattva** “the enlightened one” deferring Nirvana to help others. [Buddhism: Parrinder, 48]
3. **Buddha** a mortal who’s achieved Nirvana, particularly Gautama. [Buddhism: Parrinder, 53]
4. **Chloë** “fearful virgin” learns love’s delights on wedding night. [Gk. Lit.: *Daphnis and Chloë,* Magill I, 184]
5. **Gautama** sees “everything” and has “eyes on his feet.” [Buddhism: Parrinder, 110]
6. **prajna** (Sanskrit) “wisdom,” used in abstract sense or sometimes personified as a goddess. [Sanskrit: Parrinder, 222]
7. **Sanātana Dharma,** “eternal truth.” [Hinduism: Parrinder, 122]
8. **scales falling from eyes** vision restored, Saul is converted. [N.T.: Acts 9:17–19]

219. ENTRAPMENT

1. ***Fear of Flying*** metaphor for housewife Isadora Wing’s temporary inability to achieve self-awareness. [Am. Lit.: *Fear of Flying*]
2. **Frome, Ethan** chained to detestable wife and unsalable farm. [Am. Lit.: *Ethan Frome*]
3. **Loman, Willy** despite dreams of success, he is condemned to failure. [Am. Drama; *Death of a Salesman,* Payton, 397]
4. **Nora** trapped in the domesticity demanded by her husband. [Nor. Lit.: Ibsen *A Doll’s House*]
5. **Prufrock, J. Alfred** aware that his life is meaningless and empty, he struggles to rise above it, but cannot. [Br. Lit.: “The Love Song of J. Alfred Prufrock” in Payton, 548]
6. **Rochester, Edward** tied to insane wife; cannot marry Jane Eyre. [Br. Lit.: *Jane Eyre*]

220. ENVY (See also JEALOUSY.)

1. **Amneris** envious of Aïda. [Ital. Opera: Verdi, *Aïda,* Westerman, 325]
2. **Cinderella’s sisters** envious of their sister’s beauty. [Folklore: Barnhart, 246]
3. **green** symbol of envy; “the green-eyed monster.” [Color Symbolism: Jobes, 357; Br. Lit.: *Othello*]
4. **Iago** Othello’s ensign who, from malevolence and envy, persuades Othello that Desdemona has been unfaithful. [Br. Lit.: *Othello*]
5. **Joseph’s brothers** resented him for Jacob’s love and gift. [O.T.: Genesis 37:4]

6. **Lensky** envy of Onegin leads to his death in a duel. [Russ. Opera: Tchaikovsky, *Eugene Onegin,* Westerman, 395–397]
7. **Lisa** envious of Amina; tries unsuccessful stratagems. [Ital. Opera: Bellini, *The Sleepwalker,* Westerman, 128–130]
8. **Snow White's stepmother** envious of her beauty, queen orders Snow White's death. [Ger. Fairy Tale: Grimm, 184]

221. EPIC (See also SAGA.)

1. ***Aeneid*** Virgil's epic poem glorifying the origin of the Roman people. [Rom. Lit.: *Aeneid*]
2. ***Beowulf*** Old English epic poem of sixth-century Denmark. [Br. Lit.: *Beowulf*]
3. ***Divine Comedy*** Dante's epic poem in three sections: *Inferno, Purgatorio,* and *Paradiso.* [Ital. Lit.: *Divine Comedy*]
4. ***Faerie Queene*** allegorical epic poem by Edmund Spenser. [Br. Lit.: *Faerie Queene*]
5. ***Frithiof's Saga*** Esaias Tegnér's poetic version of the Norse Saga of Frithiof the Bold. [Nor. Lit.: Haydn & Fuller, 275]
6. ***Gilgamesh*** Babylonian epic of myth and folklore, centered on the king, Gilgamesh. [Babyl. Myth.: *Gilgamesh*]
7. ***Gosta Berling's Saga*** Selma Lagerlof's story of the legendary life of an early nineteenth-century character. [Swed. Lit.: *Gosta Berling's Saga* in Benét, 412]
8. ***Heimskringla*** medieval account of the kings of Norway from legendary times to the twelfth century. [Norw. Hist.: Haydn & Fuller, 322]
9. ***Iliad*** Homer's epic detailing a few days near the end of the Trojan War. [Gk. Lit.: *Iliad*]
10. ***Jerusalem Delivered*** Tasso's celebrated romantic epic written during Renaissance. [Ital. Lit.: *Jerusalem Delivered*]
11. ***Kalevala*** alliterative epic poem of Finland. [Finn. Lit.: *Kalevala*]
12. ***Laxdale Saga*** medieval account of two Icelandic families and their feud. [Icel. Lit.: Benét, 572]
13. ***Lusiad, The*** celebrates Portuguese heroes and wars. [Port. Lit.: Magill II, 608]
14. ***Mahabharata*** Indian epic poem of the struggle between the Pandavas and the Kauravas. [Indian Lit.: *Mahabharata*]
15. ***Nibelungenlied*** medieval German epic poem of Siegfried and the Nibelung kings. [Ger. Lit.: *Nibelungenlied*]

16. ***Njál Saga*** greatest of the Icelandic sagas, based on the historical adventures of two families. [Icel. Lit.: Haydn & Fuller, 524]
17. ***Odyssey*** Homer's long, narrative poem centered on Odysseus. [Gk. Lit.: *Odyssey*]
18. ***One Hundred Years of Solitude*** encompasses the sweep of Latin American history. [Lat. Am. Lit.: Gabriel Garcia Marquez *One Hundred Years of Solitude* in Weiss, 336]
19. ***Orlando Furioso*** Ariosto's romantic epic; actually a continuation of Boiardo's plot. [Ital. Lit.: *Orlando Furioso*]
20. ***Orlando Innamorato*** Boiardo's epic combining Carolingian chivalry and Arthurian motifs. [Ital. Lit.: *Orlando Innamorato*]
21. ***Paradise Lost*** Milton's epic poem of man's first disobedience. [Br. Lit.: *Paradise Lost*]
22. ***Ramayana*** epic poem of ancient India. [Indian Lit.: *Ramayana*]
23. ***Song of Igor's Campaign*** Old Russian epic poem of 12th-century Prince Igor. [Russ. Lit.: *Song of Igor's Campaign*]
24. ***Song of Roland*** chanson de geste of Roland and Charlemagne. [Fr. Lit.: *Song of Roland*]
25. ***Song of the Cid*** epic poem of Spain by an anonymous author. [Span. Lit.: *Song of the Cid*]
26. ***Terra Nostra*** combines the myths and history of twenty centuries of Western civilization. [Lat. Am. Lit.: Carlos Fuentes *Terra Nostra* in Weiss, 458]
27. ***Volsunga Saga*** cycle of Scandinavian legends, major source of *Niebelungenlied.* [Scand. Lit.: Benét, 1064]

222. EPICUREANISM (See also FEAST.)

1. **Belshazzar** gave banquet unrivalled for sumptuousness. [O.T.: Daniel 5:1–4]
2. **Finches of the Grove** eating club established for expensive dining. [Br. Lit.: *Great Expectations*]
3. **Gatsby, Jay** modern Trimalchio, wines and dines the upper echelon. [Am. Lit.: *The Great Gatsby*]
4. **Lucullus, Lucius Licinius** (110–57 B.C.) gave luxurious banquets. [Rom. Hist.: *New Century,* 650]
5. **Marius** young pagan who follows the original philosophical tenets of Epicurus in his search for an answer to life. [Br. Lit.: Pater *Marius the Epicurean* in Magill II, 630]
6. **Trimalchio** vulgar freedman gives lavish feast for noble guests. [Rom. Lit.: *Satyricon*]

223. EPILEPSY

1. **Myshkin, Prince** suffered fits from early youth, affecting his physical and mental health. [Russ. Lit.: Dostoevsky *The Idiot*]
2. **Vitus, St.** his chapel at Ulm famed for epileptic cures. [Christian Hagiog.: Brewster, 291]

224. EQUALITY (See also FEMINISM.)

1. **Augsburg, Peace of** German princes determined state religion; Lutherans granted equal rights (1555). [Ger. Hist.: *NCE,* 185]
2. **Bakke decision** "reverse discrimination" victim; entered medical school with Supreme Court's help. [Am. Hist.: *Facts* (1978), 483]
3. **Barataria** monarchy where all men are equal and the rulers share the palace chores. [Br. Opera: Gilbert and Sullivan *The Gondoliers*]
4. **Dred Scott decision** controversial ruling stating that Negroes were not entitled to "equal justice." [Am. Hist.: Payton, 203]
5. **Equal Employment Opportunity Commission** U.S. government agency appointed to promote the cause of equal opportunity for all U.S. citizens. [Am. Hist.: Payton, 224]
6. **Equal Rights Amendment (ERA)** the proposed 27th Amendment to the U.S. Constitution, stating that men and women must be treated equally by law. [Am. Hist.: Payton, 224]
7. **Equality State** nickname of Wyoming, first state to give women the right to vote. [Am. Hist.: Payton, 224]
8. **NAACP** (National Association for the Advancement of Colored People) vanguard of Negro fight for racial equality. [Am. Hist.: Van Doren, 548–549]
9. **Nantes, Edict of** granted Protestants same rights as Catholics in France (1598). [Fr. Hist.: *EB,* VII: 184]
10. **Nineteenth Amendment** granted women right to vote (1920). [Am. Hist.: Van Doren, 409]
11. ***We Shall Overcome*** anthem of civil rights movement, rallying song of black Americans. [Am. Pop. Cult.: Misc.]

225. EROTICISM

1. ***Aphrodite*** novel of Alexandrian manners by Pierre Louys. [Fr. Lit.: Benét, 783]
2. ***Ars Amatoria*** Ovid's treatise on lovemaking. [Rom. Lit.: Magill IV, 45]
3. **Barbarella** frequently semi-nude heroine of sexy French comicstrip. [Comics: Berger, 211]

4. **Daphnis and Chloë** their idyll reconciles naïveté and sexual fulfillment. [Gk. Lit.: Magill I, 184]
5. ***Delta of Venus*** stories of sexual adventure including incest, perversion, prostitution, etc. [Am. Lit.: Anaïs Nin *Delta of Venus* in Weiss, 124]
6. **Hill, Fanny** narrator of Cleland's 18th-century novel of erotic experiences. [Br. Lit.: Cleland *Memoirs of Fanny Hill*]
7. ***Kama-Sutra*** detailed Hindu account of the art of lovemaking. [Ind. Lit.: Benét, 538]
8. **O** a beautiful woman willing to undergo every form of sexual manipulation at the bidding of her lover. [Fr. Lit.: Pauline Réage *The Story of O* in Weiss, 445]
9. ***Perfumed Garden, The*** Arabian manual of sexual activity. [Arab. Lit.: *EB* (1963) IV, 448]
10. ***Playboy*** monthly magazine renowned for nude photographs. [Am. Pop. Cult.: Misc.]

226. ERROR

1. **Breeches Bible, the** the Geneva Bible, so dubbed because it stated that Adam and Eve made themselves breeches. [Br. Hist.: Brewer *Dictionary*, 101]
2. **Cortez** alluded to in a poem by Keats, mistaken for Balboa, as discoverer of Pacific Ocean. [Br. Poetry: "On First Looking into Chapman's Homer"]
3. **Wicked Bible, the** misprinted a commandment as "Thou shalt commit adultery." [Br. Hist.: Brewer *Dictionary*, 102]
4. **seacoast of Bohemia** Shakespearean setting in a land with no seacoast. [Br. Drama: Shakespeare *The Winter's Tale*, III,iii]

227. ESCAPE

1. **Abiathar** only son of Ahimelech to avoid Saul's slaughter. [O.T.: I Samuel 22:20]
2. **Ariadne** Minos's daughter; gave Theseus thread by which to escape labyrinth. [Gk. Myth.: Zimmerman, 31]
3. **Cerambus** transformed into beetle in order to fly above Zeus's deluge. [Gk. Myth.: Zimmerman, 55]
4. **Christian** flees the City of Destruction. [Br. Lit.: *Pilgrim's Progress*]
5. **Daedalus** escaped from Crete by flying on wings made of wax and feathers. [Gk. Myth.: Benét, 244]
6. **Dantès, Edmond** after fifteen years in the Château d'If he escapes by being thrown into the sea as another prisoner's corpse. [Fr. Lit.: Dumas *The Count of Monte Cristo*]

7. **Deucalion** on Prometheus' advice, survived flood in ark. [Gk. Myth.: Gaster, 84–85]
8. **Dunkirk** 340,000 British troops evacuated against long odds (1941). [Eur. Hist.: Van Doren, 475]
9. **Exodus** Jewish captives escape Pharaoh's bondage. [O.T.: Exodus]
10. **Fugitive, The** (Dr. Richard Kimble) tale of wrongfully-accused man fleeing imprisonment. [TV: Terrace, I, 290–291]
11. **Hansel and Gretel** woodcutter's children barely escape witch. [Ger. Fairy Tale: Grimm, 56]
12. **Hegira (Hijrah)** Muhammad's flight from Mecca to Medina (622). [Islamic Hist.: *EB,* V: 39–40]
13. **Houdini, Harry** (1874–1926) shackled magician could extricate himself from any entrapment. [Am. Hist.: Wallechinsky, 196]
14. **Ishmael** the only one to escape when the *Pequod* is wrecked by the white whale. [Am. Lit.: Melville, *Moby Dick*]
15. **Jim** Miss Watson's runaway slave; Huck's traveling companion. [Am. Lit.: *Huckleberry Finn*]
16. **Jonah** delivered from fish's belly after three days. [O.T.: Jonah 1, 2]
17. **Noah** with family and animals, escapes the Deluge. [O.T.: Genesis 8:15–19]
18. **Papillon** one of the few to escape from Devil's Island. [Fr. Hist.: *Papillon*]
19. **parting of the Red Sea** God divides the waters for Israelites' flight. [O.T.: Exodus 14:21–29]
20. **Phyxios** epithet of Zeus as god of escape. [Gk. Myth.: Kravitz, 94]
21. **Robin, John, and Harold Hensman** run away from "petticoat government" to live in forest. [Children's Lit.: *Brendon Chase,* Fisher, 306]
22. ***Strange Cargo*** prisoners escape by boat from Devil's Island, accompanied by a mysterious stranger. [Am. Cinema: *Strange Cargo*]
23. **Theseus** escapes labyrinth with aid from Ariadne. [Gk. Myth.: Zimmerman, 31]
24. **Tyler, Toby** runs away from cruel Uncle Daniel to join circus. [Children's Lit.: *Toby Tyler*]
25. **Ziusudra** Sumerian Noah. [Sumerian Legend: Benét, 1116]

228. EVANGELISM

1. **Gantry, Elmer** fire and brimstone, fraudulent revivalist. [Am. Lit.: *Elmer Gantry*]
2. **John** disciple closest to Jesus. [N.T.: John]
3. **Luke** early Christian; the "beloved physician." [N.T.: Luke]
4. **Mark** Christian apostle. [N.T.: Mark]
5. **Matthew** one of the twelve disciples. [N.T.: Matthew]

229. EVERYMAN

1. **A. N. Other** British *John Doe.* [Br. Usage: Misc.]
2. **Brother Jonathan** British slang for the typical American. [Br. Usage: Misc.]
3. **Ivan Ivanovich Ivanov** embodiment of ordinary Russian person. [Russ. Usage: *LLEI,* I: 292]
4. **Jane Doe** female counterpart of *John Doe.* [Am. Usage: Misc.]
5. **Jean Crapaud** personification of peculiarities of French people. [Fr. Usage: *LLEI,* I: 292]
6. **John Bull** any Englishman, or Englishmen collectively. [Br. Lit.: *History of John Bull,* Brewer *Dictionary,* 591]
7. **John Doe** formerly, any plaintiff; now just anybody. [Am. Pop. Usage: Brewer *Dictionary,* 329]
8. **John Q. Citizen** fictitious average man on the street. [Am. Jour.: Mathews, 910]
9. **John Q. Public** fictitious typical citizen. [Am. Jour.: Mathews, 910]
10. **John Q. Voter** fictitious typical citizen. [Am. Jour.: Mathews, 910]
11. **John a Noakes** fictitious, litigious character; used in legal proceedings. [Br. Legal Usage: Wheeler, 260]
12. **John a Styles** fictitious, litigious counterpart to John a Noakes. [Br. Legal Usage: Wheeler, 260]
13. **Richard Roe** formerly, any defendant; now just anybody. [Am. Pop. Usage: Brewer *Dictionary,* 329]

230. EVIL (See also DEMON, DEVIL, VILLAINY, WICKEDNESS.)

1. **Ahriman** represents principle of wickedness; will one day perish. [Persian Myth.: *LLEI,* I: 322; Zoroastrianism: Benét, 16]
2. **Alberich's curse** on the Rhinegold ring: possessor will die. [Ger. Opera: Wagner, *Rhinegold,* Westerman, 233]
3. **Apaches** name given to Parisian gangsters. [Fr. Hist.: Payton, 31]

4. **Apollyon** demon, personification of evil, vanquished by Christian's wholesomeness. [Br. Lit.: *Pilgrim's Progress*]
5. **Archimago** enchanter epitomizing wickedness. [Br. Lit.: *Faerie Queene*]
6. **Ate** goddess of wickedness, mischief, and infatuation. [Gk. Myth.: Parrinder, 32]
7. **Avidyā** cause of suffering through desire. [Hindu Phil.: Parrinder, 36]
8. **Badman, Mr.** from childhood to death, has committed every sin. [Br. Lit.: Bunyan *The Life and Death of Mr. Badman* in Magill III, 575]
9. **black** symbol of sin and badness. [Color Symbolism: Jobes, 357]
10. **black dog** symbol of the devil. [Rom. Folklore: Brewer *Dictionary,* 329]
11. **black heart** symbol of a scoundrel. [Folklore: Jobes, 223]
12. **black poodle** a transformation of Mephistopheles. [Ger. Lit.: *Faust*]
13. **crocodile** epitome of power of evil. [Medieval Animal Symbolism: White, 8–10]
14. **darkness** traditional association with evil in many dualistic religions. [Folklore: Cirlot, 76–77]
15. **Darth Vader** fallen Jedi Knight has turned to evil. [Am. Cinema: *Star Wars*]
16. **dragon** archetypal symbol of Satan and wickedness. [Christian Symbolism: Appleton, 34]
17. **Drug** principle of evil. [Zoroastrianism: Leach, 325]
18. **Gestapo** Nazi secret police. [Ger. Hist.: *Hitler,* 453]
19. **Golden Calf** Mephisto's cynical and demoniacal tarantella. [Fr. Opera: Gounod, *Faust,* Westerman, 187]
20. **Iago** declaims "I believe in a cruel god." [Br. Lit.: *Othello;* Ital. Opera: Verdi, *Otello;* Westerman, 329]
21. **John, Don** plots against Claudio. [Br. Lit.: *Much Ado About Nothing*]
22. **Klingsor** enemy of Grail knights. [Ger. Opera: Wagner, *Parsifal,* Westerman, 248]
23. **Kurtz, Mr.** white trader in Africa, debased by savage natives into horrible practices. [Br. Lit.: Joseph Conrad *Heart of Darkness* in Magill III, 447]
24. **lobelia** traditional symbol of evil. [Flower Symbolism: *Flora Symbolica,* 175]
25. **Loki** god of fire, evil, and strife who contrived the death of Balder. [Scand. Myth.: Brewer *Dictionary,* 560]

26. **Mephistopheles** the cynical, malicious devil to whom Faust sells his soul. [Ger. Lit.: *Faust,* Payton, 436]
27. **Miles and Flora** apparently sweet children assume wicked miens mysteriously. [Am. Lit.: *The Turn of the Screw*]
28. **Monterone** after humiliation, curses both Duke and Rigoletto. [Ital. Opera: Verdi, *Rigoletto,* Westerman, 299]
29. **o'Nell, Peg** wicked spirit claiming victim every seven years. [Br. Folklore: Briggs, 323]
30. **Pandora's box** contained all evils; opened up, evils escape to afflict world. [Rom. Myth.: Brewer *Dictionary,* 799]
31. **Popeye** degenerate gangster and murderer who rapes Temple Drake. [Am. Lit.: *Sanctuary*]
32. **Powler, Peg** wicked water-demon; lures children to death. [Br. Folklore: Briggs, 323–324]
33. **Queen of the Night** urges the murder of Sarastro, her husband, by their daughter. [Ger. Opera: Mozart *The Magic Flute* in Benét, 619]
34. **Quint, Peter** dead manservant who haunts James's story. [Am. Lit.: *Turn of the Screw*]
35. **Rasputin** immoral person of tremendous power and seeming invulnerability. [Russ. Hist.: Espy, 339–340]
36. **Satan** the chief evil spirit; the great adversary of man. [Christianity and Judaism: Misc.]
37. **Vandals** East German people known for their wanton destruction (533). [Ger. Hist.: Payton, 705]
38. **Wicked Witch of the West** the terror of Oz. [Am. Lit.: *The Wonderful Wizard of Oz*]
39. **Wolf's Glen** scene of macabre uproar. [Ger. Opera: von Weber, *Der Freischütz,* Westerman, 139–140]

231. EXAGGERATION

1. **Bunyon, Paul** legendary giant, hero of tall tales of the logging camps. [Am. Folklore: *The Wonderful Adventures of Paul Bunyon*]
2. **Jenkins' ear** trivial cause of a great quarrel. [Br. Hist.: Espy, 336]
3. **Münchhausen, Baron von** (1720–1797) soldier, adventurer, and teller of tall tales. [Ger. Hist.: *EB,* VII: 99]
4. **Madison Avenue** New York street; home of advertising companies. [Am. Culture: Misc.]

232. EXASPERATION (See also FRUSTRATION, FUTILITY.)

1. **Carter, Sergeant** Marine corps sergeant exasperated by Gomer's ceaseless stupidity. [TV: "Gomer Pyle, U.S.M.C." in Terrace, I, 319]
2. **Dagwood** comic strip character exasperated over Blondie's sale purchases. [Comics: "Blondie" in Horn, 118–119]
3. **Dithers, Mr.** Dagwood's boss; ever exasperated over Dagwood's sloppy work habits. [Comics: "Blondie" in Horn, 118–119]
4. **Gildersleeve, Throckmorton P.** comic character exasperated by nephew Leroy's antics. [Radio: "The Great Gildersleeve" in Buxton, 101]
5. **Kennedy, Edgar** film actor famous for "slow burn." [Am. Cinema: Halliwell]
6. **Kowalski, Stanley** exasperated by Blanche DuBois' affected refinement. [Am. Lit.: *A Streetcar Named Desire*]
7. **Kramden, Ralph** frustrated bus driver projects exasperation toward his wife and Ed Norton. [TV: "The Honeymooners" in Terrace, I, 365–366]
8. **Lodge, Mr.** Veronica's wealthy father driven to distraction by Archie. [Comics: Horn, 87]
9. **Moe** continually exasperated at Larry and Curly for their mischievous pranks. [TV: "The Three Stooges" in Terrace, II, 366]
10. **Ricardo, Ricky** bandleader frustrated by Lucy's mischief. [TV: "I Love Lucy" in Terrace, I, 383–384]
11. **Smith, Ranger** park manager "driven bananas" by Yogi's incorrigibility. [TV: "Yogi Bear" in Terrace, II, 448–449]

233. EXECUTION

1. **Budd, Billy** court-martialed and hanged for accidently killing a ship's officer. [Am. Lit.: Herman Melville *Billy Budd*]
2. **cigarette** final favor granted one about to die. [Pop. Cult.: Misc.]
3. **Deever, Danny** hanged by his regiment for shooting a comrade. [Br. Lit.: Kipling *Danny Deever* in Benét, 549]
4. **Derrick** famous hangman; eponym of modern hoisting apparatus. [Br. Hist.: Espy, 170]
5. **Doeg the Edomite** dispatches priests of Nob under Saul's order. [O.T.: I Samuel 22:18–19]
6. **Esmerelda** her hanging is triumphantly watched from a tower by Frollo, who is thereupon thrown from it by Quasimodo. [Fr. Lit.: Victor Hugo *The Hunchback of Notre Dame*]

7. **guillotine** invented during French Revolution as a humane method of capital punishment. [Fr. Hist.: Benét, 429]
8. **hangman's noose** characteristic knot for death by hanging. [Pop. Cult.: Misc.]
9. **Ko-Ko** appointed by the Mikado as Lord High Executioner. [Br. Opera: *The Mikado*]
10. **Lord of the Manor of Tyburn** nickname for ordinary hangman at Tyburn gallows. [Br. Hist.: Brewer *Dictionary,* 1110]
11. **Macheath, Capt.** swaggering highwayman sentenced to execution but reprieved at the last moment. [Br. Lit.: *The Beggar's Opera* in Magill I, 59; *The Threepenny Opera* in Benét, 90]
12. **Maximilian, Emperor of Mexico** executed in 1867; subject of painting by Manet. [Mex. Hist.: *NCE,* 1728; Fr. Art: *EB,* 11:440]
13. **Savonarola (1452–1498)** reformer priest, hanged and burned at the stake as a heretic. [Ital. Hist.: Benét, 900]
14. ***Seven That Were Hanged, The*** describes the fears and actions of five men and two women before their deaths on the scaffold. [Russ. Lit.: Magill II, 957]
15. **Sorel, Julien** attempts to kill his employer's wife, (his mistress), is condemned to the guillotine. [Fr. Lit.: Stendhal *The Red and the Black* in Magill I, 808]
16. **"Third of May, 1808, The"** Goya painting of Napoleon's soldiers firing on Spanish rebels. [Sp. Art: *EB,* 8:260]
17. **Tyburn** site of gallows where criminals were publicly hanged. [Br. Hist.: Brewer *Dictionary,* 920]

Exile (See **BANISHMENT.**)

234. EXPENSIVENESS

1. **Lais** charged Demosthenes 10,000 drachmas for night in bed. [Gk. Hist.: Wallechinsky, 328]
2. **100 Philistine foreskins** price David paid to marry Saul's daughter. [O.T.: I Samuel 18:25–27]
3. **Vincy, Rosamond** Lydgate's income did not meet her spendthrift habits. [Br. Lit.: *Middlemarch,* Magill I, 588–591]

235. EXPLOITATION (See also OPPORTUNISM.)

1. **Barnum, P. T.** (1810–1891) circus impressario famous for his saying, "Never give a sucker an even break." [Am. Hist.: Van Doren, 825–826]
2. **Carpetbaggers** northern exploiters whose chicanery exacerbated Reconstruction problems. [Am. Hist.: Jameson, 84]

3. **Casby, Christopher** rack-renting proprietor of slum property. [Br. Lit.: *Little Dorrit*]
4. **Stromboli** wicked puppetmaster enslaves Pinocchio aboard troupe's caravan. [Am. Cinema: *Pinocchio* in *Disney Films*, 32–37]

236. EXPLORATION (See also FRONTIER.)

1. **Balboa, Vasco Nuñez de** (1475–1517) discovered the Pacific Ocean. [Sp. Hist.: Benét, 75]
2. **Columbus, Christopher** (1446–1506) expeditions to West Indies, South and Central America; said to have discovered America in 1492. [Ital. Hist.: Jameson, 107–108]
3. **de Soto, Hernando** (c. 1500–1542) discovered the Mississippi River. [Sp. Hist.: Benét, 266]
4. **Enterprise** starship on 5-year mission to explore space. [Am. TV: *Star Trek* in Terrace]
5. **Gama, Vasco da** (c. 1460–1524) navigator who discovered route around Africa to India. [Port. Hist.: *NCE*, 1040]
6. ***Golden Hind*** ship on which Sir Francis Drake (1540–1596) became the first Englishman to sail around the world. [Br. Hist.: *EB* (1963) VII, 575]
7. **Hudson, Henry** seeking a northwest passage to the Orient, in 1609 he explored the river later named for him. [Am. Hist.: Benét, 482]
8. ***Journey to the Center of the Earth*** expedition through the core of a volcano to the earth's center. [Fr. Lit.: Verne *A Journey to the Center of the Earth* in Benét, 1055]
9. **Lewis and Clark Expedition** proved feasibility of overland route to the Pacific. [Am. Hist.: Benét, 583]
10. **Polo, Marco** (1254–1324) Venetian traveler in China. [Ital. Hist.: *NCE*, 1695]
11. **Ponce de León, Juan** (c. 1460–1521) seeking the "fountain of youth," he discovered Florida and explored its coast. [Sp. Hist.: Benét, 802]

237. EXTINCTION

1. **bald eagle** once on verge of extinction, this bird is now protected; still an endangered species. [Ecology: Hammond, 290]
2. **dinosaur** dinosaurs died out, unable to adapt to environmental change. [Ecology: Hammond, 290]
3. **dodo** large, flightless bird exterminated on Mauritius. [Ecology: Wallechinsky, 131]

4. **great auk** hunters killed such large numbers, these birds became extinct in 1840s. [Ecology: Hammond, 290]
5. **heath hen** human settlement of U.S. Atlantic Coast contributed to the extinction of these birds. [Ecology: Hammond, 290]
6. ***Last of the Mohicans, The*** novel foreseeing the extinction of various Indian tribes. [Am. Lit.: *The Last of the Mohicans*]
7. **mastodon** similar to the elephant, the mastodon is now extinct. [Ecology: Hammond, 290]
8. **moa** large ostrichlike bird, hunted chiefly for its food; it died out in 1914. [Ecology: Hammond, 290]
9. **passenger pigeon** hunted to extinction by 1914; vast numbers once darkened American skies during migratory flights. [Ecology: *EB,* VII: 786]
10. **saber-toothed tiger** wild cat that died out about 12,000 years ago. [Ecology: Hammond, 290]
11. ***Last of the Barons, The*** portrays England's brilliant aristocracy as dying breed (1470s). [Br. Lit.: *The Last of the Barons,* Magill I, 492–494]
12. **whale** many species in danger of extinction, owing to massive hunting. [Ecology: Hammond, 290]

238. EXTRAVAGANCE

1. **Bovary, Emma** spends money recklessly on jewelry and clothes. [Fr. Lit.: *Madame Bovary,* Magill I, 539–541]
2. **Cleopatra's pearl** dissolved in acid to symbolize luxury. [Rom. Hist.: Jobes, 348]

239. EXTREMISM (See also FANATICISM.)

1. **drys** advocates of Prohibition in America. [Am. Hist.: Allen, 41]
2. **Jacobins** rabidly radical faction; principal perpetrators of Reign of Terror. [Fr. Hist.: *EB,* V: 494]
3. **John Birch Society** rabid right-wing group ideologically similar to the Ku Klux Klan. [Am. Hist.: Van Doren, 576]
4. **Ku Klux Klan (KKK)** group espousing white supremacy takes law into its own hands. [Am. Hist.: *EB,* V: 935]
5. **McCarthy, Senator Joseph** (1909–1957) anti-Communist zeal frequently resulted in injustice. [Am. Hist.: Van Doren, 522]
6. **Mikado of Japan, the** demands Ko-Ko execute one person a month. [Br. Opera: *The Mikado,* Magill I, 591–592]

F

240. FADS

1. **Barbie doll** popular dress-up doll; extremely conventional and feminine. [Am. Hist.: Sann, 179]
2. **Beatle cut** hairstyle with bangs, sides trimmed just below ears; banned by many school boards (1960s). [Am Hist.: Sann, 251–254]
3. **bee-stung lips** ruby red and puckered female mouth make-up (1920s). [Am. Hist.: Griffith, 198]
4. **bobbed hair** short, curly boyish hairstyle caused shock (1920s). [Am. Hist.: Griffith, 198]
5. **bobby socks** female short socks that epitomized 1940s teen fashion. [Am. Cult.: Misc.]
6. **car-stuffing** one example: 23 people stuffed in a Volkswagen bug. (1950s–1960s). [Am. Hist.: Sann, 300]
7. **chain letters** at height in 1930s, craze crippled postal service. [Am. Hist.: Sann, 97–104]
8. **coonskin caps** raccoon cap with tail worn in recognition of Davy Crockett, Daniel Boone revival (1950s). [Am. Hist.: Sann, 30]
9. **flagpole sitting** sitting alone at the top of a flagpole; craze comes and goes. [Am. Hist.: Sann, 39–46]
10. **frisbees** tossing plastic disks was favorite pastime, especially among collegians (1970s). [Am. Hist.: Sann, 178]
11. **gold fish-swallowing** collegiate craze in 1930s. [Am. Hist.: Sann, 289–292]
12. **hip-flask** liquor bottle designed to fit into back pockets; indispensable commodity during Prohibition. [Am. Hist.: Allen, 70]
13. **hula hoops** large plastic hoops revolved around body by hip action (1950s). [Am. Hist.: Sann, 145–149]
14. **Kewpie doll** designed by Rose O'Neill and modeled on her baby brother; millions were made (starting about 1910). [Am. Hist.: *WB*, 5: 240–241]
15. **marathon dancing** dance contests, the longest of which lasted 24 weeks and 5 days (1930s). [Am. Hist.: McWhirter, 461]
16. **marathon eating** contestants consume ridiculous quantities of food; craze comes and goes. [Am. Hist.: Sann, 77–78]
17. **miniskirt** skirts hemmed at mid-thigh or higher; heyday of the leg in fashion world (1960s). [Am. Hist.: Sann, 255–263]

18. **mud baths** warm mud applied on skin supposedly to retain fresh, young complexion (1940s). [Am. Hist.: Griffith, 198]
19. **panty raids** collegiate craze in the 1940s and 1950s. [Am. Hist.: Misc.]
20. **raccoon coats** popular attire for collegians (1920s). [Am. Hist.: Sann, 175]
21. **rolled stockings** worn by flappers to achieve risqué effect (1920s). [Am. Hist.: Griffith, 198]
22. **saddle shoes** an oxford, usually white, with a saddle of contrasting color, usually brown; a favorite fad of the 1940s and 1950s. [Am. Pop. Culture: Misc.]
23. **Silly Putty** synthetic clay; uses ranging from bouncing balls to false mustaches. [Am. Hist.: Sann, 165]
24. **skateboards** mini surfboard supported on roller-skate wheels; 1960s craze enjoyed renaissance. [Am. Hist.: Sann, 151–152]
25. **telephone booth-stuffing** bodies piled on top of one another inside a telephone booth; 1950s and 1960s craze. [Am. Hist.: Sann, 297]
26. **tulipomania** tulip craze in Holland during which fortunes were lost. [Eur. Hist.: *WB,* 19: 394]
27. **yo-yo** child's toy that periodically overwhelms public's fancy. [Am. Hist.: Sann, 173]
28. **zoot suits** bizarre outfits with the "reet pleats" (1940s). [Am. Hist.: Sann, 275]

241. FAILURE

1. **Army Bomb Plot** attempted assassination of Hitler; his miraculous escape brought dreadful retaliation (1944). [Ger. Hist.: Van Doren, 500]
2. **Brown, Charlie** comic strip character for whom losing is a way of life. [Comics: "Peanuts" in Horn, 542–543]
3. **Bunion Derby** financially disastrous cross-country marathon. [Am. Hist.: Sann, 48–56]
4. **Carker, John** broken-spirited man occupying subordinate position. [Br. Lit.: *Dombey and Son*]
5. **Edsel** much bruited automobile fails on market (1950s). [Am. Hist.: Flexner, 78]
6. **English, Julian** contentious and unloved salesman; commits suicide in despair. [Am. Lit.: *Appointment in Samarra*]
7. **Gunpowder Plot** attempt to blow up the Parliament building; led to the execution of its leader, Guy Fawkes (1605). [Brit. Hist.: *EB,* IV: 70–71]

8. **Little Tramp** Chaplin's much-loved, much-imitated hapless, "I'm a failure" persona. [Am. Cinema: Griffith, 79]
9. **Loman, Willy** traveling salesman who gradually comes to realize that his life has been a complete failure; commits suicide. [Am. Lit.: *The Death of a Salesman,* Payton, 397]
10. **Mighty Casey** ignominiously strikes out in the clutch. [Am. Lit.: "Casey at the Bat" in Turkin, 642]
11. **Reardon, Edwin** very promising writer who, after unsuccessful publication, returns to clerical job. [Br. Lit.: *New Grub Street,* Magill I, 647–649]
12. **Skid Row** district of down-and-outs and bums. [Am. Usage: Brewer *Dictionary,* 1008]
13. **WIN buttons** President Ford's scheme to reduce inflation: for the American public to wear shields stating "W.I.N." (Whip Inflation Now). [Am. Hist.: Misc.]
14. **World League** "ingenious" creation of a third professional league that never materialized. [Am. Sports: Misc.]
15. **Yank** steamship stoker vainly tries to climb the social ladder, then fails in attempt to avenge himself on society. [Am. Drama: O'Neill *The Hairy Ape* in Sobel, 339]

242. FAIRY

1. **Abonde, Dame** good fairy who brings children presents on New Year's Eve. [Fr. Folklore: Brewer *Dictionary,* 3]
2. **Ariel** sprite who confuses the castaways on Prospero's island. [Br. Drama: Shakespeare *The Tempest*]
3. **fairy godmother** fulfills Cinderella's wishes and helps her win the prince. [Fr. Fairy Tale: *Cinderella*]
4. **Grandmarina** fairy who provides everything for Princess Alicia's happiness. [Br. Lit.: Dickens "The Magic Fishbone"]
5. **leprechaun** small supernatural creature associated with shoemaking and hidden treasure. [Irish Folklore: Benét, 579]
6. **Mab, Queen** fairies' midwife delivers man's brain of dreams. [Br. Legend: Benét, 610]
7. **Oberon and Titania** King and Queen of the Fairies. [Br. Drama: Shakespeare *A Midsummer Night's Dream*]
8. **Pigwiggin** his love for Queen Mab ruptures her harmony with Oberon. [Br. Poetry: *Nymphidia* in Barnhart, 824]
9. **Puck** the "shrewd and knavish sprite" who causes minor catastrophes and embarrassing situations. [Br. Drama: Shakespeare *A Midsummer Night's Dream*]

10. **Tinker Bell** fairy friend of Peter Pan. [Br. Lit.: J. M. Barrie *Peter Pan*]

243. FAITHFULNESS (See also LOYALTY.)

To God:

1. **Abdiel** seraph who refused to join Satan's rebellion. [Br. Lit.: *Paradise Lost*]
2. **Abraham** in obedience to God, would sacrifice his only son. [O.T.: Genesis 22:1–18]
3. **Becket, Thomas à** (c. 1118–70) uncompromisingly defended the rights of the Church against King Henry II. [Br. Hist.: *NCE*, 2735]
4. **Caleb** faithfully followed God in exploration of Canaan. [O.T.: Numbers 14:24–25]
5. **Canterbury bell** flower memorializing harness bells of Canterbury pilgrims. [Br. Hist.: Espy, 303]
6. **Hezekiah** brings people of Judah back to God. [O.T.: II Chronicles 29:3–11; 31:20–21]
7. **Jehoshaphat** destroyed idols; adjured men to follow God. [O.T.: II Chronicles 17:3–6; 19:9–11]
8. **Job** maintains his faith despite severe trials, is finally rewarded by God. [O.T.: Job]
9. **Josiah** tenaciously follows Moses' law; orders keeping of Passover. [O.T.: II Kings 23:21–24]
10. **Noah** saved from flood because of his faith. [O.T.: Genesis 6-10]

To Lovers:

11. **Abigail** prostrates herself before David and vows devotion. [O.T.: I Samuel 25:40–41]
12. **Akawi-ko** waits eighty years for lover to return. [Jap. Legend: Jobes, 59]
13. **Amelia** despite financial woes, remains faithful to Booth. [Br. Lit.: *Amelia*]
14. **Andromache** devoted wife of Hector. [Gk. Lit.: *Iliad; Trojan Women; Andromache;* Fr. Lit.: *Andromaque*]
15. **Aramati** name of Vedic goddess means faithfulness. [Hindu Myth.: Jobes, 117]
16. **Arsinoë** Alcmaeon's wife; continues to love husband though he is unfaithful. [Gk. Myth.: Zimmerman, 32]
17. **Brandimante** loyal to lover and leader. [Ital. Lit.: *Orlando Innamorato*]

18. **Briseis** loved Achilles despite her capture by Agamemnon. [Gk. Myth.: Walsh *Classical,* 62]
19. **Britomart** waits many years for true love, Artegall. [Br. Lit.: *Faerie Queene*]
20. **Candida** ever faithful to husband. [Br. Lit.: *Candida*]
21. **Charlotte** faithful to fiancé lost at sea. [Br. Lit.: *Fatal Curiosity*]
22. **China aster** symbol of fidelity. [Flower Symbolism: Jobes, 326]
23. **Clärchen** devoted to Egmont. [Ger. Lit.: *Egmont*]
24. **crow** faithful; does not mate again for nine generations. [Animal Symbolism: Mercatante, 161]
25. **Cynara** woman to whom Dowson is faithful in his thoughts even when consorting with others. [Br. Poetry: Barnhart, 301]
26. **de Cleves, Princess** despite her love for another, remains faithful to her husband even after his death. [Fr. Lit.: Lafayette *The Princess*]
27. **doves** faithfulness reflected in their pairing for life. [Christian Symbolism: Child, 211]
28. **Dupre, Sally** Clay Wingate's fiancée quietly waits for his return. [Am. Lit.: "John Brown's Body" in Magill I, 445–448]
29. **Enid** though falsely accused of infidelity, nurses husband through wounds. [Br. Lit.: *Idylls of the King*]
30. **Evangeline** lifelong search for lover, Gabriel. [Am. Lit.: *Evangeline*]
31. **heliotrope** symbol of lovers' faithfulness. [Flower Symbolism: *Flora Symbolica,* 174]
32. **Hypermnestra** only one of Danaides who did not murder husband on wedding night. [Gk. Myth.: Howe, 136]
33. **Imogen** spurns the advances of Iachimo, who had wagered her husband that he could seduce her. [Br. Drama: Shakespeare *Cymbeline*]
34. **ivy** traditional symbol of faithfulness. [Plant Symbolism: *Flora Symbolica,* 175]
35. **key** attribute of the personified Fidelity. [Art: Hall, 184]
36. **Laodamia** commits suicide to join husband Protesilaus in underworld. [Gk. Lit.: *Iliad;* Rom. Lit.: *Aeneid*]
37. **Leonore** disguises as Fidelio to save imprisoned husband. [Ger. Opera: Beethoven, *Fidelio,* Westerman, 109–110]
38. **Micawber, Mrs. Emma** swears she will never desert husband. [Br. Lit.: *David Copperfield*]
39. **Nanna** immolated herself on pyre with husband, Baldur. [Norse Myth.: Wheeler, 256]

40. **Penelope** Odysseus' patient wife; faithful for 20 years while waiting for his return. [Gk. Lit.: *Iliad; Odyssey*]
41. **Perseus** ever devoted to wife, Andromeda. [Gk. Myth.: Zimmerman, 200]
42. **Pietas** goddess of faithfulness, respect, and affection. [Rom. Myth.: Kravitz, 192]
43. **plum** symbol of faithfulness. [Flower Symbolism: *Flora Symbolica,* 176]
44. **Portia** takes own life after husband, Brutus's, suicide. [Rom. Hist.: *Plutarch's Lives*]
45. **red on yellow** symbol of faithfulness. [Chinese Art: Jobes, 357]
46. **Rodelinda** faithful to her deposed husband, Bertarido. [Br. Opera: Handel, *Rodelinda,* Westerman, 50–52]
47. **Roxy** tries to "save" immoral husband. [Am. Lit.: *Roxy*]
48. **Sita** princess abducted from her husband by the demon-king; she remains faithful throughout her captivity. [Indian Lit.: *Ramayana*]
49. **Sonia** young prostitute stays near prison to comfort Raskolnikov. [Russ. Lit.: *Crime and Punishment*]
50. **Valentine** a true friend and constant lover. [Br. Lit.: *Two Gentlemen of Verona*]
51. **veronica** symbol of faithfulness. [Flower Symbolism: *Flora Symbolica,* 178]
52. **violet** symbol of faithfulness. [Flower Symbolism: *Flora Symbolica,* 178; Kunz, 327]
53. **Zelda** shows devotion to Dobie, who manfully resists. [TV: "The Many Loves of Dobie Gillis" in Terrace, II, 64–66]

244. FAITHLESSNESS (See also ADULTERY, CUCKOLDRY.)

1. **Angelica** betrays Orlando by eloping with young soldier. [Ital. Lit.: *Orlando Furioso*]
2. **Camilla** falls to temptations of husband's friend. [Span. Lit.: *Don Quixote*]
3. **Carmen** throws over lover for another. [Fr. Lit.: *Carmen;* Fr. Opera: Bizet, *Carmen,* Westerman, 189–190]
4. **Coronis** princess killed by Apollo for being unfaithful to him. [Gk. Myth.: Howe, 66]
5. **Cressida** unfaithful mistress of Troilus; byword for unfaithfulness. [Br. Lit.: *Troilus and Cressida*]
6. **Dear John** letter from woman informing boyfriend that relationship is over. [Am. Usage: Misc.]

7. **Frankie and Johnnie** Johnnie, unfaithful to Frankie, is shot by her; there are nearly 500 versions of the song. [Am. Music: Misc.]
8. **Goneril and Regan** Lear's disloyal offspring; "tigers, not daughters." [Br. Lit.: *King Lear*]
9. **Manon** indifferently allows lover to be abducted. [Fr. Opera: Massenet, *Manon,* Westerman, 194–195]
10. **Shahriyar** convinced of female wantonness, marries a new wife each night, kills her in the morning. [Arab. Lit.: *Arabian Nights*]

245. FAME

1. **cardinal flower** traditional symbol of eminence. [Flower Symbolism: Jobes, 290]
2. **daphne** traditional symbol of fame. [Plant Symbolism: Jobes, 414]
3. **Grauman's Chinese Theater** famous for the imprints of movie stars' footprints in its forecourt. [Am. Cinema: Payton, 284.]
4. **Halls of Fame** national shrines honoring outstanding individuals in a particular field (baseball, football, acting, Great Americans, etc.). [Am. Culture: *WB,* 9, 22–23]
5. **Lady Fame** capriciously distributes fame and slander. [Br. Lit.: Chaucer *The House of Fame* in Benét, 479]
6. **Madame Tussaud's Waxworks** representation by a wax figure in this London museum is a sure sign of notoriety. [Pop. Culture: *EB* (1963) XXII, 634]
7. **trumpet** attribute of fame personified. [Art: Hall, 119]
8. **trumpet flower** indicates notoriety. [Flower Symbolism: *Flora Symbolica,* 178]
9. **Who's Who** biographical dictionary of notable living people. [Am. Hist.: Hart, 922]

246. FANATICISM (See also EXTREMISM.)

1. **Adamites** various sects preaching a return to life before the fall. [Christian Hist.: Brewer *Note-Book,* 8]
2. **assassins** Moslem murder teams used hashish as stimulus (11th and 12th centuries). [Islamic Hist.: Brewer *Note-Book,* 52]
3. **Fakirs** mendicant Indian sects bent on self-punishment for salvation. [Asian Hist.: Brewer *Note-Book,* 310]
4. **flagellants** various Christian sects practising self-punishment. [Christian Hist.: Brewer *Note-Book,* 331–332]

5. **Harmony Society** Harmonists, also Rappites; subscribed to austere doctrines, such as celibacy, and therefore no longer exist (since 1960). [Am. Hist.: *NCE,* 910]
6. **Hitler, Adolf** (1889–1945) German dictator tried to conquer the world. [Ger. Hist.: *Hitler*]
7. **Shakers** (or **Alethians**) received their name from the trembling produced by excesses of religious emotion; because of doctrine of celibacy, Shakers are all but extinct. [Am. Hist.: *NCE,* 1938]

247. FANTASY (See also ENCHANTMENT.)

1. **Aladdin's lamp** when rubbed, genie appears to do possessor's bidding. [Arab. Lit.: *Arabian Nights,* "Aladdin and the Wonderful Lamp"]
2. **Alice** undergoes fantastic adventures, such as dealing with the "real" Queen of Hearts. [Br. Lit.: *Alice's Adventures in Wonderland; Through the Looking Glass*]
3. **Alnaschar** dreams of the wealth he will realize from the sale of his glassware. [Arab. Lit.: Benét, 26]
4. ***Arabian Nights*** compilation of Middle and Far Eastern tales. [Arab. Lit.: Parrinder, 26]
5. ***Back to Methuselah*** England in the late twenty-second century is a bureaucracy administered by Chinese men and African women. [Br. Drama: Shaw *Back to Methuselah* in Magill III, 82]
6. **Baggins, Bilbo** Hobbit who wanders afar and brings back the One Ring of Power to The Shire. [Br. Lit.: *The Hobbit*]
7. **Bloom, Leopold** enlivens his uneventful life with amorous daydreams. [Irish Lit.: Joyce *Ulysses* in Magill I, 1040]
8. ***Chitty Chitty Bang Bang*** magical car helps track down criminals. [Children's Lit.: *Chitty Chitty Bang Bang*]
9. **Dorothy** flies via tornado to Oz. [Am. Lit.: *The Wonderful Wizard of Oz*]
10. ***Dream Children*** in a reverie, Charles Lamb tells stories to his two imaginary children. [Br. Lit.: Benét, 287]
11. ***Fantasia*** music comes to life in animated cartoon. [Am. Cinema: *Fantasia* in *Disney Films,* 38–45]
12. **Harvey** six-foot rabbit who appears only to a genial drunkard. [Am. Lit.: Benét, 444]
13. **Jurgen** regaining his lost youth, he has strange adventures with a host of mythical persons. [Am. Lit.: *Jurgen* in Magill I, 464]
14. **Land of the Giants** a *Gulliver's Travels* in outer space. [TV: Terrace, II, 10–11]

15. ***Little Prince, The*** travels to Earth from his star; fable by Antoine de Saint-Exupéry (1943). [Fr. Lit.: Benét, 889]
16. ***Lord of the Rings, The*** "feigned history" of the Hobbits; epic trilogy written by J. R. R. Tolkein. [Br. Lit.: Benét, 1013]
17. **Millionaire, The** mysterious Croesus bestows fortunes on unsuspecting individuals. [TV: Terrace, II, 97–98]
18. **Mitty, Walter** timid man who imagines himself a hero. [Am. Lit.: Benét, 1006; Am. Cinema and Drama: *The Secret Life of Walter Mitty*]
19. **Narnia** kingdom in which fantasy cycle of seven tales by C. S. Lewis takes place. [Children's Lit.: Fisher, 289–290]
20. **O'Gill, Darby** befriends dwarfdom. [Am. Cinema: *Darby O'Gill and the Little People* in *Disney Films,* 159–162]
21. **Pan, Peter** escapes to Never Never Land to avoid growing up. [Br. and Am. Drama: Benét, 778]
22. **Poppins, Mary** enchanted nanny guides her charges through fey adventures. [Children's Lit.: *Mary Poppins;* Am. Cinema: *Mary Poppins* in *Disney Films,* 226–232]
23. ***Thirteen Clocks, The*** beautiful princess is won by a disguised prince who fulfills her guardian's task with the aid of laughter that turns to jewels. [Am. Lit.: Thurber *The Thirteen Clocks* in Weiss, 462]
24. ***Wonderful Wizard of Oz, The*** adventures in land "somewhere over the rainbow." [Am. Lit.: *The Wonderful Wizard of Oz*]

248. FAREWELL

1. **Auld Lang Syne** closing song of New Year's Eve. [Music: Leach, 91]
2. **extreme unction (last rites)** anointing at the hour of death, sacrament of Orthodox Church and Roman Catholic Church. [Christianity: *NCE,* 689]
3. **gold watch** token of gratitude often bestowed on retiring employee after years of service. [Am. Pop. Culture: Misc.]
4. **golden handshake** token of gratitude bestowed on retiring employee after years of service. [Br. Pop. Culture: Misc.]
5. **kiss of death** gangsters' farewell ritual before murdering victim. [Am. Cult.: Misc.]
6. ***Last Hurrah, The*** portrays epitome of a politician's goodbye. [Am. Lit.: *The Last Hurrah*]
7. **Last Supper** Christ's final dinner with disciples before crucifixion. [N.T.: Matthew 26:26–29; Mark 14:22–25; Luke 22:14–20]

8. **MacArthur's goodbye** "Old soldiers never die; they just fade away." [Am. Hist.: Van Doren, 528]
9. **Michaelmas daisy** traditional symbol of farewell. [Flower Symbolism: Jobes, 407]

249. FARMING

1. **Aristaeus** honored as inventor of beekeeping. [Gk. Myth.: *NCE,* 105]
2. **Ashman** goddess of grain. [Sumerian Myth.: Benét, 57]
3. ***Barren Ground*** Dorinda Oakley makes her father's poor farm prosperous. [Am. Lit.: Glasgow *Barren Ground* in Magill I, 57]
4. **Bergson, Alexandra** proves her ability above brothers' to run farm. [Am. Lit.: *O Pioneers!,* Magill I, 663–665]
5. **bread basket** an agricultural area, such as the U.S. Midwest, that provides large amounts of food to other areas. [Am. Hist.: Misc.]
6. **Ceres** goddess of agriculture. [Rom. Myth.: Kravitz, 13]
7. **Chicomecoatl** goddess of maize. [Aztec Myth.: Jobes, 322]
8. **cow college** an agricultural college. [Pop. Culture: Misc.]
9. **Dea Dia** ancient Roman goddess of agriculture. [Rom. Myth.: Howe, 77]
10. **Demeter** goddess of corn and agriculture. [Gk. Myth.: Jobes, 429–430]
11. **Dionysus** god of fertility; sometimes associated with fertility of crops. [Gk. Myth.: *NCE,* 575]
12. **Fiacre, St.** extraordinary talent in raising vegetables; patron saint. [Christian Hagiog.: Attwater, 130]
13. **Freya** goddess of agriculture, peace, and plenty. [Norse Myth.: Payton, 257]
14. **Frome, Ethan** epitome of struggling New England farmer (1890s). [Am. Lit.: *Ethan Frome*]
15. **Gaea** goddess of the earth. [Gk. Myth.: *NCE,* 785]
16. ***Georgics*** Roman Vergil's poetic statement set in context of agriculture. [Rom. Lit.: Benét, 389]
17. ***Giants in the Earth*** portrayal of man's struggle with the stubborn earth. [Am. Lit.: *Giants in the Earth,* Magill I, 303–304]
18. ***Good Earth, The*** portrayal of land as only sure means of survival. [Am. Lit.: *The Good Earth*]
19. **King Cotton** term personifying the chief staple of the South. [Am. Hist.: Hart, 445]

20. **Kore** name for Persephone as symbol of annual vegetation cycle. [Gk. and Rom. Myth.: *NCE,* 1637]
21. **Odin** god of farming. [Norse Myth.: Benét, 728]
22. **Persephone** (Roman: Proserpine) goddess of fertility; often associated with crops. [Gk. and Rom. Myth.: *NCE,* 1637]
23. **Shimerda, Antonia** "like wavering grass, a child of the prairie and farm." [Am. Lit.: *My Ántonia,* Magill I, 630–632]
24. **Silvanus** god of agriculture. [Rom. Myth.: Kravitz, 13]
25. **Triptolemus** an Eleusinian who learns from Demeter the art of growing corn. [Gk. Myth.: *NCE,* 557]
26. **Walstan, St.** English patron saint of husbandmen. [Christian Hagiog.: Brewer *Dictionary,* 1138]
27. **wheat ears, garland of** to Demeter, goddess of grain. [Gk. Myth.: Jobes, 374]

250. FASCISM

1. **Cipolla** brutal magician, symbol of fascist oppression. [Ger. Lit.: *Mario and the Magician*; Haydn & Fuller, 636]
2. ***Duce, Il*** title of Benito Mussolini (1883–1945), Italian Fascist leader. [Ital. Hist.: Brewer *Dictionary*]
3. **Webley, Everard** sinister figure leads a growing Fascist movement. [Br. Lit.: Huxley *Point Counter Point* in Magill I, 760]

251. FASHION

1. **Brummel, George B. (Beau Brummel)** (1778–1840) set styles for men's clothes and manners for a quarter century. [Western Fashion: *NCE,* 926]
2. **Harper's Bazaar** leading fashion magazine. [Am. Culture: Misc.]
3. **Royal Ascot** annual horserace, occasion for great fashionable turnout. [Br. Cult.: Brewer *Dictionary,* 49]
4. **Vogue** leading fashion magazine in France and America. [Fr. and Amer. Culture: Misc.]

252. FASTIDIOUSNESS (See also PUNCTUALITY.)

1. **Fogg, Phileas** entire life tuned to precise schedule. [Fr. Lit.: *Around the World in Eighty Days*]
2. **Linkinwater, Tim** handles minutest details with order and precision. [Br. Lit.: *Nicholas Nickleby*]
3. **Morris the cat** finicky eater; eats only "9-Lives." [TV: Wallechinsky, 129]
4. **Steva** Jenufa's new scar cools his adulterous ardor. [Czech Opera: Janáček, *Jenufa,* Westerman, 407]

5. **Unger, Felix** for him, godliness is next to cleanliness. [Am. Lit.: *The Odd Couple;* Am. Cinema: *The Odd Couple;* TV: "The Odd Couple" in Terrace, II, 160–161]

253. FATE (See also CHANCE.)

1. **Adrastea** goddess of inevitable fate. [Gk. Myth.: Jobes, 35]
2. **Atropos, Clotho, and Lachesis** the three Fates; worked the thread of life. [Gk. and Rom. Myth.: Bulfinch]
3. ***Bridge of San Luis Rey, The*** catastrophe as act of divine providence. [Am. Lit.: *The Bridge of San Luis Rey*]
4. **dance of death, the** recurring motif in medieval art. [Eur. Culture: Bishop, 363–367]
5. **Destiny** goddess of destiny of mankind. [Gk. Myth.: Kravitz, 78]
6. **Fates** three goddesses who spin, measure out, and cut the thread of each human's life. Also called *Lat.* Parcae, *Gk.* Moirai. [Gk. Myth.: Benét, 757]
7. ***Jennie Gerhardt*** novel of young girl trapped by life's circumstances (1911). [Am. Lit.: *Jennie Gerhardt,* Magill III, 526–528]
8. **karma** one's every action brings inevitable results. [Buddhist and Hindu Trad.: *EB* (1963), 13: 283; Pop. Culture: Misc.]
9. **kismet** alludes to the part of life assigned one by his destiny. [Moslem Trad.: *EB* (1963), 13: 418; Pop. Culture: Misc.]
10. **Leonora** cursed by father; stabbed by brother. [Ital. Opera: Verdi, *La Forza del Destino,* Westerman, 316–317]
11. **Meleager** death would come when firebrand burned up. [Gk. Myth.: Walsh *Classical,* 186]
12. **Moirai** see **Fates.**
13. **Necessitas** goddess of the destiny of mankind. [Gk. Myth.: Kravitz, 78, 162]
14. **Nemesis** goddess of vengeance and retribution; *nemesis* has come to mean that which one cannot achieve. [Gr. Myth.: *WB,* 14: 116; Pop. Culture: Misc.]
15. **Norns** wove the fabric of human destiny. [Norse Myth.: Benét, 720]
16. **Parcae** see **Fates.**
17. **wool and narcissi, garland of** emblem of the three Fates. [Gk. Myth.: Jobes, 374]

254. FATHERHOOD

1. **Abraham** progenitor of a host of nations. [O.T.: Genesis 17:3–6]

2. **Adam** first man and progenitor of humanity. [O.T.: Genesis 5: 1–5]
3. **Dag(h)da** great god of Celts; father of Danu. [Celtic Myth.: Parrinder, 68; Jobes, 405]
4. **Dombey, Mr.** embittered by the death of his young son, neglects his daughter. [Br. Lit.: *Dombey and Son*]
5. **Goriot, Père** deprives himself of his wealth in order to ensure good marriages for his two daughters. [Fr. Lit.: Balzac *Père Goriot* in Magill I, 271]
6. **Liliom** dead for sixteen years, he is allowed to return from Heaven for a day, and attempts to please the daughter he had never seen. [Hung. Drama: Molnar *Liliom* in Magill I, 511]
7. **Priam, King of Troy** fathered fifty children, among them Hector, Paris, Troilus, and Cassandra. [Gk. Lit.: *Iliad*]
8. **Tevye** pious dairyman concerned with marrying off his seven beautiful daughters. [Yid. Lit.: *Tevye's Daughters*; Am. Musical: *Fiddler on the Roof* in *On Stage*, 468]
9. **Vatea** the first man; the father of mankind. [Polynesian Legend: *How the People Sang the Mountains Up,* 85]
10. **Zeus (Jupiter, Jove)** "Father of the gods and men"; had many legitimate and illegitimate children. [Gk. and Rom. Myth.: Benét, 1115; Bulfinch, Ch. I]

255. FATNESS

1. **Bagstock, Major** corpulent army officer. [Br. Lit.: *Dombey and Son*]
2. **Challenger, Professor** amusing and opinionated scientist of notable rotundity. [Br. Lit.: *The Lost World*]
3. **Domino, Antoine "Fats"** (1928–) popular singer of the 1950s, nicknamed for his size and shape. [Am. Music: Misc.]
4. **Double, Edmund** loves to eat; represents the Fattipuffs. [Children's Lit.: *Fattipuffs and Thinifers,* Fisher, 100–101]
5. **Eglon** obese Moabite king; sword engulfed by adiposity. [O.T.: Judges 3:17–22]
6. **Falstaff** "that swoln parcel of dropsies." [Br. Drama: Benét, 339]
7. **Five by Five, Mr.** obese subject of song by Gene DePaul and Don Raye (1942). [Am. Pop. Music: Kinkle, 1, 379.]
8. **Gleason, Jackie** (1916–) heavyweight TV comedian. [TV: "The Jackie Gleason Show," "The Honeymooners" in Terrace, I, 402]

9. **Humpty Dumpty** "egg" in Mother Goose who, among other things, alludes to fatness. [Children's Lit.: *Mother Goose*]
10. **Joe ("Fat Boy")** sole employment consists in alternately eating and sleeping. [Br. Lit.: *Pickwick Papers*]
11. **king and his ministers** "large, corpulent, oily men." [Am. Lit.: "Hop-Frog" in *Portable Poe,* 317–329]
12. **Limkins, Mr.** large gentleman with "a very round red face." [Br. Lit.: *Oliver Twist*]
13. **Minnesota Fats** (Rudolph Walter Wanderone, Jr., 1903–) world champion billiard player easily recognized by his fleshy physique. [Am. Sports: Misc.]
14. **Robbin and Bobbin** "eat more victuals than threescore men." [Nurs. Rhyme: Baring-Gould, 33]
15. **Snuphanuph, Lady** obese visitor at Bath. [Br. Lit.: *Pickwick Papers*]
16. **Tweedledum and Tweedledee** two little fat men who quickly get out-of-breath. [Br. Lit.: Lewis Carroll *Through the Looking-Glass*]
17. **Wolfe, Nero** detective whose obesity makes him reluctant to leave his office. [Am. Lit.: Herman, 119]

256. FEARSOMENESS

1. **Deimos** attendant of Ares; personification of fear. [Gk. Myth.: Howe, 77]
2. ***Dracula*** eerie tale of vampires and werewolves. [Br. Lit.: *Dracula*]
3. **Invasion from Mars** Orson Welles's broadcast; terrified a credulous America (1938). [Am. Hist.: Van Doren, 468]
4. **Iroquois** strongest, most feared of eastern confederacies. [Am. Hist.: Jameson, 250]
5. **Jaggers, Mr.** lawyer esteemed and feared by clients. [Br. Lit.: *Great Expectations*]
6. **Ko-Ko** holder of dread office of High Executioner. [Br. Opera: *The Mikado,* Magill I, 591–592]
7. ***Native Son*** portrays oppressor and oppressed as both filled with fear. [Am. Lit.: *Native Son,* Magill I, 643–645]
8. **Phobus** god of dread and alarm. [Gk. Myth.: Kravitz, 14, 84]
9. ***Seven That Were Hanged, The*** analyzes the fears of an official threatened with assassination and of seven condemned prisoners. [Russ. Lit.: Magill II, 957]
10. **Shere Khan** lame tiger who wants to devour Mowgli; causes fear throughout story. [Children's Lit.: *The Jungle Book*]

257. FEAST (See also EPICUREANISM.)

1. **Barmecide feast** a sham banquet, with empty plates, given to a beggar by wealthy Bagdad nobleman. [Arab. Lit.: *Arabian Nights,* "The Barmecide's Feast"]
2. **Belshazzar's Feast** lavish banquet, with vessels stolen from Jerusalem temple. [O.T.: Daniel, 5]
3. **Camacho's wedding** lavish feast prepared in vain, as Camacho's fiancée runs off with her love just before the ceremony. [Span. Lit.: Cervantes *Don Quixote*]
4. **Hanukkah** (Feast of Lights or Feast of Dedication) Jewish festival lasting eight days; abundance of food is characteristic. [Judaism: *NCE,* 1190]
5. **Lucullan feast** a lavish banquet; after Lucullus, roman general and gourmet. [Rom. Hist.: Espy, 236]
6. **Prospero's banquet** shown to the hungry castaways, then disappears. [Br. Drama: Shakespeare *The Tempest*]
7. **Thanksgiving** national holiday with luxurious dinner as chief ritual. [Am. Pop. Culture: Misc.]
8. **Thyestean banquet** at which Atreus served his brother Thyestes' sons to him as main course. [Gk. Myth.: *Brewer Dictionary,* 1081]
9. **Trimalchio's Feast** lavishly huge banquet given by wealthy vulgarian. [Rom. Lit.: *Satyricon*]
10. **Zeus** disguised as Amphitryon, gives a banquet at the latter's house. [Gk. Myth.: Benét, 32]

258. FEMALE POWER

1. **Boadicea** British warrior-queen who led a revolt against the Romans. [Br. Hist.: Brewer *Dictionary,* 116]
2. **Camilla** maiden-warrior who battles Aeneas' forces. [Rom. Lit.: Vergil *Aeneid*]
3. **Hippolyta** queen of the Amazons; attacked Attica but was defeated by Theseus, who then married her. [Gk. Myth.: Benét, 468]
4. **Macbeth, Lady** goads Macbeth to murder Duncan and seize power. [Br. Drama: Shakespeare *Macbeth*]
5. **Pilar** strong-minded female leader of a group of guerrillas in the Spanish Civil War. [Am. Lit.: Hemingway *For Whom the Bell Tolls*]
6. **Semiramis** warrior-queen founded Babylon; legendary conqueror, identified with the goddess Ishtar. [Asiatic Hist.: *EB* (1963) XX, 315]

7. **Valkyries** warlike virgins who ride into battle to select, from the heroes to be slain, those worthy of dining with Odin in Valhalla. [Scand. Myth.: Benét, 1046]

259. FEMININITY

1. **Belphoebe** perfect maidenhood; epithet of Elizabeth I. [Br. Lit.: *Faerie Queene*]
2. **Darnel, Aurelia** personification of femininity. [Br. Lit.: *Sir Launcelot Greaves*]
3. **Miss America** winner of beauty contest; femininity high among virtues desired. [Am. Hist.: Payton, 445]

260. FEMINISM (See also EQUALITY.)

1. **Alving, Mrs.** feminist; unconventional widow. [Nor. Lit.: *Ghosts*]
2. **Bates, Belinda** intellectual and amiable advocate of women's rights. [Br. Lit.: "The Haunted House" in Fyfe, 16]
3. **Bloomer, Amelia** (1818–1894) dress reformer; designed bloomers. [Am. Hist.: Flexner, 391]
4. **blue-stocking** female intellectual; advocates nontraditional feminine talents. [Western Folklore: Brewer *Dictionary*, 127]
5. ***Bostonians, The*** suffragists for lost causes, vulnerable to romance. [Am. Lit.: *The Bostonians*]
6. **Chancellor, Olive** devotes her life to preaching women's rights. [Am. Lit: Henry James *The Bostonians*]
7. ***Doll's House, A*** drama on the theme of women's rights. [Nor. Lit.: *A Doll's House*]
8. **Equal Rights Amendment** forbids discrimination against women. [Am. Hist.: Flexner, 397]
9. **Findlay, Maude** militant, outspoken women's libber. [TV: "Maude" in Terrace, II, 79–80]
10. **Lucy Stoners** league of feminists. [Am. Hist.: *NCE*, 2628]
11. **Lysistrata** Athenian exhorts fellow women to continence for peace. [Gk. Lit.: *Lysistrata*]
12. **Ms.** the magazine for the liberated woman. [Am. Culture: Misc.]
13. **NOW** feminist group working for social and political change. [Am. Hist.: *NCE*, 1886]
14. **Nora** rebellious heroine; leaves stultifying marriage. [Nor. Lit.: *A Doll's House*]
15. **Peel, Emma** early media manifestation of self-sufficient woman. [TV: "The Avengers" in Terrace, I, 71–73]

16. **Virginia Slims** cigarette trademark marketed to "independent women." "You've come a long way, baby," as slogan. [Trademarks: Crowley *Trade,* 630]
17. **Wisk, Miss** lady with a mission. [Br. Lit.: *Bleak House*]
18. **Women's Liberation Movement** appellation of modern day women's rights advocacy. [Am. Hist.: Flexner, 396]
19. **Wonder Woman** female comic strip heroine to offset Superman; she does everything a man can do and more. [Comics: Horn, 480]

261. FERRYING

1. **Charon** ferries dead across the river Styx. [Gk. and Rom. Myth.: Hall, 147; Ital. Lit.: *Inferno.*]
2. **Christopher, St.** took the Christ child and the weak across river. [Christian Hagiog.: Hall, 68]
3. **Julian the Hospitaler** carries leper across river. [Christian Hagiog.: Hall, 181]
4. **Phlegyas** conveyed Dante and Virgil through Stygian marsh. [Ital. Lit.: *Inferno*]
5. **Siddharta** "one who has attained goal," personified in ferryman role. [Ger. Lit.: *Siddharta*]
6. **Tuck, Friar** jolly member of Robin Hood's gang; carries Robin over stream but dumps him coming back. [Br. Lit.: *Robin Hood*]

262. FERTILITY (See also ABUNDANCE.)

1. **antler dance** archaic animal dance, preceding mating. [Br. Folklore: Brewer *Dictionary,* 1]
2. **Anu** Irish goddess of fecundity. [Irish Folklore: Briggs, 9]
3. **Aphrodite** goddess of fecundity. [Gk. Myth.: Parrinder, 24]
4. **Astarte** goddess of fecundity. [Phoenician Myth.: Jobes, 144]
5. **Astarte's dove** emblem of fecundity. [Phoenician Myth.: Jobes, 466]
6. **Atargatis' dove** emblem of fecundity. [Hittite Myth.: Jobes, 466]
7. **Athena** Athens' patroness; goddess of war and fecundity. [Gk. Myth.: Parrinder, 33; Kravitz, 40]
8. **Baal** chief male god of Phoenicians; the generative principle. [Phoenician Rel.: Parrinder, 38]
9. **Bacchus' cup** symbolizes fecundity. [Gk. Myth.: Jobes, 397]
10. **Bona Dea** goddess of fertility; counterpart of Faunus. [Rom. Myth.: Zimmerman, 43]

11. **breast** symbol of nourishment and fecundity. [Ren. Art: Hall, 52]
12. **Cernunnos** horned deity of fecundity, associated with snakes. [Celtic Myth.: Parrinder, 58]
13. **Cerridwen** nature goddess whose magical cauldron was misused. [Celtic Myth.: Parrinder, 58]
14. **Chloë** beloved maiden, goddess of new, green crops. [Gk. Myth.: Parrinder, 62]
15. **Clothru** Irish goddess of fertility. [Irish Myth.: Jobes, 349]
16. **clover** symbolizes fecundity. [Folklore: Jobes, 350]
17. **coconut** presented to women who want to be mothers. [Ind. Folklore: Binder, 85]
18. **Cybele** nature's fruitfulness assured by orgiastic rites honoring her. [Phrygian Myth.: Parrinder, 68; Jobes, 400]
19. **Dôn** goddess of fecundity; Welsh equivalent of Irish Danu. [Brythonic Myth.: Leach, 321; Jobes, 461]
20. **Dag(h)da** god of abundance, war, healing. [Celtic Myth.: Parrinder, 68; Jobes, 405]
21. **Dagon (Dāgan)** fish-corn god symbolizing fecundity and abundance. [Babyl. Myth.: Parrinder, 71; Jobes, 405]
22. **Demeter** goddess of fecundity. [Gk. Myth.: Jobes, 429–430]
23. **double ax** emblem of fecundity. [Folklore: Jobes, 163]
24. **figs, garland of** a traditional pictorial identification of Pan, pastoral god of fertility. [Gk. Myth.: Jobes, 373]
25. **fish** signifies fecundity. [Mexican Folklore: Binder, 17]
26. **flowers and fruit, garland of** traditional headdress of Pomona, goddess of fertility. [Rom. Myth.: Jobes, 373]
27. **flowers, garland of** traditional pictorial identification of Flora, goddess of flowers and fertility. [Rom. Myth.: Jobes, 373]
28. **Freya** goddess of agriculture, peace, and plenty. [Norse Myth.: Payton, 257]
29. **grape leaves, garland of** traditional headdress of Bona Dea, goddess of fertility. [Rom. Myth.: Jobes, 373]
30. **green** symbol of fruitfulness. [Color Symbolism: Jobes, 356]
31. **horn** believed to promote fertility. [Art: Hall, 157]
32. **horse** symbolizes fecundity. [Bengali Folklore: Binder, 67]
33. **Lavransdatter, Kristin** gives birth to eight sons in ten years. [Nor. Lit.: *Kristin Lavransdatter,* Magill I, 483–486]
34. **Mylitta** goddess of fertility. [Babyl. Myth.: Leach, 776]
35. **old woman who lived in a shoe** what to do with so many children? [Nurs. Rhyme: Opie, 434]

36. **Ops** Sabine goddess of fecundity. [Rom. Myth.: Brewer *Dictionary,* 782]
37. **orange blossoms** symbolic of bride's hope for fruitfulness. [Br. and Fr. Tradition: Brewer *Dictionary,* 784]
38. **Pomona** goddess of gardens and fruit trees. [Rom. Myth.: Zimmerman, 218]
39. **pomegranate** indicates abundance. [Heraldry: Halberts, 36]
40. **rabbit** symbol of fecundity. [Animal Symbolism: Mercatante, 125–126]
41. **Rhea** worshiped orgy and fertility; mother of Zeus, Poseidon, Hera, Hades, Demeter, and Hestia. [Gk. Myth.: *NCE,* 1796]
42. **rhinoceros horn** in powdered form, considered powerful fertility agent. [Eastern Culture: Misc.]
43. **waxing moon** only effective time for sowing seeds. [Gardening Lore: Boland, 31]
44. **yellow** color of fecundity, relating to yellow sun and earth. [Eastern Color Symbolism: Binder, 78]

263. FESTIVAL, FILM

1. **Cannes** founded after WWII; the 1968 festival was the scene of demonstrations by political activists. [Cinema Hist.: *EB,* 12: 496]

264. FESTIVAL, MUSIC

1. **Bayreuth** since 1876, international center for Wagner's operas. [Opera Hist.: Thompson, 165]
2. **Berkshire Music Festival (Tanglewood)** summer home of Boston Symphony since 1934. [Music Hist.: Thompson, 202–203]
3. **Edinburgh Festival** internationally famous arts celebration since 1947. [Music Hist.: Thompson, 617]
4. **Eisteddfod** ancient congress of bards, still held annually in Wales. [Music Hist.: Benét, 305]
5. **Festival of the Two Worlds (Spoleto Festival)** founded in 1958 by Gian-Carlo Menotti and held annually in Spoleto, Italy. [Music Hist.: *NCE,* 2599]
6. **Glyndebourne Festivals** annual operatic events held in Sussex, England since 1934. [Music Hist.: *NCE,* 1097]
7. **Newport Jazz Festival** annual summer jazz celebration. [Am. Mus.: *NCE,* 1927]
8. **Woodstock** 300,000 rock music fans attended this festival held near Bethel, N.Y. (August 16, 1969). [Am. Music Hist.: *EB,* X: 741]

Fierceness (See SAVAGERY.)

265. FILTH (See also DIRTINESS.)

1. **Augean stables** held 3,000 oxen, uncleaned for 30 years; Hercules' fifth labor: washes out dung by diverting a river. [Gk. and Rom. Myth.: Hall, 149]
2. ***Jungle, The*** portrays the lack of hygiene among Chicago meatpacking plants (1906). [Am. Lit.: *The Jungle,* Payton, 356]
3. **Lake Erie** Great Lake; once so polluted, referred to as Lake Eerie. [Am. Hist.: *NCE,* 887]

266. FINANCE (See also MONEY.)

1. **Bourse** the Paris stock exchange. [Fr. Commerce: Misc.]
2. **Dow Jones** the best known of several U.S. indexes of movements in price on Wall Street. [Am. Hist.: Payton, 202]
3. **Lombard Street** London bankers' row; named for 13th-century Italian moneylenders. [Br. Hist.: Plumb, 15]
4. **Old Lady of Threadneedle Street** nickname for the Bank of England. [Br. Culture: Misc.]
5. **Praxidice** goddess of commerce. [Gk. Myth.: Kravitz, 88]
6. **Rockefeller, John D(avison)** (1839–1937) multimillionaire oil tycoon and financier, [Am. Hist.: *EB,* VIII: 623]
7. **Throgmorton Street** location of Stock Exchange; by extension, financial world. [Br. Hist.: Brewer *Dictionary,* 1079]
8. **Wall Street** N.Y.C. financial district. [Am. Hist.: Jameson, 530]

267. FIRE

1. **Agni** intermediary of the gods through sacrificial fire. [Hindu Myth.: Parrinder, 12]
2. **Armida** sorceress sets fire to her own palace when it is threatened by the Crusaders. [Ital. Lit.: *Jerusalem Delivered (Gerusalemme Liberata);* in Benét, 391]
3. **burning bush** form taken by the Angel of the Lord to speak to Moses. [O.T.: Exodus 3:2-3]
4. **Caca** goddess of the hearth. [Rom. Myth.: Kravitz, 49]
5. **Dactyli** introduced fire to Crete. [Gk. Myth.: Kravitz, 74]
6. **Etticoat, Little Nancy** candle personified: longer she stands, shorter she grows. [Nurs. Rhyme: *Mother Goose,* 39]
7. ***Fahrenheit 451*** in an America of the future the fireman's job is to burn all books that have been concealed from authorities. [Am. Lit.: Bradbury *Fahrenheit 451* in Weiss, 289]
8. **Florian** miraculously extinguished conflagration; popularly invoked against combustion. [Christian Hagiog.: Hall, 126]

9. **Great Chicago Fire** destroyed much of Chicago; it was supposedly started when Mrs. O'Leary's cow kicked over a lantern (1871). [Am. Hist.: Payton, 141]
10. **Hephaestus** Prometheus' kinsman and the god of fire. [Gk. Lit.: *Prometheus Bound,* Magill I, 786–788]
11. **lucifer** kitchen match; from Lucifer, fallen archangel. [Br. Folklore: Espy, 66]
12. **Phlegethon** river of liquid fire in Hades. [Gk. Myth.: Brewer *Dictionary*, 699]
13. **Phoenix** fabulous bird that consumes itself by fire every five hundred years and rises renewed from the ashes. [Arab Myth.: Brewer *Dictionary*, 699]
14. **Polycarp, St.** sentenced to immolation, flames unscathingly ensheathed him. [Christian Hagiog.: Attwater, 290]
15. **Prometheus** Titan who stole fire from Olympus and gave it to man. [Gk. Myth.: Payton, 546]
16. **salamander** flame-dwelling spirit in Rosicrucian philosophy. [Medieval Hist.: Brewer *Dictionary,* 956]
17. **Shadrach, Meshach, and Abednego** walk unscathed in the fire of the furnace into which Nebuchadnezzar has them thrown. [O. T.: Daniel 3:21-27]
18. **Smokey the Bear** warns "only you can prevent forest fires." [Am. Pop. Cult.: Misc.]
19. **Taberah** Israelite camp scorched by angry Jehovah. [O.T.: Numbers 11:1–3]
20. **Topheth** where parents immolated children to god, Moloch. [O.T.: II Kings 23:10; Jeremiah 7:31–32]
21. **Vesta** virgin goddess of hearth; custodian of sacred fire. [Rom. Myth.: Brewer *Dictionary,* 1127]
22. **Vulcan** blacksmith of gods; personification of fire. [Art: Hall, 128]

268. FIRSTS

1. **Adam** in the Bible, the first man. [O.T.: Genesis 1:26–5:5]
2. **Alalcomeneus** the first man. [Gk. Myth.: Zimmerman, 14]
3. **Aldine Classics** first standardized, comprehensive editions of the classics (16th century). [Ital. Hist.: Plumb, 267]
4. **Armstrong, Neil** (1930–   ) first person to set foot on the moon (July 20, 1969). [Am. Hist.: *NCE,* 172]
5. **Bannister, Roger** (1929–   ) first runner to break the four-minute mile. [Sports: *EB,* I: 795]

6. ***Bay Psalm Book, The*** first book published in U.S. (1640). [Am. Hist.: Van Doren, 784]
7. **Cabrini, St. Frances** (1850–1917) first U.S. saint; tirelessly helped new Italian Americans. [Christian Hagiog.: Attwater, 135–136]
8. **Caedmon** (b. 671) earliest English Christian poet. [Br. Hist.: Grun]
9. **Cincinnati Red Stockings** first all-professional baseball team (1869). [Am. Hist.: Van Doren, 260]
10. ***Dafue*** first true opera (Florence, 1597). [Ital. Opera: Westerman, 17]
11. **Dare, Virginia** (b. 1587) first English child born in New World. [Am. Hist.: Jameson, 131]
12. **Delaware** first colony to ratify the Constitution; thus, "the first state." [Am. Hist.: *NCE,* 738]
13. **Eve** in the Bible, the first woman. [O.T.: Genesis 1–5]
14. **Gagarin, Yury** (1934–1968) first man in space (1961). [Russ. Hist.: Wallechinsky, 116]
15. **Genesis** first book of the Old Testament. [O.T.: Genesis]
16. **Gertie the Dinosaur** first substantial animated cartoon (1909). [Am. Hist.: Van Doren, 362]
17. **Great Exhibition, the** the first industrial exhibition, promoted by Prince Albert and held in Hyde Park in Crystal Palace. [Br. Hist.: Payton, 285]
18. ***Great Train Robbery, The*** considered the first "real" movie. [Am. Cinema: Griffith, 10]
19. **Gutenberg, Johannes** (1397–1468) German printer, supposedly the first European to print with movable type (c. 1436). [Ger. Hist.: *NCE,* 1166]
20. **Harvard** the first American college (1636). [Am. Hist.: *NCE,* 1200]
21. ***Jazz Singer, The*** first talking film (1927) featured Al Jolson. [Am. Cinema: Halliwell, 213]
22. **La Navidad** first European settlement in New World (1492). [Am. Hist.: Van Doren, 2]
23. **Lindbergh, Charles** (1902–1974) U.S. aviator; made the first solo, nonstop transatlantic flight (1927). [Am. Hist.: *NCE,* 1586]
24. **Macy's** prototype of the department store. [Am. Hist.: Van Doren, 217–218]
25. **Montgolfier brothers** (Joseph, 1740–1810) (Jaques, 1745–1799) first to make practical, manned balloon flight (1783). [Fr. Hist.: *NCE,* 1821]

26. **Oberlin College** first college to admit Negroes and to give women degrees. [Am. Hist.: Hart, 612]
27. **Robinson, Jackie** (1919–1972) professional American baseball player; first Negro to play in the major leagues. [Am. Sports: *NCE,* 2335]
28. **"Steamboat Willie"** first animated cartoon with sound (Disney). [Am. Cinema: Van Doren, 431]
29. **Tom Thumb** first American steam locomotive. [Am. Hist.: Van Doren, 141]
30. **Virginia** first of the Thirteen Colonies. [Am. Hist.: *NCE,* 289]
31. **Washington, George** (1732–1799) first United States president. [Am. Hist.: Hart, 897]
32. **Wright Brothers** (Wilbur, 1867–1912) (Orville, 1871–1948) made the first controlled, sustained flight in a power-driven airplane (1903). [Am. Hist.: *NCE,* 3012]

Flamboyance (See ELEGANCE.)

269. FLATTERY

1. **Adams, Jack** toady to his employer. [Br. Lit.: *Dombey and Son*]
2. **Amaziah** fawningly complains of Amos to King Jeroboam. [O.T.: Amos 7:10]
3. **bolton** one who flatters by pretending humility. [Br. Hist.: Espy, 343]
4. **Chanticleer** cajoled by fox into singing; thus captured. [Br. Lit.: *Canterbury Tales,* "Nun's Priest's Tale"]
5. **Clumsy, Sir Tunbelly** toadies towards aristocracy. [Br. Lit.: *The Relapse,* Walsh *Modern,* 102]
6. **Collins, Mr.** priggish, servile clergyman; toady to the great. [Br. Lit.: *Pride and Prejudice*]
7. **Damocles** for his sycophancy to Dionysus, seated under sword at banquet. [Gk. Myth.: *LLEI,* I: 278]
8. **Mutual Admiration Society** circle of mutual patters on the backs. [Br. Hist.: Wheeler, 254]
9. **oreo** cookie; pejoratively refers to obsequious Black with white aspirations. [Am. Culture: Flexner, 49]
10. **Ruach** island of people sustained by insincere praise. [Fr. Lit.: *Pantagruel*]
11. **Tom, Uncle** Stowe character came to signify subservient Black. [Am. Lit.: *Uncle Tom's Cabin*]
12. **Wren, Jenny** wooed by Robin Redbreast with enticing presents. [Nurs. Rhyme: *Mother Goose,* 23]

270. FLIRTATIOUSNESS (See also SEDUCTION.)

1. **Boop, Betty** comic strip character who flirts to win over boys. [Comics: Horn, 110]
2. **can-can** boisterous and indecorous French dance designed to arouse audiences. [Fr. Hist.: Scholes, 151]
3. **Célimène** unabashed coquette wooed by Alceste. [Fr. Lit.: *The Misanthrope*]
4. **Columbine** light-hearted, flirtatious girl. [Ital. Lit.: Walsh *Classical,* 83]
5. **dandelion** traditional symbol of flirtation. [Flower Symbolism: Jobes, 413]
6. **daylily** traditional symbol of flirtation. [Flower Symbolism: *Flora Symbolica,* 175]
7. **fan** symbol of coquetry. [Folklore: Jobes, 370]
8. **Frasquita** woman character chiefly remembered for her flirtatiousness toward old Don Eugenio. [Ger. Opera: Wolf, *The Magistrate,* Westerman, 262]
9. **Habanera** Carmen's "love is a wild bird" provokes hearers. [Fr. Opera: Bizet, *Carmen,* Westerman, 189–190]
10. **Jiménez, Pepita** young widow coquettishly distracts seminarian; love unfolds. [Span. Lit.: *Pepita Jiménez*]
11. **Julie, Miss** young gentlewoman high-handedly engages servant's love. [Swed. Lit.: *Miss Julie* in *Plays by August Strindberg*]
12. **Musetta** leads on Alcindoro while pursuing Marcello. [Ital. Opera: Puccini, *La Bohème,* Westerman, 349]
13. **O'Hara, Scarlett** hot-tempered heroine-coquette who wooed Southern Gentlemen. [Am. Lit.: *Gone With The Wind*]
14. **Varden, Dolly** Watteau-style colorful costume: broad-brimmed hat and dress with deep cleavage; honors Dickens character. [Br. Costume: Misc.; Br. Lit.: *Barnaby Rudge,* Espy, 272]
15. **West, Mae** (1892–1980) actress personified as a vamp; known for her famous line, "Come up and see me some time." [Am. Cinema: Halliwell, 759]

271. FLOWER or PLANT, NATIONAL (See also FLOWER, STATE.)

1. **almond blossom** of Israel. [Flower Symbolism: *WB,* 7: 264]
2. **blue anemone** of Norway. [Flower Symbolism: *WB,* 7: 264]
3. **blue cornflower** of West Germany. [Flower Symbolism: *WB,* 7: 264]
4. **cantua** of Bolivia. [Flower Symbolism: *WB,* 7: 264]
5. **carnation** of Egypt and Spain. [Flower Symbolism: *WB,* 7: 264]

6. **cattleya** of Brazil. [Flower Symbolism: *WB,* 7: 264]
7. **ceibo** of Argentina. [Flower Symbolism: *WB,* 7: 264]
8. **chrysanthemum** of Japan. [Flower Symbolism: *WB,* 7: 264]
9. **cinchona** of Ecuador. [Flower Symbolism: *WB,* 7: 264]
10. **dahlia** of Mexico. [Flower Symbolism: *WB,* 7: 264]
11. **edelweiss** of Switzerland. [Flower Symbolism: Jobes, 490]
12. **fern** of New Zealand. [Flower Symbolism: *WB,* 7: 264]
13. **flame lily** of Rhodesia. [Flower Symbolism: *WB,* 7: 264]
14. **fleur-de-lis** of France. [Flower Symbolism: Halberts, 28]
15. **frangipani** of Laos. [Flower Symbolism: *WB,* 7: 264]
16. **golden wattle** of Australia. [Flower Symbolism: *WB,* 7: 264]
17. **hibiscus** of Malaysia. [Flower Symbolism: *WB,* 7: 264]
18. **jasmine** (also **rose**) of Indonesia. [Flower Symbolism: *WB,* 7: 264]
19. **leek** of Wales. [Flower Symbolism: Brewer *Note-Book,* 334]
20. **lily** of then city-state Florence. [Flower Symbolism: Brewer *Note-Book,* 334]
21. **lily of the valley** of Finland. [Flower Symbolism: *WB,* 7: 264]
22. **linden** of former Prussia. [Flower Symbolism: Brewer *Note-Book,* 334]
23. **lotus** of India. [Flower Symbolism: *WB,* 7: 264]
24. **maple leaf** of Canada. [Flower Symbolism: Jobes, 283]
25. **mignonette** of the former Saxony. [Flower Symbolism: Brewer *Note-Book,* 334]
26. **orchid** of Venezuela. [Flower Symbolism: *WB,* 7: 264]
27. **poppy** of Greece. [Flower Symbolism: *WB,* 7: 264]
28. **protea** of South Africa. [Flower Symbolism: *WB,* 7: 264]
29. **red rose** of England. [Flower Symbolism: Brewer *Note-Book,* 334]
30. **rhododendron** of Nepal. [Flower Symbolism: *WB,* 7: 264]
31. **rose** of Honduras. [Flower Symbolism: *WB,* 7: 264]
32. **sampaguita** of Philippines. [Flower Symbolism: *WB,* 7: 264]
33. **shamrock** of Ireland. [Flower Symbolism: Brewer *Note-Book,* 334]
34. **thistle** of Scotland. [Flower Symbolism: Halberts, 38]
35. **tulip** of Netherlands. [Flower Symbolism: *WB,* 7: 264]
36. **violet** of then city-state Athens. [Flower Symbolism: Brewer *Note-Book,* 334]
37. **white orchid** of Guatemala. [Flower Symbolism: *WB,* 7: 264]

272. FLOWER, STATE (See also FLOWER or PLANT, NATIONAL.)

1. **American pasque flower** of South Dakota. [Flower Symbolism: Golenpaul, 642]
2. **apple blossom** of Arkansas and Michigan. [Flower Symbolism: Golenpaul, 626]
3. **bitterroot** of Montana. [Flower Symbolism: Golenpaul, 636]
4. **black-eyed susan** of Maryland. [Flower Symbolism: Golenpaul, 633]
5. **bluebonnet** of Texas. [Flower Symbolism: Golenpaul, 643]
6. **camellia** of Alabama. [Flower Symbolism: Golenpaul, 625]
7. **Carolina yellow jessamine** of South Carolina. [Flower Symbolism: Golenpaul, 642]
8. **Cherokee rose** of Georgia. [Flower Symbolism: Golenpaul, 629]
9. **dogwood** of North Carolina and Virginia. [Flower Symbolism: Golenpaul, 639]
10. **flower of saguaro cactus** of Arizona. [Flower Symbolism: Golenpaul, 626]
11. **forget-me-not** of Alaska. [Flower Symbolism: Golenpaul, 625]
12. **golden poppy** of California. [Flower Symbolism: Golenpaul, 627]
13. **goldenrod** of Kentucky and Nebraska. [Flower Symbolism: Golenpaul, 632]
14. **hawthorn** of Missouri. [Flower Symbolism: Golenpaul, 635]
15. **hibiscus** of Hawaii. [Flower Symbolism: Golenpaul, 629]
16. **Indian paintbrush** of Wyoming. [Flower Symbolism: Golenpaul, 646]
17. **iris** of Tennessee. [Flower Symbolism: Golenpaul, 642]
18. **magnolia** of Louisiana and Mississippi. [Flower Symbolism: Golenpaul, 632]
19. **mayflower** of Massachusetts. [Flower Symbolism: Golenpaul, 633]
20. **mistletoe** of Oklahoma. [Flower Symbolism: Golenpaul, 640]
21. **mountain laurel** of Connecticut and Pennsylvania. [Flower Symbolism: Golenpaul, 628]
22. **orange blossom** of Florida. [Flower Symbolism: Golenpaul, 628]
23. **Oregon grape** of Oregon. [Flower Symbolism: Golenpaul, 640]
24. **peach blossom** of Delaware. [Flower Symbolism: Golenpaul, 628]
25. **peony** of Indiana. [Flower Symbolism: Golenpaul, 631]
26. **purple lilac** of New Hampshire. [Flower Symbolism: Golenpaul, 637]

27. **red clover** of Vermont. [Flower Symbolism: Golenpaul, 644]
28. **rhododendron** of Washington and West Virginia. [Flower Symbolism: Golenpaul, 644]
29. **Rocky Mountain columbine** of Colorado. [Flower Symbolism: Golenpaul, 627]
30. **rose** of New York. [Flower Symbolism: Golenpaul, 638]
31. **sagebrush** of Nevada. [Flower Symbolism: Golenpaul, 636]
32. **scarlet carnation** of Ohio. [Flower Symbolism: Golenpaul, 639]
33. **sego lily** of Utah. [Flower Symbolism: Golenpaul, 643]
34. **showy lady slipper** of Minnesota. [Flower Symbolism: Golenpaul, 634]
35. **sunflower** of Kansas. [Flower Symbolism: Golenpaul, 631]
36. **syringa** of Idaho. [Flower Symbolism: Golenpaul, 630]
37. **violet** of Illinois, New Jersey, Rhode Island, and Wisconsin. [Flower Symbolism: Golenpaul, 630]
38. **white pine cone and tassel** of Maine. [Flower Symbolism: Golenpaul, 633]
39. **wild prairie rose** of North Dakota. [Flower Symbolism: Golenpaul, 639]
40. **wild rose** of Iowa. [Flower Symbolism: Golenpaul, 631]
41. **yucca** of New Mexico. [Flower Symbolism: Golenpaul, 638]

273. FLOWERS

1. **Anthea** epithet of Hera, meaning “flowery.” [Gk. Myth.: Zimmerman, 121]
2. **Anthesteria** ancient Athenian festival, celebrating flowers and new wine. [Gk. Hist.: Misc.]
3. ***Black Tulip, The*** Dumas romance involved with tulipomania of 17th-century Holland. [Fr. Lit.: Benét, 111]
4. **Chloris** goddess of flowers. [Gk. Myth.: Kravitz, 59]
5. **Tournament of Roses** New Year’s Day flower festival and parade in Pasadena. [Am. Cult.: *WB*, C:45]
6. **Zephyr and Flora** wedded pair, scatter flowers from cornucopia. [Rom. Myth.: Hall, 125]

274. FLYING

1. **Daedalus** flew with wings of wax and feathers. [Gk. Myth.: Bulfinch]
2. **Dolor** possesses magic cloak which permits flight. [Children’s Lit.: *The Little Lame Prince*]
3. **Dumbo** little elephant’s huge ears take him up and away. [Am. Cinema: *Dumbo* in *Disney Films,* 49–53]

4. **Houssain** rode upon magic carpet that could fly. [Arab. Lit.: *Arabian Nights,* "Ahmed and Paribanou"]
5. **Icarus** Daedalus's son whose wings disintegrated in flight when approaching the sun. [Gk. Myth.: Kravitz, 126]
6. **Pegasus** winged horse. [Class. Myth.: Zimmerman, 195]
7. **Phaëthon** ill-fated driver of the chariot of sun. [Gk. Myth.: *Metamorphoses*]
8. **Seagull, Johnathan Livingston** seagull spends its time elaborating flying techniques. [Am. Lit.: Richard Bach *Jonathan Livingston Seagull*]
9. **Sindbad** a roc flies him to the Valley of Diamonds, and an eagle flies him to its nest. [Arab. Lit.: *Arabian Nights*]
10. **winged ram** bearer of the golden fleece, sent by Zeus to save the life of Phryxus, who crossed the sea on its back. [Gk. Myth.: Brewer *Dictionary*, 405]

275. FOLLY

1. **Abu Jahl** "father of folly"; opposes Mohammed. [Muslim Tradition: Koran 22:8]
2. **Alnaschar's daydream** spends profits before selling his goods. [Arab. Lit.: *Arabian Nights,* "The Barber's Fifth Night"]
3. ***Bateau, Le*** Matisse's famous painting, displayed in the Museum of Modern Art for 47 days before someone discovered it was being shown upside down. [Am. Hist.: Wallechinsky, 472]
4. **Bay of Pigs, the** disastrous U.S.-backed invasion of Cuba (1961). [Am. Hist.: Van Doren, 577]
5. **Chamberlain, Arthur Nevil** British Prime Minister attempted to avert war by policy of appeasement. [Eur. Hist.: *Collier's*, IV, 552]
6. **columbine** traditional symbol of folly. [Plant Symbolism: *Flora Symbolica,* 173]
7. **dog returning to his vomit** and so the fool to his foolishness. [O.T.: Proverbs 26:11]
8. **Fulton's Folly** the first profitable steamship, originally considered a failure. [Am. Hist.: *NCE,* 1025]
9. **Gotham** English village proverbially noted for the folly (sometimes wisely deliberate) of its residents. [Eng. Folklore: Brewer *Dictionary*, 410]
10. **Grand, Joseph** spends years writing novel; only finishes first sentence. [Fr. Lit.: *The Plague*]
11. **Hamburger Hill** bloody Viet Nam battle over strategically worthless objective (1969). [Am. Hist.: Van Doren, 631]

12. **Howard Hotel** after completing construction, the contractors installed boilers and started fires before discovering they had forgotten to build a chimney. [Am. Hist.: Wallechinsky, 470]
13. **Laputa and Lagada** lands where wise men conduct themselves inanely. [Br. Lit.: *Gulliver's Travels*]
14. **Seward's Folly** Alaska, once seemingly valueless territory which William Henry Seward bought for two cents an acre (1867), thirty years before the Klondike gold rush. [Am. Hist.: Payton, 610]

Foolishness (See DIMWITTEDNESS, STUPIDITY.)

Fools (See CLOWNS.)

276. FOPPISHNESS

1. **Acres, Bob** affected, vain, cowardly, blustery country gentleman. [Br. Lit.: *The Rivals*]
2. **Aguecheek, Sir Andrew** silly old fop, believes himself young. [Br. Lit.: *Twelfth Night*]
3. **Blakeney, Percy** rescuer of French revolution victims disguises himself as brainless fop. [Br. Lit.: *Scarlet Pimpernel*]
4. **Brummel, Beau** (George B. Brummel, 1778–1840) "prince of dandies." [Br. Hist.: *Century Cyclopedia,* 682]
5. **Flutter, Sir Fopling** witless dandy. [Br. Lit.: *The Man of Mode*]
6. **Foppington, Lord** a selfish coxcomb, most intent upon dress and fashion. [Br. Hist.: Brewer *Handbook,* 381]
7. **Kookie** teen idol of 1950s whose character was depicted by slick shirts, tight pants, and "wet look" hairstyle. [TV: "77 Sunset Strip" in Terrace, II, 282–283]
8. **Malyneaux** epitome of the British dandy. [Am. Lit.: *Monsieur Beaucaire,* Magill I, 616–617]
9. **Yankee Doodle Dandy** feather-capped dandy; "handy" with the girls. [Nurs. Rhyme: Opie, 439]

277. FORGERY (See also FRAUDULENCE, HOAX.)

1. **Acta Pilati (Acts of Pilate)** apocryphal account of Crucifixion. [Rom. Hist.: Brewer *Note-Book,* 7]
2. **Altamont, Col. Jack** convicted of forgery; sentenced to transportation; escapes. [Br. Lit.: *Pendennis*]
3. **Caloveglia, Count** creates a bronze statue of a Greek faun and sells it as an authentic antique. [Br. Lit.: *South Wind* in Magill II, 988]
4. **Chatterton** boy poet produced poems allegedly by 15th-century monk. [Br. Hist.: Brewer *Note-Book,* 164]

5. **Constitutum Constantini** so-called Donation of Constantine, a document in which Constantine gave Rome authority over his capital at least a decade before his capital was founded. [Rom. Hist.: Wallechinsky, 45]
6. **Mr. X** by definition, the identity of the greatest forger of all time. [Pop. Culture: Wallechinsky, 47]
7. ***Protocols of the Elders of Zion*** tract purporting to reveal a Jewish conspiracy to control the world. [Jew. Hist.: Wigoder, 170]
8. **Raspigliosi cup** masterpiece attributed to Cellini, discovered in 1984 to have been forged by Reinhold Vasters, 19th-century goldsmith. [Ital. Art: *N. Y. Times*, Feb. 12, 1984]
9. **Rowley poems** the work of Thomas Chatterton (1752–1770), who said they were written by a 15th-century priest. [Br. Hist.: Brewer *Dictionary*, 371]
10. **Vermeer** successful fakes of his paintings went undetected for many years. [Dutch Hist.: Brewer *Dictionary*, 371]

278. FORGETFULNESS (See also CARELESSNESS.)

1. **Absent-Minded Beggar, The** ballad of forgetful soldiers who fought in the Boer War. [Br. Lit.: "The Absent-Minded Beggars" in Payton, 3]
2. **absent-minded professor** personification of one too contemplative to execute practical tasks. [Pop. Culture: Misc.]
3. **jujube** causes loss of memory and desire to return home. [Classical Myth.: Leach, 561–562]
4. **Lethe** river of Hades which induced forgetfulness. [Gk. Myth.: Brewer *Dictionary*, 687; Br. Lit.: *Paradise Lost*; Rom. Lit.: *Aeneid*]
5. **limbo** place or condition of neglect and inattention (from Dante). [Western Folklore: Espy, 124]
6. **Lotophagi** African people, eaters of an amnesia-inducing fruit. [Gk. Lit.: *Odyssey;* Br. Lit.: "The Lotus-Eaters" in Norton, 733–736]
7. **Madison, Percival Wemys** character who no longer remembers his name. [Br. Lit.: *Lord of the Flies*]
8. **soma** drug that induces forgetfulness. [Br. Lit.: *Brave New World*]
9. **Winkle, Rip Van** awakening from 20 years' sleep, forgets how things have changed. [Am. Lit.: *Sketch Book*, Payton, 574]

279. FORGIVENESS

1. **Angelica, Suor** is forgiven by the Virgin Mary for ill-considered suicide. [Ital. Opera: Puccini, *Suor Angelica,* Westerman, 364]
2. **Bishop of Digne** character who forgives Jean Valjean when latter steals the bishop's valuables. [Fr. Lit.: *Les Misérables*]
3. **Christ** forgives man for his sins. [Christianity: Misc.]
4. **fatted calf** killed to celebrate return of prodigal son. [N.T.: Luke 15:23]
5. **Matthias** of his brother, for twenty years' false imprisonment. [Ger. Opera: Kienzl, *The Evangelist,* Westerman, 264]
6. **Melibee** shepherd who pardons his enemies. [Br. Lit.: *Canterbury Tales,* "Tale of Melibee"]
7. **Myriel, Bishop** saintly cleric befriends Jean Valjean after the latter steals his candlesticks. [Fr. Lit.: Victor Hugo *Les Misérables*]
8. **Porgy** of Bess's promiscuity with Crown. [Am. Opera: Gershwin, *Porgy and Bess,* Westerman, 555]
9. **prodigal son** received with open arms by loving father. [N.T.: Luke 15:20–21]
10. **Tannhäuser** unexpectedly absolved by the Pope for sinning in the Venusberg. [Ger. Myth.: Brewer *Dictionary,* 932]
11. **Timberlane, Cass** receives Jinny after her extramarital venture. [Am. Lit.: *Cass Timberlane*]
12. **Titus** Roman emperor pardons those attempting his destruction. [Ger. Opera: Mozart, *La Clemenza di Tito,* Westerman, 100–101]

280. FORTITUDE (See also BRAVERY.)

1. **Asia** despite torture, refuses to deny Moses. [Islam: Walsh *Classical,* 35]
2. **Calantha** fulfills wifely and queenly duties despite losses. [Br. Lit.: *The Broken Heart*]
3. **Corey, Giles** martyred without flinching. [Am. Lit.: *New England Tragedies,* Walsh *Modern,* 106]
4. **helmeted warrior** representation in painting of cardinal virtue. [Art: Hall, 127]
5. **lion** personification of intrepidity. [Animal Symbolism: Hall, 193]
6. **Valley Forge** proving ground of American mettle. [Am. Hist.: Jameson, 519]

Fratricide (See **MURDER**.)

281. FRAUDULENCE (See also FORGERY, HOAX.)

1. **Cagliostro** lecherous peasant posing as count. [Ital. Hist.: Espy, 335]
2. **Confidence Man, the** an imposter who gulls passengers on a Mississippi steamboat. [Am. Lit.: Melville *The Confidence Man* in Magill III, 221]
3. **Duke and the King, the** a pair of charlatans exposed by Huckleberry Finn. [Am. Lit.: Mark Twain *Huckleberry Finn*]
4. **Gantry, Elmer** personifies hypocrisy and corruption in America's religious practices. [Am. Lit.: *Elmer Gantry*]
5. ***Inspector General, The*** pretending to be a government inspector, Khlestakov takes bribes and woos the mayor's wife and daughter. [Russ. Lit.: *The Inspector General*]
6. **Krull, Felix** lives a double life, passing himself off under various identities. [Ger. Lit.: Mann *The Confessions of Felix Krull* in Magill III, 218]
7. ***Medium, The*** Menotti opera about a fraudulent medium haunted by her own hoax. [Am. Opera: Benét, 653]
8. **Mississippi Bubble, the** land speculation scam; ultimately backfired on creators. [Am. Hist.: Jameson, 326]
9. **Pathelin, Master** small-town lawyer cheats his draper, who cheats a shepherd, who hires Pathelin and then cheats him out of his fee. [Fr. Drama: Haydn & Fuller, 466]
10. **Peters, Jeff** made a career out of schemes for bamboozling the public. [Am. Lit.: O. Henry "The Gentle Grafter"]
11. **Sabbatai Zevi** false messiah, head of Kabbalic movement in mid-1600s. [Jew. Hist.: Wigoder, 544]
12. **Schicchi, Gianni** effects a fraudulent will on the pretence that he is the testator. [Ital. Hist. and Opera: *Gianni Schicchi* in *Collier's*]
13. **Sludge, Mr.** medium pretends to greater powers and deceives many people. [Br. Lit.: Browning *Dramatis Personae* in Magill IV, 250]
14. **Tchitchikov** attempts to make a fortune by buying up landlords' titles to dead serfs in order to mortgage them for capital. [Russ. Lit.: Gogol *Dead Souls*]
15. **Tichborne case** false claimant to the Tichborne baronetcy sentenced to fourteen years' imprisonment. [Br. Hist.: Brewer *Dictionary*, 898]
16. **wooden nickel** cheap counterfeits circulating in 1850s America. [Am. Hist.: Brewer *Dictionary*, 1164]

17. **wooden nutmeg** sold by dishonest Connecticut peddlers as real thing. [Am. Hist.: Brewer *Dictionary,* 1164]

282. FREEDOM (See also DELIVERANCE.)

1. **Areopagitica** pamphlet supporting freedom of the press. [Br. Lit.: Benét, 46]
2. **Berihah** 1940s underground railroad for Jews out of East Europe. [Jew. Hist.: Wigoder, 80]
3. **Bill of Rights** (1791) term popularly applied to first 10 Amendments of U.S. Constitution. [Am. Hist.: Payton, 78]
4. **Declaration of Human Rights** (1948) declaration passed by the United Nations; the rights are the individual freedoms usually associated with Western democracy. [World Hist.: Payton, 186]
5. **Declaration of Independence** (1776) document declaring the independence of the North American colonies. [Am. Hist.: Payton, 186]
6. **Declaration of Indulgence** (1672) Charles II's attempt to suspend discrimination against Nonconformists and Catholics. [Br. Hist.: Payton, 186]
7. **Declaration of the Rights of Man** (1789) proclaimed legal equality of man. [Fr. Hist.: Payton, 186]
8. **eagle** widely used as national symbol. [Animal Folklore: Jobes, 213]
9. **Eleutherius** epithet of Zeus, meaning "god of freedom." [Gk. Myth.: Zimmerman, 292]
10. **Fourth of July** American independence day. [Am. Culture: Misc.]
11. **Great Emancipator, The** sobriquet of Abraham Lincoln. [Am. Hist.: Hart, 329]
12. **Henry, Patrick** (1736–1799) famous American patriot known for his statement: "Give me liberty or give me death." [Am. Hist.: Hart, 367]
13. **Jubilee year** fiftieth year; liberty proclaimed for all inhabitants. [O.T.: Leviticus 25:8–13]
14. **Magna Charta** symbol of British liberty. [Br. Hist.: Bishop, 49–52, 213]
15. **Monroe Doctrine** consolidated South American independence; stonewalled European intervention. [Am. Hist.: Jameson, 329–330]
16. **Phrygian cap** presented to slaves upon manumission. [Rom. Hist.: Jobes, 287]

17. **Rütli Oath** legendary pact establishing independence of Swiss cantons (1307). [Swiss Hist.: *NCE,* 2384]
18. **Rienzi** liberator of Rome from warring Colonna and Orsini families. [Ger. Opera: Wagner, *Rienzi,* Westerman, 203]
19. **Runnymede** site of Magna Charta signing (1215). [Br. Hist.: Bishop, 49–52, 213]
20. **Statue of Liberty** perhaps the most famous monument to independence. [Am. Hist.: Jameson, 284]
21. **Underground Railroad** effective means of escape for southern slaves. [Am. Hist.: Jameson, 514]
22. **water willow** indicates independence. [Flower Symbolism: *Flora Symbolica,* 178]

283. FRENZY

1. **Beatlemania** term referring to the Beatles' (rock musicians) immense popularity; manifested by screaming fans in the 1960s. [Pop. Culture: Miller, 172–181]
2. **Big Bull Market** speculation craze precipitated stock market crash (1929). [Am. Hist.: Allen, 205–226]
3. **Gold Rush** lure of instant riches precipitated onslaught of prospectors (1848, 1886). [Am. Hist.: Jameson, 203]
4. **Klondike, the** scene of wild rush for riches (1886). [Am. Hist.: Jameson, 269]
5. **Old Woman of Surrey** "morn, noon, and night in a hurry." [Nurs. Rhyme: *Mother Goose,* 117]
6. **Valentino's funeral** overwhelmed with grief, fans rioted. [Am. Hist.: Sann, 317–327]
7. **White Rabbit** agitated rabbit in a perpetual hurry. [Br. Lit.: *Alice's Adventures in Wonderland*]
8. **White Queen** in a perpetual dither. [Br. Lit.: *Through the Looking-glass*]

284. FRIENDSHIP (See also LOYALTY.)

1. **acacia** traditional symbol of friendship. [Flower Symbolism: *Flora Symbolica,* 172]
2. **Achilles and Patroclus** beloved friends and constant companions, especially during the Trojan War. [Gk. Myth.: Zimmerman, 194]
3. **Amos and Andy** dim-witted Andy Brown and level-headed partner Amos Jones, owners of the Fresh Air Taxi Cab Company. [Radio and TV: "The Amos and Andy Show" in Terrace, I, 54]

4. **Amys and Amylion** the Pylades and Orestes (q.v., below) of the feudal ages. [Medieval Lit.: *LLEI,* I: 269]
5. **Biddy and Pip** "friends for life." [Br. Lit.: *Great Expectations*]
6. **Castor and Pollux** twin brothers who lived and died together. [Gk. Myth.: Zimmerman, 52]
7. **Chingachgook and Natty Bumppo** Chingachgook as Natty Bumppo's constant sidekick and advisor. [Am. Lit.: *The Pathfinder,* Magill I, 715–717]
8. **Damon and Pythias** each agreed to die to save the other. [Gk. Hist.: Espy, 48]
9. **Diomedes and Sthenelus** Sthenelus was the companion and charioteer of Diomedes. [Gk. Myth.: Zimmerman, 248]
10. **Fannie and Edmund Bertram** while others ignored Fannie, he comforted her. [Br. Lit.: *Mansfield Park,* Magill I, 562–564]
11. **Fred and Ethel** the Ricardos' true-blue pals. [TV: "I Love Lucy" in Terrace, I, 383–384]
12. **Friday and Robinson Crusoe** Friday was Robinson Crusoe's sole companion on desert island. [Br. Lit.: *Robinson Crusoe*]
13. **ivy leaves** symbolic of strong and lasting companionship. [Heraldry: Halberts, 31]
14. **Jane Frances de Chantal and Francis de Sales, Sts.** two of most celebrated in Christian annals. [Christian Hagiog.: Attwater, 183]
15. **Jonathan and David** swore compact of love and mutual protection. [O.T.: I Samuel 18:1-3; 20:17]
16. **Lightfoot, Martin and Hereward** Hereward's companion during various wanderings. [Br. Lit.: *Hereward the Wake,* Magill I, 367–370]
17. **Nisus and Euryalus** fought bravely together; Nisus dies rescuing Euryalus. [Rom. Hist.: Wheeler, 259; Rom. Lit.: *Aeneid*]
18. **Peggotty, Clara, and David Copperfield** lifelong friends. [Br. Lit.: *David Copperfield*]
19. **Petronius and Nero** Petronius as nobleman and intimate friend of Nero. [Polish Lit.: *Quo Vadis,* Magill I, 797–799]
20. **Philadelphia** nicknamed "City of Brotherly Love." [Am. Hist.: *NCE,* 2127]
21. **Pylades and Orestes** Pylades willing to sacrifice life for Orestes. [Gk. Lit.: *Oresteia,* Kitto, 68–90]
22. **Standish, Miles and John Alden** best friends, despite their love for Priscilla. [Am. Lit.: "The Courtship of Miles Standish" in Magill I, 165–166]

23. **Theseus and Pirithoüs** Pirithoüs, King of Lapithae, was intimate friend of Theseus, Athenian hero. [Gk. Myth.: Zimmerman, 195]
24. **Three Musketeers, The** three comrades known by motto, "All for one, and one for all." [Fr. Lit.: *The Three Musketeers*]
25. **Tiberge and the Chevalier** Tiberge as ever-assisting shadow of the chevalier. [Fr. Lit.: *Manon Lescaut*]
26. **Wilbur and Charlotte** spider and pig as loyal companions. [Children's Lit.: *Charlotte's Web*]

285. FRIVOLITY

1. **Blondie** the gaffe-prone, frivolous wife of Dagwood Bumstead. [Comics: Horn, 118]
2. **Dobson, Zuleika** charming young lady who unconcernedly dazzles Oxford undergraduates. [Br. Lit.: Magill II, 1169]
3. **Golightly, Holly** madcap New York playgirl, indulges in wacky escapades. [Am. Lit.: Capote *Breakfast at Tiffany's* in Hart, 133]
4. **grasshopper** sings instead of storing away food. [Animal Symbolism: Mercatante, 108]
5. **Lescaut, Manon** amorally chooses luxury above loyalty. [Ital. Opera: Puccini, *Manon Lescaut,* Westerman, 346]
6. **Merry Mount** colonists frolic around Maypole, causing Morton's arrest. [Am. Hist.: Hart, 543]
7. **Misanthrope** exposes frivolity and inconsistency of French society (1600s). [Fr. Lit.: *Le Misanthrope*]
8. **Nickleby, Mrs.** forever introducing inapposite topics into conversations. [Br. Lit.: *Nicholas Nickleby*]
9. **Yorick, Mr.** traveling on the Continent, he and his servant engage in a series of casual love affairs. [Br. Lit.: Sterne *A Sentimental Journey* in Magill I, 879]

286. FRONTIER

1. **Boone, Daniel** (1734–1820) American frontiersman in coonskin cap. [Am. Hist.: Hart, 90]
2. **Bowie, Jim** (1799–1836) frontiersman and U.S. soldier; developed large hunting knife named after him. [Am. Hist.: Payton, 95]
3. **Bumppo, Natty** also known as Leatherstocking, a tough backwoodsman. [Am. Lit.: *Deerslayer; Pathfinder*]
4. **California Joe** (Moses Embree Milner, 1829–1876) frontiersman and scout. [Am. Hist.: *NCE,* 424]

5. ***Virginian, The*** up-and-coming cowpuncher defends his honor, espouses justice, and gains responsibility and a bride. [Am. Lit.: *The Virginian* in Magill I, 1072]

287. FRUSTRATION (See also EXASPERATION, FUTILITY.)

1. **Akaki** poor government clerk saves to buy a new overcoat, only to have it stolen. [Russ. Lit.: Gogol *The Overcoat* in Magill II, 790]
2. **Angstrom, Harry "Rabbit"** former basketball star frustrated by demands of adult life. [Am. Lit.: *Rabbit, Run,* Magill IV, 1042–1044]
3. **Barataria** dishes removed before Sancho tasted them. [Span. Lit.: *Don Quixote*]
4. **Bundren, Addie** family continually thwarted in 9-day attempt to bury her. [Am. Lit.: *As I Lay Dying*]
5. ***Catch-22*** Air Force captain's appeal to be grounded for insanity not granted because desire to avoid combat proves sanity. [Am. Lit.: Joseph Heller *Catch-22*]
6. **coyote** foiled in attempts to enjoy prey. [Am. Ind. Folklore: Mercatante, 77–78]
7. **Henderson the Rain King** character's frustration shown by his continually saying, "I want, I want." [Am. Lit.: *Henderson the Rain King*]
8. **Joseph K** accused of a mysterious crime, fails in his attempts to seek exoneration, and is executed. [Ger. Lit.: Kafka *The Trial*]
9. **K.** continually hindered from gaining entrance to mysterious castle. [Ger. Lit.: *The Castle*]
10. **Old Mother Hubbard** foiled at all attempts to care for dog. [Nurs. Rhyme: Baring-Gould, 111–113]
11. **Raven, The** answer for quests of longing: "Nevermore." [Am. Lit.: "The Raven" in Hart, 656]
12. **Sharpless** frustrated in attempt to prepare Cio-Cio-San for disappointment. [Ital. Opera: Puccini, *Madame Butterfly,* Westerman, 358]
13. **Sisyphus** man condemned to roll up a hill a huge stone which always rolls back before he gets it to the top. [Gk. Myth.: Brewer *Dictionary,* 1006]
14. **Tantalus** condemned in Hades to thirst after receding water. [Gk. Myth.: Brewer *Dictionary,* 1062]
15. ***Three Sisters, The*** sisters live dull, provincial lives, yearning to return to the gay life of Moscow. [Russ. Drama: Benét, 1005]
16. **Watty, Mr.** bankrupt; waits years for court action. [Br. Lit.: *Pickwick Papers*]

288. FUNERAL

1. **Viking funeral** given to Michael Geste by his younger brother, as in their childhood games. [Br. Lit.: P. C. Wren *Beau Geste* in Benét, 87]

289. FUTILITY (See also DESPAIR, FRUSTRATION.)

1. ***American Scene, The*** portrays Americans as having secured necessities; now looking for amenities. [Am. Lit.: *The American Scene*]
2. **Babio** performs the useless and supererogatory. [Fr. Folklore: Walsh *Classical,* 42]
3. **Bellamy, James** character who goes through phases "playboy, war hero" to suicide. [Br. TV: *Upstairs, Downstairs*]
4. **Canute** king of England demonstrated the limits of his power by commanding waves to stand still in vain. [Eng. Legend: Benét, 165]
5. **Danaides** fifty daughters, forty-nine of whom are condemned to Hades to collect water in sieves. [Rom. Myth.: *LLEI,* I: 326]
6. ***Fall, The*** tale of the monotonous life and indifference of modern man. [Fr. Lit.: *The Fall*]
7. **Grandet, Eugénie** lacking everything but wealth, she is indifferent to life. [Fr. Lit.: *Eugénie Grandet,* Magill I, 258–260]
8. **Henry, Frederic** loses lover and child; nothing left. [Am. Lit.: *A Farewell to Arms*]
9. **Moreau, Frederic** law student whose amatory attachments all come to nothing, concludes that existence is futile. [Fr. Lit.: Flaubert *A Sentimental Education* in Magill I, 876]
10. **"Necklace, The"** having lost a borrowed diamond necklace, M. and Mme. Loisel suffer ten years of privation to purchase a duplicate, then find that the original was paste. [Fr. Lit.: Maupassant "The Necklace"]
11. **Ocnus, the cord of** eaten by ass as quickly as it is made. [Gk. and Rom. Myth.: Wheeler, 767]
12. ***Of Mice and Men*** story of George Milton and Lennie Small's futile dream of having their own farm. [Am. Lit.: *Of Mice and Men*]
13. **Partington, Dame** tried to turn back tide with mop. [Br. Hist.: Brewer *Dictionary,* 807]
14. **pearls before swine** Jesus adjures one not to waste best efforts. [N.T.: Matthew 7:6]
15. ***Sun Also Rises, The*** story of American expatriates living a futile existence in Europe. [Am. Lit.: *The Sun Also Rises*]

16. ***Tobacco Road*** tale of Jeeter Lester and other oppressed, degraded lives. [Am. Lit.: *Tobacco Road*]
17. **Tregeagle** condemned to bail out Dozmary Pool with leaky shell. [Br. Legend: Brewer *Dictionary*, 1099]

G

290. GAIETY (See also CHEERFULNESS, JOVIALITY, JOY.)

1. **butterfly orchis** symbol of gaiety. [Plant Symbolism: *Flora Symbolica,* 172]
2. **Gay 90s** the 1890s, a decade of carefree and exciting days in America. [Am. Hist.: Flexner, 162]
3. **"L'Allegro"** pastoral idyll celebrating gaiety and cheerfulness. [Br. Lit.: Milton "L'Allegro"]
4. **Mardi Gras** festive day celebrated at the close of the pre-Lenten season in France and in New Orleans. [Fr. and Am. Trad.: *EB,* VI, 608]
5. **Roaring Twenties, the** the 1920s decade of the Jazz Age and the boom years before the depression. [Am. Hist.: Payton, 515]
6. **shamrock** indicates light-heartedness. [Flower Symbolism: *Flora Symbolica,* 177]

Gallantry (See **CHIVALRY.**)

291. GAMBLING

1. **Atlantic City** New Jersey city has become the Las Vegas of the East. [Am. Hist.: Misc.]
2. **Balibari, Chevalier de** professional gambler and adventurer. [Br. Lit.: *Barry Lyndon*]
3. **Beaujeu, Monsieur de** known for his betting. [Br. Lit.: *Fortunes of Nigel*]
4. **Bet-a-million Gates** wealthy American industrialist John Warne Gates (1855–1911). [Am. Culture: Misc.]
5. **Brady, "Diamond Jim"** (1856–1917) diamond-attired rail magnate and financier who loved to gamble. [Am. Hist.: Payton, 192]
6. **Camptown Races** Foster's ode to betting. [Pop. Music: Van Doren, 192]
7. **Cincinnati Kid, the** "one of the shrewdist gamblers east of the Mississippi." [Cinema: Halliwell, 462]
8. **Clonbrony, Lord** absentee landlord is compulsive gambler. [Br. Lit.: *The Absentee*]
9. **Consus** ancient Roman god of horse-racing and counsel. [Rom. Myth.: Zimmerman, 68]

10. **Detroit, Nathan** his obsession with crap games so persistent that it even keeps him from getting married. [Musical Comedy: Damon Runyon *Guys and Dolls* in *On Stage*, 322]
11. **devil's bones** epithet for dice. [Folklore: Jobes, 436]
12. **Google, Barney** hopelessly in love with the ponies. [Comics: Horn, 99–100]
13. **Ivanovich, Alexei** irrevocably drawn to betting tables. [Russ. Lit.: *The Gambler*]
14. **Las Vegas** city in Nevada notorious for its gambling casinos since 1945. [Am. Hist.: Payton, 382]
15. **Lucky, Mr.** alias Joe Adams, gambler who owns the *Fortuna*, fancy supper club and gambling yacht. [TV: Terrace, II, 117]
16. **Maverick** family name of two brothers, Bret and Bart; self-centered and untrustworthy gentlemen gamblers. [TV: Terrace, II, 80]
17. **Minnie** plays poker to save Jack Johnson's life. [Ital. Opera: Puccini, *Girl of the Golden West*, Westerman, 361]
18. **Monte Carlo** town in Monaco principality, in southeast France; a famous gambling resort. [Fr. Hist.: *NCE*, 1819]
19. **Mutt and Jeff** hapless punters always looking for a quick buck. [Comics: Horn, 508–509]
20. **Pit, the** Board of Trade's cellar, where all bidding occurs. [Am. Lit.: *The Pit*. Magill I, 756–758]
21. **Queen of Spades, The** Aleksandr Pushkin's short story about the downfall of the gambler Germann. [Russ. Lit.: Benét, 833]
22. **Smiley, Jim** bets his frog can outjump any other; loses by sabotage. [Am. Lit.: *The Celebrated Jumping Frog of Calaveras County*]

292. GANGSTERISM (See also OUTLAWRY.)

1. **Black Hand, the** sobriquet for the Mafia. [Am. Hist.: *NCE*, 1657]
2. **Capone, Al "Scarface"** (1899–1947) Chicago mobster, famous gangland bootleg king. [Am. Hist.: Flexner, 73]
3. **Cosa Nostra** secret organization akin to the Mafia; operates in the U.S. [Am. Hist.: Misc.]
4. **Detroit Purple Gang** gangster mob of the 1920s. [Am. Hist.: *NCE*, 2018]
5. **Godfather** "father figure" to the Mafia. [Am. Lit.: *The Godfather;* Am. Cinema: Halliwell, 297]
6. **Krik, Benya** tough Jewish gangster of Odessa. [Russ. Lit.: *Benya Krik, the Gangster*]

7. **Little Caesar** archetypal gangster. [Am. Cinema: Griffith, 269]
8. ***M*** criminals are so revolted by the murder of several children that they search and capture the murderer. [Ger. Cinema: Halliwell, 256]
9. **Mafia** sinister crime syndicate promotes violence to achieve goals. [Am. Hist.: *NCE,* 1657]
10. **Syndicate** organized crime unit throughout major cities of the United States. [Am. Hist.: *NCE,* 2018]

293. GENERATION GAP

1. ***Fathers and Sons*** Turgenev novel depicts conflicts of politics and generations. [Russ. Lit.: Benét, 341]
2. **Pontifex, Theobald** domineering father disinherits his unworldly son. [Br. Lit.: Butler *The Way of All Flesh* in Magill I, 1097]
3. **Wynne, Hugh** never wins the understanding or favor of his stern Quaker father. [Am. Lit.: *Hugh Wynne, Free Quaker*; Magill I, 390]

294. GENEROSITY (See also AID, ORGANIZATIONAL; KINDNESS.)

1. **Abbé Constantin** self-sacrificing priest; curé of Longueral. [Fr. Lit.: *The Abbé Constantin,* Walsh *Modern,* 105]
2. **Amelia** takes interest in Paul. [Br. Lit.: *Dombey and Son*]
3. **Antonio** lends money gratis. [Br. Lit.: *Merchant of Venice*]
4. **Appleseed, Johnny** (John Chapman, 1774–1845) gave settlers apple seeds and a helping hand. [Am. Hist.: Hart, 146]
5. **Baboushka** female Santa Claus on Feast of Epiphany. [Russ. Folklore: Walsh *Classical,* 50]
6. **Befana** female Santa Claus who comes at Epiphany. [Ital. Legend: Walsh *Classical,* 50]
7. **Bountiful, Lady** benevolent, beneficent, but a bit overbearing. [Br. Lit.: *Beaux' Stratagem,* Espy, 129]
8. **buffalo** heraldic symbol of unselfishness. [Heraldry: Halberts, 21]
9. **bull** heraldic symbol of magnanimity. [Heraldry: Halberts, 21]
10. **Burchell, Mr.** gave to the poor. [Br. Lit.: *Vicar of Wakefield*]
11. **Cinderella** feeds beggar whom sisters scorn. [Ital. Opera: Rossini, *Cinderella,* Westerman, 120–121]
12. **Dāna** almsgiving to poor, giftgiving to priests. [Hindu Rel.: Parrinder, 72]
13. **Ephron** tried unsuccessfully to give Abraham free burial-ground. [O.T.: Genesis 23:10–16]
14. **Hood, Robin** robbed rich to help poor. [Br. Lit.: *Robin Hood*]

15. **Maecenas** to poets, esp. Virgil, as a patron. [Rom. Hist.: Espy, 123]
16. **Nicholas, St.** bringer of presents to children on Christmas. [Folklore: Wheeler, 327]
17. **Rosie** could not deny love to anyone. [Br. Lit.: *Cakes and Ale*]
18. **Salvation Army** (officially called Volunteers of America) organization devoted to helping unfortunates. [Am. Hist.: Jameson, 443]
19. **Santa Claus** gives gifts to children on Christmas. [Folklore: Walsh *Classical,* 50]
20. **shmoo** ham-shaped beast that laid eggs, provided milk, and happily gave its flesh to the hungry. [Am. Comics: *Li'l Abner*]
21. **Trot, Tommy** sold bed to buy wife a mirror. [Nurs. Rhyme: Opie, 416]
22. **Twelve Days of Christmas** presents increase with each day of Yuletide. [Am. Music: "Twelve Days of Christmas" in Rockwell]
23. **Twm Shon Catti** Welsh Robin Hood. [Welsh Hist.: Brewer *Dictionary,* 1110]
24. **Unferth** offers Beowulf finest sword in kingdom. [Br. Lit.: *Beowulf*]
25. **Vincent de Paul, St.** worked and gave prodigiously of himself to poor. [Christian Hagiog.: Attwater, 337]
26. **widow's mite** poor woman's contribution of all she had. [N.T.: Mark, 12: 42–44; Luke 21:2–4]

295. GENIUS (See also WISDOM.)

1. **Aquinas, St. Thomas** (1225–1274) preeminent mind of medieval church. [Eur. Hist.: Bishop, 273–274]
2. **Aristotle** (384–322 B.C.) famous Greek philosopher of *a priori* reasoning. [Gk. Hist.: *NCE,* 147]
3. **Aronnax, Prof.** scholarly mental giant; Capt. Nemo's captive guest. [Fr. Lit.: *Twenty Thousand Leagues Under the Sea*]
4. **Jean-Christophe** musical prodigy who, in an adventurous life, becomes a world-famous musician. [Fr. Lit.: Romain Rolland *Jean-Christophe*; Magill I, 439]
5. **Leverkühn, Adrian** a composer who imagines he has made a pact with the devil, and achieves greatness. [Ger. Lit.: Thomas Mann *Doctor Faustus*]
6. **Nemo, Captain** epitome of the genius in science fiction; inventor and creator of fabulous submarine, *Nautilus*. [Fr. Lit.: *Twenty Thousand Leagues Under the Sea*]

296. GENOCIDE (See also BRUTALITY, MASSACRE.)

1. **Auschwitz** largest Nazi extermination camp; more than 1,000,000 deaths there. [Ger. Hist.: *Hitler*, 958–959, 970, 1123]
2. **Babi Yar** ravine near Kiev where Nazis slaughtered 10,000 Jews. [Russ. Hist.: Wigoder, 56]
3. **Bergen-Belsen** Nazi slave labor and extermination camp. [Ger. Hist.: *Hitler*, 1187, 1188]
4. **Buchenwald** showcase of Nazi atrocities. [Ger. Hist.: *Hitler*, 1055]
5. **Dachau** primarily work camp, experienced share of Nazi horrors. [Ger. Hist.: *Hitler*, 1055]
6. **Final Solution** Nazi plan decided fate of 6,000,000 Jews. [Ger. Hist.: *Hitler*, 1037–1061]
7. **Holocaust** Nazi attempt at extermination of European Jewry (1933–1945). [Jew. Hist.: Wigoder, 266–267]
8. **Lublin** Nazi extermination camp. [Ger. Hist.: *Hitler*, 970]
9. **Majdanek** Nazi extermination camp. [Ger. Hist.: Wigoder, 113]
10. **My Lai** American army division annihilates population of entire Vietnamese hamlet (March 16, 1968). [Am. Hist.: Kane, 450]
11. **Ravensbrueck** women's concentration camp in Germany. [Ger. Hist.: Shirer, 1275]
12. **Sachsenhausen** Nazi concentration camp. [Ger. Hist.: Shirer, 375]
13. **Six Million Jews** their deaths a testimony to Nazi "Final Solution." [Eur. Hist.: *Hitler*, 1123]
14. **Treblinka** Nazi extermination camp. [Ger. Hist.: *Hitler*, 970]
15. **Wannsee Conference** "Final Solution" plotted and scheduled. [Ger. Hist.: Wigoder, 619]
16. **Zyklon B** hydrogen cyanide; used by Nazis for mass extermination in concentration camps. [Ger. Hist.: *Hitler*, 970]

297. GENTLENESS

1. **Brown, Matilda** meek, mild heroine. [Br. Lit.: *Cranford*]
2. **Casper the Friendly Ghost** meek little ghost who desires only to make friends. [Comics: Horn, 162]
3. **Cordelia** gentle daughter of Lear. [Br. Lit.: *King Lear*]
4. **Eliante** her kind heart contrasted with Celimene's caustic wit. [Fr. Lit.: *Le Misanthrope*]
5. **Gentle Ben** massive but extremely tame bear. [TV: Terrace, I, 302]
6. **mallow** traditional symbol of gentleness or mildness. [Plant Symbolism: *Flora Symbolica*, 175]

7. **March, Beth** the domestic, sensitive, sweater-knitting March daughter. [Am. Lit.: *Little Women*]
8. **Virgilia** meek, gentle wife of Coriolanus. [Br. Lit.: *Coriolanus*]
9. **Wilkes, Melanie** gentle, mild-mannered, dutiful Southern wife. [Am. Lit.: *Gone With the Wind*]

298. GENUINENESS

1. **acid test** test of genuineness for gold; not destructive of genuine metal. [Assaying: Brewer *Dictionary,* 7]
2. **Bible** name used for Scriptures; "the real source of truth." [Christianity: *NCE,* 291]
3. **Gospel** one of the four biographies of Jesus Christ that begin the New Testament; thus, "the real beginning of Christianity." [Christianity: *NCE,* 1112]
4. **Pure, Simon** young quaker who Colonel Feignwell impersonates to marry Pure's ward. [Am. Lit.: *A Bold Stroke for a Wife,* Brewer *Handbook,* 1008]
5. **Real McCoy, the** probably originally McKay, a Scotch whisky; the term now alludes to the "first or best of its kind" or "the actual one." [Pop. Culture: Payton, 409]
6. **To Tell the Truth** question-and-answer probe to determine which of three people is the "the real McCoy." [TV: Terrace, II, 383]

299. GHOST

1. **Akakyevich, Akakii** his ghost steals coats off people's backs. [Russ. Lit.: Gogol *The Overcoat*]
2. **Alfonso** the murdered prince returns as a ghost to frustrate the usurper and proclaim the true heir. [Br. Lit.: Walpole *The Castle of Otranto* in Magill I, 124]
3. **Alonzo the Brave** appears as ghost to lover. [Br. Lit.: "Alonzo the Brave" in Walsh *Modern,* 14]
4. **Andrea** ghost returns to the Spanish court to learn of the events that followed his death. [Br. Drama: *The Spanish Tragedy* in Magill II, 990]
5. **Angels of Mons** a spectral army of angels that supposedly came between German and British forces (1914). [Br. and Fr. Hist.: Wallechinsky, 447]
6. **Banquo** his ghost appears to Macbeth at a banquet, sitting in Macbeth's own seat. [Br. Drama: Shakespeare *Macbeth*]
7. **Bhta** haunter of cemeteries; attendant of Shiva. [Hindu Myth.: Parrinder, 45]

8. ***Blithe Spirit*** ghost of witty first wife returns to mock her husband and his second wife. [Br. Drama: Noel Coward *Blithe Spirit* in *On Stage*, 236]
9. **Caesar's ghost** warns Brutus that he and Caesar will meet again at Phillipi. [Br. Lit.: Shakespeare *Julius Caesar*]
10. **Canterville ghost** after haunting an English house for three centuries, disappeared forever when new American owners refused to take him seriously. [Br. Lit.: Oscar Wilde "The Canterville Ghost"]
11. **Casper** meek little ghost who desires only to make friends. [Am. Comics: "Casper the Friendly Ghost" in Horn, 162]
12. ***Devil and Daniel Webster, The*** Webster defends his client before a jury of the ghosts of American villains. [Am. Lit.: Haydn & Fuller, 382]
13. **Drury Lane Theater Ghost** said to bring great acting success to those who see it. [Br. Folklore: Wallechinsky, 446]
14. **Epworth Poltergeist** supposedly invaded the house of Rev. Samuel Wesley. [Am. Folklore: Wallechinsky, 446]
15. **Flying Dutchman** ghost ship off Cape of Good Hope; sighting it forbodes disaster. [Folklore: Brewer *Note-Book*, 335]
16. ***Ghost and Mrs. Muir, The*** New England cottage haunted by the spirit of its 19th-century owner. [Am. TV: Terrace]
17. ***Ghost Goes West, The*** merry Scottish ghost follows his castle when it is moved to America. [Am. Cinema: Halliwell]
18. **Ghost of Charles Rosmer, the** itinerant peddler returns to the property where he was murdered. [Folklore: Wallechinsky, 446]
19. **Ghost of Christmas Past, the** Scrooge's first monitor; spirit presenting past. [Br. Lit.: *A Christmas Carol*]
20. **Ghost of Christmas Present, the** Scrooge's second monitor; spirit presenting present. [Br. Lit.: *A Christmas Carol*]
21. **Ghost of Christmas Yet to Come, the** Scrooge's third monitor; spirit presenting future. [Br. Lit.: *A Christmas Carol*]
22. **Ghost of Hamlet's Father, the** appears to the prince, states he was murdered by Claudius and demands revenge. [Br. Lit.: *Hamlet*]
23. **Ghost's Walk, the** spirit and step of Lady Morbury Dedlock. [Br. Lit.: *Bleak House*]
24. **Glas, Bodach** ghostly bearer of evil tidings. [Br. Lit.: *Waverley*]
25. **Headless Horseman, the** phantom who scares Ichabod Crane out of his wits. [Am. Lit.: *The Legend of Sleepy Hollow and Other Stories*]
26. **Homunculus** formless spirit of learning. [Ger. Lit.: *Faust*]

27. **Kirby, George and Marian** ghosts who occupy Topper's house. [TV: "Topper" in Terrace II, 381]
28. **Ligeia** months after her own death and the narrator's remarriage, she materializes upon the death of his second wife. [Am. Lit.: Poe *Ligeia*]
29. **Marley** the friendly ghost who helps Ebenezer Scrooge become more benevolent. [Br. Lit.: *A Christmas Carol*]
30. **Mauthe Doog** ghostly black spaniel that haunted Peel Castle. [Br. Folklore: Benét, 649]
31. **Morland, Catherine** terrified by imagined ghosts at the medieval abbey where she is a guest. [Br. Lit.: *Northanger Abbey* in Benét, 720]
32. **Nighe, Bean** ghost of a woman who died in childbirth. [Scot. Folklore: Briggs, 15–16]
33. ***Phantom of the Opera, The*** deformed man haunts opera house for vengeance. [Am. Cinema: Halliwell, 562]
34. **Phantom, The** mysterious, ghostlike foe of injustice in a mythical African-Asian country. [Am. Comics: Horn, 551]
35. **Quint, Peter and Miss Jessel** former lovers return to haunt house. [Am. Lit.: *The Turn of the Screw*]
36. **Richard III** visited by the ghosts of all his victims. [Br. Lit.: Shakespeare *Richard III*]
37. ***Ruddigore*** the ghosts of his ancestors confront the current baronet and change his life. [Br. Opera: Gilbert and Sullivan *Ruddigore*]
38. **Samuel** his spirit appears to Saul through the witch of Endor. [O.T.: I Samuel 28:24]
39. **Short Hoggers of Whittinghame** ghost of baby murdered by his mother cannot rest because he is "nameless." [Br. Folklore: Briggs, 363–364]
40. **Topper** house he purchases is haunted by the young couple who owned it previously and their dog. [Am. Lit., Cin., TV: *Topper* in Halliwell, 718]
41. **Vermilion Phantom** ghost rumored to have appeared at various times in French history, such as before deaths of Henry IV and Napoleon. [Fr. History: Wallechinsky, 445]
42. **White House Ghost** several people supposedly saw Abraham Lincoln's ghost there. [Am. Folklore: Wallechinsky, 447]
43. **White Lady** ghost seen in different castles and palaces belonging to Prussia's royal family. [Prussian Folklore: Brewer *Handbook*, 1207]

44. **White Lady of Avenel** "a tutelary spirit." [Br. Lit.: *The Monastery,* Brewer *Handbook,* 1208]
45. **White Lady of Ireland** the domestic spirit of a family; intimates approaching death with shrieks [Irish Folklore: Brewer *Handbook,* 1208]
46. **Wild Huntsman** spectral hunter with dogs who frequents the Black Forest. [Ger. Folklore: Brewer *Handbook,* 1207]

300. GIANTISM (See also TALLNESS.)

1. **Albion** son of Neptune and ancestor of England. [Br. Lit.: *Faerie Queene*]
2. **Alcyoneus** one of the Titans. [Gk. Myth.: Kravitz, 17]
3. **Aloeidae** name given to twins Otus and Ephialtes. [Gk. Myth.: Kravitz, 17]
4. **Anakim** race of tall men routed by Joshua. [O.T.: Numbers 13:32–33]
5. **Antaeus** colossal wrestler slain by Hercules. [Gk. Myth.: Brewer *Dictionary,* 38]
6. **Antigonus** giant nicknamed the Hand-Tosser. [Belgian Legend: Walsh *Classical,* 25]
7. **Ascapart** thirty feet tall; defeated by Sir Bevis. [Medieval Romance: Walsh *Classical,* 34]
8. **Atlas** Titan condemned to support world on his shoulders. [Gk. Myth.: Brewer *Handbook,* 13]
9. **Babe, the Blue Ox** Paul Bunyan's gigantic animal-of-all-work. [Am. Folklore: Spiller, 720]
10. **Balan** strong and courageous colossus. [Span. Lit.: *Amadis de Gaul*]
11. **Balor** Formorian giant with evil eye. [Irish Myth.: Benét, 76]
12. **Beaver, Tony** equals mythical exploits of Paul Bunyan. [Am. Lit.: *Up Eel River*]
13. **Bellerus** a Cornish giant. [Br. Lit.: Brewer *Handbook,* 108]
14. **Blunderbore** nursery tale giant killed by Jack. [Br. Lit.: Brewer *Dictionary,* 128]
15. **Brobdingnag** country of people twelve times the size of men. [Br. Lit.: *Gulliver's Travels*]
16. **Bunyan, Paul** legendary lumberjack who accomplished prodigious feats. [Am. Folklore: Brewer *Dictionary,* 163]
17. **Cardiff giant** a gypsum statue passed off as a petrified prehistoric man till revealed as a hoax (1869). [Am. Hist.: *EB* (1963), 9: 533]
18. **Clytius** son of Uranus and Gaea. [Gk. Myth.: Kravitz, 64]

19. **Colossos** a gigantic brazen statue 126 ft. high executed by Charês for the harbor at Rhodes. [Gk. Hist.: Brewer *Handbook*, 226]
20. **Cormoran** nursery tale giant felled by Jack. [Br. Lit.: Brewer *Dictionary*, 262]
21. **Cyclopes** race of one-eyed, gigantic men. [Gk. Lit.: *Odyssey;* Arab. Lit.: *Arabian Nights,* "Sindbad the Sailor," Third Voyage]
22. **Egil** giant who watched over Thor's goats. [Norse Myth.: *LLEI*, I: 327]
23. **Enceladus** powerful giant whose hisses cause volcanic eruptions. [Gk. Myth.: Kravitz, 88]
24. **Ephialtes and Otus** nine fathoms tall; threatened to battle Olympian gods. [Gk. Myth.: Leach, 39; Gk. Lit.: *Iliad*]
25. **Ferragus** the Portuguese giant who took the empress Bellisant under his care. [Br. Lit.: "Valentine and Orson" in Brewer *Handbook*, 364]
26. **Foawr** stone-throwing slaughterer of cattle. [Br. Folklore: Briggs, 178]
27. **Galapos** giant slain by King Arthur. [Br. Lit.: *History of Arthur*, Brewer *Handbook*, 400]
28. **Gargantua** royal giant who required 17,913 cows for personal milk supply. [Fr. Lit.: *Gargantua and Pantagruel*]
29. **Glumdalca, Queen** captive giantess in love with Tom. [Br. Lit.: *Tom Thumb*]
30. **Gog and Magog** two Cornish giants taken captive by Brutus, legendary founder of Britain. [Br. Legend: Brewer *Dictionary*, 471]
31. **Goliath** towering Philistine giant slain by youthful David. [O.T.: I Samuel 17:49–51]
32. **Jack-in-Irons** gigantic figure that attacks lonely wayfarers. [Br. Folklore: Briggs, 237]
33. **Jolly Green Giant** trademark comes alive in animated commercials. [Am. Advertising: Misc.]
34. **Jotunn** race of giants frequently in conflict with gods. [Norse Myth.: Leach, 559]
35. **King Kong** giant ape brought to New York as "eighth wonder of world." [Am. Cinema: Payton, 367]
36. **Long Meg of Westminster;** 16th-century giantess. [Br. Hist.: Espy, 337]
37. **Lubbard Fiend** brownie of gigantic size. [Br. Folklore: Briggs, 270–272]

38. **Miller, Maximilian Christopher** the Saxon giant. [Br. Hist.: Brewer *Handbook*, 706]
39. **Mimir** gigantic god of primeval ocean. [Norse Myth.: Leach, 728]
40. **Morgante** ferocious giant converted to Christianity. [Ital. Lit.: *Morgante Maggiore*, Wheeler, 248]
41. **Nephilim** race dwelling in Canaan before Israelites. [O.T.: Genesis 6:4]
42. **Og** giant who attacked Israelites. [O.T.: Deuteronomy 3:2]
43. **Orgoglio** a hideous giant, as tall as three men; son of Earth and Wind. [Gk. Myth.: Brewer *Handbook*, 780]
44. **Orion** colossus of great beauty and hunting skill. [Gk. and Rom. Myth.: Wheeler, 271]
45. **Pantagruel** gigantic, virtuous king who needed 4,600 cows to nurse him. [Fr. Lit.: *Gargantua and Pantagruel*]
46. **Polyphemus** cruel monster; one of the Cyclopes. [Gk. Lit.: *Odyssey;* Rom. Lit.: *Aeneid*]
47. **Titans** lawless children of Uranus and Gaea. [Gk. Myth.: Brewer *Dictionary*, 1086]
48. **Tityus** son of Zeus; body covered nine acres. [Gk. and Rom. Myth.: Wheeler, 368]
49. **Typhon** fire-breathing colossus. [Gk. and Rom. Myth.: Wheeler, 373]
50. **Utgard** residence of colossi. [Norse Myth.: Brewer *Dictionary*, 1120]
51. **Ymir** father of the giant race. [Norse Myth.: Wheeler, 395]

301. GLOOMINESS

1. **Cimmerians** dwellers in the land beyond Ocean, where the sun never shone. [Gk. Myth.: *Odyssey* XI:14]
2. **Nilfheim** region of everlasting night and endless cold. [Scand. Myth.: Brewer *Dictionary*, 642]

302. GLUTTONY (See also GREED.)

1. **Belch, Sir Toby** gluttonous and lascivious fop. [Br. Lit.: *Twelfth Night*]
2. **Biggers, Jack** one of the best known “feeders” of eighteenth-century England. [Br. Hist.: Wallechinsky, 377]
3. **Ciacco** Florentine damned to the third circle of Hell for gluttony. [Ital. Lit.: Dante *Inferno*]
4. **crab** loves to devour oysters. [Medieval Animal Symbolism: White, 210–211]

5. **Dagwood** relieves tensions by making and eating gargantuan sandwiches. [Comics: "Blondie" in Horn, 118]
6. **Fat Freddy** character who loves food more than anything else. [Comics: "The Fabulous Furry Freak Brothers" in Horn, 239–240]
7. **Gargantua** enormous eater who ate salad lettuces as big as walnut trees. [Fr. Lit.: Brewer Handbook, 406]
8. **Gastrolaters** people worshiped food in the form of Manduce. [Fr. Lit.: *Pantagruel*]
9. **hedgehog** attribute of gourmandism personified. [Animal Symbolism: Hall, 146]
10. **Jones, Nicely Nicely** Damon Runyon's Broadway glutton. [Am. Lit. and Drama: *Guys and Dolls*]
11. **Jughead** character renowned for his insatiable hankering for hamburgers. [Comics: "Archie" in Horn, 87]
12. **Laphystius** epithet of Zeus, meaning "gluttonous." [Gk. Myth. Zimmerman, 292–293]
13. **Lucullus** Roman epicure chiefly remembered for his enormous consumption of food. [Rom. Hist.: Payton, 406]
14. **lupin** traditional symbol of voracity. [Plant Symbolism: *Flora Symbolica,* 175]
15. **Manduce** idol worshiped by the Gastrolaters. [Fr. Lit.: *Pantagruel*]
16. **Pantagruel** son of Gargantua noted for his continual thirst. [Fr. Lit.: Jobes, II, 1234]
17. **Snorkel, Sergeant** character devoted to God, country, and belly. [Comics: "Beetle Bailey" in Horn, 106]
18. **Sobakevitch** huge, bearlike landowner astonishes banquet guests by devouring an entire sturgeon. [Russ. Lit.: Gogol *Dead Souls*]
19. **Stivic, Michael "Meathead"** Archie's son-in-law; has insatiable appetite. [TV: "All in the Family" in Terrace, I, 47]
20. **Willey, Walter** servant who achieved fame through his public gluttony. [Br. Hist.: Wallechinsky, 378]
21. **Wimpy, J. Wellington** Popeye's companion, a corpulent dandy with a tremendous capacity for hamburgers. [Comics: "Thimble Theater" in Horn, 657–658]
22. **Winnie-the-Pooh** lovable, bumbling devourer of honey. [Children's Lit.: *Winnie-the-Pooh*]
23. **Wood, Nicholas** his gastronomic abilities inspired poems and songs; at one historic sitting, he consumed all the edible meat of a sheep. [Br. Hist.: Wallechinsky, 378]

24. **Wood, Willy** "ate up cream cheese, roast beef, piecrust"; incessant eater. [Nurs. Rhyme: Baring-Gould, 158]
25. **Yogi Bear** character with insatiable appetite; always stealing picnic baskets from visitors to Jellystone Park. [Am. Comics: Misc.; TV: Terrace, II, 448–449]

303. GOD

1. **Abba** title of reverence for God the Father. [N.T.: Mark 14:36; Romans 8:15]
2. **Adonai** spoken in place of the ineffable Yahweh. [Judaism: *NCE,* 22]
3. **Aesir** the Teutonic pantheon. [Norse Myth.: Leach, 17]
4. **Ahura Mazda (Ormuzd, Ormazd)** the spirit of good and creator of all things. [Zoroastrianism: Payton, 11]
5. **Allah** Arabic name of the Supreme Being. [Islam: Benét, 24]
6. **Amen-Ra** national and chief god of Egyptians. [Egypt. Myth.: Leach, 42]
7. **Ancient of Days** scriptural epithet for God. [O.T.: Daniel 7:9]
8. **Assur** principal god. [Assyrian Myth.: Benét, 59]
9. **Brahman** supreme soul of the universe. [Hindu Phil.: Parrinder, 50]
10. **Buddha** "the Enlightened One"; mystical supremacy. [Hinduism: Payton, 108]
11. **Creator, the** common sobriquet for God. [Pop. Usage: Misc.]
12. **El** rare Biblical appellation of the Lord. [Judaism: Wigoder, 169]
13. **Elohim** spoken in place of the ineffable Yahweh. [Judaism: *NCE,* 22]
14. **Huitzilopochtli** supreme war god of the Aztecs. [Aztec Religion: *NCE,* 1286]
15. **Jehovah** the ancient Hebrew name for God. [Heb. Lang.: *NCE,* 1407]
16. **Manitou** supreme deity of Algonquin and neighboring tribes. [Am. Indian Religion: *Collier's,* X, 91]
17. **Marduk** warrior god, chief of the Babylonian pantheon; creator of heaven, earth, and man. [Babylonian Myth.: Benét, 634]
18. **Ormuzd** supreme deity and embodiment of good. [Persian Myth.: Wheeler, 272]
19. **Osiris** supreme deity and ruler of eternity. [Ancient Egyptian Myth.: Benét, 745]
20. **Quetzalcoatl** god of the Toltecs. [Toltec Religion: *NCE,* 2258]

21. **rays, garland of** emblem of God the Father. [Christian Iconog.: Jobes, 374]
22. **Sat Nam** true name of the one God inclusive of all others. [Indian Religion: *Collier's*, XVII, 304]
23. **Shekinah** equivalent for Lord in Aramaic interpretation of Old Testament. [Targumic Lit.: Brewer *Dictionary*, 991]
24. **Tetragrammaton** Hebrew word for Lord: YHWH; pronunciation forbidden. [Judaism: Wigoder, 593]
25. **Yahweh** reconstruction of YHWH, ancient Hebrew name for God. [Heb. Lang.: *NCE*, 3019]

304. GOODNATUREDNESS (See also CHEERFULNESS.)

1. **Booth, Amelia** good-natured heroine. [Br. Lit.: *Amelia*]
2. **Boythorn, Laurence** amiable, pleasant character. [Br. Lit.: *Bleak House*]
3. **Cadwallader, Rev. Mr.** pleasant and cheery rector. [Br. Lit.: *Middlemarch*]
4. **Cheshire Cat** imperturbable cat with perpetual grin. [Br. Lit.: *Alice's Adventures in Wonderland*]
5. **Coverley, Sir Roger de** soul of amiability. [Br. Lit.: *The Spectator*, Walsh *Modern*, 108]
6. **Good Joe** personification for a good-hearted, obliging person. [Pop. Culture: Payton, 278]
7. **Herf, Jimmy** newspaper reporter as everybody's friend. [Am. Lit.: *The Manhattan Transfer*]
8. **jasmine** traditional representation of a pleasant nature. [Flower Symbolism: *Flora Symbolica*, 175]
9. **white mullein** indicates amiability. [Flower Symbolism: *Flora Symbolica*, 178]

Goodness (See **KINDNESS.**)

305. GOSSIP (See also SLANDER.)

1. **assembly of women** symbolizes gossip in dream context. [Dream Lore: Jobes, 143]
2. **Blondie and Tootsie** two characters continually gossiping from morning to night. [Comics: "Blondie" in Horn, 118]
3. **Duchess of Berwick** rumor-jabbering woman upsets Lady Windermere. [Br. Lit.: *Lady Windermere's Fan*, Magill I, 488–490]
4. **Norris, Mrs.** Fanny's aunt, the universal type of busybody. [Br. Lit.: *Mansfield Park*, Magill I, 562–564]

5. **Peyton Place** New Hampshire town where everyone knows everyone else's business. [Am. Lit.: *Peyton Place,* Payton, 523]
6. **Sneerwell, Lady** leader of a group that creates and spreads malicious gossip. [Br. Drama: Sheridan *The School for Scandal*]

Gourmandism (See **EPICUREANISM, GLUTTONY.**)

Graciousness (See **COURTESY, HOSPITALITY.**)

306. GRATITUDE

1. **agrimony** traditional symbol for gratitude. [Flower Symbolism: *Flora Symbolica,* 172]
2. **Androcles** because he had once extracted a thorn from its paw, the lion refrained from attacking Androcles in the arena. [Rom. Lit.: Brewer *Dictionary,* 33]
3. **Canticle of the Sun, The** St. Francis of Assisi's pantheistic hymn of thanks. [Christian Hagiog.: Bishop, 296]
4. **Hannah** jubilantly thankful to God for giving son.
5. **Magwitch, Abel** amply repays Pip for having helped him when in desperate straits. [Br. Lit.: Dickens *Great Expectations*]
6. **Noah's altar** built to thank God for safe landing. [O.T.: Genesis 8:20–21]
7. **Thanksgiving Day** American holiday acknowledging God's favor. [Am. Culture: Brewer *Dictionary,* 1071]

307. GREED (See also STINGINESS.)

1. ***Almayer's Folly*** lust for gold leads to decline. [Br. Lit.: *Almayer's Folly*]
2. **Alonso** Shakespearean symbol of avarice. [Br. Lit.: *The Tempest*]
3. **Béline** fans husband's hypochondria to get his money. [Fr. Lit.: *Le Malade Imaginaire*]
4. **Barak's wife** agrees to sell shadow, symbol of her fertility. [Aust. Opera: R. Strauss, *Woman Without a Shadow,* Westerman, 432]
5. **Brown, Joe** turns in partner Joe Christmas for reward money. [Am. Lit.: *Light in August*]
6. ***Common Lot, The*** the get-rich-quick club. [Am. Lit.: *The Common Lot,* Hart, 369]
7. **Crawley, Pitt** inherits, marries, and hoards money. [Br. Lit.: *Vanity Fair*]
8. **Eugénie Grandet** wealth as raison d'être. [Fr. Lit.: *Eugénie Grandet,* Magill I, 258–260]

9. ***Financier, The*** riches as raison d'être. [Am. Lit.: *The Financier,* Magill I, 280–282]
10. **Gehazi** behind master's back, takes money he declined. [O.T.: II Kings 5:21–22]
11. **Griffiths, Clyde** insatiable desire for wealth causes his downfall. [Am. Lit.: *An American Tragedy*]
12. **Hoard, Walkadine** hastily marries courtesan posing as wealthy widow. [Br. Lit.: *A Trick to Catch the Old One*]
13. **Kibroth-hattaavah** Hebrew place name: where greedy were buried. [O.T.: Numbers, 11:33–35]
14. **Lucre, Pecunious** duped into succoring profligate nephew by lure of a fortune. [Br. Lit.: *A Trick To Catch the Old One*]
15. **Mammon** avaricious fallen angel. [Br. Lit.: *Paradise Lost*]
16. **Mammon, Sir Epicure** avaricious knight; seeks philosopher's stone for Midas touch. [Br. Lit.: *The Alchemist*]
17. ***Mansion, The*** shows material advantages of respectability winning over kinship. [Am. Lit.: *The Mansion,* Hart, 520]
18. **Midas** greedy king whose touch turned everything to gold. [Classical Myth.: Bulfinch, 42–44]
19. **Montgomery** mercenary chief proverbially kept for himself all the booty. [Fr. Hist.: Brewer *Dictionary,* 618]
20. **Naboth's Vineyard** another's possession gotten, by hook or crook. [O.T.: I Kings, 21]
21. ***New Grub Street*** place of ruthless contest among moneymongers. [Br. Lit.: *New Grub Street,* Magill I, 647–649]
22. **Osmond, Gilbert** marries Isabel Archer for her money. [Am. Lit.: *The Portrait of a Lady,* Magill I, 766–768]
23. **Overreach, Sir Giles** grasping usurer, unscrupulous and ambitious. [Br. Lit.: *A New Way to Pay Old Debts,* Wheeler, 275]
24. **Pardoner's Tale** three brothers kill each other for treasure. [Br. Lit.: *Canterbury Tales,* "Pardoner's Tale"]
25. **pig** medieval symbol of avarice. [Art: Hall, 247]
26. **Putnam, Abbie** marries old man in anticipation of inheritance. [Am. Lit.: *Desire Under the Elms*]
27. **Scrooge, Ebenezer** byword for greedy miser. [Br. Lit.: *A Christmas Carol*]
28. **Sisyphus** condemned to impossible task for his avarice. [Gk. Myth.: Wheeler, 1011]

308. GRIEF

1. **Adonais** Shelley's elegy for John Keats. [Br. Lit.: "Adonais" in Benét, 10]

2. **Aedon** changed to nightingale for murdering son; her song funereal. [Gk. Legend: *NCE,* 24]
3. **Aegiale** (**Aegle**) her tears of grief become amber. [Gk. Myth.: Kravitz, 6]
4. **All Souls' Day** holy day of prayer for repose of departed souls. [Christianity: Brewer *Dictionary,* 1021]
5. **arms reversed** visual symbol of grieving. [Heraldry: Jobes, 128]
6. **Artemisia** (fl. 4th century B.C.) built Mausoleum to commemorate husband. [Gk. Hist.: Walsh *Classical,* 32]
7. **Balder** (**Baldur**) when he was slain, all things on earth wept. [Scand. Myth: Brewer *Dictionary,* 70]
8. **Canens** Janus's daughter; cried herself to death over disappearance of husband, Picus. [Rom. Myth.: Zimmerman, 49]
9. **Ceres** grieving over the loss of her daughter Persephone, she withholds her gifts from the earth, thus bringing on winter. [Gk. Myth.: Hamilton *Mythology,* 49]
10. **Clementine** forty-niner's drowned daughter; "lost and gone forever." [Am. Music: Leach, 236]
11. **cypress** symbol of mourning. [Flower Symbolism: Jobes, 402]
12. **dandelion** symbol of grief. [Flower Symbolism: Jobes, 413]
13. **Eos** inconsolably weeps for slain son, Memnon. [Gk. Myth.: Brewer *Dictionary,* 1065]
14. ***Grief*** Adams memorial by St.-Gaudens in Washington, D. C. [Am. Art: *EB,* VIII: 781]
15. **Hecuba** mourns the death of her children. [Gk. Drama: Benét, 450]
16. **Hyacinthus** beautiful youth, accidentally killed; from his blood sprang flower marked with letters AI, a lament. [Gk. Myth: Howe, 134]
17. ***In Memoriam*** Tennyson's tribute to his friend, A. H. Hallam. [Br. Lit.: Harvey, 808]
18. **Kaddish** a prayer said for a close relative. [Judaism: Jobes, II, 901]
19. **Kinah** woeful dirge recited on Tishah b'Av. [Judaism: Wigoder, 342]
20. **Kumalo, Rev. Stephen** Zulu clergyman saddened by fate of fellow blacks. [South African Lit.: *Cry, the Beloved Country*]
21. **Libbeus the Apostle** gentlest apostle, dies from despair at Christ's death. [Ger. Lit.: *The Messiah*]
22. ***Lycidas*** Milton's elegy for his friend, Edward King (1637). [Br. Lit.: *NCE,* 1781]

23. **marigold** symbol of grief. [Flower Symbolism: *Flora Symbolica,* 175]
24. **Niobe** weeps unceasingly for her murdered children. [Gk. Myth.: Wheeler, 259]
25. ***O Captain! My Captain!*** Whitman's elegy commemorating Lincoln's death. [Am. Lit.: Benét, 726]
26. **On My First Son** Ben Jonson's short poem mourning the death of his first son. [Br. Lit.: Norton, 243]
27. ***Pietà*** representation of sorrowing Virgin with dead Christ. [Art: Hall, 246]
28. **poppy** symbol of consolation. [Flower Symbolism: *Flora Symbolica,* 176; Kunz, 329]
29. **Rachel** massacre of innocents fulfills prophecy that she will weep. [N.T.: Matthew 2:18; Jeremiah 31:15]
30. **red on blue** symbol of death and mourning. [Chinese Art: Jobes, 357]
31. **shivah** seven days of grieving following close relative's burial. [Judaism: Wigoder, 550]
32. **swallow** bird that cried "consolation" at Lord's crucifixion. [Animal Symbolism: Brewer *Dictionary,* 1050]
33. **Tishah be'Av** (9th of Av) Jewish day of lamentation for destruction of Temple. [Judaism: Wigoder, 51]
34. **Wailing Wall** Western wall where Jews lament the destruction of the Second Temple of Jerusalem. [Judaism: *EB,* X: 627]
35. **weeping willow** symbolizes grief at loss. [Flower Symbolism: *Flora Symbolica,* 178]
36. ***When Lilacs Last in the Dooryard Bloom'd*** Whitman poem mourns the death of Lincoln. [Am. Lit.: Benét, 1085]

309. GROWTH

1. **acorn** used to symbolize the beginning of growth. [Pop. Culture: Misc.]
2. **mustard seed** kingdom of Heaven thus likened; for phenomenal development. [N.T.: Matthew 13:31–32]

310. GUARDIANSHIP (See also PROTECTIVENESS.)

1. **Argus** hundred-eyed giant guarding Io. [Gk. Myth.: Leach, 72]
2. **Argus Panoptes** all-seeing herdsman with one hundred eyes. [Gk. Myth.: Walsh *Classical,* 29]
3. **battle ax** symbol of wardship. [Western Folklore: Jobes, 163]
4. **beefeater** popular name for a Yeoman of the Guard or Yeoman Warder of the Tower of London. [Br. Hist.: Payton, 88]

5. **Bodhisattva** enlightened one deferring Nirvana to help others. [Buddhism: Parrinder, 48]
6. **Cardea** protects children from witches. [Rom. Myth.: Leach, 191]
7. **Cerberus** three-headed dog, guards gate to Hades. [Gk. Myth.: Zimmerman, 55]
8. **cherubim** defended tree of life with flaming swords. [O.T.: Genesis 3:24]
9. **cock** watchful church-tower sitter. [Christian Symbolism: Appleton, 21]
10. **Cybele** protector of cities and mother-goddess. [Phrygian Myth.: Avery, 345]
11. **Delphyne** half-woman, half-beast; guarded Zeus while imprisoned by Typhon. [Gk. Myth.: Howe, 78]
12. **Egil** giant who watched over Thor's goats. [Norse Myth.: *LLEI*, I: 327]
13. **Erytheis** stood vigil over golden apples of Hesperides. [Gk. Myth.: *LLEI*, I: 327]
14. **eunuch** castrated guardian of Eastern harems. [Arab. Culture: Jobes, I, 530–531]
15. **Fafnir** dragon guarding the Nibelung's gold. [Ger. Opera: Wagner, *Siegfried*, Westerman, 240–241]
16. **fairy godmother** mythical being who guards children from danger and rewards them for good deeds. [Folklore: Misc.]
17. **Faithful Eckhardt** old man; warns people of death procession on Maundy Thursday. [Ger. Folklore: *LLEI*, I: 281]
18. **Ferohers** tutelary angels. [Persian Myth.: *LLEI*, I: 328]
19. **fiery swords** brandished by cherubim safeguarding tree of life. [O.T.: Genesis 3:24]
20. **Fisher King** guardian of the Grail. [Ger. Legend, *Parzival;* Arthurian Legend: Walsh *Classical*, 227]
21. **Fylgie** guardian spirit assigned to each human for life. [Norse Myth.: *LLEI*, I: 328]
22. **Garm** ferocious watchdog at gate of Hell. [Norse Myth.: *LLEI*, I: 328]
23. **guardian angel** term for Christian namesake who watches over a young child. [Christianity: Misc.]
24. **Heimdall** guardian of Bifrost; distinguished for acute vision and hearing. [Norse Myth.: Leach, 488]
25. **Ladon** hundred-headed dragon; guarded apples of the Hesperides. [Rom. Myth.: Zimmerman, 145]
26. **lion** sleeps with eyes open. [Christian Symbolism: Appleton, 59]

27. **Mahub Ali** horse-dealer in charge of Kim. [Br. Lit.: *Kim*]
28. **Nana** gentle old dog; guards the Darling children. [Br. Lit.: *Peter Pan*]
29. **Palace Guard, the** sobriquet for the zealous spokesmen-defenders of the Nixon Administration. [Am. Hist.: *The Palace Guard*]
30. **palladium** a "safeguard"; Troy believed safe while statue of Pallas Athene remained. [Gk. Lit.: *Iliad;* Espy, 40]
31. **raven** guardian of the dead. [Christian Folklore: Mercatante, 159]
32. **Swiss Guards** papal praetorian guard instituted by Julius II. [Ital. Hist.: Plumb, 218, 254]
33. **wyvern** protector of treasure and wealth. [Heraldry: Halberts, 40]

311. GUIDANCE (See also COUNSEL.)

1. ***Analects, The*** emphasize human relationships, the golden rule, and usefulness to the state and society. [Chin. Lit.: *The Analects of Confucius* in Benét, 33]
2. **Anthony, Mr.** gave guidance to supplicants on radio show. [Am. Radio: "Ask Mr. Anthony" in Buxton, 99]
3. **Baloo** bear who teaches Mowgli jungle law. [Br. Lit.: *The Jungle Books*]
4. **Dear Abby** column of moral or psychological advice; syndicated since 1956. [Pop. Culture: Payton, 185]
5. **Deborah** under her aegis, Barak routed the Canaanites. [O.T.: Judges 4:4–10]
6. **Dix, Dorothea** (1870–1951) syndicated columnist who gave advice to the lovelorn. [Am. Pop. Culture: Misc.]
7. **Dooley, Mr.** Irish saloonkeeper in Chicago who sagely and humorously dispenses folk philosophy. [Am. Humor: Hart, 240]
8. **lamp** Word of God showing the way. [Christian Symbolism: O.T.: Psalms 119:105]
9. **Landers, Ann** (1918–   ) syndicated columnist who gives advice on personal problems. [Pop. Culture: Misc.]
10. **Mentor** Odysseus's friend and advisor. [Gk. Lit.: *Odyssey*]
11. **Ten Commandments** God's precepts for man's life. [O.T.: Exodus 20:3–17; Deuteronomy 5:7–21]

312. GUIDE

1. **Akela** leader of wolfpack. [Br. Lit.: *The Jungle Books*]
2. **Anchises** Aeneas' guide in Elysium. [Rom. Lit.: *Aeneid*]

3. **Anubis** "Pathfinder"; conducted dead to judgment before Osiris. [Egyptian Myth.: Jobes, 105]
4. **Baedeker** series of guidebooks for travelers. [Travel: *NCE,* 207]
5. **Beatrice** Dante's beloved's soul; directs him in Paradise. [Ital. Lit.: *Divine Comedy*, Magill I, 211–213]
6. **Cumaean sibyl** famous prophetess; leads Aeneas through underworld. [Rom. Lit.: *Aeneid*]
7. **dolphin** transported blessed souls to islands of dead. [Gk. and Rom. Myth.: Appleton, 31]
8. **Jack the Porpoise** led ships through treacherous strait off New Zealand. [Br. Hist.: Wallechinsky, 128]
9. **Judas goat** a goat used to lead sheep to slaughter. [Eur. Culture: Misc.]
10. **lighthouse at Pharos** 400 ft. tall; beacon visible 300 miles at sea. [World Hist.: Wallechinsky, 257]
11. **Palinurus** pilot of Aeneas. [Rom. Lit.: *Aeneid*]
12. **pillar of cloud, pillar of fire** Jehovah leads way to promised land. [O.T.: Exodus 13:21–22]
13. **star of Bethlehem** guiding light to Jesus for the Magi. [Christian Symbolism: N.T.: Matthew, 2:9]
14. **Tiphys** pilot of the Argonauts. [Rom. Myth.: Brewer *Dictionary,* 1085]
15. **Vergil** Dante's guide in Hell and Purgatory. [Ital. Lit.: *Divine Comedy*, Magill I 211–213]

313. GULLIBILITY (See also DUPERY.)

1. **Big Claus** foolishly falls for Little Claus's falsified get-rich-quick schemes. [Dan. Lit.: *Andersen's Fairy Tales*]
2. **Emperor** orders a new outfit from weavers who claim it will be invisible to anyone unworthy of his position. [Dan. Lit.: Andersen "The Emperor's New Clothes" in *Andersen's Fairy Tales*]
3. **Georgette** Mary Richards' coworker and Ted Baxter's wife; epitomizes gullibility. [TV: "The Mary Tyler Moore Show" in Terrace, II, 70]
4. **Oswald** believes Edmund's false charges against Edgar. [Br. Lit.: *King Lear*]
5. **Othello** "thinks men honest that but seem to be so." [Br. Lit.: *Othello*]
6. **Peachum, Polly** among others, believes she is Macheath's wife. [Br. Opera: *The Beggar's Opera*]

7. **Quixote, Don** completely taken in by all the tales and plans of his squire and others who humor his delusions. [Span. Lit.: Cervantes *Don Quixote*]
8. **Simple Simon** credulous booby. [Nurs. Rhyme: Opie, 387]
9. **Tenderfoot** told that cowpunching is a cinch, is badly hurt when he tries it and is tossed. [Am. Balladry: "The Tenderfoot"]
10. **Urfe, Nicholas** trusts in the specious sincerity of the actors in Conchis's psychological experiments on him. [Br. Lit.: John Fowles *The Magus* in Weiss, 279]

H

314. HAIR

1. **Absalom** hair entangled in branches, he was left dangling. [O.T.: II Samuel 18:9]
2. **Aslaug** used hair as cloak to meet king. [Norse Myth.: Walsh *Classical,* 35]
3. **Beatles** famous English rock group whose initial appeal was derived partly from their moplike haircuts. [Br. Hist.: *NCE,* 253]
4. **Bes** shaggy-haired, shortlegged god with tail. [Egyptian Myth.: Leach, 138]
5. **Buffalo Bill** (William F. Cody, 1846–1917) American cowboy and showman whose image was fortified by his long blond hair. [Am. Hist.: *NCE,* 390]
6. **Cousin Itt** Addams's relative; four feet tall and completely covered with blond hair. [TV: "The Addams Family" in Terrace, I, 29]
7. **Custer, General George** (1839–1876) American army officer whose image included long, yellowish hair. [Am. Hist.: *NCE,* 701]
8. **Enkidu** hirsute companion of Gilgamesh. [Babyl. Myth.: *Gilgamesh*]
9. **Godiva, Lady** (d. 1057) Leofric's wife who rode through Coventry clothed only in her long, golden hair. [Br. Hist.: Payton, 274]
10. **Gruagach** "the hairy one"; fairy lady. [Scot. Folklore: Briggs, 206–207]
11. **hippies** 1960s "dropouts of American culture" usually identified with very long hair adorned with flowers. [Popular Culture: Misc.]
12. ***Hair*** rock musical celebrating youthful exuberance as evidenced by growing long hair. [Am. Mus.: *On Stage,* 517]
13. **Mullach, Meg** long-haired and hairy-handed brownie. [Scot. Folklore: Briggs, 284–285]
14. **Rapunzel** her golden tresses provide access to tower loft. [Ger. Fairy Tale: *Rapunzel*]
15. **Samson** the Hercules of the Israelites; rendered powerless when Delilah cut off his hair. [O.T.: Judges 13–16]

Happiness (See **JOY.**)

315. HARMONY

1. **Concordia** goddess of harmony, peace, and unity. [Rom. Myth.: Kravitz, 65]
2. **Harmony** child of ugly Hephaestus and lovely Aphrodite; union of opposites. [Gk. Myth.: Espy, 25]
3. **Polyhymnia** muse of lyric poetry; presided over singing. [Gk. Myth.: Brewer *Dictionary,* 849]
4. **yin-yang** complementary principles that make up all aspects of life. [Chinese Trad.: *EB,* X: 821]

316. HARSHNESS

1. **Pharaoh** imposed cruel burdens of labor on the Hebrews. [O.T.: Exodus 5]
2. **draconian laws** included severe punishments prescribed by Draco, their codifier. [Gk. Hist.: *NCE,* 791]

317. HATRED

1. **Ahab, Captain** main character whose monomania is an expression of hatred. [Am. Lit.: *Moby Dick*]
2. **basil flower** flower representing hatred of the other sex. [Flower Symbolism: Jobes, 184]
3. **Bigger Thomas** possesses a pathological hatred of white people. [Am. Lit.: *Native Son,* Magill I, 643–645]
4. **Claggart** dislikes Billy Budd so that he falsely accuses him of fomenting mutiny. [Am. Lit: Herman Melville *Billy Budd*]
5. **Esau** despised brother for stealing Isaac's blessing. [O.T.: Genesis 27:41–42]
6. **Eteocles and Polynices** their hatred extended to the funeral pyre where even their flames would not mingle. [Gk. Myth.: "The Seven Against Thebes" in Benét, 917]
7. **Feverel, Sir Austin** after wife left him, he became a woman-hater. [Br. Lit.: *The Ordeal of Richard Feverel* Magill I, 692–695]
8. **Frithiof** kills proud sea-kings, saves a king and queen from death, and defeats her brothers in battle. [Nor. Lit.: Haydn & Fuller, 275]
9. **Grimes, Peter** a community hounds a man to his death. [Br. Opera: Britten, *Peter Grimes,* Westerman, 536–539]
10. **Medea** legendary sorceress whose hatred came of jealousy. [Gk. Myth.: Payton, 433]

11. **St. John's wort** indicates animosity. [Flower Symbolism: *Flora Symbolica,* 177]
12. **Styx** river of aversion. [Br. Lit.: *Paradise Lost*]
13. **Tulliver, Mr.** instructs children to despise Mr. Wakem. [Br. Lit.: *The Mill on the Floss,* Magill I, 593–595]

Haughtiness (See **ARROGANCE.**)

318. HEADLESSNESS (See also DECAPITATION.)

1. **Acephali** fabled Libyan nation of men without heads. [Rom. Hist.: Leach, 6]
2. **Alban, St.** carries his head in his hands. [Christian Hagiog.: Brewer *Dictionary,* 18]
3. **Denis of Paris, St.** French patron; carried severed head to burial. [Christian Hagiog.: Attwater, 104–105]
4. **Headless Horseman** spectral figure haunts Ichabod Crane. [Am. Lit.: *The Legend of Sleepy Hollow*]

319. HEALING (See also MEDICINE.)

1. **Achilles' spear** had power to heal whatever wound it made. [Gk. Lit.: *Iliad*]
2. **Agamede** Augeas' daughter; noted for skill in using herbs for healing. [Gk. Myth.: Zimmerman, 11]
3. **Ahmed, Prince** possessed apple of Samarkand; cure for all diseases. [Arab. Lit.: *Arabian Nights*]
4. **Amahl** cripple cured by accompanying Magi to the Christ child. [Am. Opera: *Amahl and the Night Visitors,* Benét, 28]
5. **Ananias** Lord's disciple restores Saul's vision. [N.T.: Acts 9:17–19]
6. **balm in Gilead** metaphorical cure for sins of the Israelites. [O.T.: Jeremiah 8:22]
7. **Bethesda** Jerusalem pool, believed to have curative powers. [N.T.: John 5:2–4]
8. **copper** Indian talisman to prevent cholera. [Ind. Myth.: Jobes, 369]
9. **coral** cures madness; stanches blood from wound. [Gem Symbolism: Kunz, 68]
10. **emerald** relieves diseases of the eye. [Gem Symbolism: Kunz, 370]
11. **Jesus's five cures** he makes blind beggars see. [N.T.: Matthew 9:27–31, 20:31–34; Mark 10:46–52; Luke 18:35–43; John 9:1–34]

12. **sweet fennel** said to remedy blindness and cataracts. [Herb Symbolism; *Flora Symbolica,* 164]

320. HEALTH

1. **agate** symbolizes health; supposed to relieve snake and scorpion bites. [Class. and Medieval Legend: Leach, 27]
2. **Asclepius' cup** symbolizes well-being. [Gk. Myth.: Jobes, 397]
3. **Carna** goddess of physical fitness. [Rom. Myth.: Leach, 192]
4. **Damia** goddess of health. [Gk. Myth.: Jobes, 409]
5. **Hygeia** goddess of health; daughter and personification of Asclepius. [Gk. Myth.: Kravitz, 123]
6. **Hygeia's cup** symbol of fertility and fitness. [Gk. Myth.: Jobes, 396–397]

321. HEARTLESSNESS (See also CRUELTY, RUTHLESSNESS.)

1. **Chester, Sir John** towards son's love affair. [Br. Lit.: *Barnaby Rudge*]
2. **Clare, Angel** cannot forgive Tess's past. [Br. Lit.: *Tess of the D'Urbervilles*]
3. **Estella** trained by Miss Havisham to take advantage of men. [Br. Lit.: *Great Expectations*]
4. **Ettarre** encourages knight's love to gain his tournament prize. [Br. Lit.: *Idylls of the King,* "Pelleas and Ettarre"]
5. **Gabler, Hedda** ruthlessly debases and cruelly deceives a former lover, driving him to suicide. [Swed. Drama: Isben *Hedda Gabler*]
6. **Gerard, Lieutenant Philip** unfeeling in singleminded pursuit of Kimble. [TV: "The Fugitive" in Terrace, I, 290]
7. **Gessler** sentenced Tell to shoot apple off son's head. [Swiss Legend: Brewer *Dictionary,* 1066; Ital. Opera: Rossini, *Wilhelm Tell*]
8. **Hatto** for hardheartedness to poor during famine, eaten by mice. [Ger. Legend: *LLEI,* I: 290]
9. **Infanta** laughs at the death of the little Dwarf who can no longer dance for her. [Br. Lit.: Oscar Wilde "The Birthday of the Infanta"]
10. **Javert** coldhearted in his relentless pursuit of Valjean. [Fr. Lit.: *Les Misérables*]
11. **La Belle Dame Sans Merci** cruel and heartless lady. [Br. Lit.: "La Belle Dame Sans Merci" in Walsh *Modern,* 51]
12. **Sanine** has no pity for others' sufferings. [Russ. Lit.: Magill III, 921]

13. **Turandot** in revenge for dishonor to ancestor. [Ital. Opera: Puccini, *Turandot,* Westerman, 368]

322. HEAVEN (See also PARADISE.)

1. **Aaru** abode of blessed dead and gods. [Egyptian Myth.: Benét, 1]
2. **Abraham's bosom** reward for the righteous. [N.T.: Luke 16:23]
3. **animals in heaven** Jonah's whale and Balaam's ass are among the ten animals allowed to enter paradise. [Muslim Legend: Benét, 37]
4. **Anu (An)** Babylonian god of heaven. [Babyl. Myth.: Benét, 41]
5. **Asgard** abode of the gods. [Norse Myth.: Walsh *Classical,* 34]
6. **Avalon** the blissful otherworld of the dead. [Celtic Myth.: *NCE,* 194]
7. **Beulah** allegorical name for Israel. [O.T.: Isaiah 62:4–5]
8. **Dilmun** dwelling of gods where sun rose. [Sumerian Myth.: Gaster, 24]
9. **Elysian Fields** home of the blessed after death. [Gk. Myth.: Kravitz, 88]
10. **Elysium** abode of the blessed after death. [Gk. Myth.: Zimmerman, 94; Gk. Lit.: *Odyssey*]
11. **Fortunate Isles (Happy Isles)** otherworld for heroes favored by gods. [Gk. Myth.: *NCE,* 861]
12. **garden of the Hesperides** in this garden grew a tree with golden apples. [Gk. Myth.: Zimmerman, 109]
13. **Happy Hunting Ground** translation of Indian name for heaven. [North Am. Indian Myth.: Misc.]
14. **Holy City** poetical name for heaven. [World Rel.: *NCE,* 1213]
15. **Land of the Leal** abode of the blessed dead. [Scot. Myth.: Misc.]
16. **Mount Zion** celestial city. [Br. Lit.: *Pilgrim's Progress*]
17. **New Jerusalem** new paradise; dwelling of God among men. [N.T.: Revelation 21:2]
18. **Olympus** abode of the chief gods. [Gk. Myth.: Espy, 22]
19. **Paradise** poetic name for heaven. [World Rel.: *NCE,* 1213]
20. **seventh heaven** formed of indescribable divine light; inhabitants are supremely happy, all chanting of God. [Islamic Religion: Benét, 449]
21. **Valhalla** celestial banquet hall for departed war heroes. [Norse Myth.: Brewer *Dictionary,* 1122]

Height (See **GIANTISM, TALLNESS.**)

323. HELL (See also **UNDERWORLD.**)

1. **Abaddon** place of destruction. [N.T.: Revelation 9:11; Br. Lit.: *Paradise Lost*]
2. **Gehenna** place of eternal suffering. [O.T.: II Kings 23:10]
3. **Hades** the great underworld. [Gk. Myth.: *NCE,* 1219]
4. **Hinnom** valley of ill repute that came to mean hell. [Judaism: *NCE,* 1244]
5. **Naraka** realm of torment for deceased wicked people. [Buddhism, Hindu Myth.: Brewer *Dictionary,* 745]
6. **Pandemonium** chief city of Hell. [Br. Lit.: *Paradise Lost*]
7. **Sheol** (or **Tophet**) gloomy place of departed, unhappy souls. [Judaism: *NCE,* 1219]

324. HELPFULNESS (See also **KINDNESS.**)

1. **Bauchan** hobgoblin often helpful to man. [Scot. Folklore: Briggs, 19]
2. **Bodachan Sabhaill** barn brownie who threshed for old men. [Scot. Folklore: Briggs, 29]
3. **bwbachod** Welsh equivalent of brownies; helpful domestically. [Welsh Folklore: Briggs, 55–56]
4. **Dorcas** made garments for widows. [N.T.: Acts 9:39]
5. **Good Samaritan** man who helped half-dead victim of thieves after a priest and a Levite had "passed by." [N.T.: Luke 10:33]
6. **Killmoulis** brownie that haunted mill, helping miller. [Br. Folklore: Briggs, 246–247]
7. **Phynnodderee** benevolent Manx brownie of great strength. [Manx Folklore: Brewer *Dictionary,* 830]
8. **Robin Round-cap** domestic spirit who helped with chores. [Br. Folklore: Briggs, 344]
9. **Simon the Cyrenian** made to help bear Christ's cross to Calvary. [N.T.: Matthew 27:32; Luke 23:26]

325. HENPECKED HUSBANDS

1. **Belphegor** fiend turned man; henpecked by wife. [Ital. Lit.: *Belphegor,* Walsh *Classical,* 53]
2. **Dithers, Mr.** Dagwood's irascible boss; fears only his demanding wife. [Comics: "Blondie" in Horn, 118]
3. **Fondlewife** old banker, dotingly submissive to wife. [Br. Lit.: *The Old Bachelor*]
4. **Jiggs** nouveau riche; forever ducking nagging wife Maggie's rolling pin. [Comics: "Bringing Up Father" in Horn, 132]

5. **Mitty, Walter** daydreaming, henpecked husband. [Am. Lit.: "The Secret Life of Walter Mitty" in Cartwell, 606–610]
6. **Syntax, Doctor** harried and hectored clergyman takes off for the good life. [Br. Lit.: *Doctor Syntax,* LLEI, 1: 279]
7. **Tesman, George** Hedda's scholarly husband; jumps at her command. [Nor. Lit.: *Hedda Gabler*]

Heresy (See **APOSTASY.**)

326. HEROISM (See also BRAVERY.)

1. **Achilles** Greek hero without whom Troy could not have been taken. [Gk. Lit.: *Iliad*]
2. **Aeneas** Trojan hero; legendary founder of Roman race. [Rom. Lit.: *Aeneid*]
3. **Argonauts** those accompanying Jason to fetch Golden Fleece. [Gk. Myth.: Parrinder, 26]
4. **Arjuna** hero of the civil war between two royal houses of ancient India. [Hindu Lit.: *Mahabharata*]
5. **Arthur** king and hero of Scotland, Wales, and England. [Arthurian Legend: Parrinder, 28]
6. **Bagradian, Gabriel** leads heroic defense by a group of Armenians against the besieging Turks; is killed by a Turkish bullet. [Ger. Lit.: *The Forty Days of Musa Dagh* in Magill I, 291]
7. **Bellerophon** rider of Pegasus; conquered monsters and Amazons. [Gk. Myth.: Parrinder, 42; Kravitz, 43]
8. **Beowulf** saved Danes from monster Grendel. [Br. Lit.: *Beowulf*]
9. **Cid** Spanish knight renowned for exploits against Moors. [Span. Hist.: *EB,* 4: 615–616]
10. **Cuchulain** "the Achilles of the Gael." [Irish Myth.: Benét, 239–240]
11. **D'Artagnan** challenges horseman, rescues a lady, and earns fame as a doughty soldier. [Fr. Lit.: Dumas *The Three Musketeers*]
12. **David** boy who slew Goliath. [O.T.: Samuel: 18:4–51]
13. **Durward, Quentin** seeking his fortune abroad, he saves the life of King Louis XI, wards off attacks by the king's enemies, and distinguishes himself in a seige. [Br. Lit.: *Quentin Durward*]
14. **Edricson, Alleyne** knighted for chivalry by the Black Prince. [Br. Lit.: *The White Company* in Magill I, 1108]
15. **Frithiof** kills proud sea-kings, saves a king and queen from death, and defeats her brothers in battle. [Nor. Lit.: Haydn & Fuller, 275]

16. **Grettir the Strong** Viking adventurer whose exploits are related in *The Grettisaga*. [Icelandic Lit.: Magill I, 335]
17. **Hanuman** monkey deity, conqueror of demons, builder of a stone bridge from India to Ceylon. [Hindu Myth.: *Collier's*, IX, 214]
18. **Harmodius** slew Hipparchus, brother of the tyrant Hippias. [Gk. Hist.: *EB* (1963) XI, 198]
19. **Hector** King Priam's son; dies fighting for Troy. [Gk. Lit.: *Iliad*]
20. **Hercules** completed tasks requiring great bravery, strength, and ingenuity. [Gk. Myth.: Brewer *Dictionary*, 448]
21. **Hereward the Wake** last of the English; dies defending homeland. [Br. Lit.: *Hereward the Wake*, Magill I, 367–370]
22. **Hornblower, Captain Horatio** victorious captain of HMS *Lydia* and HMS *Sutherland*. [Br. Lit.: *Captain Horatio Hornblower*]
23. **Jason** leader of the Argonauts. [Gk. Myth.: Payton, 347]
24. **Judith** saved her city from the onslaught of Holofernes by beheading him during a drunken sleep. [Apocrypha: Judith 13:4-10]
25. **Leonidas** Spartan king held off thousands of Persians at Thermopylae with a few hundred men. [Gk. Hist.: Benét, 578]
26. **Prometheus** stole divine fire for man's sake. [Gk. Myth.: Espy, 33]
27. **Richard the Lion-Hearted** (1157–1199) nicknamed the Black Knight; performer of valorous deeds. [Br. Hist: *EB*, VIII: 566; Br. Lit.: *Ivanhoe*]
28. **Rogers, Buck** 25th-century adventurer who combats menacing aliens and other villains in order to save the world. [Comics: Berger, 93]
29. **Roland** chief paladin of Charlemagne; renowned for his prowess. [Fr. Lit.: *NCE*, 2344]
30. **Samson** hero of Israel. [O.T.: Judges 13–16]
31. **Siegfried** killed many great heroes, won the fabulous hoard of the Nibelungs, and was made invisible by the blood of a dragon he had slain. [Ger. Myth.: *Nibelungenlied* in Magill I, 653]
32. **Tancred** crusader renowned for his fighting helps capture Jerusalem from the infidels. [Ital. Lit.: *Jerusalem Delivered*; Ital. Opera: Rossini *Tancredi*]
33. **Theseus** hero of Attica who slew the Minotaur, conquered the Amazons, and helped drive off the Centaurs. [Gk. Myth.: Hamilton *Mythology*, 152]

34. **Worthies, the Nine** nine heroes — three each from the Bible, from the classical period, and from medieval romance — who were frequently grouped together. [Pop. Culture: Brewer *Dictionary*, 694]

327. HIGHSPIRITEDNESS

1. **Gashouse Gang** boisterous Cardinals ballclub of the 1930s. [Am. Sports: Shankle, 167]
2. **Gay Nineties (Naughty Nineties)** the 1890s; the *fin-de-siècle* epoch when traditional Victorian religiosity was flouted. [Am. and Br. Hist.: Payton, 264]
3. **Hal, Prince** led boisterous life in the company of Falstaff. [Br. Lit.: *I Henry IV*]
4. **Nickleby, Nicholas** adventurous student facing adversities of life. [Br. Lit.: *Nicholas Nickleby*]
5. **Roaring Twenties** decade of exuberance (1920s). [Am. Hist.: Flexner, 309]

328. HIGHWAYMEN (See also OUTLAWRY, THIEVERY.)

1. **Band of Merry Men** Robin Hood's brigands. [Br. Lit.: *Robin Hood*]
2. **Beane, Sawney** English highwayman whose gang slew and ate their victims. [Brit. Folklore: Misc.]
3. **Duval, Claude** 17th-century British highwayman; subject of ballads. [Br. Legend: Harvey, 256]
4. **Faggus, Tom** stole, especially from the Doone clan. [Br. Lit.: *Lorna Doone,* Magill I, 524–526]
5. **Highwayman, the** loves an innkeeper's daughter, who vainly tries to save him from capture. [Br. Poetry: Noyes "The Highwayman"]
6. **Hood, Robin** outlaw; stole from rich to give to poor. [Br. Lit.: *Robin Hood*]
7. **King, Tom** the "Gentleman Highwayman"; associate of Dick Turpin. [Br. Hist.: Brewer *Note-Book,* 363]
8. **Macheath, Captain** highwayman hero of the opera. [Br. Lit.: *Beggar's Opera*]
9. **Moon's men** highwaymen; worked their crimes by night. [Br. Lit.: *I Henry IV*]
10. **Rob Roy** Robin Hood of Scotland. [Br. Lit.: *Rob Roy*]
11. **Turpin, Dick** (1706–1739) enjoyed short and brutal career as horsestealer and highwayman. [Br. Hist.: *NCE,* 2808]
12. **Twitcher, Jemmy** treacherous and crafty brigand. [Br. Lit.: *Beggar's Opera*]

329. HOAX

1. ***Balloon Hoax, The*** news story in 1844, reporting the transatlantic crossing of a balloon with eight passengers. [Am. Lit.: *The Balloon Hoax* in Poe]
2. **Piltdown man** missing link turned out to be orangutan. [Br. Hist.: Wallechinsky, 46; *Time,* October 13, 1978, 82]

330. HOLY DAYS and PERIODS

1. **ember days** certain days of fasting and prayer occuring in each of the four seasons. [Christian Tradition: *NCE,* 862]
2. **Ramadan** holy month of the Muslim year. [Islamic Religion: Brewer *Dictionary,* 747]
3. **Sabbath** the seventh day of the week, prescribed as a day of rest and worship. [Judaism: Brewer *Dictionary,* 788]

331. HOMECOMING

1. ***Odyssey*** concerning Odysseus's difficulties in getting home after war. [Gk. Myth.: *Odyssey*]
2. ***You Can't Go Home Again*** revisiting his home town, a writer is disillusioned by what he sees. [Am. Lit.: Thomas Wolfe *You Can't Go Home Again*]

332. HOMOSEXUALITY

1. **Albertine** discovery of her promiscuous lesbianism breaks up her impending marriage to Marcel. [Fr. Lit.: Proust *Remembrance of Things Past*]
2. **Bilitis** putative singer of Sapphic lyrics. [Fr. Lit.: *Les Chansons de Bilitis, NCE,* 1621]
3. ***Cage aux Folles, La*** farce, with serious overtones, about a night-club owner and his homosexual lover and employee. [Fr. Cinema: *La Cage aux Folles*]
4. **Charlus, Baron de** fails to conceal his homosexual relations with a young tailor and a talented violinist. [Fr. Lit.: Proust *Remembrance of Things Past*]
5. **Christopher Street** magazine for homosexuals. [Am. Pop. Culture: Misc.]
6. ***City and the Pillar, The*** portraying a young gay separated from "normal" people. [Am. Lit.: *The City and the Pillar*]
7. ***Death in Venice*** aging successful author loses his lifelong self-discipline in his love for a beautiful Polish boy. [Ger. Lit: *Death in Venice*]

8. **Edward II** weak English king whose love for Gaviston, Earl of Cornwall, so arouses the anger of the nobles that he loses the crown and is murdered. [Br. Drama: Marlowe *Edward II* in Magill II, 286]
9. **Ganymede** beautiful shepherd entrances Jupiter. [Rom. Lit.: *Metamorphoses*]
10. **gay liberation** organization that supports equal rights in jobs, housing, etc. for homosexuals. [Am. Pop. Culture: Misc.]
11. **lambda** Greek letter adopted as symbol by gay liberation movement. [Am. Pop. Cult.: Misc.]
12. **Molinier, Oliver** loved by two writers, his uncle Edouard and Count Robert de Passavant. [Fr. Lit.: Gide *The Counterfeiters* in Magill I, 160]
13. **Oglethorpe, John** his sexual preference causes marital problems. [Am. Lit.: *The Manhattan Transfer*]
14. **Sappho** Greek poetess from Lesbos; hence, *lesbian.* [Gk. Hist.: Brewer *Dictionary,* 962]
15. **Sodomites** insisted on having sexual intercourse with angels disguised as men. [O.T.: Gen. 19]
16. **Venable, Sebastian** his homosexuality and morbid fascination with vice are revealed by a witness to his horrible death. [Am. Drama: Tennessee Williams *Suddenly Last Summer* in Weiss, 448]
17. ***Well of Loneliness, The*** novel about female homosexuality; once banned, but defended by eminent authors. [Br. Lit.: Barnhart, 530]
18. **Willard, Jim** his first homosexual fulfillment at seventeen, adheres to his erotic life-style. [Am. Lit.: Gore Vidal *The City and the Pillar*]

333. HONESTY (See also RIGHTEOUSNESS, VIRTUOUSNESS.)

1. **Alethia** ancient Greek personification of truth. [Gk. Myth.: Zimmerman, 18]
2. **Better Business Bureau** nationwide system of organizations investigating dishonest business practices. [Am. Commerce: Misc.]
3. **bittersweet** traditional symbol of truth. [Plant Symbolism: *Flora Symbolica,* 172]
4. **Boffin, Nickodemus** despite personal loss, endows patron's son. [Br. Lit.: *Our Mutual Friend*]
5. **Bunker, Edith** her uprightness frequently conflicts with Archie's opportunism. [TV: "All in the Family" in Terrace, I, 47–48]

6. **cherry tree** young George Washington's admission of chopping it down was proof of his honesty. [Am. Legend: Misc.]
7. **chrysanthemum** symbol of truth. [Flower Symbolism: *Flora Symbolica,* 173; Kunz, 330]
8. **Cordelia** though it costs her an inheritance, she refuses to say that she could love her father exclusively. [Br. Drama: Shakespeare *King Lear*]
9. **Cranmer, Thomas** a meek, patient, honest churchman. [Br. Lit.: *Henry VIII*]
10. **Diogenes** (c. 412–323 B.C.) philosopher; fabled lantern-carrying searcher for an honest man. [Gk. Hist.: Hall, 104]
11. **Edgar** truthful, straightforward character; does no evil. [Br. Lit.: *King Lear*]
12. **John of Gaunt** overly blunt uncle of Richard II. [Br. Lit.: *Richard II*]
13. **Lenox, John** his straight-forward dealings win Harum's approval. [Am. Lit.: *David Harum*]
14. **Lincoln, Abraham** (1809–1865) 16th U.S. president; nicknamed "Honest Abe." [Am. Hist.: Kane, 525]
15. **Melantius** honest soldier; trusts everyone until shown otherwise. [Br. Lit.: *The Maid's Tragedy*]
16. **open book** signified spreading of truth by text and doctrine. [Christian Symbolism: Appleton, 13]
17. **Pure, Simon** character in Centlire play (1718). [Br. Lit.: *Bold Stroke for a Wife*]
18. **Trelawney, Squire** sincere, genuine ship-owner; benevolent authority. [Br. Lit.: *Treasure Island*]
19. **Truman, Harry** (1884–1972) 33rd U.S. president who, despite much controversy over his policies, is remembered for impeccable honesty and plain speaking. [Am. Hist.: *NCE,* 2793]
20. **truth serum** drug inducing one to speak uninhibitedly. [Science: Brewer *Dictionary,* 1105]
21. **Una** personification of honesty; leads lamb and rides white ass. [Br. Lit.: *Faerie Queene*]
22. **Washington, George** (1732–1799) first U.S. president; reputed to have said, "Father, I cannot tell a lie." [Am. Hist.: *NCE,* 2933]
23. **white chrysanthemum** traditional symbol of truth. [Flower Symbolism: Jobes, 333]

334. HOPE (See also OPTIMISM.)

1. **anchor** emblem of optimism; steadfastly secured the soul in adversity. [N.T.: Hebrews, 6:18–19]
2. **cinquefoil** traditional representation of hope. [Flower Symbolism and Heraldry: Jobes, 341]
3. ***Emigrants, The*** shows Norwegians in Dakota wheatlands striving for better life. [Nor. Lit.: *The Emigrants,* Magill I, 244–246]
4. **flowering almond** symbol of spring; blooms in winter. [Flower Symbolism: Jobes, 71]
5. **Great Pumpkin, the** awaited each Halloween by Linus. [Comics: "Peanuts" in Horne, 542]
6. **hawthorn** symbol of optimism. [Flower Symbolism: *Flora Symbolica,* 174; Kunz, 328]
7. ***Iceman Cometh, The*** "The lie of the pipe dream is what gives life." [Am. Lit.: *The Iceman Cometh*]
8. ***Of Mice and Men*** portrays a philosophy that humans are made of hopes and dreams. [Am. Lit.: *Of Mice and Men*]
9. **rainbow** God's assurance He would not send another great flood. [O.T.: Genesis, 9:12–16]
10. **snowdrop** symbol of optimism. [Flower Symbolism: *Flora Symbolica,* 177; Kunz, 326]

Hopelessness (See DESPAIR.)

335. HORROR

1. **Addams, Charles** (1912–) famed cartoonist of the macabre. [Am. Comics: *NCE,* 19]
2. **Bhairava** (m), **Bhairav** (f) terrible forms of Shiva and spouse. [Hindu Myth.: Parrinder, 44]
3. **Black Death, the** plague whose unprecedented mortality was incomprehensible to medieval mind. [Eur. Hist.: Bishop, 379–382]
4. **Bosch, Hieronymus** (c. 1450–1516) paintings contain grotesque representations of evil and temptation. [Art Hist.: Osborne, 149]
5. ***Cabinet of Dr. Caligari, The*** thrilling horror story told by a madman. [Ger. Cinema: Halliwell, 119]
6. ***Danse Macabre*** Saint-Saëns' musical depiction of a dance of the dead. [Music Hist.: Thompson, 1906]
7. ***Disasters of War*** Goya's violent protest against French occupation of Spain. [Art. Hist.: Osborne, 497]
8. **Dracula, Count** vampire terrifies Transylvanian peasants and London circle. [Br. Lit.: *Dracula*]

9. **dragonwort** traditional representation of horror. [Flower Symbolism: Jobes, 469]
10. ***Exorcist, The*** supernatural horror story about a girl possessed by the devil (1974). [Am. Cinema: Halliwell, 247]
11. ***Jaws*** box office sensation about a killer shark (1975). [Am. Cinema: Halliwell, 380]
12. **mandrake** traditional representation of horror. [Plant Symbolism: *Flora Symbolica,* 175]
13. ***Phantom of the Opera, The*** story of an angry, disfigured composer who haunts the sewers beneath the Paris Opera House. [Am. Cinema: Halliwell, 562]
14. **Pit and the Pendulum, The** study in bone-chilling terror. [Am. Lit.: "The Pit and the Pendulum" in *Portable Poe,* 154–173]
15. ***Psycho*** Hitchcock's classic horror film. [Am. Cinema: *NCE,* 1249]
16. **snakesfoot** indicates shocking occurrence. [Flower Symbolism: *Flora Symbolica,* 177]
17. ***Tell-Tale Heart, The*** mad murderer dismembers victim, mistakes ticking watch for dead man's heart, and confesses. [Am. Lit.: Poe *The Tell-Tale Heart*]

336. HORSE

1. **Al Borak** white horse Muhammad rode to the seven heavens. [Islam: Leach, 172]
2. **Arion** fabulous winged horse; offspring of Demeter and Poseidon. [Gk. Myth.: Zimmerman, 31]
3. **Arundel** Bevis's incomparable steed. [Br. Lit.: *Bevis of Hampton*]
4. **Assault** famous horse in history of thoroughbred racing. [Am. Hist.: *NCE,* 1273]
5. **Balius** immortal steed of Achilles. [Gk. Myth.: Kravitz, 44]
6. **Bavieca** the Cid's horse. [Sp. Legend: Brewer *Dictionary*, 80]
7. ***Black Beauty*** story of a horse has become a children's classic. [Br. Lit.: *Black Beauty,* Payton, 80]
8. **Black Bess** belonged to the notorious highwayman, Dick Turpin. [Br. Hist.: Benét, 103]
9. **Bucephalus** wild steed, broken by Alexander to be his mount. [Gk. Hist.: Leach, 167]
10. **centaur** beast that is half-horse, half-man. [Gk. Myth.: Mercatante, 201–202]
11. **Citation** famous horse in history of thoroughbred racing. [Am. Hist.: *NCE,* 1273]

12. **Clavileño** legendary wooden horse on which Don Quixote and Sancho Panza think they are taking a journey through the air. [Span. Lit.: Benét, 205]
13. **Flicka** a paragon of horses. [TV: "My Friend Flicka" in Terrace, II, 125]
14. **Four Horsemen of the Apocalypse, The** ride white, red, black, and pale horses, symbolizing, respectively, invasion, civil strife, scarcity and famine, and pestilence and death. [N.T.: Revelation 6:1-8]
15. **Gallant Fox** famous horse in history of thoroughbred racing. [Am. Hist.: *NCE,* 1273]
16. **Gilpin, John** his borrowed horse carries him at a mad pace for miles to its owner's home, then turns and runs back. [Br. Poetry: *John Gilpin's Ride*]
17. **Grane** Brünnhilde's war horse, presented to Siegfried. [Ger. Opera: Wagner, *Götterdämmerung,* Westerman, 244]
18. **Gringalet** Gawain's steed. [Br. Lit.: *Sir Gawain and the Green Knight*]
19. **Gunpowder** Ichabod Crane's favorite steed. [Am. Lit.: Washington Irving "The Legend of Sleepy Hollow"]
20. **Hambletonian** famous trotting horse after which race for three-year-old trotters is named. [Am. Culture; Mathews, 769]
21. **Harum, David** would rather trade horses than eat or sleep. [Am. Lit.: *David Harum* in Magill I, 192]
22. **Hippolytus, St.** patron saint of horses. [Christian Hagiog.: Brewster, 367]
23. **Houyhnhnms** race of horses that represent nobility, virtue, and reason. [Br. Lit.: *Gulliver's Travels*]
24. **Man o' War ("Big Red")** famous racehorse foaled at Belmont Stables. [Am. Hist.: Payton, 421]
25. **Meg (Maggie)** Tam O'Shanter's gray mare that lost her tail to the witch. [Scot. Poetry: Burns "Tam O'Shanter"]
26. **Mr. Ed** the talking horse. [TV: Terrace, II, 116–117]
27. **Native Dancer** famous horse in history of thoroughbred racing. [Am. Hist.: *NCE,* 1273]
28. **Pegasus** winged mount of Bellerophon. [Gk. Myth.: Hall, 238]
29. **roan stallion** tramples its owner to death and is shot by his wife, though she had been seduced by the stallion's beauty. [Am. Poetry: Robinson Jeffers *The Roan Stallion* in Magill I, 835]
30. **Rosinante** Don Quixote's mount. [Span. Lit.: *Don Quixote*]

31. **Scout** Tonto's horse. [TV: "The Lone Ranger" in Terrace, II, 34; Radio: "The Lone Ranger" in Buxton, 143]
32. **Seabiscuit** famous horse in history of thoroughbred racing. [Am. Hist.: *NCE,* 1273]
33. **Seattle Slew** famous horse in history of thoroughbred racing. [Am. Hist.: *NCE,* 1273]
34. **Secretariat** famous horse in history of thoroughbred racing. [Am. Hist.: *NCE,* 1273]
35. **Shadowfax** great horse of the wizard Gandalf. [Br. Lit.: J. R. R. Tolkien *Lord of the Rings*]
36. **Silver** the Lone Ranger's trusty steed. [Radio: "The Lone Ranger" in Buxton, 143–144; TV: Terrace, II, 34–35]
37. **Sleipnir** Odin's eight-legged gray horse. [Norse Myth.: Benét, 937]
38. **Tony** Tom Mix's "Wonder Horse." [Radio: "Tom Mix" in Buxton, 241–242]
39. **Topper** Hopalong Cassidy's faithful horse. [Cinema and TV: "Hopalong Cassidy" in Terrace, I, 369]
40. **Trigger** Roy Roger's horse. [TV: "The Roy Rogers Show" in Terrace, II, 260]
41. **Whirlaway** famous horse in history of thoroughbred racing. [Am. Hist.: *NCE,* 1273]

337. HORSERACE

1. **Derby** classic annual race at Epsom Downs. [Br. Cult.: Brewer *Dictionary*, 276]
2. **Kentucky Derby** classic annual race in Louisville. [Am. Cult.: Brewer *Dictionary*, 516]
3. **Palio, the** race with medieval trappings, held annually at Siena. [Ital. Hist.: *EB* (1963) XX, 620]
4. **Royal Ascot** England's fashionable annual event. [Br. Cult.: Brewer *Dictionary*, 49]
5. **Triple Crown** premier achievement in U.S. racing, to win Kentucky Derby, Preakness and Belmont Stakes. [Amer. Cult.: *WB*, 16:59]

338. HOSPITALITY

1. **Abigail** undoes husband's unneighborliness with fare for David's troops. [O.T.: I Samuel 25:23–27]
2. **Abraham** graciously receives and treats three wayfarers. [O.T.: Genesis 18:1–15]
3. **Acestes** Sicilian king; entertains Aeneas. [Rom. Lit.: *Aeneid*]

4. **Alcandre** Polybus' wife; entertains Helen and Menelaus on their way home from Troy. [Gk. Lit.: *Odyssey*]
5. **Bailley, Harry** "Mr. Congeniality." [Br. Lit.: *Canterbury Tales*]
6. **Boniface** jovial innkeeper; name became generic for restaurateur. [Br. Drama: *The Beaux' Stratagem;* Espy, 129]
7. **fatted calf, the** best calf killed for feast to celebrate return of prodigal son. [N.T.: Luke 15:13]
8. **Gatsby, Jay** character who serves nothing but the best to his guests. [Am. Lit.: *The Great Gatsby*]
9. **Glorious Appollers, the** known for their cordiality and sociability. [Br. Lit.: *Old Curiosity Shop*]
10. **Julian the Hospitaler** set up famed hospice for weary travelers. [Medieval Romance: Hall, 181]
11. **Lot** treated and feted two disguised angels. [O.T.: Genesis, 19:1–3]
12. **Lycus** by hospitably entertaining Hercules, earned his gratitude and military assistance. [Gk. Myth.: Zimmerman, 156]
13. **oak** symbol of graciousness. [Flower Symbolism: *Flora Symbolica,* 176]
14. **Phaeacians** island people befriend and aid both Odysseus and the Argonauts. [Gk. Myth.: Benét, 780]
15. **Philemon and Baucis** poor couple welcomes disguised gods refused by rich households. [Rom. Lit.: *Metamorphoses*]

339. HOUSES, FATEFUL

1. **Manderley** place of Maxim de Winter's unhappy marriage, and of his happy one, goes up in flames. [Br. Lit.: D. duMaurier *Rebecca* in Magill I, 806]
2. **Northanger Abbey** medieval house where Catherine Morland imagines dungeons, ghosts, and mysterious events. [Br. Lit.: Austen *Northanger Abbey* in Magill II, 750]
3. **Satis House** scene of Miss Havisham's reclusive life and fiery death. [Br. Lit.: Dickens *Great Expectations*]
4. **Tara** plantation home of Scarlett O'Hara. [Am. Lit.: Margaret Mitchell *Gone With The Wind*]
5. **Thornfield Hall** home where Jane Eyre met Mr. Rochester and where he perishes in a fire. [Br. Lit.: Charlotte Brontë *Jane Eyre*]
6. **Wuthering Heights** remotely situated home where Heathcliff nurses his vengeful plans. [Br. Lit.: Emily Brontë *Wuthering Heights* in Magill I, 1137]

Hugeness (See GIANTISM.)

340. HUMBUGGERY (See also FRAUDULENCE, TRICKERY.)

1. **Barnum, P. T.** (1810–1891) circus owner whose sideshows were sometimes fraudulent; wrote *Humbugs of the World.* [Am. Hist.: *NCE,* 234]
2. **Bilko, Sergeant** bunco artist extraordinaire. [TV: "You'll Never Get Rich" in Terrace II, 452–453]
3. **Face** cunning butler, sets up scam in master's absence. [Br. Lit.: *The Alchemist*]
4. **Mandeville** supposed author of an exaggerated travelogue. [Br. Lit.: *Voyage of Sir John Mandeville,* Harvey, 511]
5. **Subtle** charlatan, posing as alchemist, bilks hapless victims. [Br. Lit.: *The Alchemist*]
6. **Wizard of Oz** false wizard takes up residence in Emerald City. [Am. Lit.: *The Wonderful Wizard of Oz*]

341. HUMILITY (See also MODESTY.)

1. **Bernadette Soubirous, St.** humble girl to whom Virgin Mary appeared. [Christian Hagiog.: Attwater, 65–66]
2. **Bonaventura, St.** washes dishes even though a cardinal. [Christian Hagiog.: Hall, 50]
3. **broom** traditional representation of humility. [Plant Symbolism: *Flora Symbolica,* 167]
4. **Bruno, St.** pictured with head bent as sign of humbleness. [Christian Hagiog.: Hall, 53]
5. **cattail** used by da Vinci as symbol of humility. [Plant Symbolism: Embolden, 25]
6. **Elizabeth of Hungary, St.** meek princess renounced world, cared for sick. [Christian Hagiog.: Attwater, 112]
7. **Job** abases self in awe of the Lord. [O.T.: Job 40:3–5; 42:1–6]
8. **John the Baptist** feels unworthy before Christ. [N.T.: Mark 1:7; Luke 3:16]
9. **small bindweed** traditional representation of humility. [Plant Symbolism: *Flora Symbolica* 172]

Humorousness (See WITTINESS.)

342. HUNGER

1. **Bangladesh** suffered devastating famine in 1970s. [World Hist.: *NCE,* 224]

2. **Biafra** secessionist state of western Africa in which, during war with Nigeria, more than 1,000,000 people died of starvation (1968). [African Hist.: *NCE,* 290]
3. **Erysichthon** condemned by Demeter to perpetual insatiety. [Gk. Myth.: Kravitz, 93]
4. **Lazarus** the beggar full of sores. [N.T.: Luke 16:19–31]
5. **Potato Famine** estimated 200,000 Irish died (1846). [Irish Hist.: Brewer *Note-Book,* 705]
6. **Tantalus** punished with ceaseless hunger for food just beyond his reach. [Gk. Myth.: Hamilton, 346]
7. **Twist, Oliver** asks workhouse-master for more gruel. [Br. Lit.: *Oliver Twist*]

343. HUNTING

1. **Agraeus** epithet of Apollo, meaning "hunter." [Gk. Myth.: Zimmerman, 26]
2. **Agrotera** epithet of Artemis, meaning "huntress." [Gk. Myth.: Zimmerman, 32]
3. **Artemis** (Rom. **Diana**) moon goddess; virgin huntress. [Gk. Myth.: Kravitz, 36]
4. **Atalanta** famous huntress; slew the Centaurs. [Gk. Myth.: Leach, 87]
5. **Britomartis** Cretan nymph; goddess of hunters and fishermen. [Gk. Myth.: Zimmerman, 43]
6. **Calydonian boar hunt** famed hunt of Greek legend. [Class. Myth: *Metamorphoses*]
7. ***Green Hills of Africa*** portrays big game-hunting coupled with literary digressions. [Am. Lit.: *Green Hills of Africa*]
8. **Hubert, St.** patron saint; encountered stag with cross in horns. [Christian Hagiog.: Brewster, 473–474]
9. **Jorrocks** irrepressible pseudo-aristocratic cockney huntsman. [Br. Lit.: *Jorrock's Jaunts and Jollies*]
10. **NRA** (National Rifle Association of America) organization that encourages sharpshooting and use of firearms for hunting. [Am. Pop. Culture: *NCE,* 1895]
11. **Nimrod** Biblical hunter of great prowess. [O.T.: Genesis 10:9; Br. Lit.: *Paradise Lost*]
12. **Orion** hunter who pursued the Pleiades. [Classical Myth.: Zimmerman 184–185]
13. **Sagittarius** the Archer of the Zodiac; used occasionally to symbolize hunting. [Astrology: Payton, 594]

14. **Stymphalian birds** venomous Arcadian flock shot by Hercules; sixth Labor. [Gk. and Rom. Myth.: Hall, 149]
15. **"tally ho"** traditional rallying cry in English fox hunts. [Pop. Cult.: Misc.]

344. HYPOCHONDRIA

1. **Argan** character who suffers imaginary ills; determined to be an invalid. [Fr. Lit.: *Le Malade Imaginaire*]
2. **Usher, Roderick** hypochondriac who invites friend to visit and comfort him. [Am. Lit.: "Fall of the House of Usher" in Benét, 338]

345. HYPOCRISY (See also PRETENSION.)

1. **Alceste** judged most social behavior as hypocritical. [Fr. Lit.: *Le Misanthrope*]
2. **Ambrosio** self-righteous abbot of the Capuchins at Madrid. [Br. Lit.: *Ambrosio, or The Monk*]
3. **Angelo** externally austere but inwardly violent. [Br. Lit.: *Measure for Measure*]
4. **Archimago** enchanter, disguised as hermit, wins confidence of Knight. [Br. Lit.: *Faerie Queene*]
5. **Arsinoé** false prude. [Fr. Lit.: *The Misanthrope*]
6. **Atar Gul** trusted domestic; betrays those he serves. [Fr. Lit.: *Atar Gul,* Walsh *Modern,* 32]
7. **Bigotes** 12th-century French order regarded as hypocritical. [Fr. Hist.: Espy, 99]
8. **Blifil** Allworthy's nephew; talebearer and consummate pietist. [Br. Lit.: *Tom Jones*]
9. **Blood, Col. Thomas** (1628–1680) false in honor and religion. [Br. Lit.: *Peveril of the Peak,* Walsh *Modern,* 61]
10. **Boulanger, Ralph** Emma's lover pretends repentance to avoid commitment. [Fr. Lit.: *Madame Bovary*]
11. **Boynton, Egeria** religious charlatan. [Am. Lit.: *Undiscovered Country*]
12. **Buncombe County** insincere speeches made solely to please this constituency by its representative, 1819–1821. [Am. Usage: Misc.]
13. **Célimène** ridicules people when absent; flatters them when present. [Fr. Lit.: *Le Misanthrope*]
14. **Cantwell, Dr.** lives luxuriously by religious cant. [Br. Lit.: *The Hypocrite,* Brewer *Handbook,* 175]
15. **Chadband, Rev.** pharisaic preacher; thinks he's edifying his hearers. [Br. Lit.: *Bleak House*]

16. **Christian, Edward** conspirator; false to everyone. [Br. Lit.: *Peveril of the Peak,* Walsh *Modern,* 96]
17. **crocodile tears** crocodile said to weep after devouring prey. [Western Folklore: Jobes, 383; Mercatante, 9–10]
18. **Dimmesdale, Arthur** acted the humble minister for seven years while former amour suffered. [Am. Lit.: *The Scarlet Letter*]
19. **Gallanbiles, the** pretend piety on Sabbath but demand dinner. [Br. Lit.: *Nicholas Nickleby*]
20. **Gantry, Elmer** ranting preacher succumbs to alcohol, fornication, theft, and cowardice. [Am. Lit.: *Elmer Gantry*]
21. **Gashford** humble manner masks sly, shirking character. [Br. Lit.: *Barnaby Rudge*]
22. **Goneril and Regan** to inherit their father's possessions they falsely profess great love for him. [Br. Drama: Shakespeare *King Lear*]
23. **Haskell, Eddie** gentleman with adults, troublemaker behind their backs. [TV: "Leave it to Beaver" in Terrace, II, 18–19]
24. **Heep, Uriah** the essence of insincerity. [Br. Lit.: *David Copperfield*]
25. **Honeythunder, Luke** his philanthropy hid animosity. [Br. Lit.: *Edwin Drood*]
26. **Manders** self-righteous pastor agrees to blackmail. [Nor. Lit.: *Ghosts*]
27. **Martext, Sir Oliver** a "most vile" hedge-priest. [Br. Lit.: *As You Like It*]
28. **Mawworm** sanctimonious preacher. [Br. Lit.: *The Hypocrite,* Brewer *Handbook,* 687]
29. **Mr. By-ends** embraces religion when it is easy to practice and to his advantage. [Br. Lit.: Bunyan *Pilgrim's Progress*]
30. **newspeak** official speech of Oceania; language of contradictions. [Br. Lit.: *1984*]
31. **Pecksniff** pretentious, unforgiving architect of double standards. [Br. Lit.: *Martin Chuzzlewit*]
32. **Pharisees** sanctimonious lawgivers do not practise what they preach. [N.T.: Matthew 3:7; 23:1–15; Luke 18:9–14]
33. **Potemkin village** false fronts constructed to deceive. [Russ. Hist.: Espy, 339]
34. **Sainte Nitouche** sanctimonious and pretentious person (Fr. *n'y touche*). [Fr. Usage: Brewer *Dictionary,* 760]
35. **Snawley** sanctimonious hypocrite; placed stepsons in Dotheboys Hall. [Br. Lit.: *Nicholas Nickleby*]

36. **Square, Mr.** Tom's tutor; spouts hypocritically about the beauty of virtue. [Br. Lit.: *Tom Jones*]
37. **Surface, Joseph** pays lip service to high principles while engaging in treacherous intrigues. [Br. Drama: Sheridan *The School for Scandal*]
38. **Tartuffe** swindles benefactor by pretending religious piety. [Fr. Lit.: *Tartuffe*]
39. **Vicar of Bray** changes religious affiliation to suit reigning monarch. [Br. Folklore: Walsh *Classical*, 61]
40. **Walrus** wept in sympathy for the oysters he and the Carpenter devoured. [Br. Lit.: Lewis Carroll *Through the Looking-Glass*]
41. **Whelp, the** nickname for hypocritical Tom Gradgrind. [Br. Lit.: *Hard Times*]
42. **whited sepulchres** analogy in Jesus's denunciation of Pharisees' sanctimony. [N.T.: Matthew 23:27]

I

346. IDEALISM

1. **Stockmann, Dr. Thomas** sacrifices his career to show that the public baths are a health menace. [Nor. Lit.: *An Enemy of the People*; Magill II, 292]

347. IDENTIFICATION

1. **Emmaus** where two disciples discover identity of Jesus. [N.T.: Luke 24:13–35]
2. **Euryclea** Ulysses' nurse; recognized him by scar on thigh. [Gk. Lit.: *Odyssey*]
3. **Longinus** centurion finally sees Christ as son of God. [N.T.: Matthew 27:54; Mark 15:39; Luke 23:47; Christian Legend: Hall, 193]
4. **Orestes** recognized by Iphigenia at the moment of his sacrifice. [Gk. Lit.: *Iphigenia in Tauris,* Kitto, 327–347]
5. **Passover** Jewish festival; blood of sacrificed lambs placed on houses of the Israelites to prevent death of their firstborn. [O.T.: Exodus 12:3–13]
6. **Sakuntala** (fl. 40) recognized as queen on return of lost ring. [Sanskrit Lit.: *Abhijnanasakuntala,* Brewer *Dictionary,* 955]
7. **shibboleth** word used by Gileadites to identify Ephraimites who could not pronounce *sh.* [O.T.: Judges 12:4–6]
8. **Simeon** recognizes young Jesus as messiah. [N.T.: Luke 2:22–34]
9. **Stanley, Henry** (1841–1904) American journalist finds explorer, Dr. Livingstone, in Africa (1871). [Am. Hist.: Van Doren, 263]
10. **Ulysses' bow** Penelope recognizes husband by his ability to bend Ulysses' bow. [Gk. Lit.: *Ulysses*]

348. IDOLATRY

1. **Aaron** responsible for the golden calf. [O.T.: Exodus 32]
2. **Ashtaroth** Canaanite deities worshiped profanely by Israelites. [O.T.: Judges 2:12]
3. **Baalim** Canaanite deities worshiped profanely by Israelites. [O.T.: Judges 2:11]
4. **Baphomet** fabled image; allegedly a Templar fetish. [Medieval Legend: Walsh *Classical,* 46]
5. **golden calf** idol made by Aaron in Moses's absence. [O.T.: Exodus 32:2–4]

6. **David** King of Israel who was held in reverence after he slew Goliath. [O.T.: Samuel 17:4–51]
7. **Jehu** obliterates the profane worship of Baal. [O.T.: II Kings 10:29]
8. **Jeroboam** forsook worship of God; made golden calves. [O.T.: I Kings 12:28–33]
9. **Moloch** deity to whom parents sacrificed their children. [O.T.: II Kings 23:10]
10. **Parsis** religious community of India; worship fire along with other aspects of nature. [Hindu. Rel.: *NCE,* 2075]

349. IGNORANCE (See also STUPIDITY.)

1. **Am ha-Arez** those negligent in or unobservant of Torah study. [Judaism: Wigoder, 26]
2. **avidya** ignorance as cause of suffering through desire. [Hindu Phil.: Parrinder, 36]
3. **Deane, Lucy** unaware of fiancé Stephen's obvious relationship with Maggie. [Br. Lit.: *The Mill on the Floss*]
4. **Dunsmen** opposers of Renaissance learning (14th century); hence, *dunce.* [Br. Hist.: Espy, 116]
5. **Islayev, Arkady** so entrenched in work, oblivious to wife's infidelities. [Russ. Lit.: *A Month in the Country*]
6. **It Pays to Be Ignorant** panelists fail to answer such questions as "Which player on a baseball team wears a catcher's mask?" [Am. Radio: Buxton, 120]
7. **Lennie** big, strong, simple-minded ranch hand. [Am. Lit.: *Of Mice and Men,* Magill I, 672–674]
8. **Newman, Alfred E.** cartoon character personifying ignorance as bliss: "What, me worry?" [Comics: "Mad" in Horn, 442]
9. **Parable of the Cave** cave dwellers see only the shadows of reality. [Gk. Phil.: *Republic*]
10. **Peppermint Patty** cartoon character habitually stumped by teacher and forever failing exams. [Comics: "Peanuts" in Horn, 543]
11. **Scarecrow** goes to Wizard of Oz to get brains. [Am. Lit.: *The Wonderful Wizard of Oz*]
12. **Schweik** cheerful, feeble-minded character; the antithesis of German militarism. [Czech Lit.: *The Good Soldier: Schweik,* Magill IV, 390–392]
13. **Sweat Hogs** class of incorrigible students majoring in remedial education. [TV: "Welcome Back, Kotter" in Terrace, II, 423]

350. ILLEGITIMACY

1. **bend sinister** supposed stigma of illegitimate birth. [Heraldry: Misc.]
2. **Clinker, Humphry** servant of Bramble family turns out to be illegitimate son of Mr. Bramble. [Br. Lit.: *Humphry Clinker*, Payton, 324]
3. **Edmund** illegitimate son of Earl of Gloucester; conspires against father. [Br. Hist.: *King Lear*]
4. **Jones, Tom** revealed to be Squire Allworthy's sister Bridget's illegitimate son. [Br. Lit.: Fielding *Tom Jones*]

351. ILLUSION (See also APPEARANCES, DECEIVING.)

1. **Barmecide feast** imaginary feast served to beggar by prince. [Arab. Lit.: *Arabian Nights*, "The Barmecide's Feast"]
2. **Emperor's New Clothes** supposedly invisible to unworthy people; in reality, nonexistent. [Dan. Lit.: *Andersen's Fairy Tales*]
3. **Fata Morgana** esp. in the Straits of Messina: named for Morgan le Fay. [Ital. Folklore: Espy, 14]
4. **George and Martha** as an imaginary compensation for their childlessness, pretend they have a son, who would now be twenty-one. [Am. Drama: Edward Albee *Who's Afraid of Virginia Woolf?* in *On Stage*, 447]
5. ***Glass Menagerie, The*** drama of St. Louis family escaping reality through illusion (1945). [Am. Lit.: *The Glass Menagerie*, Magill III, 418–420]
6. **Herbert, Niel** Mrs. Forrester's affairs destroyed his image of her. [Am. Lit.: *A Lost Lady*]
7. **Hudibras** English Don Quixote; opponent of repressive laws. [Br. Lit.: *Hudibras*, Espy, 204]
8. **Marshland, Jinny** saw philanderer Brad Criley as true lover. [Am. Lit.: *Cass Timberlane*]
9. **mirage** something illusory, such as an imaginary tree and pond in the midst of a desert. [Pop. Usage: Misc.]
10. **Mitty, Walter** imagines self in brilliant and heroic roles. [Am. Lit.: "The Secret Life of Walter Mitty" in Cartwell, 606–610]
11. **Quixote, Don** attacks windmills thinking them giants. [Span. Lit.: *Don Quixote*]
12. **Snoopy** imaginative dog. [Comics: "Peanuts" in Horn, 542–543]

13. **Xanadu** place appearing in Coleridge's dream; where Kubla Khan "did/A stately pleasure-dome decree." [Br. Lit.: "Kubla Khan" in Payton, 744]

352. IMMORTALITY (See also AGELESSNESS.)

1. **Admetus** granted everlasting life when wife Alcestis dies in his place. [Gk. Myth.: *NCE,* 54]
2. **amber axe** symbol of everlasting life. [Western Folklore: Jobes, 82]
3. **ambrosia** food of gods; bestows immortality. [Gk. Myth.: Brewer *Dictionary*]
4. **amrita** beverage conferring immortality. [Hindu Myth.: Parrinder, 19]
5. **ankh** talisman ensuring everlasting life. [Egyptian Myth.: Jobes, 99]
6. **apples of perpetual youth** admit Norse gods to eternal life. [Norse Myth.: Benét, 43]
7. **Calypso** promises Odysseus eternal youth and immortality if he will stay with her forever. [Gk. Myth.: Brewer *Dictionary,* 166]
8. **cedar** symbol of everlasting life. [Western Folklore: Jobes, 301]
9. **Chiron** immortal centaur. [Gk. Myth.: Kravitz, 58]
10. **cicada** symbol of eternal life. [Chinese Folklore: Jobes, 338]
11. **cypress** symbol of eternal life. [Flower Symbolism: Jobes, 402]
12. **cypress coffin** symbolizes everlasting life; used for burials of heroes. [Gk. and Egyptian Folklore: Leach, 272]
13. **fan palm** emblem of eternal life among early Christians. [Plant Symbolism: Embolden, 25–26]
14. **globe amaranth** flower of immortality. [Flower Symbolism: *Flora Symbolica,* 172]
15. **greybeard-grow-young** magical lake plant; its scent conferred everlasting life. [Babyl. Myth.: *Gilgamesh*]
16. **ichor** flows through the veins of gods instead of blood. [Gk. Myth.: Brewer *Dictionary*]
17. **Luggnagg** imaginary island; inhabitants immortal but lack immortal health. [Br. Lit.: *Gulliver's Travels*]
18. **nectar** drink of gods; bestows eternal life. [Gk. and Rom. Myth.: Brewer *Dictionary,* 75)]
19. **nightingale** immortal bird whose voice has been heard from time immemorial. [Br. Poetry: Keats "Ode to a Nightingale"]
20. **scarab** dung-beetle; said to carry secret of eternal life. [Egyptian Legend: Brewer *Dictionary,* 967]
21. **serpent** sheds skin to renew its life. [Gk. Myth.: Gaster, 37]

22. **Struldbrugs** race "cursed" with gift of deathlessness. [Br. Lit.: *Gulliver's Travels*]
23. **Tithonus** given eternal life but not eternal youth. [Gk. Myth.: Brewer *Dictionary,* 1087]
24. **tree of life** eat of its fruit and live forever. [O.T.: Genesis, 3:22]
25. **Utnapishtim** blessed by Enlil with everlasting life. [Babyl. Myth.: *Gilgamesh*]
26. **Wandering Jew** doomed to live forever for scorning Jesus. [Fr. Lit.: *The Wandering Jew*]
27. **Xanthus and Balius** Achilles' divine horses. [Gk. Lit.: *Iliad*]
28. **yew** traditionally planted in churchyards; symbol of deathlessness. [Br. Legend: Brewer *Dictionary,* 1171]

353. IMPERIALISM

1. **White Man's Burden** imperialist's duty to educate the uncivilized. [Br. Hist.: Brewer's *Dictionary,* 1152]

354. IMPERSONATION

1. **Patroclus** wore the armor of Achilles against the Trojans to encourage the disheartened Greeks. [Gk. Lit.: *Iliad*]
2. ***Prisoner of Zenda, The*** Englishman impersonating his distant relative King Rudolf is crowned in his stead. [Br. Lit.: *The Prisoner of Zenda*]
3. **Schicci, Gianni** dressed to resemble the dying testator in order to dictate a fraudulent will. [Ital. Hist. and Opera: *Gianni Schicci* in *Collier's*]
4. **Tichborne case** claimant to the Tichborne baronetcy impersonated the missing heir; proved a perjuror and imprisoned. [Br. Hist.: Brewer *Dictionary,* 898]
5. **Zeus** assumes the appearance of her husband Amphitryon in order to seduce Alcmene. [Fr. Drama: Molière *Amphitryon*]

355. IMPERTINENCE

1. **Bunny, Bugs** cartoon character who is impertinent toward everyone. [Comics: Horn, 140]
2. **McCarthy, Charlie** dummy who is impertinent toward master, Edgar Bergen. [Radio: "The Edgar Bergen and Charlie McCarthy Show" in Buxton, 76–77]
3. **Pierce, Hawkeye** wisecracking medic with an insult for everyone. [TV: "M*A*S*H" in Terrace, II, 71–72]

Impetuousness (See RASHNESS.)

356. IMPOSSIBILITY (See also UNATTAINABILITY.)

1. **belling the cat** mouse's proposal for warning of cat's approach; application fatal. [Gk. Lit.: *Aesop's Fables*]
2. **east and west** since one direction is relative to the other, "never the twain shall meet." [Pop. Usage: Misc.]
3. **leopard's spots** beast powerless to change them. [O.T.: Jeremiah 13:23]

357. IMPOTENCE

1. **Chatterly, Sir Clifford** paraplegic from the war, unable to satisfy his wife sexually. [Br. Lit.: D. H. Lawrence *Lady Chatterly's Lover* in Benét, 559]

358. IMPRISONMENT (See also ISOLATION.)

1. **Alcatraz Island** former federal maximum security penitentiary, near San Francisco; "escapeproof." [Am. Hist.: Flexner, 218]
2. **Altmark, the** German prison ship in World War II. [Br. Hist.: Brewer *Dictionary*, 27]
3. **Andersonville** in southwest Georgia; imprisoned Union soldiers died under wretched conditions. [Am. Hist.: *NCE*, 99]
4. **Attica** well-known prison in Attica, New York; remembered for its riot (1971). [Am. Hist.: *NCE*, 182]
5. **Bajazeth** Turkish emperor confined to a cage by Tamburlaine. [Br. Drama: *Tamburlaine the Great* in Magill I, 950]
6. **ball and chain** originally penological, now generalized symbol. [Western Folklore: Jobes, 176]
7. **Bastille** Paris prison stormed on July 14, 1789. [Fr. Hist.: Worth, 21]
8. **Birdman of Alcatraz** Robert F. Stroud (1890–1963), convicted murderer, became ornithologist in prison. [Am. Culture: Misc.]
9. **Black Hole of Calcutta** Indian dungeon in which overcrowding suffocated prisoners. [Br. Hist.: Harbottle, 45–46]
10. **Bok, Yakov** held in prison for two years under dreadful conditions. [Am. Lit.: Bernard Malamud *The Fixer*]
11. **Cereno, Benito** captain held captive by mutinous slaves. [Am. Lit.: *Benito Cereno*]
12. **Count of Monte Cristo** Edmond Dantès; wrongly imprisoned in the dungeons of Château D'If. [Fr. Lit.: *The Count of Monte Cristo*, Magill I, 158–160]

13. **Denisovitch, Ivan** struggles to stay alive in a Soviet prison camp. [Russ. Lit.: Solzhenitzyn *One Day in the Life of Ivan Denisovitch*]
14. **Devil's Island** Guiana island penal colony (1852–1938); Alfred Dreyfus among famous prisoners there. [Fr. Hist.: *NCE,* 754]
15. **Droma** chain forged to fetter wolf, Fenris. [Norse Myth.: *LLEI,* I: 326]
16. ***Enormous Room, The*** portrays three months behind bars in France. [Am. Lit.: *The Enormous Room*]
17. **Falconer** prison where former professor Farragut, who had killed his brother, witnesses the torments and chaos of the penal system. [Am. Lit.: Cheever *Falconer* in Weiss, 151]
18. **Fortunato** walled up to die in catacomb niche. [Am. Lit.: "The Cask of Amontillado" in *Portable Poe,* 309–316]
19. **Fotheringay** Mary Stuart's final prison and place of execution (1587). [Br. Hist.: Grun, 260]
20. **Hogan's Heroes** incarcerated in Stalag 13, unlikeliest of POW camps. [TV: Terrace, I, 357–358]
21. ***House of the Dead, The*** account of four years in the fortress-prison of Omsk. [Russ. Lit.: Dostoevsky *The House of the Dead* in Benét, 480]
22. **Ibbetson, Peter** imprisoned for life, spends all his nights in blissful dreams of existence with his beloved. [Br. Lit. & Am. Opera: G. du Maurier *Peter Ibbetson* in Magill I, 736]
23. **Leavenworth** the oldest military prison (est. 1874); also the name of a state penitentiary. [Am. Hist.: *NCE,* 984]
24. **Little Dorrit** born and grew up in the prison where for twenty years her father is incarcerated for debt. [Br. Lit.: Dickens *Little Dorrit*]
25. **Man in the Iron Mask** mystery prisoner; legendary contender for Louis XIV's throne. [Fr. Hist.: Brewer *Note-Book,* 460, 555]
26. **Manette, Dr.** lost memory during 18-year term in France. [Br. Lit.: *A Tale of Two Cities*]
27. **Marshalsea** ancient London prison, long used for incarcerating debtors. [Br. Hist.: Benét, 640]
28. **Newgate** famed jail of London in centuries past. [Br. Hist.: Brewer *Dictionary,* 754]
29. **Pickwick, Mr. (Samuel)** imprisoned for refusing to pay damages in a breach-of-promise suit. [Br. Lit.: Dickens *Pickwick Papers*]
30. ***Prisoner of Chillon, The*** poem by Lord Byron; based on imprisonment of François de Bonnivard. [Br. Lit.: Benét, 817]

31. **Rubashov, Nicholas** political prisoner held in isolation and brutally questioned. [Br. Lit.: Arthur Koestler *Darkness at Noon* in Magill I, 187]
32. **San Quentin** famous western California prison (established in 1852); the subject of many songs. [Am. Hist.: *NCE,* 2419]
33. **Sing Sing** notoriously harsh state prison at Ossining, New York. [Am. Hist.: Flexner, 219]
34. **Torquilstone** Front de Boeuf's castle, where he imprisoned Rowena, Rebecca, and Isaac. [Br. Lit.: Walter Scott *Ivanhoe*]
35. **Tower of London** famed as jail. [Br. Hist.: Brewer *Dictionary,* 1094]
36. **Ugolino** treacherous 13th-century count of Pisa, imprisoned and starved to death with his sons and grandsons. [Ital. Poetry: *Inferno*]
37. **Valjean, Jean** spent nineteen years in prison for stealing loaf of bread. [Fr. Lit.: *Les Misérables*]

359. INCEST

1. **Amnon** ravishes his sister, Tamar. [O.T.: II Samuel 13:14]
2. **Antiochus** sexually active with daughter. [Br. Lit.: *Pericles*]
3. **Canace** Aeolus's daughter; committed suicide after relations with brother. [Gk. Myth.: Zimmerman, 49]
4. **Cenci, Count Francesco** old libertine ravishes his daughter Beatrice. [Br. Lit.: Shelley *The Cenci,* Magill I, 131]
5. **Clymenus** Arcadian who violated his daughter, Harpalyce. [Gk. Myth.: Zimmerman, 65]
6. **Compson, Quentin** his only passion is for his sister Candace. [Am. Lit.: Faulkner *The Sound and the Fury* in Magill I, 917]
7. **Electra** bore great, passionate love for father, Agamemnon. [Gk. Myth.: Zimmerman, 92; Gk. Lit.: *Electra, Orestes*]
8. **Engstrand, Regina** Oswald's half-sister and chosen lover. [Nor. Lit.: *Ghosts*]
9. **Giovanni and Annabella** brother-sister romance. [Br. Lit.: *'Tis Pity She's a Whore*]
10. **Harpalyce** bears child by father, Clymenus. [Gk. Myth.: Howe, 114]
11. **Jocasta** unknowingly marries her son, Oedipus. [Gk. Lit.: *Oedipus Rex*]
12. **Judah** unknowingly has relations with daughter-in-law. [O.T.: Genesis 38:15–18]
13. **Lot** impregnates his two daughters. [O.T.: Genesis 19:36]

14. **Myrrha** mother of Adonis; daughter of Adonis's father. [Gk. Myth.: Brewer *Dictionary,* 741]
15. **Niquee and Anasterax** sister and brother live together in incest. [Span. Lit.: *Amadis de Gaul*]
16. **Oedipus** unknowingly marries mother and fathers four sons. [Gk. Lit.: *Oedipus Rex*]
17. **Sieglinde and Siegmund** twin brother and sister passionately in love. [Ger. Lit.: Mann "The Blood of the Walsungs"]
18. **Tamar** seduces her brother and her father. [Am. Lit.: Robinson Jeffers *Tamar* in Magill I, 948]
19. **Tower, Cassandra (Cassie)** had relations with Dr. Tower, her father. [Am. Lit.: *King's Row,* Magill I, 478–480]
20. **Warren, Nicole** suffers after having had sexual relations with father. [Am. Lit.: *Tender Is the Night*]

Incompetence (See INEPTITUDE.)

360. INCOMPLETENESS

1. ***Unfinished Symphony, The*** Schubert's eighth symphony of two movements instead of the customary four. [Ger. Music: Thompson]
2. ***Venus de Milo*** classic sculpture, discovered in 1820 with arms missing. [Gk. Art: Brewer *Dictionary*]

Incorruptibility (See HONESTY.)

361. INDECISION

1. **Buridan's ass** unable to decide between two haystacks, he would starve to death. [Fr. Philos.: Brewer *Dictionary,* 154]
2. **Cooke, Ebenezer** his irresolution usually leads to catatonia. [Am. Lit.: *The Sot-Weed Factor*]
3. **Graduate, the** college man with absolutely no direction. [Am. Lit.: *The Graduate*]
4. **Hamlet** Tragic hero who tarries and broods over revenge and suicide. [Br. Lit.: *Hamlet*]
5. **Libra** 7th constellation of the Zodiac; those born under Libra may be indecisive. [Astrology: Payton, 389]
6. **Panurge** unable to decide whether to marry, he consults many people and undertakes a long voyage to visit an oracle. [Fr. Lit.: Rabelais *Gargantua and Pantagruel*]
7. **Penelope** put off a decision on which suitor to marry by secretly unraveling the shroud she said she must first complete. [Gk. Lit.: *Odyssey*]

8. **Theramenes** shilly-shallying oligarch; nicknamed Cothurnus, i.e., ambipedal boot. [Gk. Hist.: Brewer *Dictionary*, 960]
9. ***Waiting for Godot*** tramps are torn between waiting for Godot to solve their problems and hanging themselves. [Anglo-French Drama: Samuel Beckett *Waiting for Godot* in Magill III, 1113]
10. **Whiffle, Peter** would-be writer, cursed with indecision, accomplishes nothing. [Am. Lit.: *Peter Whiffle*, Magill I, 739–741]
11. **hung jury** cannot decide guilt or innocence. [Am. Hist.: Misc.]

362. INDEPENDENCE

1. **Bastille Day** July 14; French national holiday celebrating the fall of the Bastille prison (1789). [Fr. Hist.: *NCE*, 245]
2. **Declaration of Independence** by delegates of the American Thirteen Colonies announcing U.S. independence from Great Britain (1776). [Am. Hist.: *NCE*, 733]
3. **Huggins, Henry** self-reliant boy; earns money for toys. [Children's Lit.: *Henry Huggins*]
4. **Independence Day** Fourth of July; U.S. patriotic holiday celebrating the Declaration of Independence. [Am. Hist.: *NCE*, 990]
5. **Maine** often thought of as the state of "independent Yankees." [Pop. Culture: Misc.]
6. **Mugwumps** Republican party members who voted independently. [Am. Hist.: Jameson, 337]
7. **Quebec** Canada's French-speaking province has often attempted to attain independence from rest of country. [Canadian Hist.: *NCE*, 2555]
8. **Tree of Liberty** symbolic post or tree hung with flags and other devices and crowned with the liberty cap. [Misc.: Brewer *Dictionary*, 911]
9. **white oak** indicates self-sufficiency. [Flower Symbolism: *Flora Symbolica*, 178]

363. INDIFFERENCE

1. **Antoinette, Marie** (1755–1793) queen of France to whom is attributed this statement on the solution to bread famine: "Let them eat cake." [Fr. Hist.: *NCE*, 1696]
2. **Bastienne** unsuccessful ploy to win back Bastien. [Ger. Opera: Mozart, *Bastien and Bastienne*, Westerman, 83]
3. **Defarge, Madame** feigned indifference; knitted while executions were taking place. [Br. Lit.: *A Tale of Two Cities*]

4. **Laodicean** inhabitant of ancient Greek city, Laodicea; people noted for indifferent attitude toward religion. [Gk. Hist.: *NCE,* 1529]
5. **Nero** (37–68) Roman Emperor who is reported to have fiddled while Rome burned. [Rom. Hist.: Misc.]
6. **New York City** often thought of as a metropolis of cold, uncaring people. [Pop. Culture: Misc.]
7. **Oblomov** passed life in torpor; symbolically, died sleeping. [Russ. Lit.: *Oblomov*]
8. **senvy** indicates apathy and noncaring. [Flower Symbolism: *Flora Symbolica,* 177]

364. INDIVIDUALISM (See also EGOTISM.)

1. **Beaumont, Ned** gambler-detective solves murder case in unorthodox manner. [Am. Lit.: *The Glass Key,* Magill I, 307–308]
2. **Different Drummer** Thoreau's eloquent prose poem on the inner freedom and individualistic character of man. [Am. Lit.: *NCE,* 2739]
3. **Longstocking, Pippi** eccentric young girl who sets her own standards. [Children's Lit.: *Pippi Longstocking*]

365. INDUCEMENT

1. **Electra** incited brother, Orestes, to kill their mother and her lover. [Gk. Myth.: Zimmerman, 92; Gk. Lit.: *Electra, Orestes*]
2. **Hezekiah** exhorts Judah to stand fast against Assyrians. [O.T.: II Chronicles 32:6–8]
3. **Lantier, Etienne** exhorts fellow miners to massive strike. [Fr. Lit.: *Germinal*]
4. **Mannon, Lavinia** 20th-century Electra in New England. [Am. Lit.: *Mourning Becomes Electra*]
5. **Salome** beguilingly prompts decapitation of John the Baptist. [N.T.: Mark 6:22–28]
6. **Tricoteuses** sobriquet of battle-exhorting women at French Convention. [Fr. Hist.: Brewer *Dictionary,* 1100]
7. **Tyrtaeus** (fl. 7th century B.C.) elegist; roused Spartans to Messenian triumph. [Gk. Hist.: Brewer *Dictionary,* 1111]

366. INDUSTRIOUSNESS

1. **ant** works hard to prepare for winter while grasshopper plays. [Gk. Lit.: *Aesop's Fables,* "The Ant and the Grasshopper"]
2. **beaver** perpetually and eagerly active. [Western Folklore: Jobes, 192]

3. **bee** proverbial busyness refers to ceaseless activity of worker bees. [Western Folklore: Jobes, 445]
4. **beehive** heraldic and verbal symbol. [Western Folklore: Jobes, 193]
5. **grindstone** or grind common metaphor for industriousness. [Pop. Culture: Misc.]
6. **red clover** symbolic of diligence. [Flower Symbolism: Jobes, 350]
7. **Saturday's child** works hard for his living. [Nurs. Rhyme: Opie, 309]
8. **Stakhanov, Aleksey** (1905–) Russian worker who "overachieved"; increased daily output enormously. [Russ. Hist.: *NCE,* 2606]
9. **third little pig** builds his house of bricks while his two brothers fritter away their time. [Children's Lit.: *The Three Little Pigs*]

367. INEPTITUDE (See also AWKWARDNESS.)

1. **Brown, Charlie** meek hero unable to kick a football, fly a kite, or win a baseball game. [Comics: "Peanuts" in Horn, 543]
2. **Capt. Queeg** incompetent commander of the minesweeper *Caine.* [Am. Lit. and Cinema: Wouk *The Caine Mutiny* in Benét, 157]
3. **Dogberry** officious, inept constable. [Br. Lit.: *Much Ado About Nothing*]
4. **Fife, Barney** deputy who can't be trusted with loaded gun. [TV: "The Andy Griffith Show" in Terrace, I, 55–56]
5. **George of the Jungle** bungling do-gooder. [TV: Terrace, I, 305–306]
6. **Gilligan** whose every action reeks of incompetence. [TV: "Gilligan's Island" in Terrace, I, 312–313]
7. **Gordon, Dr.** called a "butcher" for his needless and bungled operations. [Am. Lit.: *King's Row*; Magill I, 478]
8. **Hagar the Horrible** soft-hearted, unkempt Viking whose raids yield minuscule plunder. [Comics: Horn, 299]
9. **Halftrack, General** the ultimate in inept officers. [Comics: "Beetle Bailey" in Horn, 105–106]
10. **Hound, Huckleberry** bungler trying to find niche; always fails. [TV: "The Huckleberry Hound Show" in Terrace, I, 367–377]
11. **Klink, Colonel** naive official in charge of prisoner-of-war camp. [TV: "Hogan's Heroes" in Terrace, I, 357–358]
12. **Lucky Eddie** Hagar's chinless aide, bungles the simplest assignments. [Comics: *Hagar the Horrible* in Horn, 299]

13. **Marplot** actions are well-meant, but his continual interference ruins lovers' plans. [Br. Drama: *The Busybody* in Barnhart, 185]
14. **Orbaneja** obliged to label painted objects for identification. [Span. Lit.: *Don Quixote*]
15. **Peter Principle, The** book stating, "in a Hierarchy, every employee tends to rise to the level of his incompetence." [Am. Lit.: *The Peter Principle,* Payton, 522]
16. **Sad Sack** who can't do anything right. [Comics: "The Sad Sack" in Horn, 595–596]
17. **Scarecrow** can't live up to his name. [Am. Lit.: *The Wonderful Wizard of Oz;* Am. Cinema: Halliwell, 780]
18. **Schultz, Sergeant** bumbling assistant to Colonel Klink at Stalag 13. [TV: "Hogan's Heroes" in Terrace, I, 357–358]
19. **Slop, Dr.** country doctor attends Tristram Shandy's birth and crushes the infant's nose with his forceps. [Br. Lit.: *Tristram Shandy* in Magill I, 1027]
20. **three men in a boat** inexperience makes their trip on the Thames become a series of misfortunes. [Br. Lit.: Jerome *Three Men in a Boat* in Magill II, 1018]
21. **Toody and Muldoon** twin antitheses of "New York's Finest." [TV: "Car 54, Where Are You?" in Terrace, I, 138–139]
22. **Tumbleweeds** world's most incompetent sheriff. [Comics: Horn, 673]
23. **White Knight** invents clever objects that never work. [Br. Lit.: Lewis Carroll *Through the Looking-Glass*]

368. INEXPENSIVENESS

1. **bargain basement** sale of old stock at highly discounted prices. [Pop. Culture: Misc.]
2. **Five and Ten** popular sobriquet for various department stores, which at one time sold no item for more than a dime. [Pop. Culture: Misc.]
3. **flea market** yard sale of used items at low prices. [Pop. Culture: Misc.]
4. **Louisiana Purchase** about one third the area of the U.S. bought from Napoleon for $15 million (1803). [Am. Hist.: Jameson, 293]
5. **Manhattan** Manhattan Indians sold the island to Dutch West India Company supposedly for about $24 worth of merchandise (1626). [Am. Hist.: Jameson, 305]

6. **Mickey Mouse** squeaky-voiced cartoon hero; the term is often used in alluding to things of minor significance or expense. [Am. Cinema: *EB, VI:* 862; Am. Pop. Culture: Misc.]
7. **Seward's Folly** Alaska, purchased from Russia by Henry Seward for 2 cents an acre (1867). [Am. Hist.: Payton, 610]
8. **tag sale** yard sale of used items, usually at very low prices. [Pop. Culture: Misc.]
9. **Woolworth's** international five-and-dime store. [Am. Commerce: *NCE,* 3004]

369. INEXPERIENCE (See also INNOCENCE, NAÏVETÉ.)

1. **Bowes, Major Edward** (1874–1946) originator and master of ceremonies of the Amateur Hour on radio. [Am. Radio: Buxton, 149–150]
2. **Gong Show, The** variety show in which beginners try to prove their abilities. [TV: Misc.]
3. **greenhorn** a raw, inexperienced person; especially a new cowboy. [Pop. Culture: Misc.]
4. **Mack, Ted** (1904–1976) host of a television show starring amateurs. [TV: "Ted Mack and the Original Amateur Hour" in Terrace, II, 347]
5. **Newcome, Johnny** any unpracticed youth, especially new military officers. [Br. Folklore: Wheeler, 258]
6. **plebe** (plebeian) first or lowest class, especially at U.S. Military and Naval Academies. [Pop. Culture: Misc.]
7. **rookie** a novice; often an athlete playing his first season as a member of a professional sports team. [Sports: Misc.]

370. INFANTICIDE

1. **Astyanax** Hector's infant son, thrown from the walls of Troy by the Greeks. [Gk. Myth.: Hamilton, 289]
2. **Cronos** warned that a son would dethrone him, swallowed all his children at birth. [Gk. Myth.: Benét, 237]
3. **Sorrel, Hetty** leaves her illegitimate infant to die. [Br. Lit.: Eliot *Adam Bede*]

Infertility (See BARRENNESS.)

Infidelity (See ADULTERY, CUCKOLDRY, FAITHLESSNESS.)

371. INFORMER

1. **Battus** revealed theft by Mercury; turned to touchstone. [Gk. and Rom. Myth.: Walsh *Classical,* 47]

2. **Cenci, Count Francesco** old libertine ravishes his daughter Beatrice. [Br. Lit.: Shelley *The Cenci*; Magill I, 131]
3. **Chambers, Whittaker** (1901–1961) chief witness in perjury trial of Alger Hiss (1949). [Am. Hist.: *NCE,* 501]
4. **Dean, John W., III** (1938–) chief witness and informer against Nixon in the Watergate hearings. [Am. Hist.: *NCE,* 2939]
5. **Judas Iscariot** led armed band to Gethsemane and showed them which one was Jesus. [N.T.: Matthew 26:46–50; Mark 14:42–45; Luke 22:47–48; John 18:1–8]
6. **Morgan le Fay** reveals Lancelot and Guinevere's affair to Arthur. [Arthurian Legend: Harvey, 559]
7. **Nolan, Gypo** betrays friend to police for subsistence money. [Irish Lit.: *The Informer*]
8. **Peachum, Mr.** informer and fence for stolen goods. [Br. Lit.: *The Beggar's Opera*]
9. **Teresa, Vincent** wrote a book in which he revealed inner workings of the Mafia. [Am. Lit.: *My Life in the Mafia*]
10. **Valachi, Joe** (1903–1971) New York gangster who revealed the inner operations of the Mafia. [Am. Hist.: *Facts* (1971), 436]

372. INGRATITUDE

1. **Anastasie and Delphine** ungrateful daughters do not attend father's funeral. [Fr. Lit.: *Père Goriot*]
2. **Glencoe, Massacre of** Campbell clan, having accepted hospitality of the MacDonalds for more than a week, attacked their hosts, killing 38. [Scot. Hist.: *EB,* IV: 573]
3. **Goneril and Regan** two evil daughters of King Lear; their monstrous ingratitude upon receiving his kingdom drives him mad. [Br. Lit.: *King Lear*]
4. **Lucius** enjoyed Timon's generosity; refuses him loan when poor. [Br. Lit.: *Timon of Athens*]
5. **Lucullus** Timon's false friend; forgets all too easily his generosity. [Br. Lit.: *Timon of Athens*]
6. **Sempronius** shared in Timon's bounty; denies him loan when poor. [Br. Lit.: *Timon of Athens*]
7. **ten lepers** of the ten lepers cleansed by Jesus, only one returned to thank him. [N.T.: Luke 11–19]

373. INHOSPITALITY

1. **Nabal** rudely refuses David's messengers' request for food. [O.T.: I Samuel 25:10–11]

374. INJUSTICE

1. **American concentration camps** 110,000 Japanese-Americans incarcerated during WWII. [Am. Hist.: Van Doren, 487]
2. **Bassianus** murdered after being falsely accused. [Br. Lit.: *Titus Andronicus*]
3. **Bean, Judge Roy** (1825–1904) his brand of justice was the only "law west of the Pecos." [Am. Hist.: *WB,* 2, 137]
4. **Ben Hur** wrongly accused of attempted murder. [Am. Lit.: *Ben Hur,* Hart, 72]
5. ***Bleak House*** a fortune is dissipated by the long legal battle of Jarndyce vs. Jarndyce, and the heir dies in misery. [Br. Lit.: Dickens *Bleak House*]
6. **Bligh, William** (1754–1817) naval officer accused of practising unfair and illegal cruelties. [Br. Hist.: *EB,* II: 82; Am. Lit.: *Mutiny on the Bounty*]
7. **Bok, Yakov** Jew falsely accused of ritual murder in Russia. [Am. Lit.: *The Fixer*]
8. **Budd, Billy** courtmartialed and unjustly hanged as mutineer and murderer. [Am. Lit.: *Billy Budd*]
9. **Child of the Cord** defendants brought before the *Vehmgerichte.* [Ger. Hist.: Brewer *Note-Book,* 166]
10. **Dred Scott decision** majority ruling by Supreme Court that a slave is property and not a U.S. citizen (1857). [Am. Hist.: Payton, 203]
11. **Dreyfus, Capt. Albert** (1859–1935) imprisoned on Devil's Island on falsified espionage charges. [Fr. Hist.: Wallechinsky, 60]
12. **Eurydice** Orpheus's wife; taken to underworld before her time. [Gk. Myth.: Magill I, 700–701]
13. **Falder, Justice** law clerk commits forgery for an unselfish purpose, is imprisoned, barred from work, eventually commits suicide. [Br. Lit.: Galsworthy *Justice*; Magill I, 466]
14. **Furry Lawcats** name given to a rapacious breed in Rabelais's violent satire on the venality of the courts. [Fr. Lit.: Rabelais *Gargantua and Pantagruel*]
15. **Hippolytus** falsely accused by stepmother of rape after he rejected her advances. [Rom. Lit.: *Aeneid; Metamorphoses*]
16. **hops** symbol of injustice. [Flower Symbolism: *Flora Symbolica,* 174; Kunz, 330]
17. **Jedburgh Justice** Scottish version of lynch law. [Scot. Hist.: Brewer *Note-Book,* 468]

18. **Jim Crow laws** among other rulings, prevented interstate travel by Negroes. [Am. Hist.: Van Doren, 485]
19. **Joseph K.** though innocent of any crime, he is arrested, condemned, and executed. [Ger. Lit.: Kafka *The Trial* in Benét, 1023]
20. **kangaroo court** moblike tribunal, usually disregarding principles of justice. [Pop. Culture: Misc.]
21. **Lydford law** "hang first; try later." [Br. Hist.: Espy, 160]
22. **Lynch, Judge** (1736–1796) personification of mob law, summary execution. [Am. Hist.: Leach, 561]
23. **Martius and Quintus** falsely accused of Bassianus' murder. [Br. Lit.: *Titus Andronicus*]
24. **Mohicans** Indian tribe driven off homeland. [Am. Hist.: Hart, 515]
25. ***Ox-Bow Incident, The*** in revenge for having supposedly rustled cattle and killed a man, three suspects are lynched. [Am. Lit.: *The Ox-Bow Incident*]
26. **Queen of Hearts** "first the sentence, and then the evidence!" [Br. Lit.: *Alice's Adventures in Wonderland*]
27. **Rubashov, Nicholas** punished for crimes he never committed. [Br. Lit.: *Darkness at Noon*]
28. **Sacco and Vanzetti** accused and executed for murder (1927); their guilt has been largely disputed. [Am. Hist.: Allen, 59–61]
29. **Stamp Act** unfair revenue law imposed upon American colonies by Britain (1765). [Am. Hist.: Jameson, 475]
30. **Valjean, Jean** imprisoned nineteen years for stealing loaf of bread. [Fr. Lit.: *Les Misérables*]
31. **Vehmgerichte** medieval Westphalian tribunals; judges abused juridical powers. [Ger. Hist.: Brewer *Dictionary*, 1124]

375. INNOCENCE (See also INEXPERIENCE, NAÏVETÉ.)

1. **Adam and Eve** naked in Eden; knew no shame. [O.T.: Genesis 2:25]
2. **Arjuna** Sanskrit name means sinless. [Hindu Myth.: Benét, 50]
3. ***Babes in the Wood*** innocent children are lost in the wood and die. [Br. Lit.: *Babes in the Wood*, Walsh *Classical*, 42]
4. **basin and ewer** Pilate's guiltlessness signified by washing of hands. [N.T.: Matthew 27:24]
5. **Budd, Billy** friendly sailor; held in warm affection by crew. [Am. Lit.: *Billy Budd*]
6. **Christabel** free of evil. [Br. Lit.: "Christabel" in Walsh *Modern*, 95]

7. **Cinderella** with fairy godmother's aid, poor maligned girl wins prince's heart. [Fr. Fairy Tale: *Cinderella*]
8. **Cio-Cio-San** believes marriage to Pinkerton is real. [Ital. Opera: Puccini, *Madama Butterfly,* Westerman, 357]
9. **daisy** symbol of blamelessness. [Flower Symbolism: *Flora Symbolica,* 173; Kunz, 328]
10. **Delano, Amasa** naive, goodhearted captain rescues captive captain from mutineers. [Am. Lit.: *Benito Cereno*]
11. **Desdemona** blamelessness martyred through slander. [Br. Lit.: *Othello*]
12. **Hallyard, St.** Norwegian martyred in defense of guiltless woman. [Christian Hagiog.: Attwater, 165]
13. **Heidi** has instinct for goodness. [Children's Lit.: *Heidi*]
14. **Imogen** chaste wife unjustly suspected by Postumus of unfaithfulness. [Br. Drama: Shakespeare *Cymbeline*]
15. **lamb** attribute of young woman; personification of guiltlessness. [Art: Hall, 161]
16. **Minnie** female saloonkeeper in mining town; never been kissed. [Ital. Opera: Puccini, *Girl of the Golden West,* Westerman, 360–361]
17. **Pedro** in marrying former mistress of enemy. [Ger. Opera: d'Albert, *Tiefland,* Westerman, 371–374]
18. **Pinch, Tom** guileless, with unbounded goodness of heart. [Br. Lit.: *Martin Chuzzlewit*]
19. **Rima** beautiful jungle girl, lover of birds and animals, knows neither evil nor guile. [Br. Lit.: Hudson *Green Mansions* in Magill I, 333]
20. **Susanna** unjustly condemned for adultery; later acquitted. [Apocrypha: Daniel and Susanna]

Inquisitiveness (See **CURIOSITY.**)

Insanity (See **MADNESS.**)

376. INSECT

1. **archy** literary cockroach that cannot reach shift-key on the typewriter. [Am. Lit.: *archy and mehitabel*; Benét, 46]
2. **bread-and-butter-fly** its body is a crust; lives on weak tea. [Br. Lit.: Lewis Carroll *Through the Looking-glass*]
3. ***Charlotte's Web*** story of a spider who saves a young girl's pet pig. [Am. Lit.: E. B. White *Charlotte's Web*]
4. **gnat** chicken-sized insect that tells Alice all about other strange insects. [Br. Lit.: Lewis Carroll *Through the Looking-glass*]

5. ***Metamorphosis*** Gregor Samsa turned into a huge insect. [Ger. Lit.: Kafka *Metamorphosis*]
6. **rocking-horse-fly** wooden insect feeds on sap and sawdust. [Br. Lit.: Lewis Carroll *Through the Looking-glass*]
7. **snap-dragon-fly** has a body of plum pudding and lives on mince pie. [Br. Lit.: Lewis Carroll *Through the Looking-glass*]

377. INSECURITY

1. **Hamlet** introspective, vacillating Prince of Denmark. [Br. Lit.: *Hamlet*]
2. **Linus** cartoon character who is lost without his security blanket. [Comics: "Peanuts" in Horn, 542–543]

Inseparability (See **FRIENDSHIP.**)

Insolence (See **ARROGANCE.**)

378. INSPIRATION

1. **Aganippe** fountain at foot of Mt. Helicon, consecrated to Muses. [Gk. Myth.: *LLEI,* I: 322]
2. **angelica** traditional representation of inspiration. [Herb Symbolism: *Flora Symbolica,* 164]
3. **Calliope** Muse of heroic poetry. [Gk. Myth.: Zimmerman, 47]
4. **Castalia** Parnassian spring; regarded as source of inspiration. [Gk. Myth.: Zimmerman, 52]
5. **Clio** Muse of history. [Gk. Myth.: Zimmerman, 64]
6. **dove** source of afflatus. [Art: Hall, 161]
7. **Dulcinea (del Toboso)** country girl, whom Quixote apotheosizes as guiding light. [Span. Lit.: *Don Quixote*]
8. **Erato** Muse of lyric poetry, love poetry, and marriage songs. [Gk. Myth.: Zimmerman, 97]
9. **Euterpe** Muse of music and lyric poetry. [Gk. Myth.: Zimmerman, 105]
10. **Hippocrene** Mt. Helicon spring regarded as source of poetic inspiration. [Gk. Myth.: *NCE,* 1246]
11. **lactating breast** representation of poetic and musical impulse. [Art: Hall, 161]
12. **Melpomene** Muse of tragedy (tragic drama). [Gk. Myth.: Zimmerman, 163]
13. **palm, garland of** traditional identification of a Muse. [Gk. Myth.: Jobes, 374]
14. **Pegasus** steed of the Muses; symbolizes poetic inspiration. [Gk. Myth.: Espy, 32]

15. **Pierian spring** fountain in Macedonia, sacred to the Muses, believed to communicate inspiration. [Gk. Myth.: Benét, 787]
16. **Polyhymnia** or **Polymania** Muse of sacred song, oratory, lyric, singing, and rhetoric. [Gk. Myth.: Zimmerman, 216]
17. **Stroeve, Blanche** her body inspired Strickland to paint nude portrait. [Br. Lit.: *The Moon and Sixpence,* Magill I, 621–623]
18. **Terpsichore** Muse of choral song and dancing. [Gk. Myth.: Zimmerman, 260]
19. **Thalia** Muse of comedy. [Gk. Myth.: Zimmerman, 261]
20. **tongues of fire** manifestation of Holy Spirit's descent on Pentecost. [N.T.: Acts 2:1–4]
21. **Urania** Muse of astronomy. [Gk. Myth.: Zimmerman, 284]

379. INTELLIGENCE (See also WISDOM.)

1. **Alexander the Great** looses the Gordian knot by cutting it with his sword. [Gk. Legend: Brewer *Dictionary,* 409]
2. **IQ** (intelligence quotient) controversial measurement of intelligence by formula which compares mental age with chronological age. [Western Education.: *EB,* V: 376]
3. **Mensa International** organization whose members have IQs in the top two percent of the general population. [Am. Pop. Culture: *EB,* VI: 793]
4. **Stanford-Binet Intelligence Scale** test used to measure IQ; designed to be used primarily with children. [Am. Education: *EB,* IX: 521]

Intemperance (See DRUNKENNESS.)

Intimidation (See BULLYING.)

Intoxication (See DRUNKENNESS.)

380. INTRIGUE (See also CONSPIRACY.)

1. **Borgias** 15th-century family who stopped at nothing to gain power. [Ital. Hist.: Plumb, 59]
2. **Ems dispatch** Bismarck's purposely provocative memo on Spanish succession; sparked Franco-Prussian war (1870). [Ger. Hist.: *NCE,* 866]
3. **Machiavelli, Nicolò** (1469–1527) author of book extolling political cunning. [Ital. Hist.: *The Prince*]
4. **Mannon, Lavinia** undoes adulterous mother by brainwashing brother. [Am. Lit.: *Mourning Becomes Electra*]
5. **Mission Impossible** team of investigators with Byzantine *modus operandi.* [TV: "Mission Impossible" in Terrace, II, 100–101]

6. **Paolino** has cohort woo his covertly wed wife. [Ital. Opera: Cimarosa, *The Secret Marriage*, Westerman, 63]
7. **Phormio** slick lawyer finagles on behalf of two men. [Rom. Lit.: *Phormio*]
8. **Ruritania** imaginary pre-WWI kingdom, rife with political machinations. [Br. Lit.: *Prisoner of Zenda*]
9. **X Y Z Affair** thinly disguised extortion aroused anti-French feelings (1797–1798). [Am. Hist.: Jameson, 564]

381. INVENTIVENESS

1. **Archimedes** (287–212 B.C.) invented military engine which saved Syracuse. [Gk. Hist.: Hall, 31]
2. **Bell, Alexander Graham** (1847–1922) inventor of telephone (1876). [Am. Hist.: Jameson, 46]
3. **Connecticut Yankee, the** made mechanical devices in the sixth century. [Am. Lit.: *A Connecticut Yankee in King Arthur's Court*]
4. **Dictynna** invented fishermen's nets. [Gk. Myth.: Kravitz, 79]
5. **Edison, Thomas Alva** (1847–1931) inventor of many electrical devices. [Am. Hist.: Jameson, 157]
6. **Erechtheus** inventor of chariots. [Gk. Myth.: Kravitz, 91]
7. **Franklin, Benjamin** (1706–1790) gave us lightning rod, bifocals, efficient stove, etc. [Am. Hist.: Jameson, 836]
8. **Goldberg, Rube** (1883–1970) designed elaborate contraptions to effect simple results. [Am. Hist.: Espy, 111]
9. **Gumbrill, Theodore, Jr.** designs trousers with built-in air-cushion seat. [Br. Lit.: Aldous Huxley *Antic Hay* in Benét, 39]
10. **Leonardo da Vinci** (1452–1519) created prototypes for parachutes, submarines, tanks, helicopters. [Ital. Hist.: Plum, 185–200]
11. **McVey, Hugh** invents and builds successful machines for farm and mine operators. [Am. Lit.: Anderson *Poor White* in Magill I, 762]

382. INVINCIBILITY

1. **Great Boyg, the** shapeless, unconquerable troll, representing the riddle of existence. [Nor. Drama: Ibsen *Peer Gynt* in Magill I, 722]

383. INVISIBILITY

1. **Abaris** magic arrow made him invisible. [Gk. Myth.: Benét, 1]
2. **agate** confers this power. [Rom. Folklore: Brewer *Dictionary*, 15]

3. **Ariel** invisible spirit plays tricks on the castaways. [Br. Drama: Shakespeare *The Tempest*]
4. **Cheshire cat** vanishes at will; grin the last feature to go. [Br. Lit.: *Alice's Adventures in Wonderland*]
5. **chrysoprase** put in mouth, renders bearer invisible. [Gem Symbolism: Kunz, 67–68]
6. **Emperor's New Clothes** supposed to be invisible to anyone unworthy of his post. [Dan. Lit.: Andersen "The Emperor's New Clothes" in *Andersen's Fairy Tales*]
7. **fern seed** makes bearer invisible. [Western Folklore: Brewer *Dictionary*, 406]
8. **glory, hand of** severed hand of hanged man renders bearer invisible. [Western Folklore: Leach, 477]
9. **Gyges's ring** confers this power. [Gk. Folklore: Brewer, *Dictionary*, 497]
10. **Harvey** six-foot rabbit invisible to everyone but the play's protagonist. [Am. Lit.: Benét, 444]
11. **heliotrope** effective if drunk with proper invocations. [Medieval Folklore: Boland, 43]
12. **Invisible Man** (Griffin) character made invisible by chemicals. [Br. Lit.: *Invisible Man*]
13. **Mambrino's Helmet** golden helmet makes wearer invisible. [Span. Lit.: *Don Quixote*]
14. **Perseus's helmet** made him invisible when he killed Medusa. [Gk. Myth.: *Metamorphoses*]
15. **Reynard the Fox's ring** when ring becomes green, Reynard is invisible. [Medieval Lit.: *Reynard the Fox*]
16. **tarnhelm** golden helmet that allowed its wearer to assume any form or even become invisible. [Ger. Opera: Wagner *The Ring of the Nibelung*]
17. **tarnkappe** cloak taken from the Nibelungs by Siegfried grants the wearer invisibility and strength. [Ger. Lit.: *Nibelungenlied*]

384. IRASCIBILITY (See also ANGER, EXASPERATION, SHREWISHNESS.)

1. **Caius, Dr.** irritable physician. [Br. Lit.: *Merry Wives of Windsor*]
2. **Donald Duck** cantankerousness itself. [Comics: Horn, 216–217]
3. **Elisha** sics bears on boys for their jibing. [O.T.: II Kings 2:23–24]

4. **Findlay, Maude** out-spoken, oft-married, liberated woman. [TV: "Maude" in Terrace, II, 79–80]
5. **Granny** cantankerous matriarch of the Clampett family. [TV: "The Beverly Hillbillies" in Terrace, I, 93–94]
6. **Hotspur** Sir Henry Percy, so named for his fiery character. [Br. Lit.: *I Henry IV*]
7. **Houlihan, Hot Lips** resident termagant of M*A*S*H 4077. [TV: "M*A*S*H" in Terrace, II, 70–71]
8. **Nipper, Susan** sharp-tongued nurse of Florence Dombey. [Br. Lit.: *Dombey and Son*]
9. **Tybalt** irascible foil to peacemaking Benvolio. [Br. Lit.: *Romeo and Juliet*]
10. **yellow bile** humor effecting temperament of irritability. [Medieval Physiology: Hall, 130]

385. IRONY (See also LAST LAUGH.)

1. **Alvaro** attempt to disarm accidentally causes opponent's death. [Ital. Opera: Verdi, *La Forza del Destino,* Westerman, 316]
2. **Arrigo** fight for freedom means opposing new found father. [Ital. Opera: Verdi, *Sicilian Vespers,* Westerman, 308–309]
3. **Artemidorus** presents Caesar with scroll outlining conspiracy; it remains unopened. [Br. Lit.: *Julius Caesar*]
4. **Barabas** perishes in trap he set for Turks. [Br. Lit.: *The Jew of Malta*]
5. ***Barnaby Rudge*** Dennis, the public hangman, is sentenced to be hanged on his own scaffold. [Br. Lit.: Dickens *Barnaby Rudge*]
6. **Bazaroff** reformed radical; dies accidentally. [Russ. Lit.: *Fathers and Sons*]
7. ***Bel-Ami*** subtitled: "The History of a Scoundrel." [Fr. Lit.: *Bel-Ami*]
8. **Bigger Thomas** finds freedom through killing and life's meaning through death. [Am. Lit.: *Native Son,* Magill I, 643–645]
9. **Bishop, the** dying in a delirium, he speaks of pomp and luxury rather than salvation. [Br. Poetry: Browning "The Bishop Orders His Tomb"]
10. **Carlos, Don** loves bride he procured for his father. [Ital. Opera: Verdi, *Don Carlos,* Westerman, 319]
11. **Cassandra** true prophet, doomed to go unbelieved. [Gk. Myth.: Espy, 40]
12. ***Catch-22*** pleading insanity to leave army indicates sanity. [Am. Lit.: *Catch-22*]

13. **Claudius** emperor-scholar in soldier-worshiping nation. [Br. Lit.: *I, Claudius*]
14. ***Così fan tutte*** illustrates comically some shortcomings of feminine fidelity. [Ger. Opera: Mozart, *Così fan tutte,* Westerman, 97–98]
15. **Creon** victim of his own harsh tyranny. [Gk. Lit.: *Antigone*]
16. **Defender of the Faith** Henry VIII's pre-Reformation title, conferred by Leo X. [Br. Hist.: Benét, 258]
17. **Gaigern, Baron** attempts to rob ballerina; becomes her lover. [Ger. Lit.: *Grand Hotel*]
18. ***Gift of the Magi, The*** young couple sell their dearest possessions to buy Christmas gifts for one another, discover that the sacrifice made the gifts unusable. [Am. Lit.: O. Henry *The Gift of the Magi* in Benét, 395]
19. **Harmony Society** embraced communism and celibacy; the latter caused their extinction. [Am. Hist.: Hart, 349]
20. **John of Balue** imprisoned in an iron cage he invented. [Br. Lit.: *Quentin Durward*]
21. ***Magic Mountain, The*** sanatorium as escape from "insane world." [Ger. Lit.: *The Magic Mountain,* Magill I, 545–547]
22. ***Mayor of Casterbridge, The*** Henchard dies in care of man he tyrannized. [Br. Lit.: *The Mayor of Casterbridge,* Magill I, 571–573]
23. ***Modest Proposal, A*** essay in which Swift advises the Irish to eat their babies or sell them in order to relieve famine and reduce overpopulation. [Br. Lit.: Benét, 677]
24. **Otternschlag, Dr.** attempting suicide, discovers will to live. [Ger. Lit.: *Grand Hotel*]
25. **Pagliaccio** clown forced to be funny despite breaking heart. [Ital. Opera: Leoncavallo, *Pagliacci,* Espy, 339]
26. **Patterne, Sir Willoughby** egoist's actions lead to self-defeat. [Br. Lit.: *The Egoist,* Magill I, 241–242]
27. **Point, Jack** jester who must be funny even when events break his heart. [Br. Opera: Gilbert & Sullivan *The Yeomen of the Guard*]
28. **Polycrates** tyrant of Athens who, renowned for his continual good fortune, is ignominiously trapped and crucified by an envious ruler. [Gk. Myth.: Benét, 801]
29. **Popeye** murderer; hanged for murder he did not commit. [Am. Lit.: *Sanctuary*]
30. ***R.U.R.*** robots, manufactured for man's ease, revolt. [Czech. Lit.: *R.U.R.*]

31. **Rachel** executed as Jewess; revealed to be Christian clergyman's daughter. [Fr. Opera: Halévy, *The Jewess,* Westerman, 168]
32. **Rigoletto** arranges murder of daughter's seducer; she dies instead. [Ital. Opera: Verdi, *Rigoletto,* Westerman, 299–300]
33. **Sitzkrieg** "phony war"; lull between Polish conquest and invasion of France. [Eur. Hist.: *Hitler,* 815–819]
34. **Sohrab** unaware, engages in single combat with Rustum, the father he had been seeking, and is slain. [Br. Poetry: *Sohrab and Rustum* in Benét, 943]
35. **War of 1812** Jackson's New Orleans victory occurred after treaty was signed. [Am. Hist.: Hart, 893]

386. IRREPRESSIBILITY

1. ***Bell for Adano, A*** Joppolo's stress on democracy overcomes superior's arrogance. [Am. Lit.: *A Bell for Adano*]
2. ***Grapes of Wrath, The*** Ma cries, "We ain' gonna die out." [Am. Lit.: *The Grapes of Wrath*]
3. **Little Orphan Annie** a most irrepressible waif. [Comics: Horn, 459]
4. **March, Augie** man's "refusal to lead a disappointed life." [Am. Lit.: *The Adventures of Augie March*]

Irresolution (See **INDECISION.**)

387. IRRESPONSIBILITY (See also CARELESSNESS, FORGETFULNESS.)

1. **Alectryon** changed to cock because he forgot to warn Mars of sun's rising. [Rom. Myth.: *LLEI,* I: 322]
2. **Belch, Sir Toby** Olivia's riotous, reckless uncle. [Br. Lit.: *Twelfth Night*]
3. **Bovary, Emma** irresponsible, careless character; betrays husband. [Fr. Lit.: *Madame Bovary*]
4. **Capp, Andy** negligent of marital obligations. [Comics: Horn, 82–83]
5. **Falstaff, Sir John** misuses "the King's press damnably." [Br. Lit.: *II Henry IV*]
6. **Google, Barney** neglects wife for race horse. [Comics: Horn, 99–100]
7. **Palinurus** sleeping helmsman, falls overboard. [Rom. Lit.: *Aeneid*]
8. **Paragon, Mary Anne** careless servant of David and Dora. [Br. Lit.: *David Copperfield*]

9. **Trulliber, Parson** satire on one who does not do his job. [Br. Hist.: *Joseph Andrews,* Espy, 131]

10. **Wimpy** sloppily dressed comic strip character; always "forgets" to pay for hamburgers. [Comics: "Popeye" in Horn, 657–658]

388. IRREVERSIBILITY

1. **crossing the Rubicon** Caesar passes point of no return into Italy. [Rom. Hist.: Brewer *Dictionary,* 941]

2. **Humpty Dumpty** all the King's men failed to reassemble him. [Nurs. Rhyme: *Mother Goose,* 40]

389. ISOLATION (See also IMPRISONMENT, REMOTENESS.)

1. **Alcatraz Island** "The Rock"; former federal prison in San Francisco Bay. [Am. Hist.: Flexner, 218]

2. ***Alison's House*** reclusive woman guards secrets and poems of her dead sister. [Am. Drama: Glaspel *Alison's House* in Sobel, 18]

3. **Aschenbach, Gustave von** spiritual and emotional solitude combine in writer's deterioration. [Ger. Lit.: *Death in Venice*]

4. **Count of Monte Cristo** Edmond Dantès imprisoned in the dungeons of Château D'If for 14 years. [Fr. Lit.: *The Count of Monte Cristo,* Magill I, 158–160]

5. **Crusoe, Robinson** man marooned on a desert island for 24 years. [Brit. Lit.: *Robinson Crusoe,* Magill I, 839–841]

6. **Dickinson, Emily** (1830–1886) secluded within the walls of her father's house. [Am. Lit.: Hart, 224]

7. **Hermit Kingdom** Korea, when it alienated itself from all but China (c. 1637–c. 1876). [Korean Hist.: *NCE,* 1233]

8. **Iron Curtain** political and ideological barrier of secrecy concealing Eastern bloc. [Eur. Hist.: Brewer *Dictionary,* 490]

9. ***Magic Mountain, The*** suspended in time, which exists in flat world below. [Ger. Lit.: *The Magic Mountain,* Magill I, 545–547]

10. ***Man Without a Country, The*** story of man exiled from homeland. [Am. Lit.: *The Man Without a Country,* Magill I, 553–557]

11. **Olivia** "abjured the company and sight of men." [Br. Lit.: *Twelfth Night*]

12. **prisoner of Chillon** cast into a lightless dungeon and chained there for countless years. [Br. Lit.: Byron *The Prisoner of Chillon* in Benét, 817]

13. **Selkirk, Alexander** (1676–1721) marooned on Pacific island; thought to be prototype of Robinson Crusoe. [Scot. Hist.: *EB,* IX: 45]
14. **Sleepy Hollow** out-of-the-way, old-world village on Hudson. [Am. Lit.: "Legend of Sleepy Hollow" in Benét, 575]
15. **Stylites** medieval ascetics; resided atop pillars. [Christian Hist.: Brewer *Dictionary,* 1045]
16. **Stylites, St. Simeon** lived 36 years on platform atop pillar. [Christian Hagiog.: Attwater, 309]

J

390. JEALOUSY (See also ENVY.)

1. **adder's tongue** flower symbolizes jealousy. [Western Folklore: Jobes, 31]
2. **Anastasia and Orizella** Cinderella's two step-sisters; jealous of her beauty, they treat her miserably. [Fr. Fairy Tale: *Cinderella*]
3. **Arnolphe** representative of jealous middle age. [Fr. Lit.: *L'Ecole des Femmes*]
4. **Bartolo, Dr.** jealous and suspicious tutor. [Fr. Lit.: *Barber of Seville*]
5. **Calchas** dies from grief on encountering even wiser soothsayer. [Gk. Myth.: *LLEI,* I: 325]
6. **Callirrhoë** demands of husband former wife's necklace and robe. [Gk. Legend: *NCE, 55*]
7. **Cephalus and Procris** young married couple plagued by jealousy. [Gk. Myth.: Hall, 62]
8. **coat of many colors** Jacob's gift to Joseph; object of jealousy. [O.T.: Genesis 37:3]
9. **Deianira** kills husband Hercules for suspected affair with Iole. [Gk. Myth.: Leach, 303]
10. **Dionyza** jealously plots Marina's murder. [Br. Lit.: *Pericles*]
11. **Donald Duck** frustrated character jealous of Mickey Mouse. [Comics: Horn, 216–217]
12. **Ferrando** of Manrico's influence on Leonora. [Ital. Opera: Verdi, *The Troubadour,* Westerman, 302]
13. **Golaud** jealousy leads to the murder of his brother, Pelléas. [Fr. Opera: Debussy, *Pelléas and Mélisande,* Westerman, 196]
14. **green-eyed monster** epithet. [Br. Lit.: *Othello*]
15. **Kitelys** man and wife each laughably suspicious of the other's fidelity. [Br. Lit.: *Every Man in His Humour*]
16. **Leontes** of wife and Polixenes. [Br. Lit.: *The Winter's Tale*]
17. **Malbecco** seeing his wife living among satyrs, he is so mad with jealosy that he casts himself from a cliff. [Br. Lit.: Spenser *The Faerie Queene*; Brewer *Dictionary*, 336]
18. **Medea** sends husband Jason's new bride poisoned cloak. [Gk. Lit.: *Medea;* Fr. Lit.: *Médée*]

19. **Oberon** King of Fairies; jealous of wife's attachments. [Br. Lit.: *A Midsummer Night's Dream*]
20. **Othello** smothers Desdemona out of jealousy. [Br. Lit.: *Othello*]
21. **Polyphemus** crushes lover's lover. [Rom. Lit.: *Metamorphoses*]
22. **Pozdnishef, Vasyla** murders wife in fit of insane resentment. [Russ. Lit.: *The Kreutzer Sonata,* Magill I, 481–483]
23. **Shabata, Frank** mistrusted everyone who showed kindness to wife, Marie. [Am. Lit.: *O Pioneers!,* Magill I, 663–665]
24. **wild ass** signifies jealousy. [Animal Symbolism: Jobes, 142]
25. **yellow** color symbolizing jealousy. [Western Folklore: Jobes, 1704]
26. **yellow rose** indicates jealousy. [Flower Symbolism: *Flora Symbolica,* 177]

Jesters (See CLOWNS.)

391. JOKE, PRACTICAL (See also MISCHIEVOUSNESS.)

1. **April Fool's Day** April 1st; a day for playing practical jokes on the unsuspecting. [Western Folklore: Payton, 34]
2. **Barmecide feast** beggar given empty dishes, imaginary food. [Arab. Lit.: *Arabian Nights,* "The Barmecide's Feast"]
3. **Hop-Frog's king** "had an especial admiration for *breadth* in a jest." [Am. Lit.: "Hop-Frog" in Portable Poe, 317–329]
4. **Merygreeke, Matthew** mischievously puts Ralph up to wooing widow. [Br. Lit.: *Ralph Roister Doister*]
5. **Old Jackanapes** fills Miss Pussy's apple pies with frogs. [Children's Lit.: *The Golden Hen,* Fisher, 232–233]
6. **Panurge** conniving scoundrel whose forte was practical joking. [Fr. Lit.: *Pantagruel*]
7. **Pulver, Ensign** devised mechanisms to needle to skipper. [Am. Lit.: *Mister Roberts,* Magill I, 605–607]
8. **Robin Goodfellow** fairies' jester famous for his practical jokes. [Br. Folklore: Brewer *Dictionary,* 768]

392. JOURNEY (See also ADVENTUROUSNESS, QUEST, WANDERING.)

1. ***Beagle*** name of the ship in which Charles Darwin made his five-year voyage. [Br. Hist.: *NCE,* 721–722]
2. ***Canterbury Tales*** pilgrimage from London to Canterbury during which tales are told. [Br. Lit.: *Canterbury Tales*]
3. **Childe Harold** makes pilgrimage throughout Europe for liberty and personal revelation. [Br. Lit.: "Childe Harold's Pilgrimage" in Magill IV, 127–129]

4. **Christian** travels to Celestial City with cumbrous burden on back. [Br. Lit.: *Pilgrim's Progress*]
5. **Christopher, St.** patron saint; aided wayfarers across river. [Christian Hagiog.: Attwater, 85]
6. **Conestoga wagon** famed covered wagon taking pioneers to West before railroads. [Am. Hist.: *NCE,* 623]
7. **Dante** travels through Hell, Purgatory, Paradise. [Ital. Lit.: *Divine Comedy,* Magill I, 211–213]
8. **Everyman** makes pilgrimage to God, unaccompanied by erstwhile friends. [Br. Lit.: *Everyman*]
9. **Exodus** departure of Israelites from Egypt under Moses. [O.T.: Exodus]
10. **Hakluyt, Richard** (c. 1552–1616) English geographer and publisher of eyewitness accounts of more than 200 voyages of exploration. [Br. Hist.: *EB,* 8: 553–554]
11. ***Heart of Darkness*** adventure tale of journey into heart of the Belgian Congo and into depths of man's heart. [Br. Lit.: *Heart of Darkness,* Magill III, 447–449]
12. **Kon-Tiki** primitive raft used by Thor Heyerdahl to cross from Peru to the Tuamotu Islands (1947). [World Hist.: *Kon-Tiki;* NCE, 1238–1239]
13. **Mandeville, Sir John** (fl. 1356) English writer of travelers' voyages around the world. [Br. Hist.: *EB,* VI: 559]
14. **Mayflower** vessel of America's pilgrims (1620). [Am. Hist.: Hart, 530]
15. **Oregon Trail** long ride on horseback from St. Louis to Portland, Oregon. [Am. Hist.: *The Oregon Trail,* Magill I, 695–698]
16. **petasus** hat; emblem of ancient travelers and hunters. [Gk. Art: Hall, 145]
17. **pilgrimage to Mecca (hajj)** journey every good Muslim tries to make at least once. [Islamic Religion: *WB,* 10: 374–376]
18. ***Pilgrim's Progress*** Bunyan's allegory of life. [Br. Lit.: Eagle, 458]
19. **Polo, Marco** (1254–1324) Venetian traveler in central Asia and China. [World Hist.: *WB,* 15: 572–573; Ital. Lit.: *Travels of Marco Polo*]
20. ***Roughing It*** portrays trip from St. Louis across Nevada plains to California. [Am. Lit.: Hart, 729]
21. **Santa Maria, Pinta, and Niña** ships under Columbus in journey to New World. [Span. Hist.: *NCE,* 606]

22. **Santa Fe trail** caravan route from Missouri to New Mexico. [Am. Hist.: Hart, 743]
23. **Syntax, Doctor** leaves home in search of the picturesque. [Br. Lit.: *Doctor Syntax*]
24. ***Time Machine, The*** adventures of a man who travels through time. [Br. Lit.: Magill I, 986–988]
25. **Wilderness Road** pioneer route from eastern Virginia to Kentucky. [Am. Hist.: Hart, 924]

393. JOVIALITY (See also GAIETY.)

1. **Bob, Captain** Tahitian jailor known for his easy going merriment with prisoners. [Am. Lit.: *Omoo*]
2. **Costigan, Captain J. Chesterfield** jovial, good-humored man. [Br. Lit.: *Pendennis*]
3. **Friar Tuck** fat friar, jovial companion of Robin Hood. [Br. Legend: Benét, 371]
4. **Old King Cole** merry old soul. [Nurs. Rhyme: Opie, 134]
5. **Santa Claus** ho-ho-hoing merry gift-giver at Christmas. [Am. Pop. Cult.: Misc.]
6. **saffron crocus** indicates mirth and laughter. [Flower Symbolism: *Flora Symbolica,* 177]
7. **Tapley, Mark** jolly chief hostler at the Blue Dragon. [Br. Lit.: *Martin Chuzzlewit*]

394. JOY (See also GAIETY, HAPPINESS.)

1. **Auteb** female personification of gladness. [Egypt. Myth.: Jobes, 159]
2. **blue bird, the** symbolizes happiness sought by two poor children. [Belg. Lit.: *The Blue Bird*; Haydn & Fuller, 94]
3. **cinquefoil** indicates gladness. [Flower Symbolism and Heraldry: Jobes, 341]
4. **Euphrosyne** one of Graces; name means 'festivity.' [Gk. Myth.: Kravitz, 96]
5. **gold on red** symbol of felicity and joy. [Chinese Art: Jobes, 357]
6. **Hathor** cow-headed goddess of joy and love. [Egypt. Myth.: Leach, 484]
7. **Hyperboreans** blissful race lived beyond the North Wind in a region of perpetual Spring. [Gk. Myth.: Brewer *Dictionary,* 476]
8. **myrrh** symbol of gladness. [Flower Symbolism: *Flora Symbolica,* 176]

9. **red on green** symbol of felicity and joy. [Chinese Art: Jobes, 357]
10. ***Rubaiyat, The*** series of poems celebrating hedonism as a way of life. [Br. Poetry: Benét, 881]
11. **wood sorrel** indicates gladness. [Flower Symbolism: *Flora Symbolica,* 177]

395. JUDAISM

1. **Altneuland** Theodore Herzl's imaginative description of the future Zionist settlement in Palestine. [Jewish Hist.: *Collier's,* XIX, 79]
2. **Oppenheimer, Josef Süss** chooses Judaism even when renunciation would save him from execution. [Ger. Lit.: Feuchtwanger *Power*; Magill I, 773]

396. JUDGEMENT

1. **Monker and Nakir** hideous black angels who determine the fate of each soul after death. [Muslim Myth.: Benét, 679]

397. JUSTICE (See also LAWGIVING.)

1. **Aeacus** a judge of the dead. [Rom. Lit.: *Aeneid*]
2. **Ahasuerus** (519–465 B.C.) Persian king rectifies wrongs done to Jews. [O.T.: Esther 8:7–8]
3. **Arthur, King** trained by Merlin to become a just ruler, he endeavors all his life to establish a realm where justice prevails. [Br. Lit.: Malory *Le Mort d'Arthur*]
4. **Asha** in moral sphere, presides over righteousness. [Zoroastrianism: Jobes, 138]
5. **Astraea** goddess of justice. [Gk. Myth.: Benét, 59]
6. **Barataria** island-city where Sancho Panza, as governor, settles disputes equitably. [Span. Lit.: Cervantes *Don Quixote*]
7. **blindfold** worn by personification of justice. [Art: Hall, 183]
8. **blue** in American flag, symbolizes justice. [Color Symbolism: Leach, 242; Jobes, 356]
9. **Brown vs. Board of Education** landmark Supreme Court decision barring segregation of schools (1954). [Am. Hist.: Van Doren, 544]
10. **Cambyses, Judgment of** corrupt judge's flayed flesh provides judicial throne. [Gk. Hist.: *Herodotus*]
11. **Carlos, Don** conscience piqued, tries to lift Spanish yoke from Flemish. [Ger. Lit.: *Don Carlos*]
12. **Cauchon, Bishop** presided impartially over the ecclesiastical trial of Joan of Arc. [Fr. Hist.: *EB,* (1963) V, 60]

13. **Dike** one of Horae; personification of natural law and justice. [Gk. Myth.: Zimmerman, 85]
14. **Gideon v. Wainwright** established right of all defendants to counsel (1963). [Am. Hist.: Van Doren, 585]
15. **Hatto** during a famine he saves food for the rich by burning the poor, whom he compares to mice; mice invade his tower and devour him. [Ger. Legend: Brewer *Dictionary*, 439]
16. **Henry VII** (1457–1509) deliverer of Richard III's just deserts. [Br. Lit.: *Richard III*]
17. **International Court of Justice** main judicial organ of U.N. [World Hist.: *NCE*, 1351]
18. **Libra** sign of the balance, weighing of right and wrong. [Zodiac: Brewer *Dictionary*, 640]
19. **Minos** his justice approved even by the gods; became one of the three judges of the dead. [Gk. Myth.: Zimmerman, 168]
20. **Moran** equitable councillor to King Feredach. [Irish Hist.: Brewer *Dictionary*, 728]
21. **Moran's collar** strangled wearer if he judged unfairly. [Irish Folklore: Brewer *Dictionary*, 728]
22. **Nuremberg Trials** surviving Nazi leaders put on trial (1946). [Eur. Hist.: Van Doren, 512]
23. **Portia** as a lawyer, ingeniously interprets to Shylock the terms of Antonio's bond. [Br. Drama: Shakespeare *The Merchant of Venice*]
24. **Prince Po** settles dispute over a stolen child by asking the two claimants to pull it out of a circle of chalk by its arms. [Chin. Drama: *The Circle of Chalk* in Magill III, 193; cf. Brecht *The Caucasian Chalk Circle* in Weiss, 74]
25. **Rhadamanthus** made judge in lower world for earthly impartiality. [Gk. Myth.: Brewer *Handbook*, 911]
26. **rudbeckia** indicates fairness. [Flower Symbolism: *Flora Symbolica*, 177]
27. **scales** signify impartiality. [Art: Hall, 183]
28. **scepter** denotes fairness and righteousness. [Heraldry: Halberts, 37]
29. **Solomon** perspicaciously resolves dilemma of baby's ownership. [O.T.: I Kings 16–28]
30. **stars, garland of** emblem of equity. [Western Folklore: Jobes, 374]
31. **sword and scales** attributes of St. Michael as devil-fighter and judge. [Christian Symbolism: Appleton, 98]

32. ***Tale of Two Cities, A*** barrister London Stryver gets Charles Darnay acquitted by showing his resemblance to Sydney Carton. [Br. Lit.: Dickens *A Tale of Two Cities*]
33. **Valley of Jehoshaphat** where men will be ultimately tried before God. [O.T.: Joel 3:2]
34. **World Court** popular name for International Court of Justice which assumed functions of the World Court. [World Hist.: *NCE,* 3006–3007]
35. **Yves, St.** equitable and incorruptible priest-lawyer. [Christian Hagiog.: Attwater, 347]

K

Kidnapping (See ABDUCTION.)

Killing (See ASSASSINATION, INFANTICIDE, MURDER, PATRICIDE.)

398. KINDNESS (See also GENEROSITY.)

1. **Allworthy, Squire** Tom Jones's goodhearted foster father. [Br. Lit.: *Tom Jones*]
2. **Androcles** relieves lion of thorn in paw and is repaid in arena by lion's failure to attack him. [Rom. Lit.: *Noctes Atticae,* Leach, 55]
3. **Bachelor, the** "the universal mediator, comforter, and friend." [Br. Lit.: *Old Curiosity Shop*]
4. **Bishop of Digne** gave starving Valjean food, bed, and comfort. [Fr. Lit.: *Les Misérables*]
5. **Boaz** took benevolent custody of Ruth. [O.T.: Ruth 2:8–16]
6. **Brownlow, Mr.** rescued Oliver Twist from arrest and adopted him. [Br. Lit.: Dickens *Oliver Twist*]
7. **calycanthus** symbol of compassion. [Plant Symbolism: Jobes, 279]
8. **Carey, Louisa** Philip's loving, sensitive aunt. [Br. Lit.: *Of Human Bondage,* Magill I, 670–672]
9. **Cuttle, Captain** kindly shelters runaway, Florence Dombey. [Br. Lit.: *Dombey and Son*]
10. **Evilmerodach** Babylonian king; kind to captive king, Jehoiachin. [O.T.: II Kings 25:27–29]
11. **Finn, Huckleberry** refuses to turn in Jim, the fugitive slave. [Am. Lit.: *Huckleberry Finn*]
12. **Francis of Assisi, St.** (1182–1226) patron saint and benevolent protector of animals. [Christian Hagiog.: Hall, 132]
13. **Friday's child** loving and giving. [Nurs. Rhyme: Opie, 309]
14. **Glinda** the "Good Witch"; Dorothy's guardian angel. [Am. Lit.: *The Wonderful Wizard of Oz;* Am. Cinema: Halliwell, 780]
15. **Good Samaritan** helps out man victimized by thieves and neglected by other passers-by. [N.T.: Luke 10:30–35]
16. **heart** symbol of kindness and benevolence. [Heraldry: Halberts, 30]

17. **Hood, Robin** helps the poor by plundering the rich. [Br. Lit.: *Robin Hood*]
18. **Jesus Christ** kind to the poor, forgiving to the sinful. [N.T.: Matthew, Mark, Luke, John]
19. **Joseph of Arimathaea** retrieved Christ's body, enshrouded and buried it. [N.T.: Matthew 27:57–61; John 19:38–42]
20. **Kuan Yin** goddess of mercy. [Buddhism: Binder, 42]
21. **La Creevy, Miss** spinster painter of miniatures who devoted herself to befriending the Nicklebys. [Br. Lit.: Dickens *Nicholas Nickleby*]
22. **lemon balm** symbol of compassion. [Herb Symbolism: *Flora Symbolica,* 164]
23. **Merrick, Robert** doing good to others as *raison d'être.* [Am. Lit.: *The Magnificent Obsession,* Magill I, 547–549]
24. **Nereus** venerable sea god of great kindliness. [Gk. Myth.: *Century Classical,* 744–745]
25. **Old Woman of Leeds** "spent all her time in good deeds." [Nurs. Rhyme: *Mother Goose,* 97]
26. **ox** exhibits fellow-feeling for comrades. [Medieval Animal Symbolism: White, 77–78]
27. **Peggotty, Daniel** kindhearted bachelor who shelters niece and nephew. [Br. Lit.: *David Copperfield*]
28. **Philadelphia** "city of brotherly love." [Am. Hist.: Hart, 651]
29. **Rivers, St. John** takes starving Jane Eyre into his home. [Br. Lit.: *Jane Eyre*]
30. **Rodolph, Grand Duke** helps criminals and the poor to a better life. [Fr. Lit.: Sue *The Mysteries of Paris* in Magill I, 632]
31. **Romola** cares lovingly for her blind father, provides for her husband's mistress and children, and is kind to all who suffer. [Br. Lit.: George Eliot *Romola*]
32. **St. Martin** in midwinter, gave his cloak to a freezing beggar. [Christian Hagiog.: Brewer *Dictionary*]
33. **Strong, Doctor** "the kindest of men." [Br. Lit.: *David Copperfield*]
34. **throatwort** indicates sympathy. [Flower Symbolism: *Flora Symbolica,* 178]
35. **Veronica, St.** from pity, offers Christ cloth to wipe face. [Christian Hagiog.: Attwater, 334]
36. **Vincent de Paul, St.** French priest renowned for his charitable work. [Christian Hagiog.: *NCE,* 2896]
37. **Wenceslas, St.** Bohemian prince noted for piety and generosity. [Eur. Hist.: Brewer *Dictionary,* 1147]

L

399. LABOR

1. **A.F.L.-C.I.O.** (American Federation of Labor–Congress of Industrial Organizations) federation of autonomous labor unions in North America. [Am. Hist.: *NCE,* 84]
2. **Gompers, Samuel** (1850–1924) labor leader; organizer of American Federation of Labor. [Am. Hist.: Jameson, 203]
3. **I.W.W.** Industrial Workers of the World [Am. Hist.: Hart, 400]
4. **International Labor Organization (I.L.O.)** agency of the United Nations; aim is to improve labor and living conditions. [World Hist.: *EB,* V: 389–390]
5. **Marx, Karl** (1818–1883) chief theorist of modern socialism stimulated working class's consciousness. [Ger. Hist.: *NCE,* 1708]
6. **Meany, George** (1894–1980) former president of the A.F.L.-C.I.O. [Am. Hist.: *NCE,* 1733]
7. **National Labor Relations Board** independent agency of U.S. government, supporting labor's right to organize. [Am. Hist.: *NCE,* 1887]
8. **Solidarity (Solidarnosc)** Polish labor union movement of the 1980s. [Pol. Hist.: *WB,* P:541]
9. **Teamsters** large, powerful union of U. S. truckers. [Am. Hist.: *NCE,* 2703]
10. **U.A.W.** large American auto workers union. [Am. Hist.: *WB,* U:21]
11. **Wobblies** nickname for I.W.W. members. [Am. Hist.: Hart, 400]

400. LAMENESS (See also DEFORMITY.)

1. **Byron, Lord (1788–1824)** limped because of his club foot. [Br. Lit.: Benét, 152]
2. **Carey, Philip** schoolmates used his clubfoot as object of ridicule. [Br. Lit.: *Of Human Bondage,* Magill I, 670–672]
3. **Giles, St.** patron of cripples; accidentally hobbled, refused cures. [Christian Hagiog.: Brewster, 392]
4. **Henkies** trows (goblins) who limp when dancing. [Scot. Folklore: Briggs, 219–220]
5. **Hephaestus** blacksmith god; said to have been lamed when ejected from Olympus by Zeus. [Gk. Myth.: Zimmerman, 121]

6. **Mephibosheth** crippled in childhood when nurse dropped him. [O.T.: II Samuel, 4:4]
7. **Oedipus** lamed by Laius with a spike through his feet in infancy. [Gk. Myth.: Benét, 730]
8. **Porgy** crippled Negro beggar of Catfish Row. [Am. Lit.: *Porgy,* Magill I, 764–766]
9. **Roosevelt, Franklin Delano** (1882–1945) 32nd president of U.S.; stricken with polio and confined to wheelchair. [Am. Hist.: *NCE,* 2355]
10. **Tamerlane (1336–1405)** Mongol conqueror, his name a corruption of Timur i Long (Timur the Lame). [Asian Hist.: Benét, 985]
11. **Tiny Tim** crippled son of Bob Cratchit. [Br. Lit.: *A Christmas Carol*]

Lamentation (See GRIEF.)

401. LAST LAUGH (See also IRONY.)

1. **Alcyoneus** giant who threw stone at Hercules; killed when Hercules batted it back. [Gk. Myth.: Zimmerman, 17]
2. **Diomedes** eaten by his own horses, which he had reared on human flesh. [Gk. and Rom. Myth.: Hall, 149]
3. **Fulton's Folly** everybody scoffed at his 1807 steamboat, the "Clermont." [Am. Hist.: Jameson, 190]
4. **Hop-Frog** immolates king and court after repeated insults. [Am. Lit.: "Hop-Frog" in Portable Poe, 317–329]
5. ***Magnificent Ambersons, The*** Eugene acquires same position George fell from. [Am. Lit.: *The Magnificent Ambersons*]
6. **Mordecai and Haman** latter hanged on gallows he built for former. [O.T.: Esther 7:9–10]
7. **Palamon and Arcite** victorious jouster (Arcite) dies in fall; loser wins lady's hand. [Br. Lit.: *Canterbury Tales,* "Palamon and Arcite"]
8. **Pizarro, Don** illegally imprisons Florestan; is later imprisoned himself. [Ger. Opera: Beethoven, *Fidelio,* Westerman, 109–110]
9. **Seward's Folly** ridiculed purchase of Alaska proved wise buy (1867). [Am. Hist.: Van Doren, 254]
10. **Truman, Harry S.** (1884–1972) presidential winner; photographed with Chicago Tribune headline announcing Dewey's victory (1948). [Am. Hist.: *Plain Speaking,* 406]
11. **Tuck, Friar** cajoled to ferry Robin across stream, dumps him returning. [Br. Lit.: *Robin Hood*]

402. LAUGHTER

1. **Democritus** (c. 460–c. 370 B.C.) the laughing philosopher. [Gk. Phil.: Jobes, 430]
2. **hyena** rapacious scavenger, known for its maniacal laughter. [Zoology: Misc.]
3. **laughing gas** (nitrous oxide) sweet-smelling, colorless gas; produces feeling of euphoria. [Medicine: Misc.]
4. **Thalia** Muse of comedy [Gk. Myth.: Brewer *Dictionary,* 1071]

403. LAWGIVING (See also JUSTICE.)

1. **Draco** (fl. 621 B.C.) codified Athenian law. [Gk. Hist.: Benét, 286]
2. **Hammurabi** Babylonian king (c. 1800 B.C.); established first systematic legal code. [Classical Hist.: *EB,* 8: 598–599]
3. **Justinian** (485–565) ruler of eastern empire; codified Roman law. [Rom. Hist.: *EB,* 10: 362–365]
4. **Minos** scrupulous king and lawgiver of Crete. [Gk. Myth.: Wheeler, 244]
5. **Moses** presents God's ten commandments to Israelites. [O.T.: Exodus 20:1–12]
6. **Solon** (c. 639–c. 559 B.C.) Athenian statesman and wise legislator. [Gk. Hist.: Brewer *Dictionary,* 1018]
7. **Talmud** great body of Jewish law and tradition, supplementing scripture. [Judaism: Haydn & Fuller, 725]

404. LAZINESS (See also CARELESSNESS.)

1. **Bailey Junior** nonchalant, inefficient boardinghouse page. [Br. Lit.: *Martin Chuzzlewit*]
2. **Bailey, Beetle** goldbricking army private. [Comics: Horn, 105–106]
3. **Belacqua** too slothful in life, he repents after death. [Ital. Lit.: *Divine Comedy*]
4. **Bshyst** demon of sloth. [Zoroastrian Myth.: Leach, 175]
5. **Capp, Andy** deliberately jobless and shirks household duties. [Comics: Horn, 82]
6. **Datchery, Dick** hotel resident with no occupation. [Br. Lit.: *Edwin Drood*]
7. **Jughead** terminally indolent, save when hunger dictates. [Comics: "Archie" in Horn, 87]
8. **Krebs, Maynard G.** for whom "work" is a four-letter word. [TV: "The Many Loves of Dobie Gillis" in Terrace, II, 64–66]

9. **Lake of Idleness** whoever drank thereof, grew immediately "faint and weary." [Br. Lit.: *Faerie Queene*]
10. **Lazybones** popular song by Hoagy Carmichael (1933). [Am. Music: Kinkle, II, 268]
11. **Lester, Jeeter** hapless sharecropper too lazy to keep his large family from starving. [Am. Lit.: Caldwell *Tobacco Road*]
12. **Little Boy Blue** asleep under haystack while livestock roam. [Nurs. Rhyme: *Mother Goose,* 11]
13. **Oblomov** indolent landowner, always in robe and slippers. [Russ. Lit.: *Oblomov*]
14. **phlegm** humor effecting temperament of sluggishness. [Medieval Physiology: Hall, 130]
15. **sloth** arboreal mammal, always associated with sluggishness. [Zoology: Misc.]
16. **Speed** an "illiterate loiterer"; slow-moving servant. [Br. Lit.: *Two Gentlemen of Verona*]

Lechery (See LUST.)

405. LEFTHANDEDNESS

1. **Ehud** wielded sword sinistrally. [O.T.: Judges 3:15, 21]

406. LEXICOGRAPHY

1. **Johnson, Samuel** (1709–1784) literary scholar, creator of first comprehensive lexicographical work of English. [Br. Hist.: *EB,* V: 591]
2. **Murray, James** (1837–1915) renowned editor of the *Oxford English Dictionary.* [Br. Hist.: *Caught in the Web of Words*]
3. ***Oxford English Dictionary* (*OED*)** great multi-volume historical dictionary of English. [Br. Hist.: *Caught in the Web of Words*]
4. **Webster, Noah** (1758–1843) philologist and compiler of popular comprehensive American dictionary. [Am. Hist.: Hart, 902]
5. **"Webster's"** now used generically, synonymous in U.S. with authoritativeness in a dictionary. [Am. Cult.: Misc.]

407. LIFE

1. **Clotho** one of the three Fates, spins the thread that represents the life of each individual. [Gk. Myth.: *NCE,* 927]

408. LIGHT

1. **Apollo** god of light. [Gk. Myth.: Espy, 28]
2. **Asvins** twin gods of light. [Hindu Myth.: Benet, 60]
3. **Balder** god of light and peace. [Norse Myth.: Leach, 106]
4. **Jesus Christ** "I am the light of the world." [N.T.: John 8:12]

5. **Mithras** god of light. [Pers. Myth.: Wheeler, 246]
6. **patée cross** four spear-headed arms; symbolizes solar light. [Christian Iconog.: Brewer *Dictionary*, 280; Jobes, 386]

409. LIGHTNING (See also THUNDER.)

1. **Agni** god of fire and lightning. [Hindu Myth.: Benét, 15]
2. **double ax** variation of Jupiter's thunderbolt. [Rom. Myth.: Jobes, 163]
3. **Elicius** epithet of Jupiter as god of lightning. [Rom. Myth.: Kravitz, 87]
4. **Franklin, Benjamin** (1706–1790) flew kite in thunderstorm to prove electricity existed in lightning. [Am. Hist.: *NCE*, 1000]
5. **Jupiter Fulgurator** Jupiter as controller of weather and sender of lightning. [Rom. Myth.: Howe, 147]
6. **Thor** bravest of gods; protected man from lightning. [Norse Myth.: Brewer *Handbook*, 1099]

410. LITIGIOUSNESS

1. ***Bleak House*** a fortune is dissipated through the protracted lawsuit of Jarndyce vs. Jarndyce, and the heir dies in misery. [Br. Lit.: Dickens *Bleak House*]

Littleness (See DWARFISM, SMALLNESS.)

411. LONGEVITY (See also ENDURANCE.)

1. **Abie's Irish Rose** comedy by Anne Nichols ran for 2327 performances on Broadway. [Am. Lit.: Benét, 3]
2. ***Back to Methuselah*** by the end of the twenty-second century, mankind has extended the life span to nearly three hundred years. [Br. Drama: Shaw *Back to Methuselah* in Magill III, 82]
3. **Iguarán, Úrsula** matriarch who holds the clan together and lives to be one hundred years old. [Lat. Am. Lit.: Gabriel Garcia Marquez *One Hundred Years of Solitude* in Weiss, 336]
4. **Long Parliament** sat from outbreak of Civil War to Charles II's accession (1640–1660). [Br. Hist.: *EB*, VI: 319–320]
5. ***Meet the Press*** longest running television program; from 1947 to present. [Am. TV: McWhirter, 234]
6. **Methuselah** son of Enoch; patriarch said to have lived 969 years. [O.T.: Genesis 5:21–27]
7. ***Mousetrap, The*** London play by Agatha Christie, running since 1952. [Br. Lit.: McWhirter, 228]
8. **Roosevelt, Franklin Delano** (1882–1945) 32nd U.S. President; elected to four terms. [Am. Hist.: Hart, 726]

9. **Shangri-La** hidden Tibetan lamasery where all enjoy long life provided they remain there. [Br. Lit.: *Lost Horizon*]
10. **She (Ayesha)** beautiful African sorceress who has lived for 2000 years. [Br. Lit.: H. Rider Haggard *She* in Magill I, 886]
11. **Victoria, Queen** (1819–1901) queen of Great Britain and Ireland (1837–1901). [Br. Hist.: *NCE,* 2886]

412. LONGSUFFERING (See also PATIENCE.)

1. **Aspasia** pathetic figure bearing fate with fortitude. [Br. Lit.: *The Maid's Tragedy*]
2. **Burns, Helen** long-suffering victim of school's cruel treatment. [Br. Lit.: *Jane Eyre*]
3. **Canio** must be funny despite rage over wife's unfaithfulness. [Ital. Opera: Leoncavallo, *Pagliacci,* Westerman, 341–342]
4. **Clayhanger, Edwin** makes concessions to wife's greed and irascibility. [Br. Lit.: *The Clayhanger Trilogy*]
5. **Dodsworth, Sam** patiently endures egotism of his childish wife until marriage dissolves. [Am. Lit.: *Dodsworth*]
6. **Griselda** endures husband's cruelty nobly. [Br. Lit.: *Canterbury Tales,* "Clerk's Tale"; Ital. Lit.: *Decameron,* "Dineo's Tale of Griselda"]
7. **oxeye** symbol of long-suffering composure. [Flower Symbolism: *Flora Symbolica,* 176]
8. **Prynne, Hester** stoically endures the ostracism imposed on her for adultery. [Am. Lit.: *The Scarlet Letter*]
9. **Santa Cruz, Jacinta** passively tolerates husband's adultery; rears his bastard. [Span. Lit.: *Fortunata and Jacinta*]

Loquacity (See **TALKATIVENESS.**)

Loser (See **FAILURE.**)

413. LOUDNESS

1. **boiler factory** proverbial source of noise and confusion. [Am. Culture: Misc.]
2. **breaking of the sound barrier** boom of plane heard exceeding speed of about 750 m.p.h. or Mach 1. [Aviation: Misc.]
3. **Concorde** supersonic jet of British-French design. [Eur. Hist.: *EB,* III: 66]
4. **Joshua** Jericho walls razed by clamorous blasts from his troops' trumpets. [O.T.: Joshua 6]
5. **Krakatoa** volcanic explosion on this Indonesian island heard 3000 miles away (1883). [Asian Hist.: *NCE,* 1500]

6. **Olivant** Roland's horn, whose blast kills birds and is heard by Charlemagne, eight miles away. [Fr. Legend: Brewer *Dictionary*, 772]
7. **sonic boom** shock wave from plane breaking the speed of sound. [Aviation: Misc.]
8. **Stentor** Greek herald with voice of 50 men. [Gk. Myth.: Espy, 39]

414. LOVE

1. **Aengus** one of the Tuatha de Danaan; god of love. [Celtic Myth.: Jobes, 40]
2. **Amor** another name for Cupid. [Rom. Myth.: Kravitz, 19]
3. **Anacreon** (563–478 B.C.) Greek lyric poet who idealized the pleasures of love. [Gk. Lit.: Brewer *Dictionary*, 31]
4. **Aphrodite** goddess of love and beauty. [Gk. Myth.: Zimmerman, 25–26]
5. **Bast** cat-headed goddess of love and fashion. [Egyptian Myth.: Espy, 20]
6. **Biducht** goddess of love. [Persian Myth.: Jobes, 210]
7. **Cupid** (**Gk. Eros**) god of love. [Rom. Myth.: Kravitz, 70]
8. **diamond** token of affection, e.g., for engagement. [Gem Symbolism: Jobes, 440–441]
9. **Frigg** Scandinavian goddess of love and fertility. [Norse Myth.: Parrinder, 101]
10. ***Garden of Love, The*** Rubens painting of ladies and gallants in an amorous mood. [Flem. Art: *EB* (1963), III, 190]
11. **honeysuckle** symbol of affection. [Flower Symbolism: *Flora Symbolica*, 174; Kunz, 328]
12. **Kama** god of love; Hindu equivalent of Eros. [Hindu Myth.: Brewer *Dictionary*, 661]
13. **Krishna** god who plays flute to enamored milkmaids. [Hindu Myth.: Binder, 23]
14. **myrtle** to Renaissance, its perpetual greenness symbolized everlasting love. [Art: Hall, 219]
15. **pear** symbol of love and tenderness. [Flower Symbolism: *Flora Symbolica*, 176]
16. **red chrysanthemum** symbol of love. [Flower Symbolism: Jobes, 333]
17. **ring** worn on fourth finger, left hand, symbolizes love. [Western Folklore: Brewer *Dictionary*, 919]
18. **rose** traditional symbol of love. [Flower Symbolism: *Flora Symbolica*, 177]

19. ***Rules of Courtly Love, The*** dos and don'ts manual for medieval lovers. [Eur. Hist.: Bishop, 301]
20. **St. Valentine's Day** (February 14) day of celebration of love. [Western Folklore: Leach, 1153]
21. ***Sonnets from the Portuguese*** Elizabeth Browning's famous poems celebrating love for her husband (1850). [Br. Lit.: Magill III, 1007–1009]
22. **sorrel** indicates love and tenderness. [Flower Symbolism: *Flora Symbolica,* 177]
23. **three circles** symbol indicates affection. [Western Folklore: Jobes, 343]
24. **Venus** goddess of love and beauty. [Rom. Myth.: *Aeneid*]
25. **white lilacs** indicates initial feelings of love. [Flower Symbolism: *Flora Symbolica,* 175]

415. LOVE, MATERNAL

1. **asteria** symbol of motherly affection. [Gem. Symbolism: Jobes, 144]
2. **cinquefoil** symbol of motherly love. [Flower Symbolism: Jobes, 341]
3. **Cornelia** indicates that two sons are her jewels. [Rom. Hist.: Hall, 75]
4. **de Lamare, Jeanne** adores and indulges her son Paul despite his escapades and excessive debts. [Fr. Lit.: Maupassant *A Woman's Life* in Magill I, 1127]
5. **Delphine, Madame** denies motherhood for daughter's marriage. [Am. Lit.: *Madame Delphine,* Hart, 513]
6. **Mary** the Madonna; beatific mother of Christ. [N.T.: Matthew, Mark, Luke, John; Christian Iconography: *NCE,* 1709]
7. **red carnation** clove pink, sprung from St. Mary's tears at Calvary. [Christian Legend: Embolden, 23]
8. ***Silver Cord, The*** Mrs. Phelps's love for sons becomes pathological. [Am. Lit.: Hart, 769]
9. **Venus** provided future protection for Aeneas, her son. [Rom. Myth.: *Aeneid*]

Love, Platonic (See **LOVE, VIRTUOUS.**)

416. LOVE, SPURNED

1. **Anaxarete** princess turned to stone for scorning commoner's love. [Gk. Myth.: Zimmerman, 21]
2. **Aoi, Princess** afflicted by husband's amours; declines and dies. [Jap. Lit.: *The Tale of Genji*]

3. **Butterfly, Madame** considered herself Pinkerton's wife; actually his mistress. [Am. Lit.: *Madame Butterfly,* Hart, 513; Ital Opera, *Madama Butterfly*]
4. **Clavdia** thought Hans's proposal foolish and refused him. [Ger. Lit.: *The Magic Mountain,* Magill I, 545–547]
5. **Cloten** spurned but persistent lover of Imogen. [Br. Lit.: *Cymbeline*]
6. **Conchobar** spurned, the king murders intended's lover and his brothers. [Irish Legend: *LLEI,* I: 326]
7. **Courtly, Sir Hartley** rejected by heiress; she prefers his son. [Br. Lit.: *London Assurance,* Walsh *Modern,* 108]
8. **Dashwood, Elinor** bears rejection with dignity; eventually marries rejecter. [Br. Lit.: *Sense and Sensibility*]
9. **Hermione** rejected by Pyrrhus, who weds Andromache. [Fr. Lit.: *Andromache*]
10. **Hudson, Roderick** sculptor loses Christina Light to rich prince. [Am. Lit.: *Roderick Hudson*]
11. **Hugon, George** rejected by Nana, he stabs himself. [Fr. Lit.: *Nana,* Magill I, 638–640]
12. **Jason** Medea's lover; leaves her for Glauce. [Gk. Lit.: *Medea,* Magill I, 573–575]
13. **Laurie** long in love with Jo March, he begs her to marry him and is rejected. [Am. Lit.: Louisa May Alcott *Little Women*]
14. **Litvinoff, Grigory** Irina dallies with him for years but never yields. [Russ. Lit.: *Smoke* in Magill I, 897]
15. **Maggie** rejected by brother, lover, mother, and neighbors. [Am. Lit.: *Maggie: A Girl of the Streets,* Magill I, 543–544]
16. **Mellefont** doublecrossed by friend and rejected lover. [Br. Lit.: *The Double-Dealer*]
17. **Nemours, Count de** rejected by the Princess de Cleves, who will not betray her husband even after he dies. [Fr. Lit.: Countess de La Fayette *The Princess of Cleves* in Magill II, 856]
18. **Newcome, Clive** social conventions forbid him to pursue Ethel. [Br. Lit.: *The Newcomes,* Magill I, 650–652]
19. **Orestes** spurned suitor of Hermione. [Fr. Lit.: *Andromache*]
20. **Phaedra** feigns rape on being scorned. [Gk. Lit.: *Hippolytus*]
21. **Potiphar's wife** traduces Joseph when seduction of him fails. [O.T.: Genesis 39:7–18]
22. **Robin, Fanny** betrayed by Sergeant Troy, her betrothed. [Br. Lit.: *Far From the Madding Crowd,* Magill I, 266–268]

23. **Touchwood, Lady** dissolute matron rejected by nephew's love. [Br. Lit.: *The Double-Dealer*]
24. **Wiggins, Mahalah** her fiancé changed his mind on their wedding day. [Am. Lit.: *Peter Whiffle,* Magill I, 739–741]
25. **willow tree** emblem of rejected affection. [Plant Symbolism: "Tit-Willow," *Mikado;* "Willow Song," *Othello*]
26. **Wingfield, Laura** caller fails to reciprocate the love she secretly had for him since high-school days. [Am. Drama: *The Glass Menagerie* in Hart, 317]
27. **Zuleika** traditional name for Potiphar's wife. [Pers. Lit.: Brewer *Dictionary,* 1175]

417. LOVE, TRAGIC (See also DEATH, PREMATURE.)

1. **Abélard, Pierre** (1079–c.1144) philosopher notorious for the tragic love affair with Héloïse. [Fr. Hist.: Benét, 2]
2. **Abel and Rima** wordly Venezuelan falls passionately in love with girl who is killed by hostile Indians. [Br. Lit.: Hudson *Green Mansions* in Magill I, 333]
3. **Alfredo and Violetta** his love for the courtesan is shattered by her renunciation and fatal illness. [Ital. Opera: Verdi *La Traviata* in Benét, 1022]
4. ***An Iceland Fisherman*** Breton fisherman and his girl marry just before fleet leaves; he is lost in a storm. [Fr. Lit.: *An Iceland Fisherman* in Magill I, 410]
5. **Annabel Lee** a storm swept her away. [Am. Lit.: "Annabel Lee" in Hart, 35]
6. **Antony and Cleopatra** victims of conflict between political ambition and love. [Br. Lit.: *Antony and Cleopatra*]
7. **Archer, Newland** though attracted to his wife's cousin Ellen, he cannot act to win her. [Am. Lit.: *The Age of Innocence*]
8. ***Blessed Damozel, The*** Rossetti poem depicting the longing of a beatified maiden for her mortal lover. [Br. Poetry: *The Blessed Damozel* in Benét, 113]
9. **Cabot, Eben, and Abbie Putnam** after feuding, recognize love; each imprisoned thereafter. [Am. Lit.: *Desire Under the Elms*]
10. **Clärchen** commits suicide when beloved receives death sentence. [Ger. Lit.: *Egmont*]
11. **Deirdre** when Noisi is betrayed and slain, she kills herself. [Irish Legend: Benét, 259–260]
12. **Delphine and Leonce** she takes poison when he is shot as a traitor. [Fr. Lit.: Mme. de Staël *Delphine* in Benét, 262]

13. **Dido and Aeneas** with the gods demanding his departure, she commits suicide. [Rom. Lit.: *Aeneid;* Fr. Opera: Berlioz, *The Trojans,* Westerman, 174–176]
14. **Elizabeth** dies when Tannhäuser vows return to Venus. [Ger. Opera: Wagner, *Tannhäuser,* Westerman, 212]
15. **Elsa** loses Lohengrin on their wedding night when she disobeys his proviso that she never ask him to disclose his identity. [Ger. Legend: "Lohengrin" in Benét, 595]
16. **Evangeline and Gabriel** after years of searching, she finds him as he lay dying. [Am. Lit.: "Evangeline" in Hart, 263]
17. **Fabrizio and Clelia** archbishop and his mistress: she and their infant die, and he retires to a monastery. [Fr. Lit.: *The Charterhouse of Parma* in Magill I, 135]
18. **Fields of Mourning** place in underworld where lovers who committed suicide dwell. [Rom. Lit.: *Aeneid*]
19. **Forsyte, Fleur and Jon** their passion is foredoomed by the estrangement of her father and his mother. [Br. Lit.: *The Forsyte Saga*]
20. **Forsyte, Irene, and Philip Bosinney** she falls in love with him, her husband's architect; he dies in an accident. [Br. Lit.: *The Forsyte Saga*]
21. **Frankie and Johnnie** "sporting woman" shot her man for "doing her wrong." [Pop. Music: Leach, 415]
22. **Frome, Ethan** his thwarted love for Mattie culminates in an attempted double suicide that leaves them both crippled. [Am. Lit.: *Ethan Frome* in Benét, 324]
23. **Galatea and Acis** love shattered by latter's death. [Rom. Lit.: *Metamorphoses*]
24. **Gerard and Margaret** their marriage forbidden, he is given a false report of her death, and enters a monastery. [Br. Lit.: *The Cloister and the Hearth* in Benét, 208]
25. **Ghismonda and Guiscardo** princess's and commoner's affair fatal upon discovery. [Ital. Lit.: *Decameron*]
26. **Gilliatt** his plan for wedding Déruchette foiled by her love for another, he commits suicide by drowning. [Fr. Lit.: *Toilers of the Sea* in Magill II, 1037]
27. **Glaucus** loses love, Scylla, when she is made monster. [Rom. Lit.: *Metamorphoses*]
28. **Gráinne** second wife of Fionn, she elopes with Diarmiud; caught by Fionn, Diarmiud is killed. [Irish Legend: *Century Classical,* 509]

29. **Hero and Leander** latter drowns, former kills herself in grief. [Gk. Lit.: *Hero and Leander;* Br. Lit.: *Hero and Leander*]
30. **Hylonome** commits suicide after death of lover, Cyllarus. [Gk. Myth.: Kravitz, 72, 123]
31. **Karenina, Anna** her death destroys Count Vronsky's desire to live. [Russ. Lit.: *Anna Karenina*]
32. **Launcelot, Sir, and Queen Guinevere** exiled by King Arthur, he returns after the King's death to find Guinevere a nun. [Arthurian Legend: *Le Morte d'Arthur*]
33. **Le Sueur, Lucetta** her love for Henchard squelched by his degradation. [Br. Lit.: *The Mayor of Casterbridge,* Magill I, 571–573]
34. **Lenore** the lost love with whom the poet learns that he will nevermore be united. [Am. Poetry: Poe *The Raven*]
35. **Leonora and Alvaro** her brother must kill her for eloping with the man he mistakenly supposes has murdered their father. [Ital. Opera: *La Forza del Destino* in Osborne *Opera*]
36. **Liliom** ne'er-do-well adored by Julie, his young wife; caught in a robbery, he commits suicide, leaving her with child. [Hung. Drama: Molnar *Liliom* in Magill I, 511]
37. ***Love Story*** idyllic romance of a young couple that is shattered by the death of the woman. [Am. Lit.: Segal *Love Story*]
38. **Manrico and Leonora** supposed gypsy troubador loves the girl courted by his brother, the Count of Luna; she takes poison and he is executed. [Ital. Opera: Verdi *Il Trovatore* in Benét, 1028]
39. **Mimi** her love for Rodolfo ended by her early death. [Ital. Opera: Puccini, *La Bohème,* Westerman, 348–350]
40. **Norma and Pollio** die together as sacrifices to Druid war god. [Ital. Opera: Bellini, *Norma,* Westerman, 130–131]
41. **Olindo and Sophronia** latter condemned to stake; lover joins her. [Ital. Lit.: *Jerusalem Delivered*]
42. **Onegin, Eugene, and Tatyana** long hopelessly for each other after her marriage to another. [Russ. Lit.: *Eugene Onegin*]
43. **Orpheus and Eurydice** looking back to see if Eurydice was following him to earth, he lost her forever. [Gk. Myth.: Zimmerman, 103]
44. **Paolo and Francesca** slain by his jealous brother, her husband, Giancotto. [Ital. Lit.: *Inferno*]
45. **Pelléas and Mélisande** she married the wrong brother; dies of disappointment. [Fr. Opera: Debussy, *Pelléas and Mélisande,* Westerman, 196]

46. **Pyramus and Thisbe** thinking lover mauled, Pyramus kills himself; upon discovery, Thisbe does likewise. [Rom. Lit.: *Metamorphoses*]
47. **Romeo and Juliet** archetypal star-crossed lovers. [Br. Lit.: *Romeo and Juliet*]
48. **Saint-Preux and Julie d'Etange** passion waxes, but class strictures block marriage. [Fr. Lit.: *The New Heloïse*]
49. ***Thornbirds, The*** love between Father Ralph and Meggie remains unfulfilled because of his priestly vows. [Australian Lit.: McCullough *The Thornbirds* in Weiss, 463]
50. **tin soldier** adores a cardboard dancer, but both are consumed in a fire. [Dan Lit.: Andersen "The Steadfast Tin Soldier" in *Andersen's Fairy Tales*]
51. **Tosca and Cavaradossi** famous singer, witnessing her lover's execution, jumps to her death. [Ital. Opera: Puccini *Tosca* in Benét, 1017]
52. **Tristan and Iseult** irrevocably enamored; die because of his wife's machinations. [Medieval Legend: *Tristan and Iseult;* Ger. Opera: *Tristan and Iseult*]
53. ***West Side Story*** love of Puerto Rican girl and young New York street-gang leader is destroyed by his murder. [Am. Musical: *West Side Story*]
54. **Wray, Fay** innocent beauty drives giant gorilla, Kong, to his death. [Am. Cinema: *King Kong*]
55. ***Wuthering Heights*** Heathcliff's revenge for Catherine's supposed scorn leads to her marrying another and to his own lonely death. [Br. Lit.: Emily Brontë *Wuthering Heights* in Magill I, 1137]
56. **Zhivago, Dr. Yurii** has passionate but fleeting affair with Lara. [Russ. Lit.: *Doctor Zhivago* in Magill IV, 241]

418. LOVE, UNREQUITED

1. **Bashville** footman; has noble, unrequited affection for heiress. [Br. Lit.: *Cashel Byron's Profession*]
2. **Bede, Adam** thought only of Hetty; she loved another. [Br. Lit.: *Adam Bede*]
3. **Chastelard** died for love of Mary, Queen of Scots. [Br. Lit.: *Chastelard,* Walsh *Modern,* 92]
4. **daffodil** symbol of unrequited love. [Flower Symbolism: Jobes, 405]
5. **de Clèves, Princess** secretly loves a man other than her husband. [Fr. Lit.: *La Princesse de Clèves,* Walsh *Modern,* 100]

6. **de Vargas, Luis** seminarian falls for father's fiancée. [Span. Lit.: *Pepita Jiménez*]
7. **Dobson, Zuleika** every Oxford undergraduate falls in love with and despairs over her. [Br. Lit.: *Zuleika Dobson*]
8. **Echo** pined for Narcissus till only voice remained. [Gk. Myth.: Brewer *Dictionary*, 363; Br. Lit.: *Comus*, in Benét, 217]
9. **Elaine** nursing Lancelot, she falls in love with him, but he loves Guinevere; she dies of a broken heart. [Br. Poetry: Tennyson *Idylls of the King*]
10. **Goodwood, Casper** his suit thrice rejected by Isabel Archer. [Am. Lit.: *Portrait of a Lady* in Hart, 669]
11. **Hoffmann** thrice a loser when one girl turns out to be a mechanical doll, the second dies, and the third loves another man. [Fr. Opera: *Tales of Hoffmann* in Scholes, 1005]
12. **Krazy Kat** to Ignatz, despite his efforts to dissuade her. [Comics: Horn, 436–437]
13. **Mignon** dies from hopelessness of love for Wilhelm. [Ger. Lit.: *Wilhelm Meister's Apprenticeship*, Walsh *Modern*, 266]
14. **Nureddin** lovesick for Margiana, the Caliph's daughter. [Ger. Opera: Cornelius, *Thief of Baghdad*, Westerman, 256]
15. **O'Hara, Scarlett** marriages to three other men fail to dim her love for Ashley Wilkes. [Am. Lit.: Margaret Mitchell *Gone with the Wind*]
16. **Orsino, Count** a priest committed to celibacy; loved by Beatrice. [Br. Lit.: "The Cenci" in Magill I, 131–133]
17. **Porphyria** comes in a winter storm to show her devotion, and her lover strangles her with her own tresses. [Br. Poetry: Browning *Porphyria's Lover* in Magill IV, 247]
18. **Ray, Philip** locks deep within heart his love for Annie. [Br. Lit.: "Enoch Arden" in Magill I, 249–250]
19. **Sasha** Russian princess hopelessly loved by Orlando. [Br. Lit.: *Orlando*, Magill I, 698–700]
20. **Standish, Miles** (c. 1584–1656) declared love for Priscilla; received no response. [Am. Lit.: "The Courtship of Miles Standish" in Magill I, 165–166]
21. **striped carnation** symbol of love's denial. [Flower Symbolism: Jobes, 291]
22. **Treplev, Konstantin** aspiring novelist; hopelessly enamored of actress, commits suicide. [Russ. Lit.: *The Seagull*]
23. **Zenobia** strong-minded woman; disappointed in love, drowns self. [Am. Lit.: *Blithedale Romance*]

419. LOVE, VICTORIOUS

1. **Ada and Arindal** mortal and fairy permitted to stay together. [Ger. Opera: Wagner, *The Fairies,* Westerman, 202]
2. **Babbie** gypsy wins clergyman despite opposition of town. [Br. Lit.: *The Little Minister*]
3. **Beatrice and Benedick** witty rebels against love; become enamored. [Br. Lit.: *Much Ado About Nothing*]
4. **Bell, Laura** wins Pendennis's love despite his slavish admiration for wealth. [Br. Lit.: *Pendennis,* Magill I, 726–728]
5. **Bennet, Elizabeth** neither pride nor prejudice can cover up love for Darcy. [Br. Lit.: *Pride and Prejudice,* Magill I, 180–183]
6. **Berling, Gosta, and Countess Elizabeth** marry after many years of misunderstanding and misadventure. [Swed. Lit.: Lagerlof *Gosta Berling's Saga* in Benét, 412]
7. **Bezuhov, Pierre** long in love with Natasha Rostov; united after the deaths of his wife and her lover. [Russ. Lit.: Tolstoy *War and Peace* in Magill I, 1085]
8. **Castlewood, Lady and Henry Esmond** both undergo many trials before he realizes their love and they marry. [Br. Lit.: *Henry Esmond*]
9. **Cellini and Teresa** their love prevails, despite jealous suitors and duels. [Fr. Opera: Berlioz, *Benvenuto Cellini,* Westerman, 169–170]
10. **di Ripafratta, Cavalier** avowed woman-hater falls to innkeeper's feminine charms. [Ital. Lit.: *The Mistress of the Inn*]
11. **Dodsworth, Sam** finally leaves hypocritical wife for true love. [Am. Lit.: *Dodsworth*]
12. **Doone, Lorna** John and Lorna's love wins over many obstacles. [Br. Lit.: *Lorna Doone,* Magill I, 524–526]
13. **Elliott, Anne** nine years after her family made her give up her fiancé, they meet again and are united. [Br. Lit.: *Persuasion* in Magill I, 734]
14. **Ernesto and Norina** their schemes permit love to conquer. [Ital. Opera: Donizetti, *Don Pasquale,* Westerman, 123–124]
15. **Frithiof and Ingeborg** childhood lovers separated for years by court intrigue, finally reunited [Nor. Lit.: Haydn & Fuller, 275]
16. **Ione and Glaucus** though threatened by jealous rivals, a murder plot, and volcanic eruption, they eventually attain happiness. [Br. Lit.: *The Last Days of Pompeii*]

17. **Jones, Tom** eventually marries Sophia Western, his sweetheart from early childhood, after they have been kept apart by his adventurousness and unknown antecedents. [Br. Lit.: Fielding *Tom Jones*]

18. **Ladislaw, Will** finally marries Dorothea, despite her family's protests. [Br. Lit.: *Middlemarch*, Magill I, 588–591]

19. **Lavinia** after war, affianced to Aeneas. [Rom. Lit.: *Aeneid*]

20. **Levin and Kitty** long kept apart by her early refusal, their pride, and misunderstanding, they are eventually united. [Russ. Lit.: Tolstoy *Anna Karenina*]

21. **Lucia and Renzo** peasants whose marriage, long thwarted by the machinations of a local baron, is eventually consummated. [Ital. Lit.: Manzoni *The Betrothed* in Magill II, 88]

22. **Nanki-Poo** wins Yum-Yum despite his self-exile to defy his father's commands. [Br. Opera: Gilbert and Sullivan *The Mikado*]

23. **Nikulaussön, Erlend** despite social convention, he wins Kristin's hand. [Nor. Lit.: *Kristin Lavransdatter*, Magill I, 483–486]

24. ***Peer Gynt*** Solveig loves Peer Gynt, despite his life of wandering, and finally wins him. [Nor. Drama: Ibsen *Peer Gynt* in Sobel, 531]

25. **pierced heart** Renaissance emblem, with motto, "Love conquers all." [Art: Hall, 146]

26. **Pontmercy, Marius** despite grandfather's forbiddance, marries Cosette. [Fr. Lit.: *Les Misérables*]

27. **Prince Charming** handsome suitor fulfills a maiden's dreams. [Fr. Fairy Tale: *Cinderella*]

28. **Rowena** loved by Ivanhoe, who finally claims her hand. [Br. Lit.: *Ivanhoe*]

29. ***Taming of the Shrew, The*** Lucentio wins Bianca despite the machinations of his rivals and the objections of her father. [Br. Drama: Shakespeare *The Taming of the Shrew*]

30. **Tamino and Pamina** undergo trials and confinement before being united. [Ger. Opera: Mozart *The Magic Flute* in Benét, 619]

31. **Western, Jasper** Bumppo relinquishes his claim on Mabel to Jasper, whom Mabel loves. [Am. Lit.: *The Pathfinder*, Magill I, 715–717]

32. **Wickfield, Agnes** her love for David, long concealed, is fulfilled after his first wife dies. [Br. Lit.: Dickens *David Copperfield*]

420. LOVE, VIRTUOUS

1. **Aphrodite Urania** patron of ideal, spiritual love. [Gk. Myth.: Espy, 16]
2. **Armande** loves Clitandre platonically; values mind over senses. [Fr. Lit.: *Les Femmes Savantes*]
3. **Athelny, Sally** loves and marries Philip, despite the latter's shortcomings. [Br. Lit.: *Of Human Bondage,* Magill I, 670–672]
4. **Beatrice** object of Dante's adoration, even after death. [Ital. Lit.: *La Vita Nuova; Divine Comedy,* Walsh *Classical,* 48]
5. **Bergerac, Cyrano de** does not reveal his love for Roxane. [Fr. Lit.: *Cyrano de Bergerac*]
6. **Camille** gives up Armand for his family's sake. [Fr. Lit.: *Camille*]
7. **Cupid's golden arrow** symbolizes noble affection. [Rom. Myth.: Jobes, 397]
8. **Diotima** prophetess, teacher of Socrates, speaks of an ideal love. [Gk. Lit.: Plato *Symposium* in Brewer *Handbook*]
9. **Dulcinea** as Quixote's ideal; now, generic for 'sweetheart.' [Span. Lit.: *Don Quixote,* Espy, 128]
10. **Laura** Petrarch's perpetual, unattainable love. [Ital. Lit.: Plumb, 26–32]
11. **Lucretia** model of virtue; raped by son of Tarquin, she kills herself. [Rom. Legend: Daniel, 152]
12. **Murasaki** reared by future husband; causes his reform. [Jap. Lit.: *The Tale of Genji*]
13. **Oriana** faithful and fair beloved for Amadis. [Span. Lit.: *Amadis de Gaul*]
14. **Schouler, Marcus** sets aside love for Trina for McTeague's benefit. [Am. Lit.: *McTeague,* Magill I, 537–539]

421. LOVERS, FAMOUS

1. **Abélard and Héloïse** (Pierre, 1079–1142) (c. 1098–1164) persecuted 12th-century lovers. [Fr. Hist.: *Century Cyclopedia,* 14]
2. **Atala and Chactas** Indian lovers whose passion goes unconsummated. [Fr. Lit.: *Atala*]
3. **Aucassin and Nicolette** the love story of 12th-century France. [Fr. Lit.: *Aucassin and Nicolette*]
4. **Browning, Robert, and Elizabeth Barrett** (1812–1889) (1806–1861) 19th-century love one of most celebrated of literary romances. [Br. Lit.: Benét, 139]
5. **Celadon and Astree** bywords for lovers in pastoral poetry. [Br. Lit.: *Celadon,* Walsh *Modern,* 91]

6. **Ceyx and Halcyone** to perpetuate love, changed into kingfishers after former's drowning. [Rom. Lit.: *Metamorphoses*]
7. **Daphnis and Chloë** innocent though passionate love of two children. [Gk. Lit.: *Daphnis and Chloë,* Magill I, 184]
8. **Darby and Joan** inseparable old-fashioned couple. [Br. Lit.: Espy, 335]
9. **Deirdre and Noisi** celebrated lovers of the Ulster Cycle. [Irish Legend: Benét, 259–260]
10. **Della and Jim** each sacrifices greatly for other's Christmas present. [Am. Lit.: "The Gift of the Magi" in Benét, 395]
11. **Edward VIII** (1894–1972) **and Wallis Warfield Simpson** (1896–) British king abdicates throne to marry divorcee (1936). [Br. Hist.: *NCE,* 835]
12. **Helen and Paris** their elopement caused the Trojan war. [Gk. Myth.: *Century Classical,* 525–528, 815–817]
13. **Hero and Leander** love affair on the Hellespont tragically ends with latter's drowning. [Gk. Lit.: *Hero and Leander:* Br. Lit.: *Hero and Leander*]
14. **Jacob and Rachel** he worked fourteen years to win her hand. [O.T.: Genesis 29:18]
15. **Lescaut, Manon, and the Chevalier des Grieux** he accompanies Manon to Louisiana when she is exiled for prostitution. [Fr. Lit.: *Manon Lescaut*]
16. **lovebirds** small parrots, traditional symbol of affection. [Am. Culture: Misc.]
17. **Oliver and Jenny** rapturous college relationship leads to blissful marriage. [Am. Lit.: *Love Story*]
18. **Petrarch and Laura** lovers in spirit only. [Ital. Lit.: Plumb, 26–32]
19. **Rinaldo and Armida** virgin witch seeks revenge but falls in love. [Ital. Lit.: *Jerusalem Delivered*]
20. **Romeo and Juliet** young love springs up amidst family feud. [Br. Lit.: *Romeo and Juliet*]
21. **Tristan and Iseult** their pact of undying love has tragic consequences. [Medieval Legend: *Tristan and Iseult;* Ger. Opera: *Tristan and Iseult*]
22. **turtle doves** adoring couple, building their nest. [O.T.: Song of Songs 2:12]
23. **Zhivago, Yuri, and Lara** passion stirs between idealistic doctor and nurse during Russian revolution. [Russ. Lit.: *Doctor Zhivago*]

422. LOYALTY (See also FRIENDSHIP, PATRIOTISM.)

1. **Achates** companion and faithful friend of Aeneas. [Rom. Lit.: *Aeneid*]
2. **Adam** family retainer; offers Orlando his savings. [Br. Lit.: *As You Like It*]
3. **Aeneas** carried his father Anchises from burning Troy. [Rom. Lit.: *Aeneid*]
4. **alexandrite** type of chrysoberyl typifying undying devotion. [Gem Symbolism: Jobes, 67]
5. **Antony, Mark** Caesar's beloved friend; turns public opinion against Caesar's assassins. [Br. Lit.: *Julius Caesar*]
6. **Argus** Odysseus' dog; overjoyed at Odysseus' return, he dies. [Gk. Lit.: *Odyssey*]
7. **Balderstone, Caleb** servant true to Ravenswoods despite poverty. [Br. Lit.: *The Bride of Lammermoor*]
8. **Bevis** mastiff who "saved his master by his fidelity." [Br. Lit.: *Woodstock*]
9. **Blondel** loyal troubadour to Richard the Lion-hearted; helps him escape. [Br. Lit.: *The Talisman*]
10. **bluebell** symbol of loyalty. [Plant Symbolism: *Flora Symbolica*, 172]
11. **Byam, Roger** remains faithful to Captain Bligh after mutiny. [Am. Lit.: *Mutiny on the Bounty*]
12. **Camillo** as counsellor, exemplifies constancy. [Br. Lit.: *The Winter's Tale*]
13. **Chauvin, Nicolas** (fl. early 19th century) he followed Napoleon through everything. [Fr. Hist.: Wallechinsky, 164]
14. **Chester** Matt Dillon's lame but game sidekick. [TV: "Gunsmoke" in Terrace, I, 331–332]
15. **Chingachgook** ever-devoted to Hawkeye. [Am. Lit.: *The Last of the Mohicans*]
16. **Cordelia** faithful daughter of sea god Llyr [Celtic Myth.: Parrinder, 67]; loyal and loving daughter of King Lear. [Br. Lit.: *King Lear*]
17. **dog** ever pictured at feet of saints; "man's best friend." [Medieval Art: Brewer *Dictionary*, 332; Western Folklore: Misc.]
18. **Dolius** the loyal retainer of Odysseus and Penelope. [Gk. Lit.: *Odyssey*]
19. **Eros** Antony's freed slave; kills himself rather than harm Antony. [Br. Lit.: *Antony and Cleopatra*]
20. **Eumaeus** loyal swineherd of Odysseus. [Gk. Lit.: *Odyssey*]

21. **Faithful Johannes** loyal servant dies for king and is resurrected. [Ger. Fairy Tale: Grimm, 22]
22. **Flavius** loyal and upright steward of Timon. [Br. Lit.: *Timon of Athens*]
23. **Gloucester** faithful to Lear, he tries to save the king from his daughters' cruelty. [Br. Drama: Shakespeare *King Lear*]
24. **Gonzalo** Prospero's "true preserver and a loyal sir." [Br. Lit.: *The Tempest*]
25. **Good-Deeds** only companion who ultimately accompanies Everyman. [Medieval Lit.: *Everyman*]
26. **Horatio** true-blue friend of Hamlet. [Br. Lit.: *Hamlet*]
27. **Horton** "faithful one hundred percent," Horton sits on the Mayzie bird's egg until it is hatched. [Children's Lit.: *Horton Hatches the Egg*]
28. **Iolaus** nephew and trusted companion of Hercules. [Gk. Myth.: Howe, 141]
29. **Jonathan** stalwartly defended David; aided him in escape. [O.T.: I Samuel 20:32–34, 42; 23:16]
30. **Kato** loyal servant of the Green Hornet. [Radio: "The Green Hornet" in Buxton, 102–103]
31. **Kent** a "noble and true-hearted" courtier. [Br. Lit.: *King Lear*]
32. **Merrilies, Meg** Henry Bertram's Gypsy-nurse; thoroughly devoted and protective. [Br. Lit.: *Guy Mannering*]
33. **Moniplies, Richard** Nigel's servant; helps him out of imbroglio. [Br. Lit.: *Fortunes of Nigel*]
34. **Panza, Sancho** squire to Don Quixote. [Span. Lit.: *Don Quixote*]
35. **Passepartout** faithful valet of Phileas Fogg. [Fr. Lit.: *Around the World in Eighty Days*]
36. **Pilar** fiercely devoted leader of a loyalist guerrilla group in the Spanish Civil War. [Am. Lit.: Hemingway *For Whom the Bell Tolls*]
37. **pirates of Penzance** surrender only when charged by the police to yield in the name of their beloved Queen Victoria. [Br. Opera: Gilbert and Sullivan *The Pirates of Penzance*]
38. **Ruth** devotedly follows mother-in-law to Bethlehem. [O.T.: Ruth 1:15–17]
39. **Scipio** Gil Blas' secretary; shares his imprisonment. [Fr. Lit.: *Gil Blas*]
40. **speedwell** indicates female faithfulness. [Flower Symbolism: *Flora Symbolica,* 177]

41. **Suzuki** ever faithful to her mistress, especially in sorrow. [Ital. Opera: Puccini, *Madama Butterfly,* Westerman, 358]
42. **Titinius** Cassius' loyal follower; follows him to death. [Br. Lit.: *Julius Caesar*]
43. **Tom, Uncle** "noble, high-minded, devoutly Christian Negro slave." [Am. Lit.: *Uncle Tom's Cabin*]
44. **Tonto** the Lone Ranger's constant companion. [Radio: "The Lone Ranger" in Buxton, 143–144; Comics: Horn, 460; TV: Terrace, II, 34–35]
45. **Weller, Samuel** servant helps imprisoned Mr. Pickwick by getting himself imprisoned with him. [Br. Lit.: Dickens *Pickwick Papers*]
46. **Wiglaf** stood by Beowulf to fight dragon while others fled. [Br. Lit.: *Beowulf*]

423. LUCK, BAD

1. **albatross** killing it brings bad luck. [Br. Lit.: "Rime of the Ancient Mariner" in Norton, 597–610]
2. **black cat** because of its demonic associations. [Animal Folklore: Jobes, 297]
3. **black ox** sacrificed to Pluto; symbolic of calamity. [Gk. Myth.: Brewer *Dictionary,* 790]
4. ***Candide*** the hero and his relatives and friends stoically undergo an endless series of misfortunes. [Fr. Lit.: *Candide*]
5. **dead man's hand** two aces, two eights; hand Wild Bill Hickok held when murdered. [Am. Slang: Leach, 299]
6. **eclipse** regarded as portent of misfortune. [World Folklore: Leach, 337]
7. **Fawley, Jude** lost everything his heart desired. [Br. Lit.: *Jude the Obscure*]
8. **Flying Dutchman** ominous spectral ship; seen in storms off Cape of Good Hope. [Marine Folklore: *LLEI,* I: 285]
9. **Friday the 13th** regarded as unlucky day. [Western Folklore: Misc.]
10. **Hope diamond** largest blue diamond known; believed to bring bad luck. [Western Culture: *EB,* V: 126]
11. **Jonah** trying to escape God, brought tempest to sea. [O.T.: Jonah 1:4–12]
12. **ladder** walking under one can bring only misfortune. [Western Folklore: Leach, 598]
13. **mirror** the breaking of one brings seven years of bad luck. [Western Folklore: Cirlot, 211]

14. **Mutt** compulsive gambler who always loses. [Comics: Berger, 48]
15. **opal** unlucky stone; represents the Evil Eye. [Gem Symbolism: Kunz, 148, 320]
16. **Plornish** disaster was his specialty. [Br. Lit.: *Little Dorrit*]
17. **Ring of the Nibelungs** brought a curse on all who owned it. [Ger. Lit.: Benét, 860]
18. **Seian Horse** ownership fatal. [Rom. Legend: Brewer *Dictionary*, 978]
19. **shirt of Nessus** Centaur's bloodied shirt; given to Heracles as gift by unsuspecting wife, it caused his death. [Gk. Myth.: Benét, 708]
20. **spilt salt** courts evil. [Rom. Myth.: Brewer *Dictionary*, 958; Ital. Art: "Last Supper"]
21. **step on a crack** and break your mother's back; advice to avoid walking on cracks in pavement. [Am. Folklore: Misc.]
22. **thirteen** number attending Last Supper, including Judas; considered unlucky number. [Christian Hist.: Brewer *Dictionary*, 1075; Western Folklore: Misc.]

424. LUCK, GOOD

1. **albatross** its presence portends good luck. [Br. Lit.: "The Rime of the Ancient Mariner" in Norton, 597–610]
2. **bat** symbol of good fortune; bat flesh imparts felicity. [Eastern Folklore: Mercatante, 182]
3. **carnelian** brings luck; drives away evil. [Gem Symbolism: Kunz, 62–63]
4. **crossed fingers** said to bring good luck to a person. [Western Folklore: Misc.]
5. **four-leaf clover** indicates good luck. [Plant Symbolism: Jobes, 350]
6. **gypsum** in egg-shaped form, brings good fortune. [Gem Symbolism: Kunz, 80]
7. **horseshoe** protective talisman placed over doors of churches, stables, etc. [Western Folklore: Leach, 505]
8. **Irish sweepstakes** only lucky people win this famous lottery. [Irish Hist.: *NCE*, 1614]
9. **knock on wood** to bring good luck and ward off bad luck. [Am. Folklore: Misc.]
10. **moonstone** sacred stone; brings good fortune. [Gem Symbolism: Kunz, 97–98]

11. **new penny** placing new penny in gift of purse brings recipient good luck. [Western Folklore: Misc.]
12. **penny** finding one by chance in street brings good luck. [Western Folklore: Misc.]
13. **penny loafer** placing penny in slot at top of shoe brings good fortune. [Am. Folklore: Misc.]
14. **Polycrates** tyrant of Samos, known and feared for his proverbial good luck, though it is not permanent. [Gk. Hist.: Benét, 801]
15. **rabbit's foot** proverbial good luck charm. [Western Folklore: Misc.]
16. **red** life-granting color; worn by brides and babies. [Asian Color Symbolism: Binder, 78]
17. **seven** symbolizes good luck in ancient and modern societies. [World Culture: Jobes, 1421–1422]
18. **seventh son** always a lucky or gifted person. [Western Folklore: Leach, 999]
19. **swastika** ancient sign of good luck, often in the form of a charm or talisman. [Asiatic Culture: Brewer *Dictionary*, 1051]
20. **three** symbolizes good luck; most holy of all numbers. [World Culture: Jobes, 1563–1566]
21. ***Three Princes of Serendip*** adventures of three Ceylonese princes who continually discover things they are not looking for. [Persian Lit.: Benét, 915]
22. **white on red** symbolizes good fortune. [Chinese Art: Jobes, 357]

425. LUST (See also PROFLIGACY, PROMISCUITY.)

1. **Aeshma** fiend of evil passion. [Iranian Myth.: Leach, 17]
2. **Aholah and Aholibah** lusty whores; bedded from Egypt to Babylon. [O.T.: Ezekiel 23:1–21]
3. **Alcina** lustful fairy. [Ital. Lit.: *Orlando Furioso*]
4. **Ambrosio, Father** supposedly virtuous monk goatishly ravishes maiden. [Br. Lit.: *The Monk*]
5. **Angelo** asked by Isabella to cancel her brother's death sentence, Angelo agrees if she will yield herself to him. [Br. Drama: Shakespeare *Measure for Measure*]
6. **Aphrodite Porne** patron of lust and prostitution. [Gk. Myth.: Espy, 16]
7. **Armida's Garden** symbol of the attractions of the senses. [Ital. Lit.: *Jerusalem Delivered*]

8. **Aselges** personification of lasciviousness. [Br. Lit.: *The Purple Island,* Brewer *Handbook,* 67]
9. **Ashtoreth** goddess of sexual love. [Phoenician Myth.: Zimmerman, 32]
10. **Asmodeus** female spirit of lust. [Jew. Myth.: Jobes, 141]
11. **Balthazar B** shy gentleman afloat on sea of lasciviousness. [Am. Lit.: *The Beastly Beatitudes of Balthazar B*]
12. **Belial** demon of libidinousness and falsehood. [Br. Lit.: *Paradise Lost*]
13. **Bess** Porgy's "temporary" woman; she knew weakness of her will and flesh. [Am. Lit.: *Porgy,* Magill I, 764–766; Am. Opera: Gershwin, *Porgy and Bess*]
14. ***Brothers Karamazov, The*** family given to the pleasures of flesh. [Russ. Lit.: *The Brothers Karamazov*]
15. **Caro** loathsome hag; personification of fleshly lust. [Br. Lit.: *The Purple Island,* Brewer *Handbook,* 180]
16. **Casanova** (1725–1798) loving (and likable) libertine. [Ital. Hist.: Espy, 130]
17. **Cleopatra** (69–30 B.C.) Egyptian queen, used sex for power. [Egyptian Hist.: Wallechinsky, 323]
18. **Don Juan** literature's most active seducer: "in Spain, 1003." [Span. Lit.: Benét, 279; Ger. Opera: Mozart, *Don Giovanni,* Espy, 130–131]
19. **elders of Babylon** condemn Susanna when carnal passion goes unrequited. [Apocrypha: Daniel and Susanna]
20. **Falstaff, Sir John** fancies himself a lady-killer. [Br. Lit.: *Merry Wives of Windsor*]
21. **Fritz the Cat** a tomcat in every sense. [Comics: Horn, 266–267]
22. **goat** lust incarnate. [Art: Hall, 139]
23. **hare** attribute of sexual desire incarnate. [Art: Hall, 144]
24. **horns** attribute of Pan and the satyr; symbolically, lust. [Rom. Myth.: Zimmerman, 190; Art: Hall, 157]
25. **Hartman, Rev. Curtis** lusts after a young woman viewed at her window, but turns the experience into a hysterical sense of redemption. [Am. Lit.: *Winesburg, Ohio*]
26. **John of the Funnels, Friar** monk advocating lust. [Fr. Lit.: *Gargantua and Pantagruel*]
27. **Lilith** sensual female; mythical first wife of Adam. [O.T.: Genesis 4:16]
28. **long ears** symbol of licentiousness. [Indian Myth.: Leach, 333]

29. **Lothario** heartless libertine and active seducer. [Br. Lit.: *Fair Penitent,* Espy, 129]
30. **Malecasta** personification of wantonness. [Br. Lit.: *Faerie Queene*]
31. **Montez, Lola** (1818–1861) beguiling mistress to the eminent. [Br. Hist.: Wallechinsky, 325]
32. **Obidicut** fiend; provokes men to gratify their lust. [Br. Lit.: *King Lear*]
33. **Pan** man-goat of bawdy and lecherous ways. [Gk. Myth.: Brewer *Dictionary,* 798]
34. **Paphnutius** monk converts a courtesan but cannot overcome his lust for her. [Fr. Lit.: Anatole France *Thaïs* in Benét, 997]
35. **pig** attribute of lust personified. [Art: Hall, 247]
36. **Porneius** personification of fornication. [Br. Lit.: *The Purple Island,* Brewer *Handbook,* 865]
37. **Priapus** monstrous genitals led him on the wayward path. [Rom. Myth.: Hall, 252]
38. **Ridgeon, Sir Colenso** refrains from using his tuberculosis cure to save the life of a man whose wife he coveted. [Br. Lit.: Shaw *The Doctor's Dilemma* in Sobel, 173]
39. **Robinson, Mrs.** middle-aged lady lusts after young graduate. [Am. Lit.: *The Graduate;* Am. Music: "Mrs. Robinson"]
40. **Salome** in her provocative Dance of the Seven Veils. [Aust. Opera: R. Strauss, *Salome,* Westerman, 417]
41. **Spanish jasmine** flower symbolizing lust. [Flower Symbolism: *Flora Symbolica,* 175]
42. **Vathek** devotes his life to sexual and other sensuous indulgences. [Br. Lit.: Beckford *Vathek*]
43. **Villiers, George** first Duke of Buckingham and libidinous dandy. [Br. Lit.: *Waverley*]
44. **widow of Ephesus** weeping over her husband's corpse, she is cheered by a compassionate sentry and they become ardent lovers in the burial vault. [Rom. Lit.: *Satyricon*]
45. **Zeus** the many loves of this god have made his name a byword for sexual lust. [Gk. Myth.: Howe, 297–301]

426. LUXURY (See also WEALTH.)

1. **angora cat** behavior suggests self-indulgence. [Animal Symbolism: Jobes, 96]
2. **Babylon** ancient city on Euphrates river; famed for its magnificence and culture. [Mid. East. Hist.: *NCE,* 202]

3. **Cadillac** expensive automobile and status symbol. [Trademarks: Crowley *Trade,* 83]
4. **Cartier's** jewelry firm founded by Alfred and Louis Cartier in Paris (1898). [Fr. Hist.: *EB,* 10: 177]
5. **caviar** extremely expensive delicacy of sturgeon's roe; byword for luxurious living. [Western Culture: Misc.]
6. **chauffeur-driven car** sign of the high life. [Western Cult.: Misc.]
7. **chinchilla** one of the costliest of furs, made into luxurious coats. [Western Culture: Misc.]
8. **Chivas Regal** expensive Scotch whisky. [Trademarks: Crowley *Trade,* 106]
9. **clover** indicates wealth and ease. [Western Folklore: Jobes, 350]
10. **Cockaigne** fabled land of luxury and idleness. [Medieval Legend: *NCE,* 589]
11. **Dom Perignon** renowned vintage French champagne. [Western Cult.: Misc.]
12. **fat of the land** Pharaoh offers Joseph's family Egypt's plenty. [O.T.: Genesis 45:18]
13. **fleshpots of Egypt** where Israelites "did eat bread to the full." [O.T.: Exodus 16:3]
14. **land flowing with milk and honey** promised by God to afflicted Israelites. [O.T.: Exodus 3:8; 13:5]
15. **life of Riley** easy and troublefree existence. [Am. Usage: c. 1900 song, "Best of the House is None Too Good for Reilly"; TV: "The Life of Riley" in Terrace, II, 26]
16. **Mercedes Benz** expensive automobile and status symbol. [Trademarks: Crowley *Trade,* 368]
17. **mink coat** highly prized fur apparel; traditionally associated with wealthy ladies. [Western Culture: Misc.]
18. **Pullman car** comfortable, well-appointed railroad sleeping car named for maker. [Am. Hist.: Flexner, 210]
19. **Ritz** elegant and luxurious hotel opened in Paris in 1898 by César Ritz; hence, 'ritzy, putting on the ritz.' [Fr. Hist.: Wentworth, 429]
20. **Rolls Royce** the millionaire's vehicle. [Trademarks: Brewer *Dictionary,* 928]
21. **sable** fur of this mammal produces luxurious, soft fur coats. [Western Culture: Misc.]
22. **Savoy** sumptuous hotel in London; at the time of its opening, it set new standards of luxury. [Br. Hist.: *EB,* 8: 1118]

23. **Schlauraffenland** fantastic land of sumptuous pleasures and idleness. [Ger. Legend: Grimm "A Tale of Schlauraffenland"]
24. **silk** expensive fabric used in fine clothing. [Western Cult.: Misc.]
25. **Tiffany's** jewelry firm founded by Charles Lewis Tiffany; store in New York caters to the wealthy. [Am. Hist.: *EB*, 10: 177]

M

427. MADNESS

1. **Alcithoe** driven mad by Dionysus. [Gk. Myth.: Kravitz, 16]
2. **Alcmeon** driven mad by the Furies. [Gk. Myth.: Kravitz, 16]
3. **Ashton, Lucy** goes mad upon marriage; stabs husband. [Br. Lit.: *Bride of Lammermoor*]
4. **Bedlam** (Hospital of St. Mary of Bethlehem) first asylum for the insane in England; noted for brutal treatment of its patients. [Br. Hist.: *EB*, I: 924]
5. **Belvidera** goes mad when husband dies. [Br. Lit.: *Venice Preserved,* Benét, 1052]
6. **Bess o' Bedlam** inmate of London's lunatic asylum; female counterpart of Tom o' Bedlam. [Br. Folklore: Walsh, *Modern,* 55]
7. **Broteas** angered Artemis; she drove him mad. [Gk. Myth.: Kravitz, 47]
8. **Butes** Dionysus drove him mad. [Gk. Myth.: Kravitz, 48]
9. **Cleese, John** performs a manic comic character with persecution complex. [Br. TV: "Monty Python's Flying Circus" in Terrace, II, 108]
10. **Clementina, Lady** mentally unbalanced; vacillates between love and religion. [Br. Lit.: *Sir Charles Grandison,* Walsh *Modern,* 99]
11. **Dervish (Darwesh)** member of ascetic order; frenzied, whirling dancer. [Muslim Rel.: Parrinder, 75; Jobes, 433]
12. **Dympna, St.** curing of madness attributed to her intercession. [Christian Hagiog.: Attwater, 107]
13. **Elvira** great mad scene caused by betrayal of Arthur. [Ital. Opera: Bellini, *Puritani,* Westerman, 133–135]
14. **Erinyes (Furies)** three sisters who tormented those guilty of blood crimes, driving them mad. [Gk. Myth.: Benét, 320]
15. **Furioso, Bombastes** goes mad upon loss of betrothed. [Br. Opera: Rhodes, *Bombastes Furioso,* Walsh, *Modern,* 64–65]
16. **Gunn, Ben** half-demented castaway. [Br. Lit.: *Treasure Island*]
17. **Hieronimo** Spanish general goes mad on seeing the body of his murdered son. [Br. Drama: *The Spanish Tragedy* in Magill II, 990]
18. **King Lear** goes mad as all desert him. [Brit. Lit.: Shakespeare *King Lear*]

19. **Leverkühn, Adrian** brilliant musician attains pinnacle; rapidly deteriorates mentally. [Ger. Lit.: *Doctor Faustus*]
20. **Lucia** frustration causes her to murder husband. [Ital. Opera: Donizetti, *Lucia di Lammermoor,* Westerman, 126–127]
21. **Mad Hatter** crazy gentleman who co-hosts mad tea party. [Br. Lit.: *Alice's Adventures in Wonderland*]
22. ***Madwoman of Chaillot, The*** four eccentric women foil capitalistic exploiters. [Fr. Lit.: Benét, 618]
23. **Mahony, Dr. Richard** tries in vain to stay the insanity that eventually overwhelms him. [Australian Lit.: *The Fortunes of Richard Mahony* in Magill II, 341]
24. **March Hare** crazy rabbit who co-hosts mad tea party. [Br. Lit.: *Alice's Adventures in Wonderland*]
25. **McMurphy, Randall Patrick** brash Irishman, lobotomized in asylum after causing numerous scandals. [Am. Lit.: *One Flew Over the Cuckoo's Nest*]
26. **Myshkin, Prince** four years in sanitarium; thought mad, treated for epilepsy. [Russ. Lit.: *The Idiot*]
27. **Ophelia** goes mad after father's death. [Br. Lit.: *Hamlet*]
28. **Orlando** driven insane by lover's betrayal. [Ital. Lit.: *Orlando Furioso*]
29. **Rochester, Bertha** insane wife of Edward Rochester. [Br. Lit.: *Jane Eyre*]
30. **Tom o' Bedlam** an inmate of London's lunatic asylum. Cf. Bess o' Bedlam. [Br. Folklore: Benét, 3]
31. **Very, Jones** "monomaniac" or "profoundly sane"? [Am. Hist.: Hart, 883]
32. **Wozzeck** thought of blood drives him to murder and suicide. [Aust. Opera: Berg, *Wozzeck,* Westerman, 480–481]

428. MAGIC (See also ENCHANTMENT.)

1. **Aladdin's lamp** when rubbed, genie appears, grants possessor's wishes. [Arab. Lit.: *Arabian Nights*]
2. **Armida's girdle** enabled the enchantress to know and do whatever she willed. [Ital. Lit.: *Jerusalem Delivered*]
3. **Bleys** magician who taught Merlin arts of sorcery. [Arthurian Legend: Walsh *Classical,* 57]
4. **Gandalf** wizard with special control over fire. [Br. Lit.: J. R. R. Tolkien *Lord of the Rings*]
5. **Houdini, Harry** (1874–1926) famous turn of century American magician and escape artist. [Am. Hist.: *NCE,* 1275]

6. **magic carpet** flew King Solomon and his court wherever he commanded the wind to take it. [Moslem Legend: Brewer *Dictionary*, 177]
7. ***Magus, The*** millionaire living on a Greek island magically manipulates an unhappy young Englishman through bewildering experiences into self-awareness. [Br. Lit.: Fowles *The Magus* in Weiss, 279]
8. **Merlin** prince of magicians. [Br. Lit.: *Le Morte d'Arthur*]
9. **Open, Sesame!** formula that opens the door to the robber's cave. [Arab. Lit.: *Arabian Nights*]
10. **Prospero** uses magic to achieve ends. [Br. Lit.: *The Tempest*]
11. ***Skidbladnir*** ship large enough to hold all the gods and their possessions, yet so skillfully wrought by dwarves that it could be folded and pocketed. [Scand. Myth.: Bulfinch]
12. **wild ass's skin** assures the fulfillment of its possessor's wishes, but with a fatal result. [Fr. Lit.: Balzac *The Wild Ass's Skin* in Magill II, 1133]

Magnificence (See SPLENDOR.)

429. MANNISHNESS (See also BOYISHNESS.)

1. **Amazon** female warrior. [Gk. Myth.: Parrinder, 18]
2. **Boadicea (Boudicca)** British queen and warrior; slew 80,000 Romans. [Br. Hist.: Walsh, *Classical*, 58]
3. **Bradamant** female knight-errant. [Ital. Lit.: *Orlando Furioso*]
4. **Brass, Sally** couldn't tell her apart from brother Sampson. [Br. Lit.: *The Old Curiosity Shop*]
5. **Omphale** Lydian queen; wore Hercules' lion skin. [Gk. Myth.: Wheeler, 269]
6. **Rosie the Riveter** popular WWII song romanticizing women workers. [Am. Hist.: Flexner, 395]

430. MARKSMANSHIP

1. **Buffalo Bill** (1846–1917) famed sharpshooter in Wild West show. [Am. Hist.: Flexner, 67]
2. **Crotus** son of Pan, companion to Muses; skilled in archery. [Gk. Myth.: Howe, 70]
3. **Deadeye Dick** sobriquet of 1880s cowboy-sharpshooter, Nat Love. [Am. Hist.: Flexner, 41]
4. **Egil** Norse god, famed archer, met the same challenge as William Tell. [Norse Myth.: Brewer *Dictionary*, 323]
5. **Hawkeye** sharpshooting frontier folk hero. [Am. Lit.: *The Last of the Mohicans*]

6. **Hickok, "Wild Bill"** (1837–1876) sharpshooting stage driver and marshal of U.S. West. [Am. Hist.: Flexner, 387]
7. **Hood, Robin** famed throughout land for skill as archer. [Br. Lit.: *Robin Hood*]
8. **Oakley, Annie** (1860–1926) renowned expert gunshooter of Buffalo Bill's Wild West show. [Am. Hist.: Brewer *Dictionary*, 771]
9. **Robin-A-Bobbin** such a bad archer, killed crow while aiming for pigeon. [Nurs. Rhyme: *Mother Goose*, 33]
10. **Tell, William** shot apple off son's head with arrow. [Swiss Legend: Brewer *Dictionary*, 1066; Ital. Opera: Rossini, *William Tell*]

431. MARRIAGE

1. **American linden** symbol of marriage. [Plant Symbolism: *Flora Symbolica*, 182]
2. **Aphrodite Genetrix** patron of marriage and procreation. [Gk. Myth.: Espy, 16]
3. ***As You Like It*** its denouement has the marriages of four couples. [Br. Lit.: Shakespeare *As You Like It*]
4. **Benedick** nickname for groom; derived from Shakespeare's Benedick. [Br. Lit.: *Much Ado About Nothing*]
5. **Blondie and Dagwood** typify relationship between dominant wife and her inadequate mate. [Comics: Berger, 108]
6. **Bridal Chorus** traditional wedding song; from Wagner's *Lohengrin*. [Music: Scholes, 1113]
7. **Cana** wedding feast where Christ made water into wine. [N.T.: John 2:1–11]
8. ***Doll's House, A*** after eight years of marriage, in which Torvald Helmer has treated Nora more like a doll than a human being, she declares her independence. [Nor. Drama: Ibsen *A Doll's House*]
9. **epithalamium** poem in honor of bride and groom. [Western Lit.: *LLEI*, 1: 283]
10. **Erato** Muse of bridal songs. [Gk. Myth.: Kravitz, 90]
11. **Frome, Ethan** his loveless and unhappy marriage to Zeena remains hopeless when his love affair with Mattie comes to a pitiful end. [Am. Lit.: *Ethan Frome* in Benét, 324]
12. **Gretna Green** place in Scotland, just across the English border, where elopers could be married without formalities. [Br. Hist.: Brewer *Dictionary*, 418]

13. **Hulda** goddess of marriage and fecundity. [Ger. Myth.: Benét, 484]
14. **huppah** bridal canopy in Jewish weddings. [Judaism: Wigoder, 274]
15. ***Marriage à la Mode*** engravings in which Hogarth satirically depicts the daily lives of a countess and an earl. [Br. Art: *EB* (1963) XI, 625]
16. ***Modern Love*** dramatizes the feelings of a couple whose marriage is dying. [Br. Lit.: George Meredith *Modern Love* in Magill IV, 899]
17. **orange blossoms** traditional decoration for brides. [Br. and Fr. Tradition: Brewer *Dictionary,* 784]
18. ***Prothalamion*** Spenser's poem celebrating the double marriage of the two daughters of the Earl of Worcester. [Br. Poetry: Haydn & Fuller, 615]
19. **quince** in portraits, traditionally held by woman in wedding. [Art: Hall, 257]
20. **rice** newly married couples pelted with rice for connubial good luck. [Western Folklore: Leach, 938]
21. **St. Agnes's Eve** when marriageable girls foresee their future husbands. [Br. Lit.: "The Eve of St. Agnes" in Norton, 686–693]
22. ***These Twain*** difficult marital adjustments of Edwin Clayhanger and Hilda Lessways. [Br. Lit.: Bennett *These Twain* in Magill I, 148]
23. **tin cans** put on car of newlyweds leaving ceremony. [Am. Cult.: Misc.]
24. ***Way of the World, The*** profound analysis of the marriage relation in which Mirabell and Millamant negotiate a marriage agreement. [Br. Drama: Benét, 1077]
25. **Wedding March** popular bridal music from Mendelssohn's march in *Midsummer Night's Dream.* [Music: Scholes, 1113]
26. ***Who's Afraid of Virginia Woolf?*** marriage of George and Martha is a travesty, full of arguments, frustration, and hatred. [Am. Drama: Edward Albee *Who's Afraid of Virginia Woolf?* in Magill IV, 1282]
27. **Wife of Bath** many marriages form theme of her tale. [Br. Lit.: *Canterbury Tales,* "Wife of Bath's Tale]

432. MARTYRDOM (See also SACRIFICE.)

1. **Agatha, St.** tortured for resisting advances of Quintianus. [Christian Hagiog.: Daniel, 21]

2. **Alban, St.** traditionally, first British martyr. [Christian Hagiog: *NCE,* 49]
3. **Andrew, St.** apostle and missionary; condemned to be scourged and crucified. [Christian Hagiog.: Brewster, 4]
4. **arrow and cross** symbol of martyrdom of St. Sebastian. [Christian Iconog.: Attwater, 304]
5. **Brown, John** (1800–1859) abolitionist leader; died for antislavery cause. [Am. Hist.: Hart, 111]
6. **Callista** beautiful Greek convert; executed and later canonized. [Br. Lit.: *Callista*]
7. **Campion, Edmund** harassed and tortured by Anglicans, hanged on a false charge of treason. [Br. Lit.: *Edmund Campion* in Magill I, 237]
8. **carnelian** symbol of St. Sebastian. [Christian Hagiog.: Brewer *Handbook,* I, 411]
9. **Elmo, St.** patron saint of sailors; intestines wound on windlass. [Christian Hagiog.: Attwater, 117]
10. **Golgotha** place of martyrdom or of torment; after site of Christ's crucifixion. [Western Folklore: Espy, 79]
11. **Holy Innocents** male infants slaughtered by Herod. [Christian Hagiog.: Attwater, 179; N.T.: Matthew 2:16–18]
12. **James Intercisus, St.** cut to pieces for belief in Christianity. [Christian Hagiog.: Brewster, 2]
13. **Jesus Christ** crucified at demand of Jewish authorities. [N.T.: Matthew 27:24–61; Mark 15:15–47; Luke 23:13–56; John 19:13–42]
14. **Joan of Arc, St.** (1412–1431) burned at stake for witchcraft (1431). [Fr. Hist.: *NCE,* 1417; Br. Lit.: *I Henry VI*]
15. **John the Baptist, St.** Jewish prophet; beheaded at instigation of Salome. [N.T.: Matthew 11:1–19; 17:11–13]
16. **More, Sir Thomas** (1478–1535) statesman and humanist; beheaded for opposition to Henry VIII's Act of Supremacy [Br. Hist.: *NCE,* 1830]
17. **Nero's Torches** oil- and tar-smeared Christians implanted and set aflame. [Christian Hist.: Brewer *Note-Book,* 614]
18. **palm** appeared on martyrs' graves. [Christian Symbolism: Appleton, 73]
19. **Perpetua, St., and St. Felicity** gored by wild beasts; slain with swords. [Christian Hagiog.: Attwater, 273]
20. **Peter, St.** apostle crucified upside down in Rome. [Christian Hagiog.: Brewster, 310]

21. **Sacco and Vanzetti** (Nicola, 1891–1927) (Bartolomeo, 1888–1927) perhaps executed more for radicalism than murder (August 22, 1927). [Am. Hist.: Flexner, 311]
22. **Sebastian, St.** Roman soldier; shot with arrows and struck with clubs. [Christian Hagiog.: Brewster, 75]
23. **Stephen, St.** first martyr; stoned as blasphemer. [Christian Hagiog.: Attwater, 313]
24. **sword** instrument of decapitation of early saints. [Christian Symbolism: Appleton, 14]
25. **Thecla, St.** first woman martyr. [Christian Hagiog.: Brewer *Dictionary,* 1072]
26. **Thomas à Becket, St.** (1118–1170) brutally slain in Canterbury cathedral by king's knights. [Br. Hist.: *NCE,* 2735–2736]

433. MASSACRE (See also GENOCIDE.)

1. **Acre** after conquering city, Richard I executed 2700 Muslims (1191). [Eur. Hist.: Bishop, 83–84]
2. **Armenian Massacre** Turks decimated Armenian population, dispersed survivors (1896). [Eur. Hist.: *EB,* I: 525]
3. **Bloody Sunday** seeking audience with Czar, workers receive bullets instead (1905). [Russ. Hist.: *EB,* II: 93]
4. **Boston Massacre** skirmish between British troops and Boston crowd (1770). [Am. Hist.: *EB,* II: 180]
5. **Charge of the Light Brigade** Russians massacre English cavalry at Balaklava (1854). [Eur. Hist.: *NCE,* 212; Br. Lit.: Benét, 186]
6. **Fetterman Massacre** party of 80 frontiersmen ambushed by Indians (1886). [Am. Hist.: *NCE,* 942]
7. **Goliad** 300 slain by Santa Ana in wake of Alamo (1836). [Am. Hist.: Van Doren, 155]
8. ***Guernica*** bombing of Guernica (1937); memorialized by Picasso's painting. [Span. Hist.: *NCE,* 1158; Art Hist.: Osborne, 867]
9. **Holy Innocents** infant boys massacred in Bethlehem under Herod. [O.T.: Matthew 2:16–18]
10. **jawbone of ass** with this, Samson kills 1000 men. [O.T.: Judges 15:15]
11. **Katyn Massacre** mass murder of 4250 Polish officers during WWII (c. 1939). [Polish Hist.: *NCE,* 1457]
12. **Lawrence, Kansas** Union stronghold where Quantrill's Confederate band killed more than 150 people (1863). [Am. Hist.: *EB,* VIII: 338]

13. **Massacre of Glencoe** treated hospitably, king's men attempt annihilation of MacDonald clan (1692). [Br. Hist.: Brewer *Note-Book,* 567]
14. **Munich Olympics '72** Arab terrorists brutally killed 11 Israeli athletes. [Jew. Hist.: Wigoder, 462]
15. **My Lai Massacre** murder of 22 Vietnamese villagers by American troops under Lt. William Calley, Jr. (1968). [Am. Hist.: *Facts* (1973) 145]
16. **ox-goad** using this weapon, Shamgar slew 600 Philistines. [O.T.: Judges 3:31]
17. **Sicilian Vespers** massacre of French (Angevins) by Sicilian nationals (1282). [Ital. Hist.: *NCE,* 2511]
18. **St. Bartholomew's Day Massacre** thousands of French Huguenots murdered for their faith (1572). [Fr. Hist.: *EB,* VII: 775]
19. **St. Valentine's Day Massacre** murder of seven members of a gang of bootleggers in Chicago (1929). [Am. Hist.: *EB,* VII: 797]
20. **third of May** (1808) Murat's squads executed hundreds of Spanish citizens; memorialized in Goya's painting. [Sp. Hist. and Sp. Art: Daniel, 220]
21. **Whitman Massacre** murder of missionary Marcus Whitman and family by Cayuse Indians (1847). [Am. Hist.: *NCE,* 2972]
22. **Wounded Knee** scene of the slaughter of 200 Sioux Indians (1890). [Am. Hist.: Van Doren, 306]
23. **Wyoming Massacre** colonial militia butchered by Tory-Indian force (1776). [Am. Hist.: Jameson, 564]

434. MATCHMAKING

1. **Kecal** marriage broker whose plans are foiled by a pair of lovers. [Czech Opera: Smetana *The Bartered Bride* in Osborne *Opera,* 32]
2. **Levi, Dolly** personable marriage broker who manages to make an excellent match for herself. [Am. Lit.: Thornton Wilder *The Matchmaker*; Am. Theater: *Hello, Dolly!* in *On Stage,* 454]
3. **Woodhouse, Emma** mistakenly thinks she has a talent for finding mates for her young friends. [Br. Lit.: Jane Austen *Emma*]

Matricide (See MURDER.)

435. MEDDLESOMENESS

1. **Norris, Mrs.** interfering, spiteful, gossiping busybody. [Br. Lit.: Austen *Mansfield Park* in Magill I, 562]

2. **Werle, Gregers** interferes with the Ekdals' lives and brings about their daughter's suicide. [Nor. Drama: Ibsen *The Wild Duck* in Magill I, 1113]
3. **Whiteside, Sheridan** meddles in his host's family affairs and insults the townspeople by interfering. [Am. Drama: *The Man Who Came to Dinner* in Benét, 631]

Mediation (See **PEACEMAKING.**)

436. MEDICINE (See also HEALING.)

1. **Acesis** daughter of Asclepius; name means 'healing remedy.' [Gk. Myth.: Kravitz, 37]
2. **Angitia** goddess of healing. [Rom. Myth.: Kravitz, 24]
3. **Antony, St.** invoked against venereal diseases and erysipelas (St. Antony's fire). [Christian Hagiog.: Daniel, 28–29]
4. **Apollo (Phoebus)** patron of medicine. [Gk. Myth.: Kravitz, 28]
5. **Asclepius (Aesculapius)** god of healing. [Gk. Myth.: Kravitz, 37]
6. **Benassis, Dr.** devotes himself to the poor and miserable inhabitants of a remote village. [Fr. Lit.: Balzac *The Country Doctor*; Magill II, 185]
7. **Bull, George** ignorant physician who cannot prevent an epidemic. [Am. Lit.: Cozzens *The Last Adam* Haydn & Fuller, 409]
8. **caduceus** snake-entwined staff; emblem of medical profession. [Gk. Myth.: Kravitz, 49]
9. **Carmenta** goddess of healing. [Gk. Myth.: Kravitz, 53]
10. **Cosmas, St. and St. Damian** patron saints; brothers, practiced medicine without charge. [Christian Hagiog.: Attwater, 94]
11. **Diver, Dick** failed psychiatrist becomes a small-town general practitioner. [Am. Lit.: *Tender Is the Night*]
12. **Ferguson, George** young surgeon who goes to Vienna to become better qualified for a hospital job. [Am. Lit.: Kingsley *Men in White*; Haydn & Fuller, 183]
13. **Hippocrates** (c. 460–c. 360 B.C.) Greek physician and "Father of Medicine." [Gk. Hist.: *NCE*, 1246]
14. **Hippocratic oath** ethical code of medicine. [Western Culture: *EB*, 11: 827]
15. **Iaso** Asclepius's daughter; personification of his healing power. [Gk. Myth.: Kravitz, 37]
16. **Mayo Clinic** voluntary association of more than 500 physicians in Rochester, Minnesota. [Am. Hist.: *EB*, 11: 723]

17. **Mitchell, Parris** studies medicine in the U.S. and abroad, returns as a physician at an insane asylum. [Am. Lit.: *King's Row*; Magill I, 478]
18. **Paean** physician to the gods. [Gk. Myth.: Espy, 29]
19. **Panacea** daughter of Greek god of healing. [Gk. Myth.: Kravitz, 37]
20. **Prince, Nan** becomes a successful physician like her foster father. [Am. Lit.: Jewett *A Country Doctor*; Magill II, 183]
21. **Rieux, Dr. Bernard** works unceasingly to relieve victims of a deadly epidemic. [Fr. Lit.: Camus *The Plague*]
22. **Roch, St.** (also **St. Rock**) invoked against infectious diseases; especially in the 15th century, against plague. [Christian Hagiog.: Daniel, 198]
23. **Vitus, St.** invoked against epilepsy and chorea (St. Vitus's dance). [Christian Hagiog.: Attwater, 338]
24. **Watson, Dr. John H.** Sherlock Holmes's chronicler who had a medical practice. [Br. Lit.: Arthur Conan Doyle *Sherlock Holmes*]
25. **Welby, Marcus** avuncular doctor of impeccable ethics. [Am. TV: "Marcus Welby, M.D." in Terrace, II, 66]

437. MELANCHOLY (See also GRIEF.)

1. **Acheron** river of woe in the underworld. [Gk. Myth.: Howe, 5]
2. ***Anatomy of Melancholy*** lists causes, symptoms, and characteristics of melancholy. [Br. Lit.: *Anatomy of Melancholy*]
3. **Barton, Amos** beset by woes. [Br. Lit.: "Sad Fortunes of Amos Barton" in Walsh *Modern*, 45]
4. **black bile** humor effecting temperament of gloominess. [Medieval Physiology: Hall, 130]
5. **blues** melancholy, bittersweet music born among American Negroes. [Am. Music: Scholes, 113]
6. **Cargill, Rev. Josiah** serious, moody, melancholic minister. [Br. Lit.: *St. Ronan's Well*]
7. **Carstone, Richard** driven to gloom by collapse of expectations. [Br. Lit.: *Bleak House*]
8. **cave of Trophonius** oracle so awe-inspiring, consulters never smiled again. [Gk. Myth.: Brewer *Dictionary*, 1103]
9. **Eeyore** amusingly gloomy, morose donkey. [Children's Lit.: *Winnie-the-Pooh*]
10. ***Elegy Written in a Country Churchyard*** meditative poem of a melancholy mood. [Br. Lit.: Harvey, 266]

11. **Ellis Island** immigration center where many families were separated; "isle of tears." [Am. Hist.: Flexner, 193]
12. **Gummidge, Mrs.** "lone lorn creetur" with melancholy disposition. [Br. Lit.: *David Copperfield*]
13. **Hamlet** black mood dominates his consciousness. [Brit. Lit.: Shakespeare *Hamlet*]
14. **hare** flesh brings melancholy to those who eat it. [Animal Symbolism: Mercatante, 125]
15. ***Il Penseroso*** poem celebrating the pleasures of melancholy and solitude. [Br. Lit.: Milton *Il Penseroso* in Magill IV, 577]
16. **Jaques** "can suck melancholy out of a song." [Br. Lit.: *As You Like It*]
17. **Mock Turtle** forever weeping and bemoaning his fate. [Br. Lit.: *Alice's Adventures in Wonderland*]
18. **Mudville** no joy here when Casey struck out. [Am. Sports Lit.: "Casey at the Bat" in Turlin, 642]
19. **Orpheus** composed, sang many melancholic songs in memory of deceased Eurydice. [Gk. Myth.: *Orpheus and Eurydice,* Magill I, 700–701]
20. **Roquentin, Antoine** discomfited by his existence's purposelessness, solitarily despairs. [Fr. Lit.: *Nausea*]
21. **Sad Sack** hapless and helpless soldier; resigned to his fate. [Comics: Horn, 595–596]
22. **Valley of the Shadow of Death** life's gloominess. [O.T.: Psalms 23:4]
23. **Wednesday's child** full of woe. [Nurs. Rhyme: Opie, 309]
24. **yew tree** symbolizes grief. [Flower Symbolism: *Flora Symbolica,* 178]

438. MEMORY

1. **Aethalides** herald of the Argonauts; had perfect memory. [Gk. Myth.: Kravitz, 11]
2. **Balderstone, Thomas** knew all of Shakespeare by heart. [Br. Lit.: *Sketches by Boz*]
3. **Eunoe** river whose water sparks remembrance of kindnesses. [Ital. Lit.: *Purgatory,* 33]
4. ***Fahrenheit 451*** in a future America where books are prohibited, a group of people memorize texts in order to preserve their content. [Am. Lit.: Bradbury *Fahrenheit 451* in Weiss, 289]
5. **madeleine** cookie that awakened the stream of Marcel's recollections. [Fr. Lit.: Proust *Remembrance of Things Past*]

6. **Memory, Mr.** during his stage performance his feats of memory enable him to signal clues to a man trying to thwart England's enemies. [Eng. Cinema: *The 39 Steps*]
7. **Mneme** Boeotian wellspring which whetted the memory. [Gk. Myth.; Wheeler, 713]
8. **Mnemosyne** goddess of memory; mother of Muses. [Gk. Myth.: Espy, 20]
9. **Munin** one of Odin's ravens; regarded as embodying memory. [Norse Myth.: Leach, 761]

Mercy (See **FORGIVENESS.**)

439. MESSENGER

1. **Aethalides** herald of the Argonauts. [Gk. Myth.: Kravitz, 11]
2. **Alden, John** (1599–1687) speaks to Priscilla Mullins for Miles Standish. [Am. Lit.: "The Courtship of Miles Standish" in Hart, 188–189]
3. **caduceus** Mercury's staff; symbol of messengers. [Rom. Myth.: Jobes, 266–267]
4. **dove** sent by Noah to see if the waters were abated; returns with an olive leaf. [O.T.: Genesis 8:8–11]
5. **eagle** symbolic carrier of God's word to all. [Christian Symbolism: Appleton, 35]
6. **Gabriel** announces births of Jesus and John the Baptist. [N.T.: Luke 1:19, 26]
7. **Hermes** (Rom. **Mercury**) messenger of the gods. [Gk. Myth.: Wheeler *Dictionary*, 240]
8. **Iris** messenger of the gods. [Gk. Myth.: Kravitz, 130; Gk. Lit.: *Iliad*]
9. **Irus** real name was Arnaeus; messenger of Penelope's suitors. [Gk. Lit.: *Odyssey*]
10. **Munin and Hugin** Odin's two ravens; brought him news from around world. [Norse Myth.: Leach, 761]
11. **Nasby** nickname for U.S. postmasters. [Am. Usage: Brewer *Dictionary*, 745–746]
12. **Pheidippides** ran 26 miles from Marathon to Athens to carry news of Greek defeat of Persians. [Gk. Legend: Zimmerman, 159]
13. **Pony Express** speedy relay mail-carrying system of 1860s. [Am. Hist.: Flexner, 276]
14. **Reuters** news agency; established as telegraphic and pigeon post bureau (1851). [Br. Hist.: Benét, 852]

15. **Revere, Paul** (1735–1818) warned colonials of British advance (1775). [Am. Hist.: 425–426]
16. **staff** symbolic of a courier on a mission. [Christian Symbolism: Appleton, 4]
17. **Stickles, Jeremy** messenger for the king of England (1880s). [Br. Lit.: *Lorna Doone,* Magill I, 524–526]
18. **Strogoff, Michael** courier of the czar. [Fr. Lit.: *Michael Strogoff*]
19. **thorn** the messenger of Satan. [N.T.: II Corinthians 12:7]
20. **Western Union** company founded in 1851; provides telegraphic service in U.S. [Am. Hist.: *NCE,* 2958]

440. MIDDLE CLASS

1. **Babbitt** self-satisfied conformer to middle-class ideas and ideals. [Am. Lit: *Babbitt*]
2. **Forsyte** representative of property-owning class in early 20th century. [Br. Lit.: *The Forsyte Saga*]
3. **Podsnap, John** smugly complacent in his Britishness. [Br. Lit.: *Our Mutual Friend*]

441. MILITARISM (See also SOLDIERING.)

1. **Adrastus** leader of the Seven against Thebes. [Gk. Myth.: *Iliad*]
2. **Siegfried** killed many enemies; led many troops to victory. [Ger. Lit. *Nibelungenlied*]

442. MIMICRY

1. **chameleon** lizard able to change the color of its skin to match brown or green surroundings; has come to mean 'inconstant person.' [Western Culture: Misc.]
2. **Costard** apes Elizabethan courtly language. [Br. Lit.: *Love's Labour's Lost*]
3. **Doolittle, Eliza** slum girl taught by professor to imitate upper class. [Br. Lit.: *Pygmalion*]
4. **lyrebird** Australian bird; one of the most famous mimic species. [Ornithology: Sparks, 116]
5. **mockingbird** noted for mimicking songs of other birds; one of the world's most noted singers. [Ornithology: Sparks, 116]
6. **monkey** known to copy human actions. [Western Cult.: Misc.]
7. **myna** certain species are able to mimic human speech and other sounds. [Ornithology: Sparks]
8. **parrot** bird able to mimic human speech; hence, *parrot* 'to repeat or imitate.' [Western Culture: Misc.]

443. MIRACLE

1. **Aaron's rod** flowering rod proved him to be God's choice. [O.T.: Numbers 17:8]
2. **Agnes, St.** hair grew to cover nakedness. [Christian Hagiog.: Brewster, 76–77]
3. **Anthony of Padua, St.** believed to have preached effectively to school of fishes. [Christian Legend: Benét, 39]
4. **Cana** at wedding feast, Christ turns water into wine. [N.T.: John 2:1–11]
5. **deus ex machina** improbable agent introduced to solve a dilemma. [Western Drama: *LLEI,* I: 279]
6. **Elais** produced olive oil from ground by touch. [Gk. Myth.: Kravitz, 86]
7. **Euphemus** Argonaut; could cross water without getting wet. [Gk. Myth.: Kravitz, 95]
8. **Geppetto** his wish fulfilled when marionette becomes real boy. [Children's Lit.: *Pinocchio;* Am. Cinema: *Pinocchio* in *Disney Films,* 32–37]
9. **Holy Grail** chalice enabled Sir Galahad to heal a cripple. [Br. Lit.: *Le Morte d'Arthur*]
10. **Jesus Christ** as son of God, performed countless miracles. [N.T.: Matthew, Mark, Luke, John]
11. **loaves and fishes** Jesus multiplies fare for his following. [N.T.: Matthew 14:15–21; John 6:5–14]
12. **Lourdes** underground spring revealed to Bernadette Soubirous in visions (1858); major pilgrimage site. [Fr. Hist.: *EB,* VI: 352; Am. Lit.: *Song of Bernadette;* Am. Cinema: *The Song of Bernadette* in Halliwell, 670]
13. **Marah** undrinkably bitter waters, sweetened by Moses. [O.T.: Exodus 15:23–25]
14. ***Miracle on 34th Street*** Santa Claus comes to New York. [Am. Cinema: Halliwell, 493]
15. **parting of the Pamphylean Sea** Alexander's hosts traverse sea in Persian march. [Class. Hist.: Gaster, 238]
16. **parting of the Red Sea** divinely aided, Moses parts the waters for an Israelite escape. [O.T.: Exodus 14:15–31]
17. **rod of Moses** transforms into serpent, then back again. [O.T.: Exodus 4:24]
18. **Tannhäuser** as a sign that the Pope should absolve him, the papal scepter suddenly sprouts green leaves. [Ger. Myth.: Brewer *Dictionary,* 932]

444. MIRROR

1. **Alasnam's mirror** indicates to Alasnam a girl's virtue. [Arab. Lit.: *Arabian Nights,* "Prince Zeyn Alasnam"]
2. **Alice's looking-glass** Alice passes through this into dreamland. [Br. Lit.: *Through the Looking-Glass*]
3. **Cambuscan's mirror** warns of impending adversity; indicates another's love. [Br. Lit.: *Canterbury Tales,* "The Squire's Tale"]
4. **Lao's mirror** reflects the looker's mind and thoughts. [Br. Lit.: *Citizen of the World*]
5. **Merlin's magic mirror** allows king to see whatever concerns him. [Br. Lit.: *Faerie Queene*]
6. **Mirror, mirror** magically tells arrogant queen who is the most beautiful of all. [Ger. Fairy Tale: "Snow White" in Grimm, 184]
7. **Perseus's shield** he uses it as a mirror so that he will not have to look directly at Medusa. [Gk. Myth.: Howe, 214]
8. **Prester John's mirror** allows him to see happenings throughout his dominions. [Medieval Legend: Brewer *Handbook,* 710]
9. **Reynard's wonderful mirror** imaginary mirror; reflects doings a mile away. [Medieval Lit.: *Reynard the Fox*]
10. **Vulcan's mirror** showed past, present, and future to viewer. [Br. Lit.: *Orchestra,* Brewer *Handbook,* 710]

445. MISANTHROPY

1. **Ahab, Captain** consumed by hate, pursues whale that ripped off his leg. [Am. Lit.: *Moby Dick*]
2. **Alceste** antisocial hero. [Fr. Lit.: *Le Misanthrope*]
3. ***Confidence Man, The*** Melville's social satire castigating mankind. [Am. Lit.: *The Confidence Man,* Magill III, 221–223]
4. **Dryas** hated mankind; avoided public appearances. [Rom. Myth.: Kravitz, 84]
5. **Fuller's thistle** indicates hatred of mankind. [Flower Symbolism: *Flora Symbolica,* 178]
6. **Nemo, Captain** brilliant captain of submarine, "Nautilus"; bitter misanthropy the reason for his undersea seclusion. [Fr. Lit.: *Twenty Thousand Leagues Under the Sea*]
7. **Sub-Mariner** friend of fish, scourge of man. [Comics: Horn, 640]
8. **teasel** indicates hatred of mankind. [Flower Symbolism: *Flora Symbolica,* 178]
9. **Timon** "undone by goodness," turns misanthropic. [Br. Lit.: *Timon of Athens*]

Misbehavior (See **MISCHIEVOUSNESS.**)

446. MISCHIEVOUSNESS (See also JOKE, PRACTICAL.)

1. **Ate** goddess of evil and mischief. [Gk. Myth.: Parrinder, 33; Kravitz, 39]
2. **Beaver** mischievous ten-year-old beset by trivial troubles. [TV: "Leave It to Beaver" in Terrace, II, 18–19]
3. **Beg, Little Callum** devilish page. [Br. Lit.: *Waverley*]
4. **Brer Rabbit** clever trickster. [Children's Lit.: *Uncle Remus*]
5. **Brown, Buster** turn-of-the-century *enfant terrible.* [Comics: Horn, 145]
6. **Cercopes** apelike pygmies; tried to steal Hercules' weapons. [Gk. Myth.: Leach, 206]
7. **crocodile** symbolizes naughtiness and chicanery. [Jewish Tradition: Jobes, 382]
8. **Dennis the Menace** latter-day Buster Brown, complete with dog. [Comics: Horn, 201]
9. **Erlking** elf king who works mischief on children. [Ger. Folklore: *LLEI,* I: 283]
10. **Eulenspiegel, Till** legendary peasant known for his pranks. [Ger. Folklore: Benét, 325–326]
11. **Finn, Huckleberry** mischievous, sharp-witted boy has many adventures. [Am. Lit.: *Huckleberry Finn*]
12. **Georgie Porgie** kissed the girls and made them cry. [Nurs. Rhyme: Opie, 185]
13. **Halloween** (Allhallows Eve) youngsters play pranks on the neighbors. [Am. Folklore: Misc.]
14. **Junior (Red Skelton)** "the mean widdle kid." [Radio: "The Red Skelton Show" in Buxton, 197]
15. **Katzenjammer Kids** twin Teutonic terrors. [Comics: "The Captain and the Kids" in Horn, 156–157]
16. **Lampwick** archetypal juvenile delinquent leads Pinocchio astray. [Am. Cinema: *Pinocchio* in *Disney Films,* 32–37]
17. **Little Rascals, The** scamps unite to terrorize adults. [Am. TV: Terrace, II, 31]
18. **Merop's Son** misguided do-gooder. [Gk. and Rom. Myth.: Brewer *Dictionary,* 704]
19. **Moth** "handful of wit"; Armado's "pretty knavish page." [Br. Lit.: *Love's Labour's Lost*]
20. **Nicka-Nan Night** Shrove Tuesday eve when boys play tricks. [Br. Folklore: Brewer *Dictionary,* 756]

21. **Our Gang** group of children in comedy series: always into mischief. [Am. Cinema: Halliwell, 546; Am. TV: "The Little Rascals" in Terrace, II, 31]
22. **Peck's Bad Boy** mischievous boy plays pranks on his father. [Am. Lit.: *Peck's Bad Boy,* Hart, 642]
23. **Peter Rabbit** always ransacking farmer MacGregor's patch. [Children's Lit.: *The Tale of Peter Rabbit*]
24. **pixies** prank-playing fairies; mislead travelers. [Br. Folklore: Briggs, 328–330]
25. **pooka** wild shaggy colt that misled benighted travelers. [Br. Folklore: Briggs]
26. **Puck** knavish hobgoblin who plays pranks. [Br. Folklore & Lit.: *A Midsummer Night's Dream*]
27. **Rooney, Andy** scatterbrained gossoon; makes trouble without trying. [Irish Lit.: *Handy Andy*]
28. **Sawyer, Tom** hookey-playing, imaginative lad of St. Petersburg, Missouri. [Am. Lit.: *Tom Sawyer*]
29. **Stalky** with his two friends, devises ingenious pranks that make life miserable for the masters of the school. [Br. Lit.: Kipling *Stalky and Company*]
30. **Wag, Charlie** school-skipping delinquent of penny dreadful. [Br. Lit.: *Charlie Wag, the Boy Burglar,* Opie, 117]

447. MISERLINESS (See also STINGINESS.)

1. **Collyer brothers** (Homer, 1882–1947) (Langely, 1886–1947) wealthy brothers who lived barren and secluded lives in junk-laden Harlem mansion. [Am. Hist.: *Facts* (1947) 116; Am. Lit.: *My Brother's Keeper.*]
2. **Grandet, Monsieur** his loathsome miserliness and greed ruin the lives of his family. [Fr. Lit.: *Eugénie Grandet* in Magill I, 258]
3. **Green, Hetty** (1834–1916) "Witch of Wall Street"; financial wizard whose miserliness became legendary. [Am. Hist.: *The Day They Shook the Plum Tree*]
4. **Harpagon** his hoard of money means more to him than do his children. [Fr. Drama: Molière *The Miser*]
5. **Marner, Silas** cares only to amass gold; robbed of it, he finds new meaning in love for abandoned child. [Br. Lit.: Benét, 930]
6. **McTeague, Trina** loves to count her hoard of coins, is niggardly with her husband. [Am. Lit.: *McTeague,* Magill I, 537; Am. Cinema: *Greed,* Halliwell, 176]
7. **Plyushkin** incredibly miserly landowner serves Tchitchikov a year-old Easter cake. [Russ. Lit.: Gogol *Dead Souls*]

8. **Scrooge** "grasping old sinner" who learns that miserliness leads only to loneliness and pain. [Br. Lit.: "A Christmas Carol" in Benét, 196]

448. MISSIONARY

1. **Aubrey, Father** converts savages to Christianity. [Fr. Lit.: *Atala*]
2. **Boniface, St.** missionary to the German infidels in 8th century. [Christian Hagiog.: Brewster, 271]
3. **Davidson, Rev. Alfred** attempts to convert Sadie Thompson to religion but ends up seducing her. [Br. Lit.: "Miss Thompson" in Benét, 675; Am. Cinema: "Rain" in Halliwell, 593]
4. **Latour and Vaillant, Fathers** priests establish a diocese in New Mexico. [Am. Lit.: Cather *Death Comes for the Archbishop* in Magill I, 199]
5. **Livingstone, David** (1813–1873) explorer and missionary in Africa. [Br. Hist.: *NCE,* 1596]
6. **Patrick, St.** (c. 385–461) early missionary to and patron saint of Ireland. [Christian Hagiog.: Brewster, 138]
7. **Salvation Army** international religious organization known for its charitable and missionary work. [Christian Rel.: *NCE,* 2408–2409]
8. **Society of Jesus** Roman Catholic religious order distinguished in foreign missions. [Christian Hist.: *NCE,* 1412]
9. **Xavier, St. Francis** indefatigable pioneer converter of East Indies. [Christian Hagiog.: Attwater, 141–142]

449. MISTRESSES (See also COURTESANSHIP, PROSTITUTION.)

1. **Abra** favorite concubine of Solomon. [Br. Lit.: *Solomon on the Vanity of the World,* Benét, 3]
2. **Bains, Lulu** to Elmer Gantry. [Am. Lit.: *Elmer Gantry*]
3. **Brangwen, Ursula** living with Anton Skrebensky without marriage license causes shock. [Br. Lit.: *The Rainbow,* Magill I, 800–802]
4. **Bridehead, Sue** of Jude Fawley; two children by him. [Br. Lit.: *Jude the Obscure*]
5. **Burden, Joanna** mistress and benefactor to Joe Christmas. [Am. Lit.: *Light in August*]
6. **Gournay, Mlle. de** Montaigne's "adopted daughter." [Fr. Hist.: Brewer *Handbook,* 633]
7. **Guinevere, Queen** King Arthur's wife; Sir Launcelot's mistress. [Br. Lit.: *Le Morte d'Arthur*]

8. **Lady Chatterly** mistress of the gamekeeper Mellors. [Br. Lit.: Lawrence *Lady Chatterly's Lover* in Benét, 559]
9. **Maintenon, Marquise de** royal mistress and later wife of Louis XIV. [Fr. Hist.: Benét, 622]
10. **Merle, Mme.** Osmund's mistress, by whom he has a daughter, Pansy. [Am. Lit.: James *Portrait of a Lady* in Magill I, 766]
11. **Perdita** stage name of Mary Robinson, mistress of George IV when he was Prince of Wales. [Br. Hist.: Benét, 773]
12. **Pompadour, Marquise de** influential mistress of Louis XV. [Fr. Hist.: Benét, 802]
13. **Roxana** mistress of many before marrying one of her lovers. [Br. Lit.: *Roxana*]
14. **Simonet, Albertine** paramour of narrator. [Fr. Lit.: *Remembrance of Things Past*]

450. MOCKERY

1. **Abas** changed into lizard for mocking Demeter. [Rom. Myth: *Metamorphoses,* Zimmerman, 1]
2. **Beckmesser** pompous object of practical jokes. [Ger. Opera: Wagner, *Meistersinger,* Westerman, 226–227]
3. **crown of thorns** Christ thus ridiculed as king of Jews. [N.T.: Matthew 27:29; Mark 15:17; John 19:2–5]
4. **Ecce Homo** Pilate's presentation of Jesus to Jews. [N.T.: John 19:5]
5. **I.N.R.I.** ('Iesus Nazarenus, Rex Iudaeorum' = Jesus of Nazareth, King of the Jews) inscription fastened upon Christ's cross as a mockery. [Christianity: Brewer *Note-Book,* 450]
6. **Momus** god of blame and ridicule. [Gk. Myth.: Espy, 31]

451. MODESTY (See also CHASTITY, HUMILITY.)

1. **Bell, Laura** reserved, demure character. [Br. Lit.: *Pendennis*]
2. **Bianca** gentle, unassuming sister of Kate. [Br. Lit.: *The Taming of the Shrew*]
3. **fig leaves** used to cover Adam and Eve's nakedness. [O.T.: Genesis 3:7]
4. **pearl** emblem of discreet shyness. [Gem Symbolism: Kunz, 69]
5. **sweet violet** indicates a modest temperament. [Flower Symbolism: *Flora Symbolica,* 178]

452. MONEY (See also FINANCE.)

1. **Brink's** Boston armored car service; robbed of over one million dollars (1950). [Am. Hist.: *Facts* (1950), 24]

2. **Mammon** personification; one cannot serve him and God simultaneously. [N.T.: Matthew 6:24: Luke 16:9, 11, 13]
3. **Moneta** 'monitress'; epithet of Juno; origin of *mint.* [Rom. Myth.: Espy, 20]
4. **Newland, Abraham** governor of Bank of England; eponymously, banknote. [Br. Hist.: Wheeler, 258]

453. MONSTERS

1. **Abominable Snowman** enigmatic yeti of the Himalayas. [Tibetan Lore: Wallechinsky, 443]
2. **Aegaeon** gigantic monster with 100 arms, 50 heads. [Gk. and Rom. Myth.: Wheeler, 5]
3. **Ahuizotl** small creature with monkey hands and feet, a hand at the end of its long tail. [Mex. Myth.: Leach]
4. **Ammit** part hippopotamus, part lion, with jaws like a crocodile's. [Egypt. Myth.: Leach]
5. **Amphisbaena** two-headed monster, either scaled like a snake or feathered; one head remains awake while the other sleeps. [Roman Myth.: White]
6. **Anubis** jackal-headed god. [Egypt. Myth.: Jobes, 105]
7. **Argus** hundred-eyed giant who guarded Io. [Gk. Myth. and Rom. Lit.: *Metamorphoses*]
8. **banshee** spirit with one nostril, a large projecting front tooth, and webbed feet. [Irish Folklore: Briggs, 14]
9. **basilisk** lizard supposed to kill with its gaze. [Gk. Myth.: Brewer *Handbook*, 93]
10. **beasts of the Apocalypse** one has ten horns, seven heads, and ten crowns on the horns; the other has two horns and speaks like a dragon. [N.T.: Revelation 13:1,11]
11. **bonnacon** Asian monster with bull's head and horse's body, and fatally incendiary excrement. [Gk. & Rom. Myth.: White]
12. **bread-and-butter fly** its head is a lump of sugar, its wings are made of thin slices of buttered bread, and its body is a crust. [Br. Lit.: Lewis Carroll *Through the Looking-Glass*]
13. **Briareus, Cottus, and Gyges** the three Hecatoncheires (or Centimani), giants each having 50 heads and 100 arms. [Gk. Myth.: Zimmerman, 118]
14. **Brontes** cruel thunder-maker of the three Cyclopes. [Gk. Myth.: Parrinder, 47; Jobes, 251, 400]
15. **cactus cat** has thorny hair and ears, knifelike leg bones, and a branched tail. [Am. Folklore: Botkin]
16. **Cacus** fire-breathing giant monster. [Rom. Myth.: Kravitz, 49]

17. **Caliban** misshapen "missing link." [Br. Lit.: *The Tempest*]
18. **capricornus** half goat, half fish. [Gk. Myth.: *NCE*, 450]
19. **Cecrops** the traditional founder of Athens was half man, half serpent. [Gk. Myth.: Hamilton, 393]
20. **Cerberus** three-headed watchdog of Hades. [Gk. Myth.: Avery, 270]
21. **Charybdis** Poseidon's daughter; monster of the deep. [Gk. Lit.: *Odyssey;* Rom. Lit.: *Aeneid*]
22. **chimera** mythical creature: goat-lion-dragon; vomited flames. [Classical Myth.: *LLEI*, I: 325]
23. **cockatrice** half-serpent, half-cock; kills with glance. [Heraldry: Brewer *Dictionary*, 243]
24. **Cyclopes** Poseidon's sons, each with one eye in the center of his forehead. [Gk. Lit.: *Odyssey*]
25. **divis** devils shown as cat-headed men with horns and hooves. [Pers. Myth.: Barber & Riches]
26. **Echidna** half nymph, half snake; never grew old. [Gk. Myth.: Kravitz, 85]
27. **Fenris** frightful wolf, grew sinisterly in size and strength. [Scand. Myth.: *LLEI*, I: 328]
28. **Frankenstein's monster** created from parts of corpses. [Br. Lit.: *Frankenstein*]
29. **Geryon** celebrated monster with three united bodies or three heads. [Rom. Lit.: *Aeneid*]
30. **Gorgons** monsters with serpents for hair and brazen claws. [Gk. Myth.: Zimmerman, 114; Gk. Lit.: *Iliad*]
31. **Grendel** giant in human shape; lives in a murky pond. [Br. Lit.: *Beowulf*]
32. **griffin** fabulous animal, part eagle, part lion. [Gk. Myth. and Art: Hall, 143; Ital. Lit.: *Purgatory*]
33. **harpy** foul-smelling creature; half-vulture, half-woman. [Gk. Myth.: Mercatante, 212–213]
34. **hippocampus** fabulous marine creature; half fish, half horse. [Rom. Myth. and Art: Hall, 154]
35. **hippogriff** offspring of griffin and mare. [Ital. Lit.: *Orlando Furioso*]
36. **Hydra** seven-headed water snake; ravaged Lerna, near Argos. [Gk. and Rom. Myth.: Hall, 149]
37. **Jabberwock** frightful burbling monster with flaming eyes. [Br. Lit.: Carroll *Through the Looking-Glass*]
38. **Kirtimukha** the Face of Glory, depicted as a lion's head, without body or limbs. [Hindu Myth.: Barber & Riches]

39. **Kraken** giant snakelike sea creature. [Dan. Folklore: Mercatante, 194–195]
40. **Ladon** dragon who guarded the Apples of the Hesperides. [Gk. Myth.: Zimmerman, 145]
41. **Lamia** scaly, four-legged, hermaphrodite creature. [Br. Folklore: Briggs, 260–262]
42. **Leviathan** frighteningly powerful sea serpent. [O.T.: Job 41; Psalms 74:14; 104:26; Isaiah 27:1]
43. **Loch Ness monster** "Nessie"; sea serpent said to inhabit Loch Ness. [Scot. Folklore: Wallechinsky, 443]
44. **Medusa** the only mortal Gorgon. [Gk. Myth.: Zimmerman, 161]
45. **Midgard serpent** monstrous serpent that encircles the earth. [Norse Myth.: Leach, 723]
46. **Minotaur** beast with bull's head and man's body. [Gk. Myth.: Brewer *Dictionary,* 714]
47. **mock turtle** turtle with a calf's head, hooves, and tail. [Br. Lit.: Lewis Carroll *Alice's Adventures in Wonderland*]
48. **Naga** semi-divine beings with serpent bodies and human heads of terrible and ferocious aspect. [Hindu Myth.: Leach]
49. **Nicor** Scandinavian sea monster; whence, "Old Nick." [Br. Folklore: Espy, 44]
50. **Nidhogg** terrible beast in Nastrond; gnaws ashtree, Yggdrasil. [Norse Myth.: Wheeler, 259]
51. **nix** or **nixie** siren-like water-sprite, sometimes fish-tailed, that lured men to drown. [Teutonic Myth.: Barber & Riches]
52. **opinicus** fabulous amalgam of dragon, camel, and lion. [Heraldry: Brewer *Dictionary,* 782]
53. **Orc** monstrous sea creature; devours human beings. [Ital. Lit.: *Orlando Furioso*]
54. **Orthos** two-headed dog; brother of Cerberus. [Gk. Myth.: Zimmerman, 186]
55. **python** huge serpent which sprang from stagnant waters after the Deluge. [Gk. Myth.: Zimmerman, 227]
56. **Questing Beast** serpent-headed leopard that emitted loud noises. [Br. Lit.: Malory *Le Morte d'Arthur*]
57. **roc** white bird of enormous size. [Arab. Lit.: *Arabian Nights,* "Second Voyage of Sindbad the Sailor"]
58. **Sagittary** half man, half beast with eyes of fire. [Gk. Myth.: Brewer *Handbook,* 947]
59. **Sasquatch** giant hairy hominid said to lurk about the Pacific Northwest. [Am. Hist.: Payton, 601]

60. **Scylla** half beautiful maiden, half hideous dog. [Gk. Lit.: *Odyssey;* Rom. Lit.: *Metamorphoses*]
61. **siren** half-woman, half-bird, enticed seamen to their death with song. [Gk. Myth.: Benét, 934]
62. **666** number of the blasphemous beast with seven heads and ten horns. [N.T.: Revelation 13–14]
63. **Sphinx** head and breasts of a woman, body of a dog, and wings of a bird. [Gk. Myth.: Zimmerman, 246; Gk. Lit.: *Oedipus Rex*]
64. **Typhoeus** hundred-headed beast killed by Jovian thunderbolt. [Gk. Myth.: Brewer *Dictionary,* 1111]
65. **Typhon** tallest of the giants; his arms and legs ended in serpents. [Gk. Myth: Benét, 1034]
66. **werewolf** a man transformed into a wolf. [Eur. Folklore: Benét, 1082]

454. MOON

1. **Artemis** (Rom. **Diana**) goddess of the moon. [Gk. Myth.: Kravitz, 36; Brewer *Dictionary,* 727]
2. **Astarte** (**Ashtoreth**) personification of moon in crescent stage. [Phoenician Myth.: Brewer *Dictionary,* 726–727]
3. **Bast** cat-headed goddess representing sun and moon. [Ancient Egyptian Rel.: Parrinder, 42]
4. **Cynthia** goddess of the moon. [Gk. Myth.: Kravitz, 72]
5. **Endymion** name of man in the moon. [Gk. Myth.: Brewer *Dictionary,* 376–377]
6. **Hecate** personification of the moon before rising and after setting. [Gk. Myth.: Brewer *Dictionary,* 726–727]
7. **Luna** ancient Roman goddess personifying the moon. [Rom. Myth.: Zimmerman, 153]
8. **Nokomis** daughter of the Moon and grandmother of Hiawatha. [Am. Lit.: Longfellow *The Song of Hiawatha* in Magill I, 905]
9. **Petrus** caretaker of Heaven; makes sure moon shines on whole earth. [Ger. Opera: Orff, *The Moon,* Westerman, 115–116]
10. **Phoebe** moon as sister of sun (Phoebus). [Gk. Myth.: Brewer *Dictionary,* 726–727]
11. **Selene** the moon as lover of sleeping shepherd Endymion. [Gk. Myth.: Brewer *Dictionary,* 726–727]

455. MOTHERHOOD

1. **Asherah** mother of the gods; counterpart of Gaea. [Canaanite Myth.: Benét, 57]
2. **Cybele** Great Mother; goddess of nature and reproduction. [Phrygian Myth.: Parrinder, 68; Jobes, 400]

3. **Cynosura** Idaean nymph; nursed the infant Zeus. [Gk. Myth.: Howe, 74]
4. **Danu** (**Anu**) divine procreator and guardian of gods and mortals. [Celtic Myth.: Parrinder, 72]
5. **Devaki** virgin mother of Krishna. [Hindu Myth.: Parrinder, 76]
6. **Devi** the "great goddess," wife of Shiva; "Mother." [Hindu Myth.: Parrinder, 77]
7. **Gaea** earth and mother goddess. [Gk. Myth.: Zimmerman, 108]
8. **Mary** apotheosized as mother of Christ. [N.T.: Matthew, Mark, Luke, John]
9. **Rhea** often titled Great Mother of the Gods. [Gk. Myth.: *NCE,* 1796]
10. **Whistler's mother** popular name for the painter's "Arrangement in Grey and Black, No. 1: The Artist's Mother." [Am. Art: *EB,* 19:814–815]

Motivation (**See INDUCEMENT.**)

Mourning (**See GRIEF.**)

456. MURDER (See also ASSASSINATION, INFANTICIDE, PATRICIDE.)

1. **Abimelech** slew his 70 brothers to become ruler. [O.T.: Judges 9:5]
2. **Barnwell, George** noble motives cause him to murder uncle. [Br. Lit.: *The London Merchant;* Barnhart, 695]
3. **Beaumont, Jeremiah** kills the man who had seduced his wife; he is murdered by an enemy and his wife kills herself. [Am. Lit.: Warren *World Enough and Time* in Magill II, 1160]
4. **Bluebeard** closets away bodies of former wives. [Fr. Fairy Tale: Harvey, 97–98]
5. **Bluebeard** (**Henri Désiré Landru,** 1869–1922) executed for murders of ten women (1915–18). [Fr. Hist.: *EB* (1972), XIII, 661]
6. **Boston Strangler** (Albert De Salvo, 1932–   ) strangled thirteen women between 1962 and 1964. [Am. Hist.: Misc.]
7. **Busiris** murders predecessor to gain Egyptian throne. [Gk. Myth: Avery, 231]
8. **Cain** jealous, slays Abel. [O.T.: Genesis 4:8]
9. **Cenci, Beatrice** with brothers, arranges murder of cruel father. [Br. Lit.: *The Cenci*]
10. **Claudius** murders brother to gain throne. [Br. Lit.: *Hamlet*]

11. **Danaides** slew husbands on wedding night. [Gk. Myth.: Kravitz, 74]
12. **Donatello** throws Miriam's persecutor over cliff to death. [Am. Lit.: *The Marble Faun*]
13. **Donegild** killed by Alla for abandoning his wife and son at sea. [Br. Lit.: *Canterbury Tales,* "Man of Law's Tale"]
14. **Franceschini, Count** brutally murders his estranged young wife and her parents. [Br. Poetry: Browning *The Ring and the Book*]
15. **Gilligan, Amy Archer** poisons 48 elderly people in nursing homes. [Am. Hist.: Elizabeth S. Baxter *Newington*; Am. Drama: Kesselring *Arsenic and Old Lace*]
16. **Griffiths, Clyde** young social climber lets his pregnant mistress drown in a boating accident and is convicted of murder. [Am. Lit.: *An American Tragedy* in Hart, 30]
17. **Hagen** stabs Siegfried in back; kills Gunther. [Ger. Opera: Wagner, *Götterdämmerung,* Westerman, 245]
18. **Hines, Doc** kills Joe's father; lets mother die in childbirth. [Am. Lit.: *Light in August*]
19. **Ibbetson, Peter** a confessed murderer, yet a sensitive, romantic man. [Br. Lit.: *Peter Ibbetson,* Magill I, 736–738]
20. ***In Cold Blood*** nonfiction novel about a brutal, senseless murder in Kansas. [Am. Lit.: *In Cold Blood*]
21. **Injun Joe** stabs town doctor to death. [Am. Lit.: *Tom Sawyer*]
22. **Ixion** first murderer of a relative in classical mythology. [Gk. Myth.: Zimmerman, 142; Rom. Lit.: *Aeneid*]
23. **Jack the Ripper** killed and disemboweled 9 London prostitutes (1888–1889). [Br. Hist.: Brewer *Note-Book,* 463]
24. **Julian, St.** mistakenly kills his parents in their sleep. [Fr. Lit.: Flaubert "The Legend of St. Julian the Hospitaler"]
25. ***Kenilworth*** intrigue in the court of Elizabeth I. [Br. Lit.: Scott *Kenilworth* in Magill I, 469]
26. ***M*** motion picture about a child-murderer hunted down by organized criminal element. [Ger. Cinema: Halliwell]
27. **Macbeth** became king of Scotland through a series of ruthless murders, but was ultimately slain by his enemy, Macduff. [Br. Lit.: Shakespeare *Macbeth*]
28. **Medea** murdered her two children. [Gk. Lit.: *Century Classical,* 684–685]
29. **Michele** murders wife's lover; hides body under cloak. [Ital. Opera: Puccini, *The Cloak,* Westerman, 362–363]
30. **Modo** fiend presiding over homicide. [Br. Lit.: *King Lear*]

31. **Mordred, Sir** illegitimate son and treacherous killer of Arthur. [Br. Lit.: *Le Morte d'Arthur*]
32. **Orestes** commits matricide to avenge father's honor. [Gk. Lit.: *Electra*]
33. **Othello** believing false evidence of Desdemona's infidelity, he strangles her. [Br. Lit.: Shakespeare *Othello*]
34. **Ourang-Outang** brutally kills a mother and her daughter. [Am. Lit.: Poe *The Murders in the Rue Morgue*]
35. **Porgy** murders Crown, who tried to take Bess. [Am. Opera: Gershwin, *Porgy and Bess,* Westerman, 556]
36. **Raskolnikov** plans and carries out the murder of an old woman pawnbroker. [Russ. Lit.: *Crime and Punishment*]
37. **Rogêt, Marie** girl assaulted and murdered, her corpse thrown into the Seine. Am. Lit.: Poe *The Mystery of Marie Rogêt*]
38. **Rudge** murders master and gardener. [Br. Lit.: *Barnaby Rudge*]
39. **Sikes, Bill** hanged for killing of Nancy. [Br. Lit.: *Oliver Twist*]
40. **Smith, George Joseph** dispatched wives and lovers in bathtubs in 1910s. [Br. Hist.: Wallechinsky, 274]
41. **Spandrell** cynic opposed to fascist Everard Webley attacks and kills him, then commits suicide. [Br. Lit.: Huxley *Point Counter Point* in Magill I, 760]
42. **Sparafucile** his killing of Gilda fulfills curse against Rigoletto. [Ital. Opera: Verdi, *Rigoletto,* Westerman, 300]
43. **Thuggee** religious devotion to Kali involves human strangulation. [Indian Hist.: Brewer *Dictionary,* 1080]
44. **Tyrrel, James** at the king's behest, arranges the deaths of two young princes in the Tower. [Br. Drama: Shakespeare *Richard III*]

457. MUSIC

1. **Amphion** his music so powerful that stones for a wall are moved into place. [Gk. Myth.: Benét, 32]
2. **Apollo** god of music and fine arts. [Gk. Myth.: Zimmerman, 26]
3. **Bragi (Brage)** harpist-god; flowers bloomed, trees budded as he played. [Norse Myth.: Leach, 160]
4. **Cecilia, St.** patron of music and legendary inventor of organ. [Christian Hagiog.: Thompson, 380]
5. **Corybantes** musicians; provided music for goddesses' orgiastic dances. [Gk. Myth.: Kravitz, 67]
6. **Daphnis** shepherd; invented pastoral music to console himself. [Gk. Myth.: Parrinder, 72; Jobes, 414]

7. **Demodocus** minstrel whom Odysseus hears singing the amours of Ares and Aphrodite. [Gk. Lit.: *Odyssey* VIII]
8. ***Devil's Trill, The*** brilliant violin sonata by Tartini, said to have been revealed to him by the Devil in a dream. [Ital. Music: Tartini, Guiseppe in *NCE*, 2697]
9. **Euterpe** Muse of dramatic melody; patroness of flautists. [Gk. Myth.: Brewer *Dictionary*, 385]
10. **Grammy** award for musical achievement. [Am. Cult.: Misc.]
11. **Israfel** "none sing so wildly well." [Am. Lit.: "Israfel" in *Portable Poe*, 606]
12. **Jubal** forebear of all who play harp and pipe. [O.T.: Genesis 4:21]
13. **Linus** musician and poet; invented melody and rhythm. [Gk. Myth.: Zimmerman, 152]
14. **Muses** (Rom. **Camanae**) goddesses who presided over the arts. [Gk. Myth.: Howe, 172]
15. **Orpheus** musician, charmed even inanimate things with lyre-playing. [Gk. Myth.: Brewer *Dictionary*, 787]
16. **Polyhymnia** Muse of sacred song. [Gk. Myth.: Howe, 172]
17. **Schroeder** his only wish is to play Beethoven's music on his piano. [Comics: "Peanuts" in Horn, 542–543]
18. **Syrinx** transformed into reeds which pursuing Pan made into pipe. [Gk. Myth.: Hall, 232; Rom. Lit.: *Metamorphoses*]
19. **Tin Pan Alley** *lit.* 1650 Broadway, New York City; *fig.* fount of American popular music. [Am. Music: Thompson, 1105]

458. MUTENESS

1. **Elops** dumb serpent; gives no warning of its approach. [Br. Lit.: *Paradise Lost*]
2. **Henry** bald-headed, pugnosed and silent youngster of comic strip. [Comics: Sheridan, 200]
3. ***Painted Bird, The*** Kosinski novel about a foundling boy struck dumb by inhuman treatment. [Am. Lit.: Weiss, 345]
4. **Singer, Mr.** mute whose disability restricts his social contacts. [Am. Lit.: Carson McCullers *The Heart Is a Lonely Hunter* in Magill II, 416]

459. MUTILATION (See also BRUTALITY, CRUELTY.)

1. **Absyrtus** hacked to death; body pieces strewn about. [Gk. Myth.: Walsh *Classical*, 3]
2. **Agatha, St.** had breasts cut off. [Christian Hagiog.: Attwater, 34]

3. **Amazons** female warriors cut or burnt off their right breasts to prevent interference when drawing the bow. [Gk. Myth.: Brewer *Dictionary*, 29]
4. **Atreus** slew his brother Thyestes's sons and served them to their father at banquet. [Gk. Myth.: Jobes, 153]
5. **Dagon** Philistine idol; falls, losing head and hands. [O.T.: I Samuel 5:1–4]
6. **ear and knife** at Christ's betrayal, Peter cut off soldier's ear. [Christian Symbolism: N.T.: John 18:10]
7. **Erasmus, St.** disemboweled, windlass used to wind entrails out of his body. [Art: Daniel, 95]
8. **harem, the** besieged, the starving Janissaries cut off and eat a buttock from each woman, including Cunegonde, beloved of Candide. [Fr. Lit.: Voltaire *Candide*]
9. **Jack the Ripper** (late 19th century) dissected his victims. [Br. Hist.: Brewer *Note-Book*, 463]
10. **Lavinia** her tongue is cut out to prevent her from testifying to the evil deeds she has witnessed. [Br. Lit.: Shakespeare *Titus Andronicus*]
11. **Monkey's Paw, The** short story in which mangled son is brought back to life *as is* to greedy, foolish old couple with three wishes. [Brit. Lit.: Benét, 511]
12. **Philomela** violated by Tereus, king of Thrace; he cuts out her tongue to prevent her from revealing his conduct. [Gk. Myth.: Benét, 783]
13. **Procrustes** made travelers fit bed by stretching or lopping off their legs. [Gk. Myth.: Zimmerman, 221]
14. **Sinis** split victims by fastening them between two bent pines and then letting the pines spring upright. [Gk. Legend: Brewer *Dictionary*, 1005]
15. **Tereus** cuts off Philomela's tongue to prevent her telling he has raped her. [Gk. Myth.: Benét, 995]

Mutiny (See REBELLION.)

460. MYSTERY

1. **abominable snowmen** the yeti of Tibet; believed to exist, yet no sure knowledge concerning them. [Asian Hist.: Wallechinsky, 443–444]
2. **Bermuda Triangle** section of North Atlantic where many planes and ships have mysteriously disappeared. [Am. Hist.: *EB*, I: 1007]

3. **Big Foot (Sasquatch)** man ape similar to the yeti; reputed to have been seen in northwestern U.S. [Am. Hist.: "Yeti" in Wallechinsky, 443–444]
4. **closed book** medieval symbolism for the unknown. [Christian Symbolism: Appleton, 13]
5. **Dark Lady, The** mentioned in Shakespeare's later sonnets; she has never been positively identified. [Br. Lit.: *Century Cyclopedia,* I: 1191]
6. **$E=mc^2$** physical law of mass and energy; arcanum to layman. [Am. Hist.: Flexner, 298]
7. **Easter Island's statues** origin and meaning of more than two hundred statues remain unknown. [World Hist.: Wallechinsky, 443]
8. **Eleusinian Mysteries** ancient religious rites; its secrets have never been discovered. [Gk. Myth.: Benét, 305]
9. **Lady or the Tiger, The** Stockton's tale never reveals which fate awaits the youth who dared fall in love with the king's daughter. [Am. Lit.: Benét, 559]
10. **Loch Ness monster** supposed sea serpent dwelling in lake. [Scot. Hist.: Wallechinsky, 443]
11. **Man in the Iron Mask** mysterious prisoner in reign of Louis XIV, condemned to wear black mask at all times. [Fr. Hist.: Brewer *Note-Book,* 460]
12. **Mary Celeste** ship found in mid-Atlantic with sails set, crew missing (1872). [Br. Hist.: Espy, 337]
13. **Mona Lisa** enigmatic smile beguiles and bewilders. [Ital. Art: Wallechinsky, 190]
14. **Roanoke** fate of colony has never been established (1580s). [Am. Hist.: Jameson, 430]
15. **Sphinx** half woman, half lion; poser of almost unanswerable riddle. [Gk. Myth.: Howe, 258; Gk. Lit.: *Oedipus Rex*]
16. **Stonehenge** huge monoliths with lintels in Wiltshire, England, have long confounded modern man as to purpose. [Br. Hist.: Wallechinsky, 442]
17. **U.F.O.** unexplained and unidentified flying object. [Science: Brewer *Dictionary,* 1112]

461. MYSTICISM

1. **cabala** Jewish oral traditions, originating with Moses. [Judaism: Benét, 154]
2. **Catherine of Siena, St.** experienced visions from age seven. [Christian Hagiog.: Hall, 59]

3. **Druids** magical priests of Celtic religion; oak cult. [Celtic Rel.: Leach, 325; Jobes, 471]
4. **Hudson, Dr. Wayne** believed power obtained by good deeds and silence. [Am. Lit.: *The Magnificent Obsession*, Magill I, 547–549]
5. **mothers, the** keepers of the bodiless spirits of all who have lived; they supply Faust with an image of Helen of Troy. [Ger. Lit.: *Faust*]
6. **Ouija** letterboard reveals messages from spirits. [Am. Pop. Culture: Brewer *Dictionary*, 788]
7. **Svengali** Hungarian hypnotist, mesmerizes artist's model who becomes a famous singer under his influence. [Br. Lit.: *Trilby*]
8. **Teresa of Ávila, St.** religious contemplation brought her spiritual ecstasy. [Christian Hagiog.: Attwater, 318]
9. **voodoo** religious beliefs and practices from the West Indies. [Am. Cult.: Brewer *Dictionary*]
10. **Zen** Buddhist sect; truth found in contemplation and self-mastery. [Buddhism: Brewer *Dictionary*, 1174]
11. ***Zohar, The*** cabalistic reinterpretation of the Bible. [Judaism: Haydn & Fuller, 812]

N

462. NAÏVETÉ (See also INEXPERIENCE, INNOCENCE.)

1. **Agnes** young girl, affects to be simple and ingenuous. [Fr. Lit.: *L'Ecole des Femmes*]
2. **babes in the woods** applied to easily deceived or naive persons. [Folklore: Jobes, 169]
3. **beardlessness** traditional representation of innocence and inexperience. [Western Folklore: Jobes, 190]
4. **Carlisle, Lady Mary** couldn't determine true nobility. [Am. Lit.: *Monsieur Beaucaire,* Magill I, 616–617]
5. **Curlylocks** nursery rhyme heroine exemplifies innocence. [Folklore: Jobes, 398]
6. **Do-Right, Dudley** Canadian mountie do-gooder. [TV: "The Dudley Do-Right Show" in Terrace, I, 229–230]
7. **Dondi** foster child; confronts world with wide-eyed innocence. [Comics: Horn, 217–218]
8. **Errol, Cedric** seven-year-old believes the best of everyone. [Am. Lit.: *Little Lord Fauntleroy*]
9. **Evelina** 17-year-old ingenuously circulates through fashionable London. [Br. Lit.: *Evelina*]
10. **Georgette** Ted Baxter's pretty, ignorant wife. [TV: "The Mary Tyler Moore Show" in Terrace, II, 70–71]
11. **Little Nell** meek little girl reared by grandfather. [Br. Lit.: *The Old Curiosity Shop*]
12. **Miller, Daisy** innocent and ignorant American girl put in compromising European situations. [Am. Lit.: *Daisy Miller*]
13. **Miranda** innocent and noble-minded daughter of Prospero. [Br. Lit.: *The Tempest*]
14. **Myshkin, Prince** loved for his innocence and frankness, lack of sophistication, and kind heart. [Russ. Lit.: Dostoevsky *The Idiot*]
15. **Schlemihl, Peter** archetypal innocent; sold soul to devil. [Ger. Lit.: *Peter Schlemihl;* Fr. Opera: Westerman, *Tales of Hoffman,* 274–277]
16. **Shosha** narrator's mentally backward and utterly artless wife. [Am. Lit.: *Shosha*]
17. **Tessa** childlike young woman who thinks herself wedded to Tito and obeys his command to tell nobody of their supposed marriage. [Br. Lit.: George Eliot *Romola*]

18. **Topsy** young slave girl; completely naive. [Am. Lit.: *Uncle Tom's Cabin*]
19. **white lilac** flowers indicative of naiveté, callowness. [Flower Symbolism: *Flora Symbolica*, 175]

463. NATIVITY (See also CHRISTMAS.)

1. **Bethlehem** birthplace of Jesus. [N.T.: Matthew 2:1]
2. **Caspar, Melchior, and Balthazar** Magi of the Orient pay homage to infant Jesus. [Christianity: Hall, 6]
3. **manger** cattle trough which served as crib for Christ. [N.T.: Luke 2:7]
4. **ox and ass** always present in pictures of Christ's birth. [Christian Art: de Bles, 29; O.T.: Habakkuk 3:4]
5. **shepherds** notified by angel of the birth of the Messiah. [N.T.: Luke 2:8–17]
6. **Star of Bethlehem** star in the east which directed the Magi and shepherds to the baby Jesus. [N.T.: Matthew 2:9]
7. **swaddling clothes** in which Mary wraps her new-born infant. [N.T.: Luke 2:7]
8. **three wise men** kings of the Orient, come to worship the baby Jesus. [N.T.: Matthew 2:1–2]

Neglectfulness (See CARELESSNESS.)

Nervousness (See INSECURITY.)

464. NIGHT

1. **Apepi** leader of demons against sun god; always vanquished by morning. [Egyptian Myth.: Leach, 66]
2. **Apophis** opponent of sun god Ra. [Egyptian Myth.: Benét, 43]
3. **Ashtoreth** Moon goddess; Queen of night; equivalent of Greek Astarte. [Phoenician Myth.: Walsh *Classical*, 34–35]
4. **Cimmerians** half-mythical people dwelling in eternal gloom. [Gk. Lit.: *Odyssey*]
5. **Erebus** personification and god of darkness. [Gk. Myth.: Brewer *Dictionary*, 381]
6. **Fafnir** his slaying represents the destruction of night demon. [Norse Myth.: *LLEI*, I: 327]
7. **Nox** goddess of night. [Rom. Myth.: Wheeler, 261]
8. **owl** nocturnal bird; Night embodied. [Art: Hall, 231]

465. NIHILISM

1. **Bazaroff and Kirsanov** university students who have developed a nihilistic philosophy. [Russ. Lit.: Turgenev *Fathers and Sons*]

2. ***Possessed, The*** depicts political nihilism and genuine spiritual nihilism of Stavrogin. [Russ. Lit.: Benét, 809]

466. NOBLE SAVAGE

1. **Chactas** the "noble savage" of the Natchez Indians; beloved of Atala. [Fr. Lit.: *Atala*]
2. **Chingachgook** idealized noble Indian. [Am. Lit.: *The Deerslayer*]
3. **Daggoo** African savage and crew member of the *Pequod.* [Am. Lit.: *Moby Dick*]
4. **noble savage** concept of a simple, pure, and superior man, uncorrupted by civilization. [Western Culture: Benét, 718–719]
5. **Oroonoko** the noble savage enslaved; rebels against captors. [Br. Lit.: *Oroonoko*]
6. **Queequeg** Polynesian prince and Ishmael's comrade aboard whaling vessel, *Pequod.* [Am. Lit.: *Moby Dick*]

467. NOBLEMINDEDNESS

1. **Andrews, Joseph** epitome of the virtuous male. [Br. Lit.: *Joseph Andrews*]
2. **Banquo** principled and noble compatriot of Macbeth. [Br. Lit.: *Macbeth*]
3. **Bede, Adam** accepts beloved even after illicit affair. [Br. Lit.: *Adam Bede*]
4. **Camiola** generously pays Bertoldo's ransom. [Br. Lit.: *The Maid of Honor,* Walsh Modern, 84]
5. **Cheeryble Brothers** noble, generous twins. [Br. Lit.: *Nicholas Nickleby*]
6. **Daphnis** afraid of causing pain, does not deflower Chloë. [Gk. Lit.: *Daphnis and Chloë,* Magill I, 184]
7. **Grandison, Sir Charles** magnanimous gentleman feels honor-bound to marry an acquaintance who loves him, despite his love for another. [Br. Lit.: *Sir Charles Grandison* in Magill III, 983]
8. **Levin, Konstantine** shows compassion in dealing with peasant laborers. [Russ. Lit.: *Anna Karenina*]
9. **Lohengrin** defeats Telramund in trial by combat; spares him. [Ger. Opera: Wagner, *Lohengrin,* Westerman, 215]
10. **Lord Jim** successful in lifelong efforts to regain honor lost in moment of cowardice. [Br. Lit.: *Lord Jim*]
11. **Newman, Christopher** destroys the evidence that could wreck the man who obstructed his marriage plans. [Am. Lit.: *The American*]

12. **pirates of Penzance** never attacked weaker parties; always freed orphans. [Br. Opera: *The Pirates of Penzance*]
13. **Rienzi** pardons his would-be murderer. [Ger. Opera: Wagner, *Rienzi,* Westerman, 203]
14. **Valjean, Jean** yields to the man who has harassed him unmercifully. [Fr. Lit.: *Les Misérables*]
15. **Wilkes, Ashley** sensitive Southerner who remains true to homeland and wife. [Am. Lit.: *Gone With the Wind,* Magill III, 424–426.]

Noise (See **LOUDNESS.**)

Nonchalance (See **INDIFFERENCE.**)

468. NOSE

1. **Barabas** inventor of infernal machine; possessor of pachydermal snout. [Br. Lit.: *The Jew of Malta*]
2. **Bardolph** for red nose, known as "knight of the burning lamp." [Br. Lit.: *Merry Wives of Windsor*]
3. **Bergerac, Cyrano de** gallant Frenchman; mocked unceasingly for extremely large nose [Fr. Lit.: *Cyrano de Bergerac*]
4. **Durante, Jimmy** ("Schnozzola") (1893–1980) American pianist-comedian with huge nose. [Radio: "The Jimmy Durante Show" in Buxton, 124–125; Am. Cinema: Halliwell, 232]
5. **Kovalëv, Major** loses social eminence when nose self-detaches. [Russ. Lit.: *The Nose,* Kent, 474–497]
6. **Pinocchio** wooden boy's nose grows longer with every lie. [Ital. Lit.: *Pinocchio;*]
7. **Rudolph** his red nose lit the way for Santa and his sleigh. [Am. Pop. Music: "Rudolph the Red-Nosed Reindeer"]

Nosiness (See **GOSSIP.**)

469. NOSTALGIA

1. **Combray** village of narrator and family. [Fr. Lit.: *Remembrance of Things Past*]
2. **Give My Regards to Broadway** singer sends well-wishes to home town. [Am. Pop. Music: Fordin, 531]
3. ***Happy Days*** TV series viewed 1950s America through tinted lenses. [TV: Terrace, I, 337–338]
4. **Krapp** passes the time by listening to tapes on which he had recorded his earlier experiences and reflections. [Br. Drama: Beckett *Krapp's Last Tape* in Weiss, 244]

5. ***My Ántonia*** book in which author recalls her precious childhood years. [Am. Lit.: Magill I, 630–632]
6. **ou sont les neiges d'antan** "Where are the snows of yesteryear?" [Fr. Lit.: *Ballade des Dames du temps jadis,* "Villon" in Benét, 1061]

470. NUDITY

1. **Adam and Eve** unashamed in Eden without clothes. [O.T.: Genesis 2:25]
2. **Agnes, St.** hair grew to cover her nakedness. [Christian Hagiog.: Daniel, 21]
3. **burlesque show** stage entertainment to which was added striptease dancing. [Am. Hist.: *EB,* II: 383–384]
4. **Digambara** ascetic Jainist sect whose members went naked. [Jainism: *NCE,* 1392]
5. **Godiva, Lady** (d. 1057) rode naked through Coventry to secure tax reduction for the people. [Br. Legend: Brewer *Dictionary,* 471]
6. **Gymnosophists** ancient Indian philosophers forsook clothing. [Asian Hist.: Brewer *Note-Book,* 396]
7. **Lee, Gypsy Rose** (1914–1970) American burlesque artiste. [Am. Hist.: Halliwell, 429]
8. **Maja Desnuda** Goya's celebrated picture of woman in the nude. [Span. Art: *Spain,* 246–247]
9. **Playboy centerfold** nubile woman exhibited *au naturel* in centerfold of every issue. [Am. Magazines: *Playboy*]
10. **Venus de Milo** half-naked marble Aphrodite. [Gk. Art: Osborne, 1184]
11. **Wilberforce, Miss** English lady shocks the populace by publicly disrobing when drunk. [Br. Lit.: *South Wind* in Magill II, 988]

471. NURSING

1. **Eira** Frigga's attendant; taught science of nursing to women. [Norse Myth.: *LLEI,* I: 327]
2. **Irene** (fl. 3rd century) ministered to St. Sebastian, who was wounded by arrows. [Christian Hagiog.: Hall, 162]
3. **Lellis, St. Camillus de** improved hospitals; patroness of sick and nurses. [Christian Hagiog.: Attwater, 78–79]
4. **Nightingale, Florence** (1820–1910) English nurse; founder of modern nursing. [Br. Hist.: *NCE,* 1943.]

472. NYMPH

1. **Atlantides (Pleiades)** seven daughters of Atlas by Pleione. [Gk. Myth.: Zimmerman, 37]
2. **Camenae** fountain nymphs; identified with Greek Muses. [Rom. Myth.: Zimmerman, 49]
3. **dryads** divine maidens of the woods. [Gk. and Rom. Myth.: Wheeler, 108]
4. **hamadryads** wood nymphs. [Gk. Myth.: Howe, 113]
5. **Hyades** seven daughters of Atlas, entrusted with the care of the infant Dionysus. [Gk. Myth.: Howe, 134]
6. **limoniads** nymphs of meadows and flowers. [Gk. Myth.: Zimmerman, 152]
7. **naiads** divine maidens of lakes, streams, and fountains. [Gk. and Rom. Myth.: Wheeler, 256]
8. **Napaeae** nymphs of woodland glens and vales. [Rom. Myth.: Howe, 174]
9. **Nereids** sea nymphs of the Mediterranean. [Gk. and Rom. Myth.: Wheeler, 257]
10. **Oceanids** sea nymphs of the great oceans. [Gk. and Rom. Myth.: Wheeler, 263]
11. **oreads** divine maidens of the mountains. [Gk. and Rom. Myth.: Wheeler, 270]

O

Obesity (See **FATNESS**.)

473. OBSESSIVENESS

1. **Ahab, Captain** obsessed with whale. [Am. Lit.: *Moby Dick*]
2. **Allmers, Mrs.** obsessed with crippled son. [Nor. Lit.: *Little Eyolf*]
3. **Bounderby, Josiah** single-minded success addict. [Br. Lit.: *Hard Times*]
4. **Cardillac** goldsmith who murders to regain what he created. [Ger. Opera: Hindemith, *Cardillac*, Westerman, 487]
5. **Chillingworth, Roger** "very principle of his life [was] the systematic exercise of revenge." [Am. Lit.: *The Scarlet Letter*]
6. **Craig, Harriet** wrapped up in caring for her immaculate home, to the exclusion of all human relationships. [Am. Drama: *Craig's Wife* in Hart, 191]
7. **Defarge, Madame** "everlastingly knitting" before the guillotine as heads fell. [Br. Lit.: *A Tale of Two Cities*]
8. **Dick, Mr.** compulsively thinks, talks, and writes about King Charles's head. [Br. Lit.: Dickens *David Copperfield* in Brewer *Dictionary*, 520]
9. **Herman** only goal in life becomes winning at cards. [Russ. Opera: Tchaikovsky, *Queen of Spades*, Westerman, 401]
10. **Javert** personification of law's inexorableness; relentlessly tracks down Valjean. [Fr. Lit.: *Les Misérables*]
11. **Melford, Lydia** could not think of anything but lover Wilson. [Br. Lit.: *Humphry Clinker*, Magill I, 394–397]
12. **Nemo, Captain** mysterious submarine captain who attempts vengeance against society. [Fr. Lit.: *Twenty Thousand Leagues Under the Sea*]
13. **Séchard, David** neglects his business in unremitting effort to perfect a paper-making process. [Fr. Lit.: Balzac *Lost Illusions* in Magill II, 595]
14. **Tiberius** determined at any cost to become Emperor. [Br. Lit.: *I, Claudius*]

474. OBSTINACY

1. **Balmawhapple** bullheaded, blundering Scotch laird. [Br. Lit.: *Waverley*]

2. **Deans, Davie** stern and righteous Presbyterian. [Br. Lit.: *The Heart of Midlothian*]
3. **Gradgrind, Thomas** rigid "man of realities." [Br. Lit.: *Hard Times*]
4. **Grant, Ulysses S.** (1822–1885) 18th U.S. president; nicknamed "Unconditional Surrender." [Am. Hist.: Kane, 523]
5. **Jorkins** intractable, unyielding lawyer. [Br. Lit.: *David Copperfield*]
6. **Mistress Mary** known for being "quite contrary." [Nurs. Rhyme: Baring-Gould, 31]
7. **mule** symbol of obstinacy: "stubborn as a mule." [Folklore: Jobes, 462]
8. **Pharaoh** refuses to heed Moses's mandate from God. [O.T.: Exodus 7:13, 22–23, 8:32, 9:7, 12]

Obtuseness (See **DIMWITTEDNESS.**)

Oddness (See **ECCENTRICITY.**)

Oldness (See **AGE, OLD.**)

475. OMEN (See also PROPHECY.)

1. **Amasis' ring** discarded ring turns up predicting Polycrates' death. [Gk. Hist.: Benét, 28]
2. **handwriting on the wall** Daniel interprets supernatural sign as Belshazzar's doom. [O.T.: Daniel 5:25–28]
3. **huma** oriental bird; every head over which its shadow passes was believed destined to wear a crown. [Ind. Myth.: Brewer *Dictionary*, 472]
4. **Ides of March** 15 March; prophesied as fateful for Caesar. [Br. Lit.: *Julius Caesar*]
5. **merrow** Irish mermaid; her appearance signifies coming storms. [Irish Folklore: Briggs, 290–294]
6. **Mother Carey's chickens** stormy petrels; believed by sailors to be harbingers of storms. [Marine Folklore: Wheeler, 251]
7. **raven** often presages death or catastrophe. [Animal Folklore: Jobes, 213]
8. **waff** wraith whose appearance portends death. [Br. Folklore: Briggs, 425]
9. **white-winged crow** bird of evil omen. [Chinese Folklore: Jobes, 388]
10. **Wotan's ravens** of misfortune, usually fatal. [Ger. Opera: Wagner, *Götterdämmerung*, Westerman, 245]

476. OMNIPRESENCE (See also UBIQUITY.)

1. **Allah** supreme being and pervasive spirit of the universe. [Islam: Leach, 36]
2. **Big Brother** all-seeing leader watches every move. [Br. Lit.: *1984*]
3. **eye** God sees all things in all places. [Christian Symbolism: O.T.: Proverbs 15:3]
4. **God** transcendant over and immanent in the world. [Christianity and Judaism: *NCE,* 1098–1099]

477. OMNISCIENCE

1. **Ea** shrewd god; knew everything in advance. [Babylonian Myth.: *Gilgamesh*]
2. **God** knows all: past, present, and future. [Christianity and Judaism: *NCE,* 1098–1099]
3. **Santa Claus** he knows who has been bad or good. [Western Folklore: Misc.]
4. **Sphinx** ancient Egyptian symbol of all-knowingness. [Heraldry: Halberts, 38]

478. OPPORTUNISM

1. **Arabella, Lady** squire's wife matchmakes with money in mind. [Br. Lit.: *Doctor Thorne*]
2. **Ashkenazi, Simcha** shrewdly and unscrupulously becomes merchant prince. [Yiddish Lit.: *The Brothers Ashkenazi*]
3. **Butler, Rhett** southerner interested only in personal gain from Civil War. [Am. Lit.: *Gone With the Wind*]
4. **carpetbaggers** northern politicians who settled in the South to control the Negro vote. [Am. Hist.: Jameson, 84]
5. **Cowperwood, Frank A.** capitalist involves politicians in shady dealings. [Am. Lit.: *The Financier,* Magill I, 280–282]
6. **Nostromo** entrusted with a cargo of silver, manages to conceal some for his own gain. [Br. Lit.: Conrad *Nostromo*]
7. **Peters, Ivy** shyster lawyer capitalizing in New Frontier territory. [Am. Lit.: *A Lost Lady*]
8. **Ravenel, Gontran de** weds peasant's plain daughter to obtain land. [Fr. Lit.: *Mont-Oriol,* Magill I, 618–620]
9. **Wallingford, "Get-Rich-Quick"** ingenious rascal of high finance; quasi-lawful. [Am. Lit.: *Get-Rich-Quick Wallingford,* Hart, 150]

479. OPTIMISM (See also HOPE.)

1. **Bontemps, Roger** personification of cheery contentment. [Fr. Lit.: "Roger Bontemps" in Walsh *Modern*, 66]
2. **Candide** beset by inconceivable misfortunes, hero indifferently shrugs them off. [Fr. Lit.: *Candide*]
3. **Micawber, Mr.** sanguine gentleman, constantly "waiting for something to turn up." [Br. Lit.: *David Copperfield*]
4. **Pangloss, Dr.** Candide's incurably optimistic tutor. [Fr. Lit.: *Candide*]
5. **Pollyanna** always finds something to be glad about. [Am. Lit.: *Pollyanna;* Am. Cinema: *Pollyanna* in *Disney Films*, 170–172]

480. ORDERLINESS (See also CLEANLINESS.)

1. **Barbara** maid exemplifying personal and domestic neatness. [Br. Lit.: *Old Curiosity Shop*]
2. **Bertram, Sir Thomas** instructor and example of orderliness and moral conduct. [Br. Lit.: *Mansfield Park*, Magill I, 562–564]
3. **Eunomia** one of Horae; goddess of order and harmony. [Gk. Myth.: Kravitz, 95]
4. **Fogg, Phileas** British gentleman who regimented whole life minutely. [Fr. Lit.: *Around the World in Eighty Days*]
5. **Price, Fanny** appealing heroine keeps unstable house in order. [Br. Lit.: *Mansfield Park*, Magill I, 562–564]
6. **Robert's Rules of Order** manual of parliamentary procedure by General Robert. [Am. Hist.: Hart, 717]
7. **Unger, Felix** ultra-tidy roommate of the slovenly Oscar. [Am. Drama: *The Odd Couple;* Am. Cinema and TV: "The Odd Couple" in Terrace, II, 160–161]

481. ORPHAN (See also ABANDONMENT.)

1. **Adverse, Anthony** finally, at middle age, discovers origins. [Am. Lit.: *Anthony Adverse*]
2. **Carey, Philip** brought up by stingy uncle and kindly aunt. [Br. Lit.: *Of Human Bondage*, Magill I, 670–672]
3. **Cass, Eppie** child found and brought up by Silas Marner. [Br. Lit.: Eliot *Silas Marner* in Benét, 930]
4. **Clickett** the "orfling" from St. Luke's workhouse; Mrs. Micawber's maid-of-all-work. [Br. Lit.: *David Copperfield*]
5. **Cosette** waif indentured to the cruel Thenardiers; saved by the honorable Valjean. [Fr. Lit.: *Les Misérables*]
6. **Dondi** Italian war baby taken in by Americans. [Comics: Horn, 217]

7. **Finn, Huckleberry** his mother dead; his father dies toward end of novel. [Am. Lit.: *Huckleberry Finn*]
8. **Little Orphan Annie** feisty waif succored by paternal Daddy Warbucks. [Comics: Horn, 459]
9. **Luck, Thomas** infant adopted by miners when his prostitute mother dies. [Am. Lit.: Bret Harte "The Luck of Roaring Camp" in Magill III, 597]
10. **Pip** Philip Pirrip, orphaned as an infant. [Br. Lit.: *Great Expectations*]
11. **Twist, Oliver** foundling reared in school of hard knocks. [Br. Lit.: *Oliver Twist*]

482. **OUTLAWRY (See also HIGHWAYMEN, THIEVERY.)**

1. **Bass, Sam** (1851–1878) train robber and all-around desperado. [Am. Hist.: *NCE,* 244]
2. **Billy the Kid** (William H. Bonney, 1859–1881) infamous cold-blooded killer. [Am. Hist.: Flexner, 30]
3. **Bonnie and Clyde** (Bonnie Parker and Clyde Barrow) bank robbers and killers (1930s). [Am. Hist.: Worth, 35]
4. **Cassidy, Butch, and the Sundance Kid** (Henry Brown) (fl. late 19th century) Western outlaws made famous by popular film. [Am. Hist. and Am. Cinema: *Butch Cassidy and the Sundance Kid,* Halliwell, 116]
5. **Dalton gang** bank robbers of late 1800s; killed in shootout (1892). [Am. Hist.: Flexner, 15–16]
6. **Dillinger, John** (1902–1934) murderous gunslinging bank robber of 1930s. [Am. Hist.: Flexner, 290]
7. **Grettir** Viking adventurer, outlawed for his ruthless slayings. [Icelandic Lit.: *Grettir the Strong* in Magill I, 335]
8. **Holliday, "Doc"** (fl. late 19th century) outlaw who helped Wyatt Earp fight the Clanton gang (1881). [Am. Hist.: Misc.]
9. **James, Jesse** (1847–1882) romanticized train and bank robber. [Am. Hist.: Flexner, 219]
10. **Ringo, Johnny** (fl. late 19th century) notorious outlaw and gunfighter in the Southwest. [Am. Hist.: Misc.]
11. **Rob Roy** (Robert MacGregor, 1671–1734) Scottish Highland outlaw remembered in Sir Walter Scott's novel *Rob Roy* (1818). [Scottish Hist.: *EB,* VIII: 619]
12. **Robin Hood** (13th century) legendary outlaw of England who robbed the rich to help the poor. [Br. Hist.: *EB,* VIII: 615–616]
13. **Turpin, Dick** (1706–1739) English outlaw who robbed travelers on the road from London to Oxford. [Br. Hist.: *WB,* 19: 425]

14. **Villa, Pancho** (1878–1923) notorious Mexican bandit and revolutionary. [Mex. Hist.: *EB,* X: 435–436]

P

483. PACIFICATION

1. **Aegir** sea god, stiller of storms on the ocean. [Norse Myth.: Leach, 16]
2. **Feng** name taken by Odin in capacity of wave-stiller. [Norse Myth.: *LLEI,* I: 328]
3. **Saul and David** David plays his harp to mollify King Saul. [O.T.: I Samuel 16:16, 23]

Pain (**See SUFFERING.**)

484. PARADISE (See also HEAVEN, UTOPIA.)

1. **Bali** Indonesian island; thought of as garden of Eden. [Geography: *NCE,* 215–216]
2. **Brigadoon** magical Scottish village that materializes once every 100 years. [Am. Music: Payton, 100–101]
3. **Canaan** ancient region on Jordan river; promised by God to Abraham. [O.T.: Genesis 12:5–10]
4. **Earthly Paradise** place of beauty, peace, and immortality, believed in the Middle Ages to exist in some undiscovered land. [Eur. Legend: Benét, 298]
5. **Eden** earthly garden of luxury; abode of Adam and Eve. [O.T.: Genesis 2:8]
6. **Elysium (Elysian Fields)** abode of the blessed in afterlife. [Gk. & Rom. Myth.: Brewer *Dictionary*]
7. **Garden of the Hesperides** quiet garden of the gods where golden apples grew. [Gk. Lit.: *Hippolytus;* Gk. Myth.: Gaster, 25]
8. **Happy Hunting Ground** paradise for American Indians. [Am. Culture: Jobes, 724]
9. **Happy Valley** beautiful spot in Kashmir's Jhelum Valley. [Indian Hist.: Payton, 300]
10. **hissu** where trees bear fruits of lapis lazuli. [Babylonian Lit.: *Gilgamesh*]
11. **land of milk and honey** proverbial ideal of plenty and happiness. [Western Cult.: Brewer *Dictionary*]
12. **Land of the Lotophagi** African land where eating lotos fruit produced amnesia and indolence. [Gk. Lit.: *Odyssey;* Br. Lit.: "The Lotos-Eaters" in Norton, 733–736]

13. **Nirvana** eternal bliss and the end of all earthly suffering. [Indian Religion: Jobes, 1175]
14. **Shangri-la** utopia hidden in the Himalayas. [Br. Lit.: *Lost Horizon*]
15. **Suhkavati** garden of jeweled trees and dulcet-voiced birds. [Buddhist Myth.: Gaster, 24]
16. **Timbuktu** fabled land of wealth and splendor. [Eur. Hist.: Brewer *Dictionary,* 1084]
17. **Tlapallan** land of luxuriance and red sunrise. [Aztec Myth.: Gaster, 25]

485. PARADOX

1. **Catch-22** claim of insanity to be relieved of military duty proves sanity. [Am. Lit.: Joseph Heller *Catch-22*]
2. **Zeno's paradoxes** four philosophical arguments purporting to show the impossibility of motion. [Gk. Phil.: *NCE*, 3043]

486. PASSION OF CHRIST (See also CHRIST.)

1. **agony in the garden** Christ confronts His imminent death. [N.T.: Matthew 26:36–45; Mark 14:32–41]
2. **cock** its crowing reminded Peter of his betrayal. [N.T.: John 18:27]
3. **Cross, the** upon which Christ was crucified. [N.T.: Matthew 27:31–50]
4. **crown of thorns** placed upon Christ's head after scourging. [N.T.: John 19:2]
5. **Deposition** Christ is taken from the cross and enshrouded. [N.T.: Matthew 27:57–60; Christian Art: Appleton, 55]
6. **dice** cast by Roman guards for Christ's robe. [N.T.: Matthew 27:35]
7. **Eloi, Eloi, lama sabachthani?** "My God, my God, why hast thou forsaken me?" Jesus's cry at the ninth hour. [N.T.: Mark 15:34]
8. **Entry into Jerusalem** first scene of Passion cycle in painting. [Art: Hall, 114]
9. **gall** sponge soaked with it given to crucified Jesus. [N.T.: Matthew 26:48]
10. **Gethsemane** scene of Christ's agony over impending death. [N.T.: Matthew 26:36–45; Mark 14:32–41]
11. **Golgotha (Calvary)** site of Christ's crucifixion. [N.T.: Matthew 27:32]
12. **hammer** Christian symbol for martyrdom, crucifixion. [Christian Symbolism: Jobes, 391, 716]

13. **kiss** means by which Judas identified Jesus. [N.T.: Matthew 26:48–50]
14. **ladder** stood upon by Joseph to remove nails holding Christ to the cross. [Christian Symbolism: Appleton, 55]
15. **lantern** held by Judas, leading officers to Christ. [N.T.: John 18:3]
16. **Passion Play** dramatic presentation of Christ's Passion, notably the production at Oberammergau. [Medieval Drama: Benét, 763]
17. **Peter's denial** Peter denies Christ three times. [N.T.: Matthew 26: 67–75]
18. **pillar and cord** depicted Christ's scourging. [Christian Symbolism: Appleton, 76]
19. **scourges** instruments of Christ's flagellation. [Christian Symbolism: N.T.: Matthew 27:26]
20. **seamless robe** Christ's garment, wagered for by Roman soldiers. [N.T.: John 19:23–24]
21. **Simon the Cyrenean** bystander compelled to carry Christ's cross. [N.T.: Matthew 27:32]
22. **spear** weapon plunged into Jesus's side during crucifixion. [N.T.: John 19:34]
23. **Stations of the Cross** depictions of episodes of Christ's death. [Christianity: Brewer *Dictionary*, 1035]
24. **stigmata** wounds of Christ appearing on others. [Christian Hagiog.: Attwater, 136, 146, 211]
25. **30 pieces of silver** price Judas was paid for identifying Christ. [N.T.: Matthew 26:15]
26. **three nails** used to crucify Jesus. [Christian Symbolism: Appleton, 67]
27. **vernicle** Veronica's veil with Jesus's facial image. [Christian Symbolism: Appleton, 107]
28. **Via Dolorosa** Christ's route to Calvary. [Christianity: Brewer *Dictionary*, 112]
29. **vinegar** given to Jesus to drink. [N.T.: Matthew 26:34, 48]
30. **whipping post** scene of Christ's scourging. [N.T.: Matthew 15:15]

487. PASSION, SENSUAL

1. **Anteros** Eros's brother; avenger of unrequited love; god of passion. [Gk. Myth.: Zimmerman, 23]
2. **Cleopatra** (69–30 B.C.) alluring and romantic queen of Egypt. [Egypt. Hist.: *NCE*, 577]

3. **Eros** (Rom. **Cupid**) god of love; whence, word *erotic*. [Gk. Myth.: Zimmerman, 76]
4. **Himeros** god of erotic desire; attendant of Aphrodite. [Gk. Myth.: Howe, 131]
5. **Kama** god of erotic love. [Hindu Myth.: Leach, 569]
6. ***Kiss, The*** sculpture by French sculptor Rodin depicting passionate embrace. [Art: Osborne, 988]
7. ***Lolita*** twelve-year-old inspires lust in older man. [Am. Lit.: *Lolita*]
8. **ruby** represents intensity of feeling; July birthstone. [Gem Symbolism: Kunz, 28, 319]

488. PASSWORD

1. **Open, Sesame!** formula that opened the door to the robbers' cave. [Arab. Lit.: *Arabian Nights*]
2. **shibboleth** by its pronunciation the Gileadites could identify Ephraimite fugitives. [O. T.: Judges 12:4-6]

489. PASTORALISM

1. **Arcadia** mountainous region of ancient Greece; legendary for pastoral innocence of people. [Gk. Hist.: *NCE,* 136; Rom. Lit.: *Eclogues;* Span. Lit.: *Arcadia*]
2. **Chloë** Arcadian goddess, patronness of new, green crops. [Gk. Myth.: Parrinder, 62]
3. **Daphnis** Sicilian shepherd-flautist; invented bucolic poetry. [Rom. Myth.: *LLEI,* I:326]
4. ***Eclogues*** short pieces by Roman poet Vergil with pastoral setting. [Rom. Lit.: Benét, 1053]
5. **Granida and Daifilio** classic idyllic love between princess and shepherd. [Dutch Lit.: *Granida,* Hall, 141]
6. **Pastoral Symphony** Beethoven's Symphony No. 6 in F Major; hymn to nature. [Ger. Music: Thompson, 1634]
7. **Theocritus** poet; rhapsodized over charm of rustic life. [Gk. Lit.: Brewer *Dictionary,* 813]
8. ***Walden*** Thoreau's classic; advocates a return to nature. [Am. Lit.: Van Doren, 208]
9. ***Works and Days*** long poem by Hesiod, considered a farmers' almanac of ancient Greece. [Gk. Lit.: Benét, 1102]

490. PATIENCE (See also LONGSUFFERING.)

1. **Amelia** idealized personification of patience and perseverance. [Br. Lit.: *Amelia*]

2. **dock bloom** symbolizes patience. [Flower Symbolism: Jobes, 454]
3. **Enid** constant and patient wife of Sir Geraint. [Welsh Lit.: *Mabinogion;* Br. Lit.: "Idylls of the King"]
4. **Griselda** lady immortalized for patience and wifely obedience. [Br. Lit.: *Canterbury Tales,* "Clerk of Oxenford's Tale"]
5. **Hermione** bore Leontes' unfounded jealousy, thus gaining his love. [Br. Lit.: *The Winter's Tale*]
6. **Jacob** serves Laban for fourteen years before receiving permission to marry Rachel. [O.T.: Gen. 24:34]
7. **Job** underwent trial by God at Satan's suggestion. [O.T.: Job]
8. **Penelope** Odysseus' wife; model of feminine virtue, waits twenty years for husband's return. [Gk. Lit.: *Odyssey*]

491. PATRICIDE

1. **Adrammelech and Sharezer** murder father, Sennacherib, for Assyrian throne. [O.T.: II Kings 19:37]
2. **Borden, Lizzie** (1860–1927) woman accused of butchering father and stepmother with ax (1872). [Am. Hist.: Hart, 91]
3. **Edward** killed his father at his mother's instigation. [Br. Balladry: *Edward* in Benét, 302]
4. **Oedipus** kills father in argument not knowing his identity. [Gk. Lit.: *Oedipus Rex*]

492. PATRIOTISM (See also CHAUVINISM, LOYALTY.)

1. **America, Captain** comic-strip character known as the "protector of the American way." [Comics: Horn, 155–156]
2. **American elm** traditional symbol of American patriotism. [Tree Symbolism: *Flora Symbolica,* 182]
3. **Cincinnatus** farmer-hero who defeated Rome's enemies, returned in triumph, went back to his farm. [Rom. Hist.: *EB* (1963) V, 712]
4. **Fourth of July** "Independence Day"; day celebrating adoption of the Declaration of Independence. [Am. Hist.: Misc.]
5. **Hale, Nathan** (1755–1776) hero of American revolution; famous for "I regret I have but one life to give for my country." [Am. Hist.: Hart, 341]
6. **Joan of Arc, St.** (1412–1431) heroically followed call to save France. [Christian Hagiog.: Attwater, 187]
7. **nasturtium** symbolizes love of country. [Flower Symbolism: *Flora Symbolica,* 176]

8. **Nolan, Philip** long banished, he comes at last to passionately love the United States before his death. [Am. Lit.: Hale *The Man Without a Country* in Magill I, 553]
9. **Uncle Sam** personification of U.S. government. [Am. Folklore: Misc.]

493. PATRONAGE (See also PHILANTHROPY.)

1. **Alidoro** fairy godfather to Italian Cinderella. [Ital. Opera: Rossini, *Cinderella,* Westerman, 120–121]
2. **Alphonso, Don** supports Blas in return for political favors. [Fr. Lit.: *Gil Blas*]
3. **Dionysus** inspired men through wine; considered a patron of the arts. [Gk. Myth.: *NCE,* 767]
4. **Fairy Godmother** maternal fairy abets Cinderella in ball preparations. [Fr. Fairy Tale: "Cinderella"]

494. PEACE

1. **Beulah, Land of** resting-place of pilgrims after crossing river of Death. [Br. Lit.: *Pilgrim's Progress*]
2. **Concordia** ancient Roman goddess of peace and domestic harmony. [Rom. Myth.: Zimmerman, 68]
3. **dove** emblem of peace, tenderness, innocence, and gentleness. [Folklore: Brewer *Dictionary,* 340]
4. **Geneva** site of peace conferences (1955, 1960); seat of League of Nations (1920–1946). [Swiss Hist.: *NCE,* 1058]
5. **Goshen, Land of** place of peace and prosperity. [O.T.: Genesis 14:10]
6. **Irene** goddess of peace and conciliation. [Gk. Myth.: Espy, 21]
7. **Jesus Christ** prince of peace in Christian beliefs. [N.T.: Matthew; Mark; Luke; John]
8. **laurel** traditional emblem of peace. [Plant Symbolism: Jobes, 374]
9. **olive branch** symbol of peace and serenity. [Gk. and Rom. Myth.: Brewer *Handbook;* O.T.: Genesis, 8:11]
10. **Pax** goddess of peace. [Rom. Myth.: Zimmerman, 194]
11. **peace pipe** pipe of North American Indians; smoked at conclusion of peace treaties. [Am. Hist.: *NCE,* 427]
12. **Quakers** nonmilitant, gentle, religious sect. [Am. Hist.: Jameson, 189]

495. PEACEMAKING (See also ANTIMILITARISM.)

1. **Agrippa, Menenius** Coriolanus's witty friend; reasons with rioting mob. [Br. Lit.: *Coriolanus*]

2. **Antenor** percipiently urges peace with Greeks. [Gk. Lit.: *Iliad*]
3. **Benvolio** tries to stop Mercutio's fatal clash with Tybalt. [Br. Lit.: *Romeo and Juliet*]
4. **Lysistrata** leads women to use wifely continence to secure peace between countries. [Gk. Lit.: *Lysistrata*]

496. PEDANTRY

1. **Blimber, Cornelia** "dry and sandy with working in the graves of deceased languages." [Br. Lit.: *Dombey and Son*]
2. **Casaubon, Edward** dull pedant; dreary scholar who marries Dorothea. [Br. Lit.: *Middlemarch*]
3. **Caxton, Austin** erudite bookworm. [Br. Lit.: *The Caxtons*]
4. **Choakumchild, Mr.** pedantic master of Gradgrind's school. [Br. Lit.: *Hard Times*]
5. **Conseil** taxonomically talented servant of Prof. Aronnax. [Fr. Lit.: *Twenty Thousand Leagues Under the Sea*]
6. **Dalgetty, Rittmaster Dugald** garrulous pedant. [Br. Lit.: *A Legend of Montrose*]
7. **Fluellen** pedantic Welsh captain and know-it-all. [Br. Lit.: *Henry V*]
8. **Holofernes** shameless pedagogue-schoolmaster. [Br. Lit.: *Love's Labour's Lost*]
9. **Sampson, Dominie** old-fashioned, donnish scholar. [Br. Lit.: *Guy Mannering*]
10. **Scriblerus, Martinus** learned fool. [Br. Lit.: Benét, 909]
11. **Thwackum** selfish and ill-humored clerical pedagogue. [Br. Lit.: *Tom Jones*]

497. PENITENCE

1. **Act of Contrition** prayer of atonement said after making one's confession. [Christianity: Misc.]
2. **Agnes, Sister** former Lady Laurentini; a penitent nun. [Br. Lit.: *The Mysteries of Udolpho*, Freeman, 4]
3. **Ancient Mariner** telling his tale is penance for his guilt. [Br. Poetry: Coleridge "The Rime of the Ancient Mariner"]
4. **Canossa** site of Henry IV's submission to Pope Gregory VII (1077). [Eur. Hist.: Grun, 140]
5. **Dimmesdale, Arthur** Puritan minister publicly atones for sin of adultery. [Am. Lit.: *The Scarlet Letter*]
6. **Dismas (Dysmas)** in the Apocryphal gospels, the penitent thief. [Christianity: Benét, 274]

7. **Elul** sixth month of Jewish year; month of repentance. [Judaism: Wigoder, 174]
8. **Flagellants** groups of Christians who practised public flagellation as penance. [Christian Hist.: *NCE*, 959]
9. **Henry IV (1050–1106)** Holy Roman Emperor who begged forgiveness from the Pope at Canossa. [Eur. Hist.: Benét, 456]
10. **Julian, St., the Hospitaler** for having mistakenly killed his parents, atones by becoming a beggar and helping the wretched. [Christ. Leg.: Attwater]
11. **Mary Magdalene** abjectly cleans Jesus's feet with tears; dries them with her hair. [N.T.: Luke 7:37–50]
12. **Nineveh** townspeople repented for wickedness by fasting and donning sackcloth. [O.T.: Jonah 3:5–10]
13. **Pelagius the Repentant, St.** dancing-girl converts to solitary, saintly ways. [Christian Hagiog.: Attwater, 272]
14. **penance** Catholic sacrament, whereby the penitent is absolved of sins by the confessor. [Christianity: *NCE*, 2096]
15. **sable** black fur represents repentance. [Heraldry: Halberts, 37]
16. **sackcloth and ashes** traditional garb of contrition. [O.T.: Jonah 3:6; Esther 4:1–3; N.T.: Matthew 11:21]
17. **scapegoat** sent into wilderness bearing sins of Israelites. [O.T.: Leviticus 16:8–22]
18. **Scarlet Sister Mary** seeks divine forgiveness in night of wild prayer. [Am. Lit.: *Scarlet Sister Mary*]
19. **skull** always present in pictures of Mary Magdalene repenting. [Christian Art: de Bles, 29]
20. **Tannhäuser** seeking salvation, takes pilgrimage to Rome. [Ger. Opera: Wagner, *Tannhäuser*, Westerman, 211]
21. **Tenorio, Don Juan** after sinful lifetime, eleventh-hour repentance saves his soul. [Span. Lit.: *Don Juan Tenorio*]
22. **Theodosius** (346–395) Roman Emperor; did public penance before St. Ambrose. [Rom. Hist.: *EB*, 18:272–273]
23. **Twelve Labors of Hercules** undertaken as penance for slaying his children. [Gk. and Rom. Myth.: Hall, 148]
24. **violet** Christian liturgical color; worn during Lent and Advent. [Color Symbolism: Jobes, 357]
25. **Yom Kippur** most sacred Hebrew holy day; the day of atonement. [Judaism: *NCE*, 182]

498. PERFECTION

1. **Giotto's O** perfect circle drawn effortlessly by Giotto. [Ital. Hist.: Brewer *Dictionary*, 463]

2. **golden mean** or **section** a proportion between the length and width of a rectangle or two portions of a line, said to be ideal. [Fine Arts: Misc.]
3. **Grosvenor, Archibald** poet who has no earthly rival in his claim to being quite perfect. [Br. Opera: Gilbert and Sullivan *Patience*]
4. **hole in one** score of one stroke for a hole in golf. [Sports: *Webster's Sports,* 215]
5. **Jesus Christ** son of God; personification of human flawlessness. [Christian Hist.: *NCE,* 1412]
6. **perfect cadence** where the dominant passes into the harmony of the tonic chord. [Music: Thompson, 333]
7. **perfect contrition** sorrow for sin, coming from a love of God for His own perfections. [Christianity: Misc.]
8. **perfect game** baseball game in which all opposing batters are put out in succession. [Sports: *Webster's Sports,* 311]
9. **perfect number** equal in value to the sum of those natural numbers that are less than the given number but that also divide (with zero remainder) the given number. [Math.: *EB,* VII: 872]
10. **royal flush** best possible hand in poker; one-suited hand from ten to ace. [Cards: Brewer *Dictionary,* 940]
11. **Superman** Nietzsche's ideal being, a type that would arise when man succeeds in surpassing himself. [Ger. Phil.: *Thus Spake Zarathustra* in Magill III, 1069]
12. **300 game** bowling game of twelve consecutive strikes, scoring maximum 300 points. [Sports: *Webster's Sports,* 311]

499. PERJURY (See also DECEIT.)

1. **Hiss, Alger** (1904–) imprisoned for perjury during espionage hearings. [Am. Hist.: *NCE,* 1247]
2. **Oakes** rancher, remembered for his untrustworthy court testimony. [Australian Hist.: Brewer *Dictionary,* 771]
3. **Philip, King** worships "tickling Commodity"; perjures himself. [Br. Lit.: *King John*]

500. PERMANENCE

1. **law of the Medes and Persians** Darius's execution ordinance; an immutable law. [O.T.: Daniel 6:8–9]
2. **leopard's spots** there always, as evilness with evil men. [O.T.: Jeremiah 13:23; Br. Lit.: *Richard II*]
3. **Nubian's skin** permanently black, as evildoer is permanently evil. [O.T.: Jeremiah 13:23]

501. PERSECUTION

1. **Albigenses** medieval sect suppressed by a crusade, wars, and the Inquisition. [Fr. Hist.: *NCE*, 53]
2. **Camisards** uprising of Protestant peasantry after the revocation of Edict of Nantes in 1685 was brutally suppressed by the royal army. [Fr. Hist.: *NCE*, 434]
3. **Huguenots** Protestants of France, much persecuted from the 16th century onward. [Fr. Hist.: *NCE*, 1285]
4. ***Quo Vadis*** novel of Rome under Nero, describing the imprisonment, crucifixion, and burning of Christians. [Pol. Lit.: Magill I, 797]
5. **Spanish Inquisition** harsh tribunal established in 1478 to dispose of heretics, Protestants, and Jews. [Eur. Hist.: *Collier's*, X, 259]

502. PERSEVERANCE (See also DETERMINATION.)

1. **Ainsworth** redid dictionary manuscript burnt in fire. [Br. Hist.: Brewer *Handbook*, 752]
2. ***Call of the Wild, The*** dogs trail steadfastly through Alaska's tundra. [Am. Lit.: *The Call of the Wild*]
3. **canary grass** traditional symbol of perseverance. [Plant Symbolism: *Flora Symbolica*, 183]
4. **Cato the Elder (234–149** B.C.) for his last eight years said in every Senate speech, "Carthage must be destroyed." [Rom. Hist.: *EB* (1963) V, 43]
5. **Deans, Jeanie** by resourcefulness and an arduous journey, manages eventually to obtain a pardon for her sister. [Br. Lit.: *The Heart of Midlothian*]
6. **Goodwood, Caspar** eternal American pursuer of Isabel Archer's hand. [Am. Lit.: *The Portrait of a Lady*, Magill I, 766–768]
7. **Little Engine That Could** pint-sized locomotive struggles long and hard to surmount hill before succeeding. [Children's Lit.: *Little Engine That Could*]
8. **Moses** Hebrew lawgiver; led his quarrelsome people out of bondage in Egypt. [O.T.: Exodus; Leviticus]
9. **Mutt** though usually thwarted in his schemes, he remains determined to triumph someday. [Comics: Berger, 48]
10. **Penelope** foils suiters for twenty years while awaiting return of Odysseus. [Gk. Myth.: Kravitz, 182]
11. **Rembrandt to Rembrandt** artist continues to work despite financial failures. [Am. Lit.: "Rembrandt to Rembrandt" in Hart, 703–704]

12. **Santiago** attempts to subdue large fish through harshness of sea and weather. [Am. Lit.: *The Old Man and the Sea*]
13. **snail** symbol of deliberation and steadfastness. [Heraldry: Halberts, 38]
14. **tortoise** perseverance helps him succeed where those inclined to dawdle fail. [Folklore: Jobes, 1590]
15. **Zarechnaya, Nina** sacrifices everything to further career as actress. [Russ. Lit.: *The Seagull*]

503. PERVERSION (See also BESTIALITY.)

1. **bondage and domination (B & D)** practices with whips, chains, etc. for sexual pleasure. [Western Cult.: Misc.]
2. **Humbert, Humbert** middle-aged gentleman crisscrosses America staying in motels with 12-year-old "nymphet." [Am. Lit.: *Lolita*]
3. **Imp of the Perverse** perversity as motive for men's actions. [Am. Lit.: "Imp of the Perverse" in Hart, 402]
4. **Onan** Judah's son; spilled seed upon ground. [O.T.: Genesis 38: 9–10]
5. **Sacher-Masoch, Leopold von** (1836–1895) author who derived pleasure from being tortured. [Aust. Hist.: Wallechinsky, 165]
6. **Sade, Marquis de** (1740–1814) jailed for sexual crimes; wrote of sexual cruelty. [Fr. Hist.: Wallechinsky, 165]

504. PESSIMISM (See also CYNICISM, SKEPTICISM.)

1. **Calamity Jane** (Martha Jane Canary or Martha Burke, 1852–1903) frontierswoman; mannish prophetess of doom. [Am. Hist.: Flexner, 71]
2. **Cassandra** no credence ever given to her truthful prophecies of doom. [Gk. Myth.: Zimmerman, 51]
3. ***City of Dreadful Night, The*** expresses a passionate faith in pessimism as the only sensible philosophy. [Br. Poetry: James Thomson *The City of Dreadful Night* in Benét, 202]
4. **Gerontion** old man who deplores aging, aridity, and spiritual decay and despairs of civilization. [Br. Poetry: Benét, 391]
5. **Gloomy Gus** one with a pessimistic outlook on the world. [Am. Usage: Misc.]
6. **Heraclitus** (535–475 B.C.) "Weeping Philosopher"; grieved over man's folly. [Gk. Hist.: Brewer *Dictionary*, 1146]
7. **Micaiah** always prophesied misfortune for King Ahab. [O.T.: I Kings 22:8]
8. **Murphy's Law** "If anything can go wrong, it will." [Am. Culture: Wallechinsky, 480]

9. **Schopenhauer, Arthur** (1788–1860) German philosopher known for philosophy of pessimism. [Ger. Hist.: *NCE,* 2447]

505. PHILANTHROPY (See also GENEROSITY, PATRONAGE.)

1. **Appleseed, Johnny** nickname of John Chapman (c. 1775–1847), who traveled through the Ohio Valley giving away apple seeds and caring for orchards. [Am. Hist.: *Collier's,* IV, 569]
2. **Carnegie, Andrew** (1835–1919) steel magnate who believed the rich should administer wealth for public benefit. [Am. Hist.: Jameson, 83]
3. **Guggenheim** 19th- and 20th-century family name of American industrialists and philanthropists. [Am. Hist.: *NCE,* 1159]
4. **Mellon, Andrew** (1855–1937) financier and public official; left large sums for research and art. [Am. Hist.: *NCE,* 1743]
5. **Rhodes, Cecil** (1853–1902) British imperialist; left millions of pounds for public service; notably, the Rhodes scholarships. [Br. Hist.: *NCE,* 2316]
6. **Rockefeller, John D(avison)** (1839–1937) American multimillionaire; endowed many institutions. [Am. Hist.: Jameson, 431]

506. PHILISTINISM

1. **Babbitt** anti-intellectual, bourgeois conformist. [Am. Lit.: *Babbitt*]
2. ***Grand Hotel*** pictures European bourgeoisie in Berlin between wars. [Ger. Lit.: *Grand Hotel*]
3. **Philistines** perennial rivals of Israel in Biblical times; looked upon as uncultured by Israelites. [Jewish Hist.: *NCE,* 2132]

507. PHILOSOPHY

1. **Aristotle** (384–322 B.C.) eminent Greek philosopher. [Gk. Hist.: *NCE,* 147]
2. **Confucius** (c. 551–479 B.C.) classic Chinese sage. [Chinese Hist.: *NCE,* 625]
3. **Plato** (427–347 B.C.) founder of the Academy; author of *Republic.* [Gk. Hist.: *NCE,* 2165]
4. **Socrates** (469–399 B.C.) Athenian philosopher, propagated dialectic method of approaching knowledge. [Gk. Hist.: *NCE,* 2553]

508. PIANO

1. **Baldwin** famous name in concert pianos. [Am. Cult.: Misc.]
2. **Schroeder** compulsively plays the works of Beethoven on his toy piano. [Comics: "Peanuts" in Horn, 543]
3. **Steinway** famous name in concert pianos. [Am. Cult.: Misc.]

Piety (See RIGHTEOUSNESS.)

509. PIRACY

1. **Barbary Coast** Mediterranean coastline of former Barbary States; former pirate lair. [Afr. Hist.: *NCE,* 229]
2. **Blackbeard** (Edward Teach, d. 1718) colorful, albeit savage, corsair. [Br. Hist.: Jameson, 495]
3. **Conrad, Lord** proud, ascetic but successful buccaneer. [Br. Lit.: *The Corsair,* Walsh *Modern,* 104]
4. **Drake, Sir Francis** (1540–1596) British navigator and admiral; famed for marauding expeditions against Spanish. [Br. Hist.: *NCE,* 793]
5. **Fomorians** mythical, prehistoric, giant pirates who raided and pillaged Irish coast. [Irish Legend: Leach, 409]
6. **Hawkins, Sir John** (1532–1595) British admiral; led lucrative slave-trading expeditions. [Br. Hist.: *NCE,* 1206]
7. **Hook, Captain** treacherous pirate in Never-Never Land. [Br. Lit.: *Peter Pan*]
8. **Jolly Roger** black pirate flag with white skull and crossbones. [World Hist.: Brewer *Dictionary,* 926]
9. **Jonsen, Captain** boards ship taking seven children to England, seizes its valuables, and sails off with the children, who have their own piratical plans. [Br. Lit.: *The Innocent Voyage (High Wind in Jamaica)* in Magill II, 488]
10. **Kidd, Captain William** (1645–1701) British captain; turned pirate. [Br. Hist.: *NCE,* 1476]
11. **Lafitte, Jean** (1780–1826) leader of Louisiana band of privateers and smugglers. [Am. Hist.: *NCE,* 1516]
12. **Morgan, Sir Henry** (1635–1688) Welsh buccaneer; took over privateer band after Mansfield's death. [Br. Hist.: *NCE,* 1832]
13. **Silver, Long John** one-legged corsair; leads mutiny on *Hispaniola.* [Br. Lit.: *Treasure Island*]
14. **Singleton, Captain** buccaneer acquires great wealth depredating in West Indies and Indian Ocean. [Br. Lit.: *Captain Singleton*]

Pitilessness (See HEARTLESSNESS, RUTHLESSNESS.)

Plague (See DISEASE.)

510. POETRY (See also INSPIRATION.)

1. **Bragi** god of verse. [Norse Myth.: Parrinder, 50]
2. **Calliope** Muse of epic poetry. [Gk. Myth.: Kravitz, 159]

3. **Castalia** Parnassian fountain; endowed drinker with poetic creativity. [Gk. Myth.: *LLEI,* I: 325]
4. **Daphnis** creator of bucolic poetry. [Gk. Myth.: Kravitz, 75]
5. **Erato** Muse of love lyrics. [Gk. Myth.: Kravitz, 159]
6. **Euterpe** Muse of lyric poetry. [Gk. Myth.: Kravitz, 159]
7. **Homer** legendary author of the *Iliad* and the *Odyssey*. [Gk. Lit.: Benét, 474]
8. **Parnassus** mountains sacred to Muses; hence, abode of poetry. [Gk. Myth.: Hall, 234]
9. **Pléiade, The** 16th century poets sought to revitalize French literature. [Fr. Hist.: Benét, 795]
10. **Sappho** (c. 620–c. 565 B.C.) lyric poet sometimes called the "tenth muse." [Gk. Lit.: Benét, 896–897]
11. **White Goddess, the** goddess of ancient fertility and the moon whose worship is claimed by Robert Graves to be the origin of poetry. [Br. Lit.: Benét, 1087]

511. POISON

1. **unicorn** its horn used to test liquids for poison. [Medieval Legend: *EB* (1963) XXII, 702]

512. POISONING

1. **Randall, Lord** killed by eating eels poisoned by his sweetheart. [Br. Balladry: *Lord Randall*]

Politeness (See COURTESY.)

Politeness, Excessive (See COURTESY, EXCESSIVE.)

513. POLITICS

1. **Eatanswill** town where party politics arouses fierce oppositions and loyalties. [Br. Lit.: Dickens *Pickwick Papers*]
2. ***Prince, The*** handbook of advice on acquiring and using political power. [Ital. Lit.: Machiavelli *The Prince*]
3. **Skeffington, Frank** old-time machine politician loses mayoralty and dies on election night. [Am. Lit.: Edwin O'Connor *The Last Hurrah* in Hart, 457]

514. POLYGAMY

1. **Bluebeard** chevalier slays his six wives; seventh evades similar fate. [Fr. Fairy Tale: Harvey, 96–97]
2. **David** had many wives. [O.T.: I Samuel 25:43–44; II Samuel 3:2–5]

3. **Draupadi** princess won by Arjuna, brings her home as the wife of all five brothers. [Hindu Lit.: *Mahabharata*]
4. **Islam** religion permits four wives. [Islam: *WB*, A:549]
5. **Lamech** first man to have two wives. [O.T.: Genesis 4:19–20]
6. **Mongut of Siam, King** 9000 wives and concubines. [Thai. Hist.: Wallechinsky, 279]
7. **Mormons** religious sect; once advocated plural marriage. [Am. Hist.: *NCE,* 1833]
8. **Muhammad** had a total of ten wives and ten or fifteen concubines. [Islam: Brewer *Dictionary*, 614]
9. **Solomon** 700 wives, princesses, and 300 concubines. [O.T.: I Kings 11:1–8]

515. POMPOSITY

1. **Aldiborontephoscophornio** nickname from play by Carey, given by Scott to his pompous publisher, James Ballantyne. [Br. Lit.: Barnhart, 23]
2. **Chrononhotonthologos** bombastic, pompous king of Queerumania. [Br. Drama: Benét, 197]
3. **Malvolio** pompous, conceited steward who aspires to his mistress's love. [Br. Drama: Shakespeare *Twelfth Night*]

516. POSSESSION (See also ENCHANTMENT.)

1. **Gadarene swine** Jesus sends demons from man to pigs. [N.T.: Matthew 8:28–32; Mark 5:1–13; Luke 8:26–33]
2. **Legion** man controlled by devils; exorcised by Jesus. [N.T.: Mark 5:9; Luke 8:30]
3. **Regan** young girl gruesomely infested with the devil. [Am. Lit.: *The Exorcist*]

517. POVERTY

1. **Aglaus** poorest man in Arcadia, but happier than king. [Gk. Myth.: Kravitz, 13]
2. **Appalachia** West Virginia coal mining region known for its abysmal poverty. [Am. Hist.: *NCE,* 160]
3. **Apple Annie** apple seller on street corners during Depression. [Am. Hist.: Flexner, 11]
4. **bare feet** symbol of impoverishment. [Folklore: Jobes, 181]
5. **Barnardo Home** one of many homes founded for destitute children. [Br. Hist.: *NCE,* 233]
6. **Bashmachkin, Akakii Akakiievich** poor clerk saves years for overcoat that is soon stolen. [Russ. Lit.: "The Overcoat" in *The Overcoat and Other Stories*]

7. **Bonhomme, Jacques** nickname for poor French peasants. [Fr. Folklore: Walsh *Classical,* 59]
8. **Booth, Captain** continually in and out of debtor's prison. [Br. Lit.: *Amelia*]
9. **Buddha** religious leader exchanges wealth for the robe of an ascetic mendicant. [Buddhism: *NCE*, 387]
10. **Bung** experiences modified and extreme levels of want. [Br. Lit.: *Sketches by Boz*]
11. **Clare of Assisi, St.** lived entirely on alms; founded "Poor Clares." [Christian Hagiog.: Attwater, 87]
12. **Cratchit, Bob** Scrooge's poorly paid clerk. [Br. Lit.: *A Christmas Carol*]
13. **Crawley, Rev. Josiah** debt-maddened clergyman. [Br. Lit.: *Last Chronicle of Barset*]
14. **Francis, St. (1182–1226)** renounced his worldly life and possessions, extolled the virtue of poverty. [Christian Hagiog.: Brewer *Dictionary*, 375]
15. ***Grapes of Wrath, The*** about the Joad family; jobless, facing starvation. [Am. Lit.: *The Grapes of Wrath*]
16. **Great Depression** economic crisis of 1929–1939, unprecedented in length and widespread poverty. [Am. Hist.: *NCE,* 1132]
17. **Grub Street** London street; home of indigent writers. [Br. Hist.: Brewer *Note-Book,* 394]
18. **Hell's Kitchen** section of midtown Manhattan; notorious for slums and high crime rate. [Am. Usage: Misc.]
19. **Hooverville** Depression shantytown arising during Hoover administration. [Amer. Hist.: Flexner, 118]
20. **Hubbard, Old Mother** had not even a bone for her dog. [Nurs. Rhyme: Opie, 317]
21. **Job** lost everything he owned to Satan. [O.T.: Job]
22. **Job's turkey** one-feathered bird even more destitute than its owner. [Can. and Am. Usage: Brewer *Dictionary,* 589]
23. **Lazarus** satisfied with table scraps; dogs licked sores. [N.T.: Luke 16:19–22]
24. **Micawber, Wilkins** optimistic, though chronically penniless and in debt. [Br. Lit.: *David Copperfield*]
25. **Okies** itinerant dust bowl farmers (1930s). [Am. Hist.: Van Doren, 455; Am. Lit.: *The Grapes of Wrath*]
26. **War on Poverty** U.S. government program of 1960's to aid the needy. [Am. Hist.: *WB,* J:120]

27. **Yellow Kid, the** grotesque unchildish slum-child, one of the impoverished inhabitants of Hogan's Alley. [Comics: Berger, 25]

518. POWER

1. **Force, The** mystical source of a Jedi Knight's righteous power. [Am. Cinema: *Star Wars* and sequels]

519. PRECOCIOUSNESS

1. ***Franny and Zooey*** former child prodigies' lives are misshapen by their early exploitation. [Am. Lit.: J. D. Salinger *Franny and Zooey*]
2. ***Tin Drum, The*** mental developement of Oskar Matzerath is complete at birth; has extraordinary mental and physical powers. [Ger. Lit.: Magill IV, 1220]

520. PREDICAMENT

1. **Dancy, Captain Ronald** must persecute friend to save own skin. [Br. Lit.: *Loyalties,* Magill I, 533–534]
2. **Gordian knot** inextricable difficulty; Alexander cut the original. [Gk. Hist.: Espy, 49]
3. ***Lady or the Tiger, The*** hero must choose one of two doors. [Am. Lit.: *The Lady or the Tiger*]
4. **Marta** loves husband; forced into adultery by patron. [Ger. Opera: d'Albert, *Tiefland,* Westerman, 373]
5. **Scylla and Charybdis** two equally dangerous alternatives. [Gk. Lit.: *Odyssey,* Espy, 41]
6. **Symplegades** cliffs at Black Sea entrance; clashed together as ships passed through. [Gk. Myth.: Zimmerman, 251]

521. PRETENSION (See also HYPOCRISY.)

1. **Absolon** vain, officious parish clerk. [Br. Lit.: *Canterbury Tales,* "Miller's Tale"]
2. **Armado, Don Adriano de** his language inordinately disproportionate to his thought. [Br. Lit.: *Love's Labour's Lost*]
3. **Chrononhotonthologos** king whose pomposity provoked a fatal brawl with his general. [Br. Lit.: Walsh *Modern,* 96]
4. **Copper, Captain** pretends to great wealth; jewels are counterfeit. [Br. Lit.: *Rule a Wife and Have a Wife,* Walsh *Modern,* 105]
5. **Coriolanus** stiff-necked Roman aristocrat; contemptuous of the common people. [Br. Lit.: *Coriolanus*]
6. **Dodsworth, Fran** shallow industrialist's wife ostentatiously gallivants about Europe. [Am. Lit.: *Dodsworth*]

7. **Dogberry** ostentatiously and fastidiously examines prisoners. [Br. Lit.: *Much Ado About Nothing*]
8. **euphuism** style overly rich with alliteration, figures, and Latinisms. [Br. Lit.: *Euphues,* Espy, 127]
9. **Isle of Lanterns** inhabited by pretenders to knowledge. [Fr. Lit.: *Pantagruel*]
10. **Jourdain, Monsieur** parvenu grandiosely affects gentleman's mien. [Fr. Lit.: *The Bourgeois Gentilhomme*]
11. **Madelon and Cathos** their suitors had to be flamboyant. [Fr. Lit.: *Les Précieuses Ridicules*]
12. **Melody, Cornelius** self-deluded tavern-keeper boasts about his upper-class past to maintain a show of importance. [Am. Drama: Eugene O'Neill *A Touch of the Poet* in Benét, 737]
13. **morning glory** symbol of affectation; flower of September. [Flower Symbolism: *Flora Symbolica,* 175; Kunz, 330]
14. **Parolles** boastful villain of affected sentiment and knowledge. [Br. Lit.: *All's Well That Ends Well*]
15. **Pendennis** enters university "posing as moneyed aristocrat." [Br. Lit.: *Pendennis*]
16. **Verdurin, M. & Mme.** nouveau-riche couple strive for social eminence. [Fr. Lit.: Proust *Remembrance of Things Past*]
17. **willow herb** indicates affectation. [Flower Symbolism: *Flora Symbolica,* 178]
18. **Yvetot, King of** affects grandeur; kingdom is but a village. [Fr. Legend: Brewer *Dictionary,* 1173]

Prey (See **QUARRY.**)

Pride (See **BOASTFULNESS, EGOTISM, VANITY.**)

522. PRIZE

1. **Achsah** Caleb's daughter; promised in marriage to conqueror of Debir. [O.T.: Joshua 15:16–19; Judges 1:12–15]
2. **blue ribbon** denotes highest honor. [Western Folklore: Brewer *Dictionary,* 127]
3. **Bollingen** annual prize for highest achievement in American poetry. [Am. Lit.: Hart, 88]
4. **Emmy** awarded annually for best achievements in television programing and performance. [TV: Misc.]
5. **Enrico Fermi Award** given for "exceptional and altogether outstanding achievement" in atomic energy. [Am. Hist.: Misc.]
6. **Eva** to marry winner of singing contest. [Ger. Opera: Wagner, *Meistersinger,* Westerman, 225–228]

7. **gold medal** traditional first prize. [Western Cult: Misc.]
8. **Goncourt** annual award for best French fiction. [Fr. Lit.: *NCE*, 1106]
9. **Grammy** awarded by the National Academy of Recording Arts and Sciences for the best in the recording field. [Am. Hist.: Misc.]
10. **Guggenheim** annual fellowships for creative work. [Am. Hist.: Hart, 337]
11. **Heisman Trophy** awarded to the outstanding college football player of the year by New York Athletic Club. [Am. Sports: Misc.]
12. **laurel wreath** ancient award for victory. [Western Cult.: Brewer *Dictionary*]
13. **Medal of Freedom** highest award given a U.S. citizen; established 1963. [Am. Hist.: Misc.]
14. **National Book Award** given by the American Academy and Institute of Arts and Letters to outstanding works. [Am. Hist.: Misc.]
15. **Newbery-Caldecott Medal** awarded by the American Library Association for outstanding children's books. [Am. Hist.: Misc.]
16. **Nobel** monetary awards for outstanding contributions benefiting mankind. [World. Hist.: Wheeler, 718]
17. **Oscar** gold statuette awarded to film actors, directors, writers, technicians, etc. [Am. Cinema: Brewer *Dictionary*, 788]
18. **Pulitzer** awards made in letters, music, and journalism. [Am. Hist.: Wheeler, 824]
19. **Silken Threads** the three great prizes of honor in Lilliput. [Br. Lit.: *Gulliver's Travels*]
20. **Tony (Antoinette Perry Award)** presented annually for outstanding work in the Broadway theater. [Am. Hist.: Misc.]

Prodigality (See DISSIPATION.)

523. PROFLIGACY (See also DEBAUCHERY, LUST, PROMISCUITY.)

1. **Arrowsmith, Martin** simultaneously engaged to Madeline and Leona. [Am. Lit.: *Arrowsmith*]
2. **Bellaston, Lady** wealthy profligate; keeps Tom as gigolo. [Br. Lit.: *Tom Jones*]
3. **Booth, Captain** pleasure-loving prodigal; lacks discipline. [Br. Lit.: *Amelia*]
4. **Casanova, Giovanni Jacopo** (1725–1798) myriad amours made his name synonymous with philanderer. [Ital. Hist.: Benét, 172]

5. **Don Juan** internationally active profligate and seducer. [Span. Lit.: Benét, 279; Ger. Opera: Mozart, *Don Giovanni,* Westerman, 93–95]
6. **Flashman, Harry** British soldier wenches his way around world. [Br. Lit.: *Flashman*]
7. **Genji, Prince** Emperor's dashing and talented bastard woos many. [Jap. Lit.: *The Tale of Genji*]
8. **Iachimo** scorns and craftily tests feminine virtue. [Br. Lit.: *Cymbeline*]
9. **Jones, Tom** manly but all too human young man; has numerous amorous adventures. [Br. Lit.: *Tom Jones*]
10. **Karamazov, Dmitri** lusty and violent in most of his actions. [Russ. Lit.: Dostoevsky *The Brothers Karamazov*]
11. **Lothario** young rake and seducer. [Br. Lit.: *The Fair Penitent*]
12. **Lyndon, Barry** from bully to dissipative rake and cruel husband. [Br. Lit.: *Barry Lyndon*]
13. **Macheath, Captain** gambler and robber; has scores of illegitimate offspring. [Br. Opera: *The Beggar's Opera*]
14. ***Rake's Progress, A*** Hogarth prints illustrating the headlong career and sorry end of a libertine. [Br. Art: *EB* (1963) XI, 625]
15. **Santa Cruz, Juanito** loses his wife, lover, and esteem by philandering. [Span. Lit.: *Fortunata and Jacinta*]
16. **Scales, Gerald** sales representative known for lavish living, gambling, amorality. [Br. Lit.: *The Old Wives' Tale,* Magill I, 684–686]
17. **Venusberg** magic land of illicit pleasure where Venus keeps court. [Ger. Myth.: Brewer *Dictionary*, 932]
18. **Zeus** supreme of Greek gods; extramarital affairs were countless. [Gk. Myth.: Zimmerman, 292]

524. PROLIFICNESS

1. **Abraham** promised countless descendants by God. [O.T.: Genesis 13:16]
2. **Aegyptus** fathered 50 sons, who married the daughters of his twin brother Danaus. [Gk. Myth.: Benét, 11]
3. **Danaus** fathered 50 daughters, who married the sons of his twin brother Aegyptus. [Gk. Myth.: Benét, 11]
4. **Flanders, Moll** adventuress bears a dozen children to various mates. [Br. Lit.: *Moll Flanders* in Magill I, 614]
5. **Lester, Jeeter and Ada** hapless sharecroppers with seventeen children. [Am. Lit.: Caldwell *Tobacco Road*]

6. **old woman who lived in a shoe** "had so many children she didn't know what to do." [Nursery Rhyme: Baring-Gould, 85]
7. **rabbit** progenitor of many offspring at short intervals. [Zoology: Misc.]

525. PROMISCUITY (See also PROFLIGACY.)

1. **Anatol** constantly flits from one girl to another. [Aust. Drama: Schnitzler *Anatol* in Benét, 33]
2. **Aphrodite** promiscuous goddess of sensual love. [Gk. Myth.: Parrinder, 24]
3. **Ashley, Lady Brett** forever falling in love with young men. [Am. Lit.: *The Sun Also Rises*]
4. **Barbarella** scantily dressed, sex-loving, blonde astronaut. [Comics: Horn, 96]
5. **Camille** "a woman of Paris." [Fr. Lit.: *Camille*]
6. **Compson, Candace** gave herself freely to every man she met; her illegitimate daughter became equally promiscuous. [Am. Lit.: Faulkner *The Sound and the Fury* in Magill I, 917]
7. **Forrester, Mrs. Marian** traveling husband not enough to fulfill desires. [Am. Lit.: *A Lost Lady*]
8. **Ganconer** fairy who makes love with, then abandons, women. [Br. Folklore: Briggs, 183–184]
9. **Gomer** Hosea's wanton wife. [O.T.: Hosea 1:1–3]
10. ***Looking for Mr. Goodbar*** Theresa Dunn haunts singles bars in a compulsive quest for the ideal lover. [Am. Lit.: Weiss, 267]
11. **Messalina** wife of Emperor Claudius of Rome. [Rom. Hist.: Brewer *Handbook*, 701]
12. **Rogers, Mildred** though a wanton, Philip loved her above all else. [Br. Lit.: *Of Human Bondage;* Magill I, 670–672]

526. PROPAGANDA

1. **Axis Sally** [Mildred Elizabeth Sisk, (1900–) or Rita Louise Zucca, (1912–)] Nazi broadcaster who urged American withdrawal from WWII. [Am. Hist.: Flexner, 449]
2. **Haw-Haw, Lord** (William Joyce, 1906–1946) British citizen becomes German propagandist in WWII. [Br. Hist.: *NCE*, 1435]
3. **Tokyo Rose** (Iva Ikuko Toguri D'Aquino, 1916–) Japanese broadcaster who urged U.S. troops to surrender during WWII. [Am. Hist.: Flexner, 449]

527. PROPHECY (See also OMEN.)

1. **Ancaeus** prophecy that he would not live to taste the wine from his vineyards is fulfilled. [Gk. Myth.: Brewer *Dictionary*, 32]
2. **augurs** Roman officials who interpreted omens. [Rom. Hist.: Parrinder, 34]
3. **Balaam** vaticinally speaks with Jehovah's voice. [O.T.: Numbers 23:8–10; 24:18–24]
4. **banshee** Irish spirit who foretells death. [Irish Folklore: Briggs, 14–16]
5. **Belshazzar's Feast** disembodied hand foretells Belshazzar's death. [O.T.: Daniel 5]
6. **Brave New World** picture of world's condition 600 years from now. [Br. Lit.: *Brave New World*]
7. **Calamity Jane** (Martha Jane Canary or Martha Burke, 1852–1903) mannish prophetess of doom. [Am. Hist.: Flexner, 71]
8. **Calchas** declares that Iphigenia must be sacrificed to appease Artemis and ensure the Greeks' safe passage to Troy. [Gk. Myth.: Hamilton, 261]
9. **Calpurnia** sees bloody statue of Julius in dream. [Br. Lit.: *Julius Caesar*]
10. **Carmen** the cards repeatedly spell her death. [Fr. Opera: Bizet, *Carmen*, Westerman, 189–190]
11. **Cassandra** always accurate but fated to be disbelieved, predicts doom of Troy to brother, Hector. [Br. Lit.: *Troilus and Cressida;* Gk. Myth.: Parrinder, 57]
12. **Cumaean sibyl** to discover future, leads Aeneas to Hades. [Gk. Lit.: *Aeneid*]
13. **Delphi** ancient oracular center near Mt. Parnassus. [Gk. Myth.: Parrinder, 74; Jobes, 428]
14. **Dodona** oldest oracle of Zeus in Greece. [Gk. Myth.: Kravitz, 83]
15. **Ezekiel** priest and prophet to the Jews during Babylonian captivity. [O.T.: Ezekiel]
16. **Golden Cockerel** its crowing predicts either peace or disaster. [Russ. Opera: Rimsky-Korsakov, *Coq d'Or,* Westerman, 392]
17. **Guardian Black Dog** sinister omen of death. [Br. Folklore: Briggs, 207–208]
18. **haruspices** ancient Etruscan seers who divined the future from the entrails of animals. [Rom. Hist.: *EB,* IV: 933]
19. **Huldah** tells of impending disaster for the idolatrous. [O.T.: II Kings 22:14–19]

20. ***I Ching*** a book of divination and speculations. [Chinese Lit.: *I Ching*]
21. **Isaiah** foretells fall of Jerusalem; prophet of doom. [O.T.: Isaiah]
22. **Jeremiah** the Lord's herald. [O.T.: Jeremiah]
23. **John the Baptist** foretells the coming of Jesus. [N.T.: Luke 3:16]
24. **Joseph** predicted famine from Pharaoh's dreams. [O.T.: Genesis 41:25–36]
25. **Mopsus** seer who interpreted the words of the Argo's talking prow. [Gk. Myth.: Benét, 684]
26. **Muhammad** (570–632) the prophet of Islam. [Islam. Hist.: *NCE,* 1854]
27. **Nostradamus** (1503–1566) startlingly accurate French astrologer and physician. [Fr. Hist.: *NCE,* 1969]
28. **pythoness** priestess of Apollo, the Delphic Oracle, endowed with prophetic powers. [Gk. Hist.: *Collier's,* VII, 682]
29. ***Rocking-Horse Winner, The*** a small boy predicts winners in horse races through the medium of a demonic rocking horse. [Br. Lit.: D. H. Lawrence *The Rocking-Horse Winner* in Benét, 866]
30. **Sibyllae** women endowed with prophetic powers who interceded with gods for men. [Gk. Myth.: Zimmerman, 239]
31. **Sibylline Books** nine tomes foretelling Rome's future. [Rom. Leg.: Brewer *Dictionary*]
32. **Smith, Joseph** Mormon prophet; professed visions of new faith. [Am. Hist.: Jameson, 467]
33. **Smith, Valentine Michael** messianic Martian shows earthlings the way. [Am. Lit.: *Stranger in a Strange Land*]
34. **sortes (Homericae, Virgilianae, Biblicae)** fortune-telling by taking random passages from a book (as *Iliad*, *Aeneid*, or the Bible). [Eur. Culture: *Collier's,* VII, 683]
35. **Sosostris, Madame** "the wisest woman in Europe," cleverly interprets the Tarot cards. [Br. Poetry: T. S. Eliot "The Waste Land"]
36. **Tarot cards** used to tell fortunes. [Magic: Brewer *Dictionary,* 1063]
37. **Tiresias** blind and greatest of all mythological prophets. [Gk. Myth.: Zimmerman, 255; Gk. Lit.: *Antigone; Odyssey; Oedipus Tyrannus*]
38. **Ulrica** foretells Gustavus' murder by his friend Anckarström. [Ital. Opera: Verdi, *Masked Ball,* Westerman, 313–315]

39. **voice . . . crying in the wilderness** John the Baptist, in reference to his prophecy of the coming of Christ. [N.T.: Matthew 3:3]
40. **Weird Sisters** three witches who set Macbeth agog with prophecies of kingship. [Br. Lit.: *Macbeth*]

Prosperity (See **SUCCESS.**)

528. PROSTITUTION (See also COURTESANSHIP, MISTRESSES.)

1. **Adriana** comely girl becomes prostitute to support herself. [Ital. Lit.: *The Woman of Rome*]
2. **Brattle, Carrie** returns home reconciled after life in gutter. [Br. Lit: *The Vicar of Bullhampton*]
3. **Celestina** old, evil procuress hired as go-between. [Span. Lit.: *Celestina*]
4. **Dolores and Faustine** provide Swinburne with masochistic pleasure. [Br. Poetry: *Poems and Ballads* in Magill IV, 704]
5. ***Harlot's Progress, The*** Hogarth engravings tracing a prostitute's miserable career to its degraded end. [Br. Art: *EB* (1963) XI, 624]
6. **Hill, Fanny** frankly erotic heroine of frankly erotic novel. [Br. Lit.: *Memoirs of Fanny Hill.*]
7. **La Douce, Irma** leading French prostitute on Pigalle. [Am. Cinema: Halliwell, 460]
8. **Lulu** keeper of two others on her earnings. [Aust. Opera: Berg, *Lulu,* Westerman, 484]
9. **Maggie** innocent girl, corrupted by slum environment, becomes a prostitute. [Am. Lit.: *Maggie: A Girl of the Streets,* Hart, 514]
10. **Mary Magdalene** repentant prostitute who anointed Jesus's feet. [N.T.: Luke 7:36–50]
11. **Nana** beautiful lady who thrived on a troop of men. [Fr. Lit.: *Nana,* Magill I, 638–640]
12. **Overdone, Mistress** "a bawd of eleven years' continuance." [Br. Lit.: *Measure for Measure*]
13. **Rahab** harlot of Jericho who protected Joshua's two spies. [O.T.: Joshua 2]
14. **Tearsheet, Doll** violent-tempered prostitute, an acquaintance of Falstaff. [Br. Lit.: Shakespeare *II Henry IV*]
15. **Thaïs** notorious harlot in Malebolge, Hell's eighth circle. [Ital. Lit.: *Inferno*]
16. **Toast, Joan** a most saintly whore. [Am. Lit.: *The Sot-Weed Factor*]

17. **Warren, Mrs.** raises daughter in comfort and refinement on her bedside earnings. [Br. Lit.: *Mrs. Warren's Profession* in *Plays Unpleasant*]

529. PROTECTION (See also CHARMS.)

1. **aegis** protective mantle of Zeus given to Athena. [Gk. Myth.: Brewer *Dictionary*]
2. **alum** charm against evil eye. [Egyptian Folklore: Leach, 40]
3. **amethyst** preserved soldiers from harm; gave them victory. [Gem Symbolism: Kunz, 58]
4. **bennet** excludes the devil; used on door frames. [Medieval Folklore: Boland, 56]
5. **blood of the lamb** used to mark houses of the Israelites so they could be passed over. [O.T.: Exodus 12:3–13]
6. **chrysoberyl** guards against evil spirits. [Gem Symbolism: Kunz, 65]
7. **cross** used to frighten away devils and protect from evil. [Christian Iconog.: Leach, 265]
8. **daisy** provides protection against fairies. [Flower Symbolism: Briggs, 87]
9. **horseshoe** hung on buildings as defense against fairies. [Br. Folklore: Briggs, 225]
10. **jacinth** guards against plague and wounds. [Gem Symbolism: Kunz, 81]
11. **kolem** rice designs drawn to attract guardianship of gods. [Hinduism: Binder, 61]
12. **magic flute** Tamino's guard against black magic. [Ger. Opera: Mozart, *Magic Flute*, Westerman, 102–104]
13. **malachite** guards wearer from evil spirits, enchantments. [Gem Symbolism: Kunz, 97]
14. **mark of Cain** God's safeguard for Cain from potential slayers. [O.T.: Genesis 4:15]
15. **moly** herb given by Hermes to Odysseus to ward off Circe's spells. [Gk. Myth.: *Odyssey*]
16. **rowan** ash tree which guards against fairies and witches. [Br. Folklore: Briggs, 344]
17. **St. Benedict's cross** charm against disease and danger. [Christian Iconog.: Jobes, 386]
18. **St. Christopher medal** to protect travelers. [Christian Hist.: *NCE*, 552]
19. **St. John's wort** defense against fairies, evil spirits, the Devil. [Br. Folklore: Briggs, 335–336]

20. **sard** guards against incantations and sorcery. [Gem Symbolism: Kunz, 107]
21. **serpentine** guards against bites of venomous creatures. [Gem Symbolism: Kunz, 108]
22. **wood** knocking on it averts dire consequences. [Western Culture: Misc.]

530. PROTECTIVENESS (See also GUARDIANSHIP.)

1. **Adams, Parson Abraham** bookish, unworldly protector of the weak and innocent. [Br. Lit.: *Joseph Andrews*]
2. **Darius** (d. 486 B.C.) Persian king; permits and guarantees rebuilding of temple. [O.T.: Ezra 6:6–12]
3. **Douglas, the Widow** caretaker of Huck Finn. [Am. Lit.: *Huckleberry Finn*]
4. **Epona (Bubona)** goddess; watched over cattle and horses. [Rom. Myth.: Kravitz, 90]
5. **Evelyn, Aunt** uses influence to keep nephew from war front. [Br. Lit.: *Memoirs of an Infantry Officer,* Magill I, 579–581]
6. **Genevieve, St.** saved Paris from marauders by intercession. [Christian Hagiog.: Attwater, 147]
7. **Hendon, Miles** disinherited knight takes urchin-prince under wing. [Am. Lit.: *The Prince and the Pauper*]
8. **Ida** nymph who guarded infant Zeus from being eaten by father, Cronus. [Gk. Myth.: Zimmerman, 134]
9. **Jehosheba** secretes future king, Joash, from Athaliah's slaughter. [O.T.: II Kings 11:2; II Chronicles 22:11]
10. **Knights Templar** society formed to guard pilgrims to Jerusalem. [Medieval Hist.: Brewer *Dictionary,* 1066]
11. **Kuan Yin** protectress of fishermen and housemaids. [Buddhism: Binder, 42]
12. **Magwitch, Abel** saved by Pip; dedicates himself to Pip's future. [Br. Lit.: *Great Expectations*]
13. **Mannering, Guy** paternal helper of friend's daughter and tutor. [Br. Lit.: *Guy Mannering*]
14. **Michael, St.** guardian archangel. [O.T.: Daniel 10:13, 21; 12:1]
15. **Nicholas, St.** protector of sailors; patron saint of schoolboys. [Christian Hagiog.: Brewster, 12–13]
16. **Old Yeller** friend and watchdog assumes houndly nobility. [Am. Cinema: *Disney Films,* 145–146]
17. **Palladium** colossal statue whose presence insured Troy's safety. [Rom. Legend: Brewer *Dictionary,* 796]

18. **Quasimodo** creature hides Esmeralda in sanctuary to save her. [Fr. Lit.: *The Hunchback of Notre Dame*]
19. **Rahab** conceals two Israelite spies from Jericho authorities. [O.T.: Joshua 2:2–6]
20. **ravens** during drought, Elijah is fed by them. [O.T.: I Kings 17:1–6]
21. **Secret Service** provides security for U.S. presidents. [Am. Hist.: *NCE,* 2466]
22. **Swiss Guard** traditional papal escort. [Rom. Cath. Hist.: Brewer *Dictionary*]
23. **Wells Fargo** armored carriers of bullion. [Am. Hist.: Brewer *Dictionary,* 1147]

531. PRUDENCE

1. **five wise virgins** brought lamp oil in case groom arrived late. [N.T.: Matthew 25:1–13]
2. **jacinth** endows owner with discretion. [Gem Symbolism: Kunz, 82]
3. **Metis** goddess of caution and discretion. [Rom. Myth.: Wheeler, 242]
4. **mountain ash** symbol of prudence. [Tree Symbolism: *Flora Symbolica,* 176]

532. PRUDERY

1. **Grundy, Mrs.** Ashfields' straitlaced neighbor whose propriety hinders them. [Br. Lit.: *Speed the Plough*]
2. **nice Nelly** excessively modest or prudish woman. [Am. Usage: Misc.]
3. **Quakers** pacifist religious sect, often associated with puritanical behavioral standards. [Am. Hist.: *NCE,* 1017]
4. **Shakers** sect believing in virgin purity. [Christian Hist.: Brewer *Note-book,* 819]
5. **Victorian** one reflecting an unshaken confidence in piety and temperance, as during Queen Victoria's reign. [Am. and Br. Usage: Misc.]

533. PUGILISM

1. **Balboa, Rocky** lower-class Philadelphia boxer wins golden opportunity to fight in prize bout. [Am. Cinema: *Rocky*]
2. **Byron, Cashel** prizefighter; gives up boxing for wealthy lady. [Br. Lit.: *Cashel Byron's Profession*]
3. **Dares** one of Aeneas's companions; noted for his boxing skill. [Rom. Lit.: *Aeneid*]

4. **Entellus** powerful Sicilian boxer; won match for Anchises against Dares. [Rom. Lit.: *Aeneid*]
5. **Eryx** great boxer; killed at own game by challenger, Hercules. [Gk. Myth.: Howe, 97]
6. **Golden Boy** violinist turns boxer for fame, wealth. [Am. Lit.: *Golden Boy*]
7. **Great White Hope** 1910 personification of white peoples' aspirations for a white heavyweight champion. [Am. Hist.: Misc.]
8. **Palooka, Joe** comicdom's great white hope. [Comics: Horn, 343–344]
9. **Queensberry, Marquis of** (Sir John Douglas, 1844–1900) established basic rules of boxing. [Br. Hist.: *NCE,* 2257]

534. PUNCTUALITY

1. **Fogg, Phileas** completes world circuit at exact minute he wagered he would. [Fr. Lit.: *Around the World in Eighty Days*]
2. **Gilbreths** disciplined family brought up to abide by strict, punctual standards. [Am. Lit.: *Cheaper by the Dozen*]
3. **Jones, Casey** legendary railroad engineer; crashes in attempt to arrive in "Frisco" on time. [Am. Folklore: Hart, 431]
4. **Linkinwater, Tim** "punctual as the Counting House Dial." [Br. Lit.: *Nicholas Nickleby*]
5. **Old Faithful** well-known geyser in Yellowstone Park; erupts every 64.5 minutes. [Am. Hist.: *NCE,* 3023]

535. PUNISHMENT (See also TORTURE, TRANSFORMATION.)

1. **Abijah** Jeroboam's child; taken by God for father's wickedness. [O.T.: I Kings 14:12]
2. **Adam** condemned to survive by sweat of brow. [O.T.: Genesis 3:19]
3. **Amfortas** sinful life led to perpetual suffering. [Arth. Legend: Walsh *Classical,* 20; Ger. Opera: *Parsifal*]
4. **Ammit** half-hippopotamus, half-lion monster of underworld; ate the sinful. [Egyptian Myth.: Leach, 50]
5. **Ashura** land of punishment for those who die angry. [Jap. Myth.: Jobes, 140]
6. **Atlas** Titan condemned to bear world on shoulders. [Gk. Myth.: Walsh *Classical,* 38]
7. **Battus** Arcadian shepherd who revealed Mercury's theft of sheep; he was punished by being turned to stone. [Gk. and Rom. Myth.: Walsh *Classical,* 71]

8. **Born, Bertrand de** Dante has him carry his head as lantern. [Ital. Lit.: *Inferno;* Walsh *Classical,* 55]
9. **Cambyses** had a venal judge put to death and the body skinned as covering for his judgment seat. [Gk. Hist.: Herodotus in Magill III, 479]
10. **Dirae** the Furies; punished crimes and avenged wrongs. [Gk. Myth.: Kravitz, 82, 91–92]
11. **Don Juan** for murder, devoured by fire. [Span. Lit.: Benét, 279; Ger. Opera: Mozart, *Don Giovanni,* Westerman, 95]
12. **Erinyes (Furies)** three sisters who pursue those guilty of blood crimes and drive them mad. [Gk. Myth.: Benét, 320]
13. **Eve** for disobeying God, would suffer in childbirth. [O.T.: Genesis 3:16]
14. **flood** for his evilness, man perishes by inundation. [O.T.: Genesis 6: 5–8; 7:4]
15. **Herod Agrippa I** was eaten by worms for playing god. [N.T.: Acts 12:23]
16. **Herodias** lived for nineteen centuries as punishment for her crime against John the Baptist. [Fr. Lit.: Eugène Sue *The Wandering Jew*]
17. **iron maiden** hollow iron figure in the shape of a woman, lined with spikes that impaled the enclosed victim. [Ger. Hist.: Brewer *Dictionary*, 491]
18. **Ixion** Thessalian king bound to fiery wheel by Zeus. [Gk. and Rom. Myth.: Zimmerman, 142; Rom. Lit.: *Metamorphoses*]
19. **Laocoön** Trojan priest offends Athena, is strangled to death by two sea serpents. [Gk. Myth.: Benét, 565]
20. **Nadab and Abihu** destroyed by God for offering Him "alien fire." [O.T.: Leviticus 10:1–3]
21. **Papageno** for lying, has mouth padlocked. [Ger. Opera: Mozart, *The Magic Flute,* Westerman, 102–104]
22. **Peeping Tom** struck blind for peeping at Lady Godiva. [Br. Legend: Brewer *Dictionary*, 403]
23. **plagues on Egypt** God visits Egypt with plagues and epidemics to show his power. [O.T.: Exodus 8, 12]
24. **Prometheus** for rebelliousness, chained to rock; vulture fed on his liver which grew back daily. [Rom. Myth.: Zimmerman, 221–222]
25. **Prynne, Hester** pilloried and sentenced to wear a scarlet "A" for her sin of adultery. [Am. Lit.: *The Scarlet Letter*]

26. **Sisyphus** condemned in Hades to roll boulder uphill which would immediately roll down again. [Gk. Myth.: Zimmerman, 244; Gk. Lit.: *Odyssey;* Rom. Lit.: *Aeneid*]
27. **Tantalus** for his crimes, sentenced to Hades to be within reach of water he cannot drink. [Gk. Myth.: Zimmerman, 253; Gk. Lit.: *Odyssey*]
28. **Tell, William** ordered to shoot apple placed on son's head for refusing to salute governor's hat. [Ger. Lit.: *William Tell;* Ital. Opera: Rossini, *William Tell;* Westerman, 121–122]
29. **Thyestes** unknowingly eats sons served by vengeful brother. [Rom. Lit.: *Thyestes*]
30. **Tyburn tree** site of the London gibbet. [Br. Hist.: Espy, 169]
31. **Vale of Achor** site of lapidation of Achan, Israelite troublemaker. [O.T.: Joshua 7:24–26]
32. **Vathek** condemned to eternal flames for seeking forbidden knowledge. [Br. Lit.: Beckford *Vathek*]

536. PURIFICATION

1. **Circe** purified Jason and Medea after their murder of Apsyrtus. [Gk. Myth.: Benét, 201]

537. PURITANISM

1. **Alden, Oliver** too inhibited by his puritanical background to enjoy the normal life of a young man. [Am. Lit.: Santayana *The Last Puritan* in Magill I, 497]
2. **Brother Jonathan** 17th-century British nickname for Puritans. [Am. Hist.: Hart, 110]
3. **Brush, George Marvin** strait-laced salesman tries to impose his rules of conduct on others. [Am. Lit.: Wilder *Heaven's My Destination* in Magill I, 357]

538. PURITY (See also MODESTY.)

1. **almond** symbol of the Virgin Mary's innocence. [O.T.: Numbers 17: 1–11; Art: Hall, 14]
2. **crystal** its transparency symbolizes pureness. [Folklore: Jobes, 391]
3. **Galahad, Sir** sole knight who could sit in siege perilous. [Br. Lit.: *Le Morte d'Arthur; Idylls of the King*]
4. **Ivory soap** 99.44% pure. [Trademarks: Crowley *Trade,* 289]
5. **Karamazov, Alyosha** pure at heart, with compassion for his erring and tortured family. [Russ. Lit.: Dostoevsky *The Brothers Karamazov*]

6. **lily** emblematic of the Blessed Virgin Mary. [Christian Symbolism: Appleton, 39]
7. **long unbound hair** custom for unmarried women, virgin saints, brides. [Art: Hall, 144]
8. **sedge** used as symbol of purity in da Vinci paintings. [Plant Symbolism: Embolden, 25]
9. **snow** "pure as the driven snow." [Western Folklore: Misc.]
10. **Star of Bethlehem** indicates pureness. [Flower Symbolism: *Flora Symbolica,* 183]
11. **Virgin Mary** immaculately conceived; mother of Jesus Christ. [N.T.: Matthew 1:18–25; 12:46–50; Luke 1:26–56; 11:27–28; John 2; 19:25–27]
12. **water** archetypal symbol. [Christian Symbolism: Appleton, 109]
13. **water-lily** symbol of innocence of heart; flower of July. [Flower Symbolism: *Flora Symbolica,* 178; Kunz, 329]
14. **white** symbol of virginity; in American flag, purity. [Color Symbolism: Leach, 242]

Q

539. QUACKERY

1. **barber-surgeon** inferior doctor; formerly a barber performing dentistry and surgery. [Medicine: Misc.]
2. **Dulcamara, Dr.** offered bad burgundy as panacea for lovelessness. [Ital. Opera: Donizetti, *Elixir of Love; EB,* 5: 953–954]
3. **Rezio, Dr.** Baratarian court physician; practically starves Sancho Panza in the interest of diet. [Span. Lit.: *Don Quixote*]
4. **Rock, Dr. Richard** fat, 18th-century quack; professed to cure every imaginable disease. [Br. Hist.: Brewer *Handbook,* 888]
5. **Sangrado, Dr.** ignorant physician; believed blood not necessary for life. [Fr. Lit.: *Gil Blas*]
6. **Walker, Dr.** great 18th-century quack, forever advising against disreputable doctors. [Br. Hist.: Brewer *Handbook,* 888]

540. QUARRY

1. **Cerynean stag** captured by Hercules as third Labor. [Gk. and Rom. Myth.: Hall, 149]
2. **Cretan bull** savage bull caught by Hercules as seventh Labor. [Gk. and Rom. Myth.: Hall, 149]
3. **Erymanthian boar** Hercules' fourth Labor: to take this ravaging beast alive. [Gk. and Rom. Myth.: Hall, 149]
4. **fetching Cerberus** Hercules' twelfth Labor: capture the Hadean watchdog. [Gk. and Rom. Myth.: Hall, 150]
5. **Moby Dick** pursued by Ahab and crew of *Pequod.* [Am. Lit.: *Moby Dick*]
6. **Nemean lion** awesome beast strangled by Hercules as first Labor. [Gk. and Rom. Myth.: Hall, 148]
7. **Old Ben** great bear; subject of annual quest by mature men. [Am. Lit.: *The Bear* in *Six Modern Short Novels*]
8. **oxen of Geryon** captured after tremendous obstacles overcome; Hercules' tenth Labor. [Gk. and Rom. Myth.: Hall, 149]
9. **snark** elusive imaginary animal. [Br. Lit.: *The Hunting of the Snark*]
10. **Wolfman** metamorphosed man hunted down by armed men as wild beast. [Am. Lit.: *Wolfman*]

541. QUEST (See also ADVENTUROUSNESS, JOURNEY, WANDERING.)

1. **Ahab, Captain** pursues Moby Dick, the great white whale, even to the point of losing his own life. [Am. Lit.: Melville *Moby Dick*]
2. ***Argo*** Jason's galley, on which the Argonauts sailed in search of the Golden Fleece. [Gk. Myth.: Benét, 47]
3. **Dorothy** young girl, lost in dream world, follows the Yellow Brick Road to find the Wizard of Oz. [Am. Lit.: *The Wonderful Wizard of Oz*]
4. **El Dorado** mythical land of gold treasures, object of Spanish expeditions. [Am. Hist.: Jameson, 159]
5. **Golden Fleece** pelt of winged ram sought by Jason and Argonauts. [Rom. Legend: Zimmerman, 113]
6. **grail** its pursuit is central theme of some Arthurian romances. [Br. Lit.: *Le Morte d'Arthur*]
7. **Hippolyta, girdle of** secured after fight with Amazon queen; Hercules' ninth Labor. [Gk. and Rom. Myth.: Hall, 149]
8. **Knights of the Round Table** set out to find the Holy Grail. [Br. Lit.: *Le Morte d'Arthur*]
9. **Pequod** ship in which Captain Ahab pursued the great white whale. [Am. Lit.: Melville *Moby Dick*]
10. **Ponce de León, Juan** (c. 1460–1521) Spanish explorer; sought the fountain of youth. [Span. Hist.: *NCE*, 2188]
11. **Santiago** old fisherman in search of marlin. [Am. Lit.: *The Old Man and the Sea*]
12. **Siege Perilous** a seat at King Arthur's Round Table for the knight destined to find the Holy Grail; it was fatal to any other occupant. [Br. Lit.: *Morte d'Arthur*; Benét, 929]
13. **Sohrab** young warrior looks everywhere for the father he has never known. [Br. Poetry: Arnold "Sohrab and Rustum"]
14. **Telemachus** relentlessly searches for father, Odysseus. [Gk. Lit.: *Odyssey*]

R

542. RANTING (See also ANGER, EXASPERATION, IRASCIBILITY.)

1. **Boiler, Boanerges** a zealous, raving preacher. [Br. Lit.: *The Uncommercial Traveller*]
2. **Gantry, Elmer** fire-breathing, hypocritical preacher. [Am. Lit.: *Elmer Gantry*]
3. **Howler, Rev. Melchisedech** ranting loudmouth. [Br. Lit.: *Dombey and Son*]

543. RAPE

1. **Amphissa** blinded by father Echetus for having been raped by Aechmodius. [Gk. Myth.: Howe, 23]
2. **Apemosyne** raped by Hermes; killed by brother for immorality. [Gk. Myth.: Zimmerman, 25]
3. **Arne** blinded by stepfather Desmontes after he learned she had been raped and was pregnant. [Gk. Myth.: Howe, 39]
4. **Aziz, Dr.** accused of attempted rape but acquitted when his supposed victim realizes she must have been hallucinating. [Br. Lit.: Forster *Passage to India* in Magill I, 713]
5. **Belinda** violated tonsorially. [Br. Lit.: *The Rape of the Lock*]
6. **Caenis** changed into a man by Poseidon after he raped her. [Gk. Myth.: Zimmerman, 46]
7. **Cassandra** raped by Ajax the Less on the night Troy fell. [Gk. Myth.: Brewer *Dictionary*, 17]
8. **Creusa** raped by Apollo; bore Janus. [Gk. Myth.: Kravitz, 68]
9. **Cunegonde** ravished in her father's castle by two Bulgarian soldiers. [Fr. Lit.: *Candide*]
10. **Danaë** Zeus raped her, posing as a golden shower. [Gk. Myth.: Kravitz, 74]
11. **Drake, Temple** provocative co-ed whose actions invite the rape she both fears and desires. [Am. Lit.: Faulkner *Sanctuary*]
12. **Elvira** peasant girl raped by lusting nobleman. [Span. Lit.: *The King, the Greatest Alcalde*]
13. **Europa** seduced by Jupiter as bull; raped when he changes back. [Rom. Lit.: *Metamorphoses;* Gk. Myth.: Hall, 259]
14. **Lavinia** raped and mutilated by Demetrius and Chiron. [Br. Lit.: *Titus Andronicus*]
15. **Leda** raped by Zeus in form of swan. [Class. Myth.: Zimmerman, 149; Rom. Lit.: *Metamorphoses;* Br. Lit.: *Faerie Queene*]

16. **Lucretia** blackmailed into sex by despicable Sextus; commits suicide afterwards. [Rom. Lit.: *Fasti; Livy;* Br. Lit.: "The Rape of Lucrece"; Art: Hall, 259]
17. **Philomela** raped by Tereus, who cut out her tongue to prevent her from revealing the act. [Gk. Myth.: Benét, 783]
18. **Tamar** raped by her half-brother, Amnon. [O.T.: II Samuel 13:11–14]

544. RASHNESS

1. **Charge of the Light Brigade** ill-advised British assault at Balaklava, Crimea (1854). [Br. Hist.: Harbottle, 25]
2. **Gilpin, John** rides uncontrollably on fresh steed. [Br. Lit.: *John Gilpin's Ride*]
3. **Icarus** artificial wings destroyed by flying too close to sun. [Gk. Myth.: Kravitz, 126]
4. **Lear** headstrong and "full of changes." [Br. Lit.: *King Lear*]
5. **Uzzah** rashly grabs for Ark of Covenant, a transgression. [O.T.: II Samuel 6:6–8]

545. REBELLION

1. **Absalom** conspires to overthrow father, David. [O.T.: II Samuel 15:10–18:33]
2. **Bastille Day** celebration of day Paris mob stormed prison; first outbreak of French Revolution (1789). [Fr. Hist.: *EB,* I: 866]
3. **Beer Hall Putsch** early, aborted Nazi coup (1923). [Ger. Hist.: *Hitler,* 198–241]
4. **Boston Tea Party** irate colonists, dressed as Indians, pillage three British ships (1773). [Am. Hist.: Jameson, 58, 495]
5. **Boxer Rebellion** xenophobic Chinese Taoist faction rebelled against foreign intruders (1900). [Chinese Hist.: Parrinder, 50]
6. ***Caine Mutiny, The*** sailors seize command from the pathological and incompetent Capt. Queeg. [Am. Lit.: Wouk *The Caine Mutiny* in Benét, 157]
7. **Christian, Fletcher** (fl. late 18th century) leader of mutinous sailors against Captain Bligh (1789). [Am. Lit.: *Mutiny on the Bounty*]
8. **Easter Rising** unsuccessful Irish revolt against British (1916). [Irish Hist.: *EB,* III: 760–761]
9. **Gunpowder Plot** Guy Fawkes's aborted plan to blow up British House of Commons (1605). [Br. Hist.: *NCE,* 1165]
10. **Harpers Ferry** scene of Brown's aborted slave uprising. [Am. Hist.: John Jameson, 220]

11. **Hungarian Revolt** iron-curtain country futilely resisted Soviet domination (1956). [Eur. Hist.: Van Doren, 553]
12. **Jacquerie** French peasant revolt, brutally carried out and suppressed (1358). [Fr. Hist.: Bishop, 372–373]
13. **Jeroboam** with God's sanction, establishes hegemony over ten tribes of Israel. [O.T.: I Kings 11:31–35]
14. **Korah** rose up against Moses; slain by Jehovah. [O.T.: Numbers 16:1–3]
15. **Kralich, Ivan** fugitive from Turkish law; firebrand for Bulgarian independence of Ottoman rule. [Bulgarian Lit.: *Under the Yoke*]
16. ***Mutiny on the Bounty*** activities of mutineers, Captain Bligh, island wanderings (1789). [Am. Lit.: *Mutiny on the Bounty*]
17. **Peasants' Revolt, the** English villeins' attempt to improve their lot (1381). [Br. Hist.: Bishop, 220–221, 373–374]
18. **Pilot, the** Mr. Gray successfully carries out many assignments for the rebels and thwarts the British [Am. Lit.: Cooper *The Pilot*]
19. **Sepoy Rebellion** Indian soldiers' uprising against British rule in India (1857–1858). [Br. Hist.: *NCE*, 1328]
20. **Sheba** led an aborted revolt against King David. [O.T.: II Samuel 20: 1–2]
21. **Spina, Pietro** returns from exile disguised as a priest and engages in antifascist activities. [Ital. Lit.: *Bread and Wine*]

546. REBELLIOUSNESS

1. **Caulfield, Holden** schoolboy at odds with a "phoney" society. [Am. Lit.: *The Catcher in the Rye*]
2. **Dedalus, Stephen** "heretical" youth rebels against Irish politics and religion. [Irish Lit.: *Portrait of the Artist as a Young Man*]
3. **Finn, Huckleberry** unconventional and resourceful runaway boy. [Am. Lit.: *Huckleberry Finn*]
4. **Maheu, Vincent** peaceful coalminer forced into striking for justice. [Fr. Lit.: *Germinal*]
5. **Satan (Lucifer)** the Devil; cast from heaven for rebelling against God. [O.T.: Isaiah 14:12; N.T.: Revelation 12:7–9; Br. Lit.: *Paradise Lost*]
6. **Scales, Sophia Baines** announcing her desire to be a teacher causes shock (1864). [Br. Lit.: *The Old Wives' Tale*, Magill I, 684–686]

Recognition (See **IDENTIFICATION.**)

547. REDHEADEDNESS

1. **Cortés, Hernando** (1485–1547) conquistador received by Montezuma as god because of height and red hair. [Mex. Hist.: *NCE,* 662]
2. **Esau** Isaac's son. [O.T.: Genesis 25:25]
3. **Judas Iscariot** so depicted in art. [Christian Icon.: Gaster, 165]
4. **Little Orphan Annie** heroine of comic strip. [Comics: Horn, 459]
5. **Red-Headed League, the** non-existent club used to draw a redhead away from where he could interfere with a bank robbery. [Br. Lit.: "The Red-Headed League" in *Sherlock Holmes*]

548. REFORMED, THE

1. **Arkadi** turns from the idea of obtaining power through wealth to a less materialistic goal. [Russ. Lit.: Benét, 843]
2. **Hal, Prince** transformation from rakish prince to responsible king. [Br. Lit.: *II Henry IV*]
3. **Knave of Hearts** vowed he'd steal no more tarts. [Nurs. Rhyme: Baring-Gould, 152]
4. **La Sacristaine** repents of sin and rejoins convent. [Medieval Legend: Walsh *Classical,* 48]
5. **Moses the Black, St.** rascally thief; converted, became ordained priest. [Christian Hagiog.: Attwater, 247–248]
6. **Saul** becomes Christian proselytizer after Lord's visitation. [N.T.: Acts 9:1–22]
7. **Scrooge, Ebenezer** Christmas becomes a merry affair when he abandons his miserliness. [Br. Lit.: *A Christmas Carol*]
8. **Thaïs** Alexandrian courtesan; converted to Christianity. [Medieval Legend: Walsh *Classical,* 307]
9. **Vinicus** lustful Roman becomes devout Christian. [Polish Lit.: *Quo Vadis,* Magill I, 797–799]

549. REFORMERS

1. **Kennicott, Carol** idealist of social reform, especially village improvement. [Am. Lit.: *Main Street*]
2. **Luther, Martin** (1483–1546) German leader of the Protestant Reformation. [Ger. Hist.: *NCE,* 1631]

550. REFUGE (See also CONCEALMENT.)

1. **Adullam** cave where David hid from Saul. [O.T.: I Samuel 22:1]
2. **Alsatia (white friars)** London monastery; former refuge for lawless characters. [Br. Hist.: Walsh *Modern*, 15]
3. **Bezer-in-the-wilderness** one of the appointed cities of sanctuary for unintentional murderers. [O.T.: Joshua 20:8]
4. **Golan** appointed city of sanctuary for unintentional murderers. [O.T.: Joshua 20:8]
5. **Kedesh** city of sanctuary for unintentional murderers. [O.T.: Joshua 20:7]
6. **Kiriath-arba** city of sanctuary for unintentional murderers. [O.T.: Joshua 20:7]
7. **Noah's Ark** preserves Noah's family and animals from flood. [O.T.: Genesis 6:7–9]
8. **Ramoth** city of sanctuary for unintentional murderers. [O.T.: Joshua 20:8]
9. **Schechem** city of sanctuary for unintentional murderers. [O.T.: Joshua 20:7]

551. REGRET (See also REMORSE.)

1. **Epimetheus** Pandora's husband; regretted opening box. [Gk. Myth.: Kravitz, 90]
2. **Hale, Nathan** (1755–1776) American Revolutionary spy, hanged by British; regretted only having one life to give for country. [Am. Hist.: *NCE*, 1176]
3. **Moses** led his people to threshold of promised land but could not enter. [O.T.: Deuteronomy 34:1–4]
4. **Nebo, Mt.** from which Moses views promised land he cannot enter. [O.T.: Deuteronomy 34:1–4]
5. **raspberry** symbol of regret and grief. [Flower Symbolism: *Flora Symbolica*, 177]

552. REINCARNATION

1. **Dalai Lama** attains his position at birth by absorbing the spirit of his dying predecessor. [Buddhism: *NCE*, 2745 (Tibetan Buddhism)]

553. REJUVENATION

1. **Aeson** in extreme old age, restored to youth by Medea. [Rom. Myth.: *LLEI*, I: 322]

2. **apples of perpetual youth** by tasting the golden apples kept by Idhunn, the gods preserved their youth. [Scand. Myth.: Brewer *Dictionary*, 41]
3. **Bimini** Bahamas island whose fountain conferred eternal youth. [Western Folklore: Brewer *Dictionary*, 373]
4. **Dithyrambus** epithet of Dionysus, in allusion to his double birth. [Gk. Myth.: Zimmerman, 88]
5. **Faust** rejuvenated by Mephistopheles at the price of his soul. [Ger. Lit.: Goethe *Faust*]
6. **Fountain of Youth** fabulous fountain believed to restore youth to the aged. [Western Folklore: Brewer *Handbook*, 389]
7. **Heidegger, Dr.** gives his aged friends water drawn from the Fountain of Youth, but its effects are temporary. [Am. Lit.: Hawthorne "Dr. Heidegger's Experiment" in Hart, 229]
8. **Ogier the Dane** hero at the age of 100 restored to ripe manhood by Morgan le Fay. [Medieval Romance: Brewer *Dictionary*, 656]
9. **sage** a rejuvenator; said to stop gray hair. [Herb Symbolism: *Flora Symbolica*, 165]

554. REMORSE (See also REGRET.)

1. ***Ayenbite of Inwit (Remorse of Conscience)*** Middle English version of medieval moral treatise, c. 1340. [Br. Lit.: Barnhart, 74]
2. **Deianira** commits suicide out of remorse for unwittingly having killed husband, Hercules. [Gk. Myth.: Benét, 709]
3. **Hermione** commits suicide upon the funeral pyre of her beloved Pyrrhus for having instigated his murder. [Fr. Drama: Racine *Andromaque*]
4. **Jocasta** commits suicide when she realizes she has married son, Oedipus. [Gk. Lit.: *Oedipus Rex*]
5. **Lord Jim** tormented by his memory of having saved himself from a sinking ship with 800 Muslims aboard. [Br. Lit.: Joseph Conrad *Lord Jim* in Magill I, 522]
6. **Manfred** magician, living alone in an Alpine castle, broods on his alienation from mankind and on his destruction of the woman he loved. [Br. Poetry: Byron "Manfred"]
7. **Mannon, Orin** crazed by guilt for inciting mother's suicide. [Am. Lit.: *Mourning Becomes Electra*]
8. **Oedipus** blinds self upon learning of his crimes. [Gk. Lit.: *Oedipus Rex*]
9. **Othello** commits suicide from guilt for wife's murder. [Br. Lit.: *Othello*]

555. REMOTENESS (See also ISOLATION.)

1. **Antarctica** continent surrounding South Pole. [Geography: *NCE,* 113–115]
2. **Dan to Beersheba** from one outermost extreme to another. [O.T.: Judges 20:1]
3. **Darkest Africa** in European and American imaginations, a faraway land of no return. [Western Folklore: Misc.]
4. **end of the rainbow** the unreachable end of the earth. [Western Folklore: Misc.]
5. **Everest, Mt.** Nepalese peak; highest elevation in world (29,028 ft.). [Geography: *NCE,* 907]
6. **Great Divide** great ridge of Rocky Mountains; once thought of as epitome of faraway place. [Am. Folklore: Misc.]
7. **John O'Groat's House** traditionally thought of as the northernmost, remote point of Britain. [Geography: Misc.]
8. **Land's End** the southwestern tip of Britain. [Geography: Misc.]
9. **moon** earth's satellite; unreachable until 1969. [Astronomy: *NCE,* 1824]
10. **North and South Poles** figurative ends of the earth. [Geography: Misc.]
11. **Outer Mongolia** desert wasteland between Russia and China; figuratively and literally remote. [Geography: Misc.]
12. **Pago Pago** capital of American Samoa in South Pacific; thought of as a remote spot. [Geography: Misc.]
13. **Pillars of Hercules** promontories at the sides of Straits of Gibraltar; once the limit of man's travel. [Gk. Myth.: Zimmerman, 110]
14. **Siberia** frozen land in northeastern U.S.S.R.; place of banishment and exile. [Russ. Hist.: *NCE,* 2510]
15. **Tierra del Fuego** archipelago off the extreme southern tip of South America. [Geography: Misc.]
16. **Timbuktu** figuratively, the end of the earth. [Am. Usage: *NCE,* 2749]
17. **Ultima Thule** to Romans, extremity of the world, identified with Iceland. [Rom. Legend: *LLEI,* I: 318]
18. **Yukon** northwestern Canadian territory touching on the Arctic Ocean. [Geography: Misc.]

Repentance (See **PENITENCE.**)

Reproof (See **CRITICISM.**)

556. RESCUE

1. **Abishai** saves David from death by Benob. [O.T.: II Samuel 21:17]
2. **Andromeda** saved by Perseus from sea monster. [Gk. Myth: Hall, 239; Rom. Lit.: *Metamorphoses*]
3. **Ararat** traditional resting place of Noah's ark after the Flood. [O.T.: Genesis 8:4]
4. **Arion** thrown overboard; carried safely to land by dolphins. [Gk. Myth.: *LLEI,* I: 323; Br. Lit.: *Faerie Queene*]
5. **Barry** St. Bernard dog; saved over 40 snowbound people in Alps. [Swiss Hist.: Wallechinsky, 126]
6. **Charlotte** spider that saves Wilbur the pig from slaughter. [Am. Lit.: E. B. White *Charlotte's Web*]
7. **Deucalion** survived Zeus's flood in ark. [Gk. Myth.: Zimmerman, 85]
8. **Diana's statue** saved by Orestes from Scythian thieves. [Gk. Lit.: *Iphigenia in Tauris*]
9. **Dunkirk** combined military-civilian operation rescued 340,000 British troops (1940). [Br. Hist.: Van Doren, 475]
10. **Entebbe** daring Israeli raid freed airline hostages at Ugandan airport (1977). [World Hist.: *Facts* (1977), 487]
11. **Hercules** rescues Alcestis from Hades after her self-sacrifice. [Gk. Lit.: *Alcestis;* Ger. Opera: Gluck, *Alceste,* Westerman, 73–75]
12. **Iphigenia** rescued at the moment of her sacrificial stabbing. [Gk. Myth.: Gayley, 80–81]
13. **Isaac** "saved" from being sacrificed by angel of the Lord. [O.T.: Genesis 22:2–13]
14. **Jonah** saved from drowning in belly of great fish. [O.T.: Jonah 1:17]
15. **Macheath** saved from hanging by the king's reprieve. [Ger. Opera: Weill, *Threepenny Opera,* Westerman, 497]
16. **Mignon** rescued by Wilhelm Meister from gypsies. [Fr. Opera: Thomas, *Mignon,* Westerman, 187]
17. **Noah** with his sons, deemed by God worth saving from His destructive flood. [O.T.: Genesis 6–10]
18. **Rahab and family** spared from Jericho's destruction for aid rendered to Joshua's army. [O.T.: Joshua 6:25]

19. **Sanang** used magic powers to rescue Marco Polo. [Irish Lit.: *Messer Marco Polo,* Magill I, 584–585]
20. **Tinker Bell** fairy saved by the faith of the audience after she drinks a lethal potion. [Br. Drama: J. M. Barrie *Peter Pan* in Magill II, 820]
21. **oak leaves** used in crown awarded to one who saves a life. [Rom. Tradition: Wheeler, 765]

557. RESOURCEFULNESS

1. **Buck** clever and temerarious dog perseveres in the Klondike. [Am. Lit.: *Call of the Wild*]
2. **Crichton, Admirable** butler proves to be infinite resource for castaway family on island. [Br. Lit.: *The Admirable Crichton*]
3. **Crusoe, Robinson** inventive when shipwrecked on an island. [Br. Lit.: *Robinson Crusoe*]
4. **duck** from ingeniousness of duck in .eluding enemies. [Heraldry: Halberts, 26]
5. **Fogg, Phileas** burns his boat's superstructure and decks for fuel and thus reaches London on time. [Fr. Lit.: Jules Verne *Around the World in Eighty Days*]
6. **Swiss Family Robinson** shipwrecked family carves hospitable life from wilderness. [Children's Lit.: *Swiss Family Robinson*]
7. **Thoreau, Henry David** (1817–1862) example of man's ability to build his own life in the wilderness. [Am. Hist.: *NCE,* 2738]

558. RESURRECTION

1. **Adonis** vegetation god, reborn each spring. [Gk. Myth.: Benét, 10]
2. **Alcestis** after dying in place of her husband, she is brought back from the dead by Heracles. [Gk. Drama: *Alcestis*]
3. **Amys and Amyloun** sacrificed children are restored to life. [Medieval Legend: Benét, 31]
4. **Bran** god whose cauldron restored the dead to life. [Welsh Myth.: Jobes, 241]
5. **Dorcas** raised from the dead by St. Peter. [N.T.: Acts 9:36–42]
6. **Drusiana** restored to life by John the Evangelist. [Christian Hagiog.: *Golden Legend*]
7. **Dumuzi** god of regeneration and resurrection. [Sumerian Myth.: Jobes, 476]
8. **egg** symbol of Christ's resurrection. [Art: Hall, 110]
9. **Elijah** breathes life back into child. [O.T.: I Kings 17:18]

10. **Fisher King** old, maimed king whose restoration symbolizes the return of spring vegetation. [Medieval Legend: T. S. Eliot *The Waste Land* in Norton *Literature*]
11. **Jairus' daughter** Christ raises her from the dead. [N.T.: Matthew 9:18–19; Mark 5:21–24; Luke 8:40–42]
12. **Jesus Christ** arose from the dead three days after His crucifixion. [N.T.: Matthew 28; Mark 16; Luke 24; John 20]
13. **Lazarus** Jesus calls him back to life from the tomb. [N.T.: John 11:43–44]
14. **McGee, Sam** Tennessee native freezes to death in Alaska but is brought back to life in the cremation furnace. [Am. Poetry: Service "The Cremation of Sam McGee"]
15. **phoenix** fabled bird, rises from its ashes. [Gk. Legend: Brewer *Dictionary,* 829; Christian Symbolism: Appleton, 76]
16. **pomegranate** bursting with seed, it symbolizes open tomb. [Christian Symbolism: Appleton, 77]
17. **scarab** symbol for Ra, sun-god; reborn each day. [Animal Symbolism: Mercatante, 180]
18. **Thammuz** god died annually and rose each spring. [Babyl. Myth.: Brewer *Dictionary,* 1071]
19. **widow's son of Nain** touched by mother's grief, Christ brings him back to life. [N.T.: Luke 7:11–17]

559. REUNION

1. **Arafat, Mt.** Adam and Eve met here after 200 years. [Muslim Legend: Benét, 44]
2. **chickweed** flower symbolizing a rejoining. [Flower Symbolism: Jobes, 322]
3. **Esau and Jacob** after many years, they are reconciled. [O.T.: Genesis 33:1–4]
4. **Eurydice and Orpheus** reunited despite his backward look. [Ger. Opera: Gluck, *Orpheus and Eurydice,* Westerman, 72]
5. **Joachim and Anna** separated spouses joyfully meet at Jerusalem gate on news of her pregnancy. [Ital. Lit.: *Golden Legend*]
6. **Mary and Elizabeth** the two pregnant women meet after many years and rejoice. [N.T.: Luke 1:39–56]
7. **prodigal son and his father** repentant son returns home to a joyous welcome. [N.T.: Luke 15:11–32]

560. REVELRY

1. **Bacchanalia** festival in honor of Bacchus, god of wine. [Rom. Religion: *NCE,* 203]

2. **Boar's Head Tavern** scene of Falstaff's carousals. [Br. Lit.: *I Henry IV; II Henry IV*]
3. **Comus** hard-drinking god of festive mirth; whence, *comic.* [Gk. Myth.: Espy, 31]
4. **Dionysia** celebrations honoring the wine god, Dionysus. [Gk. Religion: Avery, 399, 404–408; Parrinder, 80]
5. **Dionysus** (Rom. **Bacchus**) god of wine and revelry. [Gk. Myth.: Parrinder, 39]
6. ***Fête Champêtre*** erotically tinged painting of picnic scene. [Fr. Art: Daniel, 102]
7. **Goliards** wandering scholar-poets of satirical Latin verse celebrating sensual pleasure. [Medieval Hist.: *NCE*, 1105]
8. **grapes, garland of** traditional headdress of Dionysus (Bacchus). [Gk. and Rom. Myth.: Jobes, 373]

Revenge (See **VENGEANCE.**)

Reward (See **PRIZE.**)

561. RIBALDRY

1. ***Decameron, The*** Boccaccio's bawdy panorama of medieval Italian life. [Ital. Lit.: Bishop, 314–315, 380]
2. ***Droll Tales*** Balzac's Rabelaisian stories, told in racy medieval style and frequently gross. [Fr. Lit.: *Contes Drolatiques* in Benét, 222]
3. **Fescennia** Etrurian town noted for jesting and scurrilous verse (Fescennine verse). [Rom. Hist.: *EB*, IV: 112]
4. ***Gargantua and Pantagruel*** Rabelais's farcical and obscene 16th-century novel. [Fr. Lit.: Magill I, 298]
5. ***Golden Ass, The*** tale of Lucius and his asininity, with a number of bawdy episodes. [Rom. Lit.: Apuleius *Metamorphoses* or *The Golden Ass* in Magill I, 309]
6. **Goliards** scholar-poets interested mainly in earthly delights. [Medieval Hist.: Bishop, 292–293]
7. **Iambe** girl who amused Demeter with bawdy stories. [Gk. Myth.: Howe, 136]
8. ***LaFontaine, The Tales of*** ribald stories in verse, adapted from Boccaccio and others. [Fr. Lit.: *Contes en Vers* in Benét, 222]
9. ***Miller's Tale, The*** lusty story told by the drunken Miller. [Br. Lit.: *Canterbury Tales* in Magill II, 131]
10. ***Reeve's Tale, The*** Oswald the Reeve retaliates in kind to *The Miller's Tale.*[Br. Lit.: *Canterbury Tales* in Benét, 919]

Ridicule (See MOCKERY.)

562. RIGHTEOUSNESS (See also VIRTUOUSNESS.)

1. **Amos** prophet of righteousness. [O.T.: Amos]
2. **Astraea** goddess of righteousness. [Gk. Myth.: Walsh *Classical*, 36]
3. **Benedetto, Don** Catholic teacher of moral precepts. [Ital. Lit.: *Bread and Wine*]
4. **Dharma** multi-faceted concept of morality, truth, doctrine. [Hindu Rel.: Parrinder, 77]
5. **Do-Right, Dudley** Canadian mountie who can do no wrong. [TV: "The Dudley Do-Right Show" in Terrace, I, 229–230]
6. **Enoch** traditionally seen as paragon of upright man. [O.T.: Genesis 5:21–24]
7. ***Everyman*** medieval play demonstrating man's salvation dependent on his righteousness. [Br. Lit.: *Everyman*]
8. **Josiah** virtuously reforms Jerusalem's evil ways. [O.T.: II Kings 23:1–20]
9. **Noah** only devout man of time; saved from flood. [O.T.: Genesis 6: 9–22]
10. **Stockmann, Dr. Thomas** despite attempted bribery and intimidation, refuses to suppress evidence that the public baths are a health menace. [Norwegian Lit.: *An Enemy of the People*; Magill II, 292]
11. **Zosima** elder monk; preaches message of love and forbearance. [Russ. Lit.: *Brothers Karamazov*]

563. RING, MAGIC

1. **Agramant's ring** given to dwarf, Brunello, and stolen. [Ital. Lit.: *Orlando Furioso*]
2. **Aladdin's ring** given him by the African magician to protect him from all harm. [Arab. Lit.: *Arabian Nights*: "Aladdin and the Wonderful Lamp"]
3. **Andvari's ring** he gave up magic ring to gain liberty. [Norse Myth.: Benét, 35]
4. **Draupnir** Odin's ring; symbol of fertility. [Norse Myth.: *LLEI*, I: 326]
5. **fairy rings** rings found in grassy meadows, once believed to have been produced by dancing fairies. [Br. Myth.: Brewer *Dictionary*, 345]
6. **Gyges' ring** found in a chasm, it renders him invisible and thus able to gain Candaules' wife and kingdom. [Gk. Myth.: Brewer, 425]

7. **Luned's ring** rendered its wearer invisible. [Welsh Lit.: *Mabinogion*]
8. **One Ring, the** forged by the Dark Lord, it gave invisibility and long life but corrupted its users. [Br. Lit.: J. R. R. Tolkien *The Lord of the Rings* in Magill IV, 326]
9. **Polycrates' ring** thrown into the sea to ward off misfortune, it is miraculously returned in the belly of a fish, and tragedy ensues. [Gk. Myth.: Brewer *Dictionary*, 714]
10. **Reynard's wonderful ring** tricolored; each color performed different feat. [Medieval Lit.: *Reynard the Fox*]
11. **Ring of the Nibelungs** made from the Rhine gold, brought a curse on all who owned it. [Ger. Lit.: Benét, 860]
12. **steel ring** enabled wearer to read the secrets of another's heart. [Br. Lit.: Brewer *Handbook*, 916]

564. RIOT

1. **Attica** city in New York housing state prison; one of the worst prison riots in American history occurred there (1971). [Am. Hist.: *NCE*, 182]
2. **Birmingham riots** melee resulting from civil rights demonstrations (1963). [Am. Hist.: Van Doren, 585–586]
3. **Boston Massacre** civil uprising fueled revolutionary spirit (1770). [Am. Hist.: Jameson, 57]
4. **Boston Tea Party** colonists rioted against tea tax (1773). [Am. Hist.: *NCE*, 341]
5. **Chicago riots** "police riot" arguably cost Democrats election (1968). [Am. Hist.: Van Doren, 625]
6. **Donnybrook Fair** former annual Dublin county fair; famous for rioting and dissipation. [Irish Hist.: *NCE*, 784]
7. ***Germinal*** conflict of capital vs. labor: miners strike *en masse.* [Fr. Lit.: *Germinal*]
8. **Gordon, Lord George** leader of the anti-Catholic riots of 1780, in which the idiot Barnaby is caught up. [Br. Lit.: Dickens *Barnaby Rudge*]
9. **Haymarket Riot** Chicago labor dispute erupted into mob scene (1886). [Am. Hist.: Van Doren, 297]
10. **Kent State** Ohio university where antiwar demonstration led to riot, resulting in deaths of four students (1971). [Am. Hist.: *NCE*, 1466]
11. **Little Rock** capital of Arkansas; federal troops sent there to enforce ruling against segregation (1957). [Am. Hist.: *NCE*, 1594]

12. **Luddites** British workers riot to destroy labor-saving machines (1811–1816). [Br. Hist.: *NCE,* 1626]
13. **Molly Maguires** antilandlord organization; used any means to combat mine owners (1860s, 1870s). [Am. Hist.: Van Doren, 272]
14. **New York Draft Riots** anticonscription feelings resulted in anarchy and bloodshed (1863). [Am. Hist.: Jameson, 429]
15. **Riot Act, the** reading it to unruly crowds, sheriffs under George I could force them to disperse or be jailed. [Br. Hist.: Brewer *Dictionary,* 767]
16. **Shays' Rebellion** armed insurrection by Massachusetts farmers against the state government (1786). [Am. Hist.: *NCE,* 2495]
17. **Watts** district in Los Angeles where black Americans rioted over economic deprivation and social injustices (1965). [Am. Hist.: *NCE,* 1612–1613]
18. **Whiskey Rebellion** uprising in Pennsylvania over high tax on whiskey and scotch products (1794). [Am. Hist.: *NCE,* 2967]

565. RIVALRY

1. **Brom Bones and Ichabod Crane** bully and show-off compete for Katrina's hand. [Am. Lit.: *The Legend of Sleepy Hollow*]
2. **Capulets and Montagues** bitter feud between these two houses leads to tragedy. [Br. Lit.: *Romeo and Juliet*]
3. **Diomedes and Troilus** rivals for hand of Cressida. [Br. Lit.: *Troilus and Cressida*]
4. **Esau and Jacob** struggled even in mother's womb. [O.T.: Genesis 25:22]
5. **Eteocles and Polynices** brothers battle for Theban throne. [Gk. Lit.: *Seven Against Thebes*]
6. **Gingham Dog and Calico Cat** stuffed animals eat each other up. [Am. Lit.: "The Duel" in Hollowell]
7. **Guelphs and Ghibellines** perennial medieval Italian feuding political factions. [Ital. Hist.: Plumb, 42–43]
8. **Hatfields and McCoys** 19th-century mountain families carried on endless feud in southern U.S. [Am. Hist.: *NCE,* 942]
9. **Jets and Sharks** teenage gangs fight for supremacy amid the New York tenements. [Am. Lit. and Cinema: *West Side Story*]
10. **Kilkenny cats** contentious felines fight to the death. [Nurs. Rhyme: *Mother Goose*]
11. **Percys and Douglases** the perennial Scottish border feud; recounted in famous ballad "Chevy Chase." [Scot. Hist.: Payton, 141]

12. **Proitus and Acrisius** fought in womb; contended for father's realm. [Gk. Myth.: Gaster, 164]
13. **Richard the Lion-Hearted and Saladin** Christian and Saracen leaders part friends after Crusade. [Br. Lit.: *The Talisman*]
14. **Sohrab and Rustum** champions of the Tartars and Persians, respectively, engage in mortal combat, unaware that one is the other's son. [Br. Poetry: Arnold *Sohrab and Rustum* in Magill III, 1002]

Robbery (See THIEVERY.)

Rudeness (See COARSENESS.)

566. RUFFIANISM

1. **Brown shirts (S.A.)** Nazi militia who terrorized citizens. [Germ. Hist.: *WB*, H:238]
2. **droogs** Alex's rough and tough band of hooligans. [Br. Lit.: *A Clockwork Orange*]
3. **Hawkubites** London toughs; terrorized old men, women, and children (1711–1714). [Br. Hist.: Brewer *Note-Book*, 406]
4. **Jackmen** medieval para-military thugs. [Br. Hist.: Brewer *Note-Book*, 463]
5. **Jets and Sharks** hostile street gangs. [Am. Lit. and Cinema: *West Side Story*]
6. **Mohocks** bullies terrorizing London streets in 18th century. [Br. Hist.: Brewer *Dictionary*, 720]
7. **Scowerers** London hooligans, at turn of the 18th century. [Br. Hist.: Brewer *Dictionary*, 972]
8. **Tityre Tus** young bullies in late 17th-century London. [Br. Hist: Brewer *Dictionary*, 1087]

567. RUSTICITY

1. ***American Gothic*** Grant Wood's painting of stern Iowan farming couple. [Am. Art: Osborne, 1215]
2. **Audrey** awkward rural wench who jilts a countryman for a clown. [Br. Drama: Shakespeare *As You Like It*]
3. **Caudill, Boone** epitome of the mountain man. [Am. Lit.: *The Big Sky*]
4. ***Compleat Angler, The*** fishing, hunting, and philosophizing in rural surroundings. [Br. Lit.: Izaac Walton *The Compleat Angler*]
5. **Currier and Ives** makers of colorful lithographs of scenes of nature and outdoor recreation. [Am. Hist.: *NCE*, 699]

6. **North Woods** forest and lake region; setting for lumberjack legends. [Am. Lit.: Hart, 607]
7. **Petticoat Junction** farce set in rural America. [TV: Terrace, II, 205–206]
8. **shtetl** any small-town Jewish settlement in East Europe. [Jewish Hist.: Wigoder, 552]

568. RUTHLESSNESS (See also BRUTALITY, CRUELTY, HEARTLESSNESS.)

1. **Borgia, Cesare** (1476–1507) prototype of Machiavelli's "Prince": intelligent and ruthlessly opportunistic. [Ital. Hist.: Plumb, 59]
2. **Caligula** (12–41) Roman emperor known for terror and cruel autocracy. [Rom. Hist.: *NCE,* 425]
3. **Ivan the Terrible** (1533–1584) his reign was characterized by murder and terror. [Russ. Hist.: *EB,* 9: 1179–1180]
4. **Larsen, Wolf** captain of the *Ghost*; terrorizes his crew. [Am. Lit.: London *The Sea Wolf* in Magill I, 874]
5. **Nero** (37–68) demented Roman emperor; initiated persecutions against the Christians. [Rom. Hist.: *NCE,* 1909]
6. **Robespierre, Maximilien Marie Isidore** (1758–1794) architect of the Reign of Terror (1793–1794). [Fr. Hist.: *EB,* 15: 907–910]
7. **Snopes** family of unscrupulous climbers, horse thieves, lechers, and murderers in Faulkner novels. [Am. Lit.: Benét, 940]
8. **Snopes, Flem** works his way up from obscurity to riches by ruining all his associates and relatives. [Am. Lit.: Wm. Faulkner *The Hamlet* in Magill II, 398, *The Town* in Magill III, 1074, and *The Mansion* in Magill IV, 591]
9. **Vathek** sacrifices children, seduces a betrothed girl, and commits many other crimes to satisfy his desires. [Br. Lit.: *Vathek* in Magill II, 1095]

S

569. SACRED OBJECTS

1. **Ark of the Covenant** gilded wooden chest in which God's presence dwelt when communicating with the people. [O.T.: Exodus 25:10]
2. **Black Stone, the** sacred stone at Mecca worshiped since ancient times. [Islamic Religion: Brewer *Dictionary*, 112]
3. **Holy Grail** cup said to have been used by Jesus at the Last Supper. [Christian Tradition: Brewer *Dictionary*, 412]
4. **bactyl, baetylus** stone fallen from heaven, regarded as sacred. [Antiquity: *EB* (1963) II, 920]
5. **zaïmph** mysterious veil of the Carthaginian moon-goddess Tanit. [Fr. Lit.: Flaubert *Salammbô* in Magill I, 860]

570. SACRED PLACES

1. **Alph** sacred river in Xanadu. [Br. Poetry: Coleridge "Kubla Kahn"]
2. **Delphi** shrine sacred to Apollo and site of temple and oracle. [Gk. Myth.: Brewer *Dictionary*, 274]
3. **Ganges** river sacred to the Hindus, who are freed from sin by bathing in it. [Hinduism: Brewer *Dictionary*, 385]
4. **Holy Bottle** oracle consulted by Panurge to ascertain whether he should marry. [Fr. Lit.: Rabelais *Gargantua and Pantagruel*]
5. **Kaaba** central shrine at Mecca. [Islamic Religion: Brewer *Dictionary*, 513]
6. **Mecca** holy city where Muhammad was born. [Islamic Religion: Brewer *Dictionary*, 596]
7. **Medina** holy city to which Muhammad fled from Mecca. [Islamic Religion: Brewer *Dictionary*, 596]
8. **Monsalvat** the mountain of salvation where the Holy Grail is guarded by knights. [Ger. Opera: Wagner *Parsifal* in Benét, 761]
9. **Nemi** lake in Italy, sacred to the cult of Diana and site of human sacrifices. [Rom. Myth.: *EB*, XVI, 211]
10. **Zem Zem** sacred well in Mecca where Hagar revived Ishmael. [Moslem Tradition: Brewer *Dictionary*, 969]

571. SACRIFICE (See also MARTYRDOM, SELF-SACRIFICE.)

1. **Adrammelech and Anammelech** Sepharvaite gods to whom children were immolated. [O.T.: II Kings 17:31]

2. **Akedah** biblical account of God commanding Abraham's offerings. [Jewish Hist.: Wigoder, 17]
3. **Burghers of Calais** they sacrificed themselves to save city from British siege after Battle of Crécy (1346). [Fr. Hist.: *EB*, II: 447]
4. **Idomeneus** Cretan king sacrifices his son to fulfill a vow. [Gk. Myth.: Benét, 492]
5. **Iphigenia** slain to appease Artemis' wrath. [Gk. Myth.: Walsh *Classical*, 156]
6. **Moloch** god to whom idolatrous Israelites immolated children. [O.T.: II Kings 23:10; Jeremiah 7:31–32, 32:35]
7. **Moriah** site intended for Abraham's offering up of Isaac. [O.T.: Genesis 22:2]
8. **Norma** priestess betrays her vows and sacrifices herself in atonement. [Ital. Opera: Bellini *Norma* in Benét, 720]
9. **Tophet** site of propitiatory immolations to god, Moloch. [O.T.: II Kings 23:10; Jeremiah 7:31–32]
10. **suttee** former practice of self-immolation by widow on husband's pyre. [Hinduism: Brewer *Dictionary*, 1049]

572. SACRILEGE

1. **abomination of desolation** epithet describing pagan idol in Jerusalem Temple. [O.T.: Daniel 9, 11, 12; N.T.: Mark 13:14; Matthew 24:15]
2. **Aepytus** Arcadian king; entering Poseidon's sanctuary, forbidden to mortals, he is blinded. [Gk. Myth.: Zimmerman, 9]
3. **Beaufort, Cardinal** (1377–1447) haughty churchman; dies execrating God. [Br. Lit.: *II Henry VI*]
4. **cleansing of the temple** sacrilegious money-changers driven out of temple by Christ. [N.T.: Matthew, 21:12–13; Mark, 11:15–18]
5. **Heliodorus** Syrian official attempted to loot Solomon's temple. [Apocrypha: II Maccabees 3]
6. **Hophni and Phinehas** contemptuously abused holiness of sacrifices. [O.T.: I Samuel 2:12–17]
7. **Simon Magus** tried to purchase apostolic powers; whence, *simony*. [N.T.: Acts 8:18–24]

Sadness (See **MELANCHOLY.**)

573. SALVATION (See also DELIVERANCE.)

1. **Esther, Queen** intercedes with king for cessation of extermination of Jews. [O.T.: Esther 7:8]

2. **Faerie Queene (Gloriana)** gives a champion to people in trouble. [Br. Lit.: *The Faerie Queene*]
3. **Jesus Christ** as savior of souls. [Christian Tradition: Jobes, 330]
4. **Moses** led his people out of bondage. [O.T.: Exodus]

Sanctimony (See HYPOCRISY.)

Sanctuary (See REFUGE.)

574. SATIRE

1. **Arbuthnot, Mr.** cliché expert who spoke exclusively in the clichés of each subject on which he was interviewed. [Am. Lit.: Frank Sullivan columns in *The New Yorker*]
2. ***Clouds, The*** attacks Socrates and his philosophy. [Gk. Drama: Haydn & Fuller, 144]
3. ***Frogs, The*** lampoons the plays of Euripides and his advanced thinking. [Gk. Drama: Haydn & Fuller, 276]
4. ***Joseph Andrews*** satirizes the sentimentality of contemporary fiction. [Br. Lit.: Fielding *Joseph Andrews*]
5. ***Knight of the Burning Pestle, The*** play by Beaumont and Fletcher burlesques the excesses of tales of chivalry. [Br. Drama: Haydn & Fuller, 399]
6. ***M*A*S*H*** medical farce on the horrors of war. [Am. Cinema and TV: Halliwell, 474]
7. ***Pogo*** comic strip rife with political satire. [Comics: Berger, 172]
8. ***Praise of Folly, The*** uses tongue-in-cheek praise to satirize contemporary customs, institutions, and beliefs. [Dutch Philos.: Erasmus *The Praise of Folly* in Haydn & Fuller, 607]
9. **Scourge of Princes** Pietro Aretino (1492-1556), wrote wicked satires on nobles and notables. [Ital. Lit.: Benét, 47]
10. **Teufelsdrockh, Herr** fictitious professor, Carlyle's mouthpiece for criticism of Victorian life. [Br. Lit.: *Sartor Resartus*]
11. ***Troilus and Cressida*** Homer's heroes are reduced in character and satirized. [Br. Drama: Shakespeare *Troilus and Cressida*]
12. ***Ubu Roi*** burlesques bourgeois values through outlandish political adventurism, including assassination, mock heroics, and buffoonery. [Fr. Drama: Alfred Jarry *Ubu Roi* in Benét, 1036]
13. ***Zuleika Dobson*** burlesques sentimental novels of the Edwardian era. [Br. Lit.: Magill II, 1169]

575. SAVAGERY

1. **Apache Indians** once fierce fighting tribe of American West. [Am. Hist.: *NCE*, 123]

2. **bandersnatch** imaginary wild animal of great ferocity. [Br. Lit.: "Jabberwocky" in *Through the Looking-Glass*]
3. **berserkers** ancient Norse warriors; assumed attributes of bears in battle. [Norse Myth.: Leach, 137]
4. **Comanche Indians** warlike tribe of American West. [Am. Hist.: *NCE,* 607]
5. **Crommyonian sow** ravager of the Corinthian countryside. [Gk. Myth.: Benét, 237]
6. **Erymanthian boar** ravaged Arcadian countryside until capture by Hercules. [Gk. Myth.: Jobes, 523]
7. **Huns** Mongolian invaders of western Europe until 453. [Eur. Hist.: Espy, 167]
8. **Magua** a renegade Huron who scalps white men. [Am. Lit.: *The Pathfinder,* Magill I, 715–717]
9. **mares of Diomedes** lived on human flesh; their capture was Hercules' eighth labor. [Gk. and Rom. Myth.: Hall, 149]
10. **Taras Bulba** savage yet strangely devoted Cossack leader. [Russ. Lit.: *Taras Bulba,* Walsh *Modern,* 77]
11. **Tartars** 13th-century rapacious hordes of Genghis Khan. [Medieval Hist.: Brewer *Dictionary,* 1064]
12. **tiger** aims at annihilating mankind. [Animal Symbolism: Mercatante, 55]
13. **Vandals** 5th-century sackers of Rome and its art. [Ital. Hist.: Espy, 168]

576. SCANDAL (See also CONTROVERSY.)

1. **Abélard, Peter** (1079–c. 1144) French theologian takes Héloïse, abbess, as lover; marries her in secret. [Fr. Hist.: *EB,* I: 18]
2. **Black Sox Scandal** Chicago White Sox baseball players accused of taking bribes to lose the 1919 World Series. [Sports: *EB,* II: 66]
3. **Chappaquiddick** car driven by Senator Edward Kennedy plunges off bridge; woman companion dies (1969). [Am. Hist.: *Facts* (1969), 452]
4. **Edward VIII** (1894–1972) King of Britain whose decision to marry a divorcee forced him to abdicate throne (1936). [Br. Hist.: *NCE,* 835–836]
5. **$64,000 Question, The** game show discovered to be fixed (1958). [TV: Terrace, II, 295–296]
6. **South Sea Bubble** fraud is exposed in British South Sea Company (1720). [Br. Hist.: *EB,* IX: 383]

7. **Teapot Dome** government oil reserves fraudulently leased to private concerns (1922). [Am. Hist.: Flexner, 353]
8. **Watergate** scandals involving Nixon's administration (1972). [Am. Hist.: Kane, 460–462]

Scapegoat (See DUPERY.)

577. SCHOLARLINESS

1. **Angelic Doctor** soubriquet of St. Thomas Aquinas (c. 1225–1274), scholastic philosopher. [Ital. Hist.: Benét, 44]
2. **Bardo** blind antiquarian wrapped up in his scholarly annotations of the classics. [Br. Lit.: George Eliot *Romola*]
3. **Sixte, Adrien** secluded philosopher, totally preoccupied with theoretical considerations. [Fr. Lit.: Paul Bourget *The Disciple* in Magill I, 209]
4. **Thaumaste** English scholar who debated with Panurge by gesture alone. [Fr. Lit.: *Gargantua and Pantagruel*]

578. SEA

1. **Aegir** god of the seas. [Norse Myth.: Brewer *Dictionary,* 12]
2. **Amphitrite** queen of the sea; Poseidon's wife. [Gk. Myth.: *NCE,* 94]
3. **Bowditch** standard navigational work, *American Practical Navigator;* so called from its compiler, Nathaniel Bowditch. [Am. Hist.: Hart, 97]
4. **Clement the First, St.** drowned bound to anchor; invoked in marine dedications. [Christian Hagiog.: Attwater, 88]
5. **Cuchulain** mad with grief, he battles the sea. [Irish Myth.: Benét, 239]
6. **Dylan** god of waves, which continually mourn him. [Celtic Myth.: Leach, 332; Jobes, 480]
7. **Jones, Davy** personification of the ocean. [Br. and Am. Marine Slang: Leach, 298]
8. **Manannan** Irish god of the sea. [Irish Folklore: Briggs, 280]
9. **mermaid** half-woman, half-fish; seen by sailors. [Western Folklore: Misc.]
10. **Nereids** fifty daughters of Nereus; attendants of Poseidon. [Gk. Myth.: Zimmerman, 174]
11. **Nereus** son of Oceanus; father of the Nereids. [Gk. Myth.: Zimmerman, 174; Gk. Lit.: *Iliad*]
12. **Njorthr** Scandinavian god; protector of sailors and ships. [Norse Myth.: Brewer *Dictionary,* 760]

13. **Oceanids** three thousand daughters of Oceanus and Tethys. [Gk. Myth.: Zimmerman, 178]
14. **Oceanus** Titan and father of the river gods and Oceanids. [Gk. Myth.: Zimmerman, 178]
15. **Poseidon** (Rom. **Neptune**) god of the oceans and all waters. [Gk. Myth.: Wheeler, 257]
16. **Salacia** consort of Neptune and goddess of springs. [Rom. Myth.: Kravitz, 208]
17. **Tethys** goddess-wife of Oceanus. [Gk. Myth.: Brewer *Dictionary,* 1070]
18. **Thetis** sea deity and mother of Achilles. [Gk. Myth.: Zimmerman, 269; Gk. Lit.: *Odyssey*]
19. **Tiamat** primeval sea represented as a dragon goddess, mother of all the gods. [Babylonian Myth.: Benét, 1007]
20. **trident** three-pronged fork; attribute of Poseidon. [Gk. Myth.: Hall, 309]
21. **Triton** gigantic sea deity; son and messenger of Poseidon. [Gk. Myth.: Zimmerman, 277; Rom. Lit.: *Aeneid*]
22. **Varuna** god over the waters. [Vedic Myth.: Leach, 1155]

Season (See **AUTUMN, SPRING, SUMMER, WINTER.**)

579. SEDUCTION (See also FLIRTATIOUSNESS.)

1. **Armida** modern Circe; sorceress who seduces Rinaldo. [Ital. Lit.: *Jerusalem Delivered*]
2. **Aurelius** Dorigen's nobleminded would-be seducer. [Br. Lit.: *Canterbury Tales,* "The Franklin's Tale"]
3. **Bathsheba** Uriah's wife, seduced by King David. [O.T.: II Samuel 11:4]
4. **Circe** enchantress who turned Odysseus's men into swine; byword for irresistibly fascinating woman. [Gk. Lit.: *Odyssey;* Rom. Lit.: *Aeneid*]
5. **Delilah** fascinating and deceitful mistress of Samson. [O.T.: Judges 16]
6. **Dragon Lady** beautiful Chinese temptress. [Comics: "Terry and the Pirates" in Horn, 653]
7. **Europa** seduced by Zeus in form of a white bull. [Gk. Myth.: Kravitz, 96]
8. **Harlowe, Clarissa** seduced and raped by Lovelace. [Br. Lit.: Richardson *Clarissa Harlowe* in Benét, 203]
9. **Hautdesert, Lady de** tries to seduce Gawain to test his faithfulness. [Br. Lit.: *Sir Gawain and the Green Knight*]

10. **Io** seduced by Jupiter in form of a cloud. [Rom. Myth.: *Metamorphoses*]
11. **Juan, Don** handsome Spanish lad seduces many women. [Eur. legend: Benét, 279]
12. **Leucosia, Ligeia, and Parthenope** sirens; tried to lure Odysseus and his men to destruction. [Gk. Lit.: *Odyssey*]
13. **Little Em'ly** though engaged to Ham, is seduced and runs off with Steerforth. [Br. Lit.: Dickens *David Copperfield*]
14. **Lorelei** siren; lured ships to destruction with singing. [Ger. Folklore: Benét, 599]
15. **Mirandolina** innkeeper artfully seduces misogynist for sport. [Ital. Lit.: *The Mistress of the Inn*]
16. **Rustico** convinces Alibech that the way to serve God is by sexual intercourse. [Ital. Lit.: Boccaccio *Decameron*]
17. **Sorrel, Hetty** seduced by Arthur Donnithorne. [Br. Lit.: *Adam Bede*]

Selfishness (See CONCEIT, STINGINESS.)

580. SELF-SACRIFICE (See also SACRIFICE, SUICIDE.)

1. **Aïda** dies with her beloved Radames. [Ital. Opera: Verdi, *Aïda*, Westerman, 325]
2. **Alcestis** offered self up to die in the stead of Admetus. [Gk. Myth.: Leach, 11]
3. **Anderson, Parson** self-sacrificing captain of New England rebels. [Br. Lit.: Shaw *The Devil's Disciple* in Benét, 267]
4. **Benedetto** monk gives up everything to serve others and reform the Church. [Ital. Lit.: *The Saint* in Magill II, 929]
5. **Brooke, Dorothea** gives up Casaubon's fortune for Ladislaw's affection. [Br. Lit.: *Middlemarch*, Magill I, 588–591]
6. **Camille** gives up Armand so as not to endanger his career. [Fr. Lit.: *La Dame aux Camélias*]
7. **Carton, Sydney** permits himself to be guillotined in place of Darnay. [Br. Lit.: Dickens *A Tale of Two Cities*]
8. **Colamartini, Christina** dies in wilderness attempting to help Paolo. [Ital. Lit.: *Bread and Wine*]
9. **de Posa, Marquis** clears prince's name in conspiracy by indicting himself. [Ger. Lit.: *Don Carlos*]
10. ***Deputy, The*** Father Fontana accompanies deported Jews to Auschwitz and dies with them in the gas chambers. [Ger. Drama: Weiss, 124]
11. **Din, Gunga** water-carrier killed as he rescues narrator of story. [Br. Lit.: "Gunga Din" in Benét, 430]

12. **Dounia** intends to marry Svidrigailov to relieve her brother's poverty. [Russ. Lit.: *Crime and Punishment*]
13. **Dudgeon, Dick** to save rebel leader Parson Anderson from the gallows, the reprobate Dudgeon allows himself to be arrested and sentenced to death. [Br. Drama: Shaw *The Devil's Disciple* in Benét, 267]
14. **Eponine** during fight, gives his life to save Marius. [Fr. Lit.: *Les Misérables*]
15. **Fantine** woman becomes prostitute to support daughter. [Fr. Lit.: *Les Misérables*]
16. **Gift of the Magi, The** husband and wife each give up own treasure to buy the other's Christmas present. [Am. Lit.: "The Gift of the Magi" in Benét, 395]
17. **Gilda** sacrifices self to save her beloved Duke's life. [Ital. Opera: Verdi, *Rigoletto,* Westerman, 300]
18. **Grieux, des** accompanies banished Manon to exile in Louisiana. [Fr. Lit.: *Manon Lescaut*]
19. **Hansa, Per** dies in storm on errand of mercy. [Nor. Lit.: *Giants in the Earth,* Magill I, 303–304]
20. **innkeeper's daughter** Highwayman's sweetheart, shoots herself to help him avoid capture. [Br. Poetry: Noyes "The Highwayman"]
21. **Jephthah's daughter** accepts father's vow to God to die in exchange for his victory. [O.T.: Judges 11:30–40]
22. **Jesus Christ** died on cross to save mankind. [N.T.: Matthew 27:24–61]
23. **Jordan, Robert** young American teacher in Spain who gives his life helping the Loyalist guerrillas. [Am. Lit.: Hemingway *For Whom the Bell Tolls*]
24. **Kamikaze** WWII Japanese suicide pilots; embodiment of "death before dishonor." [Jap. Hist.: Fuller, III, 618–619]
25. **little mermaid, the** sacrifices her own life to save her beloved prince. [Dan. Lit.: *Andersen's Fairy Tales*]
26. **Madeleine** executed with lover Andrea. [Ital. Opera: Giordano, *Andrea Chénier,* Westerman, 370–371]
27. **Myshkin, Prince** his desire for martyrdom makes him willing to marry a neurotic woman of easy virtue. [Russ. Lit.: Dostoevsky *The Idiot*]
28. **Oakhurst, John** kills himself so that three other outcasts may survive. [Am. Lit.: *The Outcasts of Poker Flat*]
29. **Ona** becomes a prostitute to support family. [Am. Lit.: *The Jungle*]

30. **pelican** tears open breast to feed young. [Christian Symbolism: de Bles, 29]
31. **Susanin, Ivan** leads Poles astray to safeguard tsar; executed. [Russ. Opera: Glinka, *A Life for the Tsar,* Westerman, 379]
32. **Violetta** courtesan renounces her lover in order to save his family from scandal. [Ital. Opera: Verdi *La Traviata* in Benét, 1022]

Sensuality (See **BEAUTY, SENSUAL.**)

581. SENTIMENTALITY

1. **Checkers** dog given as gift to Nixon; used in his defense of political contributions during presidential campaign (1952). [Am. Hist.: Wallechinsky, 126]
2. **Dondi** comic strip in which sentimentality is the main motif. [Comics: Horn, 217–218]
3. **Fauntleroy, Little Lord** impossibly kind and unselfish child is loved by all and reforms selfish grandfather. [Am. Lit.: Benét, 591]
4. **Five Little Peppers** saccharine story of five orphans. [Am. Lit.: Harriet Lothrop *Five Little Peppers and How They Grew* in Hart, 495]
5. **Goody Two Shoes** mawkish girl, overpleased to have two shoes, exclaims her fortune to all. [Nurs. Rhyme: "Little Goody Two Shoes" in Barnhart, 502]
6. **Hardy, Andy** protagonist of 1930s series of sentimental "family" movies. [Am. Cinema: Griffith, 300]
7. **Little Nell** death scene of sweet child epitomizes sentimentality. [Br. Lit.: *Old Curiosity Shop*]
8. **Mary Magdalene** portrayed traditionally in art as weeping; whence, *maudlin.* [Art: Misc.]
9. **Orsino** plays role of languishing lover. [Br. Lit.: *Twelfth Night*]
10. **Sentimental Tommy** forever playing the hero, he fails to be the faithful lover and husband of his adoring Grizel. [Br. Lit.: J. M. Barrie *Sentimental Tommy* in Benét, 914]
11. **sob sister** journalist who handles advice to lovelorn column. [Am. Journalism: Brewer *Dictionary,* 1016]
12. **Sweet Adeline** tune of a man's former romance, usually sung in barbershop harmony. [Am. Music: Hart, 823]
13. **Waltons, The** television show of depression-era America softened by nostalgia. [TV: Terrace, II, 418–419]

14. **Werther** artistic young man whose ultra-romantic life is filled with hopeless passions. [Ger. Lit.: *The Sorrows of Young Werther* in Magill I, 915]

582. SERVANT (See also BUTLER.)

1. **Abigail** helpmeet of King David; traditional name for handmaiden. [O.T.: I Samuel 25]
2. **Albert** popular servant's name: assistant, manservant, page-boy. [Br. Lit.: *Loving; By The Pricking of My Thumbs; A Damsel in Distress*]
3. **Brighella** prototype of interfering servant; meddles and gossips. [Ital. Drama: Walsh *Classical*, 62]
4. **Despina** her stratagems control and resolve the plot. [Ital. Opera: Mozart, *Così fan tutte*, Scholes, 259]
5. **Figaro** valet who outwits everyone by his cunning. [Fr. Lit.: *Marriage of Figaro*]
6. **Friday** young Indian rescued by Crusoe and kept as servant and companion. [Br. Lit.: *Robinson Crusoe*]
7. **Ganymede** mortal lad, taken by Zeus to be cupbearer to the gods. [Gk. Myth.: Howe, 106]
8. **golem** automaton homunculus performs duties not permissible for Jews. [Jew. Legend: Jobes, 674]
9. **Hazel** meddling maid in the Baxter house. [TV and Comics: Terrace, I, 343]
10. **Hebe** cupbearer to the gods; succeeded by Ganymede. [Gk. Myth.: Zimmerman, 117]
11. **Ithamore** purchased by Barabas to betray Governor of Malta. [Br. Drama: *The Jew of Malta*]
12. **Jeeves** stereotypical English valet of Wodehouse stories. [Brit. Lit.: *NCE*, 2997]
13. **Lichas** Hercules' attendant; unknowingly delivers poisoned robe to him. [Rom. Lit.: *Metamorphoses*]
14. **Notburga, St.** Bavarian patroness of domestics; beneficent, though poor. [Christian Hagiog.: Attwater, 257]
15. **Passepartout** Phileas Fogg's rash valet. [Fr. Lit.: *Around the World in Eighty Days*]
16. **Thing** Addams family servant; a disembodied right hand. [TV: "The Addams Family" in Terrace, I, 29]
17. **Xanthias** carries Bacchus's heavy bundles. [Gk. Lit.: *The Frogs*]
18. **Zita, St.** devout and generous domestic; patron saint. [Christian Hagiog.: Attwater, 348]

583. SEWING and WEAVING

1. **Arachne** skilled weaver; changed into spider for challenging Athena to weaving contest. [Gk. Myth.: Zimmerman, 27]
2. **Athena** goddess of spinning and weaving. [Gk. Myth.: Howe, 45]
3. **Marner, Silas** hand-loom weaver who comes, friendless, to Raveloe. [Br. Lit.: Benét, 930]
4. **Penelope** weaves shroud for 20 years, unraveling it each night. [Gk. Lit.: *Odyssey*]
5. **Prynne, Hester** ostracized, sewing becomes her daily preoccupation. [Am. Lit.: *The Scarlet Letter*]
6. **Rumpelstiltskin** dwarf who spun gold from straw to help imprisoned girl. [Ger. Fairy Tale: *Rumpelstiltskin*]
7. ***Weavers, The*** depicts plight of Silesian weavers. [Ger. Lit.: Benét, 1078]

584. SEX SYMBOLS (See BEAUTY, SENSUAL; BUXOMNESS.)

1. **Conrad** dazzling, sexually irresistible pirate, typical Byronic hero. [Br. Lit.: Byron *The Corsair* in Benét, 226]
2. **Lace, Miss** 1940s armed forces' pin-up girl from comic strip. [Comics: "Male Call" in Horn, 475]
3. **Petty girl** airbrushed beauty, scantily clad in Esquire's pages. [Am. Lit.: Misc.]
4. **"10"** fantasy of the ideal female sex object. [Am. Cinema: "*10*"]
5. **Vargas girl** originally appeared in *Esquire,* later in *Playboy;* created by Alberto Vargas. [Am. Art: *Vargas*]

585. SEXUALITY

1. ***Flowers of Evil, The*** thoroughly explore the possibilities of vice, depravity, and sin. [Fr. Poetry: Baudelaire *The Flowers of Evil* in Magill III, 399]
2. **Hite Report** surveys men's sexual habits and performance. [Amer. Pop. Cult.: Misc.]
3. ***Ideal Marriage*** Van de Velde study of the physiology and technique of marital sex. [Pop. Cult.: Misc.]
4. ***Joy of Sex, The*** popular 20th-century sex manual. [Misc.: Dr. Alex Comfort *The Joy of Sex* in Weiss, 239]
5. **Kinsey reports** pioneer explorations of sexual behavior based on interviews with 100,000 men and women. [Pop. Cult.: Misc.]
6. **Masters and Johnson** published a study of sexual performance under laboratory conditions. [Sexology: Masters and Johnson *Human Sexual Response* in Weiss, 214]

7. **Morel, Paul** his Oedipus complex makes erotic fulfillment impossible. [Br. Lit.: D. H. Lawrence *Sons and Lovers* in Magill I, 913]
8. ***Psychology of Sex, The*** seven-volume Ellis work revolutionized attitudes toward sex and sexual problems. [Pop. Cult.: Misc.]

586. SHEPHERD

1. **Corin** the faithful shepherdess; called "the Virgin of the Grove." [Br. Lit.: "The Faithful Shepherdess" in Brewer *Handbook*, 234]
2. **Daphnis** guards sheep; creator of bucolic poetry. [Gk. Myth.: Kravitz, 75]
3. **Jabal** father of herdsmen. [O.T.: Genesis 4:20]
4. **Jesus Christ** the Good Shepherd. [N.T.: John 10:11–14]
5. **Little Bo-peep** young shepherdess; searches everywhere for lost flock. [Nurs. Rhyme: Opie, 93]
6. **Little Boy Blue** asleep while his sheep are in the field. [Nurs. Rhyme: Baring-Gould, 46]

587. SHIPWRECK

1. **Spens, Sir Patrick** sets sail in a deadly storm, his ship founders, and he is drowned with his crew. [Scot. Balladry: *Sir Patrick Spens* in Benét, 935]
2. ***Tempest, The*** ship bearing the King of Naples and his company is wrecked near Prospero's island. [Br. Drama: Shakespeare *The Tempest*]

588. SHREWISHNESS (See also IRASCIBILITY.)

1. **Caudle, Mrs. Margaret** nagging, complaining wife. [Br. Lit.: *The Curtain Lectures*, Walsh *Modern*, 90]
2. **Dollallolla, Queen** even King Arthur feared his uxorial virago. [Br. Lit: *Tom Thumb the Great*]
3. **farmer's wife** makes hell too hot even for the devil, who sends her back home. [Am. Balladry: "The Devil and the Farmer's Wife"]
4. **Frome, Zenobia (Zeena)** Ethan Frome's hypochondriacal, nagging, belittling wife. [Am. Lit.: *Ethan Frome*]
5. **Galatea** 19th-century version: nags Pygmalion. [Aust. Operetta: von Suppé, *Beautiful Galatea*, Westerman, 285]
6. **Gargery, Mrs.** vixenish wife; keeps husband in thrall. [Br. Lit.: *Great Expectations*]
7. **Katherine** "intolerably curst and shrewd and froward." [Br. Lit.: *The Taming of the Shrew*]

8. **Lisa, Dame** Jurgen's petulant wife taken from him in gratitude by the Prince of Darkness. [Am. Lit.: *Jurgen* in Magill I, 464]
9. **MacStinger, Mrs.** widow; miserable to everyone. [Br. Lit.: *Dombey and Son*]
10. **Momus** personification of censoriousness, constantly carping, grumbling, and finding fault. [Gk. Myth.: *EB* (1963) XV, 685]
11. **Peninnah** continually harassed co-wife Hannah about her barrenness. [O.T.: I Samuel 1:6]
12. **Proudie, Mrs.** aggressive, domineering wife of Bishop Proudie. [Br. Lit.: Trollope *Barchester Towers* in Magill I, 55]
13. **Sofronia** Norina, disguised for mock marriage, pretends to be virago. [Ital. Opera: Donizetti, *Don Pasquale,* Westerman, 123–124]
14. **Tabitha** Mr. Bramble's virago sister; bent on matrimony. [Br. Lit.: *Humphry Clinker*]
15. **Termagant** tumultuous Muslim deity (male); today, a virago. [Medieval Lit.: Espy, 125]
16. **Xanthippe** Socrates' peevish, quarrelsome wife. [Gk. Hist.: Espy, 114]

Shyness (See **TIMIDITY.**)

Similarity (See **TWINS.**)

Sinfulness (See **WICKEDNESS.**)

589. SINGER

1. **Lorelei** siren whose singing lured ships to their destruction. [Ger. Lit.: Benét, 599]
2. **sirens** their singing so sweet, it lured sailors to their death. [Gk. Myth.: Hamilton, 48]

590. SINGER, OPERATIC

1. **Caruso, Enrico** (1873–1921) world's most celebrated tenor. [Opera Hist.: *NCE,* 469]
2. **Kronberg, Thea** leaves Colorado home to study music and becomes an international success as a diva. [Am. Lit.: *The Song of the Lark* in Benét, 944]

591. SKEPTICISM (See also CYNICISM, PESSIMISM.)

1. **Bothwell, Sergeant** believes in nothing. [Br. Lit.: *Old Mortality*]
2. **Dawes, Jabez** mischievous brat ridicules Santa's existence. [Am. Lit.: "The Boy Who Laughed at Santa Claus" in Rockwell]

3. **mushroom** symbol of suspicion. [Plant Symbolism: *Flower Symbolica,* 310]
4. **Naaman** at first doubts efficacy of leprosy cure. [O.T.: II Kings 5:11–14]
5. **Thomas, St.** wouldn't believe Christ's resurrection until he saw Him; hence, *Doubting Thomas.* [N.T.: John 20:24–25]
6. **Windermere, Lady** doesn't believe husband's "virtuous" generosity toward Mrs. Erlynne. [Br. Lit.: *Lady Windermere's Fan,* Magill I, 488–490]
7. **Zacharias** struck dumb for doubting Gabriel's birth annunciation. [N.T.: Luke 1:18–20]

Skinniness (See THINNESS.)

592. SLANDER (See also GOSSIP.)

1. **Basile** calumniating, niggardly bigot. [Fr. Lit.: *Barber of Seville; Marriage of Figaro*]
2. **Blatant Beast** monster with 100 tongues; calumnious voice of world. [Br. Lit.: *Faerie Queene*]
3. **Candour, Mrs.** the most energetic calumniator. [Br. Lit.: *School for Scandal*]
4. **cobaea vine** symbol of slander. [Flower Symbolism: *Flora Symbolica,* 173]
5. **hellebore** symbol of slander. [Flower Symbolism: *Flora Symbolica,* 174]
6. **Iago** malignant Venetian commander; slanders Cassio to Othello. [Br. Lit.: *Othello*]
7. **Kay, Sir** ill-mannered, mean-spirited, but above all, scurrilous. [Br. Lit.: *Le Morte d'Arthur; Idylls of the King*]
8. **Miriam** made leprous for maligning Moses's marriage to Cushite. [O.T.: Numbers 12:9–10]
9. **Shimei** vilifies David, implying he stole Saul's throne. [O.T.: II Samuel 16:7–8]
10. **Thersites** dedicated to denigrating his betters. [Gk. Lit.: *Iliad;* Br. Lit.: *Troilus and Cressida*]

Slaughter (See MASSACRE.)

593. SLEEP

1. **Amina** in her sleep, walks on a dangerous bridge, complaining of her unhappiness. [Ital. Opera: *La Sonnambula* in Osborne *Opera*]
2. **Cupid** while sleeping, revealed by Psyche's lamp as her lover. [Gk. Myth.: Benét, 822]

3. **Deiphobus** while sleeping, he is betrayed by Helen and slain by Menelaus. [Rom. Lit.: *Aeneid VI*]
4. **dormouse** snoozes all through the mad tea-party. [Br. Lit.: *Alice's Adventures in Wonderland*]
5. **Endymion** man kept immortally youthful through eternal sleep. [Gk. Myth.: Howe, 91]
6. **Epimenides** philosopher nods off for 57 years in cave. [Gk. Legend: *LLEI,* I: 283]
7. **hypnale** asp which kills by inducing sleep. [Medieval Animal Symbolism: White, 174]
8. **Hypnos** god of slumber. [Gk. Myth.: Hall, 250]
9. **Joe (Fat Boy)** "Damn that boy, he's gone to sleep again." [Br. Lit.: Dickens *Pickwick Papers*]
10. **Lady Macbeth** while sleepwalking, discloses her terrible deeds. [Br. Drama: Shakespeare *Macbeth*]
11. **land of Nod** mythical land of sleep; humorous reference to biblical land in Genesis. [Am. and Br. Usage; O.T.: Genesis 4:16]
12. **Morpheus** Hypno's son and god of dreams. [Gk. Myth.: Howe, 172]
13. **poppy** attribute of Hypnos, Greek god of sleep. [Art: Hall, 250]
14. **Sandman** induces sleep by sprinkling sand in children's eyes. [Folklore: Brewer *Dictionary,* 966]
15. **Seven Sleepers** youths who fled Decian persecution; slept for more than 200 years. [Christian and Muslim Tradition: Benét, 918]
16. **Sleeping Beauty** enchanted heroine awakened from century of slumber by prince's kiss. [Fairy Tale: Brewer *Dictionary,* 1011]
17. **Snow White** poisoned apple induces her sleep; prince awakens her. [Children's Lit.: Bettelheim, 213]
18. **Somnus** god of sleep; son of Nox. [Rom. Myth.: Wheeler, 349]
19. **Van Winkle, Rip** slept for 20 years, thereby missing war. [Am. Lit.: "Rip Van Winkle" in Hart, 714]
20. **Winkie, Wee Willie** made sure all the children were asleep. [Nurs. Rhyme: Opie, 424]

594. SLEUTHING (See also CRIME FIGHTING.)

1. **Alleyn, Inspector** detective in Ngaio Marsh's many mystery stories. [New Zealand Lit.: Harvey, 520]
2. **Archer, Lew** tough solver of brutal crimes. [Am. Lit.: Herman, 94–96]

3. **Brown, Father** Chesterton's priest and amateur detective. [Br. Lit.: Herman, 20–21]
4. **Bucket, Inspector** shrewd detective solves a murder and uncovers Lady Dedlock's past. [Br. Lit.: *Bleak House* in Benét, 144]
5. **Campion, Albert** unpretentious cerebral detective. [Br. Lit.: Herman, 31–33]
6. **Carrados, Max** blind detective in stories by Ernest Bramah. [Br. Lit.: Barnhart, 159]
7. **Carter, Nick** turn-of-the-century flatfoot. [Radio: "Nick Carter, Master Detective" in Buxton, 173–174]
8. **Chan, Charlie** imperturbable Oriental gumshoe. [Am.Lit.: *Herman*, 36–37; Comics: Horn, 165–166]
9. **Charles, Nick** urbane and witty private detective. [Am. Lit.: *The Thin Man*]
10. **Clouseau, Inspector Jacques** bungling French detective; inexplicably and with great asininity gets his man. [Am. Cinema: "The Pink Panther"]
11. **Columbo** untidy, cigar-smoking mastermind. [TV: "NBC Mystery Movie" in Terrace, II, 141]
12. **Cuff, Sergeant** first detective in English fiction. [Br. Lit.: *The Moonstone* in Benét, 683]
13. **Drew, Nancy** teenage girl supersleuth. [Children's Lit.: *The Hidden Staircase*]
14. **Drummond, Bulldog** patriotic Englishman, hero of stories by Sapper. [Br. Lit.: Payton, 108]
15. **Dupin, Auguste** ratiocinative solver of unsolvable crimes. [Am. Lit.: Poe "The Murders in the Rue Morgue"; "The Mystery of Marie Roget"; "The Purloined Letter"]
16. **Fell, Dr. Gideon** fat, astute detective in John Dickson Carr's mysteries. [Am. Lit.: Benét, 170]
17. **Fosdick, Fearless** square-jawed, low-paid detective of questionable expertise and unquestionable obtuseness. [Comics: "Li'l Abner" in Horn, 450]
18. **Hardy Boys** teenagers solve crimes and mysteries with detective father. [Children's Lit.: *Clue in the Embers; Twisted Claw; Tower Treasure*]
19. **Hawkshaw** implacable detective with photographic memory. [Br. Lit.: *The Ticket-of-Leave Man*, Barnhart, 546]
20. **Holmes, Sherlock** the great detective; famous for deductive reasoning. [Br. Lit.: Payton, 316]
21. **inverness** coat with cape; emblem of Sherlock Holmes. [Br. Costume and Lit.: Espy, 267]

22. **Lane, Drury** Barney Ross's deaf ex-actor and amateur detective. [Am. Lit.: Herman, 105]
23. **Lecoq, Monsieur** meticulous detective; pride of French Sureté. [Fr. Lit.: *Monsieur Lecoq*]
24. **Lestrade** bungling Scotland Yard foil to Sherlock Holmes. [Br. Lit.: Payton, 387]
25. **Lupin, Arsène** murderer turned detective. [Fr. Lit.: Herman, 20]
26. **magnifying glass** traditional detective equipment; from its use by Sherlock Holmes. [Br. Lit.: Payton, 473]
27. **Maigret, Inspector** studiously precise detective; bases his work solidly on police methods. [Fr. Lit.: Herman, 114]
28. **Mannix** private eye with unorthodox style. [TV: Terrace, II, 62]
29. **Marlowe, Philip** hard-boiled but engaging private eye. [Am. Lit.: *The Big Sleep; Farewell, My Lovely; The Long Goodbye*]
30. **Marple, Miss** sweet old lady, tougher than she seems. [Br. Lit.: Herman, 51–55]
31. **Mason, Perry** attorney busier with detection than law. [Am. Lit.: Herman, 71–74]
32. **Mayo, Asey** the "codfish Sherlock." [Am. Lit.: Herman, 122–124]
33. **McGee, Travis** tough private eye and tougher private avenger. [Am. Lit.: Herman, 92–94]
34. **Moto, Mr.** clever Japanese detective. [Am. Cin.: Halliwell, 494]
35. **Pinkertons** famous detective agency; founded in 1850. [Am. Hist.: Jameson, 392]
36. **Poirot, Hercule** brainy, dandified genius in Christie mysteries. [Br. Lit.: Herman, 51–55]
37. **Pollifax, Mrs.** redoubtable widow joins the C.I.A. [Am. Lit.: *A Palm for Mrs. Pollifax*]
38. **Pudd'nhead Wilson** lawyer uses fingerprint evidence to win his client's acquittal and expose the true murderer. [Am. Lit.: Mark Twain *Pudd'nhead Wilson*; Benét, 824]
39. **Queen, Ellery** dilettantish private investigator. [Am. Lit.: Herman, 105]
40. **Rabbi, the** Rabbi David Small solves crimes using his Talmudic training. [Am. Lit.: *Friday the Rabbi Slept Late*]
41. **Saint, the** dashing diviner of knotty puzzles. [Radio: Buxton, 206; TV: Terrace, II, 264]
42. **Spade, Sam** hard-boiled private eye. [Am. Lit.: Herman, 79–82]
43. **Strangeways, Nigel** urbane solver of intricate crimes. [Br. Lit.: Herman, 37–38]

44. **Thatcher, John Putnam** charming, civilized, urbane detective. [Am. Lit.: Herman, 86–87]
45. **Tibbs, Virgil** California's brilliant, black detective. [Am. Lit.: *In the Heat of the Night*]
46. **Tracy, Dick** square-chinned detective of police comic strip. [Comics: Horn, 206]
47. **Vance, Philo** impressively learned, polished, and urbane detective. [Am. Lit.: Herman, 22, 126–127]
48. **Wimsey, Lord Peter** Shakespeare-quoting gentleman turned amateur detective. [Br. Lit.: Herman, 113–114]
49. **Wolfe, Nero** corpulent, lazy, but persevering crime-solver. [Am. Lit.: Herman, 119–122]

595. SMALLNESS (See also DWARFISM.)

1. **Alice** nibbles a magic cake to become a pygmy. [Br. Lit.: *Alice's Adventures in Wonderland*]
2. **Alphonse** petite page to Mr. Wititterly. [Br. Lit.: *Nicholas Nickleby*]
3. **Andorra** small state of 191 square miles, between France and Spain. [Eur. Hist.: *NCE,* 100]
4. **Anon, Mr.** a deformed and hunchbacked midget. [Br. Lit.: *Memoirs of a Midget,* Magill I, 577–579]
5. **hop-o'-my-thumb** generic term for a midget or dwarf. [Folklore: Brewer *Dictionary,* 544]
6. **Liechtenstein** central European principality, comprising 65 square miles. [Eur. Hist.: *NCE,* 1578]
7. **Lilliputians** race of pygmies living in fictitious kingdom of Lilliput. [Br. Lit.: *Gulliver's Travels*]
8. **Little Tich** midget music-hall comedian of late 1800s. [Br. Hist.: Brewer *Dictionary,* 1082]
9. **Luxembourg** duchy of 999 square miles in Western Europe. [Eur. Hist.: *NCE,* 1632]
10. **Miss M.** perfectly formed midget leads the pleasant social life of a young lady but disappears mysteriously. [Br. Lit.: Walter de la Mare *Memoirs of a Midget* in Magill I, 577]
11. **Mowcher, Miss** kindhearted hairdresser of small stature. [Br. Lit.: *David Copperfield*]
12. **Pepin the Short** first Frankish king; progenitor of Carolingian dynasty. [Eur. Hist.: Bishop, 20, 25]
13. **Quilp, Daniel** small man with giant head and face. [Br. Lit.: *Old Curiosity Shop*]

14. **Rhode Island** smallest of the fifty states; nicknamed "Little Rhodie." [Am. Hist.: *NCE,* 2315]
15. **Stareleigh, Justice** "a most particularly short man." [Br. Lit.: *Pickwick Papers*]
16. **Thumb, Tom** (1838–1883) stage name for the midget, Charles Sherwood Stratton. [Am. Hist.: Benét, 1016]
17. **Thumbelina** tiny girl, rescued by a swallow, marries the tiny king of the Angels of the Flowers. [Dan. Lit.: *Andersen's Fairy Tales*]
18. **Zacchaeus** little man took to tree to see Christ. [N.T.: Luke 19:3–4]

596. SMILING

1. ***Mona Lisa ("La Gioconda")*** her mysterious smile enchants the beholder. [Ital. Art: Benét 397]

Snobbery (See ARROGANCE, PRETENSION.)

597. SOCIAL PROTEST

1. ***Germinal*** portrays the sufferings of workers in the French mines. [Fr. Lit.: Zola *Germinal*]
2. ***Jungle, The*** novel exposed harrowing moral, economic, and hygienic conditions in the meat-packing industry. [Am. Lit.: Upton Sinclair *The Jungle*]
3. ***Tin Drum, The*** Grass's surreal novel of 20th-century madness. [Ger. Lit.: Magill IV, 1220]
4. ***Weavers, The*** textile workers revolt against their employer and wreck the factory. [Ger. Drama: Haydn & Fuller, 792]

598. SOLDIERING (See also MILITARISM.)

1. ***All Quiet on the Western Front*** youth Paul Baumer suffers the miseries of the first World War. [Ger. Lit.: Remarque *All Quiet on the Western Front*]
2. **Atkins, Tommy** nickname for English soldiers. [Br. Folklore: Walsh *Modern,* 33]
3. **Bailey, Beetle** hapless private who resists authority and seeks easy way out. [Comics: Horn, 105–106]
4. **Ellyat, Jack** from Connecticut: Union trooper undergoes many hardships. [Am. Lit.: "John Brown's Body" in Magill I, 445–448]
5. **Fuzzy-Wuzzy** name for bushy-haired Sudanese warriors celebrated in a Kipling ballad. [Br. Lit.: Kipling *Barrack-Room Ballads* in Benét, 81]
6. **G.I. Joe** any American soldier. [Am. Military Slang: Misc.]

7. **Good Soldier Schweik** simple, innocent Czech soldier in the Austrian army during World War I. [Czech Lit.: *The Good Soldier: Schweik,* Magill IV, 390–392]
8. **Gurkhas** Nepalese mercenaries, renowned for valor. [Nepalese Hist.: *NCE,* 1165]
9. **Janissaries** elite Turkish infantry. [Turk. Hist.: Fuller, I, 499, 508]
10. ***Red Badge of Courage, The*** young Civil War recruit Henry Fleming receives his baptism of fire. [Am. Lit.: Stephen Crane *The Red Badge of Courage*]
11. **Sad Sack** whose travails reflect those of all soldiers. [Comics: Horn, 595–596]
12. **Sherston, George** involved in the heavy action of World War I. [Br. Lit.: *Memoirs of an Infantry Officer* in Magill I, 579]
13. **Uncle Toby and Corporal Trim** inarticulate ex-soldier and his loquacious orderly reconstruct campaigns on small bowling green. [Br. Lit.: *Tristram Shandy* in Magill I, 1027]
14. **Wingate, Clay** from Georgia: Confederate counterpart of Jack Ellyat. [Am. Lit.: "John Brown's Body" in Magill I, 445–448]

599. SONG, PATRIOTIC

1. **America the Beautiful** patriotic song by Katherine Bates glorifying national ideals (1893). [Am. Music: Scholes, 30]
2. **Battle Hymn of the Republic** Union's Civil War rallying song. [Am. Music: Van Doren, 228]
3. **Deutschland über Alles** German national anthem. [Ger. Music: Misc.]
4. **God Save the Queen** official national anthem of the British Commonwealth. [Br. Music: Scholes, 408]
5. **John Brown's Body** Union rallying hymn during Civil War. [Am. Music: Jameson, 257]
6. **Maple Leaf Forever!** Canadian national song (1867). [Can. Music: Scholes, 597]
7. **Marseillaise** French national anthem. [Fr. Music: Misc.]
8. **Maryland, My Maryland** song expressing sentiments of Southern cause during Civil War (1861). [Am. Music: Scholes, 602]
9. **O Canada!** national song of Canada, popular among French Canadians. [Can. Music: Scholes, 699]
10. **O Deutschland, Hoch in Ehren!** war song of the Germans in 1914. [Ger. Music: Scholes, 700]
11. **Over There** George M. Cohan's song of American entry into WWI. [Am. Music: Flexner, 417]

12. **Rule, Britannia!** patriotic British song (1740). [Br. Music: Scholes, 897–898]
13. **Star-Spangled Banner, The** national anthem of the United States. [Am. Music: Scholes, 980]
14. **Tipperary** war song popular in British Army in World War I. [Br. Music: Scholes, 1025]
15. **Watch on the Rhine, The** (Die Wacht am Rhein) popular national song of Germany. [Ger. Music: Scholes, 1111]
16. **Wearing of the Green, The** patriotic song of Ireland (1797). [Irish Music: Scholes, 1111]
17. **When Johnny Comes Marching Home** Southern Civil War rallying song. [Am. Music: Van Doren, 228–229]
18. **Yankee Doodle** Revolutionary War paean of American glory. [Nurs. Rhyme: Opie, 439]

600. SORCERY

1. **sorcerer's apprentice** finds a spell that makes objects do the cleanup work. [Fr. Music: Dukas *The Sorcerer's Apprentice*]

Sorrow (See GRIEF.)

601. SOUTHERN STATES (U.S.)

1. **Confederacy** government of 11 Southern states that left the Union in 1860. [Am. Hist.: *EB,* III: 73]
2. **Dixie** popular name for Southern states in U.S. and for song. [Am. Hist.: *EB,* III: 587]
3. ***Gone With the Wind*** archetypal novel about the South. [Am. Lit.: *Gone With the Wind*]
4. **gray** color of the uniform of the Confederate soldier. [Am. Hist.: *NCE,* 566]
5. **grits** coarsely ground hominy served in traditional Southern breakfast. [Am. Culture: Misc.]
6. **Johnny Reb** a Confederate soldier or a resident of the Confederate states. [Am. Usage: Misc.]
7. **Mason-Dixon Line** boundary between Pennsylvania and Maryland that came to divide the slave (southern) states from the free (northern) states. [Am. Hist.: *NCE,* 1714]
8. **Spanish moss** silvery gray plant whose threadlike fronds hang from trees in the South. [Am. Culture: *EB,* IX: 400–401]
9. **Stars and Bars** flag of the Confederate States of the U.S. [Am. Hist.: *EB,* III: 73]
10. **wisteria** woody vine found in Southern gardens. [Am. Culture: *EB,* X: 716]

602. SPECTACLE

1. ***Aïda*** opera renowned for its scenic grandeur; sometimes played with on-stage elephants. [Ital. Opera: Verdi *Aïda* in Benét, 16]
2. **Barnum and Bailey circus** "greatest show on earth," famed for outstanding displays. [Am. Culture: *Collier's*, V, 110]
3. ***Birth of a Nation, The*** D. W. Griffith's monumental Civil War film. [Am. Cinema: Halliwell, 51]
4. **Ziegfeld Follies** elaborate New York musical entertainment (1907–1931) with gorgeous settings and dancers. [Am. Theater: *NCE*, 3045]
5. **Folies Bergère** opulent musical show in Paris featuring dancers, rich costumes and scenery. [Fr. Theater: *EB* (1972 ed.), IX, 515]

Speed (See **SWIFTNESS.**)

603. SPINSTERHOOD

1. **Forsyte, June** jilted by her fiancé, becomes an old maid. [Br. Lit.: *The Forsyte Saga*]
2. **Grundy, Miss** prim and proper schoolteacher, continually vexed by her students' antics. [Comics: "Archie" in Horn, 87]
3. **Havisham, Miss** old spinster; always wore her bridal dress though jilted on wedding day. [Br. Lit.: *Great Expectations*]
4. **Lovell, Charlotte** rather than reveal that an orphan girl is her own child, she spends her life as an old maid. [Am. Lit.: Edith Wharton *The Old Maid* in Magill I, 679]
5. **Sloper, Catherine** becomes an old maid rather than marry a man interested in her inheritance. [Am. Lit.: *Washington Square* in Hart, 899]
6. **Throssel, Miss Phoebe** a spinster with marriage continually on her mind. [Br. Lit.: *Quality Street,* Magill I, 793–795]

604. SPIRITUALISM

1. **Arcati, Madame** medium who materializes her client's two successive wives. [Br. Drama: Noel Coward *Blithe Spirit* in *On Stage*, 236]
2. ***Medium, The*** Menotti's opera of a medium haunted by her own hoax. [Am. Opera: Benét, 653]

605. SPLENDOR

1. **Aladdin's palace** built of marble, gold, silver, and jewels. [Arab. Lit.: *Arabian Nights*]

2. **Alhambra, the** palatial 13th-century Moorish citadel in Granada, noted for its lofty situation, beautiful courts, and fountains. [Span. Hist.: Benét, 24]
3. **baths of Caracalla and Diocletian** massive public buildings of imperial Rome, the latter having accommodations for 3,200 bathers. [Rom. Arch.: *EB* (1963) XIX, 392]
4. **Bucentaur** opulent Venetian ship of state. [Ital. Hist.: Plumb, 257]
5. **Crystal Palace** huge museum and concert hall made of iron and glass at Great Exhibition (1851). [Br. Hist.: *NCE,* 692]
6. **dahlia** symbol of splendor. [Plant Symbolism: *Flora Symbolica,* 168]
7. **Hanging Gardens of Babylon** Nebuchadnezzar's huge terraces, built to placate wife. [World Hist.: Wallechinsky, 255]
8. **Khan, Kubla** (1215–1294) splendors of imperial court dazzled Polo entourage. [Asian Hist.: *EB,* 10: 541–543]
9. **magnolia** symbol of magnificence. [Flower Symbolism: *Flora Symbolica,* 175]
10. **Mont-St.-Michel** abbey, church, and fortress; one of the finest examples of medieval French architecture. [Fr. Hist.: *NCE,* 1824]
11. **Parthenon** magnificent temple of Athena, dominating the Acropolis of Athens. [Gk. Hist.: Benét, 761]
12. **Sainte-Chapelle, the** 13th-century chapel, called the most beautiful building in France for its architecture and stained glass. [Fr. Architecture: *NCE,* 2396]
13. **Taj Mahal** fabulous tomb of Shah Jahan's wife. [Indian Hist.: Wallechinsky, 317]
14. **Tutankhamun's tomb** full of treasures of Egyptian pharaoh (c. 1350 B.C.). [Egypt. Hist.: Osborne, 1164]
15. **Versailles** luxurious palace of French kings; outside Paris. [Fr. Hist.: Brewer *Dictionary,* 1127]
16. **Xanadu** site of Kubla Khan's "stately pleasure dome". [Br. Lit.: *Kubla Khan* in Payton, 744]

606. SPLIT PERSONALITY

1. **Haller, Harry** middle-aged man battles two selves. [Ger. Lit.: *Steppenwolf*]
2. **Jekyll, Dr., and Mr. Hyde** upright physician reduced to animality by potion. [Br. Lit.: *Dr. Jekyll and Mr. Hyde*]
3. ***Three Faces of Eve, The*** story of woman with three distinct personalities. [Am. Cinema: Bawden, 757 (Woodward, Joanne)]

607. SPRING

1. **Flora** goddess of this season. [Rom. Myth.: Hall, 130]
2. **flowers** represent this season. [Art: Hall, 129]
3. **garlanded girl** personification of spring. [Art: Hall, 130]
4. **peep frogs** their voices welcome the season. [Am. Culture: Misc.]
5. **Persephone** personification of spring. [Gk. Myth.: Cirlot, 252]
6. **robin** harbinger of spring. [Western Culture: Misc.]
7. **swallow** harbinger of the spring season. [Animal Symbolism: Mercatante, 164]
8. **turtle doves** "voice of the turtle is heard." [O.T.: Song of Songs 2:12]
9. **Venus** goddess of this season. [Rom. Myth.: Hall, 130]
10. **Ver** personification; portrayed as infantile and tender. [Rom. Myth.: *LLEI*, I: 322]

608. SPYING

1. **Birch, Harvey** a double spy, secretly in the employ of George Washington. [Am. Lit.: Cooper *The Spy*]
2. **Bond, James** Agent 007: super spy, super hero. [Br. Lit.: Herman, 27]
3. **C.I.A.** (Central Intelligence Agency) U.S. intelligence agency. [Am. Hist.: *NCE*, 492]
4. **Cheka** early Soviet secret police charged with guarding against counterrevolutionary activity. [Russ. Hist.: Benét, 190]
5. **Cly, Roger** old servant of Darnay; became a spy. [Br. Lit.: *A Tale of Two Cities*]
6. **Hannay, Richard** opponent of foreign evil. [Br. Lit.: *The Thirty-Nine Steps* in Herman, 38–39]
7. **Hushai the Archite** sent by David to inveigle Absalom's confidence. [O.T.: II Samuel 15:34]
8. **KGB** the Committee of State Security, USSR agency (begun 1954) with responsibility for espionage and counter–espionage. [*EB*, V; 780]
9. **Kuryakin, Illya** taciturn, blond partner of Solo from U.N.C.L.E. [TV: "The Man from U.N.C.L.E." in Terrace, II, 60]
10. **Leamas** British Secret Service agent torn between duty and the desire to give up espionage. [Br. Lit.: Le Carré *The Spy Who Came In from the Cold* in Weiss, 440]
11. **Mata Hari** (1876–1917) courtesan executed by French for German espionage (1917). [Ger. Hist.: *EB*, VI: 683]

12. **Muir, Lieutenant Davy** garrison quartermaster discovered to be French spy. [Am. Lit.: Magill I, 715–717]
13. **NKVD** People's Commisariat of Internal Affairs, USSR police agency (1934–1943) that carried out purges of the 1930s. [*EB*, VII: 366]
14. **OGPU** secret police agency, successor to the Cheka. [Russ. Hist.: Benét, 190]
15. **Palmer, Harry** anti-hero of *The Ipcress File.* [Am. Cinema: Herman, 28–29]
16. **Polonius** spies on Hamlet and Gertrude. [Br. Drama: Shakespeare *Hamlet*]
17. ***Secret Agent, The*** Conrad's novel of the intrigues of a foreign secret agent (1907). [Br. Lit.: Magill III, 949–951]
18. **Smersh** acronym for Smert Shpionam (Death to Spies), a section of the KGB. [*EB*, IX: 283]
19. **Smiley, George** British Secret Service hero. [Br. Lit.: Le Carré in Drabble, 558]
20. **Solo, Napoleon** suave and debonair agent for U.N.C.L.E. [TV: "The Man from U.N.C.L.E." in Terrace, II, 60]

609. STIGMA

1. **mark of Cain** God's mark on Cain, a sign of his shame for fratricide. [O. T.: Genesis 4:15]
2. **scarlet letter** the letter "A" for "adultery" sewn on Hester Prynne's garments. [Am. Lit.: Hawthorne *The Scarlet Letter*]

610. STINGINESS (See also GREED, MISERLINESS.)

1. **Benny, Jack** (1894–1974) the king of penny pinchers. [Radio: "The Jack Benny Program" in Buxton, 122–123; TV: Terrace, 402]
2. **Carey, William** Philip's penny-pinching, smugly religious uncle. [Br. Lit.: Magill I, 670–672]
3. **Euclio** parsimonious and distrustful man hoards gold treasure. [Rom. Lit.: *The Pot of Gold*]
4. **Pitt, Crawley** inherits, marries, and hoards money. [Br. Lit.: *Vanity Fair*]
5. **Sieppe, Trina** begrudged every penny she spent. [Am. Lit.: *McTeague*]

Stoicism (See LONGSUFFERING.)

611. STORYTELLING

1. **Aesop** semi-legendary fabulist of ancient Greece. [Gk. Lit.: Harvey, 10]

2. **Münchäusen, Baron** traveler grossly embellishes his experiences. [Ger. Lit.: Harvey, 565]
3. **Mother Goose** originally a fictitious nursery rhyme spinner from Perrault, later a Bostonian authoress. [Fr. Lit.: Brewer *Handbook*, 732]
4. **Odysseus** wily teller of tales. [Gk. Legend: *Odyssey*]
5. **Ovid** (Publius Ovidius Naso, 43 B.C.–A.D. 17) great storyteller of classical mythology. [Rom. Lit.: Zimmerman, 187]
6. **Remus, Uncle** narrator of animal tales in Old South. [Am. Lit.: *Nights with Uncle Remus*]
7. **Sandy** told endless tales as she and Boss traveled. [Am. Lit.: *A Connecticut Yankee in King Arthur's Court*]
8. **Scheherazade** forestalls her execution with 1,001 tales. [Arab. Lit.: *Arabian Nights*]
9. **Watson, Dr. John H.** chronicles Sherlock Holmes's cases. [Br. Lit.: Arthur Conan Doyle *Sherlock Holmes*]

612. STRENGTH (See also BRAWNINESS.)

1. **acorn** heraldic symbol of strength. [Heraldry: Jobes, 27]
2. **Atlas** Titan condemned to bear heavens on shoulders. [Gk. Myth.: Walsh *Classical*, 38]
3. **Atlas, Charles** (1892–1972) 20th-century strongman; went from "98-pound weakling" to "world's strongest man." [Am. Sports: Amory, 38–39]
4. **Babe** Paul Bunyan's blue ox; straightens roads by pulling them. [Am. Lit.: Fisher, 270]
5. **Bionic Man** superman of the technological age. [TV: "The Six Million Dollar Man" in Terrace, II: 294–295]
6. **buffalo** heraldic symbol of power. [Heraldry: Halberts, 21]
7. **Bunyan, Paul** legendary woodsman of prodigious strength. [Am. Folklore: *Paul Bunyan*]
8. **Cyclopes** one-eyed giants; builders of fortifications. [Gk. Myth.: Avery, 346]
9. **Hercules** his twelve labors revealed his godlike powers. [Rom. Myth.: Howe, 122]
10. **Katinka, the Powerful** a female Man Mountain Dean. [Am. Comics: "Toonerville Folks" in Horn, 668]
11. **Little John** oak of a man in Robin Hood's band. [Br. Lit.: *Robin Hood*]
12. **meginjardir** Thor's belt; doubled his power. [Norse Myth.: Brewer *Dictionary*, 1076]
13. **Milo of Croton** renowned athlete. [Gk. Myth.: Hall, 209]

14. **Polydamas** huge athlete who killed a fierce lion with his bare hands, stopped a rushing chariot, lifted a mad bull, and died attempting to stop a falling rock. [Gk. Myth.: Benét, 801]
15. **Samson** possessed extraordinary might which derived from hair. [O.T.: Judges 16:17]
16. **Superman** caped superhero and modern-day Hercules. [Comics: Horn, 642–643]

Strife (See **DISCORD.**)

Stubbornness (See **OBSTINACY.**)

613. STUPIDITY (See also DIMWITTEDNESS, IGNORANCE.)

1. **Abdera** maritime city whose inhabitants were known proverbially for their stupidity. [Gk. Folklore: Benét, 2]
2. **Boeotians** inhabitants of rural Greek district; considered by Athenians to be dolts. [Gk. Folklore: Brewer *Dictionary*, 124]
3. **Chelm** mythical place inhabited by amiable simpletons. [Jew. Folklore: Rosten, 84]
4. **donkey** chooses cuckoo's singing over nightingale's. [Ger. Folklore and Poetry: Brentano and Arnim, *Des Knaben Wunderhorn; NCE,* 363]
5. **Dull, Anthony** archexample of stupidity. [Br. Lit.: *Love's Labour's Lost*]
6. **Elbow** ignorant, blundering constable. [Br. Lit.: *Measure for Measure*]
7. **Gimpel** a baker, foolish to the point of saintliness, is cuckolded and mocked, becomes a Wandering Jew. [Jewish Lit.: Singer *Gimpel the Fool* in Weiss, 174]
8. **Mendel, Menachem** hopeless schlemiel who devises impossible enterprises. [Yid. Lit.: Sholem Aleichem in Haydn & Fuller, 685]
9. **pomegranate** symbol of foolishness. [Flower Symbolism: *Flora Symbolica,* 176]
10. **Simple Simon** simpleton of bumptious ways. [Nurs. Rhyme: Opie, 385]
11. **Slender** "though well-landed, an idiot." [Br. Lit.: *Merry Wives of Windsor*]
12. **Smith, Knucklehead** dummy with self-referring name. [TV: "Winchell and Mahoney" in Terrace, II, 190–192]
13. **Snerd, Mortimer** a real dummy. [Radio: "The Edgar Bergen and Charlie McCarthy Show" in Buxton, 76–77]

14. **Stephen** simpleton; made gapingstock by all. [Br. Lit.: *Every Man in His Humour*]

15. **three wise men of Gotham** fools momentarily afloat in a light bowl. [Nurs. Rhyme: Opie, 193]

614. SUBJUGATION

1. **Cushan-rishathaim** Aram king to whom God sold Israelites. [O.T.: Judges 3:8]

2. **Gibeonites** consigned to servitude in retribution for trickery. [O.T.: Joshua 9:22–27]

3. **Ham** Noah curses him and progeny to servitude. [O.T.: Genesis 9:22–27]

4. **Jabin** Canaanite king to whom God sold Israelites. [O.T.: Judges 4:1]

5. **Nebuchadnezzar** Babylonian king, plunders Jerusalem; carries people into exile. [O.T.: II Kings 24:10–16]

6. **Svengali** mesmerizes artist's model, making her a famous singer under his influence. [Br. Lit.: George DuMaurier *Trilby*]

615. SUBMISSION

1. **Elliott, Anne** reluctantly gives up her fiancé on her family's advice. [Br. Lit.: Jane Austen *Persuasion* in Magill I, 734]

616. SUBSTITUTION

1. **Arsinoë** put her own son in place of Orestes; her son was killed and Orestes was saved. [Gk. Myth.: Zimmerman, 32]

2. **Barabbas** robber freed in Christ's stead. [N.T.: Matthew 27:15–18; Swed. Lit.: *Barabbas*]

3. **Canty, Tom** young beggar takes to throne in prince's stead. [Am. Lit.: *The Prince and the Pauper*]

4. **Edward, Prince of Wales** kingling becomes urchin in clothing exchange. [Am. Lit.: *The Prince and the Pauper*]

5. **George, Tobey** after Marcus's death, replaces him in his family. [Am. Lit.: *The Human Comedy*]

6. **Hagar** thinking herself barren, Sarah offers slave to Abraham. [O.T.: Genesis 16:1–4]

7. **Leah** deceptively substituted for Rachel in Jacob's bed. [O.T.: Genesis 29:22–25]

8. **whipping boy** surrogate sufferer for delinquent prince. [Eur. Hist.: Brewer *Note-Book*, 942]

617. SUCCESS

1. **Alger, Horatio** (1834–1899) writer of boys' stories where young men are instantly rewarded for honesty, perseverance, etc. [Am. Hist.: Hart, 19]
2. **Browndock, Miss** "made her fortune in no time at all." [Br. Lit.: *Nicholas Nickleby*]
3. **McVey, Hugh** from poor white to leading manufacturer. [Am. Lit.: *Poor White,* Magill I, 762–764]
4. **O Pioneers!** realistic success story of those who fathered nation. [Am. Lit.: *O Pioneers!,* Magill I, 663–665]
5. **Porter, Sir Joseph** became First Lord of the Admiralty by sticking to desk jobs and never going to sea. [Br. Opera: Gilbert and Sullivan *H.M.S. Pinafore*]
6. **Ragged Dick** hero of Alger's rags-to-riches epic. [Am. Lit.: Van Doren, 807]
7. **white cloud** indicates high achievement. [Western Folklore: Jobes, 350]
8. **wolf** symbol of success on coats of arms. [Heraldry: Halberts, 16]

618. SUFFERING

1. **aloe** symbol of suffering. [Flower Symbolism: Jobes, 71]
2. **Andersonville** horrible Civil War prison where 12,926 Union soldiers died. [Am. Hist.: Jameson, 18]
3. **Bataan** site of U.S.-Filipino army "death march" (1943). [Am. Hist.: *EB,* I: 867–868]
4. **Black hole of Calcutta** 146 Britishers imprisoned in small, stifling room (1756). [Br. Hist.: Harbottle, 45–46]
5. **Chiron** centaur, gave up his immortality in order to end the intolerable suffering accidentally inflicted by one of Heracles' poisoned arrows. [Gk. Myth.: Benét, 194]
6. **Concentration Camps** where millions of Jews were starved, experimented on, and exterminated by Nazis (1939–1945). [Eur. Hist.: Misc.]
7. **Gethsemane** garden east of Jerusalem where Jesus suffered in anguished fatigue. [N.T.: Matthew 26:36; Mark 14:32]
8. **Hiroshima** where the atomic bomb was dropped (August 6, 1945). [Am. Hist.: Fuller, III, 626]
9. **Io** having been changed into a heifer by Zeus, pestered by gadfly sent by Hera. [Gk. Myth.: Espy, 292]
10. ***J.B.*** Job's trials in modern setting and idiom. [Am. Lit.: *J.B.*]
11. **Job** beset with calamities. [O.T.: Job 1:13–22; 2:6–10]

12. **Mauperin, Renée** undergoes lingering and anguished death from guilt. [Fr. Lit.: *Renée Mauperin*]
13. **Orestes** persecuted and tormented by Furies. [Gk. Myth.: Wheeler, 271; Gk. Lit.: *The Eumenides*]
14. **Philoctetes** Greek hero, bitten by a serpent, suffers agonies for ten years. [Gk. Drama: Sophocles *Philoctetes* in Magill III, 741]
15. **prisoner of Chillon** chained for years in a damp, dark dungeon with his brothers, watches them die. [Br. Lit.: Byron *The Prisoner of Chillon* in Benét, 817]
16. **Prometheus** chained to rock while vulture fed on his liver. [Gk. Myth.: Zimmerman, 221]
17. ***Raft of the Medusa, The*** realistically portrays anguished ship's crew. [Fr. Art: Daniel, 166]
18. **Smith, Winston** beaten and tortured with rats for conspiring against the totalitarian regime. [Br. Lit.: George Orwell *1984*]
19. **Tantalus** condemned to Tartarus with food and water always just out of reach; hence, *tantalize*. [Gk. Myth.: Zimmerman, 253]
20. **Valley Forge** winter quarters of Washington's underfed, underclothed Continental army (1778). [Am. Hist.: Jameson, 519]

619. SUICIDE (See also REMORSE, SELF-SACRIFICE.)

1. **Achitophel** hanged himself when his advice went unheeded. [O.T.: II Samuel 17:23]
2. **Aegeus** throws himself into the sea believing that his son, Theseus, has come to harm. [Gk. Myth.: Brewer *Dictionary*, 12]
3. **Ajax (the Greater)** kills himself in rage over loss of Achilles' armor. [Rom. Lit.: *Aeneid*]
4. **Antigone** imprisoned, kills herself in despair. [Gk. Lit.: *Antigone*]
5. **Antony, Mark** thinking Cleopatra is dead, he falls upon his sword. [Br. Lit.: Shakespeare *Antony and Cleopatra*]
6. **Bart, Lily** social climber takes poison when all her scheming comes to naught. [Am. Lit.: *The House of Mirth* in Hart, 385]
7. **Brand, Ethan** acknowledging "the unpardonable sin," throws himself into a lime kiln. [Am. Lit.: Hawthorne "Ethan Brand" in Hart, 261]
8. **Butterfly, Madama (Cio-cio-san)** stabs herself when her American lover returns with his lawful wife. [Ital. Opera: *Madama Butterfly* in Osborne *Opera*, 192]
9. **Calista** stabs herself on disclosure of adultery. [Br. Lit.: *The Fair Penitent*]

10. **Cassandra** commits suicide to escape the Athenians. [Fr. Opera: Berlioz, *The Trojans,* Westerman, 174]
11. **Charmian** kills herself after mistress Cleopatra's death. [Br. Lit.: *Antony and Cleopatra*]
12. **Chuzzlewit, Jonas** wicked murderer, found out, takes poison. [Br. Lit.: Dickens *Martin Chuzzlewit*]
13. **Cleopatra** kills herself rather than being led through Rome in defeat. [Br. Lit.: Shakespeare *Antony and Cleopatra*]
14. **Compson, Quentin** unable to prevent the marriage of his sister, he drowns himself on her wedding day. [Am. Lit.: Faulkner *The Sound and the Fury* in Magill I, 917]
15. **Deianira** accidentally kills husband, Hercules; kills herself out of guilt. [Gk. Myth.: Kravitz, 76]
16. **Dido** kills herself when Aeneas abandons her. [Rom. Myth.: Avery, 392–393; Rom. Lit.: *Aeneid*]
17. **Dobson, Zuleika** Oxford undergraduates commit suicide when she spurns them. [Br. Lit.: Magill II, 1169]
18. **Eden, Martin** disgusted by society snobbery, he drowns himself. [Am. Lit: *Martin Eden*]
19. **Ekdal, Hedvig** heartbroken by her father's rejection, puts a bullet through her breast. [Nor. Drama: Ibsen *The Wild Duck* in Magill I, 1113]
20. **Enobarbus** kills himself for deserting Antony. [Br. Lit.: *Antony and Cleopatra*]
21. **Erigone** hangs himself in grief over father's murder. [Gk. Myth.: Kravitz, 91]
22. **Evadne** immolates herself on husband's funeral pyre. [Gk. Myth.: Kravitz, 100]
23. **Gabler, Hedda** shoots herself upon realizing that she is in the power of a man aware that she drove another man to suicide. [Swed. Drama: Ibsen *Hedda Gabler*]
24. **Goneril** stabs herself when her murder plot is discovered. [Br. Drama: Shakespeare *King Lear*]
25. **Hero** grief-stricken when her beloved Leander drowns while swimming the Hellespont, she drowns herself. [Gk. Myth.: Brewer *Dictionary*, 450]
26. **Iseult (Yseult, Isolde) of Ireland** arriving too late to save Tristram (Tristan) from death, she kills herself. [Medieval Legend: Brewer *Dictionary*, 913]
27. **Javert** French inspector drowns himself to escape self-perpetuating torment. [Fr. Lit.: *Les Misérables*]

28. **Jonestown** in Guyana; scene of mass-murder and suicides. [Am. Hist.: *Facts* (1978), 889–892]
29. **Julie, Miss** compromised by a clandestine affair and thwarted in her plans to run away, she decides to kill herself. [Swed. Drama: Strindberg *Miss Julie* in Magill II, 675]
30. **Juliet** stabs herself on seeing Romeo dead. [Br. Lit.: Shakespeare *Romeo and Juliet*]
31. **Kamikaze** WWII Japanese pilot corps plunge own planes into enemy ships in banzai attacks. [Jap. Hist.: Fuller, III, 618–619]
32. **Karenina, Anna** throws herself in front of approaching train. [Russ. Lit.: *Anna Karenina*]
33. **Little Father Time** solemn child hangs his foster-brothers and himself because of the family's misfortunes. [Br. Lit.: Hardy *Jude the Obscure*]
34. **Loman, Willy** crashes his car to bring insurance money to his family. [Am. Drama: Arthur Miller *Death of a Salesman*]
35. **Mannon, Christine** when her lover is killed she shoots herself. [Am. Drama: Eugene O'Neill *Mourning Becomes Electra*]
36. **Nickleby, Ralph** learning that poor Smike is his own son, hangs himself. [Br. Lit.: Dickens *Nicholas Nickleby*]
37. **Ophelia** driven insane by Hamlet's actions, she drowns herself. [Br. Drama: Shakespeare *Hamlet*]
38. **Panthea** kills herself upon death of lover, Abradates. [Gk. Lit.: Walsh *Classical*, 3]
39. **Paul** deluded youth kills himself when his grandiose yearnings come to nothing. [Am. Lit.: Willa Cather "Paul's Case"]
40. **Phaedra** Athenian queen drinks poison after confessing guilt. [Fr. Lit.: *Phaedra*,Magill I, 741–742]
41. **Romeo** thinking that Juliet's sleep is death, he drinks poison. [Br. Lit.: Shakespeare *Romeo and Juliet*]
42. **Rudolf, Archduke** crown prince of Austria (1858–1889) died in suicide pact with his mistress at Mayerling. [Aust. Hist.: *Collier's*, XVI: 606]
43. **Saul** falls on sword to avoid humiliation of capture. [O.T.: I Samuel 31:4–6]
44. **Sophonisba** Carthaginian who took poison to avoid falling into Roman hands. [Rom. Hist.: Benét, 947]
45. **Suicide Club** members wishing to die are chosen by lot, as are those who are to effect their deaths. [Br. Lit.: Stevenson "The Suicide Club"]
46. **Vane, Sibyl** young actress kills herself after Dorian's betrayal. [Irish Lit.: *The Picture of Dorian Gray*, Magill I, 746–748]

620. SUMMER

1. **Aestas** personification of summer; portrayed as youthful and sprightly. [Rom. Myth.: *LLEI*, I: 322]
2. **Ceres** goddess of the season. [Rom. Myth.: Hall, 130]
3. **cricket** symbol of summer; weather prognosticator. [Insect Symbolism: Jobes, 382]
4. **naked girl with fruit** personification of summer. [Art: Hall, 130]
5. **sickle and sheaf of corn** representational of the season. [Art: Hall, 129]

621. SUN (See also LIGHT.)

1. **Apollo** sun god; his chariot ride spanned morning to night. [Gk. Myth.: Benét, 42]
2. **Aton (Aten)** solar deity worshiped as the one god by Amenophis IV. [Egypt. Myth.: Parrinder, 33]
3. **Bast** cat-headed goddess representing sun and moon. [Egypt. Myth.: Parrinder, 41]
4. **Belenus** sun god. [Celtic Myth.: Parrinder, 42]
5. **Buto** goddess and mother of the sun and moon. [Egypt. Myth. Kravitz, 48]
6. **cock** Helios's sacred bird; sacrificed to the sun in Mexico. [Rom. and Mex. Myth.: Leach, 239]
7. **Cuchulain** sun-figure and powerful fighter. [Irish Myth.: Parrinder, 68]
8. **double ax** symbol of the sun. [Hindu and Western Folklore: Cirlot, 22]
9. **eagle** symbol represents the sun. [Gk. Myth.: Brewer *Dictionary*, 358]
10. **fire** representation of the sun. [Western Symbolism: Cirlot, 105–106]
11. **gold** color of the sun's rays. [Color Symbolism: Jobes, 357]
12. **Helios** sun in its astronomic aspects; aspect of Apollo. [Gk. Myth: Espy, 28]
13. **Horus** solar deity, portrayed as a hawk-headed man. [Egypt. Myth.: Benét, 478]
14. **Hyperion** Titan and father of the sun. [Gk. Myth.: Zimmerman, 132]
15. **lion** symbol of the sun gods; corresponds to the sun. [Western Symbolism: Cirlot, 189–190]
16. **Mithra (Mithras)** god of sunlight. [Persian Myth.: *EB*, VI: 944–945]

17. **Phaëthon** Apollo's son; foolishly attempted to drive sun chariot. [Gk. Myth.: Zimmerman, 202]
18. **Phoebus** epithet of Apollo as the sun god. [Gk. Myth.: Benét, 42]
19. **Ra** personification of the sun. [Egypt. Myth.: Parrinder, 235]
20. **Sol** the sun god. [Rom. Myth.: Zimmerman, 245]

622. SUPERNATURAL

1. ***Twilight Zone, The*** tales of weird events involving ordinary people. [Am. Radio, TV, & Cinema: *The Twilight Zone* in Terrace]

623. SURPRISE

1. **Henry, O.** his plots characterized by unexpected dénouements. [Am. Lit.: Benét, 457]
2. **Operation Z** Japanese plan for Pearl Harbor attack. [Jap. Hist.: Toland, 177–178, 183–187]
3. **Pearl Harbor** site of surprise attack on American fleet by the Japanese (December 7, 1941). [Am. Hist.: Fuller, III, 455–456]
4. **thief in the night** analogy to the Lord's unexpected coming. [N.T.: I Thessalonians 5:2]
5. **truffle** indicates the unexpected. [Flower Symbolism: *Flora Symbolica,* 178]

624. SURVIVAL (See also ENDURANCE.)

1. ***Alive*** story of the survivors of plane crash in the Andes. [Am. Lit.: *Alive*]
2. **Comanche** horse; sole survivor of Little Big Horn massacre (1876). [Am. Hist.: Wallechinsky, 126]
3. **Crusoe, Robinson** only survivor of shipwreck. [Br. Lit.: *Robinson Crusoe*]
4. **Deucalion** survives flood that destroys human race. [Gk. Myth.: Howe, 80]
5. **Donner Party** survivors of group of emigrants to California (1846–1847). [Am. Hist.: *NCE,* 783–784]
6. **Lot** allowed by God to escape the conflagration of Sodom and Gomorrah. [O.T.: Genesis 13:1–12]
7. **Mellitias, St.** of "Forty Martyrs," the only one to survive icy ordeal. [Christian Hagiog.: Attwater, 133–134]
8. **Noah** chosen by God to escape the deluge. [O.T.: Genesis 5–9]
9. **Pilgrim, Billy** survives the fire-bombing of Dresden and is the only passenger to survive a domestic air-crash. [Am. Lit.: Kurt Vonnegut *Slaughterhouse-Five*]

10. **Robinsons** shipwrecked family learns to cope with nature on a desert island. [Children's Lit.: *Swiss Family Robinson*]

625. SUSTENANCE

1. **Amalthaea** goat who provided milk for baby Zeus. [Gk. Myth.: Leach, 41]
2. **ambrosia** food of the gods; bestowed immortal youthfulness. [Gk. Myth.: Kravitz, 19]
3. **locusts and wild honey** John the Baptist's meager fare in wilderness. [N.T.: Matthew 3:4; Mark 1:6]
4. **manna** given by the Lord to the Israelites. [O.T.: Exodus 16: 14–15]

626. SWIFTNESS

1. **Acestes** shoots an arrow with such force that it catches fire from friction with the air. [Rom. Lit.: *Aeneid* V, 525]
2. **Al Borak** horse who carried Muhammad from Mecca to Jerusalem overnight. [Muslim Tradition: Walsh *Classical*, 13–14]
3. **Argo** swift, magic ship of the Argonauts. [Gk. Myth.: Avery, 145]
4. **Atalanta** heroine; fleet of foot; defeated by trickery. [Gk. Myth.: Walsh *Classical*, 36–37; Br. Lit.: *Atalanta*]
5. **Bayard** swiftest horse in the world. [Medieval and Renaissance Legend: Brewer *Dictionary*, 86]
6. **Camilla** Volscian queen; could run over cornfield without bending blades. [Rom. Lit.: *Aeneid*]
7. **cheetah** fastest four-footed animal alive; can reach 60 mph. [Zoology: Misc.]
8. ***Cutty Sark*** clipper ship, built in 1869, broke speed records in the tea trade. [Br. Hist.: *EB*, (1963) V, 830]
9. **Hermes** (Rom. **Mercury**) messenger god; ran on the wings of the wind. [Gk. Myth.: Zimmerman, 124]
10. **Jehu** Israelite king noted for his rapid chariot driving. [O.T.: II Kings 9]
11. **Laelaps** hound so swift, it always overtook its quarry. [Gk. Myth.: Howe, 149]
12. **Pacolet's horse** enchanted steed of unparalleled quickness. [Fr. Lit.: *Valentine and Orson; LLEI,* 1: 304]
13. **Pheidippides** (fl. 490 B.C.) ran 26 miles to Athens to announce Greek victory over Persians at Marathon. [Gk. Legend: Zimmerman, 159]

14. **Road Runner** foxy bird who continually zooms out of the coyote's reach. [TV: "The Road Runner Show" in Terrace, 247]
15. **Superman** superhero; faster than a speeding bullet. [Comics: Horn, 642; TV: "Adventures of Superman" in Terrace, I, 37–38]
16. **winged petasus** Mercury's cap; symbolic of speed. [Gk. and Rom. Myth.: 145]

627. SWORD

1. **Almace** sabre of Turpin. [Fr. Lit.: *The Song of Roland*]
2. **Angurvadel** of Frithjof; blazed in war, gleamed dimly in peace. [Norse Myth.: *LLEI*, I: 323]
3. **Balisarda** made by sorceress for killing Orlando. [Ital. Lit.: *Orlando Furioso*, Benét, 75]
4. **Balmung** mighty sword belonging to Siegfried. [Ger. Lit.: *Nibelungenlied*]
5. **Barbamouche** Climborin's sabre. [Fr. Lit.: *The Song of Roland*]
6. **Colada** El Cid's two-hilted, solid gold sword. [Span. Lit.: *Song of the Cid*]
7. **Damocles, sword of** sword hung by a single hair over his head. [Rom. Lit.: Brewer *Handbook*, 257]
8. **Durindana (Durendal)** Orlando's unbreakable sword. [Ital. Lit.: *Morgante Maggiore*, Brewer *Handbook*, 309]
9. **Excalibur** Arthur's enchanted sword; extracting it from stone won him crown. [Br. Lit.: *Le Morte d'Arthur*]
10. **Fragarach** the "Answerer"; Lug's mighty blade could pierce any armor. [Irish Myth.: Leach, 415]
11. **Gram** belonged to Sigmund; broken by Odin. [Norse Lit.: *Volsung Saga*]
12. **Gramimond** Valdabrun's sabre. [Fr. Lit.: *The Song of Roland*]
13. **Hauteclaire** Oliver's trusty sabre. [Fr. Lit.: *The Song of Roland*]
14. **Joyeuse** Charlemagne's sword; buried with him. [Fr. Lit.: Brewer *Dictionary*, 594]
15. **Marmorie** Grandoyne's sabre. [Fr. Lit.: *The Song of Roland*]
16. **Merveilleuse** Doolin of Mayence's remarkably sharp sword. [Fr. Lit.: Wheeler, 241]
17. **Mimung** magic sword lent by Wittich to Siegfried. [Norse. Myth.: Wheeler, 244]
18. **Mordure** Arthur's all-powerful sword, made by Merlin. [Br. Lit.: *Faerie Queene*]
19. **Morglay** Bevis's sword. [Br. Lit.: *Bevis of Hampton*]
20. **Murgleys** Ganelon's sabre. [Fr. Lit.: *The Song of Roland*]

21. **Notung** Sigmund's promised sword, found in ash tree; later, Siegfried's. [Ger. Opera: Wagner, *Valkyrie*, Westerman, 236]
22. **Precieuse** sabre of the pagan, Baligant. [Fr. Lit.: *The Song of Roland*]
23. **Rosse** Alberich's gift to Otwit; frighteningly fine-edged. [Norse Myth.: Brewer *Dictionary*, 936]
24. **Sanglamore** Braggadocio's big, bloody glaive. [Br. Lit.: *Faerie Queene*]
25. **Sautuerdu** Malquiant's sabre. [Fr. Lit.: *The Song of Roland*]
26. **Sword of Justice** held by the personification of Justice. [Rom. Trad.: Jobes II, 898]
27. **Tizona** dazzling, golden-hilted sword of the Cid. [Span. Lit.: *Song of the Cid*]
28. **Zulfagar** sword of Ali, Muhammad's son. [Islamic Legend: Brewer *Handbook*, 1066]

Sycophancy (See **FLATTERY.**)

T

628. TACITURNITY

1. **Barkis** warmhearted but taciturn husband of Peggoty. [Br. Lit: *David Copperfield*]
2. **Bartleby the Scrivener** "I prefer not to" was his constant refrain and all he ever said. [Am. Lit.: "Bartleby the Scrivener"]
3. **Bert and I** taciturn "down-Easterners." [Am. Culture: Misc.]
4. **Coolidgc, Calvin** (1872–1933) 30th U.S. president; nicknamed "Silent Cal." [Am. Hist.: Frank, 99]
5. **Laconian** inhabitant of ancient country of Laconia; people noted for pauciloquy. [Gr. Hist.: *NCE,* 1514]

629. TALKATIVENESS

1. **Balwhidder** kind but loquacious Presbyterian clergyman. [Br. Lit.: *Annals of the Parish*]
2. **Bates, Miss** goodhearted purveyor of trivia and harmless gossip. [Br. Lit.: *Emma*]
3. **Bernstein, Baroness** (Beatrix Esmond) loquaciously amusing, venomous, or coarse character. [Br. Lit.: *The Virginians*]
4. **blarney stone** whoever kisses the stone "will never want for words." [Irish Folklore: Leach, 147]
5. **Brigidda, Monna** unstoppable talker and gossiper. [Br. Lit.: George Eliot *Romola*]
6. **cicada** symbol of talkativeness because of its constant, strident noise. [Folklore: Jobes, 338]
7. **daisies** the flowers chatter incessantly at Alice. [Children's Lit.: *Through the Looking-Glass*]
8. **Echo** beautiful nymph who, by her constant talk, kept Hera away from Zeus. [Gk. Myth.: Howe, 89]
9. **Kenge, Mr.** garrulous soldier; nicknamed "conversation Kenge." [Br. Lit.: *Bleak House*]
10. **Old Woman of Gloucester** talkative woman displeased with her more talkative parrot. [Nurs. Rhyme: *Mother Goose,* 112]
11. **parrot** chattering bird; mimics human speech. [Animal Symbolism: Mercatante, 157]
12. **Polonius** wordy, "wretched, rash, intruding fool." [Br. Lit.: *Hamlet*]

13. **Trim, Corporal** dutiful attendant of Uncle Toby; distinguished for volubility. [Br. Lit.: *Tristram Shandy*]

630. TALLNESS (See also GIANTISM.)

1. **Alice** drinking a magic potion, she grows so tall that she fills an entire room. [Br. Lit.: Lewis Carroll *Alice's Adventures in Wonderland*]
2. **Chrysler Building** in New York City; one of the tallest buildings in the world. [Architecture: Misc.]
3. **Colossus of Rhodes** statue of Apollo; wonder of ancient world. [Gk. Hist.: Osborne, 256]
4. **Eiffel Tower** built in 1889 in Paris. [Architecture: *NCE,* 843]
5. **elevator shoe** shoe with insole designed to increase wearer's height. [Am. Pop. Culture: Misc.]
6. **Empire State Building** New York's famous skyscraper. [Architecture: *NCE,* 865]
7. **giraffe** tallest of animals. [Zoology: *NCE,* 1088]
8. **redwoods** giant trees (sequoias) of Pacific Coast. [Botany: *NCE,* 2477]
9. **Sears Tower** in Chicago; one of America's tallest buildings. [Architecture: Misc.]
10. **Woolworth Building** in New York City; erected by Frank Woolworth in 1913; tallest building until Empire State Building (1930–1931). [Architecture: *NCE,* 3004]
11. **World Trade Center** New York's giant twin edifices. [Architecture: Payton, 742]

631. TARDINESS

1. **Dagwood** comic strip character; chronically late at the office. [Comics: "Blondie" in Horn, 118]
2. **ten o'clock scholar** schoolboy who habitually arrives late. [Nurs. Rhyme: Opie, 378]
3. **White Rabbit** pocket watch-carrying rabbit. [Br. Lit.: *Alice's Adventures in Wonderland*]

632. TEACHING (See also EDUCATION.)

1. **Aristotle** (384–322 B.C.) Greek philosopher who tutored Alexander the Great. [Gk. Hist.: *NCE,* 147]
2. **Arnold, Dr.** wise headmaster of Rugby shows his understanding of youth. [Br. Lit.: *Tom Brown's School Days*; Magill II, 1039]

3. **Auburn schoolmaster** learned and severe yet kind master of the village school. [Br. Poetry: Goldsmith *The Deserted Village* in Norton *Literature*]
4. **Bhaer, Professor** teaches writing to Jo; eventually marries her. [Am. Lit.: *Little Women*]
5. **Brooks, Miss** (Connie) popular TV show features a harried Miss Brooks as high school teacher. [TV: "Our Miss Brooks" in Terrace, II, 174]
6. **Chips, Mr.** lovable and didactic schoolteacher. [Br. Lit.: *Goodbye, Mr. Chips*]
7. **Chiron** knowledgeable Centaur; instructed Achilles, Jason, and Asclepius. [Gk. Myth.: Parrinder, 62]
8. **Grundy, Miss** Archie's grumpy high school teacher. [Am. Comics: "Archie" in Horn, 87]
9. **Hartsook, Ralph** backwoods schoolteacher has severe problems with boisterous older pupils. [Am. Lit.: *The Hoosier Schoolmaster*; Magill I, 373]
10. **Hicks, Miss** history teacher, antiquated but wise, impassioned, and just to her pupils. [Am. Lit.: Saroyan *The Human Comedy* in Magill I, 392]
11. **Kotter, Gabe** teacher of Special Guidance Remedial Academics. [TV: "Welcome Back, Kotter" in Terrace, II, 423]
12. **Leonowens, Mrs. Anna** young Welsh widow, tutors children and women of King of Siam. [Br. Lit.: Landon *Anna and the King of Siam*; Am. Musical: Rodgers and Hammerstein *The King and I* in *On Stage*, 333]
13. **Moffat, Miss** teacher in Welsh mining town. [Br. Lit.: *The Corn Is Green; NCE,* 2982]
14. **Pangloss** character who taught Candide "metaphysico-theologo-cosmolonigology." [Fr. Lit.: *Candide*]
15. **Phillotson, Mr.** Jude's former schoolmaster. [Br. Lit.: Thomas Hardy *Jude The Obscure*]
16. **Porpora** famous music master of Consuelo and Haydn. [Fr. Lit.: *Consuelo,* Magill I, 156–158]
17. **Silenus** knowledgeable tutor of Bacchus. [Rom. Myth.: Daniel, 213]
18. **Socrates** (469–399 B.C.) Greek philosopher; tutor of Plato. [Gk. Hist.: *NCE,* 2553]
19. **Squeers, Wackford** dismally ignorant schoolmaster, cruel to his charges. [Br. Lit.: Dickens *Nicholas Nickleby*]

20. **Swift, Kate** stern schoolteacher, takes pains to encourage any signs of genius. [Am. Lit.: Anderson *Winesburg, Ohio* in Benét, 1095]

21. **village schoolmaster** stern yet kind; the rustics wondered "that one small head could carry all he knew." [Br. Poetry: Goldsmith *The Deserted Village* in Magill IV, 823]

633. TEENAGER (See also ADOLESCENCE.)

1. ***Ah, Wilderness!*** high-school senior has problems with girls and his father. [Am. Drama: O'Neill *Ah, Wilderness!* in Sobel, 15]
2. **Aldrich, Henry** teenaged film character of the 1940s. [Am. Cinema: Halliwell, 337]
3. **American Bandstand** durable and popular TV show; teenagers are featured performers. [TV: Terrace, I, 52]
4. **Archie** the eternal comic-book teenager. [Comics: Horn, 87]
5. **Baxter, William Sylvanus** adolescent in the throes of first love. [Am. Lit.: Booth Tarkington *Seventeen* in Benét, 918]
6. **Caulfield, Holden** sensitive, troubled teenager. [Am. Lit.: *Catcher in the Rye*]
7. **Dedalus, Stephen** undergoes all the trials, troubles, fears, and embarrassments of a teenager. [Irish Lit.: Joyce *Portrait of the Artist as a Young Man*]
8. **Gidget** archetypal teenage girl. [TV: Terrace, I, 311–312]
9. **Gillis, Dobie** 1950s and 1960s teenager struggling to postpone adulthood. [TV: "The Many Loves of Dobie Gillis" in Terrace, II, 64–66]
10. **Hardy, Andy** teenaged son of a "typical family" in a small midwestern town. [Am. Cinema: Halliwell, 323]

634. TEMPERANCE

1. **Alcoholics Anonymous (AA)** organization founded to help alcoholics (1934). [Am. Culture: *EB*, I: 448)
2. **amethyst** provides protection against drunkenness; February birthstone. [Gem Symbolism: Kunz, 58–59]
3. **Anti-Saloon League** successfully led drive for Prohibition (1910s). [Am. Hist.: Flexner, 357]
4. **Jonadab** enjoined his people to abstinence. [O.T.: Jeremiah 35: 5–11]
5. **Nation, Carry** (Amelia Moore) (1846–1911) hatchet-wielding saloon wrecker. [Am. Hist.: Flexner, 253]
6. **Prohibition** (1919–1933) period when selling and consuming liquor was against the law. [Am. Hist.: *NCE*, 2710]

7. **Rechabites** pastoral people who abstained from all wines. [O.T.: Jeremiah 35:5–19]
8. **Samson** consecrated to God in abstinence. [O.T.: Judges 13:4–5]
9. **Volstead Act** 18th Amendment, passed by Congress to enforce Prohibition (1919). [Am. Hist.: Flexner, 286]
10. **Woman's Christian Temperance Union** society of militant housewives against drinking (20th century). [Am. Hist.: Flexner, 357]

635. TEMPTATION

1. **apple** as fruit of the tree of knowledge in Eden, has come to epitomize temptation. [O.T.: Genesis 3:1–7; Br. Lit.: *Paradise Lost*]
2. **forbidden fruit** God prohibits eating from Tree of Knowledge. [O.T.: Genesis 2:16–17]
3. **Potiphar's wife** tried to induce Joseph to lie with her. [O.T.: Gen. 39]
4. **quince** symbol of temptation [Flower Symbolism: *Flora Symbolica,* 176]
5. **Satan** offers world to Jesus in exchange for His obeisance. [N.T.: Matthew 4:8–11]
6. **serpent** coaxes Eve to eat forbidden fruit. [O.T.: Genesis 3:1–5]
7. **Zuleika** name given in Arabian legend to Potiphar's wife, who vainly tempted Joseph. [Arab. Legend: Benét, 1117]

Terror (See **HORROR.**)

636. TERRORISM

1. **Al Fata** Palestine Liberation movement's terrorist organization. [Arab. Hist.: Wigoder, 186]
2. **Baader-Meinhof gang** German terrorists. [Ger. Hist.: *Facts* (1978), 114–115]
3. **Black Panthers** militant black revolutionists and civil-rightists. [Am. Hist.: Flexner, 46]
4. **Gestapo** Nazi secret police; executors of "Final Solution." [Ger. Hist.: Wigoder, 211]
5. **IRA** the Irish Republican Army; long history of terror and violence. [Irish Hist.: *NCE,* 1365–1366]
6. **Ku Klux Klan** post-Civil War white supremacist organization used terrorist tactics against blacks. [Am. Hist.: *NCE,* 1505]
7. **Nazis** (National Socialism) spread fear and terror throughout Hitler's Germany. [Ger. Hist.: *NCE,* 1894]

8. **Red Brigade** Italian terrorist group; assassinated Aldo Moro (1978). [Ital. Hist.: *Facts* (1978), 133]
9. **Reign of Terror** (1793–1794) revolutionary government made terror its means of suppression, by edict (September 5, 1793). [Fr. Hist.: *EB,* IX: 904]
10. **Symbionese Liberation Army** small terrorist group that kidnapped Patty Hearst (1974–1975). [Am. Hist.: *Facts* (1974), 105]
11. **Weathermen** American terrorist group against the "Establishment." [Am. Hist.: *Facts* (1972), 384]

637. TEST

1. **Abraham** his faith is tested when God demands the sacrifice of his son Isaac. [O.T.: Genesis 22:13]
2. **Arthur, King** (c. 950–1000) becomes King of England by pulling sword from stone. [Arth. Legend: *NCE,* 159]
3. **Carmel, Mt.** site of contest between Elijah and Baal priests. [O.T.: I Kings 18:19–40]
4. **Cuban missile crisis** President Kennedy called Krushchev's bluff, forcing dismantling of missile sites (1962). [Am. Hist.: Van Doren, 581–582]
5. **J.B.** testing of contemporary Job. [Am. Lit.: *J.B.*]
6. **Job** tormented to test devoutness. [O.T.: Job 1, 2]
7. **Judgment of God** medieval trial by combat or ordeal. [Eur. Hist.: Leach, 561]
8. **K'ung Fu** Confucian-based sect demands rigid tests for membership. [TV: Terrace, I, 448]
9. **ordeal by fire** noble accused of crime holds red-hot iron or walks blindfolded and barefoot over red-hot plowshares to prove his innocence. [Br. Hist.: Brewer *Handbook,* 779]
10. ***Turandot*** solver of riddles wins Turandot; failure brings death. [Ital. Opera: Puccini, *Turandot,* Westerman, 367–368]

638. THEATER

1. **Abbey Theatre** home of famed Irish theatrical company. [Irish Hist.: *NCE,* 3]
2. **Bolshoi** Moscow's premier ballet company. [Russ. Hist.: *NCE,* 327]
3. **Broadway** famous theatrical district at New York's Times Square. [Am. Hist.: Hart, 107]
4. **Carnegie Hall** New York's venerable theater for concert-goers. [Am. Hist.: *NCE,* 460]

5. **Comédie-Française** (Théâtre-Français) world's oldest established national theater. [Fr. Hist.: *EB,* III: 33]
6. **Drury Lane** London street famed for theaters; the theatrical district. [Br. Hist.: Herbert, 1321]
7. **Federal Theater** provided employment for actors, directors, writers, and scene designers (1935–1939). [Am. Hist.: *NCE,* 932]
8. **Garrick Theatre** famous London playhouse; named for David Garrick. [Br. Lit.: *NCE,* 1048]
9. **Globe Theatre** playhouse where Shakespeare's plays were performed. [Br. Lit.: *NCE,* 1094]
10. **Habima Theater** national theater of Israel; its troupe is famous for passionate acting style. [Israeli Hist.: *NCE,* 1170]
11. **La Scala (Teatro alla Scala)** "Theater at the Stairway"; Milan opera house; built 1776. [Ital. Hist.: *EB,* VI: 57]
12. **Lincoln Center** New York's modern theater complex. [Am. Hist.: *NCE,* 1586]
13. **Metropolitan Opera House** famous theater in New York City; opened in 1883. [Am. Hist.: *NCE,* 1761]
14. **Old Vic** London Shakespeare theater (1914–1963). [Br. Hist.: *NCE,* 1999]
15. **Radio City Music Hall** New York City's famous cinema; home of the Rockettes. [Am. Hist.: *NCE,* 2338]
16. **Shubert Alley** heart of Broadway; named after the three Shubert brothers. [Am. Hist.: Herbert, 1322]
17. **Winter Garden** a famous old theater in New York City. [Am. Hist.: Payton, 738]

639. THIEVERY (See also GANGSTERISM, HIGHWAYMEN, OUTLAWRY.)

1. **Alfarache, Guzmán de** picaresque, peripatetic thief; lived by unscrupulous wits. [Span. Lit.: *The Life of Guzmán de Alfarache*]
2. **Armstrong, Johnnie** Scottish Robin Hood; robbed only the English. [Br. Hist.: Walsh *Classical,* 31–32]
3. **Artful Dodger** tricky thief; pupil of Fagin. [Br. Lit.: Dickens *Oliver Twist*]
4. **Autolycus** master robber. [Gk. Myth.: Leach, 96]
5. **Barabbas** thief released instead of Jesus to appease crowd. [N.T.: Matthew 27:16–26; Mark 15:7–15; John 18:40]
6. **Cacus** Vulcan's three-headed, thieving son. [Rom. Myth.: Benét, 154]

7. **Compeyson** accomplished criminal; swindles, forges, and steals. [Br. Lit.: *Great Expectations*]
8. **Crackit, Toby** a housebreaker; burglarizes Chertsey. [Br. Lit.: *Oliver Twist*]
9. **Dawkins, John** London pickpocket and thief. [Br. Lit.: *Oliver Twist*]
10. **Fagin** he trained young boys to become thieves. [Br. Lit.: *Oliver Twist*]
11. **Gradgrind, Tom** thief; robbed Bounderby's Bank. [Br. Lit.: *Hard Times*]
12. **Hood, Robin** took from the rich and gave to the poor. [Br. Lit.: *Robin Hood*]
13. **Knave of Hearts** "stole the tarts" made by Queen of Hearts. [Nurs. Rhyme: Baring-Gould, 152]
14. **Lockhart, Jamie** a backwoods bandit with heroic qualities, chosen by a rich planter to be his daughter's husband. [Am. Lit.: Eudora Welty *The Robber Bridegroom* in Weiss, 124]
15. **Mak** sheep stealer succeeds by waiting till the shepherds fall asleep. [Br. Lit.: *The Second Shepherd's Play*]
16. **Mercury** god of thieves. [Gk. Myth.: Wheeler, 240]
17. **Nicholas's Clerks** slang for thieves. [Br. Usage: Brewer *Handbook*, 754; Br. Lit.: *I Henry IV; II Henry IV*]
18. **Nym** humorous thief and rogue. [Br. Lit.: *Merry Wives of Windsor; Henry V*]
19. **Raffles** leading Victorian criminal-hero. [Br. Lit.: Herman, 19–20]
20. **Sikes, Bill** Fagin's thieving associate. [Br. Lit.: *Oliver Twist*]
21. **Taffy** Welshman who "stole a piece of beef." [Nurs. Rhyme: Baring-Gould, 72–73]
22. **Turpin, Dick** (1706–1739) English housebreaker and highwayman. [Br. Hist.: Brewer *Dictionary*, 1108]
23. **Valentine, Jimmy** a romanticized burglar. [Am. Lit: *Alias Jimmy Valentine*, Espy, 337]
24. **Valjean, Jean** stole a loaf of bread; sentenced to 19 years in jail. [Fr. Lit.: *Les Misérables*]

640. THINNESS

1. **Crane, Ichabod** Sleepy Hollow's gaunt schoolmaster. [Am. Lit.: *Legend of Sleepy Hollow*]
2. **Dartle, Rosa** Mrs. Steerforth's gaunt companion. [Br. Lit.: *David Copperfield*]
3. **Oyl, Olive** Popeye's skinny girlfriend. [Comics: "Thimble Theater" in Horn, 657–658]

4. **Sprat, Jack** "He could eat no fat." [Nurs. Rhyme: Opie, 238]

641. THIRST

1. **Ancient Mariner** he and his crew nearly die of thirst. [Br. Poetry: Coleridge *The Ancient Mariner*]

642. THUNDER (See also LIGHTNING.)

1. **Bromius** epithet of Dionysus, meaning 'thunder.' [Gk. Myth.: Zimmerman, 43]
2. **Brontes** cruel Cyclops who controls the weather; able to cause great thunder. [Gk. Myth.: Parrinder, 47; Jobes, 241, 400]
3. **Donar** god of thunder; corresponds to Thor. [Ger. Myth.: Leach, 321]
4. **Indra** thunder god and controller of weather. [Vedic Myth.: Leach, 521]
5. **Mjolnir** Thor's hammer. [Norse Myth.: Brewer *Dictionary,* 1076]
6. **Thor** god of thunder. [Norse Myth.: Leach, 1109]

643. TIME

1. **Antevorta** goddess of the future. [Rom. Myth.: Kravitz, 24]
2. **Cronos** (Rom. **Saturn**) Titan; god of the world and time. [Gk. and Rom. Myth.: Kravitz, 69]
3. **dance of Shiva** symbolizes the passage of time. [Hindu Tradition: Cirlot, 76]
4. **Father Time** classic personification of time with scythe and hourglass. [Art: Hall, 119]
5. **Marcel** the fast ebbing of time impels him to devote his life to recording it. [Fr. Lit.: Proust *Remembrance of Things Past*]
6. **ring** represents the cyclical nature of time. [Pop. Culture: Cirlot, 273–274]
7. **river** represents the irreversible passage of time. [Pop. Culture: Cirlot, 274]
8. **Skulda** Norn of future time. [Norse Myth.: Wheeler, 260]
9. **Urda** Norn of time past. [Norse Myth.: Wheeler, 260]
10. **Verdandi** Norn of time present. [Norse Myth.: Wheeler, 260]
11. **white poplar** traditional symbol of time. [Flower Symbolism: *Flora Symbolica,* 178]
12. ***Years, The*** the seven decades of Eleanor Pargiter's life. [Br. Lit.: Benét, 1109]

Timelessness (See **AGELESSNESS, IMMORTALITY.**)

644. TIME TRAVEL

1. **Connecticut Yankee, the** struck on the head, he awakens to find himself in 6th-century England. [Am. Lit.: Mark Twain *A Connecticut Yankee in King Arthur's Court*]
2. ***Looking Backward*** Julian West awakens more than a century later to enjoy a new life in the Boston of A.D. 2000. [Am. Lit.: *Looking Backward* in Magill I, 520]
3. **Pilgrim, Billy** taught time-traveling by the Tralfamadorian space creatures. [Am. Lit.: Kurt Vonnegut *Slaughterhouse-Five*]
4. ***Time Machine, The*** Englishman voyages through millions of years to mankind's future. [Br. Lit.: Magill I, 980]

645. TIMIDITY (See also COWARDICE.)

1. **Alden, John** (c. 1599–1687) too timid to ask for Priscilla's hand in marriage. [Am. Lit.: "The Courtship of Miles Standish" in Benét, 230]
2. **Bergson, Emil** could only express love for Marie in secret thoughts. [Am. Lit.: *O Pioneers!,* Magill I, 663–665]
3. **Blushington, Edward** upon taking marriage vows, he needs wine to say "I do." [Br. Lit.: *The Bashful Man,* Walsh *Modern,* 62–63]
4. **Cowardly Lion** timid king of beasts. [Am. Lit.: *The Wonderful Wizard of Oz*]
5. **Crane, Ichabod** timorous schoolteacher. [Am. Lit.: *The Legend of Sleepy Hollow*]
6. **cyclamen** traditional symbol of timidity. [Flower Symbolism: Jobes, 400]
7. **Florimel** feared "the smallest monstrous mouse that creeps on floor." [Br. Lit.: *Faerie Queene*]
8. **Kent, Clark** mild-mannered reporter whose dynamic alter ego is Superman. [Comics: Berger, 146]
9. **Little Dorrit** withdrawn, self-effacing seamstress. [Br. Lit.: *Little Dorrit*]
10. **Little Miss Muffet** frightened away by a spider. [Nurs. Rhyme: Opie, 323]
11. **Milquetoast, Casper** the timid soul; easily controlled by others. [Comics: *The Timid Soul,* Espy, 141]
12. **Mitty, Walter** timid, henpecked husband. [Am. Lit.: Payton, 448]
13. **Peepers, Mr.** shy character in TV series. [TV: Terrace, II, 118–119]
14. **peony** symbol of shyness and timidity. [Flower Symbolism: *Flora Symbolica,* 176]

15. **Piglet** diffident little pig; tremulously courageous. [Children's Lit.: *Winnie-the-Pooh*]
16. **Prufrock, J. Alfred** indecisive man, too shy and evasive to make a proposal. [Br. Poetry: T. S. Eliot "The Love Song of J. Alfred Prufrock"]
17. **rush** indicates docility and diffidence. [Flower Symbolism: *Flora Symbolica,* 177]
18. **Wingfield, Laura** crippled girl so shy that she has withdrawn into her own confined world. [Am. Drama: Williams *The Glass Menagerie* in Benét, 400]

646. TORTURE

1. **Marsyas** flute player who challenges Apollo, loses, and is flayed alive for his presumption. [Gk. Myth.: Brewer *Dictionary*, 588]
2. **St. Bartholomew** martyr flayed alive before being crucified. [Hagiog.: *Collier's*, III, 77]

647. TOTALITARIANISM

1. ***Animal Farm*** animals revolt against the despotism of Farmer Jones, but their leader sets up an equally totalitarian regime. [Br. Lit.: Orwell *Animal Farm*]
2. ***Clockwork Orange, A*** depicts a future state that enforces conformity and crushes all heresy and rebellion. [Br. Lit.: Anthony Burgess *Clockwork Orange*]
3. ***Darkness at Noon*** Communists accused of having betrayed party principles are imprisoned, tortured, and executed. [Br. Lit.: Weiss, 117]
4. **Oceania** totalitarian state dominated by Big Brother's omnipresence. [Br. Lit.: George Orwell *1984*]

648. TOUGHNESS

1. **Kojak** tough, New York City plainclothes detective. [TV: Terrace, 445]
2. **Nolan, Jim** hard-bitten, he rouses fellow migrant workers to strike. [Am. Lit.: *In Dubious Battle*]

649. TOURING

1. ***Expedition of Humphrey Clinker, The*** describes Bramble family coach trip around 18th-century England. [Br. Lit.: Benét, 486]
2. ***Innocents Abroad, The*** tour of Europe satirizes the pretentiousness of foreign culture. [Am. Lit.: Haydn & Fuller, 370]

650. TRANSFORMATION

1. **Actaeon** surprised Artemis bathing and was changed by her into a stag. [Gk. Myth.: Jobes, 28]
2. **Adonis** killed by a boar, he was changed into an anemone by Venus. [Gk. Lit.: *Metamorphoses*]
3. **Alectryon** changed into rooster by angry Ares for neglecting to warn against approach of the sun; doomed forever to announce its arrival. [Gk. Myth.: Zimmerman, 17]
4. **Alpheus** hunter pursuing Arethusa is turned into a river. [Gk. Myth.: Brewer *Dictionary*, 26]
5. **Arachne** won weaving contest against Athena, who then changed her into a spider. [Gk. Myth.: Jobes, 116]
6. **Arethusa** changed into stream by Artemis to save her from river god, Alpheus. [Gk. Myth.: Zimmerman, 29]
7. **Argus** hundred-eyed giant ordered slain by Zeus, changed by Hera into a peacock with a tail full of "eyes." [Gk. Myth.: Benét, 48]
8. **Ascalaphus** turned into an owl by Demeter. [Gk. Myth.: Kravitz, 37]
9. **Atys** beloved of Cybele, who changed him into a pine tree as he was about to commit suicide. [Gk. Myth.: Brewer *Dictionary*, 55]
10. **Bottom, Nick** Puck turns his head into that of an ass. [Br. Drama: Shakespeare *A Midsummer Night's Dream*]
11. ***Breast, The*** literature professor transformed into a 155-pound breast topped by a football-size nipple. [Am. Lit.: Philip Roth *The Breast* in Weiss, 55]
12. **Cadmus** sows dragon's teeth that turn into armed men. [Gk. Myth.: Brewer *Dictionary*, 180]
13. **Callisto** nymph that Zeus transformed into a bear. [Gk. Myth.: Walsh *Classical*, 28]
14. **Ceyx and Halcyone** royal couple are changed into sea-birds. [Gk.Myth.: Bulfinch]
15. **Chelone** changed into tortoise for refusing to attend wedding of Zeus and Hera. [Gk. Myth.: Zimmerman, 59]
16. **Circe** seductive sorceress who turned Odysseus' companions into swine. [Gk. Myth.: Benét, 201]
17. **Clytie** ocean nymph, in love with Apollo, was changed into a heliotrope. [Gk. Myth.: Brewer *Dictionary*]
18. **Crocus** distressed by unrequited love, changed by Hermes into a saffron plant. [Gk. Myth.: Avery, 338]
19. **Cyane** turned by Hades into a fountain (or river). [Gk. Myth.: Kravitz, 70]

20. **Daphne** turned into laurel tree to escape Apollo. [Gk. Myth.: Kravitz, 75]
21. **Derceto** nature deity; became mermaid when Mopsus pursued her. [Philistine Myth.: Jobes, 433; Avery, 389]
22. **Dirce** changed by gods into a fountain. [Gk. Myth.: Zimmerman, 88]
23. **Doolittle, Eliza** Cockney flower-girl, trained by a professor, gains admission to polite society. [Br. Drama: G. B. Shaw *Pygmalion*; Am. Musical: *My Fair Lady* in *On Stage*, 373]
24. **Duchess's baby** ill-treated infant turns into a pig. [Br. Lit.: Lewis Carroll *Alice's Adventures in Wonderland*]
25. **Eurydice** transformed into a bacchante to suit enamored Zeus. [Fr. Operetta: Offenbach, *Orpheus in Hades,* Westerman, 271–272]
26. **frog prince** transformed by a witch, he is turned back into a prince by favor of a princess. [Ger. Fairy Tale: Grimm]
27. **Galatea** statue of woman fashioned by Pygmalion and brought to life by Aphrodite. [Gk. Myth.: Jobes, 623]
28. **Hermine** her body is shrunk to figurine size. [Ger. Lit.: Herman Hesse *Steppenwolf*]
29. **Hippomenes and Atalanta** changed into a lion and a lioness for failing to honor Venus after their legendary race. [Gk. Myth.: Bulfinch]
30. **Hulk, the** the monster that David Banner becomes when angered. [Comics and TV: Horn, 324]
31. **Io** changed into heifer by Zeus because of Hera's jealousy. [Gk. Myth.: Zimmerman, 137]
32. **Jekyll, Dr. Henry** by means of a drug, changes himself into a repulsive, evil creature. [Br. Lit.: Stevenson *Dr. Jekyll and Mr. Hyde* in Magill I, 214]
33. **Jurgen** middle-aged pawnbroker turned into a young man ready for amorous adventure. [Am. Lit.: *Jurgen* in Magill I, 464]
34. **Lawford, Arthur** dozing in a graveyard, his body – but not his mind – is replaced by one of the dead. [Br. Lit.: Walter de la Mare *The Return* in Magill II, 896]
35. **Lot's wife** disobeyed God's order not to look back; she became a pillar of salt. [O.T.: Genesis 19:26]
36. **Lucius** metamorphosed into an ass, has a series of adventures. [Rom. Lit.: Apuleius *Metamorphoses* or *The Golden Ass* in Magill I, 309]
37. **Lycaon** king turned into a wolf for having served human flesh. [Gk. Myth.: Brewer *Dictionary*, 570]

38. **Medusa** her face was so hideous that any who saw it were turned to stone. [Gk. Myth.: Brewer *Dictionary*, 596]
39. **Midas** everything he touched turned to gold. [Gk. Myth.: Zimmerman, 167]
40. **Myrmidons** originally ants, turned into human beings by Zeus to populate the island of Oenone. [Gk. Myth.: Benét, 697]
41. **Narcissus** enamored of his own reflection in a pool, he pines away and is turned into a flower. [Gk. Myth.: Benét, 701]
42. **Niobe** her children slain, she is turned to stone by Zeus at her own request. [Gk. Myth.: Benét, 717]
43. **Odysseus' crew** turned into swine by Circe. [Gk. Lit.: *Odyssey*]
44. **Orion** slain by Diana, giant hunter becomes a constellation. [Gk. Myth.: Brewer *Dictionary*, 664]
45. **Orlando** born a man in 1588, dies a woman in 1928. [Br. Lit. *Orlando,* Magill I, 698–700]
46. **Periclymenus** had the power to assume any form. [Gk. Myth.: Zimmerman, 199]
47. **Petrouchka** clown puppet that comes to life. [Russ. Ballet: *Petrouchka* in Thompson, 1657]
48. **Philemon and Baucis** couple turned into an oak and a linden so that they are together in death. [Gk. Myth.: Brewer *Dictionary*, 698]
49. **Philomela (Philomena)** changed by gods into nightingale. [Gk. Myth.: Zimmerman, 205–206]
50. **Phoulca** bogey-beast taking many forms; e.g., horse, bat, eagle. [Irish Folklore: Briggs, 326–327]
51. **Pinocchio** changed from mischievous puppet to loving boy. [Ital. Lit.: *Pinocchio*]
52. **portrait of Dorian Gray** becomes more hideous as Gray grows more vicious. [Br. Lit.: Oscar Wilde *The Picture of Dorian Gray*]
53. **Proteus** has ability to change shape. [Gk. Myth.: Kravitz, 201]
54. **pumpkin** turned into coach by Cinderella's fairy godmother. [Fr. Fairy Tale: *Cinderella*]
55. **Red Queen** shaken by Alice, she turns into a kitten. [Br. Lit.: Lewis Carroll *Through the Looking-Glass*]
56. ***Rhinoceros*** Berenger discovers that Jean is turning into a rhinoceros like all the other townspeople. [Fr. Drama: Weiss, 394]
57. **Samsa, Gregor** young man wakes up one day to find that he has turned into an enormous insect. [Ger. Lit.: Kafka *The Metamorphosis* in Benét, 663]
58. **Syrinx** nymph, pursued by Pan, was changed into a reed, from which Pan made his pipes. [Gk. Myth.: Brewer *Dictionary*, 876]

59. **tarnhelm** golden helmet that allowed its wearer to assume any form or even become invisible. [Ger. Opera: Wagner *The Ring of the Nibelung*]
60. **Tebrick, Silvia Fox** changed from dignified woman into wild fox. [Am. Lit.: *Lady into Fox,* Magill I, 486]
61. **Tippetarius** boy changed into Ozma, Queen of Oz. [Children's Lit.: *The Land of Oz*]
62. **Tiresias** saw two snakes copulating and was changed into a woman. [Gk. Myth.: Jobes, 1576]
63. **Tithonus** unable to remove him from the earth because of his immortality, Eos changes him into a grasshopper. [Gk. Myth.: Brewer *Dictionary,* 901]
64. **transubstantiation** changing of bread to body of Christ. [Christian Theol.: Brewer *Dictionary,* 1097]
65. **Veretius** Welsh king changed into wolf by St. Patrick. [Br. Legend: Brewer *Dictionary,* 1148]
66. **Zeus** assumed many forms to indulge his passions. [Zimmerman, 292–293]

651. TRANSVESTISM

1. **Klinger, Cpl.** dresses in women's clothes to try to win discharge from the army. [Am. TV: *M*A*S*H* in Terrace]

652. TREACHERY (See also TREASON.)

1. **Aaron** plots downfall of Titus. [Br. Lit.: *Titus Andronicus*]
2. **Achitophel** traitorous Earl of Shaftesbury. [Br. Lit.: *Absalom and Achitophel*]
3. **Agravain, Sir** traitorous with Modred against Arthur. [Br. Lit.: *Le Morte d'Arthur*]
4. ***Animal Farm*** allegory in which the leader of the pigs turns their revolutionary cause of equality into a government of privilege for the "more equal". [Br. Lit.: George Orwell *Animal Farm*]
5. **Antenor** assigned to hell for actions defeating Troy. [Gk. Myth.: Avery, 106; Ital. Lit.: Dante, *Inferno,* Walsh *Classical,* 24]
6. **Antonio** schemes against his brother Prospero. [Br. Lit.: *The Tempest*]
7. **Ascalaphus** Hadean gardener; informs on Persephone, learning of her potential departure. [Gk. Myth.: Zimmerman, 33]
8. **Baanah and Rechab** Ishbosheth's captains decapitate him in bed. [O.T.: II Samuel 4:5–7]
9. **Bellerophon letter** letter, given in pretended friendship, denounces bearer. [Folklore: Walsh *Classical,* 52]

10. **Brutus, Decius** committed treachery against friend Caesar. [Br. Lit.: *Julius Caesar*]
11. **Cantwell, Dr.** treacherous towards Lady Lambert; arrested as swindler. [Br. Lit.: *The Hypocrite,* Walsh *Modern,* 85–86]
12. **Charrington, Mr.** antique-store keeper sets up lovers for captors. [Br. Lit.: *1984*]
13. **Chuzzlewit, Jonas** tries to poison father. [Br. Lit.: *Martin Chuzzlewit*]
14. **Claudius** plotted to kill Hamlet's father and marry his mother. [Br. Lit.: *Hamlet*]
15. **cock crow** before third crowing, Peter thrice denies Christ. [N.T.: Matthew 26:34, 74–75]
16. **Cortés, Hernando** (1485–1547) repaid Montezuma's courtesy by murdering him. [Span. Hist.: *EB,* 5: 194–196]
17. **David** orders Uriah to be exposed in battle so he may marry Uriah's wife Bathsheba. [O.T.: II Samuel 11:6]
18. **Delilah** divulged secret of Samson's strength to Philistines. [O.T.: Judges 16:19–20]
19. **Ephialtes** Greek betrayer of Spartans at Thermopylae. [Gk. Hist.: Kravitz, 89]
20. **Ganelon** the Judas among Charlemagne's paladins. [Fr. Lit.: *Song of Roland; LLEI,* I: 286; Ital. Lit.: *Inferno*; Br. Lit.: *Canterbury Tales,* "Nun's Priest's Tale"]
21. **Iago** soldier discredits Desdemona's fidelity. [Br. Lit.: *Othello*]
22. **Joab** murders two fellow commanders; sides with usurper, Adonijah. [O.T.: I Kings 2:32]
23. **Judas Iscariot** betrayer of Jesus. [N.T.: Matthew 26:14–16, 20–25, 47–56; 27:3–10]
24. **Maskwell** cunning doublecrosser; betrays friend and lover. [Br. Lit.: *The Double-Dealer*]
25. **Melema, Tito** betrays his foster father, his stepfather, and his political allies. [Br. Lit.: George Eliot *Romola*]
26. **Modred** revolted against King Arthur. [Arth. Legend: Brewer *Handbook,* 714–715; Br. Lit.: *Idylls of the King*]
27. **Morgan le Fay** tricks Accolon into stealing Excalibur. [Arth. Legend: *Le Morte d'Arthur,* Walsh *Classical,* 3]
28. **Pearl Harbor** Japan, while negotiating in Washington, bombs Hawaii (December 7, 1941). [Am. Hist.: Fuller, III, 455–456]
29. **perfidious Albion** Napoleon's epithet for England, "perfide Albion." [Fr. Hist.: Misc.]
30. **Phaedra** in a letter written before her suicide, falsely accuses Hippolytus of attempting to ravish her. [Gk. Drama: *Hippolytus*]

31. **Polymestor** slays Priam's youngest son Polydorus, who had been entrusted to his care. [Gk. Drama: Euripides *Hecuba* in Benét, 450]
32. **Potiphar's wife** spurned by Joseph, she falsely accuses him of trying to seduce her. [O.T.: Gen. 39]
33. **Ptolemy** captain of Jericho invites Simon Maccabeus and his sons to a banquet and then slays them. [O.T.: I Maccabees, 16:16]
34. **redheadedness** from Judas Iscariot; so depicted in art. [Christian Iconog.: Gaster, 165]
35. **Rosencrantz and Guildenstern** Hamlet's traitorous friends; "adders fang'd." [Br. Lit.: *Hamlet*]
36. **Saturninus** connives and plots politically; kills Titus. [Br. Lit.: *Titus Andronicus*]
37. **Schoolmaster of Falerii** Etruscan teacher, after delivering children to Romans, is rebuffed. [Rom. Hist.: Hall, 119]
38. **Sebastian** plots to murder Alonso and Gonzalo. [Br. Lit.: *The Tempest*]
39. **Thermopylae** shown the back door, Persians destroyed Spartans (480 B.C.). [Gk. Hist.: Harbottle, 248]
40. **30 pieces of silver** price paid Judas to deliver Jesus. [Christian Symbolism: N.T.: Matthew 26:15]
41. **Ugolino** 13th-century count of Pisa who treacherously deserted his own party and then twice joined the enemies of his own city. [Ital. Hist.: Brewer *Dictionary*, 921]
42. **Uriah letter** Uriah carries David's letter ordering his own death. [O.T.: II Samuel 11:15]
43. **whale** lures fish to mouth with sweet breath. [Animal Symbolism: Mercatante, 27]
44. **woman in red** Dillinger's mysterious girl friend; alerted FBI to his whereabouts. [Am. Hist.: Flexner, 291]
45. **yellow** color marking doors of convicted traitors. [Fr. Legend: Brewer *Dictionary*, 1171]

653. TREASON (See also TREACHERY.)

1. **Arnold, Benedict** (1741–1801) American Revolutionary general who plotted surrender of West Point to British. [Am. Hist.: Benét, 52]
2. **Burgundy, Duke of** fights for English, then joins French. [Br. Lit.: *I Henry VI*]
3. **Carne, Caryl** traitor to country. [Br. Lit.: *Springhaven*]
4. **Christian, Colonel William** executed for treason. [Br. Lit.: *Peveril of the Peak*, Walsh *Modern*, 96]

5. **Edmund** "a most toad-spotted traitor." [Br. Lit.: *King Lear*]
6. **Nolan, Philip** deserts the U.S. Army to join Burr's conspiracy. [Am. Lit.: Hale *The Man Without a Country* in Magill I, 553]
7. **Quisling, Vidkun** (1887–1945) Norwegian fascist leader; persuaded Hitler to attack Norway. [Nor. Hist.: Flexner, 444]
8. **Vichy** seat of collaborationist government after German occupation (1941). [Fr. Hist.: Brewer *Dictionary,* 1128]
9. **Wallenstein, Count** powerful German general in Thirty Years' War who corresponded with the Swedish enemy. [Ger. Drama: Schiller *Wallenstein* in Magill II, 1119]

654. TREASURE

1. **Ali Baba** uses magic to find thieves' storehouse of booty. [Arab. Lit.: *Arabian Nights,* "Ali Baba and the Forty Thieves"]
2. **Comstock Lode** richest silver vein in world. [Amer. Hist.: Flexner, 177]
3. **Dantès, Edmond** digs up the treasure revealed to him by a dying fellow prisoner. [Fr. Lit.: Dumas *The Count of Monte Cristo*]
4. **El Dorado** legendary land of gold in South America. [Span. Myth.: *NCE,* 846]
5. **Fort Knox** U.S. depository of gold bullion. [Am. Hist.: *NCE,* 984]
6. **forty-niners** participants in California gold rush of 1849. [Am. Hist.: *LLEI,* I: 270]
7. **Golconda** fabled Indian city, meaning "source of great wealth." [Indian Hist.: *NCE,* 1101]
8. **gold bug** leads to finding of Captain Kidd's buried treasure. [Am. Lit.: Poe "The Gold Bug"]
9. **Golden Fleece** fleece of pure gold from a winged ram, stolen from Colchis by Jason and the Argonauts. [Gk. Myth.: Benét, 406]
10. **Kidd, Captain** (c. 1645–1701) pirate captures prizes and buries treasure. [Am. Lit.: Hart, 444]
11. **King Solomon's mines** in Africa; search for legendary lost treasure of King Solomon. [Br. Lit.: *King Solomon's Mines*]
12. **Legrand, William** uncovers chest of gold by deciphering parchment. [Am. Lit.: Poe "The Gold Bug"]
13. **Mother Lode** name applied to gold-mining region of California. [Am. Hist.: Hart, 569]
14. **Nibelung, the** more gold and jewels than wagons could carry. [Ger. Lit.: *Nibelungenlied*]
15. **Nostromo** inadvertently gains hoard of silver ingots. [Br. Lit.: *Nostromo*]

16. **Ophir** Red Sea area noted for gold. [O.T.: I Kings 9:28; 10:11; 22:48]
17. **Sutter's Mill** site of first strike precipitating Gold Rush. [Am. Hist. Flexner, 175]
18. ***Treasure Island*** search for buried treasure ignited by discovery of ancient map. [Br. Lit.: *Treasure Island*]
19. ***Treasure of the Sierra Madre, The*** in Mexico, written by the reclusive, pseudonymous B. Traven. [Am. and Mex. Lit.: *The Treasure of the Sierra Madre*]

655. TREES

1. **Birnam wood** apparently comes to Dunsinane, fulfilling a prophecy misinterpreted by Macbeth. [Br. Drama: Shakespeare *Macbeth*]
2. **Bo-tree** tree of perfect knowledge under which Gautama attained enlightenment and so became the Buddha. [Buddhism: Benét, 124]
3. **Charter Oak** ancient white oak where the Connecticut charter was secreted in 1687 to avoid its seizure by the royal governor. [Am. Hist.: *NCE*, 515]
4. **Chestnuts, The** tree apartment, home of Owl. [Br. Lit.: A. A. Milne *Winnie-the-Pooh*]
5. **Druids** conducted their rites in oak groves and venerated the oak and the mistletoe. [Celtic Relig.: Benét, 289]
6. **Ents** treelike creatures who shelter and defend the friends of Frodo. [Br. Lit.: J. R. R. Tolkien *Lord of the Rings*]
7. **laurel tree** sacred to Apollo; a wreath of laurel, or bay, protected the wearer from thunderstorms. [Roman Myth.: Brewer *Dictionary*, 81]
8. **oak** considered more likely to be struck by lightning, sacred to the god of thunder and venerated by the Druids. [Br. Legend: Brewer *Dictionary*, 652]
9. **upas** juice contains a poison used for tipping arrows; its vapor was believed capable of killing all who came within miles. [Eur. Myth.: Brewer *Dictionary*, 926]
10. **yew** symbol of immortality; hence, planted in churchyards and near Druid temples. [Br. Legend: Brewer *Dictionary*, 967]
11. **Ygdrasil** the great ash tree that supported the universe, having sprung from the body of the giant Ymir. [Norse Myth.: Benét, 111]

656. TRIAL

1. **Bardell vs. Pickwick** trial for breach of promise results in imprisonment of both parties for not paying damages and costs. [Br. Lit.: Dickens *Pickwick Papers*]
2. ***Trial by Jury*** trial of a breach-of-promise suit is dismissed when the judge decides to marry the plaintiff. [Br. Opera: Gilbert and Sullivan *Trial by Jury*]
3. ***Trial, The*** Joseph K. is tried by a strange court for an unspecified crime. [Ger. Lit.: Kafka *The Trial*]

657. TRICKERY (See also CUNNING, DECEIT, HUMBUGGERY.)

1. **Bunsby, Captain Jack** trapped into marriage by landlady. [Br. Lit.: *Dombey and Son*]
2. **Camacho** cheated of bride after lavish wedding preparations. [Span. Lit.: *Don Quixote*]
3. **Delilah** tricks Samson into revealing secret of his strength. [O.T.: Judges 16:6–21]
4. **gerrymander** political chicanery aimed at acquiring votes. [Am. Hist.: Jameson, 199]
5. **Gibeonites** obtained treaty with Joshua under false pretenses. [O.T.: Joshua 9:3–15]
6. **Hippomenes** outraced Atalanta by tossing golden apples to distract her. [Gk. Myth.: Bulfinch]
7. **Jacob** through guile, obtained blessing intended for Esau. [O.T.: Genesis 27:18–29]
8. **Joseph's coat** dipped in the blood of a kid and shown to Jacob as proof of Joseph's death. [O.T.: Gen. 37:31-33]
9. **Laban** substitutes Leah for Rachel on Jacob's wedding night. [O.T.: Genesis 29:16-26]
10. **Loge (Loki)** enables Wotan to overpower Alberich, gain Rhinegold. [Ger. Opera: Wagner, *Das Rheingold*, Westerman, 232]
11. **Malatesta** schemes outwit miser; enable young lovers to wed. [Ital. Opera: Donizetti, *Don Pasquale*, Westerman, 123–124]
12. **Rebekah** encouraged son Jacob to deceive father for blessing. [O.T.: Genesis 27:5–17]
13. **Serpina** dupes bachelor employer into marrying her. [Ital. Opera: Pergolesi, *La Serva Padrona*, Westerman, 61]

658. TRINITY

1. **botonné cross** symbolizes Father, Son, and Holy Ghost. [Christian Iconog.: Jobes, 386]
2. **equilateral triangle** perfect geometrical representation of triune God. [Christian Symbolism: Appleton, 102]

3. **fleur-de-lis** symbol of the trinity; resembles lily. [Christian Symbolism: *EB,* IV: 182]
4. **iris** emblem of the trinity in da Vinci's "Madonna of the Rocks." [Plant Symbolism: Embolden, 26]
5. **shamrock** St. Patrick's legendary symbol of triune God. [Christian Symbolism: Appleton, 87]
6. **Sign of the Cross** signifying Father, Son, and Holy Ghost. [Christianity: *NCE,* 2786]
7. **trefoil (clover)** emblem of the Trinity. [Christian Symbolism: Cirlot, 50–51]
8. **Trimurti** Hindu triad of Brahma, Vishnu, and Siva. [Hinduism: Brewer *Dictionary,* 1101]

659. TRUMPET

1. **Gabriel** angel who will blow the trumpet to announce the coming of Judgment Day. [Christian Trad.: *Century Cyclopedia,* 1667]

Truth (See HONESTY.)

660. TURNING POINT

1. **Alamogordo** site of first A-bomb explosion; heralded atomic age (1945). [Am. Hist.: Flexner, 11]
2. **Barbarossa** disastrous invasion of Russia; sealed Nazi fate (1941–1943). [Eur. Hist.: *Hitler,* 888–921, 922–955]
3. **Caesar crosses Rubicon** defying Roman law, Caesar moves to consolidate power (49 B.C.). [Rom. Hist.: *EB,* 3: 575–580]
4. **Cannonade of Valmy** dawn of modern warfare (1792). [Eur. Hist.: Fuller, II, 346–369]
5. **Crécy** first European use of gunpowder (by British) in battle (1346). [Eur. Hist.: Bishop, 382–385]
6. **D-Day** Allied invasion of France during WWII (June 6, 1944). [Eur. Hist.: Fuller, III, 562–567]
7. **El Alamein** "Desert Fox" outfoxed; Allies gained upper hand (1943). [Eur. Hist.: Fuller, III, 494–502]
8. **Fall of Constantinople** associated with end of Middle Ages (1453). [Eur. Hist.: Bishop, 398]
9. **Gettysburg, Battle of** the deathblow of the Confederacy (1863). [Am. Hist.: Jameson, 199]
10. **Golden Spurs, Battle of** early victory of infantry over mounted knights (1302). [Eur. Hist.: *EB,* IV: 608]
11. **Hastings, Battle of** Norman conquest; last successful invasion of Britain (1066). [Br. Hist.: Harbottle, 107]

12. **Khe Sanh** savage siege marks turning point in Vietnam (1968). [Am. Hist.: Van Doren, 620]
13. **Magna Charta** beginning of British democratic system (1215). [Br. Hist.: Bishop, 49–52, 213]
14. **Marston Moor** deciding battle of British Civil War (1644). [Br. Hist.: Harbottle, 154]
15. **Midway** decisive American victory over Japanese in WWII (1942). [Am. Hist.: Fuller, III, 470–477]
16. **Moon Landing** astronauts Armstrong and Aldrin make history (1969). [Am. Hist.: *NCE,* 2579–2581]
17. **95 Theses** Martin Luther presented his theses at Wittenberg (1517). [Eur. Hist.: *EB,* 11: 188–196]
18. ***Origin of Species*** Darwin's revolutionary theory of human evolution (1859). [Science: *NCE,* 721–722]
19. **Spanish Armada** Britain supplanted Spain as master of the sea. [Br. Hist.: Harbottle, 19]
20. **Tours** Arab onslaught halted by Franks under Charles Martel (732). [Eur. Hist.: Bishop, 19]
21. **theory of relativity** Einstein's contribution to the space-time relationship. [Science: *NCE,* 843–844]

661. TWINS (See also DOUBLES.)

1. **Alcmena's sons** born in single delivery but conceived by two men. [Rom. Lit.: *Amphitryon*]
2. **Antipholus** identically named sons of Aegeon and Emilia. [Br. Lit.: *Comedy of Errors*]
3. **Apollo and Artemis** twin brother and sister; children of Leta and Zeus. [Gk. Myth.: *NCE,* 125–126]
4. **Bobbsey Twins** two sets of twins share adventures. [Children's Lit.: *Bobbsey Twins' Mystery at Meadowbrook*]
5. **Castor and Pollux** sons of Leda and Zeus, placed in heaven as constellation Gemini. [Gk. Myth.: Zimmerman, 52]
6. ***Comedy of Errors*** based on Plautus's *Menaechmi,* with two sets of twins. [Br. Lit.: *Comedy of Errors*]
7. **de Franchi, Lucien and Louis** one twin instinctively feels what happens to other. [Fr. Lit.: *The Corsican Brothers*]
8. **Dioscuri (Castor and Pollux)** Spartan brothers. [Gk. Myth.: Avery, 408; Leach, 314]
9. **Donny, the Misses** twin principals of Greenleaf boarding school. [Br. Lit.: *Bleak House*]
10. **Dromio** Dromio of Ephesus; Dromio of Syracuse. [Br. Lit.: *Comedy of Errors*]

11. **Gemini** (**Castor and Pollux**) zodiacal twins; [Gk. Myth.: *NCE*, 1056]
12. **Katzenjammer Kids** early comic strip featured incorrigible twins. [Comics: "The Captain and the Kids" in Horn, 421]
13. **Man in the Iron Mask** Bastille prisoner learns that he is the twin brother of Louis XIV; conspirators planned to substitute him for the king. [Fr. Lit.: Dumas *Vicomte de Bragellonne* in Magill I, 1063]
14. ***Menaechmi*** comedy, by Plautus, about mistakes involving identical twins. [Rom. Lit.: *Menaechmi*]
15. **Mike and Ike** short lookalike twins with derbies. [Comics: Horn, 492]
16. **Perez and Zerah** born to Tamar; conceived by father-in-law, Judah. [O.T.: Genesis 38:29–30]
17. **Romulus and Remus** suckled by she-wolf; founded Rome. [Rom. Myth.: Wheeler, 320]
18. **Siamese twins** Eng and Chang (1814–74), the original pair, were connected at the chest. [Medical Hist.: Brewer *Dictionary*, 828]
19. **Tweedledum and Tweedledee** identical characters in children's fantasy. [Br. Lit.: *Through the Looking-Glass*]
20. **two circles** symbol of twins; in particular, Castor and Pollux [Gk. Myth.: Jobes, 343]

662. TYRANNY

1. **Big Brother** omnipresent leader of a totalitarian nightmare world. [Br. Lit.: *1984*]
2. **Creon** rules Thebes with cruel decrees. [Gk. Lit.: *Antigone*]
3. **Gessler** Austrian governor treats Swiss despotically; shot by Tell. [Ital. Opera: Rossini, *William Tell*, Westerman, 121–122]
4. **Jones, Brutus** former porter sets himself up as dictator of a West Indies island and rules the natives with an iron hand. [Am. Drama: O'Neill *Emperor Jones*]
5. **Necho, Pharaoh** oppresses Jerusalem by exaction of harsh taxes. [O.T.: II Kings 23: 33–35]
6. **pig** mean, sadistic tyrant; epitome of human horridness. [Br. Lit.: *Animal Farm*]
7. **Queen of Hearts** dictatorial ruler who orders subjects' heads chopped off. [Br. Lit.: *Alice's Adventures in Wonderland*]
8. **Rehoboam** bitterly repressed his people. [O.T.: I Kings 12:12–16]

9. **salamander** Francis I's symbol of absolute dictatorial power. [Animal Symbolism: Mercatante, 19]

U

663. UBIQUITY (See also OMNIPRESENCE.)

1. **Burma-Shave** their signs seen as “verses of the wayside throughout America.” [Am. Commerce and Folklore: Misc.]
2. **Coca-Cola** soft drink found throughout the world. [Trademarks: Crowley *Trade*, 115]
3. **Gideon Bible** bible placed in hotel rooms and other establishments throughout the world. [Am. Hist.: *NCE*, 291]
4. **Howard Johnson's** restaurant-motel chain throughout America; buildings recognized by their bright orange roofs. [Trademarks: Crowley *Trade*, 274]
5. **Kilroy** fictitious American soldier; left inscription, “Kilroy was here,” everywhere U.S. soldiers were stationed (1940s). [Am. Mil. Folklore: Misc.]
6. **McDonald's** fast-food restaurant chain throughout the world; recognized by golden arches. [Am. Culture: Misc.]

664. UGLINESS

1. **Avagddu** ugly child of Tegid Voel and Cerridwen. [Celtic Folklore: Parrinder, 35]
2. **Balkis** hairy-legged type of Queen of Sheba. [Talmudic Legend: Walsh *Classical*, 45]
3. **Bendith Y Mamau** stunted, ugly fairies; kidnapped children. [Celtic Folklore: Briggs, 21]
4. **Berchta** beady-eyed, hook-nosed crone with clubfoot and stringy hair. [Ger. Folklore: Leach, 137]
5. **Black Annis** cannibalistic hag with blue face and iron claws. [Br. Folklore: Briggs, 24]
6. **Duessa** witch, stripped of lavish disguise, found to be hideous hag. [Br. Lit.: *Faerie Queene*]
7. **Ethel** buck-toothed, gangly teenager in love with idler, Jughead. [Comics: “Archie” in Horn, 37]
8. **Euryale and Stheno** the immortal Gorgons; had serpents for hair and brazen claws. [Gk. Myth.: Zimmerman, 114]
9. **Frankenstein's monster** ugly monster. [Br. Lit.: *Frankenstein*, Payton, 254]
10. **gargoyles** medieval European church waterspouts; made in form of grotesque creatures. [Architecture: *NCE*, 1046]

11. **Gorgons** snake-haired, winged creatures of frightful appearance. [Gk. Myth.: Howe, 108]
12. **Gross, Allison** repulsive witch "in the north country." [Scot. Ballad: *Childe Ballads*]
13. **Medusa** creature with fangs, snake-hair, and protruding tongue. [Gk. Myth.: Hall, 206]
14. **Quasimodo** "Nowhere on earth a more grotesque creature." [Fr. Lit.: *The Hunchback of Notre Dame*]
15. **Spriggans** grotesque fairies; "dourest and most ugly set of sprights." [Br. Folklore: Briggs, 380–381]
16. **Ugly Duchess** repulsive woman with pocket-shaped mouth. [Br. Lit.: *Alice's Adventures in Wonderland*]
17. **Ugly Duckling** ugly outcast until fully grown. [Fairy Tale: Misc.]
18. **Witch of Wookey** repulsive hag curses boys and girls. [Br. Legend: Brewer *Dictionary,* 1164]

665. UNATTAINABILITY (See also IMPOSSIBILITY.)

1. **Elixir of Life** fabulous potion conferring immortality. [Medieval Legend: Brewer *Dictionary,* 371]
2. **Fountain of Youth** legendary fountain of eternal youth. [World Legend: Brewer *Dictionary,* 432]
3. **perpetual motion machine** machine operating of itself forever. [World Legend: Brewer *Dictionary,* 823]
4. **Philosopher's Stone** substance supposed to convert base metal to gold. [Medieval Legend: Brewer *Dictionary,* 829]

666. UNDERWORLD (See also HELL.)

1. **Aidoneus** epithet of Hades. [Gk. Myth.: Zimmerman, 14]
2. **Amenti** hidden world where the sun sets. [Egypt. Myth.: Leach, 42]
3. **Anunnaki** lesser Sumerian underworld deities. [Sumerian Myth.: Benét, 41]
4. **Aornum** entrance through which Orpheus descended to Hades. [Gk. Myth.: Zimmerman, 25]
5. **Aralu** desolate land of no return. [Babyl. Myth.: Leach, 69]
6. **Avernus, Lake** entrance to the maw. [Rom. Lit.: *Aeneid;* Art: Hall, 147]
7. **Dis** god of nether world; identified with Pluto. [Rom. Myth.: Leach, 315]
8. **Duat** one of the Egyptian abodes of the dead. [Egypt. Myth.: Benét, 290]

9. **Erebus** god of underground darkness. [Gk. Myth.: Benét, 319]
10. **Ereshkigal** queen of underworld; Persephone equivalent. [Sumerian Myth.: Benét, 319–320]
11. **Hades** realm of departed spirits. [Gk. Myth.: Brewer *Dictionary*, 499]
12. **Hel** ruled over world of the dead. [Norse Myth.: Leach, 488]
13. **Nergal** god ruling the world of dead. [Sumerian and Akkadian Myth.: Parrinder, 203]
14. **Niflheim** region of perpetual cold and darkness; afterworld. [Norse Myth.: Wheeler, 259]
15. **oak leaves, garland of** emblem of Hecate, goddess of the underworld. [Gk. Myth.: Jobes, 374]
16. **Orcus** nether world of the dead. [Rom. Myth.: Wheeler, 270]
17. **Pluto** god of underworld. [Gk. Myth.: Howe, 224]
18. **Sheol** abode of the dead. [Hebrew Theology: Brewer *Dictionary*, 499]
19. **Styx** river of Hades across which souls of dead must travel. [Gk. Myth.: Howe, 259]
20. **Tartarus** infernal regions. [Gk. Myth.: Hall, 147]

Unfaithfulness (See FAITHLESSNESS.)

Ungratefulness (See INGRATITUDE.)

Unkindness (See CRUELTY, INHOSPITALITY.)

667. UNSCRUPULOUSNESS (See also TRICKERY.)

1. **Blas, Gil** educated rogue on warpath for self-gain. [Fr. Lit.: *Gil Blas*]
2. **Brass, Sampson** unprincipled attorney. [Br. Lit.: *Old Curiosity Shop*]
3. **Bray, Walter** to clear his debts to old Gride, arranges to have Gride marry his daughter. [Br. Lit.: *Nicholas Nickleby*]
4. **Butler, Rhett** war profiteer; morality not a concern. [Am. Lit.: *Gone With the Wind*]
5. **Claudio** asks sister to sacrifice her virtue to save his life. [Br. Lit.: *Measure for Measure*]
6. **Dodson and Fogg** unscrupulous lawyers who file breach-of-promise suit against Mr. Pickwick. [Br. Lit.: Dickens *Pickwick Papers*]
7. **Duroy, George** climbs to wealth by exploiting wife's disgrace. [Fr. Lit.: *Bel-Ami*]

8. **Hajji Baba** clever rogue travels around Persia taking glamorous jobs for illicit gain. [Fr. Lit.: *Hajji Baba of Ispahan* in Magill I, 343]
9. **Henchard, Michael** when drunk offers wife and child for sale. [Br. Lit.: *The Mayor of Casterbridge*]
10. **Livia** she poisoned whoever interfered with her plans. [Br. Lit.: *I, Claudius*]
11. ***Prince, The*** practicality in power; end justifies means. [Ital. Lit.: *The Prince*]
12. **Steele, Lucy** jilts Edward for his brother Robert to take advantage of a switch of their inheritance. [Br. Lit.: *Sense and Sensibility*]
13. **Tweed, William Marcy "Boss"** (1823–1878) corrupt politico; controlled New York City government (1863–1871). [Am. Hist.: Jameson, 511]
14. **Winterset, Duke de** commonly described as "an English scoundrel." [Am. Lit.: *Monsieur Beaucaire,* Magill I, 616–617]

668. UNSELFISHNESS (See also DEDICATION.)

1. **Arden, Enoch** returned castaway; keeps identity secret from wife to preserve her "new life" happiness. [Br. Lit.: *Enoch Arden*]
2. **Bartholomea Capitanio and Vincentia Gerosa, Sts.** founded order to nurse sick, teach young. [Christian Hagiog.: Attwater, 58]
3. **Bergerac, Cyrano de** composed eloquent love letters for another. [Fr. Lit.: *Cyrano de Bergerac*]
4. **Carton, Sydney** allows himself to be guillotined in place of Charles Darnay. [Br. Lit.: Dickens *A Tale of Two Cities*]
5. **Cratchit, Bob** ill-paid clerk; uncomplainingly supports large family. [Br. Lit.: *A Christmas Carol*]
6. **Goriot, Père** generosity to daughters caused his own poverty. [Fr. Lit.: *Père Goriot*]

669. UNSOPHISTICATION (See also NAÏVETÉ.)

1. **Adams, Parson** industrious curate; good-naturedly unsophisticated. [Br. Lit.: *Joseph Andrews*]
2. **Agnès** ignorant girl; unaware of world's and guardian's wiles. [Fr. Lit.: *L'Ecole des Femmes*]
3. ***Barefoot Boy*** adventures of rural boyhood. [Am. Lit.: Hart, 57]
4. **Beverly Hillbillies** the rustication of California's wealthy Beverly Hills. [TV: Terrace, I, 93–94]

5. **brown ass** traditional symbol signifying lack of culture. [Animal Symbolism: Jobes, 142]
6. **Dogpatch** town of illiterate country folk. [Comics: "Li'l Abner" in Horn, 450]
7. **Donn, Arabella** Jude's wife; a vulgar country girl. [Br. Lit.: *Jude the Obscure*]
8. **Geese of Brother Philip** sheltered lad believes father's explanation of girls. [Ital. Lit.: *Decameron,* Hall, 135]
9. **Grand Ole Opry** country-western music performance hall and radio show; "back-country" motif. [Radio: Buxton, 100–101]
10. **Grand Fenwick, Duchy of** minuscule backward European kingdom that "bites the world's tail." [Am. Lit.: *The Mouse That Roared*]
11. **Green, Verdant** callow Oxford freshman; victim of practical jokes. [Br. Lit.: *The Adventures of Mr. Verdant Green,* Brewer *Dictionary,* 1126]
12. **Kadiddlehopper, Clem** character who epitomizes naiveness. [Radio: "The Red Skelton Show" in Buxton, 197]
13. **Li'l Abner** naive comic strip character. [Comics: Horn, 450–451]
14. **Miller, Daisy** her American ways caused scandal in Rome. [Am. Lit.: *Daisy Miller*]
15. **Okies** Californians' derogatory name for Oklahoma immigrants; meaning "ignorant tramps." [Am. Lit.: *The Grapes of Wrath*]
16. **Pyle, Gomer** innocent character in Marine Corps situation comedy. [TV: "Gomer Pyle, U.S.M.C." in Terrace, I, 319]
17. **Snerd, Mortimer** ventriloquist's dummy personifies unsophistication. [Radio: "The Edgar Bergen and Charlie McCarthy Show" in Buxton, 7–77]

Unworldliness (See ASCETICISM.)

Uselessness (See FUTILITY.)

670. USURPATION

1. **Adonijah** presumptuously assumed David's throne before Solomon's investiture. [O.T.: I Kings 1:5–10]
2. **Anschluss** Nazi takeover of Austria (1938). [Eur. Hist.: *Hitler,* 590–627]
3. **Athaliah** steals throne by killing all royal line. [O.T.: II Kings 11:1]
4. **Claudius** usurped throne of Hamlet's father. [Br. Lit.: *Hamlet*]

5. **Frederick** arrogated dominions of his brother. [Br. Lit.: *As You Like It*]
6. **Glorious Revolution** James II deposed; William and Mary enthroned (1688). [Br. Hist.: *EB,* 3: 248]
7. **Godunov, Boris** (c. 1551–1605) cunningly has tsarevich murdered; gallantly accepts throne. [Russ. Lit.: *Boris Godunov;* Russ. Opera: Moussorgsky, *Boris Godunov*]
8. **Menahem** murders Shallum and enthrones himself. [O.T.: II Kings 15:14]
9. **Otrepyev, Grigory** baseborn monk assumes dead tsarevich's identity and throne. [Russ. Lit.: *Boris Gudonov;* Russ. Opera: Moussorgsky, *Boris Godunov*]

671. USURY

1. **Fledgeby** cowardly and deceitful moneylender. [Br. Lit.: *Our Mutual Friend*]
2. **Gride, Arthur** extorting moneylender. [Br. Lit.: *Nicholas Nickleby*]
3. **Milo** loaned gold for huge interest rates and sexual favors. [Gk. Lit.: *The Golden Ass*]
4. **Nickleby, Ralph** avaricious and ungentlemanly moneylender. [Br. Lit.: *Nicholas Nickleby*]
5. **Shylock** shrewd, avaricious moneylender. [Br. Lit.: *Merchant of Venice*]

672. UTOPIA (See also **HEAVEN, PARADISE, WONDERLAND.**)

1. **Abbey of Thelema** Rabelais' vision of the ideal society. [Fr. Lit.: *Gargantua,* Plumb, 394]
2. **Altneuland** future Jewish state; "if willed, no fairytale." [Hung. Lit.: *Altneuland,* Wigoder, 21]
3. **Altruria** equalitarian, socialist state founded on altruistic principles. [Am. Lit.: *A Traveler from Altruria* in Hart, 860]
4. **Amaurote** chief city in Utopia. [Br. Lit.: *Utopia*]
5. **Annfwn** land of perpetual beauty and happiness where death is unknown. [Welsh Myth.: Leach, 91]
6. **Atlantis** legendary island; inspired many Utopian myths. [Western Folklore: Misc.]
7. **Brook Farm** literary, socialist commune intended to be small utopia (1841–1846). [Am. Hist.: Jameson, 63]
8. **Castalia** founded by intellectuals to form a synthesis of arts and sciences, symbolized in the Glass Bead Game. [Ger. Lit.: Hesse *Magister Ludi* in Weiss, 278]
9. **Cloud Cuckooland** (See **Nephelococcygia,** below.)

10. ***Coming Race, The*** depicts a classless society of highly civilized people living deep under the earth's surface. [Br. Lit.: Barnhart, 268]
11. **El Dorado** legendary place of fabulous wealth. [Am. Hist.: Espy, 335]
12. **Erewhon** utopia–anagram of "nowhere." [Br. Lit.: *Erewhon*]
13. **Golden Age** legendary period under the rule of Cronus when life was easy and blissful for all. [Gk. Myth.: *NCE*, 33]
14. **Helicon Home Colony** socialist community founded by Upton Sinclair. [Am. Hist.: *NCE*, 2524]
15. ***Looking Backward, 2000–1887*** utopian novel (1888). [Am. Lit.: Benét, 598]
16. **Nephelococcygia** ethereal wonderland of castles; secure from gods. [Gk. Lit.: *The Birds*]
17. **Never Never Land** fictional home. [Br. Lit.: *Peter Pan*, Espy, 339]
18. ***New Atlantis, The*** Sir Francis Bacon's 1627 account of a visit to the island of Bensalem, which abounds in scientic discoveries. [Br. Lit.: Haydn & Fuller, 515]
19. **New Harmony** cooperative colony founded by Robert Owen in Indiana (1825). [Am. Hist.: *EB*, X: 315]
20. ***News from Nowhere*** account of a Socialist Utopia based on craftsmanship, love, and beauty. [Br. Lit.: Drabble, 695]
21. **Oneida** founded by John Humphrey Noyes in New York; based on extended family system. [Am. Hist.: *EB*, X: 315]
22. **Perelandra** used of the planet Venus, where life has been newly created and the atmosphere has the innocent beauty of Eden. [Eng. Lit.: Lewis *Perelandra; The Space Trilogy* in Weiss, 437]
23. ***Republic, The*** Plato's dialogue describes the ideal state. [Gk. Lit.: Benét, 850]
24. **Saint-Simonism** sociopolitical theories advocating industrial socialism. [Fr. Hist.: Brewer *Dictionary*, 955]
25. **Seven Cities of Cibola** the land of the Zuñis (New Mexico); great wealth sought by Coronado. [Mex. Myth.: Payton, 614]
26. **Shangri-la** earthly paradise in the Himalayas. [Br. Lit.: *Lost Horizon*]
27. ***Utopia*** More's humanistic treatise on the ideal state (1516). [Br. Lit.: *Utopia*]

V

Valor (See **BRAVERY.**)

673. **VANITY** (See also **CONCEIT, EGOTISM.**)

1. **Barnabas, Parson** conceited and weak clergyman. [Br. Lit.: *Joseph Andrews*]
2. **Bottom, Nick** self-important weaver. [Br. Lit.: *A Midsummer Night's Dream*]
3. **Cassiopeia** claimed her beauty was greater than that of the Nereids. [Gk. Myth.: Leach, 196]
4. **Eglantine, Madame** distinguished by her feminine delicacy and seeming worldliness. [Br. Lit.: *Canterbury Tales,* "The Prioress's Tale"]
5. **March, Amy** beautiful, vain, spoiled girl. [Am. Lit.: *Little Women*]
6. **mirror** attribute of vainglory. [Art: Hall, 211]
7. **Narcissus** fell in love with own image. [Gk. Myth.: Howe, 174]
8. **peacock** conceit personified. [Animal Symbolism: Hall, 239]
9. **Turveydrop, Mr.** conceited father of Prince. [Br. Lit.: *Bleak House*]
10. **Zion, Daughters of** Lord reacts harshly to their wanton finery. [O.T.: Isaiah 3:16–26]

674. **VENGEANCE**

1. **Absalom** kills half-brother, Amnon, for raping sister, Tamar. [O.T.: II Samuel 13:28–29]
2. **Acamas** Aeneas's companion; kills Promachus to avenge brother's murder. [Gk. Lit.: *Iliad*]
3. **Acarnan and Amphoterus** enabled by Zeus to grow to manhood in single day to avenge father's murder. [Gk. Myth.: Zimmerman, 2]
4. **Achilles** avenges Patroclus's death by brutally killing Hector. [Gk. Lit.: *Iliad*]
5. **Agag** mutilated by Samuel to requite Israelite slaughter. [O.T.: I Samuel 15:33]
6. **Ahab, Captain** seeks revenge on whale. [Am. Lit.: *Moby Dick*]
7. **Alastor** epithet applied to Zeus and others as avenger. [Gk. Myth.: *NCE,* 49]

8. **Alfio** takes vengeance on Turiddu for adultery with his wife. [Ital. Opera: Mascagni, *Cavalleria Rusticana,* Westerman, 338–339]
9. **Atreus** cuckolded by brother, serves him his sons for dinner. [Rom. Lit.: *Thyestes,* Brewer *Dictionary,* 1081]
10. **Balfour, Ebenezer** takes vengeance on David, whose father stole Ebenezer's woman. [Brit. Lit.: *Kidnapped*]
11. **Barabas** his house and riches seized by the governor, murders the governor's son and others, and betrays the city to the Turks. [Br. Drama: Marlowe *The Jew of Malta* in Benét, 521]
12. **Calvo, Baldassare** Tito's aged benefactor, robbed and betrayed by Tito, eventually denounces and strangles him. [Br. Lit.: George Eliot *Romola*]
13. **Chillingworth, Roger** tortures Dimmesdale for adultery. [Am. Lit.: *The Scarlet Letter*]
14. **Colomba** will not rest until father's murder is avenged. [Fr. Lit.: *Colomba*]
15. **Coppelius** destroys Olympia because of bad check. [Fr. Opera: Offenbach, *Tales of Hoffmann,* Westerman, 275]
16. **Cousin Bette** deprived of her lover by Baron Hulot, she eventually manages to ruin the family. [Fr. Lit.: Balzac *Cousin Bette* in Magill I, 166]
17. **cry of blood** innocent victim's blood calls for justice. [O.T.: Genesis 4:10; Br. Lit.: *Richard II*]
18. **Dantès, Edmond** uses his wealth to punish those who betrayed him. [Fr. Lit.: Dumas *The Count of Monte Cristo*]
19. **Dirae** avenging goddesses or Furies. [Rom. Myth.: *LLEI,* I: 326]
20. **Don Carlos** takes vengeance upon Alvaro, alleged murderer of his father. [Ital. Opera: Verdi, *La Forza del Destino,* Westerman, 316–317]
21. **Electra** wreaks vengeance on her father's murderers. [Gk. Lit.: *Electra*]
22. **Epigoni, the** sons of the chiefs killed in the siege of Thebes avenge their fathers' deaths by razing the city. [Gk. Myth.: Benét, 318]
23. **eye for an eye** Moses's *lex talionis.* [O.T.: Exodus 21:23–25; Leviticus 24:20; Deuteronomy 19:21]
24. **Falke, Dr.** avenges his public humiliation by Eisenstein. [Aust. Operetta: J. Strauss, *Die Fledermaus,* Westerman, 278]
25. **Furies** horrible avengers of crimes. [Gk. Myth.: Brewer *Dictionary,* 381]

26. **golden cockerel, the** warns the king whenever enemies approach, but kills him when he breaks his promise of a reward. [Russ. Ballet: *Coq d'Or* in Goode, 78]
27. **Hamlet** spurred on by his father's ghost, avenges murder of his father. [Br. Lit.: *Hamlet*]
28. **Hecuba** kills Polymestor's children and blinds him for his treacherous murder of her son Polydorus. [Gk. Drama: Euripides *Hecuba* in Benét, 450]
29. **Herodias** spitefully effects decapitation of John the Baptist. [N.T.: Mark 6:19–26]
30. **Hiawatha** adventurous avenger of his father's wickedness to his mother. [Am. Lit.: Longfellow *The Song of Hiawatha* in Magill I, 905]
31. **Hieronimo** stages a play that gives him the opportunity to kill his son's murderers. [Br. Drama: *The Spanish Tragedy* in Magill II, 990]
32. **Hope, Jefferson** to avenge the murder of his sweetheart by two Mormons, trails them from Utah to London and kills both. [Br. Lit.: Doyle *A Study in Scarlet* in *Sherlock Holmes*]
33. **Joab** kills Abner, murderer of his brother. [O.T.: II Samuel 3:27]
34. **Kentucky Tragedy** noted tale of retribution, inspired many works. [Am. Hist.: Benét, 544]
35. **Lisbeth (Cousin Bette)** swears to get back at the Hulots. [Fr. Lit.: *Cousin Bette,* Magill I, 166–168]
36. ***Malta, The Jew of*** Christian-hating merchant's betrayal of Malta. [Br. Lit.: *The Jew of Malta*]
37. **Medea** uses poisoned nightgown to kill Jason's new wife. [Fr. Opera: Cherubini, *Medea,* Westerman, 81]
38. **Montresor** redresses insult by entombing insulter in catacomb niche. [Am. Lit.: Poe "The Cask of Amontillado"]
39. **Nemesis** daughter of Night, brought retribution upon haughty. [Gk. Myth.: Hall, 221]
40. **Orestes** killed his mother and her lover for having murdered his father. [Gk. Myth.: Benét, 741]
41. **Pied Piper, the** refused his promised reward for ridding Hamelin of rats, he lures the children away. [Ger. Legend: Benét, 787]
42. **Rigoletto** wreaks vengeance on daughter-seducing Duke of Mantua. [Ital. Opera: Verdi, *Rigoletto,* Westerman, 300]

43. **Samson** brings down the temple of the Philistines to avenge their blinding of him and dies in the process. [O.T.: Judges 16:28-30]

44. **Sextus** kills Ptolemy for the murder of Pompey. [Br. Opera: *Julius Caesar in Egypt,* Westerman, 52–53]

45. **Tamora** plots to avenge son by murdering the Andronicus family. [Br. Lit.: *Titus Andronicus*]

46. **Titus Andronicus** exacts revenge for crimes against his family. [Br. Lit.: *Titus Andronicus*]

47. **Todd, Sweeney** barber returns to England; takes revenge for false conviction by slitting throats of customers. [Br. Folklore: Misc; Br. Lit.: *Sweeney Todd;* Am. Musical Theater: *Sweeney Todd, the Demon Barber of Fleet Street,* in *Facts* (1979), 292.]

48. **trefoil** traditional symbol of vengeance. [Flower Symbolism: *Flora Symbolica,* 178]

49. **Zachanassian, Claire** a multi-millionairess, she bribes the villagers to execute the man who was responsible for her shame. [Swiss Drama: Duerrenmatt *The Visit* in Benét, 1063]

675. VERBOSITY

1. ***Clarissa Harlowe*** longest novel in the English language, totalling one million words. [Br. Lit.: Benét, 203]

2. ***Mahabharata*** epic poem of Ancient India runs to some 200,000 verses. [Hindu Lit.: Benét, 620]

3. ***War and Peace*** Tolstoy masterwork of exceeding length. [Russ. Lit.: Benét, 1071]

676. VERSATILITY

1. **Franklin, Benjamin** (1706–1790) American statesman, inventor, printer, author, scientist. [Am. Hist.: Benét, 366]

2. **George** Georges d'Amboise (1460–1510), conjectural eponym of "Let George do it," made premier and cardinal by Louis XII, who found him capable of any task. [Fr. Hist.: Brewer *Dictionary,* 392]

3. **jack-of-all-trades** epitome of the versatile worker of trades. [Pop. Culture: Misc.]

4. **Jefferson, Thomas** (1743–1826) writer of Declaration of Independence; inventor, scholar, president. [Am. Hist.: Jameson, 256–257]

5. **Leonardo da Vinci** (1452–1519) painter, sculptor, architect, musician, scientist, engineer. [Ital. Hist.: *NCE,* 1561–1562]

677. VICTORY

1. **Arc de Triomphe** arch built in Paris by Napoleon to celebrate his conquests (1806–1836). [Fr. Hist.: Misc.]
2. **Arch of Trajan** triumphal monument by emperor (c. 100). [Rom. Hist.: Misc.]
3. **bay leaves** wreath used as victor's crown. [Heraldry: Halberts, 20]
4. **Beethoven's 5th** symphony's first four notes are Morse code for *V*, symbolizing victory. [Western Culture: Misc.]
5. **Greek cross** symbol of Christ's triumph over death. [Christian Iconog.: Jobes, 386]
6. **laurel wreath** traditional symbol of victory, recognition, and reward. [Gk. and Rom. Hist.: Jobes, 374]
7. **Nike (Victoria)** winged goddess of triumph. [Gk. Myth.: Brewer *Dictionary,* 757]
8. **palm** sign of triumph. [N.T.: Revelation 7:9]
9. **V-E Day** Allies accept Germany's surrender in WWII (May 8, 1945). [World Hist.: Van Doren, 506]
10. **V-J Day** Allies accept Japan's surrender in WWII (August 15, 1945). [World Hist.: Van Doren, 507]

678. VILLAINY (See also EVIL, WICKEDNESS.)

1. **d'Acunha, Teresa** portrait of devilish Spanish servant and kidnapper. [Br. Lit.: *The Antiquary*]
2. **Bligh, Captain** (1754–1817) sadistic, heavy-handed captain of the *Bounty* [Am. Lit.: *Mutiny on the Bounty*]
3. **Bluto (Brutus)** Popeye's archenemy. [Comics: "Thimble Theater" in Horn, 657–658]
4. **Boris and Natasha** duo of dirty dealers. [TV: "Rocky and His Friends" in Terrace, II, 252–253]
5. **Dalgarno, Lord** young profligate nobleman; betrays Lady Hermione, slanders Nigel. [Br. Lit.: *Fortunes of Nigel*]
6. **Dastardly, Dick** popular personification of a villain. [TV: "Dastardly and Mutley" in Terrace, I, 185]
7. **deVille, Cruella** witchlike rich lady dognaps 99 dalmatians for coat-making. [Am. Cinema: *101 Dalmatians* in *Disney Films,* 181–184]
8. **Fagin** iniquitous old man; employs youngsters as thieves. [Br. Lit.: *Oliver Twist*]
9. **Foulfellow, J. Worthington** sly fox cajoles Pinocchio onto stage. [Am. Cinema: *Pinocchio* in *Disney Films,* 32–37]

10. **Iago** slanders Desdemona; precipitates tragedy. [Br. Lit.: *Othello*]

11. **Legree, Simon** cruel slavemaster of Uncle Tom. [Am. Lit.: *Uncle Tom's Cabin*]

12. **Lovelace, Robert** nefariously seduces the honorable, virtuous Clarissa. [Br. Lit.: Richardson *Clarissa Harlowe* in Magill I, 143]

13. **Mime** tries to poison Siegfried and get Nibelung treasure. [Ger. Opera: Wagner, *Siegfried,* Westerman, 241]

14. **Montoni, Signor** imprisons and mistreats his wife, tries to force his niece into marriage, and terrorizes the area. [Br. Lit.: Radcliffe *The Mysteries of Udolpho* in Magill I, 635]

15. **Montserrat, Conrade de** attempts to assassinate king; detected by Kenneth's hound. [Br. Lit.: *The Talisman*]

16. **Moriarty, Professor** arch-criminal, foe of Sherlock Holmes. [Br. Lit.: Doyle *Sherlock Holmes*]

17. **Mother St. Agatha** prioress abets lustful monk's plot to punish runaway. [Br. Lit.: *The Monk*]

18. **Murdour** reprehensible scoundrel; cuckolds and kills Bevis's father. [Br. Lit.: *Bevis of Hampton*]

19. **Oil Can Harry** a study in dastardliness. [Comics: "Mighty Mouse" in Horn, 492; TV: "The Mighty Mouse Playhouse" in Terrace, II, 96]

20. **Pizarro, Don** illegally imprisons and starves Florestan; plans murder. [Ger. Opera: Beethoven, *Fidelio,* Westerman, 109–110]

21. **Plantagenet, Richard** murders Somerset. [Br. Lit.: *II Henry VI*]

22. **Queen, the** "a crafty devil"; "hourly coining plots." [Br. Lit.: *Cymbeline*]

23. **Scarpia** offers mock execution for Tosca's affections. [Ital. Opera: Puccini, *Tosca,* Westerman, 352–354]

24. **Sheriff of Nottingham** traditional badman; thwarted in attempts to capture Robin Hood. [Br. Lit.: *Robin Hood*]

25. **Tello, Don** lustful nobleman; sates his passion on Elvira. [Span. Lit.: *The King, the Greatest Alcalde*]

26. **Wild, Jonathan** ambitious knave, schemer, and robber, whose "greatness" is satirized. [Br. Lit.: Fielding *Jonathan Wild the Great* in Magill II, 516]

Vindictiveness (See **VENGEANCE.**)

Violence (See **BRUTALITY, CRUELTY.**)

679. VIOLIN

1. **Nero** (37–68) emperor said to have fiddled while Rome burned (64). [Rom. Hist.: Misc.]
2. **Stradivarius** renowned hand-crafted instruments, rare and highly prized. [Western Music: *NCE,* 2631]

680. VIRGINITY (See also CHASTITY, PURITY.)

1. **Agnes, St.** patron saint of virgins. [Christian Hagiog.: Brewer *Dictionary,* 16]
2. **Atala** Indian maiden learns too late she can be released from her vow to remain a virgin. [Fr. Lit.: *Atala*]
3. **Athena** goddess who had no love affairs and never married, called Parthenos, 'the Virgin.' [Gk. Myth.: Benét, 60]
4. **Cecilia, St.** consecrated self to God, bridegroom followed suit. [Christian Hagiog.: Attwater, 81–82]
5. **Chrysanthus and Daria, Sts.** sexless marriage for glory of God. [Christian Hagiog.: Attwater, 86]
6. **Drake, Temple** chastity makes her the object of attacks. [Am. Lit.: *Sanctuary*]
7. **garden, enclosed** wherein grow the red roses of chastity. [Christian Symbolism: *De Virginibus,* Appleton, 41]
8. **Josyan** steadfastly retains virginity for future husband. [Br. Lit.: *Bevis of Hampton*]
9. **Lygia** foreign princess remains chaste despite Roman orgies. [Polish Lit.: *Quo Vadis,* Magill I, 797–799]
10. **lily** symbol of Blessed Virgin; by extension, chastity. [Christian Symbolism: Appleton, 57–58]
11. **ostrich egg** symbolic of virgin birth. [Art: Hall, 110]
12. **red and white roses, garland of** emblem of virginity, esp. of the Virgin Mary. [Christian Iconog.: Jobes, 374]
13. **Vestals** six pure girls; tended fire sacred to Vesta. [Rom. Hist.: Brewer *Dictionary,* 1127]
14. **Virgin Mary, Blessed** mother of Jesus. [Christianity: *NCE,* 1709]

681. VIRILITY (See also BEAUTY, MASCULINE; BRAWNINESS)

1. **Fury, Sergeant** archetypal he-man. [Comics: "Sergeant Fury and His Howling Commandos" in Horn, 607–608]

2. **Henry, John** a "natchal man" from Black River country. [Am. Lit.: Hart, 428]
3. **Macomber, Francis** Hemingway's hero assumes manhood by assertive act. [Am. Lit.: *The Short Happy Life of Francis Macomber,* Magill IV, 1130–1133]
4. **Marlboro Man** cigarette advertising campaign established new symbol of virility. [Am. Pop. Culture: Misc.]
5. **Priapus** male generative power personified. [Gk. Myth.: Espy, 27, 224]
6. **rooster** symbol of maleness. [Folklore: Binder, 85]
7. **stag** symbol of maleness. [Animal Symbolism: Mercatante, 59–60]
8. **Sweeney** in poems by T. S. Eliot, symbolizes the sensual, brutal, and materialistic 20th-century man. [Br. Poetry, Benét, 978]

682. VIRTUOUSNESS (See also HONESTY, RIGHTEOUSNESS.)

1. **Amelia** faithful wife of William Booth, often in debtors' prison, saved by her purity from the men who prey upon her. [Br. Lit.: *Amelia*]
2. **Andrews, Pamela** servant who, despite threats, attempted seduction, and imprisonment by her master, remains chaste till their marriage. [Br. Lit.: Richardson *Pamela*]
3. **Andromache** thinks only of family; rejects king's advances. [Fr. Lit.: *Andromache*]
4. **Apostrophia** epithet of Aphrodite, meaning "rejecter of sinful passion." [Gk. Myth.: Misc.]
5. **Christian** John Bunyan's virtuous, well-traveled hero. [Br. Lit.: *Pilgrim's Progress*]
6. **Erlynne, Mrs.** gains socially admirable title of "good woman." [Br. Lit.: *Lady Windermere's Fan,* Magill I, 488–490]
7. **Galahad, Sir** noblest and purest knight of the Round Table. [Br. Lit.: *Le Morte d'Arthur*]
8. **Guyon, Sir** embodiment of virtuous self-control. [Br. Lit.: *Faerie Queene*]
9. **Marina** "a piece of virtue." [Br. Lit.: *Pericles*]
10. **Nickleby, Kate** pure-minded sister of Nicholas; repulses all advances. [Br. Lit.: *Nicholas Nickleby*]
11. **Pamela** sweet maidservant who chastely repels disgraceful advances, marries her aristocratic pursuer, and attempts to reform him. [Br. Lit.: Richardson *Pamela*]
12. **Susanna** rejects advances of elderly men. [Apocrypha: Susanna]

13. **Thirty-Six Righteous Men** the minimum number of anonymous individuals in each generation believed to have the virtues and humility to which the world owes its continued existence. [Jew. Legend: *Encyclopedia Judaica,* X, 1367]
14. **Tuesday's child** full of grace. [Nurs. Rhyme: Opie, 309]
15. **Wilkes, Melanie** virtuous, long-suffering wife of Ashley. [Am. Lit.: *Gone With the Wind*]

683. VISIONS and VOICES

1. **Bernadette Soubirous** had a vision in a grotto of the Blessed Virgin. [Ger. Lit.: *The Song of Bernadette*; Magill I, 903]
2. **Wieland** driven by mysterious voices, he kills his wife and children. [Am. Lit.: Magill II, 1131]

Voluptuousness (See **BEAUTY, FEMININE; BUXOMNESS; SEX SYMBOLS.**)

Voracity (See **GLUTTONY.**)

684. VOYEURISM (See also EAVESDROPPING.)

1. **Actaeon** turned into stag for watching Artemis bathe. [Gk. Myth.: Leach, 8]
2. **elders of Babylon** watch Susanna bathe. [Apocrypha: Susanna; Art: Daniel, 217]
3. **Gyges** king's bodyguard requested secretly to view queen undressing. [Gk. Lit.: Avery, 507–508]
4. **Peeping Tom** illicitly glanced at the naked Godiva. [Br. Legend: Brewer *Dictionary,* 815]
5. **Roberts, Mr.** takes advantage of unshaded hospital window to watch nurses taking baths. [Am. Lit.: Heggen *Mister Roberts* in Sobel, 479]

685. VULNERABILITY

1. **Achilles** warrior vulnerable only in his heel. [Gk. Myth.: Zimmerman, 4]
2. **Antaeus** only vulnerable if not touching ground. [Gk. and Rom. Myth.: Hall, 151]
3. **Balder** conquerable only with mistletoe. [Norse Myth.: Walsh *Classical,* 43]
4. **Diarmuid** Irish Achilles, killed through cunning Fionn's deceit. [Irish Myth.: Jobes, 443; Parrinder, 79]
5. **Maginot Line** French fortification zone along German border; thought impregnable before WWII. [Fr. Hist.: *NCE,* 1658]

6. **Samson** strength derived from his hair; betrayed by Delilah. [O.T.: Judges 16]
7. **Siegfried** vulnerable in only one spot on his back. [Ger. Opera: Wagner, *Götterdämmerung,* Westerman, 245]
8. **Siegfried Line** German fortification zone opposite the Maginot Line between Germany and France. [Ger. Hist.: *WB,* 17: 370]
9. **Superman** invulnerable except for Kryptonite. [TV: "The Adventures of Superman" in Terrace, I, 38; Comics: Horn, 642]

Vulgarity (See **COARSENESS.**)

W

686. WANDERING (See also ADVENTUROUSNESS, BOHEMIANISM, JOURNEY, QUEST.)

1. **Ahasuerus** German name for the Wandering Jew. [Ger. Lit.: Benét, 1071]
2. **Ancient Mariner** Coleridge's wandering sailor. [Br. Lit.: "The Rime of the Ancient Mariner" in Norton, 597–610]
3. **Aniara** spaceship condemned to perpetual earth orbit. [Swed. Opera: Blomdahl, *Aniara,* Westerman, 562]
4. **Argonauts** sailed with Jason in search of Golden Fleece. [Gk. Myth.: Howe, 36]
5. **Bedouin** a nomadic desert Arab. [Br. Folklore: Espy, 98]
6. **Bloom, Leopold** Jewish advertising salesman whose wanderings around Dublin are ironic parallels of Ulysses' voyages. [Irish Lit.: James Joyce *Ulysses*]
7. **Cain** punished by God to life of vagrancy. [O.T.: Genesis 4:12]
8. **Candide** a wanderer in search of best of all possible worlds. [Fr. Lit.: *Candide*]
9. **Cocytus** Hadean river where unburied were doomed to roam for 100 years. [Gk. Myth.: Benét, 210]
10. **Eulenspiegel, Till** roams Low Countries as soldier and deliverer. [Ger. Folklore: Benét, 325–326]
11. ***Flying Dutchman*** spectral ship doomed to eternal wandering. [Marine Folklore: Benét, 355]
12. **Goedzak, Lamme** accompanies Eulenspiegel on his circumambulations. [Ger. Folklore: Benét, 325–326]
13. **Goliards** wandering scholar-poets of 12th-century Europe. [Medieval Hist.: *NCE,* 1105]
14. **Gulliver, Lemuel** visits fabulous lands. [Br. Lit.: *Gulliver's Travels*]
15. **Gynt, Peer** Norwegian farmer drifts around without purpose. [Nor. Lit.: *Peer Gynt,* Magill I, 722–724]
16. **Gypsy** member of nomadic people who usually travel in small caravans. [Eur. Hist.: *NCE,* 1168]
17. **Harold, Childe** seeking an end to disappointment in love, he wanders about Europe. [Br. Poetry: Byron *Childe Harold's Pilgrimage* in Magill IV, 127]

18. **Herodias** condemned to wander the world for centuries for her part in the execution of John the Baptist. [Fr. Lit.: Eugène Sue *The Wandering Jew*]
19. **Ishmael** "the wanderer" aboard Ahab's ship. [Am. Lit.: *Moby Dick*]
20. **Kwai Chang Caine** Shaolin priest wanders throughout America. [TV: "Kung Fu" in Terrace I, 449]
21. **Labre, St. Benedict** itinerant holy beggar. [Christian Hagiog.: Attwater, 64]
22. **land of Nod** condemned to vagabondage, Cain settles here. [O.T.: Genesis 4:16]
23. **Meaulnes, Augustine** dreamer with a lifelong fondness for wandering into romantic adventures. [Fr. Lit.: *The Wanderer* in Magill I, 1081]
24. **Melmoth the Wanderer** to win souls, he is cursed to roam earth after death. [Br. Lit.: *Melmoth the Wanderer*]
25. **Moses** led his people through the wilderness for forty years. [O.T.: Pentateuch]
26. **Mother Courage** shrewd old woman who makes her living by following the armies of the Thirty Years' War selling her wares to the soldiers. [Ger. Drama: Brecht *Mother Courage and Her Children* in Benét, 690]
27. **Nolan, Philip** transferred from ship to ship; never lands. [Am. Lit.: "The Man Without a Country" in Benét, 632]
28. **Odysseus (Ulysses)** hero of the Trojan War wanders for seven years before returning home. [Gk. Lit.: *Odyssey*]
29. **Omoo** Polynesian word for an island rover. [Am. Lit.: *Omoo*]
30. **Ossian** a legendary, wandering Irish bard. [Irish Lit.: Harvey, 603]
31. **Route 66** adventure series of two young men wandering along highway Route 66. [TV: Terrace, II, 259]
32. **Rugg, Peter** wanders on horseback for fifty years, trying to find his way home. [Am. Lit.: Austin "Peter Rugg, the Missing Man" in Hart, 48]
33. **Siddhartha** character who wanders in search of "inner truth." [Ger. Lit.: Hesse, *Siddhartha*]
34. ***Travels with Charley*** accompanied by his poodle, Steinbeck drives 10,000 miles through 40 states to discover America. [Am. Lit.: Steinbeck *Travels with Charley* in Benét, 961]
35. ***Travels with a Donkey*** R. L. Stevenson's wanderings through the mountains of southern France, accompanied by a donkey. [Br. Lit.: Magill I, 1014]

36. **Wandering Jew** condemned to eternal wandering for mocking Christ. [Christian Legend: *NCE,* 2926; Fr. Lit.: *Wandering Jew*]
37. **Yorick, Mr.** in a leisurely trip through 18th-century France, he meets a variety of people and enjoys the company of the fair sex. [Br. Lit.: Sterne *A Sentimental Journey* in Benét, 914]

687. WAR (See also BATTLE.)

1. **Amazons** race of female warriors. [Gk. Myth.: Zimmerman, 19]
2. **Ares** (**Mars**) god of war. [Gk. Myth.: Kravitz, 31]
3. **Athena** (Rom. **Minerva**) goddess of war. [Gk. Myth.: Howe, 44]
4. **battle ax** symbol of military conflict. [Western Folklore: Jobes, 163]
5. **Bellona** Mars's charioteer and sister. [Rom. Myth.: Leach, 135]
6. **Durga** malignant goddess of war. [Hinduism: Leach, 330]
7. **Enyo** goddess of battle and attendant of Ares. [Gk. Myth.: Howe, 91]
8. **Guernica** painting by Picasso depicting horror of war. [Art: Osborne, 866–867]
9. **Huitzilopochtli** war god of ancient Mexicans. [Mex. Myth.: Harvey, 403]
10. ***Iliad*** Homer's poetic account set during the legendary Trojan war. [Gk. Poetry: *The Iliad*]
11. ***Mahabharata*** lengthy narrative poem about the great war supposed to have taken place in India about 1400 B.C. [Sanskrit Lit.: Haydn & Fuller, 451]
12. **Myrmidon** one of the fierce Thessalonians who fought in the Trojan War under their king, Achilles. [Gk. Myth.: *Iliad*]
13. **Neman** form of Irish war goddess, Badb (also Morrigan or Macha). [Irish Folklore: Briggs, 308]
14. **Odin** god who presided over feasts of slain warriors. [Norse Myth.: Brewer *Dictionary,* 774]
15. **red cloud** indicates military conflict. [Eastern Folklore: Jobes, 350]
16. **Tyr** god of victory in war. [Norse Myth.: Leach, 1147]
17. **Valkyries** Odin's warrior maidens. [Norse Myth.: Leach, 1154]

688. WARNING

1. **Canterbury bells** fairies' church bells; relied on for vigilance. [Flower Symbolism: *Flora Symbolica,* 167]
2. **Capitoline geese** squawked obstreperously at sight of invader mounting rampart. [Rom. Hist.: Benét, 166]

3. **cock** crows at trespassers; morning call routs evil spirits. [Folklore: White, 150; Mercatante, 173–175]
4. **crow's cry** warning of death or illness. [Western Folklore: Jobes, 388]
5. **fiery cross** traditional Highlands call to arms. [Scot. Hist.: Brewer *Note-Book*, 324–325]
6. **Laocoön** Trojan priest warns citizens not to accept wooden horse. [Rom. Lit.: *Aeneid*]
7. **Olivant** Roland's ivory horn; sounded to summon Charlemagne. [Fr. Lit.: *The Song of Roland*]
8. **Revere, Paul** (1735–1818) famous American patriot who warned, "The British are coming" (1775). [Am. Hist.: Jameson, 425–426]

689. WATER

1. **Adad** storm god; helped cause the Flood. [Babyl. Myth.: Benét, 7]
2. **Adam's ale** water; only drink in Paradise. [Folklore: Brewer *Dictionary*, 9]
3. **Alpheus** river god. [Gk. Myth.: Zimmerman, 18]
4. **Apsu** personification of fresh water. [Babyl. Myth.: Benét, 4]
5. **Arethusa** changed into stream by Artemis to save her from Alpheus. [Gk. Myth.: Zimmerman, 29]
6. **Cyane** turned into a fountain by Hades. [Gk. Myth.: Kravitz, 70]
7. **Dirce** turned into a fountain at death. [Gk. Myth.: Kravitz, 82–83]
8. **Galatea** grieving, turned into a fountain. [Gk. Myth.: *Metamorphoses*]
9. **Jupiter Pluvius** dispenser of rain. [Rom. Myth.: Espy, 22]
10. **Neptune** in allegories of the elements, personification of water. [Art: Hall, 128]
11. **undine** female water spirit. [Medieval Hist.: Brewer *Dictionary*, 1115]

690. WEAKNESS (See also TIMIDITY, VULNERABILITY.)

1. **Gertrude** "Frailty, thy name is woman!" [Br. Lit.: *Hamlet*]
2. **Henry VI** dominated by queen and vassal; shirks responsibilities. [Br. Lit.: *Henry VI*]
3. **John, King** without grandeur, strength, or any regal quality. [Br. Lit.: *King John*]

4. **Milquetoast, Casper** the original "Timid Soul"; afraid of calling soul his own. [Comics: Horn, 663]
5. **Mitty, Walter** epitome of weak-spirited man. [Am. Lit.: "The Secret Life of Walter Mitty" in Payton, 448]
6. **musk** traditional symbol of weakness. [Plant Symbolism: *Flora Symbolica,* 176]
7. **Pilate, Pontius** yields to clamoring of Jews, hands Jesus over. [N.T.: Matthew 27:24–26; Luke 23:16–25; John 19:1–16]
8. **Warren, Nicole** relies on Dick for stability and identity. [Am. Lit.: *Tender Is the Night*]

691. WEALTH (See also LUXURY, TREASURE.)

1. **Abu Dhabi** Persian Gulf sheikdom overflowing with petrodollars. [Mid-East Hist.: *NCE,* 9]
2. **Big Daddy** wealthy Mississippi landowner of humble origins. [Am. Lit.: *Cat on a Hot Tin Roof*]
3. **black and gold** symbol of financial prosperity. [Heraldry: Jobes, 222]
4. **buttercup** traditional symbol of wealth. [Plant Symbolism: *Flora Symbolica,* 167]
5. **Cave of Mammon** abode of god of riches. [Br. Lit.: *Faerie Queene*]
6. **Corinth** ancient Greek city; one of wealthiest and most powerful. [Gk. Hist. and Myth.: Zimmerman, 69]
7. **Croesus** Lydian king; name became synonymous with riches. [Gk. Myth.: Kravitz, 69]
8. **Dives** rich man who ignored poor man's plight; sent to Hell. [N.T.: Luke 16:19–31]
9. **Erichthonius** world's richest man in classical times. [Gk. Myth.: Kravitz, 91]
10. **Fortunatus' purse** luckless man receives gift of inexhaustible purse. [Ital. Fairy Tale: *LLEI,* I: 286]
11. **Fuggers** 16th-century German financiers. [Ger. Hist.: *NCE,* 1023–1024]
12. **Hughes, Howard** (1905–1976) eccentric millionaire; lived as recluse. [Am. Hist.: *NCE,* 1284]
13. **Midas** Phrygian king; whatever he touched became gold. [Gk. and Rom. Myth.: Wheeler, 24]
14. **Plutus** god of wealth: blind (indiscriminate); lame (slow to accumulate); and winged (quick to disappear). [Gk. Lit.: *Plutus*]

15. **Rockefeller, John D(avison)** (1839–1937) oil magnate; name has become synonymous with "rich." [Am. Hist.: Jameson, 431]
16. **Solomon** fabulous riches garnered from gifts and tolls. [O.T.: I Kings 10:14–25]
17. **Timon** rich Athenian; ruined by his prodigal generosity to friends. [Br. Lit.: *Timon of Athens*]
18. **turquoise** seeing turquoise after a new moon brings wealth. [Gem Symbolism: Kunz, 345]
19. **Warbucks, Daddy** adventurous soldier of fortune and richest man in world. [Comics: "Little Orphan Annie" in Horn, 459]
20. **wheat stalk** traditional symbol of wealth. [Flower Symbolism: *Flora Symbolica*, 178]

Weaving (See SEWING and WEAVING.)

692. WHITENESS

1. **ermine** winter stoat; said to die if whiteness is soiled. [Art: Hall, 115]
2. **Moby Dick** white whale pursued relentlessly by Captain Ahab; "It was the whiteness of the whale that above all things appalled me." [Am. Lit.: *Moby Dick*]
3. **pale horse** ridden by Death. [*N.T.: Revelation* 6:8]
4. **Silver** flashing white steed of the Lone Ranger. [Radio: Buxton, 143–144]
5. **white belt of wampum** giving one was giving the deepest pledge of honor. [Am. Indian Trad.: Misc.]
6. **white forked flame** holiest flame on the altar. [Persian Folklore: Misc.]
7. **White Steed of the Prairies** charger who led the wild horses before the West was tamed. [Am. Indian Legend: Misc.]
8. **white stone** marked a joyful day. [Rom. Trad.: Misc.]

693. WHOLESOMENESS

1. **Armstrong, Jack** "the all-American boy." [Radio: Buxton, 121–122]
2. **Brady Bunch, The** widower and widow marry, producing an instant, wholesome family of eight. [TV: Terrace, I, 115]
3. **Miss America** annual beauty contest features wholesome contestants. [Am. Hist.: Allen, 56–57]
4. **Ozzie and Harriet** series portraying the wholesome, American family. [TV: "The Adventures of Ozzie and Harriet" in Terrace, I, 34]

5. **Waltons, The** poor, rural family in the 1930s; they extol chastity, honesty, family unity, and love. [TV: Terrace, II, 418]

694. WICKEDNESS (See also EVIL, VILLAINY.)

1. **Admah and Zeboyim** cities destroyed by God for citizens' sinfulness. [O.T.: Deuteronomy 19:23]
2. **Ahab** honored false gods, usurped others' land; byword for baseness. [O.T.: I Kings 17:29–34; 21:25]
3. **Bluebeard** murders six wives; a personification of wickedness. [Fr. Lit.: Walsh *Classical,* 58]
4. **de Winter, Rebecca** taunts her husband with her promiscuity and plots to have him accused of her murder. [Br. Lit.: D. du Maurier *Rebecca* in Magill I, 806]
5. **Jezebel** urged husband, Ahab, to evildoing. [O.T.: I Kings 21:25]
6. **Manasseh** idolatrously and murderously leads Jerusalem astray. [O.T.: II Kings 21:2–4, 9]
7. **Sodom and Gomorrah** cities of iniquity destroyed by God's wrath. [O.T.: Genesis 19:24]
8. **Thornhill, Squire** abducts a young woman and has her kind father jailed for debt. [Br. Lit.: Goldsmith *The Vicar of Wakefield*]

695. WIDOWHOOD

1. **Douglas, Widow** adopted Huck Finn and took care of him. [Am. Lit.: Mark Twain *Huckleberry Finn*]
2. **Gummidge, Mrs.** "a lone lorn creetur," the Pegotty's housekeeper. [Br. Lit.: Dickens *David Copperfield*]
3. ***Old Wives' Tale, The*** novel of two sisters widowed young, one by death, the other by desertion. [Br. Lit.: Magill I, 684]
4. **Wadman, Widow** romantic neighbor who unsuccessfully lays siege to Uncle Toby's affections. [Br. Lit.: *Tristram Shandy*; Magill I, 1027]
5. **widow of Ephesus** weeping over her husband's corpse, she is cheered by a compassionate sentry and they become ardent lovers in the burial vault. [Rom. Lit.: *Satyricon*]
6. **Wife of Bath, the** kept her five successive husbands under her thumb by trickery. [Br. Lit.: Chaucer *Canterbury Tales*]

696. WIFELINESS (See also DOMESTICITY.)

1. **Amoret** Sir Scudamore's wife; loving and ever-devoted. [Br. Lit.: *Faerie Queene*]

2. **Arundhati** example of the ideal Hindu wife. [Hindu Legend: Benét, 56]
3. **Billy Boy** question-and-answer ballad pointing up merits of possible bride. [Br. and Am. Folklore: Leach, 139]
4. **Martha** personification of the busy housekeeper. [N.T.: Luke 10:39]
5. **Penelope** a model of wifely virtue. [Gk. Lit.: *Odyssey*]

697. WILD WEST

1. **Apache** North American Indians of Southwest who fought against frontiersmen. [Am. Hist.: *NCE,* 123]
2. **Arapaho** North American Plains Indians living along the Platte and Arkansas rivers. [Am. Hist.: *EB,* I: 477–478]
3. **Bass, Sam** (1851–1878) desperado whose career inspired ballads. [Am. Hist.: *NCE,* 244]
4. **Bean, Judge Roy** (c. 1825–1903) legendary frontier judge who ruled by one law book and a six-shooter. [Am. Hist.: *NCE,* 252]
5. ***Big Valley, The*** portraying cattle-owning aristocrats of the Wild West. [TV: Terrace, I, 99–100]
6. **Billy the Kid** (William H. Bonney, 1859–1881) Brooklyn-born gunman of the Wild West. [Am. Hist.: Worth, 27]
7. ***Bonanza*** saga of the Cartwright family. [TV: Terrace, I, 111–112]
8. **Boom Town** originally, a western town that prospered suddenly, usually because of gold mines nearby. [Am. Hist.: Misc.]
9. **boot hill** typical graveyard of gunfighters and their victims. [Am. Folklore: Misc.]
10. **Bowie knife** throwing weapon invented by James or Rezin Bowie, frontiersmen in Texas. [Am. Folklore: *EB,* II: 207]
11. ***Broken Arrow*** a series depicting Indian–white man exploits. [TV: Terrace, I, 122]
12. **Calamity Jane** (Martha Jane Canary Burke, c. 1852–1903) extraordinary markswoman and pony express rider. [Am. Hist.: *NCE,* 418]
13. **California Trail** route used by pioneers, extending from Wyoming to Sacramento. [Am. Hist.: *WB,* 21: 440f]
14. **Carson, Kit** (**Christopher**) (1809–1868) frontiersman, guide, and Indian fighter in the West and Southwest. [Am. Hist.: *NCE,* 466]
15. **Cheyenne** North American Indians who made up part of the Wild West scene. [Am. Hist.: *NCE,* 562]

16. **Cheyenne** cowboy of the strong, silent type. [TV: Terrace, I, 153–154]
17. **Chisholm Trail** route used by traders and drovers bringing cattle from Texas to Kansas. [Am. Hist.: *NCE,* 543]
18. **circuit rider** frontier Methodist preacher who served "appointments" (services) in cabins, schoolhouses, and even taverns. [Am. Hist.: *NCE,* 561]
19. **Cochise** (c. 1815–1874) Apache Indian chief who led the fight against white men in the Southwest. [Am. Hist: *NCE,* 589]
20. **Cody, "Buffalo Bill"** (1846–1917) ex-Army scout who joined and led a famous Wild West show. [Am. Hist.: *NCE,* 390]
21. **Colt .45** six-shot revolver invented by Samuel Colt and used throughout the West. [Am. Hist.: *WB,* 4: 684–685]
22. **Comanche** North American Indian tribe; often figured in Wild West stories. [Am. Hist.: *NCE,* 607]
23. **Comstock Lode** richest silver deposit in U.S.; famous during frontier days. [Am. Hist.: *NCE,* 418]
24. **Conestoga wagon** horse-drawn freight wagon; originated in the Conestoga Creek region in Pennsylvania. [Am. Hist.: *EB,* III: 72]
25. **Crazy Horse** (1842–1877) Indian chief who led Sioux against the white men in the northern plains. [Am. Hist.: *EB,* III: 225–226]
26. **Custer's Last Stand** U.S. troops led by Col. Custer are massacred by the Indians at Little Big Horn, Montana (1877). [Am. Hist.: *NCE,* 701]
27. **Deadwood Gulch** Wild West city in South Dakota where graves of Hickok and Annie Oakley are located. [Am. Hist.: *NCE,* 729]
28. ***Death Valley Days*** vignettes depicting frontier life. [TV: Terrace, I, 195]
29. **Dillon, Matt** frontier marshal of Dodge City. [TV: "Gunsmoke" in Terrace, I, 331]
30. **Dodge City** onetime rowdy cowboy town under supervision of Bat Masterson and Wyatt Earp. [Am. Hist.: *NCE,* 776]
31. **Earp, Wyatt** (1848–1929) U.S. cowboy, lawman, and gunfighter. [Am. Hist.: *NCE,* 819]
32. **Geronimo** (1829–1909) renegade Indian of the Wild West. [Am. Hist.: *NCE,* 1076]
33. **ghost town** town left vacant after gold strike; common during frontier days. [Am. Hist.: *NCE,* 1080]

34. ***Gunsmoke*** Wild West television epic with Dodge City setting. [TV: Terrace, I, 331–332]
35. **Hickok, "Wild Bill"** (1837–1876) famous marshal of the West. [Am. Hist.: Hart, 371]
36. ***High Noon*** western film in which time is of the essence. [Am. Cinema: Griffith, 396–397]
37. **Holliday, "Doc"** (fl. late 19th century) outlaw who helped Wyatt Earp fight the Clanton gang at O.K. Corral. [Am. Hist.: Misc.]
38. **"Home on the Range"** popular song about the West "where the buffalo roam" and "the deer and the antelope play." [Am. Culture: Misc.]
39. **Indian Territory** area set aside for the Indians by the U.S. government. [Am. Hist.: *NCE,* 1331]
40. **James, Jesse** (1847–1882) American outlaw of the Wild West. [Am. Hist.: *NCE,* 1395]
41. ***Lone Ranger, The*** masked hero of the Wild West. [TV: Terrace, II, 34–35; Radio: Buxton, 143–144]
42. **O.K. Corral** scene of famous gunfight between Wyatt Earp and the Clanton gang (1881). [Am. Hist.: *WB,* 6: 9]
43. **Oakley, Annie** (1860–1926) sharpshooter; major attraction of Buffalo Bill's show. [Am. Hist.: *NCE,* 1982]
44. **"Oh, Bury Me Not on the Lone Prairie"** popular song about life in the West. [Am. Culture: Misc.]
45. **Oregon Trail** wagon-train route used by pioneers, extending from Missouri to the Oregon Territory. [Am. Hist.: *NCE,* 2016]
46. **Paladin** archetypal gunman who leaves a calling card. [TV: *Have Gun, Will Travel* in Terrace, I, 341]
47. **Pecos Bill** giant folk hero famed for cowboy exploits. [Am. Lit.: Hart, 643]
48. **Pony Express** relay mail service during frontier days. [Am. Hist.: *NCE,* 2190]
49. **prairie schooner** horse-drawn wagon used by pioneers; its white canvas top resembled a schooner sailing on the prairie. [Am. Hist.: *NCE,* 2209]
50. ***Rawhide*** series depicting cowboys as cattle-punchers along the Santa Fe trail. [TV: Terrace, II, 235]
51. **Ringo, Johnny** (fl. late 19th century) notorious outlaw who fought many gun battles in the Southwest. [Am. Hist.: Misc.]
52. **Santa Fe Trail** wagon-train route extending from Independence, Missouri to Santa Fe, New Mexico. [Am. Hist.: *NCE,* 2421]

53. ***Shane*** a classic, serious western film about a pioneer family protected by a mysterious stranger. [Am. Cinema: Halliwell, 651]
54. **Sioux** confederation of North American Indian tribes; last battle fought at Wounded Knee. [Am. Hist.: *NCE,* 2527]
55. **Sitting Bull** (1831–1890) Indian chief who united the Sioux tribes against the white men. [Am. Hist.: *EB,* IX: 243–244]
56. **Slade the Terrible** stagecoach agent and desperado known for shooting his enemies dead at the drop of a hat. [Am. Lit.: Mark Twain *Roughing It* in Magill I, 858]
57. **Texas Rangers** established in 1835, a mounted fighting force to maintain law and order in the West. [Am. Hist.: *NCE,* 2723]
58. **Tombstone** Arizona town known for its outlaws, prospectors, and gun battles (1800s). [Am. Hist.: *EB,* X: 36]
59. **Wells Fargo** company that handled express service to western states; often robbed. [Am. Hist.: *NCE,* 2953]
60. **Winchester 73** repeating rifle manufactured by Oliver Winchester and widely used by the settlers of the West. [Am. Hist.: *EB,* X: 699]

698. WIND

1. **Aeolian harp** musical instrument activated by winds. [Gk. Myth.: Jobes, 40]
2. **Aeolus** steward of winds; gives bag of winds to Odysseus. [Gk. Myth: Kravitz, 10; Gk. Lit.: *Odyssey*]
3. **Afer (Africus)** southwest wind. [Gk. Myth.: Kravitz, 11]
4. **Apeliotes (Lips)** east or southeast wind. [Gk. Myth.: Kravitz, 27]
5. **Aquilo** equivalent of Boreas, the Greek north wind. [Rom. Myth.: Kravitz, 30]
6. **Argestes** name of the east wind. [Gk. Myth.: Kravitz, 32]
7. **Aura** goddess of breezes. [Gk. Myth.: Kravitz, 42]
8. **Auster** the southwest wind. [Rom. Myth.: Kravitz, 42]
9. **Boreas** god of the north wind. [Gk. Myth.: Parrinder, 49]
10. **Caicas** the northeast wind. [Gk. Myth.: Kravitz, 50]
11. **Corus** god of the north or northwest wind. [Rom. Myth.: Jobes, 374]
12. **Eurus (Volturnus)** the southeast wind. [Gk. Myth.: Kravitz, 97, 238]
13. **Favonius** ancient Roman personification of west wind. [Rom. Myth.: Howe, 103]

14. **Gentle Annis** weather spirit; controls gales on Firth of Cromarty. [Scot. Folklore: Briggs, 185]
15. **gregale (Euroclydon)** cold, northeast wind over the central Mediterranean. [Meteorology: *EB,* IV: 724; *N.T.: Acts* 27:14]
16. **Keewaydin** the Northwest Wind, to whose regions Hiawatha ultimately departed. [Am. Lit.: Longfellow *The Song of Hiawatha* in Magill I, 905]
17. **Mudjekeewis** Indian chief; held dominion over all winds. [Am. Lit.: "Hiawatha" in Benét, 466]
18. **Njord** god of the north wind. [Norse Myth.: Wheeler, 260]
19. **Ruach** isle of winds. [Fr. Lit.: *Pantagruel*]
20. **Sleipnir** Odin's eight-legged horse; symbolizes the wind that blows from eight points. [Norse Myth.: Benét, 937]
21. **Zephyrus** the west wind. [Gk. Myth.: Kravitz, 38, 242]

699. WINE

1. **Anacreon** (563–478 B.C.) Greek lyric poet who praised the effects of wine. [Gk. Lit.: Brewer *Dictionary,* 31]
2. **Andros** center for worship of Bacchus, wine god. [Rom. Myth.: Hall, 16]
3. **Bacchus** god of wine. [Rom. Myth.: Hall, 37, 142]
4. **Beaujolais** a wine-growing region in France; often a medium-dry, fruity burgundy. [Fr. Hist.: *NCE,* 2990]
5. **Bordeaux** French city whose wines (especially Médoc, Graves, Sauternes, Saint Émilion) are world-known. [Fr. Hist.: *EB,* II: 162]
6. **Burgundy** region of France that produces fine wines. [Fr. Hist.: *NCE,* 2989]
7. **Catawba** grape grown in the eastern U.S., producing a medium-dry white wine. [Am. Hist.: Misc.]
8. **Chablis** village in central France known for the white wine which bears its name. [Fr. Hist.: *NCE,* 497]
9. **chalice** cup holding wine at Eucharist. [Christian Tradition: N.T.: Mark 14:23]
10. **Champagne** province in northeastern France renowned for its sparkling wine. [Fr. Hist.: *EB,* II: 724]
11. **Chianti** the best-known Italian wine. [Ital. Hist.: *NCE,* 2990]
12. **Dionysus** god of the vine and its enlightening powers. [Gk. Myth.: Avery, 404–408; Parrinder, 80]
13. **Finger Lakes** the region in New York state where many eastern wines are made. [Am. Hist.: *NCE,* 2990]

14. **Liber and Libera** ancient Italian god and goddess of wine and vine cultivation. [Rom. Myth.: Howe, 154]
15. **Liebfraumilch** the best-known Rhine wine. [Ger. Hist.: *NCE,* 2990]
16. **Médoc** a red Bordeaux wine. [Fr. Hist.: *NCE,* 2990]
17. **Marsala** a sweet, amber wine made in Sicily. [Ital. Hist.: *NCE,* 2990]
18. **Napa Valley** greatest wine-producing region of the United States. [Am. Hist.: *NCE,* 2990]
19. **Naxian Groves** vineyards celebrated for fine vintages. [Gk. Hist.: Brewer *Handbook,* 747]
20. **Oeneus** Calydonian king; first to cultivate grapes. [Rom. Myth.: Hall, 142]
21. **port** fortified sweet wine made from grapes grown in the Douro valley in Portugal. [Port. Hist.: *NCE,* 2194]
22. **Rhine valley** region of Germany that produces fine wines. [Ger. Hist.: *NCE,* 2990]
23. **Riesling** grape grown in Germany and California, producing a dry or sweet white wine. [Ger. Hist.: Misc.]
24. **Rioja** Spain's most widely exported wine. [Span. Hist.: *NCE,* 2990]
25. **sherry** dry fortified wine, originally made from grapes grown in Andalusia, Spain. [Span. Hist.: *NCE,* 2501]
26. **Tokay** region of Hungary that produces wines. [Hung. Hist.: *NCE,* 2889]
27. **Valpolicella** a dark, rich red wine from Veneto. [Ital. Hist.: *NCE,* 2990]
28. **Vouvray** village in central France known for its medium-dry white wine. [Fr. Hist.: Misc.]

700. WINTER

1. **Boreas** the north wind; associated with winter. [Rom. Myth.: Hall, 130]
2. **crane** pictorial emblem in Buddhist tradition. [Animal Symbolism: Jobes, 378]
3. **Ded Moroz** personification of winter; "Grandfather Frost." [Russ. Folklore: Misc.]
4. **goat** zodiacally belongs to December; hence, winter. [Astrology: Hall, 139]
5. **Hiems** personification; portrayed as old and decrepit. [Rom. Myth.: *LLEI,* I: 322]
6. **Jack Frost** personification of winter. [Pop. Culture: Misc.]

7. **Old Man Winter** personification of winter. [Pop. Culture: Misc.]
8. **old man wrapped in cloak** personification of winter. [Art: Hall, 130]
9. **Persephone** the period of her stay (winter) with Hades. [Gk. Myth.: Espy, 28]

701. WISDOM (See also GENIUS.)

1. **Amenhotep** (fl. 14th century B.C.) pictured as bearded man holding papyrus roll. [Ancient Egypt. Art: Parrinder, 18]
2. **Athena** (Rom. **Minerva**) goddess of wisdom. [Gk. and Rom. Myth.: Brewer *Dictionary,* 713]
3. **Augustine, St.** (354–430) patron saint of scholars; voluminous theological author. [Christian Hagiog.: Brewster, 384–385]
4. **Balder** most beautiful, luminescent, and wise god. [Norse Myth.: Parrinder, 40]
5. **blue salvia** traditional symbol of wisdom; indicates mature judgment. [Flower Symbolism: *Flora Symbolica,* 177]
6. **Bodhi** knowledge by which one attains Nirvana. [Buddhism: Parrinder, 48]
7. **Bragi** god of wisdom, poetry, and eloquence. [Norse Myth: Parrinder, 50]
8. **Chiron** knowledgeable Centaur; instructed Achilles, Jason, and Asclepius. [Gk. Myth.: Parrinder, 62]
9. **Confucius** (551–479 B.C.) Chinese philosopher and writer. [Chinese Hist.: Parrinder, 65]
10. **Enki** god of wisdom; counterpart of Akkadian Ea. [Sumerian Myth.: Parrinder, 90]
11. **Fudo** Japanese god of wisdom. [Jap. Myth.: Leach, 427]
12. **Ganesha** wisdom god having a human body and an elephant head. [Hindu Myth.: Leach, 440]
13. **gold** symbol of sagacity. [Color Symbolism: Jobes, 356]
14. **Hiawatha** "wise man"; legendary founder of Iroquois Confederacy. [Am. Hist.: Jameson, 229; Am. Lit.: "Hiawatha" in Benét, 466]
15. **Jerome, St.** Latin doctor of Church; preeminent biblical scholar. [Christian Hagiog.: Attwater, 185]
16. **Mimir** guardian of well of wit and wisdom. [Norse Myth.: Wheeler, 244]
17. **Nebo** god of sagacity; inventor of writing. [Babyl. Myth.: Brewer *Dictionary,* 749]

18. **Nestor** sage counselor and just king of Pylos. [Gk. Hist.: Wheeler, 257; Gk. Lit.: *Iliad*]
19. **Odin** god; drank from fountain, became all-knowing. [Norse Myth.: Brewer *Dictionary,* 774]
20. **owl** associated with Athena, goddess of wisdom. [Gk. Myth.: Hall, 231]
21. **Plato** (427–347 B.C.) Greek philosopher revered for wisdom. [Gk. Hist.: *NCE,* 2165]
22. **Sarastro** High Priest represents benevolent guidance. [Ger. Opera: Mozart *The Magic Flute* in Benét, 619]
23. **scroll** early form of manuscript; symbolic of learning. [Christian Symbolism: Appleton, 85]
24. **Socrates** (469–399 B.C.) wise and respected teacher adept at developing latent ideas. [Gk. Hist.: *EB,* 16: 1001–1005]
25. **Solomon** invested by God with unprecedented sagacity. [O.T.: I Kings 3:7–13; 4:29–34]
26. **tree of the knowledge of good and evil** eat of its fruit and know all. [*O.T.: Genesis* 2:9; 3:6]
27. **white mulberry** traditional symbol of wisdom. [Tree Symbolism: *Flora Symbolica,* 176]

702. WITCHCRAFT (See also ENCHANTMENT, SORCERY.)

1. **Alcina** Circelike spellmaker; defeated by good magic. [Br. Opera: Handel, *Alcina,* Westerman, 54–55]
2. **Baba Yaga** cannibalistic crone; stone-breasted companion of devil. [Russ. Folklore: Leach, 100]
3. **Brocken** Harz peak; rendezvous for the Sabbat on Walpurgis Night. [Ger. Folklore: Leach, 165]
4. **Broom Hilda** witch as cigar-smoking, love-starved crone. [Comics: Horn, 134]
5. **Circe** turns Odysseus's men into animals. [Gk. Myth.: *Odyssey*]
6. **Cutty Sark** witch who pulls off the tail of Tam O'Shanter's mare before it has fully escaped from her power. [Scot. Poetry: Benét, 242]
7. **Esmerelda** gypsy trains a goat to dance to her tambourine, is convicted of sorcery. [Fr. Lit.: Victor Hugo *The Hunchback of Notre Dame*]
8. **Hecate** mysterious goddess of Hades; associated with sorcery. [Gk. Myth.: Howe, 115]
9. **Kundry** sorceress; ugly messenger of the Grail castle. [Ger. Legend: *Parzival;* Ger. Opera: *Parsifal*]

10. **Morgan le Fay** sorceress of Arthurian legend. [Medieval Romance: Brewer *Dictionary*, 620]
11. **Pamphile** applies ointment to change into eagle. [Rom. Lit.: *The Golden Ass*]
12. **Rosemary's baby** through witchcraft, child born with horns and tail. [Am. Lit.: *Rosemary's Baby*]
13. **Salem, Massachusetts** locale of frenzied assault on supposed witches (1692). [Am. Hist.: Jameson, 442; Am. Lit.: *The Crucible*]
14. **Samantha** good witch married to a mortal. [TV: "Bewitched" in Terrace, I, 94–95]
15. **Walpurgis Night** traditional German witches' sabbath. [Ger. Folklore: *NCE*, 2918]
16. **Weird Sisters** demon-women; predict Macbeth's fate. [Br. Lit.: *Macbeth*]
17. **Wicked Witch of the West** uses her powers to upset the plans of Dorothy and her friends. [Am. Lit. and Cin.: *The Wonderful Wizard of Oz*]
18. **Witch of Endor** conjures up Samuel for distressed Saul. [O.T.: I Samuel 28:3–25]
19. **Witches' Hammer** manual for recognizing telltale marks of witches (15th century). [Eur. Hist.: Brewer *Note-Book*, 952]

703. WITNESS

1. **cranes of Ibycus** called on by the dying poet to bear witness, the birds lead to the murderers' conviction. [Gk. Myth.: *NCE*, 1307]

704. WITTINESS

1. **Bennet, Elizabeth** lively and clever character. [Br. Lit.: *Pride and Prejudice*]
2. **Boyet** "wit's pedler" and "an ape of form." [Br. Lit.: *Love's Labour's Lost*]
3. **Mercutio** clever, comic foil to Romeo. [Br. Lit.: *Romeo and Juliet*]

705. WONDERLAND (See also HEAVEN, PARADISE, UTOPIA.)

1. **Annwn** land of joy and beauty without disease or death. [Welsh Lit.: *Mabinogion*]
2. **Atlantis** fabulous and prosperous island; legendarily in Atlantic Ocean. [Gk. Myth.: Leach, 89]

3. **Avalon** island where dead King Arthur was carried. [Arth. Legend and Br. Lit.: *Le Morte d'Arthur; Idylls of the King; The Once and Future King*]
4. **Istakhar, mountains of** lair of Eblis; beautiful treasure land. [Br. Lit.: *Vathek*]
5. **Middle-earth** an old-fashioned name for "world": scene of J. R. R. Tolkien's fantasies. [Br. Lit.: *The Hobbit; The Lord of the Rings*]
6. **Munchkinland** domain of little people in Oz. [Am. Lit.: *The Wonderful Wizard of Oz*]
7. **Narnia** scene of fantasies by C. S. Lewis. [Br. Lit.: *Prince Caspian*]
8. **Never Never Land** magic land of lost boys and Indians. [Br. Lit.: *Peter Pan*]
9. **Oz** fabulous kingdom over the rainbow. [Am. Lit.: *The Wonderful Wizard of Oz*]
10. **Xanadu** site of Kubla Khan's "pleasure dome." [Br. Lit.: "Kubla Khan" in Benét, 555]

706. WONDERS, ARCHITECTURAL

1. **Great Pyramid, the** Cheops' tomb, built 4,600 years ago, nearly 500 feet high, with bases 755 feet long. [Egypt. Arch.: Brewer *Dictionary*, 735]
2. **Great Wall of China** runs for 1,400 miles along China's north and northwest borders. [Chin. Hist.: *NCE*, 538]
3. **Hagia Sophia** supreme achievement of Byzantine architecture, noted for its great size and rising succession of domes. [Turkish Arch.: *NCE*, 1172]
4. **Leaning Tower of Pisa** belltower has stood for eight centuries despite tilt. [Ital. Arch.: Brewer *Dictionary*, 539]
5. **Pagoda of Nanking, the** unique octagonal stone structure, demolished c. 1860. [Chinese Arch.: *EB* 12:822]
6. **Stonehenge** prehistoric group of huge standing stones arranged in a circle 300 feet in diameter. [Br. Hist.: *NCE*, 2682]
7. **Temple of Artemis (Diana)** in Ephesus, Asia Minor; one of the seven wonders of the world. [Gk. Arch.: Benét, 918]

707. WRITINGS, SACRED

1. **Avesta** book of teachings of Zoroaster. [Zoroastrianism: Leach, 97]
2. **Bhagavad-Gita** part of *Mahabharata:* most important Hindu scripture. [Hindu Rel.: Parrinder, 43]

3. **Book of Mormon** supplementary bible of the Latter-Day Saints. [Am. Hist.: Payton, 455]
4. **Book of the Dead** instructions for the Art of Dying. [Ancient Egypt. Rel.: Parrinder, 49]
5. **Dead Sea Scrolls** papyrus scrolls containing texts of Old Testament, found in 1947. [Mid-East Hist.: *NCE,* 729]
6. **Eddas** bible of ancient Scandinavian religion; two separate collections. [Norse Lit.: Jobes, 490; Parrinder, 87]
7. ***Granth Sahib***, or ***Adi Granth*** bible of the Sikhs. [Indian Religion: *Collier's*, XVII, 304]
8. **Holy Bible** name for book containing the Christian Scriptures. [Christianity: *NCE,* 291]
9. **Koran (Quran)** the sacred book of Islam. [Islam: *NCE,* 1496]
10. ***Mahabharata*** long Sanskrit epic poem on theology and morals. [Indian Lit.: *Mahabharata*]
11. ***Popul Vuh*** "Book of the People", sacred book of certain Mayan tribes. [Mayan Religion: *NCE,* 2191]
12. **Talmud** Jewish civil and religious law, including the Mishna. [Judaism: Payton, 661]
13. **Torah** the Penteteuch, especially in the form of the hand-written scroll always present in the synagogue. [Jew. Hist.: Benét, 1017]
14. **Tripitaka** the ethical and doctrinal teachings of Buddha. [Buddhism: Haydn & Fuller, 759]
15. **Vedas, the** oldest scriptures of Hinduism. [Hinduism: *NCE,* 2870]

X

708. XENOPHOBIA

1. **Boxer Rebellion** Chinese rising aimed at ousting foreign interlopers (1900). [Chinese Hist.: Van Doren, 334–335]
2. **Hermit Kingdom, the** Korea; so called for 300-year closed-door policy. [Am. Hist.: Van Doren, 286]
3. **House Un-American Activities Committee** conducted investigations to purge government of foreign influences. [Am. Hist.: *NCE,* 1641]
4. **Know-Nothing Party** aimed at WASP control of government by depriving naturalized Americans and Roman Catholics of political rights. [Am. Hist.: Payton, 371]
5. **McCarthyism** from U.S. Senator Joseph McCarthy who acted out morbid fear of aliens, especially Communists. [Am. Hist.: Payton, 409]
6. **New Orleans riots** anti-Italian mobs lynched 11 immigrants after Sicilian murder trial (1891). [Am. Hist.: Van Doren, 309]
7. **Sacco and Vanzetti** (Nicola, 1891–1927) (Bartolomeo, 1888–1927) Italian anarchists convicted in controversial murder trial (1921). [Am. Hist.: Van Doren, 411]

Y

709. YOUTH (See also CHILDREN.)

1. **Agni** Vedic light god; embodies eternal youth. [Vedic Myth.: *LLEI,* I: 322]
2. **Freya** goddess of eternal youth. [Ger. Myth. and Opera: Wagner, *Rheingold,* Westerman, 232]
3. **Hebe (Juventas)** goddess of the young. [Gk. and Rom. Myth.: Hall, 146]
4. **primrose** symbol of early youth. [Flower Symbolism: *Flora Symbolica,* 176; Kunz, 327]

Z

710. ZANINESS

1. **Allen, Gracie** (1902–1964) actress who played scatterbrained wife of George Burns. [TV: "The George Burns and Gracie Allen Show" in Terrace, I, 303–304]
2. **Ball, Lucille** (1910–) American comedienne; "unchallenged queen of scatterbrains." [TV: "I Love Lucy" in Terrace, I, 383]
3. **Caesar, Sid** (1922–) pillar of zany 1950s comedy. [TV: "Your Show of Shows" in Terrace, II, 290–291]
4. ***Harvard Lampoon*** mocking, satirical periodical. [Am. Pop. Culture: Misc.]
5. ***Hellzapoppin*** Olsen and Johnson's "screamlined revue" described by one drama critic as a "demented vaudeville brawl." [Am.Theater: Misc.]
6. **Keystone Kops, the** slapstick film comedians specializing in wild chases (1912–1920). [Am. Cinema: Halliwell, 399]
7. **Krazy Kat** tremendously zany, popular comic character that delighted Jazz Age intellectuals. [Comics: Payton, 372; "Krazy Kat" in Horn, 436]
8. ***Mad* magazine** popular publication featuring zany approach to life. [Am. Pop. Culture: Misc.]
9. ***Monty Python's Flying Circus*** ingenious, satiric show that uses both live action and animation. [Br. and Am. TV: Terrace, II, 108]
10. **Sales, Soupy** (1926–) American entertainer; children's "funny man." [TV: "The Soupy Sales Show" in Terrace, II, 305]
11. **Skelton, Red** (1910–) comedian with zaniness personified in characters such as Freddie the Freeloader and Clem Kaddiddlehopper. [TV: "The Red Skelton Show" in Terrace, II, 238]
12. **Three Stooges, the** (Moe Howard, 1897–1975) (Shemp Howard, 1895–1955) (Larry Fine, 1902–1975) masters of slapstick in the extreme. [TV: Terrace, II, 366]

711. ZEAL

1. **Bows, Mr.** crippled fiddler with intense feelings. [Br. Lit.: *Pendennis*]

2. **Cedric of Rotherwood** zealous about restoring Saxon independence. [Br. Lit.: *Ivanhoe*]
3. **Faustus, Doctor** zealous for universal knowledge; sells soul to Lucifer. [Medieval Legend and Ger. Lit.: *Faust;* Br. Lit.: *Doctor Faustus*]
4. **flaming heart** attribute of St. Augustine; symbol of religious fervor. [Art: Hall, 123]
5. **Merridew, Jack** boy with lust for authority and killing. [Brit. Lit.: *Lord of the Flies*]
6. **Olsen, Jimmy** eager-beaver cub reporter and Superman's friend. [Comics: "Superman" in Horn, 341]
7. **Palace Guard** term used in alluding to Richard Nixon's zealous, ardent staff, with reference to Watergate and cover-up. [Am. Pop. Culture: Misc.]
8. **white dittany** traditional symbol of zeal. [Flower Symbolism: *Flora Symbolica,* 173]

712. ZODIAC (See also ASTROLOGY.)

1. **Aquarius** water-bearer (Jan. 20–Feb. 18). [Astrology: Hall, 314]
2. **Aries** ram (Mar. 21–Apr. 19). [Astrology: Hall, 314]
3. **Cancer** crab (June 21–July 22). [Astrology: Hall, 314]
4. **Capricorn** goat (Dec. 22–Jan. 19). [Astrology: Hall, 315]
5. **Gemini** twins (May 21–June 20). [Astrology: Hall, 314]
6. **Leo** lion (July 23–Aug. 22). [Astrology: Hall, 315]
7. **Libra** balance (Sept. 23–Oct. 22). [Astrology: Hall, 315]
8. **Pisces** fishes (Feb. 19–Mar. 20). [Astrology: Hall, 314]
9. **Sagittarius** archer (Nov. 22–Dec. 21). [Astrology: Hall, 315]
10. **Scorpio** scorpion (Oct. 23–Nov. 21). [Astrology: Hall, 315]
11. **Taurus** bull (Apr. 20–May 20). [Astrology: Hall, 314]
12. **Virgo** virgin (Aug. 23–Sept. 22). [Astrology: Hall, 315]

Bibliography

Bibliography

The Abbot
Scott, Sir Walter. *The Abbot.* Dutton, 1969.

Absalom and Achitophel
Dryden, John. *Absalom and Achitophel,* ed. James and Helen Kinsley. Oxford U.P., 1961.

The Absentee
Edgeworth, Maria. *The Absentee* in *Castle Rackrent.* Dutton, 1960.

Ackerman
Ackerman, A.S.E. *Popular Fallacies.* Gale, 1970.

Adam Bede
Eliot, George. *Adam Bede.* Washington Square Press, 1971.

The Admirable Crichton
Barrie, James M. *The Admirable Crichton* in *English Drama in Transition, 1880–1920,* ed. Henry F. Salerno. Pegasus, 1968.

Adonais
Shelley, Percy B. *Adonais, an Elegy on the Death of John Keats,* ed. Thomas J. Wise. AMS Press, 1886.

The Adventures of Augie March
Bellow, Saul. *The Adventures of Augie March.* Fawcett World, 1973.

The Adventures of Pinocchio
Collodi, Carlo. *The Adventures of Pinocchio.* Macmillan, 1972.

The Adventures of the Little Wooden Horse
Williams, Ursala. *The Adventures of the Little Wooden Horse.* Penguin, 1975.

Aeneid
Vergil. *Aeneid,* 2nd edition, tr. and ed. Frank Copley. Bobbs-Merrill, 1975.

Aesop's Fables
Aesop. *Aesop's Fables,* tr. Samuel Croxall and Roger L'Estrange. Brownlow, 1969.

Against The Grain
Huysmans, Joris Karl. *Against the Grain.* Dover, 1969.

The Age of Innocence
Wharton, Edith. *The Age of Innocence.* Scribner, 1968.

Ah Sin
Harte, Bret, and Mark Twain. *Ah Sin* in *The Complete Works of Bret Harte.* Chatto and Windus, 1880–1912.

Alastor
Shelley, Percy B. *Alastor: Or the Spirit of Solitude, and Other Poems.* ed. Bertram Dobell. AMS Press, n.d.

Alcestis
Euripides. *Alcestis,* tr. William Arrowsmith. Oxford U.P., 1915.

The Alchemist
Jonson, Ben. *The Alchemist.* Hill and Wang, 1966.

Alice's Adventures in Wonderland
Carroll, Lewis. *Alice's Adventures in Wonderland.* Viking Press, 1975.

Alive
Read, Piers P. *Alive.* Avon, 1975.

L'Allegro
Milton, John. "L'Allegro" in *L'Allegro and Il Penseroso.* Southwest Book Services, 1976.

Allen
Allen, Frederick Lewis. *Only Yesterday.* Bantam, 1959.

All for Love
Dryden, John. *All for Love,* ed. John J. Enck. Crofts, 1966.

All Quiet on the Western Front
Remarque, Erich Maria. *All Quiet on the Western Front.* Fawcett World, 1969.

All the King's Men
Warren, Robert Penn. *All the King's Men.* Random House, 1960.

All's Well That Ends Well
Shakespeare, William. *All's Well that Ends Well,* ed. G. K. Hunter. Barnes & Noble, 1966.

Almayer's Folly
Conrad, Joseph. *Almayer's Folly.* Bentley, 1971.

Amadis de Gaul
Amadis de Gaul, tr. Edwin Place and Herbert Behm. Univ. Press of Kentucky, 1974.

Ambrosio
Lewis, Matthew G. *Ambrosio, or The Monk.* Avon, 1975.

Amelia
Fielding, Henry. *Amelia.* Dutton, 1978.

The American
James, Henry. *The American,* ed. Joseph Beach and Quentin Anderson. Holt, Rinehart, and Winston, 1949.

The American Dream
Albee, Edward. *The American Dream.* Coward, 1961.

The American Scene
James, Henry. *The American Scene.* Indiana U.P., 1968.

Amory
Amory, Cleveland, ed. *International Celebrity Register.* Celebrity Register Ltd., 1959.

Amphitryon
Dryden, John. *Amphitryon* in *The Dramatic Works,* ed. M. Summers. 6 vols. Gordian, 1968.

Amphitryon
Molière, Jean B. *Amphitryon,* tr. Oscar Mandel. Spectrum, 1977.

Amphitryon
Plautus. *Amphitryon: Three Plays in New Verse Translation.* Univ. of North Carolina Press, 1974.

Amphitryon 38
Giraudoux, Jean. *Amphitryon 38* in *Giraudoux: Three Plays,* tr. La Farge and Judd. Hill and Wang, 1964.

Anatole
Titus, Eve. *Anatole.* McGraw-Hill, 1956.

Anatomy of Melancholy
Burton, Robert. *Anatomy of Melancholy.* R. West, 1923.

Andersen's Fairy Tales
Andersen, Hans Christian. *Andersen's Fairy Tales.* Macmillan, 1963.

Androcles and the Lion
Shaw, George Bernard. *Androcles and the Lion.* Penguin, 1951.

Andromache
Euripides. *Andromache,* ed. P.T. Stevens. Oxford U.P., 1971.

Andromaque
Racine, Jean B. *Andromaque,* ed. Philip Koch. Prentice-Hall, 1969.

Animal Farm
Orwell, George. *Animal Farm.* Harcourt, 1954.

Anna Karenina
Tolstoy, Leo. *Anna Karenina.* Bantam, 1977.

Annals
Tacitus. *Annals,* ed. F.R. Goodyear. Cambridge U.P., 1972.

Annals of the Parish
Galt, John. *Annals of the Parish: Or the Chronicles of Dalmailing During the Ministry of Reverend Micah Balwhidder Written by Himself,* ed. James Kinsley. Oxford U.P., 1967.

Anne Frank
Frank, Anne. *Anne Frank: Diary of a Young Girl.* Doubleday, 1967.

Anne of Green Gables
Montgomery, L.M. *Anne of Green Gables.* Bantam, 1976.

Ant and Bee
Banner, Angela. *Ant and Bee.* Franklin Watts, 1958.

Anthony Adverse
Allen, Hervey. *Anthony Adverse.* Holt, 1958.

Antigone
Anouilh, Jean. *Antigone.* Larousse, 1966.

Antigone
Sophocles. *Antigone,* tr. Richard Braun. Oxford U.P., 1973.

The Antiquary
Scott, Sir Walter. *The Antiquary.* Dutton, 1955.

Antony and Cleopatra
Shakespeare, William. *Antony and Cleopatra,* ed. C.J. Gianakaris. William C. Brown, 1969.

Apocrypha
Apocrypha. New English Bible. Oxford U.P., 1970.

Appleton
Appleton, Leroy, and Stephen Bridges. *Symbolism in Liturgical Art.* Scribner, 1959.

Appointment in Samarra
O'Hara, John. *Appointment in Samarra.* Popular Library, 1976.

Arabel's Raven
Aiken, Joan. *Arabel's Raven.* Dell, 1975.

Arabian Nights
Book of a Thousand Nights and One Night, tr. Powys Mathers. St. Martin's Press, 1972.

La Arcadia
de Vega, Lope. *La Arcadia,* ed. E.S. Morby. Castalia, c. 1975.

Arcadia
Greene, Robert. *Arcadia* in *The Life and Complete Works in Prose and Verse of Robert Greene.* Printed for private circulation, 1881–86.

Arcadia
Sannazaro, Jacopo. *Arcadia and Piscatorial Eclogues,* tr. Ralph Nash. Wayne State U.P., 1966.

Arcadia
Sidney, Philip. *Arcadia.* Penguin, 1977.

archy and mehitabel
Marquis, Don. *archy and mehitabel.* Doubleday, 1970.

The Ark
Benary-Isbert, Margot. *The Ark.* Harcourt, 1953.

Arms and the Man
Shaw, George Bernard. *Arms and the Man.* Bantam, 1968.

Around the World in Eighty Days
Verne, Jules. *Around the World in Eighty Days.* Oxford U.P., 1959.

Arrowsmith
Lewis, Sinclair. *Arrowsmith.* Harcourt, 1949.

Ars Poetica
Horace. *Ars Poetica* in *Collected Works of Horace,* tr. Dunsany and Oakley. Dutton, 1961.

Arthur Mervyn
Brown, Charles Brockton. *Arthur Mervyn,* ed. W. Bertho ff. Holt, 1966.

Ash Wednesday
Eliot, T.S. *Ash Wednesday* in *The Complete Poetry and Plays, 1909–1950.* Harcourt, 1952.

As I Lay Dying
Faulkner, William. *As I Lay Dying.* Random House, 1964.

L'Assommoir
Zola, Emile. *L'Assommoir.* Penguin, 1970.

As You Like It
Shakespeare, William. *As You Like It,* ed. Agnes Latham. Barnes & Noble, 1975.

Atala
de Chateaubriand, René. *Atala.* Prentice-Hall, 1965.

Atalanta
Swinburne, A.C. *Atalanta in Calydon.* Scholarly Press, reprint of 1923 ed.

The Atheist's Tragedy
Tourneur, Cyril. *The Atheist's Tragedy,* ed. Brian Morris and Roma Gill. Norton, 1976.

Atlas Shrugged
Rand, Ayn. *Atlas Shrugged.* New American Library, 1970.

Attwater
Attwater, Donald. *Penguin Dictionary of Saints.* Penguin, 1965.

Aucassin and Nicolette
Aucassin and Nicolette & Other Medieval Romances & Legends, ed. Eugene Mason. Dutton, 1958.

Auden
Replogle, Justin. *Auden's Poetry.* Univ. of Washington Press, 1971.

Ausubel
Ausubel, Nathan. *The Book of Jewish Knowledge.* Crown, 1964.

Avery
Avery, Catherine B. *The New Century Handbook of Greek Mythology and Legend.* Appleton-Century-Crofts, 1972.

The Awkward Age
James, Henry. *The Awkward Age.* Penguin, 1974.

Babbitt
Lewis, Sinclair. *Babbitt.* Harcourt, 1949.

Bailey
Bailey, Nathaniel. *Universal Etymological English Dictionary.* Alfred Adler Institute, 1969.

Balchin
Balchin, Nigel. "Guy Fawkes" in *British History Illustrated,* October 1975, pp. 2–13.

Ballet Shoes
Streatfeild, Noel. *Ballet Shoes.* Random House, 1950.

Balthazar B
Donleavy, J.P. *The Beastly Beatitudes of Balthazar B.* Dell, 1968.

Bambi
Salten, Felix. *Bambi.* Grosset and Dunlap, 1969.

Barabbas
Lagerkvist, Pär. *Barabbas.* Bantam, 1968.

The Barber of Seville
Beaumarchais, Pierre A. *The Barber of Seville,* tr. B.P. Ellis. AHM, 1966.

Baring-Gould
Baring-Gould, William S., and Ceil Baring-Gould. *The Annotated Mother Goose.* Bramhall House, 1962.

Barnaby Rudge
Dickens, Charles. *Barnaby Rudge.* Dutton, 1972.

Barnhart
New Century Handbook of English Literature, ed. Clarence Barnhart. Appleton-Century-Crofts, 1967.

Baron Münchhausen
Baron Münchhausen: Fifteen Truly Tall Tales. Retold by Doris Orgel. Addison Wesley, 1971.

Baron Münchhausen's Narrative
Raspe, Rudolph Erich. *Baron Münchhausen's Narrative.* Brentano's, 1907.

Barren Ground
Glasgow, Ellen. *Barren Ground.* Hill and Wang, 1957.

Barry Lyndon
Thackeray, William Makepeace. *Memoirs of Barry Lyndon, Esq.* Univ. of Nebraska Press, 1962.

Bartleby
Melville, Herman. "Bartleby the Scrivener" in *Complete Works,* ed. Howard Vincent. Hendricks House, 1947.

Bartlett
Bartlett's Familiar Quotations, 14th ed., revised E.M. Beck. Little, Brown, 1968.

Baxter
Baxter, John. *Sixty Years of Hollywood.* A.S. Barnes, 1973.

Baydo
Baydo, A. *Topical History of the United States.* Prentice-Hall, 1974.

A Bear Called Paddington
Bond, Michael. *A Bear Called Paddington.* Dell, 1968.

Beau James
Fowler, Gene. *Beau James.* Viking Press, 1949.

The Beauties of English Poesy
Goldsmith, Oliver. *The Beauties of English Poesy.* W. Griffin, 1767.

The Beaux' Stratagem
Farquhar, George. *The Beaux' Stratagem.* British Book Centre, 1975.

Beggar on Horseback
Kaufmann, George, and Marc Connelly. *Beggar on Horseback.* Scholarly Press, 1925.

Beggar's Opera
Gay, John. *The Beggar's Opera,* ed. Peter Lewis. Barnes & Noble, 1973.

Bel Ami
de Maupassant, Guy. *Bel Ami,* tr. Douglas Parmee. Penguin, 1975.

A Bell for Adano
Hersey, John. *A Bell for Adano.* Bantam, 1970.

Benét
The Reader's Encyclopedia, 2nd edition. William Rose Benét. Thomas Y. Crowell, 1965.

Benito Cereno
Melville, Herman. *Benito Cereno* in *Eight Short Novels,* ed. Dean Flower. Fawcett World, 1970.

Benvenuto Cellini
Cellini, Benvenuto. *The Autobiography of Benvenuto Cellini,* tr. John Symonds. Doubleday, 1960.

Benya Krik, the Gangster
Babel, Isaac. *Benya Krik, the Gangster and Other Stories,* ed. Avrahm Yarmolinsky. Schocken Books, 1969.

Beowulf
Beowulf, tr. Burton Raffel. New American Library, 1963.

Berger
Berger, Auther Asa. *The Comic-Stripped American.* Walker & Co., 1973.

The Bermuda Triangle
Berlitz, Charles. *The Bermuda Triangle.* Avon, 1977.

Bettelheim
Bettelheim, Bruno. *The Uses of Enchantment.* Vintage Books, 1977.

Bevis of Hampton
Unknown. *Bevis of Hampton.* Penguin, 1974.

The Big Sky
Guthrie, A.B., Jr. *The Big Sky.* Bantam, 1972.

The Big Sleep
Chandler, Raymond. *The Big Sleep.* Random House, 1976.

Billy Budd
Melville, Herman. *Billy Budd.* Doubleday, 1970.

Binder
Binder, Pearl. *Magic Symbols of the World.* Hamlyn, 1972.

Birds
Aristophanes. *Birds.* Chandler, 1968.

Birth of Tragedy
Nietzsche, Friedrich. *The Birth of Tragedy,* tr. Francis Golffing. Doubleday, 1956.

Bishop
Bishop, Morris. *The Horizon Book of the Middle Ages,* ed. Norman Kotker, et al. American Heritage, 1968.

Black Beauty
Sewell, Anna. *Black Beauty.* Macmillan, 1962.

The Black Cauldron
Alexander, Lloyd. *The Black Cauldron.* Dell, 1969.

Black Oxen
Atherton, Gertrude. *Black Oxen.* Folcroft Library, 1923.

Blanchard
Blanchard, R. H. *Handbook of Egyptian Gods and Mummy Amulets.* Attic Books, 1974.

Bleak House
Dickens, Charles. *Bleak House.* Holt, 1970.

Blue Willow
Gates, Doris. *Blue Willow.* Viking Press, 1969.

Blunt
Blunt, Rev. John Henry. *Dictionary of Sects, Heresies, Ecclesiastical Parties, and Schools of Religious Thought.* Gale, 1974.

The Blythedale Romance
Hawthorne, Nathaniel. *The Blythedale Romance* in *Works,* vol. 5. Houghton Mifflin, 1882–91.

Bobbsey Twins
Hope, Laura Lee. *Bobbsey Twins' Mystery at Meadowbrook.* Grosset and Dunlap, 1963.

Boland
Boland, Bridget. *Gardener's Magic and Other Old Wives' Lore.* Farrar, 1977.

Bold Stroke for a Wife
Centlivre, Susannah. *Bold Stroke for a Wife,* ed. Thalia Stathas. Univ. of Nebraska Press, 1968.

Bombaugh
Bombaugh, Charles C. *Gleanings for the Curious from the Harvest Fields of Literature.* Gale, 1970.

Bombaugh *Facts*
Bombaugh, Charles C. *Facts and Fancies for the Curious.* Gale, 1968.

The Book of Three
Alexander, Lloyd. *The Book of Three.* Holt, 1964.

Boris Godunov
Pushkin, Alexandre. *Boris Godunov,* tr. Philip Barbour. Greenwood Press, 1976.

The Borrowers
Norton, Mary. *The Borrowers.* Harcourt, 1965.

The Bostonians
James, Henry. *The Bostonians.* Penguin, 1974.

Le Bourgeois Gentilhomme
Molière, Jean P. *Le Bourgeois Gentilhomme* in *Oeuvres Complètes.* Gallimard, 1971.

Brand
Ibsen, Henrik. *Brand.* Dutton, 1959.

Brave New World
Huxley, Aldous. *Brave New World.* Harper & Row, 1969.

Bray
Bray, Frank Chapin. *Bray's University Dictionary of Mythology.* Apollo Editions, 1964.

Bread and Wine
Silone, Ignazio. *Bread and Wine.* Harper, 1937.

Breakfast of Champions
Vonnegut, Kurt. *Breakfast of Champions.* Dell, 1974.

Brewer *Dictionary*
Brewer, E. Cobham. *Brewer's Dictionary of Phrase and Fable,* ed. Ivor H. Evans. Harper, 1971.

Brewer *Handbook*
Brewer, E. Cobham. *The Reader's Handbook.* Gale, 1966.

Brewer *Miracles*
Brewer, E. Cobham. *A Dictionary of Miracles.* Gale, 1966.

Brewer *Note-Book*
Brewer, E. Cobham. *The Historic Note-Book.* Gale, 1966.

Brewton
Brewton, John E. and Sara W. *Index to Children's Poetry.* H.W. Wilson, 1965.

Brewster
Brewster, H. Pomeroy. *Saints and Festivals of the Christian Church.* Gale, 1974.

The Bride of Lammermoor
Scott, Sir Walter. *The Bride of Lammermoor.* Dutton, 1972.

The Bridge of San Luis Rey
Wilder, Thornton. *The Bridge of San Luis Rey.* Harper, 1967.

The Bridge Over the River Kwai
Boulle, Pierre. *The Bridge Over the River Kwai.* Bantam, 1970.

Brief Lives
Aubrey, John. *Brief Lives or Minutes of Lives,* ed. Edward G. McGehee. Oxford U.P., 1972.

Briggs
Briggs, Katherine. *An Encyclopedia of Fairies: Hobgoblins, Brownies, Bogies and Other Supernatural Creatures.* Pantheon, 1977.

The Broken Heart
Ford, John. *The Broken Heart,* ed. Brian Morris. Hill and Wang, 1966.

The Bronze Bow
Speare, Elizabeth. *The Bronze Bow.* Houghton Mifflin, 1972.

Brothers Ashkenazi
Singer, Israel Joshua. *The Brothers Ashkenazi.* Knopf, 1936.

The Brothers Karamazov
Dostoevski, Fyodor. *The Brothers Karamazov.* Bantam, 1971.

Browne
Browne, Ray B., and Marshall Fishwick, eds. *Icons of America.* Popular Press, 1978.

Bulfinch
Bulfinch, Thomas. *Age of Fable.* Dutton, 1969.

Bungalow Mystery
Keene, Carolyn. *The Bungalow Mystery.* Grosset and Dunlap, 1930.

Bussy D'Ambois
Chapman, George. *Bussy D'Ambois,* ed. Maurice Evans. Hill and Wang, 1966.

Buxton
Buxton, Frank, and Bill Owen. *The Big Broadcast: 1920–1950.* Avon, 1973.

By Love Possessed
Cozzens, James Gould. *By Love Possessed.* Fawcett World, 1973.

By the Pricking of My Thumbs
Christie, Agatha. *By the Pricking of My Thumbs.* Pocket Books, 1975.

The Cabala
Wilder, Thornton. *The Cabala.* Avon, 1975.

Cain
Byron, George. *Cain* in *Byron: Poetical Works,* ed. Frederick Page and John Jump. Oxford U.P., 1970.

Callista
Newman, John H. *Loss and Gain: The Story of a Convert, 1848,* ed. Robert L. Wolff. Garland, 1975.

Call of the Wild
London, Jack. *The Call of the Wild.* AMSCO School Publications, 1969.

Camille
Dumas, Alexandre, fils. *Camille,* tr. Matilde Heron. Books for Libraries, 1976.

Campbell *Creative*
Campbell, Joseph. *The Masks of God: Creative Mythology.* Viking Press, 1968.

Campbell *Encyclopedia*
Campbell, Oscar J. *A Shakespeare Encyclopedia.* Methuen, 1966.

Campbell *Hero*
Campbell, Joseph. *Hero With a Thousand Faces.* Princeton U.P., 1968.

Campbell *Occidental*
Campbell, Joseph. *The Masks of God: Occidental Mythology.* Viking Press, 1964.

Campbell *Oriental*
Campbell, Joseph. *The Masks of God: Oriental Mythology.* Viking Press, 1962.

Campbell *Primitive*
Campbell, Joseph. *The Masks of God: Primitive Mythology.* Viking Press, 1959.

Candida
Shaw, George Bernard. *Candida.* Penguin, 1974.

Candide
Voltaire. *Candide,* ed. G.R. Havens. Holt, 1969.

Cannery Row
Steinbeck, John. *Cannery Row.* Viking Press, 1945.

Canterbury Tales
Chaucer, Geoffrey. *The Canterbury Tales,* tr. David Wright. Random House, 1965.

Captain Brassbound's Conversion
Shaw, George Bernard. *Captain Brassbound's Conversion* in *Four Plays by Shaw.* Dell, 1957.

Captain Hatteras
Verne, Jules. *At the North Pole: The Adventures of Captain Hatteras.* Aeonian Press, 1976.

Captain Horatio Hornblower
Forester, C.S. *Captain Horatio Hornblower.* Little, Brown, 1939.

Captain Singleton
Defoe, Daniel. *Captain Singleton: The Life, Adventures & Pyracies of the Famous Captain Singleton.* Oxford U.P., 1973.

Carmen
Mérimée, Prosper. *Carmen,* ed. Pierre de Beaumont. Odyssey, 1969.

Cartwell
Cartwell, Van H., and Charles Grayson. *The Golden Argosy.* Dial, 1955.

Carved Lions
Molesworth, Mary. *The Carved Lions.* Dutton, 1964.

Case
Case, Brian, and Stan Britt. *The Illustrated Encyclopedia of Jazz.* Harmony, 1978.

Cashel Byron's Profession
Shaw, George Bernard. *Cashel Byron's Profession,* ed. Stanley Weintraub. Southern Illinois U.P., 1968.

Cass Timberlane
Lewis, Sinclair. *Cass Timberlane.* Random House, 1945.

The Castle
Kafka, Franz. *The Castle.* Random House, 1974.

Castle of Llyr
Alexander, Lloyd. *Castle of Llyr.* Holt, 1966.

The Catcher in the Rye
Salinger, J.D. *The Catcher in the Rye.* Bantam, 1970.

Catch-22
Heller, Joseph. *Catch-22.* Simon and Schuster, 1961.

Cat on a Hot Tin Roof
Williams, Tennessee. *Cat on a Hot Tin Roof.* New Directions, 1975.

Caught in the Web of Words
Murray, K.M. *Caught in the Web of Words.* Yale U.P., 1977.

The Caxtons
Bulwer-Lytton, Edward. *The Caxtons: A Family Picture.* Scholarly Press, 1971.

The Celebrated Jumping Frog of Calaveras County
Twain, Mark. *The Celebrated Jumping Frog of Calaveras County.* Gregg, 1969.

Celestina
De Rojas, Fernando. *Celestina.* Dutton, 1959.

The Cenci
Shelley, Percy B. *The Cenci,* ed. Roland A. Duerksen. Bobbs-Merrill, 1970.

Century Classical
New Century Classical Handbook, ed. C.B. Avery and J. Johnson. Appleton-Century-Crofts, 1962.

Century Cyclopedia
New Century Cyclopedia of Names, ed. Clarence L. Barnhart and William D. Halsey. Appleton-Century-Crofts, 1954.

Century English
Barnhart, Clarence L. *New Century Handbook of English Literature,* rev. ed. Appleton-Century-Crofts, 1967.

Chambers
Chambers, Robert. *The Book of Days.* Gale, 1967.

Charlotte's Web
White, E.B. *Charlotte's Web.* Harper, 1952.

Cheaper By the Dozen
Gilbreth, Frank, and Ernestine Carey. *Cheaper By the Dozen.* Crowell, 1963.

Child
Child, Heather, and Dorothy Colles. *Christian Symbols: Ancient and Modern.* Scribner, 1971.

Childe Ballads
Traditional Tunes of the Childe Ballads, ed. Bertrand H. Bronson. 4 vols. Princeton U.P., 1959 (Vol. 1), 1962 (Vol. 2), 1966 (Vol. 3), 1972 (Vol. 4).

Children of Green Knowe
Boston, Lucy M. *The Children of Green Knowe.* Harcourt, 1967.

A Child's Christmas in Wales
Thomas, Dylan. *A Child's Christmas in Wales.* New Directions, 1959.

Chitty-Chitty-Bang-Bang
Fleming, Ian. *Chitty-Chitty-Bang-Bang.* Random House, 1964.

A Christmas Carol
Dickens, Charles. *A Christmas Carol.* Dutton, 1972.

Christmas Stories
Dickens, Charles. *Christmas Stories* in *New Oxford Illustrated Dickens.* Oxford U.P., 1956.

Cinderella
Perrault, Charles. *Cinderella.* Henry Walck, 1971.

Cinq-Mars
de Vigny, Alfred. *Cinq-Mars; or, a Conspiracy under Louis XIII.* Howard Fertig, 1978.

Cirlot
Cirlot, J.E. *Dictionary of Symbols,* 2nd ed. Philosophical Library, 1972.

Citizen of the World
Goldsmith, Oliver. *Citizen of the World.* Dutton, Everyman, n.d.

The City and the Pillar
Vidal, Gore. *The City and the Pillar.* Dutton, 1965.

Clockwork Orange
Burgess, Anthony. *A Clockwork Orange.* Ballantine, 1976.

The Clouds
Aristophanes. *The Clouds,* ed. William Arrowsmith. New American Library, 1970.

Clue in the Embers
Dixon, Franklin W. *The Clue in the Embers.* Grosset and Dunlap, 1956.

A Cold Wind Blowing
Willard, Barbara. *A Cold Wind Blowing.* Dutton, 1973.

Collier's
Collier's Encyclopedia. Collier, 1949–51.
Colomba
Mérimée, Prosper. *Colomba.* French and European Pubn., 1963.
Colonel Sheperton's Clock
Turner, Philip. *Colonel Sheperton's Clock.* Collins, 1966.
Comedy of Errors
Shakespeare, William. *The Comedy of Errors,* ed. R.A. Foakes. Barnes & Noble, 1968.
Common Sense
Paine, Thomas. *Common Sense.* Penguin, 1976.
Communist Manifesto
Marx, Karl, and Friedrich Engels. *The Communist Manifesto.* Penguin, 1968.
The Compleat Angler
Walton, Izaak. *The Compleat Angler.* Dutton, Everyman, n.d.
Confessions
De Quincey, Thomas. *Confessions of an English Opium Eater.* New American Library, 1966.
Coningsby
Disraeli, Benjamin. *Coningsby: or The New Generation.* Scholarly Press, 1976.
A Connecticut Yankee in King Arthur's Court
Twain, Mark. *A Connecticut Yankee in King Arthur's Court.* Harper & Row, n.d.
The Conquest of Granada
Dryden, John. *The Conquest of Granada, or Almanzor and Almahide* in *Dryden: Three Plays,* ed. George Saintsbury. Hill and Wang, 1957.
Coriolanus
Shakespeare, William. *Coriolanus,* ed. B.H. Kemball-Cook. Oxford U.P., 1954.
Corpus Delicti
Herman, Linda, and Beth Stiel. *Corpus Delicti of Mystery Fiction.* Scarecrow Press, 1974.
Corsican Brothers
Dumas, Alexandre, père. *The Corsican Brothers.* Methuen, 1904.
Corson
Corson, Hiram. *Index of Proper Names and Subjects to Chaucer's Canterbury Tales.* Folcroft Library Editions, 1973.
Cott
Cott, Ted. *Victor Book of Musical Fun.* Simon and Schuster, 1945.
The Count of Monte-Cristo
Dumas, Alexandre, père. *The Count of Monte-Cristo.* Hart, 1975.
Cousin Pons
Balzac, Honoré de. *Cousin Pons.* French and European Pubn., 1962.
Cranford
Gaskell, Elizabeth. *Cranford,* ed. Elizabeth P. Watson. Oxford U.P., 1972.
Cricket on the Hearth
Dickens, Charles. *Cricket on the Hearth.* Frederick Warne, 1956.
Crime and Punishment
Dostoyevsky, Fyodor. *Crime and Punishment.* tr. Constance Garnett. Random House, Vintage, 1955.
Critique of Hegel's "Philosophy of Right"
Marx, Karl. *Critique of Hegel's "Philosophy of Right,"* ed. J. O'Malley. Cambridge U.P., 1970.
Crowley
Crowley, Ellen T. *Acronyms, Initialisms, and Abbreviations Dictionary,* 5th ed. Gale, 1976; annual supplements.
Crowley *Trade*
Crowley, Ellen. *Trade Names Dictionary.* Gale, 1974.
The Crucible
Miller, Arthur. *The Crucible: Text & Criticism,* ed. Gerald Weales. Viking Press, 1971.
Cry, The Beloved Country
Paton, Alan. *Cry, The Beloved Country.* Scribner, 1948.
Curious George
Rey, Hans A. *Curious George.* Houghton Mifflin, 1951.
Cyclops
Cyclops in *Euripides; The Complete Greek Tragedies,* ed. D. Grene and R. Lattimore, vol. 3. Univ. of Chicago Press, 1955 ND59.

Cymbeline
Shakespeare, William. *Cymbeline.* Oxford U.P., 1972.

Cyrano
Rostand, Edmond. *Cyrano de Bergerac,* tr. Anthony Burgess. Knopf, 1971.

Daisy Miller
James, Henry. *Daisy Miller and Other Stories.* Airmont, 1968.

La Dame aux Camélias
Dumas, Alexandre, fils. *La Dame aux Camélias.* French and European Pubn., 1955.

A Damsel in Distress.
Wodehouse, P.G. *A Damsel in Distress.* British Book Centre, 1956.

Daniel
Daniel, Howard. *Encyclopaedia of Themes and Subjects in Painting.* Thames and Hudson, 1971.

Darrel of the Blessed Isles
Bacheller, Irving A. *Darrel of the Blessed Isles.* Grosset, 1903.

Davenport
Davenport, Adams W. *Dictionary of English Literature.* Gale, 1966.

David Copperfield
Dickens, Charles. *David Copperfield.* Dutton, 1953.

Davidson
Davidson, H.R. Ellis. *Gods and Myths of Northern Europe.* Penguin, 1964.

Dawson
Dawson, Lawrence H. *Nicknames and Pseudonyms.* Gale, 1974.

The Day They Shook the Plum Tree
Lewis, Arthur H. *The Day They Shook the Plum Tree.* Pocket Books, 1975.

Dead Souls
Gogol, Nikolai. *Dead Souls.* tr. Andrew MacAndrew. New American Library, Signet, 1961.

Death in the Afternoon
Hemingway, Ernest. *Death in the Afternoon.* Scribner, 1932.

Death in Venice
Mann, Thomas. *Death in Venice.* Knopf, 1965.

Death of a Salesman
Miller, Arthur. *Death of a Salesman.* Viking Press, 1967.

de Bles
de Bles, Arthur. *How to Distinguish the Saints in Art.* Art Culture Pubn., 1925.

Decameron
Boccaccio, Giovanni. *The Decameron,* tr. G.H. McWilliam. Penguin, 1972.

The Deerslayer
Cooper, James Fenimore. *The Deerslayer.* Macmillan, 1962.

de Mille
de Mille, Agnes. *The Book of the Dance.* Golden Press, 1963.

de Purucker
de Purucker, G. *Occult Glossary.* Theosophical U.P., 1956.

Desire Under the Elms
O'Neill, Eugene. *Desire Under the Elms* in *Three Plays.* Random House, 1959.

Dictionary of Facts
The Standard Dictionary of Facts. Frontier Press, 1924.

Disney Films
Maltin, Leonard. *The Disney Films.* Bonanza Books, 1973.

Divine Comedy
Dante Alighieri. *The Divine Comedy.* Random House, 1955.

Dr. Breen's Practice
Howells, William D. *Doctor Breen's Practice.* Scholarly Press, 1970.

Doctor Faustus
Mann, Thomas. *Doctor Faustus.* Knopf, 1948.

Doctor Faustus
Marlowe, Christopher. *Doctor Faustus.* New American Library, 1969.

Doctor Syntax
Hamilton, Harlan W. *Dr. Syntax.* Kent State U.P., 1969.

Doctor Thorne
Trollope, Anthony. *Doctor Thorne.* Harcourt, 1962.

Dodsworth
Lewis, Sinclair. *Dodsworth.* New American Library, 1971.

A Doll's House
Ibsen, Henrik. *A Doll's House.* Dutton, 1954.

Dombey and Son
Dickens, Charles. *Dombey and Son.* Penguin, 1975.

Dominic
Steig, William. *Dominic.* Farrar, 1972.

Don Carlos
Schiller, Friedrich. *Don Carlos,* tr. Charles E. Passage. Ungar, 1959.

Don Juan Tenorio
Zorilla y Moral, José. *Don Juan Tenorio,* ed. Nicholson B. Adams. Prentice-Hall, 1971.

Don Quixote
Cervantes, Miguel de. *Don Quixote.* Airmont, 1967.

Don Segundo Sombra
Guiraldes, Ricardo. *Don Segundo Sombra,* tr. Angela B. Dellepiane. Prentice-Hall, 1971.

The Double-Dealer
Congreve, William. *The Double-Dealer.* British Book Centre, 1974.

Down to Earth
Wrightson, Patricia. *Down to Earth.* Harcourt, 1965.

Dr. Doolittle
Lofting, Hugh. *The Story of Dr. Doolittle.* Lippincott, 1920.

Dracula
Stoker, Bram. *Dracula.* Doubleday, 1959.

Dry Guillotine
Belbenoit, René. *Dry Guillotine.* Dutton, 1938.

Dunkling
Dunkling, Leslie. *The Guinness Book of Names.* Guinness Superlatives, 1974.

Eagle
Eagle, Dorothy, ed. *The Concise Oxford Dictionary of English Literature,* 2nd ed. Oxford U.P., 1970.

Eastman
Eastman, Mary H. *Index to Fairy Tales, Myths, and Legends.* F.W. Faxon, 1926.

EB
Encyclopaedia Britannica. Encyclopaedia Britannica, 1977. [Roman numerals refer to Micropaedia; Arabic numerals refer to Macropaedia.]

***EB* (1963)**
Encyclopaedia Britannica. Encyclopaedia Britannica, 1963.

***EB* (1978)**
1978 Book of the Year: Events of 1977. Encyclopaedia Britannica, 1978.

Eclogues
Virgil. *Eclogues,* ed. H.E. Gould. St. Martin's Press, 1967.

L'Ecole des Femmes
Molière, Jean P. *L'Ecole des Femmes.* French and European Pubn., 1964.

Edgar
Edgar, M.G., ed. *Treasury of Verse for Little Children.* Crowell, 1946.

Edwin Drood
Dickens, Charles. *Edwin Drood and Master Humphrey's Clock.* Dutton, 1970.

Eggenberger
Eggenberger, David. *A Dictionary of Battles From 1479* B.C. *to the Present.* Thomas Y. Crowell, 1967.

Egmont
Goethe, Johann W. Von. *Egmont,* tr. Willard Trask. Barron's, 1960.

The Egoist
Meredith, George. *The Egoist.* Penguin, 1979.

Electra
Euripides. *Electra,* tr. Gilbert Murray. Oxford U.P., 1905.

Eliot
Eliot, T.S., ed. *A Choice of Kipling's Verse.* Faber and Faber, 1963.

Elmer Gantry
Lewis, Sinclair. *Elmer Gantry.* New American Library, Signet, 1971.

Emboden
Emboden, W.A. *A Renaissance Botanist: Leonardo da Vinci. Hortulus Aliquando,* Winter 1975–76, pp. 13–30.

Emma
Austen, Jane. *Emma.* New American Library, 1964.

Emperor Jones
O'Neill, Eugene. *Emperor Jones.* Prentice-Hall, 1960.

Encyclopedia Judaica
Encyclopedia Judaica. Macmillan, 1972.

Enoch Arden
"Enoch Arden" in *Tennyson,* ed. Kingsley Amis. Penguin, 1973.

The Epicurean
Moore, Thomas. *The Epicurean.* Miller, 1875.

Espy
Espy, Willard R. *O Thou Improper, Thou Uncommon Noun.* Clarkson N. Potter, 1978.

Eugene Aram
Bulwer-Lytton, Edward. *Eugene Aram* in *Works.* Wanamaker, n.d.

Eugene Onegin
Pushkin, Alexander. *Eugene Onegin,* ed. Avrahm Yarmolinsky, tr. Babette Deutsch. Penguin, 1975.

The Eunuch
Terence. *The Eunuch,* tr. Frank O. Copley. Bobbs-Merrill, 1965.

Evans
Evans, Bergen. *Dictionary of Mythology, Mainly Classical.* Centennial Press, 1970.

Evelina
Burney, Fanny. *Evelina.* W.W. Norton, 1965.

Everyman
Everyman, ed. A.C. Cawley. Barnes & Noble, 1970.

Every Man in His Humour
Jonson, Ben. *Every Man in His Humour.* British Book Centre, 1974.

The Exorcist
Blatty, William P. *The Exorcist.* Harper & Row, 1971.

Faber
Faber Book of English Verse, ed. John Hayward. Faber and Faber, 1958.

Fables
Fontaine, Jean de la. *Fables,* tr. Edward Marsh. Dutton, 1966.

Facts
Facts on File. Facts on File, various years.

Faerie Queene
Spenser, Edmund. *Faerie Queene,* ed. P.C. Bayley. Oxford U.P., 1965–66.

Fair Maid of Perth
Scott, Sir Walter. *The Fair Maid of Perth* in *Complete Works.* Houghton, 1923.

The Fair Penitent
Rowe, Nicholas. *The Fair Penitent,* ed. Malcolm Goldstein. Univ. of Nebraska Press, 1969.

The Fall
Camus, Albert. *The Fall.* Knopf, 1957.

Farewell, My Lovely
Chandler, Raymond. *Farewell, My Lovely.* Random House, 1976.

Family from One End Street
Garnett, Eve. *Family from One End Street.* Vanguard, 1960.

A Farewell to Arms
Hemingway, Ernest. *A Farewell to Arms.* Scribner, 1967.

Far Out the Long Canal
De Jong, Meindert. *Far Out the Long Canal.* Harper, 1964.

Fasti
Ovid. *Fasti,* ed. Cyril Bailey. Oxford U.P., 1921.

Fatal Curiosity
Lillo, George. *Fatal Curiosity,* ed. William H. McBurney. Univ. of Nebraska Press, 1967.

Father Christmas
Briggs, Raymond. *Father Christmas.* Coward, 1973.

Fathers and Sons
Turgenev, Ivan. *Fathers and Sons,* tr. R. Edmonds. Penguin, 1975.

Faust
Goethe, Johann W. von. *Faust,* tr. Walter Kaufmann. Doubleday, 1961.

Feminine Mystique
Friedan, Betty. *The Feminine Mystique.* Norton, 1974

Les Femmes Savantes
Molière, Jean B. *Les Femmes Savantes,* ed. H. Gaston Hall. Oxford U.P., 1974.

Fentress
Fentress, Calvin. "Ram Dass, Nobody Special" in *New Times,* September 4, 1978, pp. 37–47.

Ferguson
Ferguson, George. *Signs and Symbols in Christian Art.* Oxford U.P., 1954.

Fifteen
Cleary, Beverly. *Fifteen.* William Morrow, 1956.

Finn Family Moomintroll
Jansson, Tove. *Finn Family Moomintroll.* Henry Walck, 1965.

Finnegans Wake
Joyce, James. *Finnegans Wake.* Viking Press, 1959.

Fisher
Fisher, Margery. *Who's Who in Children's Books.* Holt, 1975.

The Five Hundred Hats of Bartholomew Cubbins
Seuss, Dr. *The Five Hundred Hats of Bartholomew Cubbins.* E.M. Hale, 1938.

Five on a Treasure Island
Blyton, Enid. *Five on a Treasure Island.* Atheneum, 1972.

Five Weeks in a Balloon
Verne, Jules. *Five Weeks in a Balloon.* Aeonian Press, reprint of 1869 ed.

The Fixer
Malamud, Bernard. *The Fixer.* Dell, 1966.

Flashman
Fraser, George Macdonald. *Flashman.* New American Library, 1969.

Flexner
Flexner, Stuart Berg. *I Hear America Talking.* Van Nostrand, 1976.

Flight of the Doves
Macken, Walter. *The Flight of the Doves.* Macmillan, 1970.

Flora Symbolica
Flora Symbolica, reprinted in *Sex in the Garden,* ed. Tom Riker. Morrow, 1976.

Foerster
Foerster, Norman, ed. *American Poetry and Prose.* Houghton Mifflin, 1970.

Follow My Black Plume
Trease, Geoffrey. *Follow My Black Plume.* Vanguard Press, 1963.

Fordin
Fordin, Hugh. *The World of Entertainment! Hollywood's Greatest Musicals.* Doubleday, 1975.

The Forsyte Saga
Galsworthy, John. *The Forsyte Saga.* Scribner, 1933.

Fortunata and Jacinta
Galdos, Benito Perez. *Fortunata and Jacinta,* tr. Lester Clark. Penguin, 1975.

Fortunes of Nigel
Scott, Sir Walter. *The Fortunes of Nigel.* Dutton, 1965.

For Whom the Bell Tolls
Hemingway, Ernest. *For Whom the Bell Tolls.* Scribner, 1940.

Four Major Plays
Ibsen, Henrik. *Four Major Plays,* vol. 2, tr. Rolf Fjelde. New American Library, 1970.

Frank
Frank, Sid. *The Presidents: Tidbits & Trivia.* Hammond, 1975.

Frankenstein
Shelley, Mary W. *Frankenstein: Or, the Modern Prometheus,* ed. James H. Rieger. Bobbs-Merrill, 1974.

Franny and Zooey
Salinger, J.D. *Franny and Zooey.* Bantam, 1969.

Freeman
Freeman, William. *Dictionary of Fictional Characters,* rev. Fred Urquhart. The Writer, 1974.

Friar Bacon
Greene, Robert. *Friar Bacon and Friar Bungay.* British Book Centre, 1975.

Friday the Rabbi Slept Late
Kemelman, Harry. *Friday the Rabbi Slept Late.* Crown, 1964.

The Frogs
Aristophanes. *The Frogs and Other Plays,* tr. David Barrett. Penguin, 1964.

Fuller
Fuller, J.F.C. *A Military History of the Western World,* 3 vols. Funk & Wagnalls, 1956.

Fyfe
Fyfe, Thomas Alexander. *Who's Who in Dickens.* Gryphon Books, 1971.

The Gambler
Dostoevsky, Feodor. *The Gambler,* ed. Edward Wasiolek, tr. Victor Terras. Univ. of Chicago Press, 1972.

A Game of Dark
Mayne, William. *A Game of Dark.* Dutton, 1971.

Gardener's Dog
de Vega, Lope. *The Gardener's Dog* in *Four Plays of Lope de Vega.* Hyperion Press, 1978.

Gargantua and Pantagruel
Rabelais, François. *Gargantua and Pantagruel,* tr. John M. Cohen. Penguin, 1955.

Gaster
Gaster, Theodore, ed. *Myth, Legend, and Custom in the Old Testament.* Harper, 1969.

Gayley
Gayley, Charles Mills. *The Classic Myths in English Literature and Art.* Milford House, 1974.

Gemini
Kipling, Rudyard. *Gemini* in *Soldiers Three.* Doubleday, 1909.

Gentleman's Agreement
Hobson, Laura Z. *Gentleman's Agreement.* Simon and Schuster, 1947.

Gentlemen Prefer Blondes
Loos, Anita. *Gentlemen Prefer Blondes.* Boni and Liveright, 1925.

George
Turnbull, Agnes. *George.* E.M. Hale, 1965.

Germinal
Zola, Emile. *Germinal.* New American Library, 1970.

Ghost of Thomas Kempe
Lively, Penelope. *The Ghost of Thomas Kempe.* Dutton, 1973.

Ghosts
Ibsen, Henrik. *Ghosts.* Avon, 1965.

Gil Blas
Le Sage, Alain René. *The Adventures of Gil Blas of Santillane.* Hyperion, 1977.

Giles Goat-Boy
Barth, John. *Giles Goat-Boy.* Fawcett Crest, 1966.

Gilgamesh
Gilgamesh: A Verse Narrative, ed. Herbert Mason. New American Library, 1972.

Ginger Pye
Estes, Eleanor. *Ginger Pye.* Harcourt, 1972.

Go Down, Moses
Faulkner, William. *Go Down, Moses.* Random House, 1973.

God Bless You, Mr. Rosewater
Vonnegut, Kurt. *God Bless You, Mr. Rosewater.* Dell, 1974.

God's Little Acre
Caldwell, Erskine. *God's Little Acre.* Viking Press, 1933.

The Golden Ass
Apuleius, Lucius. *The Golden Ass,* tr. Jack Lindsay. Indiana U.P., 1962.

Golden Boy
Odets, Clifford, and William Gibson. *Golden Boy.* Atheneum, 1965.

Golden Legend
De Voragine, Jacobus. *Golden Legend.* Arno Press, 1941.

Golden Mary
Dickens, Charles. "The Wreck of the 'Golden Mary' TH" in *Christmas Stories* in *New Oxford Illustrated Dickens.* Oxford U.P., 1956.

Golden Treasury
Untermeyer, Louis, ed. *Golden Treasury of Poetry.* Golden Press, 1959.

Goldfinger
Fleming, Ian. *Goldfinger.* Macmillan, 1966.

Golenpaul
Golenpaul, Ann. *Information Please Almanac: Atlas and Yearbook, 1975.* Information Please Almanac, 1975.

The Gondoliers
in *The Complete Plays of Gilbert and Sullivan.* Norton, 1976.

Gone With the Wind
Mitchell, Margaret. *Gone With the Wind.* Avon, 1974.

The Good Earth
Buck, Pearl. *The Good Earth.* Pocket Books, 1975.

The Graduate
Webb, Charles. *The Graduate.* New American Library, 1971.

Granger
Granger, Edith. *Granger's Index to Poetry and Recitation.* Books for Libraries, 1974.

Grapes of Wrath
Steinbeck, John. *Grapes of Wrath.* Bantam Books, 1970.

Great Expectations
Dickens, Charles. *Great Expectations,* ed. Angus Calder. Penguin, 1965.

The Great Gatsby
Fitzgerald, F. Scott. *The Great Gatsby.* Scribner, 1920.

The Green Carnation
Hichens, Robert. *The Green Carnation,* ed. Stanley Weintraub. Univ. of Nebraska Press, 1970.

The Green Hills of Africa
Hemingway, Ernest. *The Green Hills of Africa.* Scribner, 1935.

Grendel
Gardner, John. *Grendel.* G.K. Hall, 1972.

Griffith
Griffith, Richard, and Arthur Mayer. *The Movies.* Simon and Schuster, 1957.

Grimm
Grimms' Tales for Young and Old, tr. Ralph Manheim. Doubleday, 1977.

Grinding It Out
Kroc, Ray, and Robert Anderson. *Grinding It Out: The Making of McDonald's.* Contemporary Publishing, 1977.

Grove
Grove's Dictionary of Music and Musicians, 5th ed. St. Martin's Press, 1954.

Grun
Grun, Bernard. *The Timetables of History.* Simon and Schuster, 1975.

Guirand
Guirand, Felix. *New Larousse Encyclopedia of Mythology.* Putnam, 1973.

Gulliver's Travels
Swift, Jonathan. *Gulliver's Travels,* ed. L.A. Landa. Houghton Mifflin, 1960.

The Guns of August
Tuchman, Barbara W. *The Guns of August.* Bantam, 1976.

Guy Mannering
Scott, Sir Walter. *Guy Mannering.* Dutton, 1954.

Guzmán de Alfarache
Aleman, Mateo. *The Life of Guzmán de Alfarache.* Knopf, 1924.

Hall
Hall, James. *Dictionary of Subjects and Symbols in Art.* Harper, 1974.

Halliwell
Halliwell, Leslie. *The Filmgoer's Companion.* Hill and Wang, 1977.

Hamlet
Shakespeare, William. *Hamlet,* ed. George Rylands. Oxford U.P., 1947.

The Happy Lion
Duvoisin, Roger. *The Happy Lion.* McGraw-Hill, 1954.

Harbottle *Battles*
Harbottle, Thomas Benfield. *Dictionary of Battles.* Gale, 1966.

Hard Times
Dickens, Charles. *Hard Times,* ed. David Craig. Penguin, 1969.

Handy Andy
Lover, Samuel. *Handy Andy; A Tale of Irish Life.* Appleton, 1904.

Hans Breitmann's Ballads
Leland, Charles G. *Hans Breitmann's Ballads.* Dover, 1914.

The Happy Hooker
Hollander, Xaviera. *The Happy Hooker.* Dell, 1972.

Harding's Luck
Nesbit, Edith. *Harding's Luck.* British Book Centre, 1974.

Hardwick
Hardwick, Michael. *A Literary Atlas and Gazetteer of the British Isles.* Gale, 1973.

Harris
Harris, Brice, ed. *Restoration Plays.* Modern Library, 1966.

Hart
Hart, James D., ed. *The Oxford Companion to American Literature,* 4th ed. Oxford U.P., 1965.

Harvey
Harvey, Sir Paul, ed. *The Oxford Companion to English Literature,* 4th edition. rev. Dorothy Eagle. Oxford U.P., 1967.

The Haunted House
Dickens, Charles. *The Haunted House* in *Christmas Stories from Household Words and All the Year Round.* n.d.

Havelok the Dane
Havelok the Dane, ed. Ian Serraillier. Walck, 1967.

Haydn & Fuller
Haydn, Hiram and Fuller, Edmund. *Thesaurus of Book Digests.* Crown, 1949.

The Heart Is a Lonely Hunter
McCullers, Carson. *The Heart Is a Lonely Hunter.* Bantam, 1970.

The Heart of Midlothian
Scott, Sir Walter. *The Heart of Midlothian.* Dutton, 1956.

The Heathen Chinee
Harte, Bret. "The Heathen Chinee," usually known as "Plain Language from Truthful James" in *The Complete Works of Bret Harte.* Chatto and Windus, 1880–1912.

Hedda Gabler
Ibsen, Henrik. *Hedda Gabler and Other Plays,* tr. Eva LeGallienne and Norman Ginsbury. Dutton, Everyman, 1976.

Heidi
Spyri, Johanna. *Heidi.* Penguin, 1971.

Helen
Euripides. *Helen,* ed. A.M. Dale. Oxford U.P., 1967.

Heloïse and Abelard
Moore, George. *Heloïse and Abelard.* Liveright, 1945.

Hemingway
Hemingway, Ernest. *Short Stories of Ernest Hemingway.* Scribner, 1938.

Henderson the Rain King
Bellow, Saul. *Henderson the Rain King.* Fawcett World, 1974.

Henry and Beezus
Cleary, Beverly. *Henry and Beezus.* William Morrow, 1952.

I Henry IV
Shakespeare, William. *I Henry IV,* ed. George L. Kittredge and Irving Ribner. John Wiley, 1966.

II Henry IV
Shakespeare, William. *II Henry IV.* Oxford U.P., 1970.

Henry V
Shakespeare, William. *Henry V.* Oxford U.P., 1971.

I Henry VI
Shakespeare, William. *I Henry VI.* Oxford U.P., 1970.

II Henry VI
Shakespeare, William. *II Henry VI.* Oxford U.P., 1970.

III Henry VI
Shakespeare, William. *III Henry VI,* ed. George L. Kittredge and Irving Ribner. John Wiley, 1969.

Henry VIII
Shakespeare, William. *Henry VIII.* Oxford U.P., 1971.

Henry Esmond
Thackeray, William M. *Henry Esmond.* Dutton, 1972.

Henry Huggins
Cleary, Beverley. *Henry Huggins.* William Morrow, 1950.

Herbert
Herbert, Ian. *Who's Who in the Theatre.* Gale, 1977.

A Herd of Deer
Dillon, Eilis. *A Herd of Deer.* Funk & Wagnalls, 1970.

Herman
Herman, Linda, and Beth Stiel. *Corpus Delicti of Mystery Fiction.* Scarecrow Press, 1974.

Hero and Leander
Marlowe, Christopher. *Hero and Leander.* Johnson Reprint, 1972.

Hero and Leander
Musaeus. *Hero and Leander,* tr. F.L. Lucas. Golden Cockerel Press, 1977.

Herzog
Bellow, Saul. *Herzog.* Fawcett World, 1974.

Hiawatha
Longfellow, Henry Wadsworth. *The Song of Hiawatha.* Tuttle, 1975.

The Hidden Staircase
Keene, Carolyn. *The Hidden Staircase.* Grosset and Dunlap, 1930.

Hippolytus
Euripides. *Hippolytus,* tr. Robert Bagg. Oxford U.P., 1973.

History of John Bull
Arbuthnot, John. *History of John Bull.* Oxford U.P., 1976.

Hitler
Toland, John. *Adolf Hitler.* Ballantine Books, 1976.

H.M.S. Pinafore
Gilbert, W. S. "H.M.S. Pinafore" in *The Complete Works of Gilbert and Sullivan.* Norton, 1976.

The Hobbit
Tolkien, J.R.R. *The Hobbit.* Houghton Mifflin, 1973.

Hollowell
Hollowell, Lillian. *A Book of Children's Literature.* Rinehart, 1950.

Hone
Hone, William. *The Table Book.* Gale, 1966.

Hone *Everyday*
Hone, William. *The Everyday Book.* Gordon, 1967.

The Hope of the Katzekopfs
Paget, Frances E., and William Churne. *The Hope of the Katzekopfs: A Fairy Tale.* Johnson Reprints, 1968.

Horn
Horn, Maurice. *The World Encyclopedia of Comics.* Chelsea House, 1976.

Horton Hatches the Egg
Seuss, Dr. *Horton Hatches the Egg.* Random House, 1940.

The Hound of the Baskervilles
Doyle, A. Conan. *The Hound of the Baskervilles.* Dell, 1959.

House of Arden
Nesbit, Edith. *House of Arden.* Dutton, 1968.

The House of Sixty Fathers
de Jong, Meindert. *The House of Sixty Fathers.* Harper, 1956.

The House of the Seven Gables
Hawthorne, Nathaniel. *The House of the Seven Gables.* Harcourt, 1970.

Howe
Howe, George, and Harrer, G. A. *A Handbook of Classical Mythology.* Gale, 1970.

How the People Sang the Mountains Up
Leach, Maria. *How the People Sang the Mountains Up.* Viking Press, 1967.

Huckleberry Finn
Twain, Mark. *The Adventures of Huckleberry Finn.* Holt, 1948.

Hugo and Josephine
Gripe, Maria. *Hugo and Josephine.* Dell, 1971.

Humphrey Clinker
Smollett, Tobias. *The Expedition of Humphrey Clinker,* ed. Lewis M. Knapp. Oxford U.P., 1966.

The Hunchback of Notre Dame
Hugo, Victor. *The Hunchback of Notre Dame.* Dutton, 1953.

The Hunting of the Snark
Carroll, Lewis. *The Hunting of the Snark.* Clarkson N. Potter, 1975.

The Iceman Cometh
O'Neill, Eugene. *The Iceman Cometh.* Random House, 1957.

I Ching
I Ching or the Book of Changes, tr. Peter Legge. Citadel Press, 1971.

I, Claudius
Graves, Robert. *I, Claudius.* Random House, Vintage, 1961.

The Idiot
Dostoyevsky, Fyodor. *The Idiot.* New American Library, Signet, 1969.

Idylls
Theocritus. *Idylls of Theocritus.* Purdue Univ. Studies, 1963.

Idylls of the King
Tennyson, Alfred, Lord. *Idylls of the King.* St. Martin's Press, 1930.

Iliad
Homer. *Iliad,* tr. Robert Fitzgerald. Doubleday, 1975.

Imagines
Philostratrus. *Imagines.* Harvard U.P., 1972.

The Importance of Being Earnest
Wilde, Oscar. *The Importance of Being Earnest.* New York Public Library, 1968.

In Cold Blood
Capote, Truman. *In Cold Blood.* New American Library, 1971.

In Dubious Battle.
Steinbeck, John. *In Dubious Battle.* Bantam, 1970.

Indian Summer
Howells, William Dean *Indian Summer.* Indiana U.P., 1972.

Inferno
Dante Alighieri. *Inferno.* Dutton, 1965.

The Informer
O'Flaherty, Liam. *The Informer.* Triangle Books, 1943.

Ingleby
Ingleby, C.M., et al. *Shakspere AllusionBook: A Collection of Allusions to Shakspere from 1591 to 1700.* Books For Libraries, 1970.

The Injustice Collectors
Auchincloss, Louis. *The Injustice Collectors.* Avon, 1974.

The Inspector General
Gogol, Nikolai. *The Inspector General.* Avon, 1976.

In the Heat of the Night
Ball, John. *In the Heat of the Night.* Harper & Row, 1965.

The Invisible Man
Wells, H.G. *The Invisible Man.* Popular Library, 1972.

Iphigenia in Tauris
Euripides. *Iphigenia in Tauris,* tr. Gilbert Murray. Oxford U.P., 1910.

Iron Giant
Hughes, Ted. *Iron Giant: A Story in Five Nights.* Harper, 1968.

The Iron Lily
Willard, Barbara. *The Iron Lily.* Dutton, 1974.

Ivanhoe
Scott, Sir Walter. *Ivanhoe.* Macmillan, 1962.

Jack
Jack, Alex. *The New Age Dictionary.* Kanthaka Press, 1976.

Jack Sheppard
Ainsworth, William. *Jack Sheppard.* Century, 1909.

Jacobowsky & Der Oberst
Werfel, Franz. *Jacobowsky & Der Oberst.* Irvington, 1961.

Jameson
Jameson, J. Franklin. *Dictionary of United States History.* Gale, 1971.

Jane Eyre
Bronte, Charlotte. *Jane Eyre.* Dutton, 1963.

J.B.
MacLeish, Archibald. *J.B.* Houghton Mifflin, 1958.

Dr. Jekyll and Mr. Hyde
Stevenson, Robert L. *Dr. Jekyll and Mr. Hyde.* Dutton, Everyman, 1962.

Jerusalem Delivered
Tasso, Torquato. *Jerusalem Delivered.* Putnam, 1963.

Jew of Malta
Marlowe, Christopher. *The Jew of Malta* in *Marlowe: Five Plays,* ed. Havelock Ellis. Hill and Wang, 1956.

Jobes
Jobes, Gertrude. *Dictionary of Mythology, Folklore, and Symbols*– Parts 1 & 2. Scarecrow Press, 1962.

John Brent
Winthrop, Theodore. *John Brent,* ed. H. Dean Propst. College and Univ. Press, 1970.

John Gabriel Borkman
Ibsen, Henrik. *John Gabriel Borkman* in *Four Major Plays,* tr. Rolf Fjelde, vol. 2. New American Library, 1970.

John Gilpin's Ride
Cowper, William. *John Gilpin's Ride.* Watts, 1967.

Johnny Tremain
Forbes, Esther. *Johnny Tremain.* Dell, 1969.

Johnson
Johnson, Rossiter. *Dictionary of Famous Names in Fiction, Drama, Poetry, History and Art.* Gale, 1974.

Jonathan Livingston Seagull
Bach, Richard. *Jonathan Livingston Seagull.* Macmillan, 1970.

Jorrock's Jaunts & Jollities
Surtees, Robert S. *Jorrock's Jaunts and Jollities*, ed. Herbert Van Thal. Dufour, 1969.

Joseph Andrews
Fielding, Henry. *Joseph Andrews*. Norton, 1958.

Josh
Southall, Ivan. *Josh*. Macmillan, 1972.

Joy
Joy, Charles Rhind. *Harper's Topical Concordance*, rev. ed. Harper, 1962.

Jude the Obscure
Hardy, Thomas. *Jude the Obscure*. St. Martin's Press, 1977.

Judgment Day
Farrell, James T. *Judgment Day*. Avon, 1973.

Julius Caesar
Shakespeare, William. *Julius Caesar*, ed. T.S. Dorsch. Barnes & Noble, 1964.

The Jungle
Sinclair, Upton. *The Jungle*. New American Library, 1973.

The Jungle Books
Kipling, Rudyard. *The Jungle Books*. Grosset and Dunlap, 1950.

Jurgi
Jurgi, E.J. *Great Religions of the Modern World*. Princeton U.P., 1946.

Kaganoff
Kaganoff, Benzion C. *A Dictionary of Jewish Names and Their History*. Schocken Books, 1977.

Kalevala
Loenrot, Elias. *Kalevala*, tr. Francis P. Magoun. Harvard U.P., 1963.

Kane
Kane, Joseph Nathan. *Facts About the Presidents*. Ace Books, 1976.

Karst
Karst, Gene, and Martin J. Jones, Jr. *Who's Who in Professional Baseball*. Arlington House, 1973.

Keddie
Keddie, William. *Cyclopaedia of Literary and Scientific Anecdote*. Gryphon, 1971.

Kent
Kent, Leonard J. *The Collected Tales and Plays of Nikolai Gogol*. Pantheon, 1964.

Kidnapped
Stevenson, Robert L. *Kidnapped*. New American Library, 1959.

Killikelly
Killikelly, Sarah H. *Curious Questions*. Gale, 1968.

King John
Shakespeare, William. *King John*, ed. E.A. Honingmann. Barnes & Noble, 1965.

King Lear
Shakespeare, William. *King Lear*, in *William Shakespeare: The Complete Works*, ed. Peter Alexander. Collins, 1951.

King of the Golden River
Ruskin, John. *King of the Golden River*. Dover, 1974.

King *Quotations*
King, William F. *Classical and Foreign Quotations*. Gale, 1968.

The King, the Greatest Alcalde
de Vega, Lope. *The King, the Greatest Alcalde*. in *Poet Lore* 29 (1918): 379–446.

King *Things*
King, Edmund F. *Ten Thousand Wonderful Things*. Gale, 1970.

Kinkle
Kinkle, Roger D. *The Complete Encyclopedia of Popular Music and Jazz, 1900–1950*. 4 vols. Arlington House, 1974.

Kipps
Wells, H.G. *Kipps*. Dell, 1968.

Kitto
Kitto, H.D.F., *Greek Tragedy: A Literary Study*. Doubleday, 1954.

Kon-Tiki
Heyerdahl, Thor. *Kon-Tiki*. Washington Square Press, 1973.

Koran
Koran, tr. N.J. Dawood. Penguin, 1964.

Kravitz
Kravitz, David. *Who's Who in Greek and Roman Mythology*. Clarkson N. Potter, 1975.

Kubla Khan
Coleridge, Samuel Taylor. "Kubla Khan, A Vision in a Dream" in *Collected Works of Samuel T. Coleridge*. Princeton U.P., 1972.

Kunz
Kunz, George Frederick. *The Curious Lore of Precious Stones*. Dover, 1971.

Kwong
Kwong, Ki Chaou. *Dictionary of English Phrases*. Gale, 1971.

The Lady or the Tiger
Stockton, Frank. *The Lady or the Tiger and Other Stories*. Mss Information Co., 1972

Lahue
Lahue, Kalton C. *World of Laughter: The Motion Picture Comedy Short, 1910–1930*. Univ. of Oklahoma Press, 1972.

The Land of Oz
Baum, L. Frank. *The Land of Oz*. Airmont, 1968.

The Lark and the Laurel
Willard, Barbara. *The Lark and the Laurel*. Harcourt, Bruce, Jovanovich, 1970.

The Last Chronicle of Barset
Trollope, Anthony. *The Last Chronicle of Barset*, ed. Arthur Mizener. Houghton Mifflin, 1964.

The Last Days of Pompeii
Bulwer-Lytton, Edward. *The Last Days of Pompeii* in *Works*. Wanamaker, n.d.

Latham
Latham, Edward. *Dictionary of Names, Nicknames, and Surnames*. Gale, 1966.

Laughlin
Laughlin, William H. *Laughlin's Fact Finder—People, Places, Things, Events*. Parker, 1969.

Leach
Leach, Maria, ed. *Funk & Wagnalls Standard Dictionary of Folklore, Mythology, and Legend*. Funk & Wagnalls, 1972.

Leaves of Grass
Whitman, Walt. *Leaves of Grass*. Norton, 1968.

The Legend of Sleepy Hollow
Irving, Washington. *The Legend of Sleepy Hollow and Other Stories*. Airmont, 1964.

A Legend of Montrose
Scott, Walter. *A Legend of Montrose* in *Complete Works*. Houghton, 1923.

Leonard
Leonard, Thomas M. *Day by Day: the Forties*. Facts on File, 1977.

Lie Down In Darkness
Styron, William. *Lie Down In Darkness*. Viking Press, 1957.

The Life of John Buncle
Amory, Thomas. *The Life of John Buncle, Esq., 1756–1766*, ed. Michael F. Shugrue. Garland, 1974.

Light in August
Faulkner, William. *Light in August*. Random House, 1967.

The Lion, the Witch, and the Wardrobe
Lewis, C.S. *The Lion, The Witch, and The Wardrobe*. Macmillan, 1970.

Little
Little, Charles. *Historical Lights: 6000 Quotations*. Gale, 1968.

Little Blue and Little Yellow
Lionni, Leo. *Little Blue and Little Yellow*. Astor-Honor, 1959.

Little Dorrit
Dickens, Charles. *Little Dorrit*, ed. John Holloway. Penguin, 1967.

The Little Engine That Could
Piper, Watty. *The Little Engine That Could*. Platt, 1976.

Little Eyolf
Ibsen, Henrik. *Little Eyolf* in *Ibsen: The Complete Major Prose Plays*. Farrar, Straus, and Giroux, 1978.

The Little House
Burton, Virginia. *The Little House*. Houghton Mifflin, 1943.

Little House in The Big Woods
Wilder, Laura Ingalls. *Little House in The Big Woods*. Harper & Row, 1953.

The Little Lame Prince
Mulock, Dinah. *The Little Lame Prince and his Travelling Cloak.* Hale, 1909.

Little Lord Fauntleroy
Burnett, Frances H. *Little Lord Fauntleroy.* Biblio Distribution Centre, 1975.

The Little Minister
Barrie, J.M. *The Little Minister.* Airmont, 1968.

Little Old Mrs. Pepperpot
Proysen, Alf. *Little Old Mrs. Pepperpot.* Astor-Honor, 1960.

Little Red Fox
Uttley, Allison. *Little Red Fox and the Wicked Uncle.* Bobbs-Merrill, 1963.

The Little Steam Roller
Greene, Grahame. *The Little Steam Roller.* Doubleday, 1975.

Little Tim
Ardizzone, Edward. *Little Tim and the Brave Sea Captain.* Henry Walck, 1955.

Little Women
Alcott, Louisa May. *Little Women.* Grosset and Dunlap, 1947.

Livy
Livy. *Livy,* ed. T.A. Dorey. Univ. of Toronto Press, 1971.

LLEI
The Lincoln Library of Essential Information. 2 vols. The Frontier Co., 1972.

Lolita
Nabokov, Vladimir. *Lolita.* Berkeley Pub. Co., 1975.

The Long Goodbye
Chandler, Raymond. *The Long Goodbye.* Ballantine, 1977.

The Long Voyage
Dickens, Charles. "The Long Voyage" in *Reprinted Pieces.* Dutton, 1970.

Look Homeward, Angel
Wolfe, Thomas. *Look Homeward, Angel.* Scribner, 1929.

Lord Jim
Conrad, Joseph. *Lord Jim.* Doubleday, 1927.

Lord of Burleigh
Tennyson, Alfred, Lord. "Lord of Burleigh" in *Poems of Tennyson,* ed. Christopher Ricks. Norton, 1972.

Lord of the Flies
Golding, William. *Lord of the Flies.* Putnam, 1959.

Lord of the Rings
Tolkien, J.R.R. *Lord of the Rings.* Houghton Mifflin, 1974.

Lost Horizon
Hilton, James. *Lost Horizon.* Washington Square Press, 1972.

A Lost Lady
Cather, Willa. *A Lost Lady.* Random House, Vintage, 1972.

The Lost World
Doyle, Arthur Conan. *The Lost World.* Random House, 1959.

Lothair
Disraeli, Benjamin. *Lothair,* ed. Vernon Bogdanor. Oxford U.P., 1975.

Louie's Lot
Hildrick, E.W. *Louie's Lot.* D. White, 1968.

Love's Labour's Lost
Shakespeare, William. *Love's Labour's Lost,* ed. Richard W. David. Barnes & Noble, 1966.

Love Story
Segal, Erich. *Love Story.* Harper & Row, 1970.

Loving
Green, Henry. *Loving.* Dufour, 1949.

Lucy Brown and Mr. Grimes
Ardizzone, Edward. *Lucy Brown and Mr. Grimes.* Henry Walck, 1971.

Lurie
Lurie, Charles N. *Everyday Sayings.* Gale, 1968.

Lusiads
Camoes, Luis de. *Lusiads.* Southern Illinois U.P., 1963.

Lysistrata
Aristophanes. *Lysistrata,* tr. Douglass Parker. New American Library, 1970.

Macbeth
Shakespeare, William. *Macbeth,* ed. R.W. Dent. William C. Brown, 1969.

Mabinogion
The Mabinogion, tr. Jeffrey Gantz. Penguin, 1976.

Macleod
Macleod, Ann, adapt. *English Fairy Tales.* Paul Hamlyn, 1965.

Madame Bovary
Flaubert, Gustave. *Madame Bovary,* ed. Charles I. Weir. Holt, 1948.

Maggie: A Girl of the Streets
Crane, Stephen. *Maggie: A Girl of the Streets.* Fawcett World, 1978.

The Magician's Nephew
Lewis, C.S. *The Magician's Nephew.* Macmillan, 1970.

Magill
Magill, Frank. *Masterpieces of World Literature in Digest Form.* 4 vols. Harper & Row, 1960.

The Magnificent Ambersons
Tarkington, Booth. *The Magnificent Ambersons.* Avon, 1973.

Mahābhārata
Mahābhārata, tr. Chakravarthi V. Narasimhan. Columbia U.P., 1973.

The Maid's Tragedy
Beaumont, Francis, and John Fletcher. *The Maid's Tragedy,* ed. Andrew J. Gurr. Univ. of California Press, 1969.

Main Street
Lewis, Sinclair. *Main Street.* Signet Classics, 1971.

Major Bradford's Town
Melville, Doris Johnson. *Major Bradford's Town: A History of Kingston.* Town of Kingston, Mass., 1976.

Le Malade Imaginaire
Molière, Jean B. *Le Malade Imaginaire.* French and European Pubn., 1964.

The Maldonado Miracle
Taylor, Theodore. *The Maldonado Miracle.* Doubleday, 1973.

The Maltese Falcon
Hammett, Dashiell. *The Maltese Falcon.* Random House, 1972.

Manhattan Transfer
Dos Passos, John. *Manhattan Transfer.* Houghton Mifflin, 1963.

Manon Lescaut
Prevost, Antoine. *Manon Lescaut,* tr. Helen Waddell. Hyperion, 1977.

Manxmouse
Gallico, Paul. *Manxmouse.* Coward, McCann and Geoghegan, 1968.

The Marble Faun
Hawthorne, Nathaniel. *The Marble Faun.* Ohio State U.P., 1968.

Marianne Dreams
Storr, Catherine. *Marianne Dreams.* Penguin, 1975.

The Marriage of Figaro
Beaumarchais, P.A. *The Marriage of Figaro,* tr. B.P. Ellis. AHM Publishing, 1966.

Martin Chuzzlewit
Dickens, Charles. *Martin Chuzzlewit,* ed. P.N. Furbank. Penguin, 1975.

Martin Eden
London, Jack. *Martin Eden.* Macmillan, 1957.

Martin Pippin
Farjeon, Eleanor. *Martin Pippin in the Apple Orchard.* Lippincott, 1961.

Martinus Scriblerus
Pope, Alexander, et al. *Memoirs of Martinus Scriblerus* in *The Works of Alexander Pope,* ed. J.W. Croker, Vol. 10. Gordian Press, 1967.

Marvin
Marvin, Frederic Rowland. *The Last Words of Distinguished Men and Women.* Gale, 1970.

Mary Poppins
Travers, Pamela L. *Mary Poppins.* Harcourt Brace Jovanovich, 1972.

Master of Ballantrae
Stevenson, Robert L. *Master of Ballantrae.* Dutton, 1972.

Mathews
Mathews, Mitford, ed. *Dictionary of Americanisms on Historical Principles.* Univ. of Chicago Press, 1951.

Mayers
Mayers, William F. *Chinese Reader's Manual.* Gale, 1968.

The Mayor of Casterbridge
Hardy, Thomas. *The Mayor of Casterbridge.* Norton, 1977.

McWhirter
McWhirter, Norris, and Ross McWhirter. *Guinness Book of World Records.* Bantam, 1975.

Measure for Measure
Shakespeare, William. *Measure for Measure,* ed. R.E. Houghton. Oxford U.P., 1970.

Medea
Euripides. *Medea,* ed. Alan Elliott. Oxford U.P., 1969.

Médée
Anouilh, Jean. *Médée.* French and European Pubn., 1953.

Meg and Mog
Nicoll, Helen. *Meg and Mog.* Atheneum, 1973.

Mein Kampf
Hitler, Adolf. *Mein Kampf,* tr. Ralph Manheim. Houghton Mifflin, 1962.

Melmoth the Wanderer
Maturin, Charles R. *Melmoth the Wanderer.* Univ. of Nebraska Press, 1961.

Memoirs of Fanny Hill
Cleland, John. *Memoirs of Fanny Hill.* New American Library, Signet, n.d.

Menaechmi
Plautus. *Menaechmi,* tr. Frank O. Copley. Bobbs-Merrill, 1956.

Mencken
Mencken, H.L. *The American Language,* abridged R.I. McDavid. Knopf, 1963.

Mercatante
Mercatante, Anthony S. *The Zoo of the Gods: Animals in Myth, Legend, and Fable.* Harper & Row, 1974.

The Merchant of Venice
Shakespeare, William. *The Merchant of Venice,* ed. John R. Brown. Barnes & Noble, 1964.

The Merry Wives of Windsor
Shakespeare, William. *The Merry Wives of Windsor,* ed. H.J. Oliver. Barnes & Noble, 1971.

Messiah
Klopstock, F.G. *Messiah.* Collyer, 1769–71.

Metamorphoses
Ovid. *Metamorphoses,* tr. Rolfe Humphries. Indiana U.P., 1955.

Michael Strogoff
Verne, Jules. *Michael Strogoff.* Airmont, 1964.

Middlemarch
Eliot, George. *Middlemarch.* Macmillan, 1966.

Midshipman Quinn
Styles, Showell. *Midshipman Quinn.* Vanguard, 1958.

A Midsummer Night's Dream
Shakespeare, William. *A Midsummer Night's Dream,* ed. Sally Freeman. Gordon and Breach, 1975.

The Mikado
in *The Complete Plays of Gilbert and Sullivan.* Norton, 1976.

Mike Mulligan
Burton, Virginia Lee. *Mike Mulligan and His Steam Shovel.* Houghton Mifflin, 1977.

Miller
Miller, Sim, ed. *The Rolling Stone Illustrated History of Rock & Roll.* Random House, 1976.

The Misanthrope
Molière, Jean B. *The Misanthrope,* tr. Bernard D. Grebanier. Barron's, 1959.

Misc.
Includes items of a proverbial nature and/or of common knowledge.

The Miser
Molière Jean B. *The Miser,* tr. Wallace Fowlie. Barron's, 1965.

Les Misérables
Hugo, Victor. *Les Misérables.* French and European Pubn., 1951.

Mistress Masham's Repose
White, Terence H. *Mistress Masham's Repose.* Putnam, 1960.

The Mistress of the Inn
Goldoni, Carlo. *The Mistress of the Inn.* Moscow Art Theater series of Russian plays, 1923.

Moby Dick
Melville, Herman. *Moby Dick,* ed. Harold Beaver. Penguin, 1975.

A Modern Midas
Jōkai, Mor. *A Modern Midas.* J.W. Lovell, 1886.

The Moffats
Estes, Eleanor. *The Moffats.* Harcourt Brace Jovanovich, 1968.

The Monastery
Scott, Sir Walter. *The Monastery.* Dutton, 1969.

The Monk
Lewis, Matthew. *The Monk.* Avon, 1975.

Monmouth
Geoffrey of Monmouth. *History of the Kings of Britain,* ed. Charles Dunn. Dutton, 1958.

Monsieur Beaucaire
Tarkington, Booth. *Monsieur Beaucaire.* McClure, Phillips, 1900.

Monsieur Lecoq
Gaboriau, Emile. *Monsieur Lecoq,* ed. E.F. Bleuler. Dover, 1975.

A Month in the Country
Turgenev, Ivan. *A Month in the Country.* French, 1957.

Moody
Moody, Sophy. *What Is Your Name* Gale, 1976.

Mopsa, The Fairy
Ingelow, Jean. *Mopsa, The Fairy.* Dutton, 1964.

Le Morte d'Arthur
Malory, Thomas. *Le Morte d'Arthur,* ed. Janet Cowen. Penguin, 1975.

Mostly Mary
Rae, Gwynneth. *Mostly Mary.* Avon, 1972.

Mother Goose
The Real Mother Goose. Rand McNally, 1955.

Mourning Becomes Electra
O'Neill, Eugene. *Mourning Becomes Electra.* Random House, 1931.

The Mourning Bride
Congreve, William. *The Mourning Bride, Poems, and Miscellanies.* Somerset Pubn., n.d.

The Mouse That Roared
Wibberley, Leonard. *The Mouse That Roared.* Little, Brown, 1955.

Mr. Polly
Wells, H.G. *The History of Mr. Polly,* ed. Gordon Ray. Houghton Mifflin, 1961.

Mrs. Easter's Parasol
Drummond, V.H. *Mrs. Easter's Parasol.* Faber and Faber, 1944.

Mrs. Frisby
O'Brien, Robert C. *Mrs. Frisby and the Rats of NIMH.* Atheneum, 1975.

Much Ado About Nothing
Shakespeare, William. *Much Ado About Nothing,* ed. Charlton Hinman. Oxford U.P., 1972.

Mulberry Street
Seuss, Dr. *And to Think That I Saw It on Mulberry Street.* E.M. Hale, 1937.

Murder in the Cathedral
Eliot, T.S. *Murder in the Cathedral.* Harcourt Brace Jovanovich, 1964.

Mutiny on the Bounty
Nordhoff, Charles B., and James N. Hall. *Mutiny on the Bounty.* Washington Square Press, 1975.

My Brother's Keeper
Davenport, Marcia. *My Brother's Keeper.* Scribner, 1954.

My Father's Dragon
Gannett, Ruth. *My Father's Dragon.* Random House, 1948.

My Friend Flicka
O'Hara, Mary. *My Friend Flicka.* Lippincott, 1973.

My Life in the Mafia
Teresa, Vincent C., with Thomas C. Renner. *My Life in the Mafia.* Doubleday, 1973.

My Side of the Mountain
George, Jean. *My Side of the Mountain.* Dutton, 1967.

Mysterious Island
Verne, Jules. *Mysterious Island.* Pendulum Press, 1974.

Mythology
Hamilton, Edith. *Mythology.* Little, Brown, 1942.

The Namesake
Hodges, C. Walter. *The Namesake: A Story of King Alfred.* Coward, McCann and Geoghegan, 1964.

Nares
Nares, Robert. *Glossary of Words, Phrases, Names, and Allusions in the Works of English Authors.* Gale, 1966.

Native Son
Wright, Richard. *Native Son.* Harper & Row, 1940.

Nausea
Sartre, Jean-Paul. *Nausea,* tr. Lloyd Alexander. New Directions, 1959.

NCE
The New Columbia Encyclopedia, ed. William H. Harris and Judith S. Levey. Columbia U.P., 1975.

A Nest of Simple Folk
O'Faolain, Sean. *A Nest of Simple Folk.* Viking Press, 1934.

The Newcomes
Thackeray, William Makepeace. *The Newcomes.* Bradbury and Evans, 1854 ND55.

New Héloise
Rousseau, Jean-Jacques. *La Nouvelle Héloise.* Penn. State U.P., 1968.

Nibelungenlied
Nibelungenlied, tr. Frank G. Ryder. Wayne State U. P., 1962.

Nicholas Nickleby
Dickens, Charles. *Nicholas Nickleby.* Dutton, 1957.

Nigger of the Narcissus
Conrad, Joseph. *The Nigger of the Narcissus.* Macmillan, 1962.

The Night Before Christmas
Moore, Clement. *The Night Before Christmas.* Grosset and Dunlap, 1970.

Nine Tailors
Sayers, Dorothy. *Nine Tailors.* Harcourt Brace Jovanovich, 1966.

1984
Orwell, George. *1984.* New American Library, 1971.

Noctes Atticae
Gellius. *Noctes Atticae,* ed. P. K. Marshall. Oxford U.P., 1968.

Noddy and His Car
Blyton, Enid. *Noddy and His Car.* British Book Centre, 1974.

Norton
Eastman, et al. *The Norton Anthology of Poetry.* Norton, 1970.

Norton *Literature*
Norton Anthology of English Literature, 3rd edition. 2 vols. Norton, 1974.

Norton *Modern*
Norton Anthology of Modern Poetry, ed. Richard Ellmann and Robert O'Clair. Norton, 1973.

Nostromo
Conrad, Joseph. *Nostromo.* Modern Library, 1951.

N.T.
New Testament. *New English Bible.* Oxford U.P., 1970.

Number One
Dos Passos, John. *Number One.* Queens House, 1977.

Oblomov
Goncharov, Ivan. *Oblomov,* tr. Natalie Duddington. Dutton, 1972.

The Odd Couple
Simon, Neil. *The Odd Couple.* Random House, 1966.

Odyssey
Homer. *Odyssey,* tr. Robert Fitzgerald. Doubleday, 1974.

Oedipus Rex
Sophocles. *Oedipus Rex,* tr. Gilbert Murray. Oxford U.P., 1948.

Oedipus Tyrannus
Sophocles. *Oedipus Tyrannus.* Norton, 1970.

Of Mice and Men
Steinbeck, John. *Of Mice and Men.* Bantam, 1970.

The Old Batchelour
Congreve, William. *The Old Batchelour.* British Book Centre, 1974.

The Old Curiosity Shop
Dickens, Charles. *The Old Curiosity Shop,* ed. A. Easson. Penguin, 1972.

The Old Man and the Sea
Hemingway, Ernest. *The Old Man and the Sea.* Scribner, 1961.

Old Mortality
Scott, Sir Walter. *Old Mortality,* ed. Angus Calder. Penguin, 1975.

Oliver Twist
Dickens, Charles. *Oliver Twist,* ed. Kathleen Tillotson. Oxford U.P., 1966.

Omoo
Melville, Herman. *Omoo.* Northwestern U.P., 1968.

On Stage
Beckerman, Bernard and Siegman, Howard. *On Stage: Selected Theater Reviews from* The New York Times. Arno Press, 1970.

On the Road
Kerouac, Jack. *On the Road.* Viking Press, 1978.

The Once and Future King
White, T.H. *The Once and Future King.* Putnam, 1958.

One Day in the Life of Ivan Denisovich
Solzhenitzyn, Alexandr. *One Day in the Life of Ivan Denisovich,* tr. Aitken Gillon. Farrar, 1971.

One Flew Over the Cuckoo's Nest
Kesey, Ken. *One Flew Over the Cuckoo's Nest.* New American Library, 1975.

Opie
Opie, Iona and Peter. *Oxford Dictionary of Nursery Rhymes.* Oxford U.P., 1951.

Orestes
Aeschylus. *Oresteia,* tr. Robert Fagles. Bantam, 1977.

Origin of the Species
Darwin, Charles. *Origin of the Species.* Macmillan, 1962.

Orlando Furioso
Ariosto, Ludovico. *Orlando Furioso,* tr. John Harrington. Oxford U.P., 1972.

Orlando Innamorato
Bojardo, Matteo Maria. *Orlando Innamorato.* Sansoni, 1892.

Oroonoko
Behn, Aphra. *Oroonoko; Or, The Royal Slave.* Norton, 1973.

Osborne
Osborne, Harold, ed. *The Oxford Companion to Art.* Oxford U.P., 1970.

Osborne *Opera*
Osborne, Charles. *The Dictionary of the Opera.* Simon and Schuster, 1983.

O.T.
Old Testament. *New English Bible.* Oxford U.P., 1970.

Othello
Shakespeare, William. *Othello,* ed. J. Leeds Barroll. William C. Brown, 1971.

Our Mutual Friend
Dickens, Charles. *Our Mutual Friend,* ed. Stephen Gill. Penguin, 1971.

The Outcasts of Poker Flat
Harte, Bret. *The Outcasts of Poker Flat and Other Tales.* New American Library, Signet, 1961.

The Overcoat
Gogol, Nikolai. *The Overcoat and Other Stories.* Knopf, 1950.

Overland Launch
Hodges, C. Walter. *The Overland Launch.* Coward, McCann and Geoghegan, 1969.

The Owl Service
Garner, Alan. *The Owl Service.* Henry Walck, 1968.

The Ox-Bow Incident
Clark, Walter van Tilberg. *The Ox-Bow Incident.* New American Library, 1943.

Oxford English Dictionary
The Oxford English Dictionary, ed. J.A. Murray, et al. Oxford U.P., 1970.

Paddle-to-the-Sea
Holling, Holling C. *Paddle-to-the-Sea.* Houghton Mifflin, 1941.

The Palace Guard
Rather, Dan, and Gary P. Gates. *The Palace Guard.* Harper & Row, 1975.

A Palm for Mrs. Pollifax
Gilman, Dorothy. *A Palm for Mrs. Pollifax.* Doubleday, 1973.

Pamela
Richardson, Samuel. *Pamela.* Norton, 1958.

Pansies
Lawrence, D.H. *Pansies.* P.R. Stephensen, 1929.

Pantagruel
Rabelais, François. *Pantagruel.* French and European Pubn., 1964.

Papillon
Charrière, Henri. *Papillon.* Pocket Books, 1973.

Paradise Lost
Milton, John. *Paradise Lost,* ed. Scott Elledge. Norton, 1975.

Parish
Parish, James Robert. *Actors' Television Credits, 1950–1972.* Scarecrow Press, 1973.

Parrinder
Parrinder, Geoffrey. *Dictionary of Non-Christian Religions.* Westminster Press, 1971.

Parzival
Von Eschenbach, Wolfram. *Parzival.* Random House, 1961.

Patience
Gilbert, W.S. "Patience" in *The Complete Plays of Gilbert and Sullivan.* Norton, 1976.

A Pattern of Roses
Peyton, K.M. *A Pattern of Roses.* Thomas Y. Crowell, 1973.

Payton
Payton, Geoffrey. *Webster's Dictionary of Proper Names.* G. & C. Merriam, 1970.

Pendennis
Thackeray, William M. *The History of Pendennis.* Harper, 1864.

Pensées
Pascal, Blaise. *Pensées,* tr. A.J. Krailsheimer. Penguin, 1966.

Pepita Jimenez
Valera, Juan. *Pepita Jimenez,* tr. Harriet De Onis. Barron's, 1965.

Perceval
de Troyes, Chrétien. *Le Roman de Perceval.* Droz, 1959.

Père Goriot
Balzac, Honoré de. *Père Goriot.* Modern Library, 1950.

Pericles
Shakespeare, William. *Pericles,* ed. F.D. Hoeniger. Barnes & Noble, 1963.

Peter Churchmouse
Austin, Margot. *Peter Churchmouse.* Dutton, 1941.

The Peterkin Papers
Hale, Lucretia. *The Peterkin Papers.* Dover, 1960.

Peter Pan
Barrie, James M. *Peter Pan.* Grosset and Dunlap, 1970.

Peter Schlemihl
Chamisso, Adelbert von. *Peter Schlemihl's Remarkable Story,* ed. Fred Honig. Arc Books, 1964.

Phormio
Terence. *Phormio,* tr. Frank O. Copley. Bobbs-Merrill, 1958.

Phyfe
Phyfe, William Henry P. *5000 Facts and Fancies.* Gale, 1966.

Pickwick Papers
Dickens, Charles. *Pickwick Papers,* ed. Robert L. Patten. Penguin, 1975.

The Picture of Dorian Gray
Wilde, Oscar. *The Picture of Dorian Gray.* Dell, 1956.

Pierce
Pierce, Gilbert Ashville. *The Dickens Dictionary.* Haskell House, reprint of 1878 ed.

Pilgrim's Progress
Bunyan, John. *Pilgrim's Progress.* Holt, 1949.

The Pilot
Cooper, James Fenimore. *The Pilot.* Townsend, 1859.

Pinky Pye
Estes, Eleanor. *Pinky Pye.* Harcourt, 1958.

Pinocchio
Collodi, Carlo. *Pinocchio,* tr. E. Harden. Penguin, Puffin, 1972.

Pippi Longstocking
Lindgren, Astrid. *Pippi Longstocking.* Viking Press, 1950.

The Pirates of Penzance
Gilbert, W.S. and Arthur Sullivan. "The Pirates of Penzance" in *The Complete Plays of Gilbert and Sullivan.* Norton, 1976.

The Pit
Norris, Frank. *The Pit: A Story of Chicago.* Bentley, 1971.

The Plague
Camus, Albert. *The Plague.* Random House, 1972.

Plain Speaking
Miller, Merle. *Plain Speaking*. Berkley, 1974.

Plays of Strindberg
Strindberg, August. *Plays of Strindberg*, tr. Michael Meyer, 2 vols. Random House, 1976.

Plays Unpleasant
Shaw, George Bernard. *Plays Unpleasant*. Penguin, 1950.

Pliny
Pliny. *Natural History*, 11 vols. Harvard U.P., 1962.

Plumb
Plumb, J.H. *The Horizon Book of the Renaissance*, ed. Richard Ketchum, et al. American Heritage, 1961.

Plutarch's Lives
Plutarch. *Plutarch's Lives*, ed. Edmund Fuller. Dell, 1968.

Plutus
Aristophanes. *Plutus*. W.B. Clive, 1889.

Poe
Poe, Edgar A. *Collected Works of Edgar Allan Poe, vol. 1: Poems*, ed. Thomas O. Mabbott. Harvard U.P., 1969.

Pollyanna
Porter, Eleanor. *Pollyanna*. A.L. Burt, 1913.

Pope
Pope, Alexander. *Poems of Alexander Pope*, ed. John Butt. Yale U.P., 1963.

Portable Poe
Poe, Edgar Allan. *The Portable Edgar Allan Poe*, ed. Philip Van Doren Stern. Viking Press, 1972.

Portrait of the Artist as a Young Man
Joyce, James. *A Portrait of the Artist as a Young Man*. Penguin, 1977.

Potiphar Papers
Curtis, George W. *The Potiphar Papers*. AMS Press, 1970.

Pot of Gold
Plautus. *The Pot of Gold and Other Plays*, tr. E.F. Watling. Penguin, 1965.

Les Précieuses Ridicules
Molière, Jean P. *Les Précieuses Ridicules*. French and European Pubn., 1965.

Pride and Prejudice
Austen, Jane. *Pride and Prejudice*. Oxford U.P., 1975.

The Prince
Machiavelli, Niccolo. *The Prince*. St. Martin's Press, 1964.

The Prince and the Pauper
Twain, Mark. *The Prince and the Pauper*. Macmillan, 1962.

Prince Caspian
Lewis, C.S. *Prince Caspian*. Macmillan, 1951.

Prince Prigio
Lang, Andrew. *Prince Prigio and Prince Ricardo*. Dutton, 1961.

The Prisoner of Zenda
Hope, Anthony. *The Prisoner of Zenda*. New American Library, 1974.

Private Lives
Coward, Noel. *Private Lives*. Doubleday, 1930.

Profiles in Courage
Kennedy, John F. *Profiles in Courage*. Harper & Row, 1964.

Psychomachia
Prudentius. "Psychomachia" in *Works*. Harvard U.P., 1942.

Puck of Pook's Hill
Kipling, Rudyard. *Puck of Pook's Hill*. Dover, 1968.

Pumping Iron
Gaines, Charles, and George Butler. *Pumping Iron*. Simon and Schuster, 1974.

Pygmalion
Shaw, George Bernard. *Pygmalion*. New American Library, 1975.

Queenie Peavy
Burch, Robert. *Queenie Peavy*. Viking Press, 1966.

Quennell
Quennell, Peter, and Hamish Johnson. *Who's Who in Shakespeare*. Weidenfeld and Nicholson, 1973.

Quentin Durward
Scott, Sir Walter. *Quentin Durward*. Dutton, 1965.

Rabbit Hill
Lawson, Robert. *Rabbit Hill.* Dell, 1968.

Racketty Packetty House
Burnett, Frances Hodgson. *Racketty Packetty House.* Lippincott, 1975.

Radford
Radford, Edwin. *Unusual Words and How They Came About.* Philosophical Library, 1946.

Ragan
Ragan, David. *Who's Who in Hollywood.* Arlington House, 1976.

Ragged Dick
Alger, Horatio. *Ragged Dick and Mark the Match Boy.* Macmillan, 1962.

Raggedy Ann Stories
Gruelle, John B. *Raggedy Ann Stories.* Volland, 1918.

The Railway Children
Nesbit, Edith. *The Railway Children.* British Book Centre, 1974.

Ralph Roister Doister
Udall, Nicholas. *Ralph Roister Doister.* J.M. Dent, 1901.

Ramage *French*
Ramage, Crauford Tait. *Familiar Quotations from French and Italian Authors.* Gale, 1968.

Ramage *German*
Ramage, Crauford Tait. *Familiar Quotations from German and Spanish Authors.* Gale, 1968.

Ramage *Greek*
Ramage, Crauford Tait. *Familiar Quotations from Greek Authors.* Gale, 1968.

Ramayana
Valmiki. *Ramayana,* tr. Chakravarti Rajagopalachari. InterCulture, 1974.

The Rape of Lucrece
Shakespeare, William. *The Rape of Lucrece.* British Book Centre, 1974.

Rape of the Lock
Pope, Alexander. *The Rape of the Lock,* ed. J.S. Cunningham. Oxford U.P., 1966.

Rapunzel
Grimm Brothers. *Rapunzel.* Crowell, 1975.

Rebecca of Sunnybrook Farm
Wiggin, Kate Douglas. *Rebecca of Sunnybrook Farm.* Macmillan, 1962.

The Red Badge of Courage
Crane, Stephen. *The Red Badge of Courage.* Macmillan, 1966.

Redburn
Melville, Herman. *Redburn.* Northwestern U.P., 1969.

The Red Pony.
Steinbeck, John. *The Red Pony.* Viking Press, 1959.

The Rehearsal
Villiers, George. *The Rehearsal.* Folcroft, 1976.

The Relapse
Vanbrugh, John. *The Relapse,* ed. Curt Zimansky. Univ. of Nebraska Press, 1970.

Reliques
Percy, Thomas. *Reliques of Ancient English Poesy,* ed. Henry B. Wheatley. Dover, 1966.

Remembrance of Things Past
Proust, Marcel. *Remembrance of Things Past.* Random House, 1934.

Renée Mauperin
de Goncourt, Edmond and Jules. *Renée Mauperin.* Fasquelle, 1920.

The Republic
Plato. *The Republic,* ed. Allan Bloom. Basic Books, 1968.

The Rescuers
Sharp, Margery. *The Rescuers.* Dell, 1974.

The Return of the Native
Hardy, Thomas. *The Return of the Native.* New American Library, Signet, 1973.

Reynard the Fox
Reynard the Fox, ed. Roy Brown. Abelard-Schuman, 1969.

RHD
The Random House Dictionary of the English Language, ed. Jess Stein, et al. Random House, 1973.

Richard II
Shakespeare, William. *Richard II.* Oxford U.P., 1966.

Richard III
Shakespeare, William. *Richard III,* ed. R.E. Houghton. Oxford U.P., 1965.

Riders to the Sea
Synge, John Millington. *Riders to the Sea.* Irish Academic Press, 1972

The Rime of the Ancient Mariner
Coleridge, Samuel Taylor. "The Rime of the Ancient Mariner" in *the Oxford Book of English Verse,* ed. A. Quiller-Couch. Oxford U.P., 1939.

The Ring and the Book
Browning, Robert. *The Ring and the Book.* Dutton, 1962.

The Ring of the Nibelung
Wagner, Richard. *The Ring of the Nibelung.* Scribner, 1975.

The Rise of Silas Lapham
Howells, William Dean. *The Rise of Silas Lapham.* Indiana U.P., 1971.

The Rivals
Sheridan, Richard B. *The Rivals.* Oxford U.P., 1968.

Rob Roy
Scott, Sir Walter. *Rob Roy.* Dutton, 1973.

Robin Hood
Robin Hood, ed. J. Ritson. Rowman, 1972.

Robinson Crusoe
Defoe, Daniel. *Robinson Crusoe,* ed. J. Donald Crowley. Oxford U.P., 1972.

Rockwell
Norman Rockwell's Christmas Book, ed. Lena Tabori Fried and Ruth Eisenstein. Abrams, 1977.

Roderick Hudson
James, Henry. *Roderick Hudson.* Houghton Mifflin, 1977.

Roderick Random
Smollett, Tobias. *Roderick Random.* New American Library, 1964.

Rogers
Rogers, May. *The Waverly Dictionary.* Gale, 1967.

Roller Skates
Sawyer, Ruth. *Roller Skates.* Dell, 1969.

Romeo and Juliet
Shakespeare, William. *Romeo and Juliet,* ed. Maynard Mack and Robert Boynton. Hayden, 1975.

Romola
Eliot, George. *Romola* in *The Complete Works of George Eliot.* Harper, n.d.

The Rose and the Ring
Thackeray, William Makepeace. *The Rose and the Ring.* Pierpont Morgan Library, 1947.

Rosie's Walk
Hutchins, Pat. *Rosie's Walk.* Macmillan, 1968.

Rosemary's Baby
Levin, Ira. *Rosemary's Baby.* Random House, 1967.

Rosten
Rosten, Leo. *The Joys of Yiddish.* McGraw-Hill, 1968.

Rovin
Rovin, Jeff. *The Great Television Series.* A.S. Barnes, 1977.

Roxana, the Fortunate Mistress
Defoe, Daniel. *Roxana, the Fortunate Mistress.* Oxford U.P., 1964.

Roxy
Eggleston, Edward. *Roxy.* Gregg Press, 1968.

The Royal Family
Kaufmann, George S., and Edna Ferber. *The Royal Family.* French, 1929.

Ruddigore
in *The Complete Plays of Gilbert and Sullivan.* Norton, 1976.

Rumpelstiltskin
Grimm Brothers. *Rumpelstiltskin.* Scholastic Book Service, 1974.

R.U.R.
Čapek, Karel. *R.U.R.* Oxford U.P., 1961.

Ship of Fools
Porter, Katherine Anne. *Ship of Fools.* Norton, 1972.

Ryland
Ryland, Frederick. *Chronological Outlines of English Literature.* Gale, 1968.

Sacco-Vanzetti Case: A Transcript
Sacco-Vanzetti Case: A Transcript of the Trial of Nicola Sacco and Bartolomeo Vanzetti in the Courts of Massachusetts and Subsequent Proceedings, 1920–27. 2nd edition. ed. Paul P. Appel. Appel, 1969.

St. Ronan's Well
Scott, Sir Walter. *St. Ronan's Well* in *Complete Works.* Houghton, 1923.

Saints and Festivals
Brewster, H. Pomeroy. *Saints and Festivals of the Christian Church.* Gale, 1974.

Samson Agonistes
Milton, John. "Samson Agonistes" in *Compact Milton,* ed. H.S. Taylor. Barron's, 1967.

Sanctuary
Faulkner, William. *Sanctuary.* New American Library, 1968.

Sann
Sann, Paul. *Fads, Follies and Delusions of the American People.* Crown Publishers, 1967.

Sartoris
Faulkner, William. *Sartoris.* Random House, 1966.

Sartor Resartus
Carlyle, Thomas. *Sartor Resartus.* Scholarly Press, 1977.

The Saturdays
Enright, Elizabeth. *The Saturdays.* Dell, 1966.

Satyricon
Petronius. *Satyricon.* New American Library, 1960.

The Scarlet Letter
Hawthorne, Nathaniel. *The Scarlet Letter: A Romance.* Oxford U.P., 1965.

The Scarlet Pimpernel
Orczy, Emmuska. *The Scarlet Pimpernel.* New American Library, 1974.

Scarlet Sister Mary
Peterkin, Julie. *Scarlet Sister Mary.* Berg, 1929.

Scholes
Scholes, Percy A., ed. *The Oxford Companion to Music,* 10th edition. rev. John Owen Ward. Oxford U.P., 1972.

The School for Scandal
Sheridan, Richard B. *The School for Scandal,* ed. C.J. Price. Oxford U.P., 1971.

The School for Wives
Molière, Jean P. *The School for Wives,* tr. Richard Wilbur. Harcourt, Brace Jovanovich, 1972.

The Seagull
Chekhov, Anton. *The Seagull,* tr. Jean-Claude Van Itallie. Harper & Row, 1977.

Second Shepherds' Play
Second Shepherds' Play in *Specimens of Pre-Shaksperian Drama,* ed. J.M. Manly, vol. 1. Dover, 1967.

The Secret Garden
Burnett, Frances H. *The Secret Garden.* Lippincott, 1962.

The Secret Language
Nordstrom, Ursula. *The Secret Language.* Harper, 1960.

Sense and Sensibility
Austen, Jane. *Sense and Sensibility.* Oxford U.P., 1975.

Septimus and the Danedyke Mystery
Chance, Stephen. *Septimus and the Danedyke Mystery.* Nelson, 1973.

Seraphina
Harris, Mary K. *Seraphina.* Faber, 1960.

Seven Against Thebes
Aeschylus. *Seven Against Thebes,* ed. Christopher Dawson. Prentice-Hall, 1970.

Sexual Politics
Millett, Kate. *Sexual Politics.* Avon, 1973.

Shamela Andrews
Baker, Sheridan. *Shamela and Joseph Andrews.* Thomas Y. Crowell, 1972.

Sharp
Sharp, Harold and Marjorie Z. *Index to Characters in the Performing Arts.* 4 vols.: Part 1—Non-Musical Plays, 1966; Part 2—Opera & Musical Productions, 1969; Part 3—Ballets A to Z and Symbols, 1972; Part 4—Radio and Television, 1973. Scarecrow Press.

Shepard
Shepard, Leslie. *History of Street Literature.* Gale, 1973.

Sheridan
Sheridan, Martin. *Comics and Their Creators.* Hyperion Press, 1971.

Sherlock Holmes
Baring-Gould, William S. *The Annotated Sherlock Holmes.* Clarkson N. Potter, 1967.

Shirer
Shirer, William L. *The Rise and Fall of the Third Reich.* Fawcett World, 1972.

Short Friday
Singer, Isaac Bashevis. *Short Friday.* Fawcett Crest, 1964.

Shosha
Singer, Isaac Bashevis. *Shosha.* Farrar, Straus & Giroux, 1978.

Siddhartha
Hesse, Hermann. *Siddhartha.* tr. Hilda Rosner. New Directions, 1951.

The Silver Chair
Lewis, C.S. *The Silver Chair.* Macmillan, 1970.

Simon
Simon, George T. *Simon Says: The Sights and Sounds of the Swing Era 1935–1955.* Galahad Books, 1971.

Simplicissimus
von Grimmelshausen, H.J.C. *Simplicissimus the Vagabond,* tr. A.T. Goodrich. Folcroft, 1978.

Sir Gawain and the Green Knight
Sir Gawain and the Green Knight in *The Age of Chaucer* [Vol. I, *Penguin Guide to English Literature*]. Penguin, 1954.

Sir Launcelot Greaves
Smollett, Tobias. *Sir Launcelot Greaves,* ed. David Evans. Oxford U.P., 1973.

Sirga
Guillot, Rene. *Sirga.* S.G. Phillips, 1959.

Six Modern Short Novels
Six Great Modern Short Novels. Dell, 1964.

The Sketch Book of Geoffrey Crayon, Gentleman
Irving, Washington. *The Sketch Book of Geoffrey Crayon, Gentleman.* Twayne, 1978.

Sketches by Boz
Dickens, Charles. *Sketches by Boz.* Dutton, 1968.

Slaughterhouse-Five
Vonnegut, Kurt. *Slaughterhouse-Five.* Dell, 1971.

The Small House at Allington
Trollope, Anthony. *The Small House at Allington.* Dutton, 1972.

Smith
Garfield, Leon. *Smith.* Pantheon, 1967.

Smithsonian
Smithsonian, November 1977.

Snark
Carroll, Lewis. *The Hunting of the Snark.* Clarkson N. Potter, 1975.

The Snowy Day
Keats, Ezra Jack. *The Snowy Day.* Viking Press, 1962.

Sobel
Sobel, Bernard. *The New Theatre Handbook and Digest of Plays.* Crown, 1959.

Soldiers of Fortune
Davis, Richard Harding. *Soldiers of Fortune.* Scholarly Press, 1971.

Song of Igor's Campaign
Song of Igor's Campaign, tr. Vladimir Nabokov. McGraw-Hill, 1975.

Song of Roland
The Song of Roland, tr. Dorothy Sayers. Penguin, 1957.

Song of the Cid
Song of the Cid, tr. J.G. Markley. Bobbs-Merrill, 1961.

Sophocles Two
Sophocles Two, ed. David Grene and Richard Lattimore. Univ. of Chicago Press, 1957.

Sordello
Browning, Robert. "Sordello" in *Poems of Robert Browning,* ed. Donald Smalley. Houghton Mifflin, 1956.

The Sot-Weed Factor
Barth, John. *The Sot-Weed Factor.* Bantam, 1969.

Southwick *Quizzism*
Southwick, Albert P. *Quizzism and Its Key.* Gale, 1970.

Southwick *Wisps*
Southwick, Albert P. *Wisps of Wit and Wisdom.* Gale, 1968.

Spain
Spain: A History in Art, ed. Bradley Smith. Doubleday, 1971.

Sparks
Sparks, John. *Bird Behavior.* Bantam, 1971.

Spevack
Spevack, Marvin. ed. *Harvard Concordance to Shakespeare.* Belknap, 1974.

Spiller
Spiller, Robert, et al. *Literary History of the United States,* 3rd ed. Macmillan, 1963.

Spoon River Anthology
Masters, Edgar Lee. *Spoon River Anthology.* Macmillan, 1968.

Sports Illustrated
"Inside the Eagle's Nest" in *Sports Illustrated,* February 15, 1979, pp. 142–143.

Springhaven
Blackmore, Richard. *Springhaven.* Harper., 1887.

The Spy
Cooper, James Fenimore. *The Spy.* Popular Library, 1971.

Stalky and Company
Kipling, Rudyard. *Stalky and Company.* Dell, 1968.

Stauffer
Stauffer, Francis H. *The Queer, the Quaint, and the Quizzical.* Gale, 1968.

Stefansson
Stefansson, Vilhjalmur. *Adventures in Error.* Gale, 1970.

Steppenwolf
Hesse, Hermann. *Steppenwolf.* Holt, Rinehart, Winston, 1970.

Stimpson
Stimpson, George W. *Nuggets of Knowledge.* Gale, 1970.

Stimpson *Questions*
Stimpson, George W. *Popular Questions Answered.* Gale, 1970.

The Stone-Faced Boy
Fox, Paula. *The Stone-Faced Boy.* Scholastic Book Service, 1972.

Stories
Cheever, John. *The Stories of John Cheever.* Knopf, 1978.

The Story About Ping
Flack, Marjorie. *The Story About Ping.* Viking, 1970.

The Story of Ferdinand
Leaf, Munro. *The Story of Ferdinand.* Viking Press, 1969.

Stranger in a Strange Land
Heinlein, Robert. *Stranger in a Strange Land.* Putnam, 1972.

Strawberry Girl
Lenski, Lois. *Strawberry Girl.* Lippincott, 1945.

A Streetcar Named Desire.
Williams, Tennessee. *A Streetcar Named Desire.* New Directions, 1947.

The Sun Also Rises
Hemingway, Ernest. *The Sun Also Rises.* Scribner, 1926.

Swiss Family Robinson
Wyss, Johann. *Swiss Family Robinson.* Grosset and Dunlap, 1970.

Sylvester and the Magic Pebble
Steig, William. *Sylvester and the Magic Pebble.* Dutton, 1973.

Sylvestre Bonnard
France, Anatole. *The Crime of Sylvestre Bonnard.* Dodd Mead, 1924.

The Tale of Benjamin Bunny
Potter, Beatrix. *The Tale of Benjamin Bunny.* Dover, 1974.

The Tale of Genji
Murasaki, Lady Shikibu. *The Tale of Genji.* Modern Library, 1960.

The Tale of Peter Rabbit
Potter, Beatrix. *The Tale of Peter Rabbit.* Dover, 1972.

A Tale of Two Cities
Dickens, Charles. *A Tale of Two Cities,* ed. George Woodcock. Penguin, 1970.

Tales of Hoffmann
Hoffmann, E.T.A. *Tales of Hoffmann,* tr. Michael Bullock. Frederick Ungar, 1963.

Tales of Terror
Poe, Edgar Allan. *Tales of Terror and Fantasy.* Dutton, 1972.

Tales of the Genii
Tales of the Genii, tr. James Ridley. Harrap, 1919.

The Talisman
Scott, Sir Walter. *The Talisman.* Dutton, 1972.

The Taming of the Shrew
Shakespeare, William. *The Taming of the Shrew,* ed. George L. Kittredge and Irving Ribner. John Wiley, 1966.

Tartarin de Tarascon
Daudet, Alphonse. *Tartarin de Tarascon.* French and European Pubn., 1965.

Tartuffe
Molière, Jean. *Tartuffe,* ed. Hallam Walker. Prentice-Hall, 1969.

Tarzan of the Apes
Burroughs, Edgar Rice. *Tarzan of the Apes.* Grosset and Dunlap, 1973.

Taylor
Taylor, Margaret Fisk. *A Time to Dance.* United Church Press, 1967.

The Tempest
Shakespeare, William. *The Tempest,* ed. Leonard Nathanson. William C. Brown, 1969.

Tender Is the Night
Fitzgerald, F. Scott. *Tender Is the Night.* Scribner, 1960.

Terrace
Terrace, Vincent. *The Complete Encyclopedia of Television Programs, 1947–1976.* 2 vols. A.S. Barnes, 1976.

Tess of the D'Urbervilles
Hardy, Thomas. *Tess of the D'Urbervilles,* ed. Scott Elledge. Norton, 1966.

Thebaid
Statius. *The Thebaid.* Adolt M. Hakkert, 1968.

The Thin Man
Hammett, Dashiell. *The Thin Man.* Random House, 1972.

This Side of Paradise
Fitzgerald, F. Scott. *This Side of Paradise.* Scribner, 1920.

Thompson
Thompson, Oscar. *International Cyclopedia of Music and Musicians,* 10th rev. ed. Dodd, 1975.

Thorne *Facts*
Thorne, Robert. *Fugitive Facts.* Gale, 1969.

The Three Musketeers
Dumas, Alexandre, père. *The Three Musketeers.* Hart, 1975.

Three Princes of Serendip
Hodges, Elizabeth J. *Three Princes of Serendip.* Atheneum, 1964.

The Three Royal Monkeys
de la Mare, Walter. *The Three Royal Monkeys.* Knopf, 1948.

The Three Toymakers
Williams, Ursula Moray. *The Three Toymakers.* Hamish Hamilton, 1945.

Through the Looking-glass
Carroll, Lewis. *Through the Looking-glass.* Random House, 1946.

Thyestes
Seneca. *Thyestes,* tr. Moses Hadas. Bobbs-Merrill, 1957.

Tiger at the Gates
Giraudoux, Jean. *Tiger at the Gates.* Oxford U.P., 1955.

Till Ulenspiegel
DeCoster, Charles T. *The Legend of the Glorious Adventures of Tyl Ulenspiegel in the Land of Flanders and Elsewhere.*Hyperion Press, 1978.

Timbs
Timbs, John. *Historic Ninepins.* Gale, 1969.

Timbs *Things*
Timbs, John. *Things Not Generally Known.* Gale, 1968.

Time of Trial
Burton, Hester. *Time of Trial.* Dell, 1970.

The Time Machine
Wells, H.G. *The Time Machine.* Bantam, 1968.

Timon of Athens
Shakespeare, William. *Timon of Athens,* ed. H.J. Oliver. Barnes & Noble, 1958.

'Tis Pity She's A Whore
Ford, John. *'Tis Pity She's A Whore.* Hill and Wang, 1969.

Titus Andronicus
Shakespeare, William. *Titus Andronicus,* ed. J.C. Maxwell. Barnes & Noble, 1968.

Tobacco Road
Caldwell, Erskine. *Tobacco Road.* New American Library, Signet, 1970.

Toby Tyler
Otis, James. *Toby Tyler.* Scholastic Book Service, 1972.

To Have and Have Not
Hemingway, Ernest. *To Have and Have Not.* Scribner, 1937.

Toland
Toland, John. *The Rising Sun.* Bantam Books, 1971.

Tom Brown's School Days
Hughes, Thomas. *Tom Brown's School Days.* Airmont, 1968.

Tom Jones
Fielding, Henry. *Tom Jones,* ed. W. Somerset Maugham. Fawcett World, 1969.

Tom Sawyer
Twain, Mark. *Tom Sawyer.* Washington Square Press, 1972.

Tom Thumb the Great
Fielding, Henry. *Tom Thumb and the Tragedy of Tragedies.* Univ. of California Press, 1970.

Tom's Midnight Garden
Pearce, Philippa. *Tom's Midnight Garden.* Lippincott, 1959.

Torrie
Johnson, Annabel and Edgar. *Torrie.* Harper & Row, 1960.

Tortilla Flat
Steinbeck, John. *Tortilla Flat.* Viking Press, 1935.

The Tower Treasure
Dixon, Franklin W. *The Tower Treasure.* Grosset and Dunlap, 1927.

Traveller
Goldsmith, Oliver. *Traveller, Or, a Prospect of Society.* British Book Centre, 1975.

Travels of Marco Polo
Polo, Marco. *Travels of Marco Polo.* Dutton, Everyman, 1954.

Treasure Island
Stevenson, Robert Louis. *Treasure Island.* Macmillan, 1962.

Treat
Treat, Roger. *The Encyclopedia of Football.* A.S. Barnes, 1977.

The Trial
Kafka, Franz. *The Trial.* Random House, 1969.

Trial by Jury
in *The Complete Plays of Gilbert and Sullivan.* Norton, 1976.

A Trick to Catch the Old One
Middleton, Thomas. *A Trick to Catch the Old One.* Univ. of California Press, 1968.

Trilby
DuMaurier, George. *Trilby.* Dutton, 1953.

Tristan
Von Strassburg, Gottfried. *Tristan,* tr. Arthur T. Hatto. Penguin, 1960.

Tristan and Isolde
Wagner, Richard. *Tristan and Isolde: Complete Orchestral Score.* Dover, 1973.

Troilus and Cressida
Shakespeare, William. *Troilus and Cressida,* ed. Arthur Quiller-Couch, et al. Cambridge U.P., 1969.

The Trojan Women
Euripides. *The Trojan Women,* tr. Gilbert Murray. Oxford U.P., 1915.

Tropic of Cancer
Miller, Henry. *Tropic of Cancer.* Ballantine, 1975.

Turkin
Turkin, Hy, and S.C. Thompson. *The Official Encyclopedia of Baseball,* 9th ed. A.S. Barnes, 1977.

Turner
Turner, Michael R., and Anthony Miall, eds. *The Parlour Song Book.* Viking Press, 1972.

The Turn of the Screw
James, Henry. *The Turn of the Screw.* Dell, 1956.

Twelfth Night
Shakespeare, William. *Twelfth Night,* ed. T.H. Howard-Hill. William C. Brown, 1969.

Twelve Famous Plays
Twelve Famous Plays of the Restoration and Eighteenth Century. Modern Library, 1933.

The Twenty-One Balloons
DuBois, William Pène. *The Twenty-One Balloons.* Dell, 1969.

Twenty Thousand Leagues Under the Sea
Verne, Jules. *Twenty Thousand Leagues Under the Sea,* tr. Mendor Brunetti. New American Library, Signet, 1969.

The Twisted Claw
Dixon, Franklin D. *The Twisted Claw.* Grosset and Dunlap, 1939.

Two Gentlemen of Verona
Shakespeare, William. *Two Gentlemen of Verona,* ed. George L. Kittredge and Irving Ribner. John Wiley, 1969.

Tyler, Wilkin, and Skee
Burch, Robert. *Tyler, Wilkin, and Skee.* Dell, 1971.

Uncle Remus
Harris, Joel C. *Uncle Remus: His Songs and Sayings.* Grosset and Dunlap, 1974.

Uncle Tom's Cabin.
Stowe, Harriet Beecher. *Uncle Tom's Cabin.* Dutton, 1961.

Uncle Vanya
Chekhov, Anton. *Uncle Vanya.* Avon, 1974.

The Uncommercial Traveller
Dickens, Charles. *The Uncommercial Traveller.* Dutton, 1970.

Understood Betsy
Fisher, Dorothy. *Understood Betsy.* Grosset and Dunlap, 1970.

Under the Yoke
Vazov, Ivan. *Under the Yoke.* Heinemann, 1912.

The Undiscovered Country
Howells, William D. *The Undiscovered Country.* Scholarly Press, 1971.

Universal Dictionary
Bailey, Nathan. *Universal Etymological English Dictionary.* Adler's Foreign Books, 1969.

Up Eel River
Montague, Margaret P. *Up Eel River.* Arno, facsimile of 1928 ed.

Upstairs, Downstairs
Hawkesworth, John. *Upstairs, Downstairs.* Ulverscroft, 1976.

Utopia
More, St. Thomas. *Utopia,* ed. Edward Surtz. Yale U.P., 1964.

V.
Pynchon, Thomas. *V.* Lippincott, 1961.

Van Doren
Van Doren, Charles, et al., eds. *Webster's Guide to American History.* G. & C. Merriam, 1971.

Vanity Fair
Thackeray, William M. *Vanity Fair.* Dutton, 1972.

Vargas
Austin, Reid, and Alberto Vargas. *Vargas.* Crown, 1980.

Vathek
Beckford, William. *Vathek.* Oxford U.P., 1970.

The Velveteen Rabbit
Williams, Margery. *The Velveteen Rabbit.* Doubleday, 1958.

The Vicar of Bullhampton
Trollope, Anthony. *The Vicar of Bullhampton.* Oxford U.P., 1975.

The Vicar of Wakefield
Goldsmith, Oliver. *The Vicar of Wakefield.* Dutton, 1956.

The Village
Bunin, Ivan. *The Village,* tr. I. Hapgood. Fertig, 1975.

Villon
Villon. *Poems,* tr. Peter Dale. St. Martin's Press, 1973.

The Virginians
Thackeray, William M. *The Virginians*. Smith, Elder, 1886.

La Vita Nuova
Dante's Vita Nuova, tr. Mark Musa. Indiana U.P., 1973.

Vizetelly
Vizetelly, Frank H., and Leander J. DeBekker. *Desk-Book of Idioms and Idiomatic Phrases in English Speech and Literature*. Gale, 1970.

Volsung Saga
Volsung Saga, tr. William Morris. Macmillan, 1962.

Voyage of the 'Dawn Treader'
Lewis, C.S. *The Voyage of the 'Dawn Treader.'* Macmillan, 1970.

Voyage to the Moon
Verne, Jules. *Voyage to the Moon*. Harmony Books, 1977.

Walden
Thoreau, Henry David. *Walden*. Macmillan, 1966.

Wallechinsky
Wallechinsky, David, et al. *The Book of Lists*. William Morrow, 1977.

Walsh *Information*
Walsh, William S. *A Handy Book of Curious Information*. Gale, 1970.

Walsh *Classical*
Walsh, William S. *Heroes and Heroines of Fiction: Classical, Medieval, Legendary*. Gale, 1966.

Walsh *Curiosities*
Walsh, William S. *A Handy Book of Literary Curiosities*. Gale, 1966.

Walsh *Modern*
Walsh, William S. *Heroes and Heroines of Fiction: Modern Prose and Poetry*. Gale, 1966.

The Wandering Jew
Sue, Eugène. *The Wandering Jew*. Modern Library, n.d.

The Water Babies
Kingsley, Charles. *The Water Babies*. Hart, 1977.

Watership Down
Adams, Richard. *Watership Down*. Macmillan, 1974.

Waverley
Scott, Sir Walter. *Waverley*. Dutton, 1969.

Webster's Sports
Webster's Sports Dictionary. G. & C. Merriam, 1976.

Weiss
Weiss, Irving and Anne D. *Thesaurus of Book Digests 1950–1980*. Crown, 1981.

Wells
Wells, Carolyn. *A Whimsey Anthology*. Gale, 1976.

Wentworth
Wentworth, Harold, and S.B. Flexner. *Dictionary of American Slang*, 2nd supplemented ed. Thomas Y. Crowell, 1975.

Werner Bischof
Capa, Cornell. *Werner Bischof*. Grossman, 1974.

Westerman
Westerman, Gerhart von. *Opera Guide*. Dutton, 1968.

West Side Story
Bernstein, Leonard, et al. *West Side Story*. Random House, 1958.

What Makes Sammy Run
Schulberg, Budd. *What Makes Sammy Run* Random House, 1941.

Wheeler
Wheeler, William A. *Dictionary of the Noted Names of Fiction*. Gale, 1966.

Wheeler *Allusions*
Wheeler, William A. *Familiar Allusions*. Gale, 1966.

Where the Wild Things Are
Sendak, Maurice. *Where the Wild Things Are*. Harper & Row, 1963.

White
White, T.H. *The Book of Beasts*. Jonathan Cape, 1954.

The White Archer
Houston, James. *The White Archer: An Eskimo Legend*. Harcourt Brace Jovanovich, 1967.

The White Devil
Webster, John. *The White Devil*. Chandler, 1961.

White Fang
London, Jack. *White Fang.* Macmillan, 1935.

White Jacket
Melville, Herman. *White Jacket.* Holt, 1967.

Wieland
Brown, Charles Brockden. *Wieland.* Harcourt Brace Jovanovich, 1969.

Wigoder
Wigoder, Geoffrey, ed. *Encyclopedic Dictionary of Judaica.* Leon Amiel, 1974.

Wild Jack
Christopher, John. *Wild Jack.* Macmillan, 1974.

William Tell
Schiller, Friedrich Von. *William Tell,* tr. Sidney E. Kaplan. Barron's, 1954.

William the Dragon
Donnison, Polly. *William the Dragon.* Coward, McCann and Geoghegan, 1973.

The Wind in the Willows
Grahame, Kenneth. *The Wind in the Willows.* Dell, 1969.

Wind, Sand and Stars
De Saint-Exupéry, Antoine. *Wind, Sand and Stars.* Harcourt Brace Jovanovich, 1967.

Winesburg, Ohio
Anderson, Sherwood. *Winesburg, Ohio.* Viking Press, 1960.

Winnie-the-Pooh
Milne, A.A. *Winnie-the-Pooh,* Dell, 1974.

The Winter's Tale
Shakespeare, William. *The Winter's Tale,* in *William Shakespeare: The Complete Works,* ed. Peter Alexander. Collins, 1951.

The Witch's Daughter
Bawden, Nina. *The Witch's Daughter.* Lippincott, 1966.

A Wizard of Earthsea
LeGuin, Ursula. *A Wizard of Earthsea.* Bantam, 1975.

The Wolfman
Dreadstone, Carl. *The Wolfman.* Berkley, 1977.

The Woman of Rome
Moravia, Alberto. *The Woman of Rome,* tr. Lydia Holland. Manor Books, 1948.

The Wonderful Adventures of Nils
Lagerlof, Selma. *The Wonderful Adventures of Nils.* Pantheon, 1947.

The Wonderful Adventures of Paul Bunyon
The Wonderful Adventures of Paul Bunyon, retold by Louis Untermeyer. Heritage, c. 1945.

The Wonderful Wizard of Oz
Baum, L. Frank. *The Wonderful Wizard of Oz.* Random House, 1972.

The Wondrous Tale of Alroy
Disraeli, Benjamin. *The Wondrous Tale of Alroy.* Carey, Lea, and Blanchard, 1833.

Woods
Woods, George Benjamin, and Jerome Buckley, eds. *Poetry of the Victorian Period.* Scott Foresman, 1955.

Woodstock
Scott, Sir Walter. *Woodstock.* Dutton, 1969.

WB
World Book Encyclopedia. World Book-Childcraft International, 1979.

Yankee Thunder
Shapiro, Irwin. *Yankee Thunder: The Legendary Life of Davy Crockett.* Julian Messner, 1944.

The Yearling
Rawlings, Marjorie K. *The Yearling.* Scribner, 1962.

The Yeoman of the Guard
in *The Complete Plays of Gilbert and Sullivan,* Norton, 1976.

You Can't Go Home Again
Wolfe, Thomas. *You Can't Go Home Again.* Harper, 1940.

The Young Manhood of Studs Lonigan
Farrell, James T. *The Young Manhood of Studs Lonigan* in *Studs Lonigan: A Trilogy.* Vanguard, c. 1932–35.

Zeely
Hamilton, Virginia. *Zeely.* Macmillan, 1971.

Zimmerman
Zimmerman, J.E. *Dictionary of Classical Mythology.* Harper & Row, 1964.

Index

Index

C

D

Index

E

F

G

H

I

J

K

L

O

Index

Q

R

S

T

U

W

X

Index